THE PAPERS OF

BENJAMIN FRANKLIN

SPONSORED BY

The American Philosophical Society

and Yale University

VIR

THE PAPERS OF

Benjamin Franklin

VOLUME I *January 6, 1706 through December 31, 1734*

LEONARD W. LABAREE, *Editor*

WHITFIELD J. BELL, JR., *Associate Editor*

Helen C. Boatfield and Helene H. Fineman, Assistant Editors

New Haven YALE UNIVERSITY PRESS, 1959

The reprinting of this volume was made possible by a grant from the Charles E. Culpeper Foundation to the Friends of Franklin, and by a grant from the National Historical Publications and Records Commission.

Library of Congress catalogue number: 59-12697.
International standard book number: 0-300-00650-0.

∞ The paper in this book meets the guidelines for permanence and durability of the Committee on Production Guidelines for Book Longevity of the Council on Library Resources.

Printed in the United States of America.

10 9 8 7 6 5 4 3 2

"Advertisement to the Public"

Throughout the long span of history, the "wise man" has been one of the most significant of human figures. To him all sorts and conditions of mankind have looked for guidance. These counsellors and leaders of thought or emotion have been most potent as contrivers of patterns of human behavior. They have generally had the capacity to catch the spirit, not only of what their fellows might wish to think, but also of what they might be capable of thinking, and to put it in language which could be grasped appreciatively and oft repeated. It was not that they invented so much as that they discovered and defined, so to speak, what was in the air.

Men of this type have been the authors of various kinds of "wisdom literature" and from age to age have been recognized as prophets or statesmen. Some of them were poets, some philosophers; occasionally journalists or politicians have risen to their ranks. Their characteristics frequently have included good common sense, deep human understanding, and shrewd powers of observation, together with a capacity for simple and effective written and spoken communication. These qualities in their sum total have produced personalities which have seemed impressive, even awe-inspiring, to many diverse elements in society. Frequently, these personalities have been underscored by an attractive and often bewildering eccentricity.

One of these wise men, the first of the few who were to grow up in the new American society, was Benjamin Franklin. Motivated by an intricate combination of interests in self-education and self-advertisement, this ambitious young man sought to collect, record, invent, and communicate aphorisms and bits of wisdom which he used as advice to himself and admonition to others. In so doing, he promoted the dissemination of his ideas most effectively as a printer and newspaper editor, at the same time that he was organizing communication, at first, by stimulating the creation of a discussion group and a library; and, later on, by scientific experimentation and by advancing the cause of higher education. Finally, as legislator, diplomat, and statesman, he put his wisdom

ix

and his talent for communicating it to most practical use in the complicated task of creating a new and experimental body politic. He and his associates contrived this state in a highly sophisticated Age of Reason whose very intellectual sophistication had a tendency to make its leaders slightly naïve, naïve in their reliance upon reason and in their discount of the force of human emotion.

The significance of Franklin's wisdom and of his capacity to communicate has long been recognized, though perhaps not as long as popularly supposed, and there have been numerous biographical studies and four significant collections of his works put into print. But new discoveries of material and a broader concept of design now make it appropriate to reconsider the means best fitted to make Franklin's wisdom more intelligible and more available.

To this end, the American Philosophical Society and Yale University, encouraged by a generous gift from *Life* Magazine, have united to offer to the public a new and more comprehensive edition of Franklin's wisdom. The first of these was an organization for the communication of ideas, in which Franklin himself was most active; the second, among the earliest of American institutions of higher education which were beginning to flourish in Franklin's lifetime, recognized him by the award of an honorary degree. The sponsors of this edition believe that they are making Franklin's thinking more immediately useful by including the letters to Franklin which so frequently give greater meaning to what he himself wrote and by preparing a comprehensive series of editorial comments which relate his writing to the times and circumstances which had so much to do in forming his thought and expression. In presenting this edition, the sponsors are motivated by a "decent respect" for the needs of the hour, believing that wisdom, now as ever, is an element vital to the continued welfare of mankind.

ROY FRANKLIN NICHOLS
Chairman, Administrative Board

Publishers' Acknowledgments

This project was born one evening in 1952 at the summer home of the president of Yale University when several alumni fell to discussing the extensive William Smith Mason collection of Franklin materials in the Sterling Memorial Library. Inevitably this led to the possibility of a new edition of Franklin's papers, an idea that seemed the more appealing in view of the successful launching of the Jefferson edition at Princeton which they greatly admired.

In New Haven that fall advice was sought from Leonard W. Labaree, of the Yale history department, who made it clear that no edition of Franklin's writings could be undertaken without the full participation of the American Philosophical Society, possessors of more than half the surviving Franklin papers; the Society, which had been engaged in amassing Franklin materials for some years, had recently published several small collections of letters and had actually considered sponsoring a comprehensive edition of his writings. Professor Labaree also called attention to the report of the National Historical Publications Commission, sponsored by President Truman, which set a new edition of Franklin's papers as a national goal.

Particularly through Julian P. Boyd and Waldo G. Leland, the possibility of a partnership of the American Philosophical Society and Yale University was explored. Meanwhile, the Yale planners sought funds to support the University's share of the venture and Henry R. Luce, appreciating at once the project's importance, gave assurances of a substantial gift in the name of *Life*. The Society responded with the balance necessary to launch the project.

Representatives of the two institutions held several meetings in Philadelphia, where, under the wise guidance of the late Justice Owen J. Roberts, then president of the Society, a working agreement was reached and the joint sponsorship of the project was formally established in 1953. The editors were selected, editorial offices established, and a public announcement made on the 248th anniversary of Franklin's birth, January 17, 1954. Work began soon afterward, and now, five years later, the first results are presented to the public.

The governors of the Yale University Press from the first took the view that nothing less than the best in design, materials, and printing would suit the publication of the papers of America's great colonial printer. The interest of Gaylord Donnelley, president of R. R. Donnelley and Sons, Chicago, and of George E. O'Connor, president of the Mohawk Paper Mills of Cohoes, N. Y., was enlisted; their personal oversight and generous gifts of services from both companies have assured the quality of this and the succeeding volumes. In addition, Bromwell Ault, Edward Byron Smith, Gilbert H. Scribner, and Gaylord Donnelley have contributed to the costs of publication. The Press is pleased and proud to acknowledge its obligations to these individuals, as well as to its own staff and that of The Lakeside Press. It is part of Benjamin Franklin's legacy that two centuries after he lived his name continues to evoke a magical response.

CHESTER KERR
Director, Yale University Press

Contents

"Advertisement to the Public," by Roy Franklin Nichols   *ix*

Publishers' Acknowledgments, by Chester Kerr   *xi*

List of Illustrations   *xix*

Introduction   *xxi*

    Note on Versions of Manuscripts   *xliv*

Genealogy   *xlix*

Genealogical Charts:

    A. The English Franklins   *lxviii*

    B. The Folger Family   *lxx*

    C(a). Descendants of Josiah Franklin (*First Marriage*)   *lxxii*

    C(b). Descendants of Josiah Franklin (*Second Marriage*)   *lxxiv*

    D. Descendants of Benjamin Franklin   *lxxvi*

Editorial Staff   *lxxix*

Editors' Acknowledgments   *lxxix*

Contributors to Volume I   *lxxxiii*

Abbreviations and Short Titles   *lxxxv*

Chronology   *lxxxvii*

1706

Record of Birth, January 6/17   3

Record of Baptism, January 6/17   3

1710

Verses from Benjamin Franklin (the Elder), July 7   3

Acrostic from Benjamin Franklin (the Elder), July 15   4

1713

Verses from Benjamin Franklin (the Elder)   5

1718

The Lighthouse Tragedy   6

1719

The Taking of Teach the Pirate   7

1722

Silence Dogood, No. 1, April 2	8
Silence Dogood, No. 2, April 16	11
Silence Dogood, No. 3, April 30	13
Silence Dogood, No. 4, May 14	14
Silence Dogood, No. 5, May 28	18
Silence Dogood, No. 6, June 11	21
Silence Dogood, No. 7, June 25	23
Silence Dogood, No. 8, July 9	27
Silence Dogood, No. 9, July 23	30
Silence Dogood, No. 10, August 13	32
Silence Dogood, No. 11, August 20	37
Silence Dogood, No. 12, September 10	39
Silence Dogood, No. 13, September 24	41
Silence Dogood, No. 14, October 8	43
[Elegy on My Sister Franklin]	46

1723

The Printer to the Reader, February 11	47
On Titles of Honor, February 18	51
[Other Courant Essays Possibly by Franklin]	52

1724

Promissory Note to John Phillips, May 5 [?]	53

1725

To Sir Hans Sloane, June 2	54
A Dissertation on Liberty and Necessity	57

1726

Journal of a Voyage	72
Plan of Conduct	99

1727

To Jane Franklin, January 6	100

xiv

1728

Articles of Belief and Acts of Religion, November 20   101
Epitaph   109

1729

Martha Careful and Caelia Shortface, January 28   111
The Busy-Body, No. 1, February 4   113
The Busy-Body, No. 2, February 11   117
The Busy-Body, No. 3, February 18   118
The Busy-Body, No. 4, February 25   122
The Busy-Body, No. 5, March 4   127
The Busy-Body, No. 8, March 27   134
The Nature and Necessity of a Paper-Currency, April 3   139
The Printer to the Reader, October 2   157
Governor Burnet and the Massachusetts Assembly, October 9   159
The Printer to the Reader, October 23   161
Affairs of Ireland, November 20   162
From the Casuist: The Case of the Trespassing Horse,
     December 16   163
Extracts from the Gazette   164

1730

Printer's Errors, March 13   169
[Two Dialogues between Philocles and Horatio,
     concerning Virtue and Pleasure, June 23, July 9]   170
To Sarah Davenport, [June?]   171
Ledger A & B, July 4   172
From Hugh Meredith: Dissolution of Partnership, July 14   175
[Public Men, September 10]   176
On Governor Belcher's Speech, September 24   176
On Conversation, October 15   177
A Witch Trial at Mount Holly, October 22   182
Extracts from the Gazette   184

1731

Advertisement of Godfrey's Almanacs, January 19   190

From James Logan, May 1   191
Observations on Reading History, May 9   192
Apology for Printers, June 10   194
To Jane Mecom, June 19   200
St. John's Lodge Account, June 24   202
Articles of Agreement with Thomas Whitmarsh, September 13   205
Joseph Breintnall to Directors of Library Company, November 8 208
Miscellaneous Business Memoranda   210
Petition to the Pennsylvania Assembly regarding Fairs   211
Doctrine to be Preached   212
Extracts from the Gazette   213

1732

Query to the Casuist: The Case of the Missing Horse, January 18 221
From the Casuist: The Case of the Missing Horse, January 25   222
The Palatines' Appeal, February 15   226
To Library Company Subscribers, March 25   229
Louis Timothée to the German Inhabitants, May 6   230
Report of a Committee on By-Laws for St. John's Lodge, [June 5] 231
[Louis Timothée?] to the Reader, June 24   233
Query to the Casuist: A Case of Conscience, June 26   234
From the Casuist: A Case of Conscience, July 3   235
Anti-Casuist: A Case of Conscience, [July 3]   235
Anthony Afterwit, July 10   237
Celia Single, July 24   240
Alice Addertongue, September 12   243
Joseph Breintnall to Peter Collinson, November 7   248
Reply to a Complaining Reader, November 9   249
Agreement between Louis Timothée and Directors of Library
    Company, November 14   250
On Colds, November 30   252
A Sea Captain's Letter   254
Standing Queries for the Junto   255
Proposals and Queries to be Asked the Junto   259
On the Providence of God in the Government of the World   264
Miscellaneous Observations   270
Extracts from the Gazette   271

1733

Poor Richard 280
Slippery Sidewalks, January 11 318
Directors of Library Company to Thomas Penn
    and Reply, May 16 320
Agreement of Directors of Library Company, May 28 321
Remarks on a South Carolina Currency Scheme, May 31 322
Receipted Bill to the Proprietors, June 25 324
A Scolding Wife, July 5 325
On Ill-Natured Speaking, July 12 327
[A Meditation on a Quart Mugg, July 19] 328
On Literary Style, August 2 328
Power of Attorney to Deborah Franklin, August 30 331
Half-Hour's Conversation with a Friend, November 16 333
Articles of Agreement with Louis Timothée, November 26 339
Extracts from the Gazette 342

1734

Poor Richard 349
Agreement between Directors of Library Company and
    William Parsons, March 14 359
Sarah Read to Benjamin and Deborah Franklin:
    Bargain and Sale, April 9 362
Sarah Read to Benjamin and Deborah Franklin:
    Release, April 10 365
Benjamin and Deborah Franklin and John and Frances
    Croker to Sarah Read: Lease, April 11 367
From a Reader to the Printer, April 11 370
Bill to Thomas Penn, May 18 371
Thomas Godfrey to the Printer of the Gazette, August 15 371
Admission of John Mifflin to Library Company, August 27 373
To the Grand Lodge of Massachusetts, November 28 373
To Henry Price, November 28 375
Extracts from the Gazette 376

Index 385

List of Illustrations

Benjamin Franklin   *Frontispiece, opposite title page*

By Joseph-Siffred Duplessis. Painted in 1778 for Franklin's friend, LeRay de Chaumont, this picture was the work of the leading portraitist of the French court, and its exhibition at the Salon of 1779, hanging near the portraits of the King and Queen, reaffirmed the official recognition of the new nation. On the frame, the snake, symbolical of wisdom, the torch of liberty, the liberty cap, and the flayed lion's skin are emblematical of Franklin's role in the war for American independence. Of the laconic characterization of Franklin on the frame, Dupont de Nemours wrote, "Il n'y a pas un trait de sa figure, ni de sa vie qui la démente." Jules Belleudy, *J.-S. Duplessis, Peintre du Roi* (Chartres, 1913), p. 87. Extolled as a masterpiece of portraiture, engraved, copied, and repeated by the artist, this picture became the best known of Franklin portraits. Reproduced by permission of The Metropolitan Museum of Art; Michael Friedsam Collection, 1931.

Franklin's Birthplace   4

By William Wood Thackara. The house stood on Milk Street, at the corner of a small alley between Marlborough and Hawley Streets; it burned down in 1810. For a history of the property, see Nathaniel B. Shurtleff, *A Topographical and Historical Description of Boston* (Boston, 1871), pp. 615–25. Thackara, a Philadelphia engraver, sketched the birthplace in his journal of a visit to Boston in 1820. "The annexed drawing is perhaps the only view of it, now in existence," he wrote under date of August 22, "and was copied from a pencil drawing, almost obliterated, which was taken on the spot, by a gentleman a short time before it was destroyed." Reproduced by courtesy of the owner, Mrs. Robert D. Crompton, Glenside, Pennsylvania.

Title-page of *Liberty and Necessity*, 1725   55

Franklin wrote this pamphlet to refute some "reasonings" in William Wollaston's *Religion of Nature Delineated*, and printed it in Samuel Palmer's shop in London. It was his first separate publication. He later considered the rationalistic essay an "erratum" and destroyed the edition. Only two copies are known to have survived, one in the Library of Congress, the other in the Yale University Library. The latter copy is here reproduced by permission.

Little Britain, Aldersgate, London — 70

Artist unknown. Franklin took lodgings here in 1724, in a house next to John Wilcox' bookshop. He worked for a year as a journeyman in Palmer's printing-house in Bartholomew's Close nearby. The street, which is near St. Paul's Cathedral, was destroyed during the Second World War. Reproduced by permission of the Trustees of the British Museum.

Franklin's Epitaph — 110

Written about 1728, the Epitaph became one of Franklin's best known compositions. It was often repeated, and he himself made copies for friends. Two of these autograph versions survive, and a third is known in a facsimile. His gravestone, however, reads simply, as his will directed, "Benjamin and Deborah Franklin 1790." Reproduced by permission of the Yale University Library.

Philadelphia about 1720 — 140

By Peter Cooper. This view from the Delaware shows Philadelphia as Franklin first saw the city in 1723 and as it appeared in the years of his young manhood. Reproduced by permission of the Library Company of Philadelphia.

Poor Richard, 1733 — 285–310

This is the first impression of the first annual almanac of Poor Richard. Photographed by Laurens H. Fritz, Merion, Pennsylvania. Reproduced by permission of The Philip H. and A. S. W. Rosenbach Foundation, Philadelphia.

Thomas Penn — 370

Mezzotint engraving by D. Martin from a painting by Davis. The second son of William and Hannah Callowhill Penn, Thomas Penn became one of the proprietors of Pennsylvania in 1727 and was "the principal Proprietor" from 1746 until his death in 1775. He lived in Philadelphia from 1732 to 1741. Reproduced by permission of the Yale University Art Gallery. The Mabel Brady Garvan Collection.

Introduction

The Papers of Benjamin Franklin is intended to be comprehensive. It cannot, of course, be complete, for there are Franklin manuscripts we have not been able to find and Franklin writings we have not identified. In a larger sense, no edition of Franklin's writings could ever be complete, for many of his papers were lost or destroyed in his lifetime, to say nothing of the vicissitudes others have suffered since. All this the history of Franklin's papers makes clear.

THE FRANKLIN PAPERS

The largest single body of Franklin manuscripts was that which he himself preserved. This consisted of letters he received, drafts and copies of essays and of letters sent, business ledgers, invoices, and receipts, even household accounts of the most trivial character. When Franklin went abroad in October 1776, he deposited a large part of these papers for safekeeping with his friend Joseph Galloway at Galloway's Bucks County house, Trevose. But Trevose was sacked in 1778, and though some of Franklin's papers were recovered, many were destroyed. Among them, Franklin wrote in distress, were "eight or ten quire or 2-quire Books of rough Drafts of my Letters, containing all my Correspondence, when in England, for near twenty Years."[1] Only one of these letterbooks survives. During the nine years he spent in France, Franklin accumulated another and greater mass of papers. These, with his remaining earlier manuscripts and most of his books, he bequeathed to his grandson William Temple Franklin. Selecting several thousand pieces, mostly of a public and scientific character, William Temple Franklin took them to London in 1791, where he intended to edit and publish an edition of his grandfather's writings. The remainder of his literary inheritance, consisting of more than 15,000 manuscripts, William Temple Franklin left with his friend, Dr. George Fox, of Champlost, near Philadelphia. Some of these manuscripts were political, many were personal letters of members of the family, but most were letters addressed

1. To Richard Bache, Sept. 13, 1781.

to Franklin during the years of his ministry in France. By his will William Temple Franklin converted the deposit into a gift to Dr. Fox; and on the latter's death in 1828, the manuscripts passed to his son, Charles Pemberton Fox.

Mr. Fox took little more interest in them than to put them in a dry place in the Champlost stable, where, though they were neglected, they were not forgotten. From time to time Mr. Fox presented autograph letters to friends as souvenirs, and he gave Dr. Franklin Bache, Franklin's great-grandson, a large number of the personal papers. Philadelphia antiquarians and other members of the American Philosophical Society and of the newly founded Historical Society of Pennsylvania knew of the collection. One of these gentlemen conducted Jared Sparks to the Champlost stable when the Harvard historian came to Philadelphia in 1831 to gather material for his edition of the writings of Washington. Sparks returned to Champlost in 1837 and was allowed to make a large selection of letters for his edition of Franklin's writings, then being published. Impressed once more with the importance of the collection, Sparks urged Mr. Fox to deposit it in an institution; and in 1840 Fox presented a mass of some 13,000 manuscripts to the American Philosophical Society.[2] Through an oversight in emptying the storage place, this gift did not include all the Champlost manuscripts. Several hundred more were uncovered in 1862 intermingled with an accumulation of Fox family papers in the process of destruction; they were given to a friend and eventually, in 1903, went to the University of Pennsylvania.[3] Still another group of Franklin papers that was almost certainly once at Champlost is now in the Historical Society of Pennsylvania. And the letters that were given to Dr. Bache became part of a collection of some 1100 pieces—the last substantial lot to remain in possession of Franklin's descendants—which the American Philosophical Society purchased in 1936.

William Temple Franklin used the papers he took to London in his edition of his grandfather's writings, which finally appeared in 1817–18. Thereafter the manuscripts had neither interest nor

2. William E. Lingelbach, "Benjamin Franklin's Papers in the American Philosophical Society," APS *Proc.*, XCIX (1955), 359–80.

3. J. G. Rosengarten, "Some New Franklin Papers. A Report ... to the Board of Trustees," Univ. of Pa., *Alumni Register*, VII (1903), 498–504.

value for him; he laid them aside and his widow abandoned them. They were discovered by chance about 1840 in a London tailor's shop where they were being cut up for use as paper patterns. Henry Stevens, the American bookseller in London, bought them in 1851, but before he could either sell or publish them he pledged the collection as security for a loan and they became inaccessible to scholars. In 1880 the executors of Stevens' creditor ordered the papers to be sold at auction; before they were dispersed in this manner, however, Stevens arranged a sale to the United States Government. For many years the collection remained in the Department of State, and is now in the Library of Congress.[4]

A second category of Franklin manuscripts is his official correspondence, whether with governmental bodies like the Pennsylvania Assembly and the Continental Congress, or with private institutions and associations. Some of Franklin's letters to the Assembly, for example, were printed in the official journals; others, preserved by the clerk, were included in the *Pennsylvania Archives*, published in the nineteenth century; most, however, were destroyed or scattered. Correspondence from Franklin and the American Commission in Paris to the Continental Congress was filed by the secretary, Charles Thomson, and by him ultimately deposited in the Department of State. There Peter Force, Francis Wharton, and Albert H. Smyth examined these documents, which now form a part of the Papers of the Continental Congress in the National Archives. Letters to the French government, together with drafts of the Foreign Minister's letters to Franklin, are preserved in the extensive file of Correspondance politique, États-Unis in the Ministère des Affaires Étrangères. Smyth was the first editor to use this archive systematically. Similarly the records of such institutions as the Pennsylvania Hospital, the Union Fire Company, and the Pennsylvania Society for Promoting the Abolition of Slavery contain letters and reports sent to or received by Franklin as a member, officer, or patron. Few if any of these materials have been printed in previous editions of Franklin's writings.

A third class of Franklin's letters are those to individuals in

4. Henry Stevens, *Benjamin Franklin's Life and Writings: A Bibliographical Essay on the Stevens' Collection of Books and Manuscripts relating to Doctor Franklin* (London, 1881); Worthington C. Ford, *List of the Benjamin Franklin Papers in the Library of Congress* (Washington, 1905), pp. 3–4.

America and abroad, on business, political, scientific, and personal affairs. He must have written to several thousand different people during his long life. Many—perhaps most—of these letters were not kept by their recipients; but many were carefully preserved and bequeathed to children and grandchildren as mementos of the great man. Letters to Catharine Ray Greene, Mme. Brillon, and the family of Bishop Shipley, for example, remained in possession of their families until the twentieth century. On the other hand, the widow of Charles W. F. Dumas, who had Franklin's letters to her husband in two bound volumes, allowed them to go out of her possession early in the nineteenth century and never recovered them. There is abundant evidence that the volumes were broken up soon afterwards and the letters scattered as single autographs. It is principally from among these private letters that most collectors and institutions have obtained the Franklin manuscripts they now possess.

Thus far we have spoken only of manuscripts. Another part of Franklin's literary output consisted of printed pamphlets and letters and essays published in newspapers. Those compositions which he signed or which can be clearly identified by references in the autobiography and letters have offered no serious problems. If the pamphlet or newspaper survives, it can usually be located, however scarce it may be. Identifying the many pieces Franklin printed himself or sent to another printer without a name or over a pseudonym has been more difficult. Verner W. Crane has performed this task for contributions to the English press between 1758 and 1775.[5] The present editors have identified others in American newspapers.

FRANKLIN'S WRITINGS IN PRINT

Long before his death in 1790 Franklin had a universal reputation as a writer. Some of his letters and essays became famous and were often reprinted in periodicals. No fewer than four collections of his works appeared during his lifetime, all with his knowledge, several with his active help.[6] The first consisted of his letters on

5. *Benjamin Franklin's Letters to the Press, 1758–1775* (Chapel Hill, [1950]).
6. Francis S. Philbrick, "Notes on Early Editions and Editors of Franklin," APS *Proc.*, XCVII (1953), 525–64.

electricity addressed to Peter Collinson, which Collinson and Fothergill arranged and saw through the press in 1751 under the title *Experiments and Observations on Electricity*. Subsequent editions of this work appeared, enlarged and corrected; Franklin himself oversaw the fourth, in 1769. In 1773 Franklin's French friend and admirer Barbeu Dubourg published a two-volume collection of Franklin's works, which is interesting for its prefaces and valuable because it contains some otherwise unavailable pieces and because Franklin advised in the translation.[7] Benjamin Vaughan brought out in London in 1779 a stout volume of Franklin's writings which contained such things as the famous epitaph and rules for the Junto, which Franklin supplied him.[8] And in 1787 Charles Dilly published a small volume of Franklin's later philosophical papers that was intended to supplement the *Experiments and Observations* and Vaughan's edition.[9]

These volumes foretold what the public might expect of William Temple Franklin's proposed edition. But he seemed indifferent to the demand for a comprehensive publication of his grandfather's works. As the years passed and he took no step to fulfill his announced intention, other collections appeared. The most important was William Duane's, which began to be published in Philadelphia in 1808.[1] As a member of the Franklin family—he had married the widow of the philosopher's grandson, Benjamin Franklin Bache—Duane had access to manuscripts and other materials which promised to give his edition a special authority. When only four volumes had appeared, however, Duane agreed with William Temple Franklin that he would print no more until the latter's edition was ready. Not until 1817 did Temple Franklin at last publish the first of his three-volume quarto edition.[2] His work

7. *Œuvres de M. Franklin ... Traduites de l'anglois sur la quatrième édition. Par M. Barbeu Dubourg. Avec des additions nouvelles et des figures en taille douce* (2 vols., Paris, 1773).

8. See Edwin Wolf, 2nd, "Benjamin Franklin's *Political, Miscellaneous and Philosophical Pieces*, 1779," [Univ. of Pa.] *Lib. Chron.*, XVI (1949–50), 50–63.

9. *Philosophical and Miscellaneous Papers. Lately written by B. Franklin, LL.D. ...* (London, 1787).

1. *The Works of Dr. Benjamin Franklin ...* [title varies] (6 vols., Phila., 1808–18).

2. *Memoirs of the Life and Writings of Benjamin Franklin, LL.D. ...* [title varies] (4to edit., 3 vols., London, 1817–18). Three editions also appeared in six volumes octavo between 1818 and 1833.

was completed in 1818, as was Duane's. Though in most respects similar, each edition included manuscripts the other omitted; and later editions of each work enlarged the contents slightly.

The next general edition of Franklin's writings was that of Jared Sparks, published at Boston in 1836–40. Already the editor of the writings of Washington and of the diplomatic correspondence of the Revolutionary period, Sparks was an intelligent, tireless, and experienced collector of manuscripts, and his achievement was impressive—nine volumes of writings and one of biography, including 465 letters and essays not previously printed in any edition of Franklin, of which three-fifths had never been printed before at all.[3]

Sparks had searched in vain for the manuscripts Temple Franklin was known to have taken to London. Not until after his *Works of Benjamin Franklin* was completed did they come to light, and only forty years after that did they become available to scholars. So important were they that a new edition of Franklin's writings was called for. It was prepared by John Bigelow in 1887–88.[4] Bigelow could submit impressive credentials as a Franklinist. As American Minister in Paris in 1865–66, he had discovered and acquired the original manuscript of Franklin's autobiography (hitherto known only in an English retranslation of a French translation of an incomplete manuscript, now lost) and had edited and published it in 1868. Among the 345 new pieces in Bigelow's edition, for example, was an important group of letters to William Strahan, which had recently been sold in London. More significant perhaps than the new material was the chronological arrangement Bigelow adopted instead of the topical order followed in all former editions.

Within fifteen years still another general edition was in preparation. The occasion was the forthcoming bicentennial observance of Franklin's birth in 1906, in which the American Philosophical Society and the University of Pennsylvania took the leading roles. Albert Henry Smyth, professor of English in Philadelphia's Central High School, was an editor of considerable ability

3. *The Works of Benjamin Franklin* . . . (10 vols., Boston, 1836–40).
4. *The Complete Works of Benjamin Franklin* . . . (10 vols., N.Y. and London, 1887–88). A "Federal Edition" with slightly differing title appeared in 12 volumes in 1904.

and boundless energy. His edition, which includes some 2,000 pieces, used for the first time the newly acquired University of Pennsylvania collection, many single letters from private collections, and a number of Franklin contributions to the press.[5] Here first appeared, for example, the Silence Dogood papers from the *New-England Courant*. For nearly half a century scholars have generally depended on Smyth's edition, I. Minis Hays' *Calendar* of Franklin papers in the American Philosophical Society (5 vols., Philadelphia, 1908), Worthington C. Ford's *List* of papers in the Library of Congress, and Paul Leicester Ford's *Franklin Bibliography* (Brooklyn, 1889).

Recently, however, several important additions have been made to the body of published Franklin writings. With the purchase of the large collection of papers from the Bache family in 1936, the American Philosophical Society adopted a policy of adding systematically to its Franklin holdings. In the past twenty years it has acquired hundreds of important documents and four notable groups of letters: Franklin's correspondence with Jane Mecom, Richard Jackson, Catharine Ray Greene, and Mary Stevenson Hewson; and has published the first three of these groups.[6] Verner W. Crane's *Benjamin Franklin's Letters to the Press, 1758–1775* has made yet another body of writings generally available.

These general editions, even when thus supplemented, no longer meet the requirements of students of Franklin and his time. Some earlier editors took liberties with the manuscripts which seem unwarrantable to twentieth-century scholars. William Temple Franklin, Sparks, Bigelow, and Smyth all had to be selective: Smyth's publishers, for example, arbitrarily stopped the edition at ten volumes, when much material of great interest remained to be printed. Moreover, none of the editors was able to search for manuscripts in smaller or out-of-the-way repositories. Finally, they printed only a few letters to Franklin, so that the letters which they edited were really only one side of a correspondence.

5. *The Writings of Benjamin Franklin* . . . (10 vols., N.Y., 1905–07).
6. *The Letters of Benjamin Franklin and Jane Mecom*, ed. Carl Van Doren (Princeton, 1950); *Letters and Papers of Benjamin Franklin and Richard Jackson, 1753–1785*, ed. Carl Van Doren (Phila., 1947); *Benjamin Franklin and Catharine Ray Greene: Their Correspondence, 1755–1790*, ed. William Greene Roelker (Phila., 1949).

Work on an edition of Franklin's writings that would meet these objections was begun in 1954 under the joint sponsorship of the American Philosophical Society and Yale University. The editors' first task was to locate and photocopy Franklin manuscripts and printed works in the scores of institutions and private collections where they are preserved. The major bodies of Franklin materials are well known to historians: the American Philosophical Society, the Library of Congress, the National Archives, the Historical Society of Pennsylvania, the University of Pennsylvania, Yale University, the Massachusetts Historical Society, and the French Foreign Office each owns more than 500 manuscripts. Scholars have long been acquainted with the Franklin papers in Harvard College Library, the William L. Clements Library, the New York Public Library, the New-York Historical Society, the Pierpont Morgan Library, the Henry E. Huntington Library, the Library Company of Philadelphia, the Pennsylvania State Records Office, and, abroad, in the British Museum, Public Record Office, Royal Society, and Bibliothèque Nationale. These twenty libraries and about a score more composed the first list of probable owners which the editors prepared when they began their work in 1954.

Obtaining photostats or microfilms from the larger libraries was, for the editors, relatively easy. (In a very few cases, for some special reason, manuscript transcripts had to be made.) By correspondence and personal visits single letters were located in smaller libraries and collections. University libraries, state and municipal libraries, and state and local historical societies were routinely canvassed. The indexes prepared by the Federal Historical Records Survey of the Works Progress Administration provided helpful information, as did, in Great Britain, the *Reports* of the Historical Manuscripts Commission. The *Catalogue Général des Manuscrits des Bibliothèques Publiques de France* led to a dozen or more provincial libraries, and the admirable centralization of library facilities in France enabled us to examine and copy these manuscripts in the Bibliothèque Nationale in Paris. The director of the National Historical Publications Commission had a search made of the Continental Congress Papers and other promising collections in the National Archives at Washington and provided microfilms. Institutions which Franklin served, like the Pennsylvania Hospital and the Associates of the late Reverend Dr. Bray, almost always had a letter or two. Colleagues and strangers reported the existence of Franklin letters in their friends' libraries or in places to which we would probably never have addressed an inquiry, like the Riverdale Country Day School. Sometimes, as in the Salem County, N.J., Historical Society and in Christ Church in Philadelphia, while searching for a manuscript we believed to be there, we found others we had not known about. No place, it turned out, was too improbable to hold a Franklin letter: there are eight at Windsor Castle (seven of them presented to the Prince of Wales, later Edward VII, during his American tour in 1860), and two (each to a president of Yale College) in the Karl Marx University at Leipzig. We began as scholars, but have become sleuths and venturesome serendipitists as well.

Descendants of Franklin and his principal correspondents, especially in Philadelphia, without exception took a lively interest in the work, as their parents and grandparents did in the work of Smyth and Sparks, and allowed copies of their manuscripts to be made, or, if they had no manuscripts themselves, sent us to aunts and cousins who did. Autograph collectors, many of them members of the Manuscript Society, also responded to our requests and cordially and promptly allowed copies to be made of their treasures. As the first volume goes to press, about 220 institutions and some 110 private owners have given permission to print their manuscripts in this edition. All seem to regard *The Papers of Benjamin Franklin,* in words J. Francis Fisher of Philadelphia used to Jared Sparks, as "a national work," which they wish to promote as they can.[7] Nor is this cooperation limited to owners in the United States. Photocopies have reached us not only from thirty-one states from Maine to Hawaii, and the District of Columbia, but also from twelve foreign countries extending from Canada to the Soviet Union. This response suggests that an edition of Franklin's writings may now be regarded as an international work.

Carrying the search to yet another level, the editors examined the published correspondence of Franklin's contemporaries, printed archival collections, the periodicals of historical societies and

7. J. Francis Fisher to Jared Sparks, June 26, 1837. Sparks MSS, Harvard Coll. Lib.

associations; and found other letters, from now lost manuscripts, printed in whole or in part in the book and autograph sales catalogues of Goodspeed, Henkels, Maggs, Parke-Bernet, and others.[8]

Even this exhaustive search is, of course, not ended. It will continue throughout the preparation of this edition, and even then manuscripts will continue to turn up. Just as Sparks, for some reason, did not or could not see the Franklin-Mecom correspondence that was preserved in Boston at the time he was working; and Smyth could find no trace of Franklin's letters to Ingenhousz, which had been sold only a few years before; so we have been unable to verify in any way a report that Franklin letters are in possession of descendants of Joseph Galloway in Eire. So the search continues, and with it an appeal to those who read these pages to inform the editors (in care of the publishers) of any Franklin manuscripts of whose existence they know.

FRANKLIN'S LITERARY LEGACY

During his long career Franklin contributed to many different areas of life and thought. He was unusually versatile, not only in his interests and activities, but also in the literary forms he used to present his ideas and to inform or persuade his fellow men. Sometimes he employed extensively the device of the newspaper essay, often but not invariably cast in the form of a letter to the printer, signed with a pseudonym. He was familiar with that vehicle of information and argument so popular in the eighteenth century, the pamphlet, and used it most effectively to enlighten or influence the public on some issue in which he was interested. Active in the establishment of various organizations for the general good, he made a number of his most useful contributions by writing himself, or joining with other men in writing, the articles of association by means of which such organizations might operate most effectively. As a member of legislative bodies or other political groups he often served on important committees; it was frequently his pen which drafted the committee reports or the bills which came out of their discussions. He also participated with varying degrees of activity in the deliberations which resulted in many of

8. The extent of Franklin's correspondence is indicated by the fact that the editorial file of photocopies contains letters to or from approximately 4200 individuals.

the important state papers of his age: the Albany Plan of Union, the Declaration of Independence, the Treaty of Alliance with France, the peace treaties with Great Britain, and the Constitution. And always, throughout his mature years, Franklin wrote letters, thousands of them, personal, scientific, political, and diplomatic—letters in which he expressed his thoughts on a great range of topics, through which he made and retained countless friendships throughout the western world, often with men he never met personally, and as a result of which he exerted an influence upon the society he lived in that cannot be measured.

Many of Franklin's interests, while persisting throughout his life, claimed his major attention only during limited periods of his career. It is natural, therefore, that the focus of his papers should shift repeatedly from one topic to another and that even the literary forms he found most useful for the expression of his ideas should change from time to time. Consequently the volumes of this edition will vary substantially in the kinds of writings which predominate in their pages. A brief summary of these changes may be serviceable to the reader.

Very few personal letters by or to Franklin survive for the first thirty years or so of his life. These were the years when the young man was learning his trade as a printer and developing his place as a journalist and businessman. A large proportion of the material from this period, therefore, consists of Franklin's writings in the newspapers of Boston and Philadelphia: the letters of Silence Dogood, the Busy-Body letters, and many essays in his own paper, *The Pennsylvania Gazette*. In this period, too, he began one of his best known and most successful undertakings, the annual publication of *Poor Richard's Almanack*. Papers connected with the earliest organizations he helped to found, the Junto and the Library Company, forecast his later activities in the establishment of other institutions, and his contributions to the Hemphill controversy in 1735 gave him his first important experience as a pamphleteer.

Franklin's surviving letters become more numerous in the 1740s, and it is in this decade that his scientific correspondence begins, at first chiefly with Cadwallader Colden of New York, later with Peter Collinson of London. The letters to Collinson, continued and expanded with other letters during the next decade, provided the central material for the several editions of Franklin's most influential scientific book, *Experiments and Observations on Electricity,* first published in 1751. The years between 1737 and 1757 witnessed his growing importance as a civic and political figure in the city and province where he made his home, and the volumes covering those years will include such papers, largely of his authorship, as the articles of association of the Union Fire Company and of the first local fire insurance company, and the history of the Pennsylvania Hospital. The pamphlet *Plain Truth,* the military association of 1747, and numerous reports of Assembly committees on which he served likewise attest his developing political influence, which became intercolonial in scope with his participation in 1754 in the Albany Congress and soon took on military importance with his labors in support of General Braddock and the defense of the Pennsylvania frontier.

When Franklin went to London in 1757 as agent for the Pennsylvania Assembly he began an extensive correspondence with political leaders at home, especially with Joseph Galloway in Philadelphia and later with Samuel Cooper and Thomas Cushing in Boston. At the same time he made new friends and gained new correspondents in the British Isles, some of them scientific, such as members of the Royal Society, others more strictly personal, such as the Scottish jurist Lord Kames, or his London landlady's daughter Polly Stevenson, or Bishop Jonathan Shipley and his daughters. As the conflict between Great Britain and her colonies deepened, Franklin's pen became active in the American cause, and the English newspapers printed many of his letters, usually disguised as to authorship, satirizing ministerial policies or expounding the colonial position.

Back in America in the spring of 1775, he actively supported the revolt as a member both of the Continental Congress and of the Provincial Congress of Pennsylvania, visiting Washington's camp at Cambridge, traveling to Canada on a vain mission to enlist the help of its French-speaking inhabitants, serving on important Congressional committees, among them those for drafting the Declaration of Independence and for Secret Correspondence. He had little time for writing private letters during the year and a half before he sailed for France, and those he did write reflect his deep absorption in public affairs to the almost complete exclusion of scientific and personal concerns.

Franklin's surviving papers for the period of his residence in France, from December 1776 to July 1785, are vastly more numerous than for any earlier period of his life, and in many respects they are very different in character. He was, for example, almost deluged during the first year or so with letters from Frenchmen and other Europeans seeking commissions in the American army or other favors. To most of these unknown correspondents he seems never even to have replied. More important was his active and extensive correspondence with French officials both before and after the negotiation of the Treaty of Alliance; with his American diplomatic colleagues in Europe, especially Silas Deane, John Adams, Arthur Lee, and John Jay; with financial and commercial agents in France and the Netherlands; with American naval officers such as John Paul Jones and privateers sailing under American commissions; and with Congress, its committees, and its civilian aides, notably Robert Morris and Charles Thomson.

But Franklin's capacity for personal friendships brought him delightful contacts and extensive correspondence with kindred spirits among the subjects of the King of France—with the Abbé Morellet and the Duc de la Rochefoucauld, for example, and with Mmes. Helvétius and Brillon. The personal letters he exchanged with such men and women as these are among the most charming in the entire collection. During these years he also wrote most of his informal essays or "bagatelles," and printed many of them privately on his own press at Passy. Until the war was over and the treaties of peace had been successfully negotiated, Franklin had little time for his scientific interests, though he did continue his correspondence with fellow scientists such as his old friend from London days, Jan Ingenhousz, now court physician in Vienna. But when peace came at last, he was able to pay some attention again to matters of interest to "philosophers," observing and reporting on the first balloon ascensions and participating with distinguished Frenchmen on the commission appointed to investigate the experiments of F. A. Mesmer with "animal magnetism."

The old man's final years in Philadelphia brought him new responsibilities: presidency of the Supreme Executive Council of Pennsylvania for three years, where he signed countless official papers, most of which were purely routine and called for almost no intellectual effort on his part, and membership in the Constitutional

Convention of 1787, where he spoke little and wrote less, but undoubtedly exercised considerable personal influence toward compromising the conflicting points of view among other delegates. Then, as he moved quietly toward the end of his life, his writings again assume a personal tone and reflect his abiding interest in the enlightenment and welfare of his fellow men: letters—essentially farewell letters—to old friends, correspondence with young men such as Noah Webster, who would become intellectual leaders of a new generation, and, as a concluding public document, a memorial to Congress on behalf of the Pennsylvania Society for Promoting the Abolition of Slavery. At this time, too, he wrote the last short installments of his memoirs, which he had begun in England in 1771. Incomplete as they remain, carrying the narrative only to 1757, they demonstrate Franklin's mastery of another literary form, the autobiography. And they link the youth and the productive middle years about which he wrote with the ripe and mellow years of his seniority, in which he looked out upon the America he had seen change so much during his long life and in the transformation of which he had taken so important a part.

PRINCIPLES OF SELECTION

This edition will present the full text of every document of Franklin's career, signed or unsigned, that we can locate and establish to our satisfaction to have been written by Franklin or by Franklin with others. There are essays in the contemporary press which he may have written, and when the weight of the evidence supports the idea of his authorship, we shall print them, indicating that evidence, but also making clear its limits and our uncertainty. Writings which previous editors have assigned to Franklin but which subsequent research has proved not to be his, or which our own study leads us to judge are not by him, will be presented only by title and location, in their chronological order, with our reasons for rejecting them.

The important state papers in which Franklin participated and which he signed will be printed in full, with annotation indicating the nature and extent of his contribution. Where his part in the drafting was substantial, we shall include such preliminary versions as will show the evolution of the document into its final form.

There are some very large volumes of records of Franklin's printing business, and of official, post office, and personal affairs. Printing these in full would take a great deal of space and would serve the purposes of none but a very few scholars of limited and highly specialized interests. We shall give the description and location of each such record book in its proper chronological place, that is, according to the date of the earliest entry. We shall indicate its nature and, when warranted, reproduce sample entries. Like treatment will be accorded groups of miscellaneous business papers, invoices, bills of exchange, and calling cards. Many legal documents will appear only in the form of abstracts.

We shall normally exclude two other categories of documents actually written by Franklin. The first consists of documents of bodies which he served as secretary or clerk, such as the Pennsylvania Assembly and, occasionally, the Library Company of Philadelphia. The journals, minutes, and addresses of such institutions, though in his autograph, are not properly parts of the Franklin Papers; and they are useful mainly in annotation. The same is true of the hundreds of routine official documents which he signed or which came to him as minister to France and as president of the Supreme Executive Council of Pennsylvania—passports, commissions, orders on the state treasurer, bankruptcy petitions, and the like. We shall print an example of each of these forms, perhaps in facsimile, and we shall present such individual pieces as derive significance from other documents in the Franklin Papers or are of general historical importance. But to include all this sort of thing would add nothing either to the interest or to the usefulness of this edition.

The ultimate test to be applied in determining whether to print any document or part of a Franklin document is whether the contents are in any sense the product of his mind.

A second major group of materials in this edition will consist of letters and other communications, personal or official, addressed to Franklin individually, or to an official body of which he was a member, such as the American Commissioners in France. In general we shall print in full all personal letters and such official ones as we deem of historical or other importance. Such communications as the hundreds of letters addressed to him in France by unknown persons seeking favors, introductions, commissions in the army, most of which seem to have remained unanswered, will be given only in abstract form, except when the individual did serve in the American Army or was otherwise important. The abstract will give the location of the manuscript, and the names of all persons mentioned in the document will appear in the index.

Finally there are the "third-party" letters, which were sent to Franklin for his information or action, or longhand copies of essays or treatises from scientist correspondents asking for comment and criticism. Some of these had covering letters from which they have become separated. The editors will use their best judgment as to which of these to print in full, in abstract, or only as the annotation of other documents, and which to omit entirely.

ARRANGEMENT

The documents will be printed in chronological sequence according to their dates when these are given, or according to the date of publication in cases of contemporary printed materials. Records such as diaries, journals, and account books which cover substantial periods will appear according to the dates of their earliest entries. When no date appears on the document itself, one will be editorially supplied. When no day within a month is given, the letter or essay will be placed after the pieces specifically dated on the last day of that month. Those dated only by year will be placed according to a similar principle. More difficult will be the placing of documents which can be assigned only to a period covering several years, such as those addressed to Franklin at Passy and relating so generally to the American Revolution that they could have been written at any time between 1777 and 1783. When a probable year is tentatively assigned, it will be placed in brackets, with a question mark, and the document will appear among those without precise dates at the end of that year. If even such tentative dating is impossible, inclusive dates in brackets will be supplied (e.g., [1777-1783]), and the document will be printed after all others of the first year of the period (e.g., 1777).

When the edition reaches its final volume, there may still remain undated and undatable papers. These will have to be printed at the end under the unsatisfactory but unavoidable rubric "n.d."

One exception to this system of dating will be *Poor Richard's Almanack,* which Franklin prepared for the years 1733 through

1758. He might announce publication of his almanac at any time between early October and mid-December of the preceding year. But since the almanacs covered particular calendar years, it seems appropriate to print the material drawn from them as the first documents of the years for which Franklin prepared them, rather than on the earlier dates when he first announced their publication.

Another exception to strict chronological arrangement has to do with miscellaneous brief news reports, notes, and advertisements in *The Pennsylvania Gazette*. These record or reflect Franklin's interests, his activities, or his sense of humor; as such they deserve to be included in this edition, but are too short or too inconsequential to justify printing as separate documents in regular chronological order. We have made selections of such items from each year of the *Gazette* from 1729 through 1747, when Franklin took a partner into his printing office; and we shall print a group of them, under the heading "Extracts from the *Gazette*," at the end of each year to which they belong. The issue in which each individual item appeared will be noted with it.

Franklin began to write his Memoirs, as he called his autobiography, in 1771. He continued them in 1784, 1788, and 1789. In this edition the Memoirs will be printed in four parts, under the four dates when Franklin wrote them.

When two or more documents have the same date, they will be arranged in the following order:

1. Those by a group of which Franklin was a member (e.g., the American Commissioners in Paris)
2. Those by Franklin individually
3. Those to a group of which Franklin was a member
4. Those to Franklin individually
5. "Third-party" and unaddressed miscellaneous writings by others than Franklin.

In the first two categories letters will be arranged alphabetically by the name of the addressee; and in the last three, by the name of the signatory. An exception to this practice will occur on the rare occasions when a letter to Franklin and his answer were written on the same day: in such cases the first letter must precede the reply. The same rules will apply to documents lacking precise dates printed together at the end of any month or year.

The document and its accompanying editorial apparatus will be presented in the following pattern:

1. *Heading* or *Caption*. Essays and formal papers will be headed by their titles, except in the case of pamphlets with very long titles, when a short form will be substituted. Where previous editors have supplied a title to a piece that had none, and this title has become familiar, we shall use it; otherwise we shall devise a suitable one.

Letters written by Franklin individually will be captioned as "To" the person or body addressed, as: To John Adams; To John Adams and Arthur Lee; To the Royal Society.

Letters to Franklin individually will be captioned as "From" the person or body who wrote them, as: From John Adams; From John Adams and Arthur Lee; From Committee of Secret Correspondence.

Letters of which Franklin was the joint author or joint recipient will be captioned with the names of all concerned, as: Franklin and Silas Deane to Arthur Lee; Arthur Lee to Silas Deane and Franklin. "Third-party" letters or those by or to a body of which Franklin was a member will be captioned with the names of both writers and addressees, as: William Franklin to Deborah Franklin; American Commissioners to David Hartley.

Documents not fitting into any of these categories will be given brief descriptive headings, as: Power of Attorney to Deborah Franklin.

2. *Source-Identification.* This will give the nature of the printed or manuscript version of the document, and, in the case of a manuscript or a rare printed work, the ownership and location of the original.

Printed sources of three different classes will be distinguished: First, a contemporary pamphlet, which will be given its full title, place and date of publication, and the location of the copy the editors have used. Second, an essay or letter appearing originally in a *contemporary* publication, which will be introduced by the words "Printed in," followed by the title, date, and inclusive page numbers, if necessary, of the publication. Third, a document, the manuscript or contemporary printed version of which is now lost, but which was printed at a later date, will be identified by the words "Reprinted from," followed by the name of the work from which the editors have reproduced it. The distinction will be apparent from the following illustrations:

> Printed in *The Pennsylvania Gazette,* October 2, 1729.
> Reprinted from Duane, *Works,* VI, 3.

A manuscript's Source-Identification will consist of a term or symbol indicating the character of the manuscript version, followed by the name of the owner of the manuscript, as: Draft: Library of Congress. Since manuscripts belonging to individuals have a tendency to migrate, we will indicate the year in which each private owner gave permission to publish his manuscript, as: MS: Morris Duane, Philadelphia, 1957.

The editors have prepared a table listing and defining the various kinds of manuscript versions in descending order of authority. The terms and symbols used in this list are described below (p. xliv). When two or more manuscript versions survive, the Source-Identification will list them in descending order according to this table, the version first listed being that followed in this edition. Important differences between the versions will be indicated in annotation, but minor variations in phraseology, spelling, capitalization, and punctuation, not affecting sense, will be ignored.

3. An editorial *Headnote* will precede many documents in this edition; it will appear between the Source-Identification and the actual text. Such a headnote will be designed to supply the background of the composition of the document, its relation to events or other writings, and any other information or general commentary on the piece as a whole which may be useful to the reader.

4. The *Text* of the document will follow the Source-Identification, or Headnote, if any. The principles guiding the rendering of eighteenth-century manuscript and print into twentieth-century type are explained in the next section of this introduction.

5. *Footnotes* to the Heading, Source-Identification, Headnote, and Text, will appear on the pages to which they pertain. References to documents to be printed in later volumes will be by description and date.

The Papers of Benjamin Franklin will follow a middle course between exact reproduction of the eighteenth-century text and complete modernization.[9] The purpose is to preserve as faithfully as possible the form and spirit in which the authors composed their documents, and at the same time to reproduce their words in a manner intelligible to the present-day reader and within the normal range of modern typographical equipment and techniques. To state this purpose, however, is not in itself to make fully clear the exact procedures to be followed in every situation that may arise. While it is unnecessary to give here in full detail all the rules which the editors follow in the transcription of documents, the most important principles are summarized below.

Printed Material:

Franklin's writings printed in his own lifetime (whether under his own direction, as in the *Pennsylvania Gazette,* or that of another) are considered as having been edited once from an original manuscript. Such writings will be presented as originally printed with the following exceptions:

a. The place and date line will be uniformly set at the beginning of a letter, regardless of where it appears in the printed version.

b. Proper nouns, such as the names of persons and places, which were conventionally printed in italics in the eighteenth century, will be printed in roman type.

c. Prefaces to pamphlets or other publications and passages of substantial length in other pieces were often printed in italics for typographical reasons that were cogent in the eighteenth century but no longer seem persuasive. These also will appear in roman type. Italics will be preserved, however, for words or phrases of emphasis and in other special cases as, for example, in some instances of dialogue or conversation.

d. Single words originally printed in full capitals for emphasis or other similar reasons will usually be printed in small capitals in harmony with modern typographical taste.

9. For a discussion of principles which the editors have in general followed, see Oscar Handlin and others, *Harvard Guide to American History* (Cambridge, Mass., 1954), pp. 95–104.

e. The signature of a letter will be printed in capitals and small capitals.

f. Obvious typographical errors will be silently corrected.

Similar rules will apply to Franklin's writings or other materials which exist only in later printed versions (as in a nineteenth-century newspaper, or Sparks' edition of the *Works*). Except for obvious misreadings and typographical errors, no attempt will be made to reconstruct the original version.

In the case of a printed form with blanks filled in longhand, the words originally in type will be set in roman and the longhand insertions in italics with spaces before and after to suggest the blanks in the form.

Manuscript Material:

a. The *spelling* of all words, including proper names, will be retained as written. When spelling is so abnormal as to obscure the meaning of a word or phrase, the correct form will be added within brackets or in a footnote. Words ending in "-ed" which was not pronounced as a separate syllable (as, for example, "looked" or "joined") were sometimes written with an apostrophe instead of an "e" ("look'd," "join'd"). We shall use either the letter or the apostrophe as we find the word written in the original. A similar rule will apply to words ending in "-ough," such as "though" and "through," which often appear as "tho'" and "thro'."

b. *Capitalization.* Franklin himself was a life-long advocate of the use of initial capitals for all substantives, as he explained in a long letter to Noah Webster, December 29, 1789, and the editors, obedient to his views, will follow his practice in printing his manuscripts. We shall likewise retain all other capitalization as written, except that we shall begin every sentence with a capital letter. Some eighteenth-century writers, however, were so erratic and the size of their initial letters often varied so much in the same manuscript, that it is sometimes uncertain whether the writer meant to use a capital or a small letter, especially with such letters as "C" and "P." In these circumstances we shall render doubtful initial letters as like letters are in the same manuscript or, such a guide failing, employ modern usage.

xli

Words underlined once in a manuscript will be printed in italics; words underlined twice or spelled out in large capitals will be printed in small capitals.

c. *Punctuation* will be retained as in the original with the following exceptions:

1. Every sentence will end with a period unless it is not clear where a sentence ends, in which case the original punctuation will be retained.

2. A dash used in place of a period, comma, or semicolon will be replaced by the appropriate mark of punctuation. If a sentence ends with both a period and a dash, the dash will be omitted.

3. Commas scattered meaninglessly through a sentence will be silently omitted.

4. When the nature of a mark of punctuation is not clear in the manuscript, or it could be read as either of two or more possible marks, that one will be used which corresponds most closely to modern usage.

5. A few documents, including some of a legal nature, almost entirely lack punctuation. This will be supplied but the fact will be indicated in the annotation.

d. *Contractions and abbreviations* will in general be expanded unless the form is retained in modern usage. Superscript letters will be lowered and the word expanded. The thorn will always be printed as "th." The tilde will be replaced by the letter or letters it represents. The ampersand will be written "and" except in the form "&c.," in the names of companies, and in a few other special cases such as the printing of financial accounts. The tailed "p" will be expanded to "per," "pre," or "pro" as the occasion may require. We shall retain abbreviations still in current usage, as, for example, in the days of the week or names of the months or in titles, such as "Fri.," "Dec.," "Mr.," and shall likewise retain contractions of proper names such as "Geo. Washington," "Benj. Rush," "Jno. Dickinson," and "Fr. Dana." The reason for this last is that, while "Geo." and "Benj." stand only for "George" and "Benjamin," "Jno." is used for "John" and sometimes also for "Jonathan," while "Fr." may mean either "Francis" or "Frederick." When weights, measures, and monetary values are spelled out, the form will be retained, but when any of a variety of symbols appears, the modern form will be substituted. Thus, "25 *li.*," "25 *l.*" and "*£25*" will uniformly be printed as "*£25.*"

e. *Omissions, mutilations, and illegible words* will be treated as follows:

1. Blanks in a manuscript which the author obviously intended to fill but did not will be left as blanks. If such a blank is of substantial length the fact will be indicated in a footnote.

2. When a word or words must be omitted because of mutilation or illegibility the omission will be indicated by an explanatory word or phrase in brackets, as: [*illegible*] or [*remainder missing*].

3. Missing or illegible digits will be indicated by suspension points in brackets, the number of points corresponding to the estimated number of digits omitted, thus: "*£25*[..]," or "12[...]6 dollars."

In all cases, however, the editors will attempt to supply omitted letters, words, and digits conjecturally, observing the following rules:

1. If not more than four letters are missing and there is no question what the word is, the missing letters will be supplied silently. Thus "George Washingt[ ]," "ind[ ]dence," "my[ ]ster Mecom" will be rendered "George Washington," "independence," "my sister Mecom."

2. If more than four letters, or one or more whole words, are missing because of the author's inadvertence or the mutilation or fading of the manuscript, the omission will be supplied by conjecture in brackets. Uncertainty as to conjecture will be indicated by a question mark within the brackets.

f. *Author's additions or corrections* will be treated as follows:

1. Interlineations will be brought down and inserted in the text as indicated, without notation. The same will be done with very brief additions placed in the margin instead of between the lines.

2. Marginal additions of substantial length, such as whole sentences or paragraphs, will be brought into the text and indicated by the words "in the margin" italicized and in brackets.

3. Ordinarily, words or groups of words struck through, as in the draft of a letter, will be omitted without notation, un-

less the correction appears to be significant as an indication of a substantial change in the author's thought in the process of composition; in the latter case deleted words will be indicated in a footnote. In the case of an important document, such as the draft of a treaty, the deleted passage will be put in the text enclosed in angle brackets *before* the words substituted.

4. Variant readings of several manuscript versions of a document, as for example between a draft letter and the communication actually sent, or occasionally between the manuscript and one of the principal printed editions of Franklin's writings, will not be noted unless the differences appear to be of substantial importance, when they will be indicated in footnotes.

g. *Editorial insertions, corrections, or descriptive interpolations* in the text will be italicized and placed within brackets unless they are of such length as to require presentation in a footnote. Any obvious slip of the pen, as, for example, "the Proposal of the the Minister," will be corrected silently.

h. *The form of a letter* will be preserved with the following exceptions:

1. The place and date will always be placed at the top.

2. The complimentary close will be set continuously with the text, regardless of how it was written.

3. The signature, set in capitals and small capitals, will be placed at the right of the last line of the text or complimentary close if there is room; if not, then on the line below.

4. The address and endorsement (or docketing), if any, will be labeled as such and printed immediately below and to the left of the signature.

NOTE ON VERSIONS OF MANUSCRIPTS

The following table lists and defines the terms used in this edition to describe the kinds of manuscripts available for publication and indicates the order of priority the editors will observe in determining which of two or more available versions to follow in printing a text.

A. *Autograph Versions*

1. ALS (*Autograph letter signed*)

ADS (*Autograph document signed*). A letter or document in the handwriting of the author or one of the joint authors, signed by him or them and sent or intended to be sent to the addressee or, if a document, made public.

2. LS (*Letter signed*)

DS (*Document signed*). The same as group 1 above except that the body of the letter or document is in the handwriting of another person, often a clerk.

3. AL (*Autograph letter, not signed*)

AD (*Autograph document, not signed*). A letter or document in the handwriting of the author or one of the joint authors but not including his or their signatures (e.g., a note written in the third person; a bill introduced into a legislative body).

4. MS, MSS (*Manuscript, manuscripts*). Other manuscript materials of highest priority not belonging to any of the above groups, such as a diary or journal, account book, or poem. When appropriate, descriptive words will be added to the designation "MS" (e.g., "MS Journal," "MS Ledger").

Note: The above four groups enjoy equal priority.

5. *Duplicate.* A letter or document textually the same as its counterpart in group 1, 2, 3, or 4, but a separate paper transmitted at the same or a later time by different conveyance, usually to offset possible loss of the original.

6. *Presscopy.* A contemporary reproduction of a letter or document made by the letterpress method on very thin dampened paper impressed onto the original to transfer some of the ink and to be read through the back. First used by BF about 1780. Sometimes badly blurred; may omit last-minute changes in the original.

7. *Printed form.* A printed document, usually governmental, legal, or financial in nature, with blanks to be filled in and places for dates and signatures. Three varieties are distinguished:

    a. Printed form, blanks unfilled

    b. Printed form, with MS insertions in blanks

    c. Printed form, with MS additions (or revisions).

B. *Later Image Reproductions*

1. *Photograph, photostat.* A reproduction of a letter or document made by photographic process, including microphotography. Also including, for convenience, some other modern direct copying processes

not strictly photographic. A valid substitute for any version in Class A when there is assurance that it reproduces the original completely, without tampering and without loss of legibility through unskillful technique, disappearance of marginal words, or the like.[1]

2. *Facsimile.* An exact (or purportedly exact) copy of a manuscript or printed page or portion thereof, imitating the form and character of the original handwriting or printing, and reproduced by engraving, lithography, line cut, or some similar process of printing. Susceptibility to manipulation in reproduction reduces the priority of a facsimile.

C. *Other Contemporary Versions*

1. *Draft.* A version of a letter or document which the author has made in the process of composition. It is normally in the author's own handwriting and has usually been amended by cancellations, erasures, and additions. It may or may not be signed.

2. *Letterbook copy.* A version of a letter or document copied into a book kept by the author, the addressee, or a third party for the purpose of maintaining a file of correspondence or other papers. Letterbook copies often omit or abbreviate full date line, salutation, complimentary close, and signature, or any of these. Last-minute changes in the original are often also omitted.

3. *Retained copy.* A version of a letter or document retained by the author in his own files as a record, but on a separate sheet or sheets, not copied into a letterbook. Often a draft served as the author's retained copy.

4. *Copy.* This term denotes, when used without qualifying word or words, a version of a letter or document made by or at the order of the author, the addressee, or some other person directly concerned with the business at hand, at the time or reasonably soon thereafter; usually intended to provide some person or body (such as a joint author, an official superior, or an interested friend) with the text of the letter or document. A *copy* is to be distinguished from a *transcript;* see below, D.1.

5. *Translation.* A copy of a letter or document translated into some other language than that in which the original was written. Possible defects in translation may reduce the accuracy of the version; on the other hand, its importance may be enhanced if, as often happens in diplomatic correspondence, the translation was the version the addressee actually read and acted upon.

---

1. In some instances photographic techniques can make legible words which cannot be deciphered in the original; hence a photograph may supplement, if not replace, the original for the purpose of establishing a text.

D. *Later Versions*

1. *Transcript.* A version of a letter or document made at a substantially later date than that on which it was first written or received, and usually by or at the order of a person *not* directly involved in the business concerned (e.g., by a clerk in some later central repository or archive, or by an editor for publication). A *transcript* is differentiated from a *copy*, first by its time of making, and second by the person responsible for its making. Capitalization, punctuation, and spelling are often modernized in a transcript. A typewritten copy of an eighteenth-century document is obviously a transcript.

2. *Extract.* A copy or transcript (as the case may be) of a portion of a letter or document. Extracts may vary in scope from quoted single sentences, or even parts of sentences, to long passages embodying the heart of the original piece.

3. *Abstract.* A summary of the contents, or of a portion, of a letter or other document. The least satisfactory of all versions; occasionally the only one surviving.

Genealogy

This genealogy is selective, concentrating on those relatives of Benjamin Franklin with whom he was most closely associated or who appear in his papers. It includes his ancestors in the direct male lines of the Franklin and Folger families back to the earliest known progenitor of each; his uncles and aunts; his brothers and sisters; his descendants to and including his great-grandchildren; most, but not all, of his nephews, nieces, and first cousins; all other relatives whose correspondence with Franklin is included in this edition or who are mentioned in it; and a few other individuals who are listed in order to make clear the lines of descent and connection of other persons included in the genealogy. Several other relatives, some of them contemporary with Benjamin, are excluded because they do not figure in his papers. For convenience the genealogy is divided into four sections, for all of which there are both charts and tables. The sections are:

A. The English Franklins and their descendants, excluding descendants of Josiah Franklin, Benjamin's father.
B. The Folger family.
C. Descendants of Josiah Franklin, excluding those of Benjamin.
D. Benjamin Franklin's descendants.

A system of letter and numeral symbols has been devised to make clear the identity and descent of each individual named. The progenitor in each section is designated simply by the letter of that section. Each child of the progenitor has a numeral added to the letter, corresponding to that individual's order among his known brothers and sisters. Each child in a subsequent generation has a symbol corresponding to that of his parent, to which is added a further numeral indicating his or her order among brothers and sisters. The letter and numerals of each symbol are separated by periods; the number of such numerals in any symbol equals the number of generations that individual is removed from the progenitor of the section concerned. Thus on Chart A and Table A, Josiah Franklin (A.5.2.9) was the ninth child of Thomas Franklin

(A.5.2), who was the second child of Henry Franklyn (A.5), who was the fifth child of Thomas Francklyne (A), the progenitor. Josiah Franklin, therefore, was three generations removed from Thomas Francklyne, his great-grandfather. Persons in any section with the same number of numerals in their symbols belong to the same generation.

Each section is subdivided into subordinate units separated by ruled lines. Within each unit the generations are shown by successive indentations. The first unit of each section carries the family only to the point at which it is important to list all children of a particular father. Their symbols, names, and dates appear in a column under the father's entry. The full entries for each of the children and his or her descendants, when they are dealt with, occupy one of the succeeding units, which is separated by ruled lines from the units that precede and follow.

In the tables the exact relation to Benjamin Franklin of each person given a symbol is indicated in italics within parentheses following his or her name. In the charts all persons belonging to the same generation appear within the same horizontal broken lines and the relationship of such persons to Benjamin Franklin is indicated in the margin of the chart.

In some instances the sources and authorities used do not make clear whether the year in a date between January 1 and March 25 before 1752 is Old Style or New Style. When no clarifying information has been found elsewhere the year is repeated here as given.

A. THE ENGLISH FRANKLINS

See Chart A

A. THOMAS FRANCKLYNE (*great-great-grandfather of* BF), fl. 1563–73, of Ecton, Northamptonshire. Wife's name unknown. Issue included:

A.5 HENRY FRANKLYN (*great-grandfather of* BF), b. Ecton, May 26, 1573; d. Ecton, Oct. 23, 1631; husbandman, blacksmith. Married, Oct. 30, 1595, AGNES JOANES or JAMES, b. ——; d. Jan. 29, 1646. Issue included:

A.5.2 THOMAS FRANKLIN (*grandfather of* BF), b. Ecton, Oct. 8, 1598; d. Banbury, Mar. 21, 1682; farmer, blacksmith. Married (1) JANE WHITE, b. *c.* 1617; d. Oct. 30, 1662; (2) ELIZABETH —— (dates unknown). Issue by wife Jane:

1

A.5.2.1 Thomas Franklin (1637–1702).
A.5.2.2 Samuel Franklin (1641–64). No issue.
A.5.2.3 John Franklin (1643–91).
A.5.2.4 Joseph Franklin (1646–83).
A.5.2.5 A twin son "Name lost died young."[2]
A.5.2.6 A twin son "Name forgot died young."[2]
A.5.2.7 Benjamin Franklin (1650–1727).
A.5.2.8 Hannah Franklin (Morris) (1654–1712).
A.5.2.9 Josiah Franklin (1657–1745).

A.5.2.1 THOMAS FRANKLIN (*uncle of* BF), b. Ecton, Mar. 11, 1637; d. Ecton, Jan. 6, 1702; schoolteacher, tobacco merchant, scrivener. Married ELEANOR or HELEN ———, b. ———; d. Mar. 14, 1711. Issue:

A.5.2.1.1 MARY FRANKLIN (FISHER) (*first cousin of* BF), b. Ecton, Oct. 24, 1673; d. Dec. 25, 1758. Married RICHARD FISHER of Wellingborough, Northamptonshire, d. Dec. 12, 1758. Issue:

A.5.2.1.1.1 ELEANOR FISHER (*first cousin once removed of* BF), b. ———; d. *c.* 1728.

A.5.2.3 JOHN FRANKLIN (*uncle of* BF), b. Ecton, Feb. 20, 1643; d. Banbury, June 7, 1691; dyer. Married ANN JEFFS of Marston, Warwickshire. Issue included:

A.5.2.3.1 THOMAS FRANKLIN (*first cousin of* BF), b. Banbury, Sept. 15, 1683; d. Birmingham, *c.* 1752; dyer; lived at Lutterworth, Leicestershire. Wife's name unknown. Issue:

A.5.2.3.1.1 THOMAS FRANKLIN (*first cousin once removed of* BF), b. ———; living in 1791 "very old"; dyer of Lutterworth. Wife's name unknown. Visited BF in London in 1766 and later. Issue:

---

2. Authority for placing the unnamed twins at this point among the children of Thomas and Jane Franklin is found in the MS "Short Account" of the family written by the twins' brother Benjamin in 1717. After listing those who lived to adulthood, with their dates of birth, he wrote: "They had two sons more, Twins, born before benjam but tis tho't they dyed unbaptized because their names are not found in the church Register at Ecton where we were all born and brought up." BF, on the other hand, placed the unnamed sons between Samuel and John in the genealogical chart he prepared about 1758 (*PMHB*, XXIII, facing p. 2) but he gave no date for John's birth. If the elder Benjamin intended the date he gave for this event, "20 Feb. 1643," to be Old Style (i.e. 1644 New Style) the twins could easily have been born between Samuel and John, but if he meant 1643 New Style, the fifteen and a half months between these brothers would appear to allow too little time for both the twins and John, as BF indicated, unless all three were very premature.

A.5.2.3.1.1.1 SARAH FRANKLIN (PEARCE) (*first cousin twice removed of* BF), b. Lutterworth, *c.* 1753; d. Oct. 22, 1781. Resided with BF in London during parts of 1766–70. Married, 1773, JAMES PEARCE. Issue: 1 son, 3 daus.

A.5.2.3.3 ANNE FRANKLIN (FARROW) (*first cousin of* BF), b. *c.* 1686; d. *c.* 1771; lacemaker at Hartwell; kept school at Castlethorpe, near Stony Stratford, Bucks. Married HENRY FARROW, d. before 1759. Issue:

A.5.2.3.3.1 HANNAH FARROW (WALKER) (*first cousin once removed of* BF), b. July 21, 1724; d. ———. Married THOMAS WALKER. Lived in Westbury, Northamptonshire. Helped financially by BF. Issue:

A.5.2.3.3.1.1 JOHN WALKER, b. Mar. 4, 1755 (*first cousin twice removed of* BF).

A.5.2.3.3.1.2 HENRY WALKER, b. Nov. 29, 1756 (*first cousin twice removed of* BF).

A.5.2.3.5 JANE FRANKLIN (PAGE) (*first cousin of* BF), b. ———; d. *c.* 1757. Married ROBERT PAGE, whom BF visited at or near Ecton, 1758, securing family letters, etc.

A.5.2.4 JOSEPH FRANKLIN (*uncle of* BF), b. Ecton, Oct. 10, 1646; d. Nov 30, 1683; carpenter. Married SARAH SAWYER. Issue: 1 son.

A.5.2.7 BENJAMIN FRANKLIN (THE ELDER or "UNCLE BENJAMIN") (*uncle of* BF), b. Ecton, Mar. 20, 1650;[3] d. Boston, Mar. 17, 1727; dyer in Ecton and London; removed to Boston, landing Oct. 10, 1715. Married, Nov. 23, 1683, HANNAH WELLES of Banbury, d. Westminster, Nov. 4, 1705. Issue: 6 sons, 4 daus., all dying young except:

A.5.2.7.1 SAMUEL FRANKLIN (*first cousin of* BF), b. Oct. 15, 1684; d. ———; cutler; removed to Boston before his father. Married (1) Aug. 13, 1719, HANNAH KELLINECK; married (2) ———. Issue by wife Hannah:

A.5.2.7.1.1 SAMUEL FRANKLIN, JR. (*first cousin once removed of* BF), b. Boston, Oct. 21, 1721; d. Boston, Feb. 21, 1775; cutler. Married (1) May 12, 1748, SARAH BEAUDRI, without issue; married (2) Jan. 22, 1756, EUNICE GREENLEAF. Issue by wife Eunice: 4 daus.

3. Benjamin Franklin the Elder gives the date thus himself in his MS "Short Account." His epitaph in the Granary Burial Ground in Boston, however, reads "Aged 76 years Decd. March the 17 1727." *New-Eng. Hist. Gen. Reg.*, IV (1850), 170. If this is correct, he must have been born in 1650 Old Style, or 1651 New Style.

A.5.2.7.6 ELIZABETH FRANKLIN (*first cousin once removed of* BF), b. Southwark, Oct. 27, 1694; d. —— (living in 1717).

A.5.2.8 HANNAH FRANKLIN (MORRIS) (*aunt of* BF), b. Ecton, Oct. 29, 1654; d. Ecton, June 24, 1712. Married JOHN MORRIS of Ecton, d. June 17, 1695; dyer. Issue:

    A.5.2.8.1 ELEANOR MORRIS (*first cousin of* BF).
    A.5.2.8.2 JANE MORRIS (*first cousin of* BF).
    A.5.2.8.3 HANNAH MORRIS (*first cousin of* BF).

A.5.2.9 JOSIAH FRANKLIN (*father of* BF), b. Ecton, Dec. 23, 1657; d. Boston, Jan. 16, 1745. *See* Table C.

B. THE FOLGER FAMILY

See Chart B

B. JOHN FOULGIER (*great-grandfather of* BF), b. Norwich, Norfolk, *c.* 1593; d. Martha's Vineyard, autumn, 1660; probably the son of Flemish refugees. Migrated to New England on ship *Abigail*, landing at Boston, Oct. 6, 1635. Lived in Dedham and Watertown; moved to Martha's Vineyard, *c.* 1648. Married MERIBAH (MERIBLE) GIBBS, d. *c.* 1664. Issue included:

    B.1 PETER FOLGER or FOULGER (*grandfather of* BF), b. Norwich, 1617; d. Nantucket, 1690. Trained as a weaver; migrated to Boston with parents, 1635; lived in Dedham and Watertown; helped to settle Martha's Vineyard, *c.* 1642; schoolmaster; removed to Portsmouth, R.I., 1662; removed to Nantucket, autumn, 1664; miller, public official. Married, *c.* 1642, MARY MORRILS (MORRILL), former bond servant of Rev. Hugh Peter, d. Nantucket, 1704. Issue:

        B.1.1 Joanna Folger (Coleman) (*c.* 1643–1719).
        B.1.2 Bethia Folger (Barnard) (?–1669).
        B.1.3 Dorcas Folger (Pratt).
        B.1.4 Eleazer Folger (1648–1716).
        B.1.5 Bathsheba Folger (Pope).
        B.1.6 Patience Folger (Harker) (?–1717).
        B.1.7 John Folger (1659–1732).
        B.1.8 Experience Folger (Swain) (1661–1739).
        B.1.9 Abiah Folger (Franklin) (1667–1752).

B.1.1 JOANNA FOLGER (COLEMAN) (*aunt of* BF), b. Martha's Vineyard, *c.* 1643; d. Nantucket, July 18, 1719. Married, *c.* 1666, JOHN COLEMAN of Nantucket, d. 1715. Issue: 6 sons, 2 daus.

B.1.2 BETHIA FOLGER (BARNARD) (*aunt of* BF), b. Martha's Vineyard, ——;

d. Nantucket, Aug. 6, 1669. Married, Feb. 26, 1668, JOHN BARNARD of Nantucket, d. Nantucket, Aug. 6, 1669. Both drowned; no issue.

B.1.3 DORCAS FOLGER (PRATT) (*aunt of* BF), b. Martha's Vineyard, dates of birth and death uncertain. Married, Feb. 12, 1674/5, JOSEPH PRATT of Charlestown, d. Dec. 24, 1712. Issue: 4 sons, 5 daus.

B.1.4 ELEAZER FOLGER (*uncle of* BF), b. Martha's Vineyard, 1648; d. Boston, 1716; shoemaker, blacksmith. Married, 1671, SARAH GARDNER. Issue: 5 sons, 2 daus. including:

B.1.4.1 ELEAZER FOLGER, JR. (*first cousin of* BF), b. Nantucket, July 2, 1672; d. Nantucket, Feb. 25, 1753; farmer, schoolteacher. Married (1) Sept. 27, 1706, BETHIA GARDNER, b. Aug. 13, 1676; d. June 20, 1716; married (2) Sept. 25, 1717, MARY MARSHALL, d. Dec. 11, 1765. Issue by wife Bethia: 3 sons; by wife Mary: 4 sons, 6 daus.

B.1.4.2 PETER FOLGER (*first cousin of* BF), b. Nantucket, Aug. 28, 1674; d. Nantucket, 1707. Married JUDITH COFFIN. Issue included:

B.1.4.2.2 DANIEL FOLGER (*first cousin once removed of* BF), b. Nantucket, Feb. 13, 1701/2; d. Vineyard Sound, Dec. 30, 1744. Married, Aug. 31, 1721, his first cousin once removed ABIGAIL FOLGER (B.1.7.7, *first cousin of* BF; *see* p. lv), dau. of John Folger (B.1.7). Issue included:

B.1.4.2.2.2 KEZIAH FOLGER (COFFIN) (through father: *first cousin twice removed of* BF; through mother: *first cousin once removed*), b. Nantucket, Dec. 9, 1723; d. Nantucket, Mar. 29, 1798. Married, Dec. 4, 1740, JOHN COFFIN, d. July 18, 1788. She was accused as Tory informer during Revolution; was the subject of J. C. Hart's novel, *Miriam Coffin.*

B.1.4.6 NATHAN FOLGER (*first cousin of* BF), b. Nantucket, 1678; d. Nantucket, Nov. 2, 1747; blacksmith, innkeeper, farmer. Married, Dec. 29, 1699, SARAH CHURCH, d. Apr. 13, 1745. Issue included:

B.1.4.6.1 ABISHA FOLGER (*first cousin once removed of* BF), b. Nantucket, Sept. 27, 1700; d. Jan. 22, 1788. Married (1) Nov. 6, 1727, SARAH MAHEW, d. July 13, 1734; married (2) Oct. 30, 1735, DINAH COFFIN (STARBUCK), d. Sept. 1, 1793. Issue by wife Sarah included:

B.1.4.6.1.3 TIMOTHY FOLGER (*first cousin twice removed of* BF), b. Nantucket, 1732; d. Milford Haven, Wales, Feb. 1814; ship's captain; BF's informant on Gulf Stream; Tory suspect during Revolution. Married, Dec. 6, 1753, ABIAH COLEMAN.

Issue by wife Dinah included:

B.1.4.6.1.7 JOHN FOLGER (*first cousin twice removed of* BF), b.

Nantucket, 1745 or 1746; d. in West Indies, 1780. Probably the Capt. John Folger involved, 1777, in Hynson's theft of BF's dispatches; but see also B.1.7.1.2. Unmarried.

B.1.5 BATHSHEBA or BETHSHUA FOLGER (POPE) (*aunt of* BF), b. Martha's Vineyard, ——; d. Danvers, ——. Married, *c.* 1676, JOSEPH POPE of Salem, d. 1712. Lived in Danvers. Issue: 5 sons, 3 daus., of whom the eldest dau. BATHSHEBA POPE was one of the "afflicted children" of the Salem witchcraft episode.

B.1.6 PATIENCE FOLGER (HARKER) (*aunt of* BF), b. Martha's Vineyard, ——; d. 1717. Married EBENEZER HARKER, and had issue: 1 son, 2 daus.

B.1.7 JOHN FOLGER (*uncle of* BF), b. Martha's Vineyard, 1659; d. Nantucket, Oct. 23, 1732; miller, farmer. Married MARY BARNARD, b. *c.* 1667; d. Oct. 1737. Issue: 6 sons, 3 daus., including:

B.1.7.1 JETHRO FOLGER (*first cousin of* BF), b. Nantucket, Oct. 17, 1689; d. Nantucket, Apr. 19, 1772. Married, Feb. 1, 1710/11, MARY STARBUCK, d. July 22, 1763. Issue: 4 sons, 4 daus., including:

B.1.7.1.2 JOHN FOLGER (*first cousin once removed of* BF), b. Nantucket, Mar. 28, 1714 or 1715; d. "abroad" ——. Married, Dec. 13, 1733, REBECCA BAKER of Barnstable, d. Aug. 1, 1746. Possibly the Capt. John Folger involved, 1777, in Hynson's theft of BF's dispatches; but see also B.1.4.6.1.9.

B.1.7.3 NATHANIEL FOLGER (*first cousin of* BF), b. Nantucket, Feb. 18, 1694/5; d. Apr. 15, 1774. Married, Nov. 18, 1718, PRISCILLA CHASE of Tisbury, d. Dec. 30, 1753. Issue: 1 son, 3 daus.

B.1.7.4 JONATHAN FOLGER (*first cousin of* BF), b. Nantucket, Apr. 10, 1696; d. Mar. 6, 1777; blacksmith. Married (1) Mar. 6, 1716/7, MARGARET GARDNER, d. July 17, 1727, issue: 2 sons, 2 daus.; married (2) Aug. 29, 1728, DEBORAH PADDOCK (BUNKER), d. June 27, 1750, without issue; married (3) Feb. 24, 1752, SUSAN GOREHAM (PADDOCK), d. July 13, 1777, without issue.

B.1.7.5 RICHARD FOLGER (*first cousin of* BF), b. Nantucket, July 14, 1698; d. Sept. 15, 1782; carpenter. Married, Oct. 11, 1722, SARAH PEASE, d. June 10, 1783. Issue: 4 sons, 4 daus.

B.1.7.6 SHUBAEL FOLGER (*first cousin of* BF), b. Nantucket, Oct. 25, 1700; d. Aug. 21, 1776. Married, Feb. 10, 1720/1, JERUSHA CLARK, d. Aug. 18, 1778. Issue: 3 sons, 4 daus.

B.1.7.7 ABIGAIL FOLGER (FOLGER, PINKHAM) (*first cousin of* BF), b. Nantucket, June 8, 1703; d. Nov. 21, 1787. Married (1) Aug. 31, 1721, her first cousin once removed DANIEL FOLGER (B.1.4.2.2, *first cousin once removed of* BF); married (2) Oct. 20, 1748, DANIEL PINKHAM.

lv

B.1.7.8 ZACCHEUS FOLGER (*first cousin of* BF), b. Nantucket, Aug. 14, 1706; d. July 20, 1779; whaling captain. Married, Nov. 20, 1728, ABIGAIL COFFIN, d. Aug. 1770. Issue: 6 sons, 3 daus.

B.1.8 EXPERIENCE FOLGER (SWAIN) (*aunt of* BF), b. Martha's Vineyard, *c.* 1661; d. Nantucket, Aug. 4 or Oct. 23, 1739. Married, *c.* 1687, JOHN SWAIN, JR., b. *c.* 1664; d. Jan. 29, 1738/9; farmer, whaler. Issue: 5 sons, 4 daus.

B.1.9 ABIAH FOLGER (FRANKLIN) (*mother of* BF), b. Nantucket, Aug. 15, 1667; d. Boston, May 8, 1752. Married, Nov. 25, 1689, JOSIAH FRANKLIN. *See* Table C.

C. DESCENDANTS OF JOSIAH FRANKLIN

See Charts C(a) and C(b)

C. JOSIAH FRANKLIN (*father of* BF), b. Ecton, Dec. 23, 1657; d. Boston, Jan. 16, 1745; learned silk-dyer's trade as apprentice of brother John (A.5.2.1) in Banbury; migrated to Boston, 1683; became tallow-chandler and soapmaker. Married (1) ANN(E) CHILD, b. Ecton, ——; d. Boston, July 9, 1689; dau. of Robert Child of Ecton; married (2) Nov. 25, 1689, ABIAH FOLGER (B.1.9) (*mother of* BF), b. Nantucket, Aug. 15, 1667; d. Boston, May 8, 1752; dau. of Peter Folger (B.1). Issue by wife Ann(e):

C.1 Elizabeth Franklin (Berry, Douse) (1678–1759).
C.2 Samuel Franklin (1681–1720).
C.3 Hannah Franklin (Eddy, Cole) (1683–1723).
C.4 Josiah Franklin (1685–c. 1715).
C.5 Anne Franklin (Harris) (1687–1729).
C.6 Joseph Franklin I (Feb. 6–11, 1688).
C.7 Joseph Franklin II (June 30–July 15, 1689).
Issue by wife Abiah:
C.8 John Franklin (1690–1756).
C.9 Peter Franklin (1692–1766).
C.10 Mary Franklin (Homes) (1694–1731).
C.11 James Franklin (1697–1735).
C.12 Sarah Franklin (Davenport) (1699–1731).
C.13 Ebenezer Franklin (Sept. 20, 1701–Feb. 5, 1703).[4]
C.14 Thomas Franklin (Dec. 7, 1703–Aug. 17, 1706).
C.15 BENJAMIN FRANKLIN (1706–90).
C.16 Lydia Franklin (Scott) (1708–58).

---

4. "Ebenezer Franklin of the South Church, a male-Infant of 16 months old, was drown'd in a Tub of Suds, Feb. 5, 1702/3." *Diary of Samuel Sewall* (5 Mass. Hist. Soc. *Colls.*, VI, 73).

C.17 Jane Franklin (Mecom) (1712–94).

C.1 ELIZABETH FRANKLIN (BERRY, DOUSE) (*half-sister of* BF), b. Ecton, Mar. 2, 1678; d. Aug. 25, 1759. Married (1) Jan. 8, 1707, JOSEPH BERRY, shipmaster; married (2) Mar. 19, 1721, RICHARD DOUSE. No issue.

C.2 SAMUEL FRANKLIN (*half-brother of* BF), b. Banbury, May 16, 1681; d. Mar. 30, 1720; blacksmith. Married, May 16, 1705, ELIZABETH TYNG. Issue:

    C.2.1 ELIZABETH FRANKLIN (COMPTON) (*niece of* BF), b. ——; d. July, 1773. Married, Sept. 22, 1732, WILLIAM COMPTON, b. ——; d. Aug. 1786. Lived in Providence, R.I. Issue: 1 son, 5 daus.

C.3 HANNAH FRANKLIN (EDDY, COLE) (*half-sister of* BF), b. Banbury, May 25, 1683; d. Apr. 3, 1723. Married (1) JOSEPH EDDY; married (2) June 22, 1710, THOMAS COLE. No issue.

C.4 JOSIAH FRANKLIN (*half-brother of* BF), b. Boston, Aug. 23, 1685; d. *c.* 1715. Went to sea, returned after nine years, shipped again and was lost. No issue.

C.5 ANN(E) FRANKLIN (HARRIS) (*half-sister of* BF), b. Boston, Jan. 5, 1687; d. Ipswich, June 16, 1729. Married, July 10, 1712, WILLIAM HARRIS, of Ipswich. Issue: 2 sons, 5 daus. including:

    C.5.2 ANNE HARRIS (FULLER) (*niece of* BF), b. Boston, Dec. 29, 1714; d. ——. Married, *c.* Oct. 1734, JACOB FULLER. Moved to Connecticut, *c.* 1743. Issue: 11 sons, 2 daus. including:

        C.5.2.5 JOSEPH FULLER (*grand-nephew of* BF), b. Lisbon, Conn., May 3, 1746; d. Providence, R.I., May 3, 1822. Married (1) PRISCILLA ——, b. *c.* 1741; d. Providence, Apr. 7, 1815; married (2) June 19, 1817, ANNE WALKER. No issue.

    C.5.3 GRACE HARRIS (WILLIAMS) (*niece of* BF), b. Aug. 3, 1718; d. Mar. 1790. Married, Mar. 23, 1746, JONATHAN WILLIAMS, SR.,[5] Boston merchant, b. June 19, 1719; d. Philadelphia, Sept. 17, 1796. Issue: 7 sons, 3 daus. including:

---

5. Jonathan Williams, Sr. (1719–1796) had a brother John Williams, inspector general of customs, or special agent to the Commissioners of Customs in Boston, sometimes called John Williams "the inspector." He in turn had a son named Jonathan, who visited his cousin Jonathan Jr. (C.5.3.2) in France in 1779 and died in 1780. Since Jonathan Sr. also had a son named John (C.5.3.5), the simultaneous existence in this Williams family of three Jonathans and two Johns has sometimes caused confusion among indexers and cataloguers.

C.5.3.1 JOSIAH WILLIAMS (*grand-nephew of* BF), b. Boston, Dec. 31, 1747; d. Boston, Aug. 1772. Went to London in 1770 with brother Jonathan (C.5.3.2) and uncle John Williams, "the inspector" (see note 5); studied music there, and returned to Boston, spring 1772. Unmarried.

C.5.3.2 JONATHAN WILLIAMS, JR. (*grand-nephew of* BF), b. Boston, May 15, 1750; d. Philadelphia, May 16, 1815. U.S. commercial agent in France, 1776; merchant in Nantes to 1785; returned to U.S. with BF; merchant in Philadelphia; superintendent of U.S. Military Academy, West Point, 1801–03; army engineer. Married, Sept. 12, 1779, MARIANNE ALEXANDER, b. Aug. 24, 1764; d. 1845. Issue, mother unknown ("a milliner"):

> C.5.3.2.1 JOSIAH WILLIAMS (*great-grand-nephew of* BF), b. 1776 or 1777.

Issue by wife Marianne:

> C.5.3.2.2 CHRISTINE WILLIAMS (BIDDLE) (*great-grand-niece of* BF).
>
> C.5.3.2.3 HENRY JONATHAN WILLIAMS (*great-grand-nephew of* BF).
>
> C.5.3.2.4 ALEXANDER JOHN WILLIAMS (*great-grand-nephew of* BF), killed at Fort Erie, 1814.

C.5.3.5 JOHN WILLIAMS (*grand-nephew of* BF), b. Boston, Apr. 3, 1756; d. ——; merchant. Married, 1778, HANNAH CHANDLER.

C.5.7 MARTHA HARRIS (JOHNSON) (*niece of* BF), b. 1729; d. ——. Married —— JOHNSON, d. by 1769. She lived in London; with her children visited BF at Craven St. Issue:

> C.5.7.1 SAMUEL ("SAMMY") JOHNSON (*grand-nephew of* BF), d. *c.* 1783.
>
> C.5.7.2 ANNE (NANCY) JOHNSON (CLARKE) (*grand-niece of* BF), b. ——; d. 1805. Married Capt. PETER CLARKE, R.N., d. *c.* 1777. Lived in Barbados and England.

C.8 JOHN FRANKLIN (*brother of* BF), b. Boston, Dec. 7, 1690; d. Boston, Jan. 20, 1756; tallow-chandler; soapmaker; deputy postmaster of Boston. Married (1) MARY GOOCH; married (2) ELIZABETH GOOCH (HUBBART or HUBBARD). Issue by wife Mary:

C.8.1 JOHN FRANKLIN (*nephew of* BF), b. June 17, 1716. Lost at sea. No issue by wife Elizabeth, but she had issue by her first husband, John Hubbart or Hubbard, 4 sons, 3 daus. including:

THOMAS HUBBART (*step-nephew of* BF) (1717–96). Married, 1747, Judith Ray, sister of BF's friend Catharine Ray (Greene).

TUTHILL HUBBART (*step-nephew of* BF) (1720–1808?). Appointed postmaster of Boston, 1756, to succeed his stepfather.

ELIZABETH HUBBART (PARTRIDGE) (*step-niece of* BF) (1728–1814). Married, Dec. 13, 1768, Capt. Samuel Partridge, shopkeeper, superintendent of Boston Alms House.

C.9   PETER FRANKLIN (*brother of* BF), b. Boston, Nov. 22, 1692; d. Philadelphia, July 1, 1766; merchant and shipmaster, Newport; appointed deputy postmaster, Philadelphia, 1763 or 1764. Married, Sept. 2, 1714, MARY HARMAN. Issue uncertain, but she writes, Aug. 21, 1747, to Deborah F. mentioning "Our Sarah," the latter's husband, unnamed, and two unnamed sons of Sarah, then aged two years and five months respectively.

C.10   MARY FRANKLIN (HOMES or HOLMES) (*sister of* BF), b. Boston, Sept. 26, 1694; d. 1731. Married, Apr. 3, 1716, ROBERT HOMES or HOLMES, d. at sea before 1743, a ship captain in coastwise trade. Issue:

   C.10.1   WILLIAM HOMES (*nephew of* BF), b. Jan. 10, 1716/7; d. July 17, 1785; gold and silversmith of Boston. Married, Apr. 24, 1740, REBECCA DAWES. Issue: 2 sons, 3 daus. including:

      C.10.1.2   WILLIAM HOMES, JR. (*grand-nephew of* BF), b. Boston, May 7, 1742; d. ——; gold and silversmith of Boston. Jane Mecom's son John was apprenticed to him. Married, Nov. 1, 1764, ELIZABETH WHITWELL. Issue: 2 sons, 1 dau.

   C.10.2   ABIAH HOMES (*niece of* BF), b. Dec. 14, 1718; d. Aug. 3, 1729.

   C.10.3   ROBERT HOMES (*nephew of* BF), b. 1720; d. before 1744.

C.11   JAMES FRANKLIN (*brother of* BF), b. Boston, Feb. 4, 1696/7; d. Newport, Feb. 4, 1735; printer, to whom BF was apprenticed. Moved to Newport, 1726. Married, Feb. 4, 1723, ANN SMITH, d. Apr. 19, 1763. Issue (exact order uncertain):

   C.11.1   ABIAH FRANKLIN (BUCKMASTER) (*niece of* BF), b. *c.* 1726; d. Newport, Oct. 15, 1754. Married, July 17, 1743, GEORGE BUCKMASTER.

   C.11.2   ANN FRANKLIN (*niece of* BF), b. *c.* 1728; d. Nov. 2, 1730.

   C.11.3   SARAH(?) FRANKLIN (HALL), (*niece of* BF), b. Newport, ——; d. ——. Married SAMUEL HALL, b. Nov. 2, 1740; d. Oct. 30, 1807; printer. He became partner of his mother-in-law after death of James Franklin (C.11.4); continued Newport business until 1768, then moved to Salem and continued printing and newspaper business there and in Boston.

   C.11.4   JAMES FRANKLIN, JR. (*nephew of* BF), b. Newport, *c.* 1730–32; d. Newport, Apr. 21, 1762; printer; apprenticed to BF in Philadelphia, 1740; returned to Newport to join mother in family business, 1748. Probably unmarried.

   C.11.5   MARY FRANKLIN (ALLEN) (*niece of* BF), b. Newport, ——; d. ——. Married, Jan. 23, 1752, WILLIAM ALLEN. Issue included:

C.11.5.1 ISAAC ALLEN (*grand-nephew of* BF), captured by British in 1781 or 1782.

C.11.6 ELIZABETH FRANKLIN (ALL) (*niece of* BF), b. Newport, ——; d. ——. Married, Mar. 19, 1761, ISAAC ALL, ship captain.

C.12 SARAH FRANKLIN (DAVENPORT) (*sister of* BF), b. Boston, July 9, 1699; d. May 23, 1731. Married, May 23, 1722, JAMES DAVENPORT (the second of his 3 wives), baker, tavernkeeper, of Boston. Issue:

C.12.1 ELIZABETH DAVENPORT (INGERSOLL) (*niece of* BF), b. 1723; d. ——. Married, Oct. 12, 1749, Col. JOSEPH INGERSOLL, d. *c.* 1789, tavernkeeper of Boston; removed to Falmouth, Me. Issue:

C.12.1.1 ELIZABETH INGERSOLL (JARVIS) (*grand-niece of* BF), b. ——; d. ——. Married —— JARVIS.

C.12.1.2 SARAH INGERSOLL (FABIAN) (*grand-niece of* BF), b. ——; d. ——. Married, before 1773, Capt. LEWIS FABIAN, R.N. Issue: at least 1 son.

C.12.2 DORCAS DAVENPORT (STICKNEY) (*niece of* BF), b. Aug. 26, 1724; d. Chester, N.H., Aug. 1774. Married, May 7, 1747, ANTHONY STICKNEY, b. 1727; d. Oct. 1774; chairmaker of Newbury. Moved to New Hampshire by 1772. Issue: 3 sons, 3 daus. including:

C.12.2.1 ANTHONY SOMERSBY STICKNEY (*grand-nephew of* BF), b. Newburyport, Mar. 2, 1747/8; d. Chester, Jan. 25, 1819. Married, Mar. 6, 1770, RUTH BROWN COFFIN. Issue: 1 son, 3 daus. including:

C.12.2.1.2 BENJAMIN FRANKLIN STICKNEY (*great-grand-nephew of* BF), b. Newburyport, Apr. 1, 1775; d. Toledo, O., Jan. 7, 1852; Indian agent; commanded left wing under Andrew Jackson at New Orleans. Married (1) Aug. 7, 1802, MARY STARK, d. 1828; married (2), 1835, MARY MATILDA WAY. Issue: 2 sons, 3 daus.

C.12.3 MARY DAVENPORT (ROGERS) (*niece of* BF), b. Mar. 9, 1725/6; d. ——. Married, Mar. 13, 1745/6, JOHN ROGERS. Issue: 3 sons, 2 daus. including:

C.12.3.2 JOHN ROGERS, JR. (*grand-nephew of* BF), b. Jan. 8, 1748; d. ——. Married, according to Jane Mecom, "in England a reputable young Lady with a Prity Litle Fourtin."

C.12.4 JOSIAH [FRANKLIN] DAVENPORT (*nephew of* BF), b. Dec. 18, 1727; d. ——. Married (1) Boston, June 29, 1749, SARAH BILLINGS, d. Apr. 1, 1751; married (2) Philadelphia, Dec. 13, 1751, ANN ANNIS. Set up as baker in Philadelphia, 1750; storekeeper in Pittsburgh, 1764; later settled in New Jersey. Added "Franklin" to his name. Issue by wife Sarah: one child, died with its mother. Issue by wife Ann: 2 sons, 2 daus. including:

C.12.4.4 FRANKLIN DAVENPORT (*grand-nephew of* BF), b. Sept. 1755; d. July 27, 1832; lawyer, military officer, U.S. Senator, 1798–99; U.S. Representative, 1799. Married, May 18, 1804, SARAH BARTON ZANTZINGER.

C.12.5 ABIAH DAVENPORT (GRIFFITH) (*niece of* BF), b. Oct. 2, 1729; d. ——. Married, June 29, 1751, JOHN GRIFFITH of Portsmouth. Issue: 1 child.

C.15 BENJAMIN FRANKLIN. *See* Table D.

C.16 LYDIA FRANKLIN (SCOTT) (*sister of* BF), b. Boston, Aug. 8, 1708; d. 1758. Married, 1731, ROBERT SCOTT, a sea captain. Issue: 1 dau. No further facts known.

C.17 JANE FRANKLIN (MECOM) (*sister of* BF), b. Boston, Mar. 27, 1712; d. Boston, May —, 1794. Married, July 27, 1727, EDWARD MECOM, saddler of Boston, b. Dec. 15, 1704; d. Boston, Sept. 11, 1765. Issue:

C.17.1 JOSIAH MECOM I (*nephew of* BF), b. June 4, 1729; d. May 18, 1730.

C.17.2 EDWARD MECOM (*nephew of* BF), b. Mar. 29, 1731; d. Dec. 7, 1758; saddlemaker. Married, July 22, 1755, RUTH WHITTEMORE. Issue: one or more children who died in infancy.

C.17.3 BENJAMIN MECOM (*nephew of* BF), b. Boston, Dec. 29, 1732; d. *c.* 1776; printer in Antigua, Boston, New York, New Haven, Philadelphia. Went insane; disappeared after battle of Trenton, Dec. 26, 1776. Married, *c.* 1757, ELIZABETH ROSS. Issue: 1 son, 4 daus., 1 unknown, including:

C.17.3.4 JANE MECOM (KINSMAN) (*grand-niece of* BF), b. Boston, *c.* 1765; d. after 1859. Lived for some years with grandmother Mecom. Married, Feb. 13, 1800, SIMEON KINSMAN, shipmaster.

C.17.4 EBENEZER MECOM (*nephew of* BF), b. Boston, May 2, 1735; d. Jan. 18, 1762; baker; lived at Gloucester. Unmarried.

C.17.5 SARAH MECOM (FLAGG) (*niece of* BF), b. June 28, 1737; d. June 12, 1764. Married, Mar. 18, 1756, WILLIAM FLAGG, d. Boston, June, 1775, laborer. Issue: 1 son, 3 daus. including:

C.17.5.1 JANE FLAGG (GREENE) (*grand-niece of* BF), b. *c.* 1757; d. Apr. 6, 1782. Married, Dec. 5, 1775, ELIHU GREENE of Potowomut, R.I.; miller, ironworker; bro. of Gen. Nathaniel Greene, cousin of William Greene. Issue: 1 son, 3 daus.

C.17.5.3 JOSIAH FLAGG (*grand-nephew of* BF), b. Nov. 12, 1760; d. Feb. 11, 1840; shoemaker; lamed as a child; clerked for BF, 1786. Moved to Lancaster, Mass. Married, June 7, 1789, DOLLY THURSTON. Issue: 3 sons, 3 daus.

C.17.6　PETER FRANKLIN MECOM (*nephew of* BF), b. May 13, 1739; d. before Feb. 14, 1779; soapmaker; apprenticed to uncle John Franklin (C.8). Became insane; BF assisted in maintenance. Unmarried.

C.17.7　JOHN MECOM (*nephew of* BF), b. Boston, Mar. 31, 1741; d. New Jersey, Sept. 30, 1770; goldsmith. Married, New Brunswick, N.J., Sept. 11, 1765, CATHERINE OUKE or OAKEY, who married (2) Thomas Turner, a British army officer. No issue.

C.17.8　JOSIAH MECOM II (*nephew of* BF), b. Boston, Mar. 26, 1743; d. 1775; saddler, whaler; served in Mass. regt. 1775. Unmarried.

C.17.9　JANE MECOM (COLLAS) (*niece of* BF), b. Boston, Apr. 12, 1745; d. 1802. Married, Mar. 23, 1773, PETER COLLAS, shipmaster. No issue.

C.17.10　JAMES MECOM (*nephew of* BF), b. Boston, July 31, 1746; d. Boston, Nov. 30, 1746.

C.17.11　MARY (POLLY) MECOM (*niece of* BF), b. Boston, Feb. 29, 1748; d. Nantucket, Sept. 19, 1767, at house of her relative Keziah Folger Coffin (B.1.4.2.2.2).

C.17.12　ABIAH MECOM (*niece of* BF), b. Boston, Aug. 1, 1751; d. Boston, Apr. 23, 1752.

D. DESCENDANTS OF BENJAMIN FRANKLIN

See Chart D

D.　BENJAMIN FRANKLIN (C.15), b. Boston, Jan. 6/17, 1705/6; d. Philadelphia, Apr. 17, 1790. Took to wife, Philadelphia, Sept. 1, 1730, DEBORAH READ (ROGERS), b. Philadelphia, 1708; d. Philadelphia, Dec. 19, 1774; dau. of JOHN READ, b. 1677; d. Sept. 2, 1724; and SARAH READ, d. Philadelphia, Dec. 7, 1761. Issue, mother unknown:
D.1　William Franklin (*c.* 1731–1813).
Issue by wife Deborah:
D.2　Francis Folger Franklin (1732–36).
D.3　Sarah Franklin (Bache) (1743–1808).

D.1　WILLIAM FRANKLIN (*son of* BF), b. *c.* 1731; d. London, Nov. 16, 1813; governor of New Jersey; loyalist; settled in London, 1782. Married (1) London, Sept. 4, 1762, ELIZABETH DOWNES, b. West Indies, ——; d. New Jersey, July 28, 1777, without issue; married (2) London, Aug. 14, 1788, MARY D'EVELIN, d. Aug. 3, 1811, without issue. Issue, mother unknown:
D.1.1　WILLIAM TEMPLE FRANKLIN (*grandson of* BF), b. London? Feb. 22, 1762;[6] d. Paris, May 25, 1823; served as BF's secretary in France, 1776–85; edited BF's writings. Married, Paris, May 6, 1823, HANNAH

---

6. Date given on his tombstone in Père Lachaise Cemetery, Paris.

or ANNA COLLYER of Barkham, Berkshire, Eng.,[7] b. ——; d. Paris, Dec. 12, 1846, without issue. Issue by "Blanchette" Caillot:

    D.1.1.1 A son, name unknown (*great-grandson of* BF), b. Paris, c. 1785.

Issue by Ellen Johnson D'Evelin:

    D.1.1.2 ELLEN FRANKLIN (HANBURY)[8] (*great-granddaughter of* BF), bapt. St. James Church, London, May 15, 1798; d. ——. Married, June 8, 1818, CAPEL HANBURY of the Royal Scots.

D.2 FRANCIS FOLGER FRANKLIN (*son of* BF), b. Philadelphia, Oct. 20, 1732; d. Philadelphia, Nov. 21, 1736, of smallpox.

D.3 SARAH (SALLY) FRANKLIN (BACHE) (*daughter of* BF), b. Philadelphia, Sept. 11, 1743; d. Philadelphia, Oct. 5, 1808. Married, Philadelphia, Oct. 29, 1767, RICHARD BACHE, merchant, b. Settle, Yorkshire, Feb. 23 or Sept. 12, 1737; d. Philadelphia, July 29, 1811, son of William and Mary Bache. Issue:

    D.3.1 BENJAMIN FRANKLIN BACHE (*grandson of* BF), b. Philadelphia, Aug. 12, 1769; d. Philadelphia, Sept. 10, 1798. Accompanied BF to France, 1776–85; publisher, 1790–98, of Philadelphia *General Advertiser*, later called the *Aurora*. Died in yellow-fever epidemic. Married, Nov. 17, 1791, MARGARET HARTMAN MARKOE, b. Nov. 7, 1770; d. May 28, 1836. She married (2) as his second wife, William Duane, b. New York, May 17, 1760; d. Philadelphia, Nov. 24, 1835, who became second editor of *Aurora;* first American editor of BF's writings. Issue of B. F. Bache and wife Margaret:

        D.3.1.1 FRANKLIN BACHE (*great-grandson of* BF) (1792–1864). *Had issue.*

        D.3.1.2 RICHARD BACHE 3D (*great-grandson of* BF) (1794–1836).

        D.3.1.3 BENJAMIN BACHE (*great-grandson of* BF) (1796–1853).

        D.3.1.4 HARTMAN BACHE (*great-grandson of* BF) (1798–1872). *Had issue.*

    D.3.2 WILLIAM BACHE (*grandson of* BF), b. Philadelphia, May 31, 1773; d. Aug. 5, 1820? Married, Nov. 28, 1797, CATHARINE WISTAR, b. Jan. 29, 1770; d. Nov. 20, 1820. Issue:

7. Mentioned in his will of 1814 as "my dear friend and companion Hannah Collyer or Anna Collyer of Berkshire England, (who has resided with me for several years and gone by my name)." The codicil of his will gives the date of marriage. Nat. Arch., Recs. of U. S. Consulate, Paris, Register D, pp. 380–6, esp. pp. 381, 383.

8. Parentage and baptism stated in William Temple Franklin's will. William Franklin appears to have raised Ellen Franklin as his own. William Franklin to Jonathan Williams, Jr., July 24, 1807, MS, Indiana Univ. Lib.

D.3.2.1 SARAH BACHE (HODGE) (*great-granddaughter of* BF) (1798–1849). *Had issue.*

D.3.2.2 BENJAMIN FRANKLIN BACHE (*great-grandson of* BF) (1801–81). *Had issue.*

D.3.2.3 EMMA MARY BACHE (*great-granddaughter of* BF) (1803–13).

D.3.2.4 CATHARINE WISTAR BACHE (*great-granddaughter of* BF) (1805–86).

D.3.3 SARAH BACHE (*granddaughter of* BF), b. Philadelphia, Dec. 1, 1775; d. Philadelphia, Aug. 17, 1776.

D.3.4 ELIZABETH or ELIZA FRANKLIN BACHE (HARWOOD) (*granddaughter of* BF), b. Philadelphia, Sept. 10, 1777; d. Jan. 13, 1820. Married, Jan. 9, 1800, JOHN EDMUND HARWOOD, b. 1770; d. Sept. 21, 1809. Issue:

D.3.4.1 BENJAMIN FRANKLIN HARWOOD (*great-grandson of* BF) (1801–02).

D.3.4.2 ANDREW ALLEN HARWOOD (*great-grandson of* BF) (1802–84). *Had issue.*

D.3.4.3 ELIZABETH HARWOOD (*great-granddaughter of* BF).

D.3.4.4 MARY HARWOOD (*great-granddaughter of* BF) (1806–15).

D.3.5 LOUIS BACHE (*grandson of* BF), b. Philadelphia, Oct. 7, 1779; d. Oct. 4, 1819. Married (1) Mar. 26, 1807, MARY ANN SWIFT, d. 1812 or 1813; married (2) Apr. 11, 1816, ESTHER EGEE, b. Sept. 7, 1801. Issue by wife Mary Ann:

D.3.5.1 ELIZABETH BACHE (BURNETT) (*great-granddaughter of* BF) (1807–37).

D.3.5.2 THEOPHYLACT BACHE I (*great-grandson of* BF) (1809–16).

D.3.5.3 WILLIAM BACHE (*great-grandson of* BF) (1811–97). *Had issue.*

Issue by wife Esther:

D.3.5.4 THEOPHYLACT BACHE II (*great-grandson of* BF) (1817–75). *Had issue.*

D.3.6 DEBORAH BACHE (DUANE) (*granddaughter of* BF), b. Philadelphia, Oct. 1, 1781; d. Feb. 12, 1863. Married, Dec. 31, 1805, WILLIAM JOHN DUANE, lawyer, Sec. of U.S. Treasury, b. Clonmel, Ireland, May 9, 1780; d. Philadelphia, Sept. 26, 1865, son of William Duane (*see under* Benjamin Franklin Bache, D.3.1) by his first wife. Issue:

D.3.6.1 WILLIAM DUANE (*great-grandson of* BF) (1808–82). *Had issue.*

D.3.6.2 SARAH FRANKLIN DUANE (*great-granddaughter of* BF) (1810–50).

D.3.6.3 MARY DUANE (WILLIAMS) (*great-granddaughter of* BF) (1812–45). *Had issue.*

D.3.6.4 CATHERINE DUANE (*great-granddaughter of* BF) (1814–36).

D.3.6.5 ELLEN DUANE (SATTERTHWAITE) (*great-granddaughter of* BF) (1816–46). *Had issue.*

D.3.6.6 FRANKLIN BACHE DUANE (*great-grandson of* BF) (1819–20).

D.3.6.7 ELIZABETH DUANE (GILLESPIE) (*great-granddaughter of* BF) (1821–1901). *Had issue.*

D.3.6.8 RICHARD BACHE DUANE (*great-grandson of* BF) (1823–75). *Had issue.*

D.3.6.9 BENJAMIN FRANKLIN DUANE (*great-grandson of* BF) (1827–93). *Had issue.*

D.3.7 RICHARD BACHE, JR. (*grandson of* BF), b. Philadelphia, Mar. 11, 1784; d. Mar. 17, 1848. Married, Apr. 4, 1805, SOPHIA BURRELL DALLAS, b. 1785; d. July 8, 1860. Issue:

D.3.7.1 ALEXANDER DALLAS BACHE (*great-grandson of* BF) (1806–67).

D.3.7.2 MARY BLECHYNDEN BACHE (WALKER) (*great-granddaughter of* BF) (1808–73). *Had issue.*

D.3.7.3 GEORGE MIFFLIN BACHE (*great-grandson of* BF) (1811–46). *Had issue.*

D.3.7.4 RICHARD BACHE 4TH (*great-grandson of* BF).

D.3.7.5 SOPHIA ARABELLA BACHE (IRWIN) (*great-granddaughter of* BF) (1816–1904). *Had issue.*

D.3.7.6 MATILDA WILKINS BACHE (EMORY) (*great-granddaughter of* BF) (1819–?). *Had issue.*

D.3.7.7 HENRIETTA CONSTANTIA BACHE (ABERT) (*great-granddaughter of* BF) (1822–87). *Had issue.*

D.3.7.8 SARAH FRANKLIN BACHE (WAINWRIGHT) (*great-granddaughter of* BF) (1824–?). *Had issue.*

D.3.7.9 MARIA BACHE (MCLANE) (*great-granddaughter of* BF).

D.3.8 SARAH BACHE (SERGEANT) (*granddaughter of* BF), b. Philadelphia, Sept. 12, 1788; d. Oct. 6, 1863. Married, Sept. 14, 1812, THOMAS SERGEANT, b. Jan. 14, 1782; d. May 5, 1860. Issue:

D.3.8.1 HENRY JONATHAN SERGEANT (*great-grandson of* BF) (1815–58).

D.3.8.2 FRANCES SERGEANT (PERRY) (*great-granddaughter of* BF) (1817–1903). *Had issue.*

D.3.8.3 THOMAS SERGEANT, JR. (*great-grandson of* BF) (1819–78).

D.3.8.4 WILLIAM SERGEANT (*great-grandson of* BF) (1821–23).

NOTE ON SOURCES

The data in this genealogy have been derived from a great variety of sources and authorities. Benjamin Franklin the Elder wrote

"A short account of the Family of Thomas Franklin of Ecton in Northamptonshire, 21 June 1717" (MS, Yale Univ. Lib.), which supplies much of the information for Table A. BF himself became much interested in his English ancestry, corresponded with relatives and local clergymen, visited Ecton and Banbury, and compiled a genealogical chart. John W. Jordan has brought together the papers resulting from this investigation in "Franklin as a Genealogist," *PMHB*, XXIII (1899), 1–22. Among official or semi-official local records, the following have been most useful: Boston Record Commissioners' *Reports: Boston Births, 1700-1800,* and *Boston Marriages, 1700-1751* and *1752-1809; Vital Records of Nantucket, Mass. to 1850* (5 vols., 1925–28); *Vital Record of Rhode Island,* vols. VIII, XIII, XIV, and XX. Such contemporary publications as the *Gentleman's Magazine* occasionally contain notices of marriages and deaths not otherwise conveniently accessible.

Several MS genealogies of the Folger family are deposited in the Nantucket Historical Society and the Nantucket Atheneum; one has been printed in *New-England Historical and Genealogical Register,* XVI (1862), 269–78. Other volumes of the *Register* provide scattered information on branches of the Franklin family. Printed genealogies of Franklin-related families have been useful, notably those of Chandler, Fuller, Gooch, Greene, Harris, Hubbard, Pope, Pratt, Stickney, and Williams. Franklin's descendants are extensively traced in a MS genealogical table compiled in 1926 by Franklin Bache and now in the possession of Miss Emily Bache of Philadelphia; in *The Descendants and Some of the Forebears of Hon. William John Duane of Philadelphia 1780-1865 . . . and of His Wife Deborah Bache Duane 1781-1863 . . .* compiled by Richard B. Duane, 2nd, December 1951 (privately printed); and in Frank Willing Leach, "Descendants of the Signers of the Declaration of Independence," MS in Collections of the Genealogical Society of Pennsylvania.

Various authors and editors include genealogical information in text or notes of their publications, especially Jared Sparks, *Works,* I, 539-46; Carl Van Doren, *The Letters of Benjamin Franklin and Jane Mecom* (1950); the same author's *Jane Mecom: Franklin's Favorite Sister* (1950); and C. E. Banks, *History of Martha's Vineyard* (3 vols., 1911-25). Many letters and other documents to be printed in this edition of *The Papers of Benjamin Franklin* contain information not found in any genealogical compilation.

Genealogical Charts

CHART A. THE ENGLISH FRANKLINS

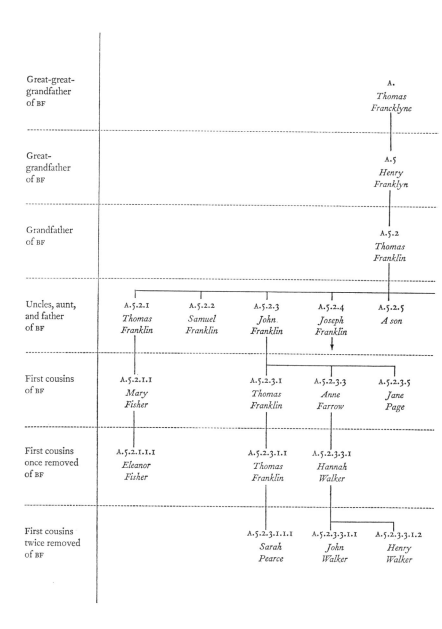

Great-great-grandfather of BF					A. *Thomas Francklyne*
Great-grandfather of BF					A.5 *Henry Franklyn*
Grandfather of BF					A.5.2 *Thomas Franklin*
Uncles, aunt, and father of BF	A.5.2.1 *Thomas Franklin*	A.5.2.2 *Samuel Franklin*	A.5.2.3 *John Franklin*	A.5.2.4 *Joseph Franklin*	A.5.2.5 *A son*
First cousins of BF	A.5.2.1.1 *Mary Fisher*		A.5.2.3.1 *Thomas Franklin*	A.5.2.3.3 *Anne Farrow*	A.5.2.3.5 *Jane Page*
First cousins once removed of BF	A.5.2.1.1.1 *Eleanor Fisher*		A.5.2.3.1.1 *Thomas Franklin*	A.5.2.3.3.1 *Hannah Walker*	
First cousins twice removed of BF			A.5.2.3.1.1.1 *Sarah Pearce*	A.5.2.3.3.1.1 *John Walker*	A.5.2.3.3.1.2 *Henry Walker*

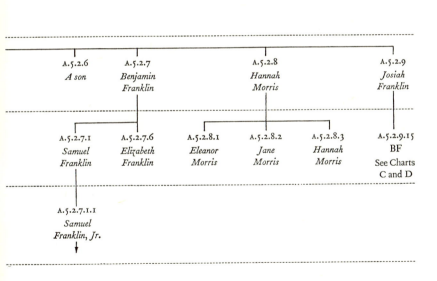

A.5.2.6
A son

A.5.2.7
*Benjamin
Franklin*

A.5.2.8
*Hannah
Morris*

A.5.2.9
*Josiah
Franklin*

A.5.2.7.1
*Samuel
Franklin*

A.5.2.7.6
*Elizabeth
Franklin*

A.5.2.8.1
*Eleanor
Morris*

A.5.2.8.2
*Jane
Morris*

A.5.2.8.3
*Hannah
Morris*

A.5.2.9.15
BF
See Charts
C and D

A.5.2.7.1.1
*Samuel
Franklin, Jr.*

CHART B. THE FOLGER FAMILY

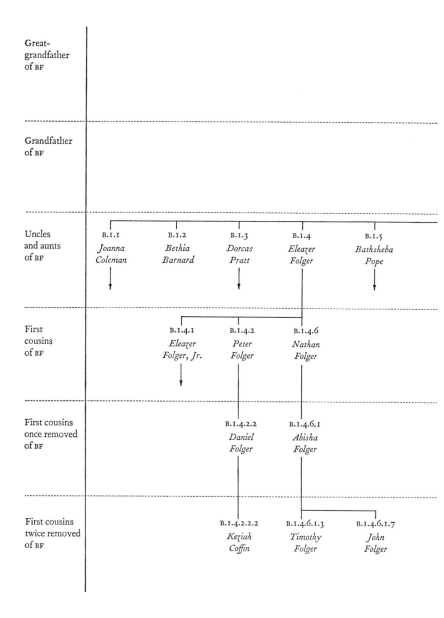

Great-
grandfather
of BF

Grandfather
of BF

Uncles
and aunts
of BF

B.I.1	B.I.2	B.I.3	B.I.4	B.I.5
Joanna *Coleman*	*Bethia* *Barnard*	*Dorcas* *Pratt*	*Eleazer* *Folger*	*Bathsheba* *Pope*

First
cousins
of BF

B.I.4.1	B.I.4.2	B.I.4.6
Eleazer *Folger, Jr.*	*Peter* *Folger*	*Nathan* *Folger*

First cousins
once removed
of BF

B.I.4.2.2	B.I.4.6.1
Daniel *Folger*	*Abisha* *Folger*

First cousins
twice removed
of BF

B.I.4.2.2.2	B.I.4.6.1.3	B.I.4.6.1.7
Keziah *Coffin*	*Timothy* *Folger*	*John* *Folger*

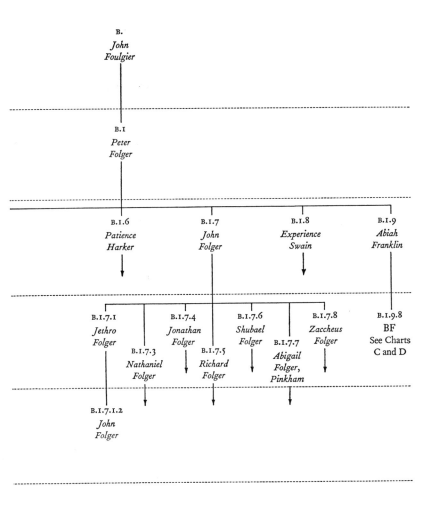

B.
John
Foulgier

B.1
Peter
Folger

B.1.6
Patience
Harker

B.1.7
John
Folger

B.1.8
Experience
Swain

B.1.9
Abiah
Franklin

B.1.7.1
Jethro
Folger

B.1.7.3
Nathaniel
Folger

B.1.7.4
Jonathan
Folger

B.1.7.5
Richard
Folger

B.1.7.6
Shubael
Folger

B.1.7.7
Abigail
Folger,
Pinkham

B.1.7.8
Zaccheus
Folger

B.1.9.8
BF
See Charts
C and D

B.1.7.1.2
John
Folger

CHART C(a). DESCENDANTS OF JOSIAH FRANKLIN (*First Marriage*)

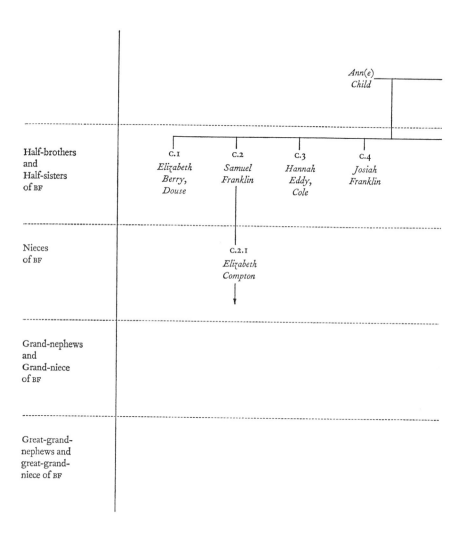

				Ann(e) *Child*

Half-brothers and Half-sisters of BF

C.1	C.2	C.3	C.4
Elizabeth Berry, Douse	*Samuel Franklin*	*Hannah Eddy, Cole*	*Josiah Franklin*

Nieces of BF

C.2.1
 Elizabeth Compton

Grand-nephews and Grand-niece of BF

Great-grand-nephews and great-grand-niece of BF

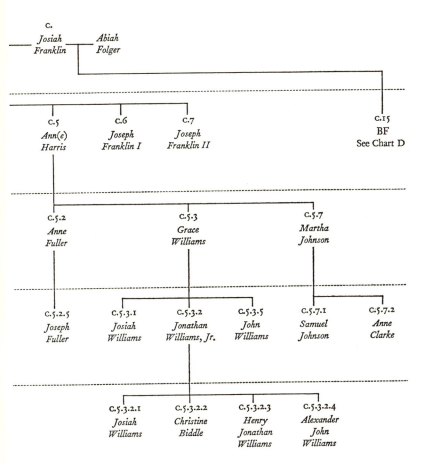

CHART C(b). DESCENDANTS OF JOSIAH FRANKLIN (*Second Marriage*)

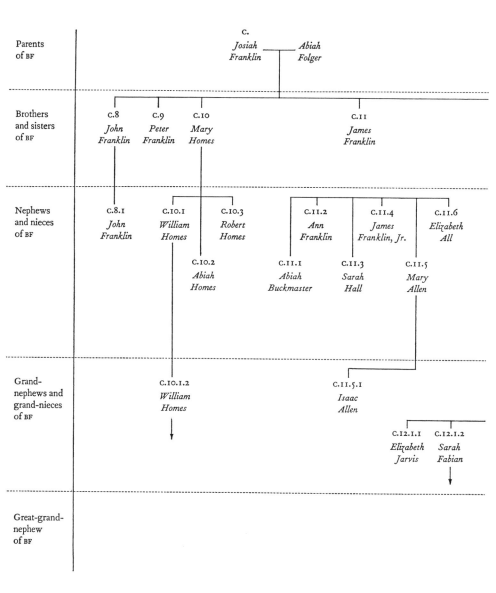

Parents of BF

C.
Josiah Franklin —— *Abiah Folger*

Brothers and sisters of BF

C.8
John Franklin

C.9
Peter Franklin

C.10
Mary Homes

C.11
James Franklin

Nephews and nieces of BF

C.8.1
John Franklin

C.10.1
William Homes

C.10.3
Robert Homes

C.11.2
Ann Franklin

C.11.4
James Franklin, Jr.

C.11.6
Elizabeth All

C.10.2
Abiah Homes

C.11.1
Abiah Buckmaster

C.11.3
Sarah Hall

C.11.5
Mary Allen

Grand-nephews and grand-nieces of BF

C.10.1.2
William Homes

C.11.5.1
Isaac Allen

C.12.1.1
Elizabeth Jarvis

C.12.1.2
Sarah Fabian

Great-grand-nephew of BF

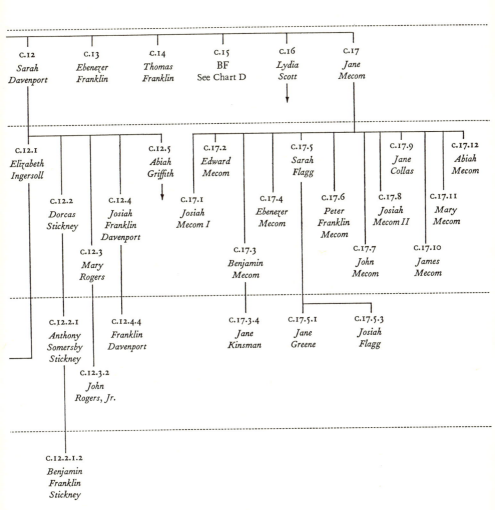

C.12
*Sarah
Davenport*

C.13
*Ebenezer
Franklin*

C.14
*Thomas
Franklin*

C.15
BF
See Chart D

C.16
*Lydia
Scott*

C.17
*Jane
Mecom*

C.12.1
*Elizabeth
Ingersoll*

C.12.2
*Dorcas
Stickney*

C.12.3
*Mary
Rogers*

C.12.4
*Josiah
Franklin
Davenport*

C.12.5
*Abiah
Griffith*

C.17.1
*Josiah
Mecom I*

C.17.2
*Edward
Mecom*

C.17.3
*Benjamin
Mecom*

C.17.4
*Ebenezer
Mecom*

C.17.5
*Sarah
Flagg*

C.17.6
*Peter
Franklin
Mecom*

C.17.7
*John
Mecom*

C.17.8
*Josiah
Mecom II*

C.17.9
*Jane
Collas*

C.17.10
*James
Mecom*

C.17.11
*Mary
Mecom*

C.17.12
*Abiah
Mecom*

C.12.2.1
*Anthony
Somersby
Stickney*

C.12.3.2
*John
Rogers, Jr.*

C.12.4.4
*Franklin
Davenport*

C.17.3.4
*Jane
Kinsman*

C.17.5.1
*Jane
Greene*

C.17.5.3
*Josiah
Flagg*

C.12.2.1.2
*Benjamin
Franklin
Stickney*

lxxv

CHART D. DESCENDANTS OF BENJAMIN FRANKLIN

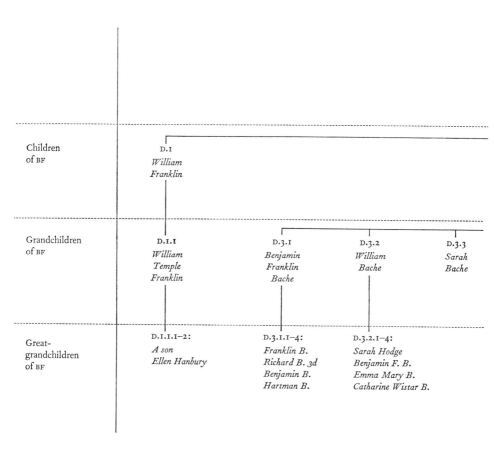

Children
of BF

D.1
*William
Franklin*

Grandchildren
of BF

D.1.1
*William
Temple
Franklin*

D.3.1
*Benjamin
Franklin
Bache*

D.3.2
*William
Bache*

D.3.3
*Sarah
Bache*

Great-
grandchildren
of BF

D.1.1.1–2:
*A son
Ellen Hanbury*

D.3.1.1–4:
*Franklin B.
Richard B. 3d
Benjamin B.
Hartman B.*

D.3.2.1–4:
*Sarah Hodge
Benjamin F. B.
Emma Mary B.
Catharine Wistar B.*

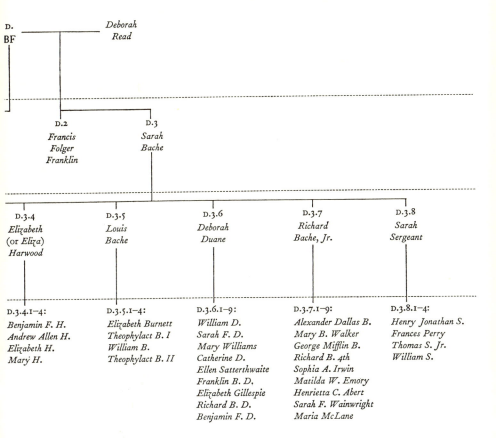

Editorial Staff

Assembling, organizing, and preparing for publication the materials for this edition has been the work of many hands. In addition to the editors named on the title page the following men and women have assisted in the work for longer or shorter periods since the opening of the editorial office in the spring of 1954, on a full- or part-time basis, in New Haven, Philadelphia, or elsewhere. To each of them the editors extend their grateful thanks.

Marie Bertha Achenbach
Jeanne Gould Bloom
Ruth Blumenfeld
Elizabeth Davies Booher
Marianna L. Carlson
Judith S. Chernaik
Jacqueline Short Corning
Maxine S. Davis
Abel Doysié
Mary A. Felton
Jonathan P. Fineman
Jonathan W. Fleming

Esther A. Freeman
Herbert Freeman
Armida Prati Hastings
Robert S. Hewett
Virginia Q. Hutchison
R. Tenney Johnson
Philip Kerr
L. Jesse Lemisch
Polly A. Lewis
Nancy Webb Lincoln
Edward Lindeman
Claude A. Lopez

Ursula McHugh
Phyllis Harris Mitchell
Yvonne Noble
James D. O'Connor
John B. Riggs
Allene M. Roche
David A. Ross
Dorris H. Skinner
Andrée Tafoya
Jack R. Wahlquist
Patricia Weed
Diana C. Woodruff

Editors' Acknowledgments

Hundreds of persons have made this edition possible, some in the course of their regular duties, others by making special efforts, but all cheerfully and willingly. Many of these colleagues we do not know personally, but only as correspondents or through the often laborious bibliographical and photographic work they have done on our behalf. Though we cannot name them all, we are grateful to each for his or her contribution.

We appreciate particularly the support and encouragement *The Papers of Benjamin Franklin* has received from the presidents of the two sponsoring institutions: the late Owen J. Roberts and

William J. Robbins of the American Philosophical Society, and A. Whitney Griswold of Yale University. The members of the Administrative Board, Editorial Advisory Committee, and Cooperating Committee have uniformly given us their support, direction, or counsel. Their names appear elsewhere in this volume. Former members of the editorial staff have made a contribution to this work that can neither be measured nor described; their names too are listed on another page.

The edition was begun with the confident assumption that institutions and private persons owning Franklin papers would make them available. That assumption has been justified in a way that has given an unexpected dividend of pleasure to all concerned in the work. On a separate page in each volume we shall record our acknowledgment to the owners of all documents printed in it.

Most of the editorial preparation is being done in the Yale University Library, where we have the extraordinary advantage of using every day the superb Franklin Collection which William Smith Mason assembled over many years and which he gave to the University in 1935. The library staffs at Yale and at the American Philosophical Society, where we have also worked extensively, have served and continue to serve our needs in countless ways, not only contributing to the accuracy and speed of our work, but adding pleasure and encouragement through their friendly interest. We would particularly mention:

In the Yale University Library: Matthew T. Blake, Miss Dorothy W. Bridgwater, Miss Ruth R. Brown, Mrs. Barbara Farrell, Archibald Hanna, Jr., Mrs. Marjorie K. Lewis, Einar Lindquist, Frederic G. Ludwig, Robert F. Metzdorf, John H. Ottemiller, Mrs. Margaret Shand, Roland W. West, Mrs. Eleanor D. Wheeler, and Miss Marjorie G. Wynne; and in the American Philosophical Society Library: Mrs. Ruth A. Duncan, Marvin Goldman, Mrs. Gertrude D. Hess, Murphy D. Smith, and Willman Spawn.

We have made frequent and often heavy calls upon the principal repositories of Franklin papers and some other agencies, and their directors and members of their staffs have responded generously to our requests for help. We have not always learned the names of those who have done most of the work for us, but we wish to express our particular thanks to the following:

Boston Public Library: John Alden, Zoltán Haraszti, and Miss Ellen M. Oldham; Columbia University Library: Roland Baughman; Harvard College

Library: William H. Bond and William A. Jackson; Haverford College Library: Thomas E. Drake and Miss Anna B. Hewitt; Historical Society of Pennsylvania: J. Harcourt Givens, Miss Catharine H. Miller, Howard T. Mitchell, Sarah A. G. Smith, and Nicholas B. Wainwright; Library Company of Philadelphia: Barney Chesnick and Edwin Wolf, 2nd; Library of Congress: Mrs. Dorothy S. Eaton, Donald C. Holmes, Robert H. Land, and Donald H. Mugridge; Massachusetts Historical Society: Stephen T. Riley; National Historical Publications Commission: Miss F. Helen Beach, Mrs. Anne Henry, and James R. Masterson; New-York Historical Society: Wayne Andrews and Wilmer R. Leech; New York Public Library: Robert W. Hill; Pennsylvania State Records Office: Henry H. Eddy and Henry J. Young; Pierpont Morgan Library: Herbert Cahoon; Princeton University Library: Alexander P. Clark and Howard C. Rice, Jr.; University of Pennsylvania Library: Thomas R. Adams (now at the John Carter Brown Library), Miss Alice R. Bruce, and Mrs. Neda M. Westlake; University of Virginia Library: Francis L. Berkeley, Jr., and Russell M. Smith.

Contributions of the most varied kinds have been made to this work by scores of others. They have directed or led us to manuscripts, patiently and informedly answered our questions, and acquainted us early with knotty problems we should try to solve; often they have gone to great personal inconvenience to supply our needs. Some individuals made available to us manuscripts which they then owned but which have since passed into other possession. With a deep sense of appreciation for their part in making this edition, we record these names:

Alfred Owen Aldridge, University of Maryland; David G. C. Allan, Royal Society of Arts; Rev. Charles A. Anderson, Presbyterian Historical Society; the late Miss Caroline D. Bache, Philadelphia; Miss Emily H. Bache, Philadelphia; the late Miss Evelin Bache, Bristol, R. I.; Miss Margaret M. Bache, Philadelphia; Jack C. Barnes, University of Maryland; Sir Gavin de Beer, British Museum (Natural History); Henri Bonnet, Paris; Mrs. Hendrik Booraem, St. Michael's, Md.; Julian P. Boyd, *The Papers of Thomas Jefferson;* Miss Frances M. Bradford, Philadelphia; James Sydney Bradford, Philadelphia; Miss Gertrude Brincklé, Historical Society of Delaware; Jasper Yeates Brinton, Cairo, Egypt; Rev. Kenneth W. Cameron, Trinity College, Hartford; Lester J. Cappon, Institute of Early American History and Culture; John H. Cary, Boston, Mass.; Harold E. Cassin, Great Neck, Long Island; Mrs. Ralph Catterall, Valentine Museum, Richmond, Va.; Miss W. D. Coats, National Register of Archives, London; A. J. Collins, British Museum; Thomas W. Copeland, University of Massachusetts; Mrs. George W. Corner, New York City; William S. Cornyn, Yale University; Harry A. Crispin, Salem, N.J.; Lewis P. Curtis, Yale University; Charles W. David, Longwood Foundation; Morris Duane, Philadelphia; A. Hunter Dupree, Gray Herbarium, Harvard University; Walter N. Eastburn, East Orange, N. J.;

J. Harold Easterby, South Carolina Archives Commission; Durand Echeverria, Brown University; Miss Rosana Eckman, Kane, Pa.; Leonard C. Faber, *The Adams Papers;* Bernard Faÿ, Fribourg, Switzerland; Robert H. Ferrell, Indiana University; Dr. Joseph E. Fields, Joliet, Ill.; Larry Fritz, Merion, Pa.; Mlle. F. Gaston-Chérau, Bibliothèque Nationale; Miss Florence M. Greim, Pennsylvania Hospital; Max R. Hall, Crestwood, N. Y.; Rt. Rev. Kenneth G. Hamilton, Archives of the Moravian Church; Thompson R. Harlow, Connecticut Historical Society; W. O. Hassell, Bodleian Library; John M. Hemphill, II, Southwestern College; Charles T. Henry, New York City; Miss Ruthanna Hindes, Historical Society of Delaware; Miss S. Madeline Hodge, Princeton, N. J.; Hajo Holborn, Yale University; George L. Howe, Washington, D. C.; the late Stuart W. Jackson, Gloucester, Va.; Henry James, Jr., Gloucester, England; Robert L. Kahn, University of Washington; Ralph L. Ketcham, *The Papers of James Madison;* David Kirschenbaum, New York City; Edward Connery Lathem, Dartmouth College Library; Kenneth A. S. Leslie, Edinburgh; Richard Maass, New York City; Richmond Maury, Richmond, Va.; William H. McCarthy, The Rosenbach Foundation; Samuel H. McVitty, Salem, Va.; C. William Miller, Temple University; E. H. Mueller, Milwaukee; John A. Munroe, University of Delaware; J. Bennett Nolan, Reading, Pa.; Amédée Outrey, Ministère des Affaires Étrangères; Antonio Pace, Syracuse University; William J. Paterson, Grand Lodge, F. and A. M., of Pennsylvania; Charles E. Peterson, National Park Service, Philadelphia; Henri Peyre, Yale University; T. Van C. Phillips, Collingswood, N. J.; the late Dr. Frank Lester Pleadwell, Honolulu; Richard R. Pleasants, Groton School; Edmund Quincy, Boston; Miss Doris M. Reed, Indiana University Library; J. Renoult, Bibliothèque Mazarine; Edward M. Riley, Colonial Williamsburg; Francis S. Ronalds, Morristown National Historical Park; Henry Schuman, New York City; Charles Coleman Sellers, Dickinson College; Miss Ellen Shaffer, The Free Library of Philadelphia; Fred Shelley, New Jersey Historical Society; Brooks Shepard, Jr., Yale University; Miss Miriam R. Small, Wells College; Robert A. Smith, Yale University; Miss Bertha Solis-Cohen, Philadelphia; Mrs. Rose Marie Stanley, Parke-Bernet Galleries; Miss Madeline E. Stanton, Yale University; Francis W. Steer, Sussex Record Office; Miss Miriam V. Studley, Newark Public Library; Arthur Swann, Parke-Bernet Galleries; Max Terrier, Compiègne, France; Frederick B. Tolles, Swarthmore College; Justin G. Turner, Los Angeles; Paul A. W. Wallace, Harrisburg; Peter Walne, Berkshire Record Office; Ralph L. Ward, Yale University; René Wellek, Yale University; A. S. Westwood, Assay Office, Birmingham; Melvin K. Whiteleather, Philadelphia; Edwin A. Willard, Washington; Mrs. Robert Williams, Jr., Paterson, N. J.; John A. Woods, London; Miss Mabel Zahn, Philadelphia.

Contributors to Volume 1

The ownership of each manuscript, or the location of the particular copy used by the editors of each contemporary pamphlet or similar printed work, is indicated where the document appears in the text. The sponsors and editors are deeply grateful to the following institutions and individuals for permission to print in the present volume manuscripts or other materials which they own:

Abbreviations and Short Titles

ADS	Autograph document signed. See p. xlv for definition.
ALS	Autograph letter signed. See p. xlv for definition.
APS	American Philosophical Society
BF	Benjamin Franklin
Bigelow, *Works*	John Bigelow, ed., *The Complete Works of Benjamin Franklin* . . . (10 vols., New York, 1887–88).
DAB	*Dictionary of American Biography*
DNB	*Dictionary of National Biography*
DS	Document signed. See p. xlv for definition.
Duane, *Works*	William Duane, ed., *The Works of Dr. Benjamin Franklin* . . . (6 vols., Philadelphia, 1808–18). Title varies in the several volumes.
Laws of Pa.	*A Collection of all the Laws of the Province of Pennsylvania: Now in Force* (Philadelphia, 1742).
Lib. Co. Phila.	Library Company of Philadelphia
LS	Letter signed. See p. xlv for definition.
MS, MSS	Manuscript(s). See p. xlv for definition.
PMHB	*Pennsylvania Magazine of History and Biography*
Pa. Arch.	Samuel Hazard and others, eds., *Pennsylvania Archives* (9 series, Philadelphia and Harrisburg, 1852–1935).
Pa. Col. Recs.	*Minutes of the Provincial Council of Pennsylvania* . . . (16 vols., Philadelphia, 1838–53). Title changes with volume 11 to Supreme Executive Council.
Pa. Gaz.	*Pennsylvania Gazette*
Par. Text edit.	Max Farrand, ed., *Benjamin Franklin's Memoirs. Parallel Text Edition* . . . (Berkeley and Los Angeles, 1949).

Parton, *Franklin*   James Parton, *Life and Times of Benjamin Franklin* (2 vols., New York, 1864).

Smyth, *Writings*   Albert H. Smyth, ed., *The Writings of Benjamin Franklin* ... (10 vols., New York, 1905–07).

Sparks, *Works*   Jared Sparks, ed., *The Works of Benjamin Franklin* . . . (10 vols., Boston, 1836–40).

Van Doren, *Franklin*   Carl Van Doren, *Benjamin Franklin* (New York, 1938).

Van Doren, *Franklin-Mecom*   Carl Van Doren, ed., *The Letters of Benjamin Franklin & Jane Mecom* (*Memoirs* of the American Philosophical Society, XXVII, Princeton, 1950).

Van Doren, *Jane Mecom*   Carl Van Doren, *Jane Mecom, the Favorite Sister of Benjamin Franklin* ... (New York, 1950).

WTF, *Memoirs*   William Temple Franklin, ed., *Memoirs of the Life and Writings of Benjamin Franklin, LL.D., F.R.S. &c.* . . . (3 vols., 4to, London, 1817–18).

Chronology

1706
January 6 (January 17, New Style): BF born in Boston.

[1718?]
BF apprenticed a printer to his brother James.

1721
August 7: James Franklin begins publication of *The New-England Courant*.

1722
April 2: First paper of Silence Dogood published in the *Courant*.
June 12: James Franklin arrested and jailed.

1723
January 24: James Franklin ordered arrested; February 12: surrenders and gives bond; May 7: discharged.
February 11: *The New-England Courant* appears over BF's name.
September-October: BF runs away from Boston to Philadelphia.
November [?]: BF employed as a journeyman by Samuel Keimer.

1724
April-May: BF visits Boston.
November 5: The *London Hope*, with BF aboard, clears for England; December 24: BF reaches London.

1725
BF writes and prints in London *A Dissertation on Liberty and Necessity*.

1726
July 21: BF sails from London in the *Berkshire;* October 11: arrives at Philadelphia.

1727
The Junto formed.

1728

BF forms a partnership with Hugh Meredith.

December 24: Samuel Keimer begins publication of *The Pennsylvania Gazette.*

1729

February 4: The Busy-Body, No. 1, published in *The American Weekly Mercury.*

April 3: BF's *A Modest Enquiry into the Nature and Necessity of a Paper-Currency* published.

October 2: BF takes over publication of *The Pennsylvania Gazette.*

1730

January 29: Franklin and Meredith appointed printers to the Pennsylvania Assembly.

July 14: Franklin and Meredith partnership dissolved.

September 1: BF takes Deborah Read Rogers to wife.

[1731?]

William Franklin born.

1731

February: BF made a Mason in St. John's Lodge, Philadelphia.

September 13: BF forms a partnership with Thomas Whitmarsh to run a printing-office in Charleston, S.C.

November 8: First meeting of the Directors of the Library Company.

1732

May 6: BF begins publication of the *Philadelphische Zeitung.*

October 20: Francis Folger Franklin born.

December 19: First annual *Poor Richard's Almanack* published.

1733

September-October: BF visits Boston.

November 26: BF forms a partnership with Louis Timothée to run a printing-office in Charleston, S.C., succeeding Thomas Whitmarsh, deceased.

1734

May 16: BF publishes *The Constitutions of the Free-Masons*, "by special Order, for the Use of the Brethren in North-America."

June 24: BF elected Grand Master of Masons of Pennsylvania.

THE PAPERS OF
BENJAMIN FRANKLIN

VOLUME I

January 6, 1706 through December 31, 1734

Record of Birth

MS Record, Boston Births, V, 113: City Registry, Boston

Benjamen Son   of Josiah Frankling & Abiah   his Wife   born
6 Janry 1706[1]

Record of Baptism

MS Baptismal Records of the Clerk of Old South Church in Boston

[1705/6]
Jan. 6.   Benjamin, of Josiah & Abiah Franklin[2]

Verses from Benjamin Franklin (the Elder)

MS Commonplace Book of Benjamin Franklin (the Elder): American Antiquarian Society

Benjamin Franklin's uncle Benjamin Franklin (1650–1727), born at Ecton in Northamptonshire, was for many years a silk-dyer in London. After years of sickness and adversity, he settled at Boston in October 1715,

> And there a Kind, kind Brother found,
> Bless't with a Wife and Num'rous Race.
>
> Four years they did me kindly Treat
> But noe Imployment did present,
> Which was to me a burden great
> And could not be to their content.

He lived four years in Josiah Franklin's household, then in November 1719 moved to the house of his son Samuel, who had preceded him to

1. This entry is taken from an official compilation, made at some later time, from the original book of record. The clerk used the year dates of the New Style calendar (adopted by Great Britain in 1752), recording the year of BF's birth as a simple 1706 instead of the technically more correct 1705/6. He did not, however, adjust the days of the month, but retained the Old Style January 6, not adding eleven days as the New Style calendar would require to make BF's birthday January 17. The clerk thus followed a not uncommon practice: in his Epitaph (below, p. 111), for example, BF himself gives his birthday as January 6, 1706; and many places, including Boston, continued until well after the American Revolution to celebrate Washington's birthday on February 11. The record is printed in facsimile in Col. Soc. Mass., *Pubs.*, X (1907), facing p. 228.
2. Printed in facsimile in Col. Soc. Mass., *Pubs.*, X (1907), facing p. 228.

America but had just married; and there he died (Genealogy, A.5.2.7).

Franklin remembered his uncle as an ingenious man, the inventor of a shorthand which he taught his nephew, a collector of books and family anecdotes. From early manhood this clever, gentle man composed poems of love, sorrow, and thanksgiving, rendered the Psalms into his own verse, and contrived acrostics, crosses, ladders, and other curious verse forms. Many of these were written for his children, nieces, and nephews; three were addressed to his "Name[sake]," though the child was in America and the old man was still in England.[3] Punctuation, largely lacking in the manuscript, has been supplied in this and the following two poems.

Sent to My Name upon a Report
of his Inclineation to Martial affaires
7 July 1710

Beleeve me Ben. It is a Dangerous Trade—
The Sword has Many Marr'd as well as Made.
By it doe many fall, Not Many Rise;
Makes Many poor, few Rich and fewer Wise;
Fills Towns with Ruin, fields with blood beside;
Tis Sloth's Maintainer, And the Shield of pride;
Fair Citties Rich to Day, in plenty flow,
War fills with want, Tomorrow, and with woe.
Ruin'd Estates, The Nurse of Vice, broke limbs and scarts
Are the Effects of Desolating Warrs.

Acrostic from Benjamin Franklin (the Elder)

MS Commonplace Book of Benjamin Franklin (the Elder): American Antiquarian Society

Sent To B.F. in N. E.   15 July 1710

Be to thy parents an Obedient son;
Each Day let Duty constantly be Done;
Never give Way to sloth or lust or pride
If free you'd be from Thousand Ills beside.

3. Other verses from this MS volume are printed in *Hist. Mag.*, III (1859), 9–12, 50–1, 86–7. A commonplace book kept by the elder Franklin at Boston and his treatise on dyeing and coloring are printed in Col. Soc. Mass., *Pubs.*, X (1907), 191–205, 206–25. For a sympathetic portrait based on these MSS see Parton, *Franklin*, I, 32–8, 41–3.

Franklin's Birthplace, Milk Street, Boston.

Above all Ills be sure Avoide the shelfe:
Mans Danger lyes in Satan, sin and selfe.
In vertue, Learning, Wisdome progress make.
Nere shrink at suffering for thy saviours sake;
Fraud and all Falshood in thy Dealings Flee;
Religious Always in thy station be;
Adore the Maker of thy Inward part:
Now's the Accepted time, Give him thy Heart.
Keep a Good Conscience, 'tis a constant Frind;
Like Judge and Witness This Thy Acts Attend.
In Heart with bended knee Alone Adore
None but the Three in One Forevermore.

Verses from Benjamin Franklin (the Elder)

MS Commonplace Book of Benjamin Franklin (the Elder): American
Antiquarian Society

To My Name 1713.

Tis time for me to Throw Asside my pen
When Hanging-sleeves Read, Write, and Rhime Like Men.
This Forward Spring Foretells a plentious crop,
For if the bud bear Graine what will the Top?
If plenty in the verdant blade Appear,
What may we not soon hope for in the Ear?
When Flow'rs are Beautifull before they'r Blown,
What Rarities will afterward be shown?
If Tree's Good fruit unoculated bear,
You May be sure 'Twill afterward be Rare.
If fruits are Sweet before th'ave time to Yellow,
How Luscious will they be when they are Mellow!
If first years Shoots such Noble clusters send,
What Laden boughs, Engedi like, May We Expect I'th End?
Goe on, My Name, and be progressive still,
Till thou Excell Great Cocker with thy Quill;[4]

4. Edward Cocker (1631–1675), author of several arithmetical works, of
poems and distichs, and of a number of quaintly titled books on calligraphy.
DNB. When he was 16, "asham'd of my Ignorance in Figures," BF took
Cocker's Arithmetic and went through the whole book "with great Ease."

Soe Imitate and's Excellence Reherse
Till thou Excell His cyphers, Writing, Verse.
And show us here that your young Western clime
Out Does all Down unto our present Time;
With choycer Measures put his poesie Down,
And I will vote for thee the Lawrell Crown.[5]

The Lighthouse Tragedy   Not found

As a lad of twelve or thirteen Franklin "took a Fancy to Poetry, and made some little Pieces." One of these was a ballad he remembered as "the *Light House Tragedy*," inspired by the drowning on November 3, 1718, of George Worthylake, keeper of the light on Beacon Island, with his wife and daughter. (In the autobiography he remembered it incorrectly as Worthylake and his two daughters.) Though "wretched Stuff, in the Grubstreet Ballad Stile," the verses "sold wonderfully"; but no authenticated copy is known to survive. On August 7, 1940, however, the *Boston Post* reported that some verses entitled "The Lighthouse Tragedy," printed in "old style English characters" on a tattered and yellowed sheet, had been discovered "in a tumbledown closet in the ruins of [an] old house" on Middle Brewster Island in Boston harbor. These verses began:

Oh! George, This wild November
We must not pass with you
For Ruth, our fragile daughter,
It's chilly gales will rue.

The manuscript proved on examination to be in a nineteenth-century hand.[6]

Without citing an authority, Worthington C. Ford declared in his edition of Cotton Mather's diary, II (7 Mass. Hist. Soc., *Colls.*, VIII), 566n, that the ballad was translated into French as "La Tragédie du Phare" and retranslated into English as "The Tragedy of Pharaoh." Neither of these versions has been found.[7]

5. This prediction became part of the Franklin family tradition. BF's sister Jane related it to Ezra Stiles in 1779. Franklin B. Dexter, ed., *The Literary Diary of Ezra Stiles* (N.Y., 1901), II, 375–6.

6. Zoltán Haraszti in *Publishers' Weekly*, CXXXVIII (Oct. 5, 1940), 1620–1.

7. A possible source of Ford's statement has been suggested by Donald H. Mugridge and Allen G. Anderson of the Library of Congress. The Buisson translation of BF's autobiography, 1791 (Par. Text edit., p. 33), correctly

The Taking of Teach the Pirate

The second ballad which Franklin wrote and hawked through the streets of Boston was "a Sailor Song on the Taking of Teach or Black-beard the Pirate." This may have been written in March 1719, after the Boston *News-Letter* carried a full account of the last fight and death of Captain Edward Teach on November 22, 1718.[8] In the middle of the nineteenth century the Boston physician George Hayward remembered a stanza which he thought was part of Franklin's ballad:

> So each man to his gun,
> For the work must be done
>   With cutlass, sword, or pistol.
> And when we no longer can strike a blow,
> Then fire the magazine, boys, and up we go!
> It's better to swim in the sea below
> Than to swing in the air and feed the crow,
>   Says jolly Ned Teach of Bristol.

In 1898 Edward Everett Hale ("Ben Franklin's Ballads," *New England Magazine*, XXIV, 505–7) suggested that the verses Franklin composed were actually those entitled "The Downfal of Pyracy," printed in *The Worcestershire Garland* (Newcastle, 1765?) and reprinted in John Ashton, ed., *Real Sailor-Songs* (London, 1891), p. 79. Nothing in the ballad is inconsistent with this view. The first stanza is:

> Will you hear of a bloody Battle,
>   Lately fought upon the Seas,
> It will make your Ears to rattle,
>   And your Admiration cease:
> Have you heard of Teach the Rover,
>   And his Knavery on the Main;
> How of Gold he was a Lover,
>   How he loved ill got Gain.

---

renders BF's recollection of the ballad's title as "*la Tragédie du Phare*." This translation of the autobiography was retranslated into English—very badly—and published in London by J. Parsons in 1793 as *The Private Life of the Late Benjamin Franklin, LL.D. . . .* , where, p. 17, the ballad is called "the *Tragedy of Pharoah*" [*sic*].

8. For the history of Blackbeard and his death see Captain Charles Johnson [Daniel Defoe], *A General History of the . . . Pirates . . .* , first published in 1724 (N.Y., 1927), pp. 45–66.

Silence Dogood, No. 1

Printed in *The New-England Courant*, April 2, 1722.

The first issue of James Franklin's *New-England Courant* appeared on August 7, 1721, at the height of the inoculation controversy in Boston.[9] Because the Mathers supported inoculation, the *Courant* opposed it; and the paper's lively, combative essays and verses were soon directed also against the clergy, the magistrates, the postmaster, Harvard College, men of wealth and property—in short, against the whole Massachusetts Establishment. The *Courant*'s literary quality alone made the paper pay, for it carried very little advertising and James Franklin had no post office business. The original material was composed by the printer and his friends, a group of "ingenious Men" which included Dr. William Douglass, Captain Taylor, John Checkley, Matthew Adams, John Eyre, and a Mr. Gardner.

Franklin's autobiography tells how he joined their company anonymously. The writers came regularly to the printing shop in Queen Street, "over against Mr. Sheaf's School." Franklin overheard them discuss their work; emboldened to try his hand, he composed a satirical essay and "put it in at Night under the Door of the Printing House." Next morning he had the "exquisite Pleasure" of hearing the warm approval of the assembled Couranteers and their flattering guesses as to who might have written the piece. His letter was printed, the author's further contributions were invited, and the sixteen-year-old apprentice wrote thirteen more essays in this way "till my small Fund of Sense for such Performances was pretty well exhausted." Then he revealed his identity.

In his autobiography Franklin failed to name these essays. Joseph T. Buckingham was the first to suggest that they were the letters of Silence Dogood; he judged them, however, to be "doubtless the work of different hands, though I think chiefly from the pen of Benjamin Franklin."[1] Parton followed Buckingham, asserting that the pseudonym, the plan, and most of the articles were Franklin's.[2] In 1868 Bigelow settled the question of authorship: in his edition of the autobiography, printed from the original manuscripts, appeared an outline of subjects Franklin meant to take up, including "My writing. Mrs. Dogoods

---

9. John B. Blake, "The Inoculation Controversy in Boston: 1721–1722," *New Eng. Quar.*, XXV (1952), 489–506. On the *Courant* generally, see Perry Miller, *The New England Mind: From Colony to Province* (Cambridge, Mass., 1953), pp. 333–44.

1. *Specimens of Newspaper Literature* (Boston, 1850), I, 64.

2. Parton, *Franklin*, I, 84.

Letters."[3] Further evidence is provided by the file of the *Courant* now in the British Museum, presumably Franklin's own. It has the authorship of most of the contributions regularly indicated—James', for example, as "Mr. J. Franklin," Adams' as "Mr. Matthew Adams," but the Dogood Letters always simply as "B.F."[4]

Franklin's essays are indebted generally to *The Spectator*, one of his models for English style;[5] but their immediate models and inspiration were the homely, unsophisticated satires of the Couranteers. Silence Dogood may be a distant relation of Sir Roger de Coverley, but she is own sister to James Franklin's Abigail Afterwit and Timothy Turnstone, to Matthew Adams' Harry Meanwell, and to Mr. Gardner's Fanny Mournful; and her letters are an integral part of the *Courant*'s spirited satirical review of society, politics, religion, and morality in Massachusetts in 1722.

To the Author of the *New-England Courant.*

Sir,

It may not be improper in the first place to inform your Readers, that I intend once a Fortnight to present them, by the Help of this Paper, with a short Epistle, which I presume will add somewhat to their Entertainment.

And since it is observed, that the Generality of People, now a days, are unwilling either to commend or dispraise what they read, until they are in some measure informed who or what the Author of it is, whether he be *poor* or *rich, old* or *young,* a *Schollar* or a *Leather Apron Man,* &c. and give their Opinion of the Performance, according to the Knowledge which they have of the Author's Circumstances, it may not be amiss to begin with a short Account of my past Life and present Condition, that the Reader may not be at a Loss to judge whether or no my Lucubrations are worth his reading.

At the time of my Birth, my Parents were on Ship-board in their Way from London to N. England. My Entrance into this troublesome World was attended with the Death of my Father, a Mis-

3. John Bigelow, ed., *Autobiography of Benjamin Franklin* (Phila., 1868), p. 61.

4. The file is fully described by Worthington C. Ford, "Franklin's New England Courant," Mass. Hist. Soc., *Proc.,* LVII (1923–24), 336–53.

5. George F. Horner, "Franklin's *Dogood Papers* Re-examined," *Studies in Philology,* XXXVII (1940), 501–23.

fortune, which tho' I was not then capable of knowing, I shall never be able to forget; for as he, poor Man, stood upon the Deck rejoycing at my Birth, a merciless Wave entred the Ship, and in one Moment carry'd him beyond Reprieve. Thus, was the *first Day* which I saw, the *last* that was seen by my Father; and thus was my disconsolate Mother at once made both a *Parent* and a *Widow*.

When we arrived at Boston (which was not long after) I was put to Nurse in a Country Place, at a small Distance from the Town, where I went to School, and past my Infancy and Childhood in Vanity and Idleness, until I was bound out Apprentice, that I might no longer be a Charge to my Indigent Mother, who was put to hard Shifts for a Living.

My Master was a Country Minister, a pious good-natur'd young Man, and a Batchelor: He labour'd with all his Might to instil vertuous and godly Principles into my tender Soul, well knowing that it was the most suitable Time to make deep and lasting Impressions on the Mind, while it was yet untainted with Vice, free and unbiass'd. He endeavour'd that I might be instructed in all that Knowledge and Learning which is necessary for our Sex, and deny'd me no Accomplishment that could possibly be attained in a Country Place; such as all Sorts of Needle-Work, Writing, Arithmetick, &c. and observing that I took a more than ordinary Delight in reading ingenious Books, he gave me the free Use of his Library, which tho' it was but small, yet it was well chose, to inform the Understanding rightly, and enable the Mind to frame great and noble Ideas.

Before I had liv'd quite two Years with this Reverend Gentleman, my indulgent Mother departed this Life, leaving me as it were by my self, having no Relation on Earth within my Knowledge.

I will not abuse your Patience with a tedious Recital of all the frivolous Accidents of my Life, that happened from this Time until I arrived to Years of Discretion, only inform you that I liv'd a chearful Country Life, spending my leisure Time either in some innocent Diversion with the neighbouring Females, or in some shady Retirement, with the best of Company, *Books*. Thus I past away the Time with a Mixture of Profit and Pleasure, having no affliction but what was imaginary, and created in my own Fancy; as nothing is more common with us Women, than to be grieving for nothing, when we have nothing else to grieve for.

As I would not engross too much of your Paper at once, I will defer the Remainder of my Story until my next Letter; in the mean time desiring your Readers to exercise their Patience, and bear with my Humours now and then, because I shall trouble them but seldom. I am not insensible of the Impossibility of pleasing all, but I would not willingly displease any; and for those who will take Offence where none is intended, they are beneath the Notice of Your Humble Servant,   SILENCE DOGOOD[6]

Silence Dogood, No. 2

Printed in *The New-England Courant*, April 16, 1722.

To the Author of the *New-England Courant*.

Sir,   [No. 2

Histories of Lives are seldom entertaining, unless they contain something either admirable or exemplar: And since there is little or nothing of this Nature in my own Adventures, I will not tire your Readers with tedious Particulars of no Consequence, but will briefly, and in as few Words as possible, relate the most material Occurrences of my Life, and according to my Promise, confine all to this Letter.

My Reverend Master who had hitherto remained a Batchelor, (after much Meditation on the Eighteenth verse of the Second Chapter of Genesis,)[7] took up a Resolution to marry; and having made several unsuccessful fruitless Attempts on the more topping Sort of our Sex, and being tir'd with making troublesome Journeys and Visits to no Purpose, he began unexpectedly to cast a loving Eye upon Me, whom he had brought up cleverly to his Hand.

There is certainly scarce any Part of a Man's Life in which he appears more silly and ridiculous, than when he makes his first

6. Directly after this essay the printer inserted the following invitation: "As the Favour of Mrs. Dogood's Correspondence is acknowledged by the Publisher of this Paper, lest any of her Letters should miscarry, he desires they may for the future be deliver'd at his Printing-House, or at the Blue Ball in Union-Street, and no Questions shall be ask'd of the Bearer." The Blue Ball in Union Street was the house of Josiah Franklin, the father of James and Benjamin.

7. "And the Lord God said, It is not good that the man should be alone: I will make him an help meet for him."

Onset in Courtship. The aukward Manner in which my Master first discover'd his Intentions, made me, in spite of my Reverence to his Person, burst out into an unmannerly Laughter: However, having ask'd his Pardon, and with much ado compos'd my Countenance, I promis'd him I would take his Proposal into serious Consideration, and speedily give him an Answer.

As he had been a great Benefactor (and in a Manner a Father to me) I could not well deny his Request, when I once perceived he was in earnest. Whether it was Love, or Gratitude, or Pride, or all Three that made me consent, I know not; but it is certain, he found it no hard Matter, by the Help of his Rhetorick, to conquer my Heart, and perswade me to marry him.

This unexpected Match was very astonishing to all the Country round about, and served to furnish them with Discourse for a long Time after; some approving it, others disliking it, as they were led by their various Fancies and Inclinations.

We lived happily together in the Heighth of conjugal Love and mutual Endearments, for near Seven Years, in which Time we added Two likely Girls and a Boy to the Family of the Dogoods: But alas! When my Sun was in its meridian Altitude, inexorable unrelenting Death, as if he had envy'd my Happiness and Tranquility, and resolv'd to make me entirely miserable by the Loss of so good an Husband, hastened his Flight to the Heavenly World, by a sudden unexpected Departure from this.

I have now remained in a State of Widowhood for several Years, but it is a State I never much admir'd, and I am apt to fancy that I could be easily perswaded to marry again, provided I was sure of a good-humour'd, sober, agreeable Companion: But one, even with these few good Qualities, being hard to find, I have lately relinquish'd all Thoughts of that Nature.

At present I pass away my leisure Hours in Conversation, either with my honest Neighbour Rusticus and his Family, or with the ingenious Minister of our Town, who now lodges at my House, and by whose Assistance I intend now and then to beautify my Writings with a Sentence or two in the learned Languages, which will not only be fashionable, and pleasing to those who do not understand it, but will likewise be very ornamental.

I shall conclude this with my own Character, which (one would think) I should be best able to give. *Know then,* That I am an

Enemy to Vice, and a Friend to Vertue. I am one of an extensive Charity, and a great Forgiver of *private* Injuries: A hearty Lover of the Clergy and all good Men, and a mortal Enemy to arbitrary Government and unlimited Power. I am naturally very jealous for the Rights and Liberties of my Country; and the least appearance of an Incroachment on those invaluable Priviledges, is apt to make my Blood boil exceedingly. I have likewise a natural Inclination to observe and reprove the Faults of others, at which I have an excellent Faculty. I speak this by Way of Warning to all such whose Offences shall come under my Cognizance, for I never intend to wrap my Talent in a Napkin. To be brief; I am courteous and affable, good humour'd (unless I am first provok'd,) and handsome, and sometimes witty, but always, Sir, Your Friend and Humble Servant, SILENCE DOGOOD

Silence Dogood, No. 3

Printed in *The New-England Courant*, April 30, 1722.

To the Author of the *New-England Courant*.

Sir, [No. 3
It is undoubtedly the Duty of all Persons to serve the Country they live in, according to their Abilities; yet I sincerely acknowledge, that I have hitherto been very deficient in this Particular; whether it was for want of Will or Opportunity, I will not at present stand to determine: Let it suffice, that I now take up a Resolution, to do for the future all that *lies in my Way* for the Service of my Countrymen.

I have from my Youth been indefatigably studious to gain and treasure up in my Mind all useful and desireable Knowledge, especially such as tends to improve the Mind, and enlarge the Understanding: And as I have found it very beneficial to me, I am not without Hopes, that communicating my small Stock in this Manner, by Peace-meal to the Publick, may be at least in some Measure useful.

I am very sensible that it is impossible for me, or indeed any *one* Writer to please *all* Readers at once. Various Persons have different Sentiments; and that which is pleasant and delightful to one, gives another a Disgust. He that would (in this Way of

13

Writing) please all, is under a Necessity to make his Themes almost as numerous as his Letters. He must one while be merry and diverting, then more solid and serious; one while sharp and satyrical, then (to mollify that) be sober and religious; at one Time let the Subject be Politicks, then let the next Theme be Love: Thus will every one, one Time or other find some thing agreeable to his own Fancy, and in his Turn be delighted.

According to this Method I intend to proceed, bestowing now and then a few gentle Reproofs on those who deserve them, not forgetting at the same time to applaud those whose Actions merit Commendation. And here I must not forget to invite the ingenious Part of your Readers, particularly those of my own Sex to enter into a Correspondence with me, assuring them, that their Condescension in this Particular shall be received as a Favour, and accordingly acknowledged.

I think I have now finish'd the Foundation, and I intend in my next to begin to raise the Building. Having nothing more to write at present, I must make the usual excuse in such Cases, of *being in haste,* assuring you that I speak from my Heart when I call my self, The most humble and obedient of all the Servants your Merits have acquir'd,   SILENCE DOGOOD[8]

Silence Dogood, No. 4

Printed in *The New-England Courant,* May 14, 1722.

An sum etiam nunc vel Graecè loqui vel Latinè docendus? Cicero.[9]

To the Author of the *New-England Courant.*

Sir,   [No. 4

Discoursing the other Day at Dinner with my Reverend Boarder, formerly mention'd, (whom for Distinction sake we will call by the Name of Clericus,) concerning the Education of Children, I ask'd his Advice about my young Son William, whether or no I had best bestow upon him Academical Learning,

8. To this letter the printer appended the following invitation: "Those who incline to favour Mrs. Dogood with their Correspondence, are desir'd to send their Letters (directed to her) to the Publisher of this Paper."
9. *De Finibus,* II, 5.

14

or (as our Phrase is) *bring him up at our College:* He perswaded me to do it by all Means, using many weighty Arguments with me, and answering all the Objections that I could form against it; telling me withal, that he did not doubt but that the Lad would take his Learning very well, and not idle away his Time as too many there now-a-days do. These Words of Clericus gave me a Curiosity to inquire a little more strictly into the present Circumstances of that famous Seminary of Learning; but the Information which he gave me, was neither pleasant, nor such as I expected.

As soon as Dinner was over, I took a solitary Walk into my Orchard, still ruminating on Clericus's Discourse with much Consideration, until I came to my usual Place of Retirement under the *Great Apple-Tree;* where having seated my self, and carelessly laid my Head on a verdant Bank, I fell by Degrees into a soft and undisturbed Slumber. My waking Thoughts remained with me in my Sleep, and before I awak'd again, I dreamt the following DREAM.

I fancy'd I was travelling over pleasant and delightful Fields and Meadows, and thro' many small Country Towns and Villages; and as I pass'd along, all Places resounded with the Fame of the Temple of LEARNING: Every Peasant, who had wherewithal, was preparing to send one of his Children at least to this famous Place; and in this Case most of them consulted their own Purses instead of their Childrens Capacities: So that I observed, a great many, yea, the most part of those who were travelling thither, were little better than Dunces and Blockheads. Alas! alas!

At length I entred upon a spacious Plain, in the Midst of which was erected a large and stately Edifice: It was to this that a great Company of Youths from all Parts of the Country were going; so stepping in among the Crowd, I passed on with them, and presently arrived at the Gate.

The Passage was kept by two sturdy Porters named *Riches* and *Poverty,* and the latter obstinately refused to give Entrance to any who had not first gain'd the Favour of the former; so that I observed, many who came even to the very Gate, were obliged to travel back again as ignorant as they came, for want of this necessary Qualification. However, as a Spectator I gain'd Admittance, and with the rest entred directly into the Temple.

In the Middle of the great Hall stood a stately and magnificent

Throne, which was ascended to by two high and difficult Steps. On the Top of it sat LEARNING in awful State; she was apparelled wholly in Black, and surrounded almost on every Side with innumerable Volumes in all Languages. She seem'd very busily employ'd in writing something on half a Sheet of Paper, and upon Enquiry, I understood she was preparing a Paper, call'd, *The New-England Courant.* On her Right Hand sat *English,* with a pleasant smiling Countenance, and handsomely attir'd; and on her left were seated several *Antique Figures* with their Faces vail'd. I was considerably puzzl'd to guess who they were, until one informed me, (who stood beside me,) that those Figures on her left Hand were *Latin, Greek, Hebrew,* &c. and that they were very much reserv'd, and seldom or never unvail'd their Faces here, and then to few or none, tho' most of those who have in this Place acquir'd so much Learning as to distinguish them from *English,* pretended to an intimate Acquaintance with them. I then enquir'd of him, what could be the Reason why they continued vail'd, in this Place especially: He pointed to the Foot of the Throne, where I saw *Idleness,* attended with *Ignorance,* and these (he informed me) were they, who first vail'd them, and still kept them so.

Now I observed, that the whole Tribe who entred into the Temple with me, began to climb the Throne; but the Work proving troublesome and difficult to most of them, they withdrew their Hands from the Plow, and contented themselves to sit at the Foot, with Madam *Idleness* and her Maid *Ignorance,* until those who were assisted by Diligence and a docible Temper, had well nigh got up the first Step: But the Time drawing nigh in which they could no way avoid ascending, they were fain to crave the Assistance of those who had got up before them, and who, for the Reward perhaps of a *Pint of Milk,* or a *Piece of Plumb-Cake,*[1] lent the Lubbers a helping Hand, and sat them in the Eye of the World, upon a Level with themselves.

1. Plum cake was traditionally served at Harvard parties. The Corporation in 1693 ordered the custom stopped (Samuel E. Morison, *Harvard College in the Seventeenth Century,* Cambridge, Mass., 1936, II, 470); but the practice continued. During the administration of President Leverett (1707–24) another effort was made to control Commencement disorders and "Extravagancies" by forbidding either "Plumb-Cake or rosted, boiled, or Baked Meats or Pyes of any kind" to be prepared or provided "by any Commencer." Col. Soc. Mass., *Pubs.,* XV (1925), 343; XVI (1925), 456, 471.

16

The other Step being in the same Manner ascended, and the usual Ceremonies at an End, every Beetle-Scull seem'd well satisfy'd with his own Portion of Learning, tho' perhaps he was *e'en just* as ignorant as ever. And now the Time of their Departure being come, they march'd out of Doors to make Room for another Company, who waited for Entrance: And I, having seen all that was to be seen, quitted the Hall likewise, and went to make my Observations on those who were just gone out before me.

Some I perceiv'd took to Merchandizing, others to Travelling, some to one Thing, some to another, and some to Nothing; and many of them from henceforth, for want of Patrimony, liv'd as poor as Church Mice, being unable to dig, and asham'd to beg, and to live by their Wits it was impossible. But the most Part of the Crowd went along a large beaten Path, which led to a Temple at the further End of the Plain, call'd, *The Temple of Theology*. The Business of those who were employ'd in this Temple being laborious and painful, I wonder'd exceedingly to see so many go towards it; but while I was pondering this Matter in my Mind, I spy'd *Pecunia* behind a Curtain, beckoning to them with her Hand, which Sight immediately satisfy'd me for whose Sake it was, that a great Part of them (I will not say all) travel'd that Road. In this Temple I saw nothing worth mentioning, except the ambitious and fraudulent Contrivances of Plagius, who (notwithstanding he had been severely reprehended for such Practices before) was diligently transcribing some eloquent Paragraphs out of Tillotson's *Works,* &c., to embellish his own.

Now I bethought my self in my Sleep, that it was Time to be at Home, and as I fancy'd I was travelling back thither, I reflected in my Mind on the extream Folly of those Parents, who, blind to their Childrens Dulness, and insensible of the Solidity of their Skulls, because they think their Purses can afford it, will needs send them to the Temple of Learning, where, for want of a suitable Genius, they learn little more than how to carry themselves handsomely, and enter a Room genteely, (which might as well be acquir'd at a Dancing-School,) and from whence they return, after Abundance of Trouble and Charge, as great Blockheads as ever, only more proud and self-conceited.

While I was in the midst of these unpleasant Reflections, Clericus (who with a Book in his Hand was walking under the

Trees) accidentally awak'd me; to him I related my Dream with all its Particulars, and he, without much Study, presently interpreted it, assuring me, *That it was a lively Representation of* HARVARD COLLEGE, *Etcetera.* I remain, Sir, Your Humble Servant,

SILENCE DOGOOD[2]

Silence Dogood, No. 5

Printed in *The New-England Courant*, May 28, 1722.

Mulier Mulieri magis congruet. Ter.[3]

To the Author of the *New-England Courant*.

Sir, [No. V.

I shall here present your Readers with a Letter from one, who informs me that I have begun at the wrong End of my Business, and that I ought to begin at Home, and censure the Vices and Follies of my own Sex, before I venture to meddle with your's: Nevertheless, I am resolved to dedicate this Speculation to the Fair Tribe, and endeavour to show, that Mr. Ephraim charges Women with being particularly guilty of Pride, Idleness, &c. wrongfully, inasmuch as the Men have not only as great a Share in those Vices as the Women, but are likewise in a great Measure the Cause of that which the Women are guilty of. I think it will be best to produce my Antagonist, before I encounter him.

To Mrs. Dogood.

"Madam,

"My Design in troubling you with this Letter is, to desire you would begin with your own Sex first: Let the first Volley of your Resentments be directed against *Female* Vice; let Female Idleness, Ignorance and Folly, (which are Vices more peculiar to your Sex

2. To this attack one of the Harvard wits, probably Samuel Mather, replied in the *Boston Gazette*, May 28. Over the signature "John Harvard," he ridiculed Mrs. Dogood as a "Rustic Couranto" for her inept allegory of students withdrawing their hands from the plow before they reached the throne of the temple, and he charged the *Courant* with several specific plagiarisms. The *Courant* scornfully rejected the charges June 4, and in the same issue printed satirical verses on Harvard which the Dogood letter had elicited. Perry Miller, *The New England Mind: From Colony to Province* (Cambridge, Mass., 1953), pp. 342–3.

3. Terence, *Phormio*, IV, v, 14.

than to our's,) be the Subject of your Satyrs, but more especially Female Pride, which I think is intollerable. Here is a large Field that wants Cultivation, and which I believe you are able (if willing) to improve with Advantage; and when you have once reformed the Women, you will find it a much easier Task to reform the Men, because Women are the prime Causes of a great many Male Enormities. This is all at present from Your Friendly Wellwisher,   EPHRAIM CENSORIOUS"

After Thanks to my Correspondent for his Kindness in cutting out Work for me, I must assure him, that I find it a very difficult Matter to reprove Women separate from the Men; for what Vice is there in which the Men have not as great a Share as the Women? and in some have they not a far greater, as in Drunkenness, Swearing, &c.? And if they have, then it follows, that when a Vice is to be reproved, Men, who are most culpable, deserve the most Reprehension, and certainly therefore, ought to have it. But we will wave this Point at present, and proceed to a particular Consideration of what my Correspondent calls *Female Vice*.

As for Idleness, if I should Quaere, Where are the greatest Number of its Votaries to be found, with us or the Men? it might I believe be easily and truly answer'd, *With the latter*. For notwithstanding the Men are commonly complaining how hard they are forc'd to labour, only to maintain their Wives in Pomp and Idleness, yet if you go among the Women, you will learn, that *they have always more Work upon their Hands than they are able to do;* and that *a Woman's Work is never done,* &c. But however, Suppose we should grant for once, that we are generally more idle than the Men, (without making any Allowance for the *Weakness of the Sex*,) I desire to know whose Fault it is? Are not the Men to blame for their Folly in maintaining us in Idleness? Who is there that can be handsomely Supported in Affluence, Ease and Pleasure by another, that will chuse rather to earn his Bread by the Sweat of his own Brows? And if a Man will be so fond and so foolish, as to labour hard himself for a Livelihood, and suffer his Wife in the mean Time to sit in Ease and Idleness, let him not blame her if she does so, for it is in a great Measure his own Fault.

And now for the Ignorance and Folly which he reproaches us with, let us see (if we are Fools and Ignoramus's) whose is the

19

Fault, the Men's or our's. An ingenious Writer, having this Subject in Hand, has the following Words, wherein he lays the Fault
wholly on the Men, for not allowing Women the Advantages of
Education.[4]

"I have (says he) often thought of it as one of the most barbarous Customs in the World, considering us as a civiliz'd and
Christian Country, that we deny the Advantages of Learning to
Women. We reproach the Sex every Day with Folly and Impertinence, while I am confident, had they the Advantages of Education equal to us, they would be guilty of less than our selves. One
would wonder indeed how it should happen that Women are
conversible at all, since they are only beholding to natural Parts for
all their Knowledge. Their Youth is spent to teach them to stitch
and sew, or make Baubles: They are taught to read indeed, and
perhaps to write their Names, or so; and that is the Heighth of a
Womans Education. And I would but ask any who slight the Sex
for their Understanding, What is a Man (a Gentleman, I mean)
good for that is taught no more? If Knowledge and Understanding had been useless Additions to the Sex, God Almighty would
never have given them Capacities, for he made nothing Needless.
What has the Woman done to forfeit the Priviledge of being
taught? Does she plague us with her Pride and Impertinence?
Why did we not let her learn, that she might have had more Wit?
Shall we upbraid Women with Folly, when 'tis only the Error of
this inhumane Custom that hindred them being made wiser."

So much for Female Ignorance and Folly, and now let us a little
consider the Pride which my Correspondent thinks is *intollerable*.
By this Expression of his, one would think he is some dejected
Swain, tyranniz'd over by some cruel haughty Nymph, who (perhaps he thinks) has no more Reason to be proud than himself.
Alas-a-day! What shall we say in this Case! Why truly, if Women
are proud, it is certainly owing to the Men still; for if they will be
such *Simpletons* as to humble themselves at their Feet, and fill
their credulous Ears with extravagant Praises of their Wit, Beauty,
and other Accomplishments (perhaps where there are none too,)
and when Women are by this Means perswaded that they are
Something more than humane, what Wonder is it, if they carry

4. Defoe, *An Essay on Projects* (London, 1697), pp. 282–4, with minor
omissions and variations in spelling and punctuation.

themselves haughtily, and live extravagantly. Notwithstanding, I believe there are more Instances of extravagant Pride to be found among Men than among Women, and this Fault is certainly more hainous in the former than in the latter.

Upon the whole, I conclude, that it will be impossible to lash any Vice, of which the Men are not equally guilty with the Women, and consequently deserve an equal (if not a greater) Share in the Censure. However, I exhort both to amend, where both are culpable, otherwise they may expect to be severely handled by Sir, Your Humble Servant,　　　　　SILENCE DOGOOD

N.B. Mrs. Dogood has lately left her Seat in the Country, and come to Boston, where she intends to tarry for the Summer Season, in order to compleat her Observations of the present reigning Vices of the Town.

Silence Dogood, No. 6

Printed in *The New-England Courant*, June 11, 1722.

Quem Dies videt veniens Superbum,
Hunc Dies vidit fugiens jacentem. Seneca.[5]

To the Author of the *New-England Courant.*

Sir,　　　　　　　　　　　　　　　　　　　　[No. VI.

Among the many reigning Vices of the Town which may at any Time come under my Consideration and Reprehension, there is none which I am more inclin'd to expose than that of *Pride.* It is acknowledg'd by all to be a Vice the most hateful to God and Man. Even those who nourish it in themselves, hate to see it in others. The proud Man aspires after Nothing less than an unlimited Superiority over his Fellow-Creatures. He has made himself a King in *Soliloquy;* fancies himself conquering the World; and the Inhabitants thereof consulting on proper Methods to acknowledge his Merit. I speak it to my Shame, I my self was a Queen from the Fourteenth to the Eighteenth Year of my Age, and govern'd the World all the Time of my being govern'd by my Master. But this speculative Pride may be the Subject of another Letter: I shall at present confine my Thoughts to what we call

5. *Thyestes*, 613–4.

Pride of Apparel. This Sort of Pride has been growing upon us ever since we parted with our Homespun Cloaths for *Fourteen Penny Stuffs,* &c. And the *Pride of Apparel* has begot and nourish'd in us a *Pride of Heart,* which portends the Ruin of Church and State. *Pride goeth before Destruction, and a haughty Spirit before a Fall:* And I remember my late Reverend Husband would often say upon this Text, That a Fall was the *natural Consequence,* as well as *Punishment* of Pride. Daily Experience is sufficient to evince the Truth of this Observation. Persons of small Fortune under the Dominion of this Vice, seldom consider their Inability to maintain themselves in it, but strive to imitate their Superiors in Estate, or Equals in Folly, until one Misfortune comes upon the Neck of another, and every Step they take is a Step backwards. By striving to appear rich they become really poor, and deprive themselves of that Pity and Charity which is due to the humble poor Man, who is made so more immediately by Providence.

This Pride of Apparel will appear the more foolish, if we consider, that those airy Mortals, who have no other Way of making themselves considerable but by gorgeous Apparel, draw after them Crowds of Imitators, who hate each other while they endeavour after a Similitude of Manners. They destroy by Example, and envy one another's Destruction.

I cannot dismiss this Subject without some Observations on a particular Fashion now reigning among my own Sex, the most immodest and inconvenient of any the Art of Woman has invented, namely, that of *Hoop-Petticoats.*[6] By these they are incommoded in their General and Particular Calling, and therefore they cannot answer the Ends of either necessary or ornamental Apparel. These monstrous topsy-turvy *Mortar-Pieces,* are neither fit for the Church, the Hall, or the Kitchen; and if a Number of them were well mounted on Noddles-Island, they would look more like Engines of War for bombarding the Town, than Ornaments of the Fair Sex. An honest Neighbour of mine, happening to be in Town some time since on a publick Day, inform'd me, that he saw four Gentlewomen with their Hoops half mounted in

6. Petticoats were further commented on in a letter to the *Courant* Aug. 20; and on Nov. 26 James Franklin advertised as "just published" an eight-page attack on *Hoop-Petticoats, Arraigned and Condemned by the Light of Nature, and Law of God.*

a Balcony, as they withdrew to the Wall, to the great Terror of the Militia, who (he thinks) might attribute their irregular Volleys to the formidable Appearance of the Ladies Petticoats.

I assure you, Sir, I have but little Hopes of perswading my Sex, by this Letter, utterly to relinquish the extravagant Foolery, and Indication of Immodesty, in this monstrous Garb of their's; but I would at least desire them to lessen the Circumference of their Hoops, and leave it with them to consider, Whether they, who pay no Rates or Taxes, ought to take up more Room in the King's High-Way, than the Men, who yearly contribute to the Support of the Government. I am, Sir, Your Humble Servant,

SILENCE DOGOOD[7]

Silence Dogood, No. 7

Printed in *The New-England Courant*, June 25, 1722.

Give me the Muse, whose generous Force,
Impatient of the Reins,
Pursues an unattempted Course,
Breaks all the Criticks Iron Chains. Watts.[8]

To the Author of the *New-England Courant*.

Sir, [No. VII.

It has been the Complaint of many Ingenious Foreigners, who have travell'd amongst us, *That good Poetry is not to be expected in New-England*. I am apt to Fancy, the Reason is, not because our Countreymen are altogether void of a Poetical Genius, nor yet because we have not those Advantages of Education which other Countries have, but purely because we do not afford that Praise and Encouragement which is merited, when any thing extra-ordinary of this Kind is produc'd among us: Upon which Con-sideration I have determined, when I meet with a Good Piece of New-England Poetry, to give it a suitable Encomium, and there-by endeavour to discover to the World some of its Beautys, in order to encourage the Author to go on, and bless the World with more, and more Excellent Productions.

7. In the next issue of the *Courant*, June 18, Hypercarpus asserted that pride of heart is the cause of pride of apparel, not a consequence of it, as Mrs. Dogood alleged. See postscript to Silence Dogood, No. 7, below, p. 26.

8. Isaac Watts, "The Adventurous Muse," in *Horae Lyricae . . . The Second Edition . . .* (1709).

There has lately appear'd among us a most Excellent Piece of Poetry, entitled, *An Elegy upon the much Lamented Death of Mrs. Mehitebell Kitel, Wife of Mr. John Kitel of Salem, &c.*[9] It may justly be said in its Praise, without Flattery to the Author, that it is the most *Extraordinary* Piece that ever was wrote in New-England. The Language is so soft and Easy, the Expression so moving and pathetick, but above all, the Verse and Numbers so Charming and Natural, that it is almost beyond Comparison,

> *The Muse disdains*
> *Those Links and Chains,*
> *Measures and Rules of vulgar Strains,*
> *And o'er the Laws of Harmony a Sovereign Queen she reigns.**

I find no English Author, Ancient or Modern, whose Elegies may be compar'd with this, in respect to the Elegance of Stile, or Smoothness of Rhime; and for the affecting Part, I will leave your Readers to judge, if ever they read any Lines, that would sooner make them *draw their Breath* and Sigh, if not shed Tears, than these following.

> *Come let us mourn, for we have lost a Wife, a Daughter, and*
> *a Sister,*
> *Who has lately taken Flight, and greatly we have mist her.*

In another Place,

> *Some little Time before she yielded up her Breath,*
> *She said, I ne'er shall hear one Sermon more on Earth.*
> *She kist her Husband some little Time before she expir'd,*
> *Then lean'd her Head the Pillow on, just out of Breath and tir'd.*

But the Threefold Appellation in the first Line

> *a Wife, a Daughter, and a Sister,*

must not pass unobserved. That Line in the celebrated Watts,

*Watts.

9. A Mehitabel Browne married John Kittle of Salem, June 17, 1718. *Vital Records of Salem, Mass.* (Salem, 1916–25), III, 564. A Mrs. Mehitabel Kittle, wife of John, died at Beverly, Sept. 15, 1718. *Vital Records of Beverly, Mass.* (Topsfield, Mass., 1906–7), II, 482. These are probably the same woman, as Beverly is next to Salem and the quoted parts of the elegy speak of the dead woman as "a Wife, a Daughter, and a Sister," but not as a mother, which this woman could not have been.

GUNSTON *the Just, the Generous, and the Young,*

is nothing Comparable to it. The latter only mentions three Qualifications of *one* Person who was deceased, which therefore could raise Grief and Compassion but for *One.* Whereas the former, *(our most excellent Poet)* gives his Reader a Sort of an Idea of the Death of *Three Persons,* viz.

a Wife, a Daughter, and a Sister,

which is *Three Times* as great a Loss as the Death of *One,* and consequently must raise *Three Times* as much Grief and Compassion in the Reader.

I should be very much straitned for Room, if I should attempt to discover even half the Excellencies of this Elegy which are obvious to me. Yet I cannot omit one Observation, which is, that the Author has (to his Honour) invented a new Species of Poetry, which wants a Name, and was never before known. His Muse scorns to be confin'd to the old Measures and Limits, or to observe the dull Rules of Criticks;

Nor Rapin gives her Rules to fly, nor Purcell Notes to sing. Watts.

Now 'tis Pity that such an Excellent Piece should not be dignify'd with a particular Name; and seeing it cannot justly be called, either *Epic, Sapphic, Lyric,* or *Pindaric,* nor any other Name yet invented, I presume it may, (in Honour and Remembrance of the Dead) be called the KITELIC. Thus much in the Praise of *Kitelic Poetry.*

It is certain, that those Elegies which are of our own Growth, (and our Soil seldom produces any other sort of Poetry) are by far the greatest part, wretchedly Dull and Ridiculous. Now since it is imagin'd by many, that our Poets are honest, well-meaning Fellows, who do their best, and that if they had but some Instructions how to govern Fancy with Judgment, they would make indifferent good Elegies; I shall here subjoin a Receipt for that purpose, which was left me as a Legacy, (among other valuable Rarities) by my Reverend Husband. It is as follows,

A RECEIPT to make a New-England Funeral ELEGY.

For the Title of your Elegy. Of these you may have enough ready made to your Hands; but if you should chuse to make it your self, you must be sure not to omit the Words *Aetatis Suae,* which will Beautify it exceedingly.

For the Subject of your Elegy. Take one of your Neighbours who has lately departed this Life; it is no great matter at what Age the Party dy'd, but it will be best if he went away suddenly, being *Kill'd, Drown'd,* or *Froze to Death.*

Having chose the Person, take all his Virtues, Excellencies, &c. and if he have not enough, you may borrow some to make up a sufficient Quantity: To these add his last Words, dying Expressions, &c. if they are to be had; mix all these together, and be sure you *strain* them well. Then season all with a Handful or two of Melancholly Expressions, such as, *Dreadful, Deadly, cruel cold Death, unhappy Fate, weeping Eyes,* &c. Have mixed all these Ingredients well, put them into the empty Scull of some *young Harvard;* (but in Case you have ne'er a One at Hand, you may use your own,) there let them Ferment for the Space of a Fortnight, and by that Time they will be incorporated into a Body, which take out, and having prepared a sufficient Quantity of double Rhimes, such as, *Power, Flower; Quiver, Shiver; Grieve us, Leave us; tell you, excel you; Expeditions, Physicians; Fatigue him, Intrigue him;* &c. you must spread all upon Paper, and if you can procure a Scrap of Latin to put at the End, it will garnish it mightily; then having affixed your Name at the Bottom, with a *Mœstus Composuit,* you will have an Excellent Elegy.

N.B. This Receipt will serve when a Female is the Subject of your Elegy, provided you borrow a greater Quantity of Virtues, Excellencies, &c. Sir, Your Servant,   SILENCE DOGOOD[1]

P.S. I shall make no other Answer to Hypercarpus's Criticism on my last Letter than this, *Mater me genuit, peperit mox filia matrem.*[2]

---

1. A contributor to the same issue of the *Courant* satirized the elegy in verse and named "the Sage and Immortal Doctor H———k," possibly Edward Holyoke, later president of Harvard, as its author. The elegy, or Mrs. Dogood's comments on it, inspired other satirical critiques of New England funerary verse and other attacks on Harvard learning. See, for example, the *Courant,* Aug. 6, Nov. 12, 1722, and subsequently, esp. Aug. 5, 1723.

2. See above, p. 23 n.

Silence Dogood, No. 8

Printed in *The New-England Courant*, July 9, 1722.

On June 11 the *Courant* had insinuated that the Massachusetts authorities were not making proper exertions to capture a pirate vessel reported to be off the coast.[3] Exasperated by this "High Affront," the latest of many, the General Court the next day ordered James Franklin to be confined in jail for the remainder of the legislative session. During his brother's imprisonment Benjamin managed the paper, and "made bold to give our Rulers some Rubs in it, which my Brother took very kindly, while others began to consider me . . . as a young Genius that had a Turn for Libelling & Satyr." The eighth and ninth letters of Mrs. Dogood were two such "Rubs."[4]

To the Author of the *New-England Courant.*

Sir,   [No. VIII.

I prefer the following Abstract from the London Journal to any Thing of my own, and therefore shall present it to your Readers this week without any further Preface.[5]

"Without Freedom of Thought, there can be no such Thing as Wisdom; and no such Thing as publick Liberty, without Freedom of Speech; which is the Right of every Man, as far as by it, he does not hurt or controul the Right of another: And this is the only Check it ought to suffer, and the only Bounds it ought to know.

"This sacred Privilege is so essential to free Governments, that the Security of Property, and the Freedom of Speech always go together; and in those wretched Countries where a Man cannot call his Tongue his own, he can scarce call any Thing else his own. Whoever would overthrow the Liberty of a Nation, must begin by subduing the Freeness of Speech; a *Thing* terrible to Publick Traytors.

"This Secret was so well known to the Court of King Charles the First, that his wicked Ministry procured a Proclamation, to

3. The offending words were: "We are advis'd from Boston, that the Government of the Massachusetts are fitting out a Ship to go after the Pirates, to be commanded by Capt. Peter Papillion, and 'tis thought he will sail sometime this Month, if Wind and Weather permit."

4. Clyde A. Duniway, *The Development of Freedom of the Press in Massachusetts* (Cambridge, Mass., 1906), pp. 99–100, 163–4; Mass. House of Reps., *Journals, 1722–1723*, pp. 23, 31, 35, 72.

5. *London Journal*, No. LXXX, Feb. 4, 1720/1.

forbid the People to talk of Parliaments, which those Traytors had laid aside. To assert the undoubted Right of the Subject, and defend his Majesty's legal Prerogative, was called Disaffection, and punished as Sedition. Nay, People were forbid to talk of Religion in their Families: For the Priests had combined with the Ministers to cook up Tyranny, and suppress Truth and the Law, while the late King James, when Duke of York, went avowedly to Mass, Men were fined, imprisoned and undone, for saying he was a Papist: And that King Charles the Second might live more securely a Papist, there was an Act of Parliament made, declaring it Treason to say that he was one.

"That Men ought to speak well of *their Governours* is true, while *their Governours* deserve to be well spoken of; but to do publick Mischief, without hearing of it, is only the Prerogative and Felicity of Tyranny: A free People will be shewing that they are *so*, by their Freedom of Speech.

"The Administration of Government, is nothing else but the Attendance of the *Trustees of the People* upon the Interest and Affairs of the People: And as it is the Part and Business of the People, for whose Sake alone all publick Matters are, or ought to be transacted, to see whether they be well or ill transacted; so it is the Interest, and ought to be the Ambition, of all honest Magistrates, to have their Deeds openly examined, and publickly scann'd: Only the *wicked Governours* of Men dread what is said of them; *Audivit Tiberius probra queis lacerabitur, atque* perculsus est.[6] The publick Censure was true, else he had not felt it bitter.

"Freedom of Speech is ever the Symptom, as well as the Effect of a good Government. In old Rome, all was left to the Judgment and Pleasure of the People, who examined the publick Proceedings with such Discretion, and censured those who administred them with such Equity and Mildness, that in the space of Three Hundred Years, not five publick Ministers suffered unjustly. Indeed whenever the *Commons* proceeded to Violence, the great Ones had been the Agressors.

"*Guilt* only dreads Liberty of Speech, which drags it out of its lurking Holes, and exposes its Deformity and Horrour to Daylight. Horatius, Valerius, Cincinnatus, and other vertuous and undesigning Magistrates of the Roman Commonwealth, had nothing

6. Tacitus, *Annales*, IV, 42.

28

to fear from Liberty of Speech. *Their virtuous* Administration, the more it was examin'd, the more it brightned and gain'd by Enquiry. When Valerius in particular, was accused upon some slight grounds of affecting the Diadem; he, who was the first Minister of Rome, does not accuse the People for examining his Conduct, but approved his Innocence in a Speech to them; and gave such Satisfaction to them, and gained such Popularity to himself, that they gave him a new Name; *inde cognomen factum Publicolae est;* to denote that he was their Favourite and their Friend. *Latae deinde leges—Ante omnes de provocatione* ADVERSUS MAGISTRATUS AD POPULUM, Livii, lib. 2. Cap. 8.

"But Things afterwards took another Turn. Rome, with the Loss of its Liberty, lost also its Freedom of Speech; then Mens Words began to be feared and watched; and then first began the *poysonous Race of Informers,* banished indeed under the righteous Administration of Titus, Narva, Trajan, Aurelius, &c. but encouraged and enriched under the *vile Ministry* of Sejanus, Tigillinus, Pallas, and Cleander: *Queri libet, quod in secreta nostra non inquirant principes, nisi quos Odimus,* says Pliny to Trajan.[7]

"The best Princes have ever encouraged and promoted Freedom of Speech; they know that upright Measures would defend themselves, and that all upright Men would defend them. Tacitus, speaking of the Reign of some of the Princes abovemention'd, says with Extasy, *Rara Temporum felicitate, ubi sentire quae velis, & quae sentias dicere licet:*[8] A blessed Time when you might think what you would, and speak what you thought.

"I doubt not but old Spencer and his Son,[9] who were the *Chief Ministers* and *Betrayers* of Edward the Second, would have been very glad to have stopped the Mouths of all the honest Men in England. They dreaded to be called *Traytors,* because they were *Traytors.* And I dare say, Queen Elizabeth's Walsingham, who deserved no Reproaches, feared none. Misrepresentation of publick Measures is easily overthrown, by representing publick Measures truly; when they are honest, they ought to be publickly known, that they may be publickly commended; but if they are knavish or

7. Pliny, *Panegyricus,* 68.
8. Tacitus, *Historiae,* I, I.
9. Hugh Le Despenser, Earl of Winchester (1262–1326), and his son, Sir Hugh Le Despenser (d. 1326).

pernicious, they ought to be publickly exposed, in order to be publickly detested." Yours, &c.,   SILENCE DOGOOD

Silence Dogood, No. 9

Printed in *The New-England Courant*, July 23, 1722.

Corruptio optimi est pessima.[1]

To the Author of the *New-England Courant*.

Sir,

It has been for some Time a Question with me, Whether a Commonwealth suffers more by hypocritical Pretenders to Religion, or by the openly Profane? But some late Thoughts of this Nature, have inclined me to think, that the Hypocrite is the most dangerous Person of the Two, especially if he sustains a Post in the Government, and we consider his Conduct as it regards the Publick. The first Artifice of a *State Hypocrite* is, by a few savoury Expressions which cost him Nothing, to betray the best Men in his Country into an Opinion of his Goodness; and if the Country wherein he lives is noted for the Purity of Religion, he the more easily gains his End, and consequently may more justly be expos'd and detested. A notoriously profane Person in a private Capacity, ruins himself, and perhaps forwards the Destruction of a few of his Equals; but a publick Hypocrite every day deceives his betters, and makes them the Ignorant Trumpeters of his supposed Godliness: They take him for a Saint, and pass him for one, without considering that they are (as it were) the Instruments of publick Mischief out of Conscience, and ruin their Country for God's sake.

This Political Description of a Hypocrite, may (for ought I know) be taken for a new Doctrine by some of your Readers; but let them consider, that *a little Religion, and a little Honesty, goes a great way in Courts*. 'Tis not inconsistent with Charity to distrust a Religious Man in Power, tho' he may be a good Man; he has many Temptations "to propagate *publick Destruction* for *Personal Advantages* and Security": And if his Natural Temper be covetous, and his Actions often contradict his pious Discourse, we

1. "So true is that old saying, *Corruptio optimi pessima." Purchas his Pilgrimage* (3d edit., London, 1617), "To the Reader."

30

may with great Reason conclude, that he has some other Design in his Religion besides barely getting to Heaven. But the most dangerous Hypocrite in a Common-Wealth, is one who *leaves the Gospel for the sake of the Law*:[2] A Man compounded of Law and Gospel, is able to cheat a whole Country with his Religion, and then destroy them under *Colour of Law:* And here the Clergy are in great Danger of being deceiv'd, and the People of being deceiv'd by the Clergy, until the Monster arrives to such Power and Wealth, that he is out of the reach of both, and can oppress the People without their own blind Assistance. And it is a sad Observation, that when the People too late see their Error, yet the Clergy still persist in their Encomiums on the Hypocrite; and when he happens to die *for the Good of his Country,* without leaving behind him the Memory of *one good Action,* he shall be sure to have his Funeral Sermon stuff'd with *Pious Expressions* which he dropt at such a Time, and at such a Place, and on such an Occasion; than which nothing can be more prejudicial to the Interest of Religion, nor indeed to the Memory of the Person deceas'd. The Reason of this Blindness in the Clergy is, because they are honourably supported (as they ought to be) by their People, and see nor feel nothing of the Oppression which is obvious and burdensome to every one else.

But this Subject raises in me an Indignation not to be born; and if we have had, or are like to have any Instances of this Nature in New England, we cannot better manifest our Love to Religion and the Country, than by setting the Deceivers in a true Light, and undeceiving the Deceived, however such Discoveries may be represented by the ignorant or designing Enemies of our Peace and Safety.

I shall conclude with a Paragraph or two from an ingenious Political Writer in the *London Journal,* the better to convince your Readers, that Publick Destruction may be easily carry'd on by *hypocritical Pretenders to Religion.*[3]

2. Probably a reference to the strongly detested Governor Joseph Dudley, who graduated from Harvard, 1665, intending to study for the ministry, but soon entered politics instead. *DAB.*

3. Thomas Gordon (d. 1750) and John Trenchard (1662–1723) began a series of letters signed "Cato" in the *London Journal* in Nov., 1720. The letter here quoted, which appeared in the issue of May 27, 1721, was written by Gordon. *DNB.*

"A raging Passion for immoderate Gain had made Men universally and intensely hard-hearted: They were every where devouring one another. And yet the Directors and their Accomplices, who were the acting Instruments of all this outrageous Madness and Mischief, set up for wonderful pious Persons, while they were defying Almighty God, and plundering Men; and they set apart a Fund of Subscriptions for charitable Uses; that is, they mercilessly made a whole People Beggars, and charitably supported a few *necessitous* and *worthless* FAVOURITES. I doubt not, but if the Villany had gone on with Success, they would have had their Names handed down to Posterity with Encomiums; as the Names of other *publick Robbers* have been! We have *Historians* and ODE MAKERS now living, very proper for such a Task. It is certain, that most People did, at one Time, believe the *Directors* to be *great and worthy Persons*. And an honest Country Clergyman told me last Summer, upon the Road, that Sir John was an excellent publick-spirited Person, for that he had beautified his Chancel.

"Upon the whole we must not judge of one another by their best Actions; since the worst Men do some Good, and all Men make fine Professions: But we must judge of Men by the whole of their Conduct, and the Effects of it. Thorough Honesty requires great and long Proof, since many a Man, long thought honest, has at length proved a Knave. And it is from judging without Proof, or false Proof, that Mankind continue Unhappy." I am, Sir, Your humble Servant,   SILENCE DOGOOD

Silence Dogood, No. 10

Printed in *The New-England Courant*, August 13, 1722.

Optimè societas hominum servabitur. Cic.[4]

To the Author of the *New-England Courant*.

Sir,   [No. X.

Discoursing lately with an intimate Friend of mine of the lamentable Condition of Widows, he put into my Hands a Book, wherein the ingenious Author proposes (I think) a certain Method for their Relief.[5] I have often thought of some such Project for

4. Cicero, *De Officiis*, I, 16.
5. Daniel Defoe, *An Essay upon Projects* (London, 1697), pp. 132–41.

their Benefit my self, and intended to communicate my Thoughts to the Publick; but to prefer my own Proposals to what follows, would be rather an Argument of Vanity in me than Good Will to the many Hundreds of my Fellow-Sufferers now in New-England.

"We have (says he) abundance of Women, who have been Bred well, and Liv'd well, Ruin'd in a few Years, and perhaps, left Young, with a House full of Children, and nothing to Support them; which falls generally upon the Wives of the Inferior Clergy, or of Shopkeepers and Artificers.

"They marry Wives with perhaps £300 to £1000 Portion, and can settle no Jointure upon them; either they are Extravagant and Idle, and Waste it, or Trade decays, or Losses, or a Thousand Contingences happen to bring a Tradesman to Poverty, and he Breaks; the Poor Young Woman, it may be, has Three or Four Children, and is driven to a thousand shifts, while he lies in the Mint or Fryars under the *Dilemma* of a Statute of Bankrupt; but if he Dies, then she is absolutely Undone, unless she has Friends to go to.

"Suppose an Office to be Erected, to be call'd *An Office of Ensurance for Widows,* upon the following Conditions;

"Two thousand Women, or their Husbands for them, Enter their Names into a Register to be kept for that purpose, with the Names, Age, and Trade of their Husbands, with the Place of their abode, Paying at the Time of their Entring 5s. down with 1s. 4d. *per* Quarter, which is to the setting up and support of an Office with Clerks, and all proper Officers for the same; *for there is no maintaining such without Charge;* they receive every one of them a Certificate, Seal'd by the Secretary of the Office, and Sign'd by the Governors, for the Articles hereafter mentioned.

"If any one of the Women becomes a Widow, at any Time after Six Months from the Date of her Subscription, upon due Notice given, and Claim made at the Office in form, as shall be directed, she shall receive within Six Months after such Claim made, the Sum of £500 in Money, without any Deductions, saving some small Fees to the Officers, which the Trustees must settle, that they may be known.

"In Consideration of this, every Woman so Subscribing, Obliges her self to Pay as often as any Member of the Society becomes a Widow, the due Proportion or Share allotted to her to Pay, to-

33

wards the £500 for the said Widow, provided her Share does not exceed the Sum of 5s.

"No Seamen or Soldiers Wives to be accepted into such a Proposal as this, on the Account before mention'd, because the Contingences of their Lives are not equal to others, unless they will admit this general Exception, supposing they do not Die out of the Kingdom.

"It might also be an Exception, That if the Widow, that Claim'd, had really, *bona fide*, left her by her Husband to her own use, clear of all Debts and Legacies, £2000 she shou'd have no Claim; the Intent being to Aid the Poor, not add to the Rich. But there lies a great many Objections against such an Article: As

"1. It may tempt some to forswear themselves.

"2. People will Order their Wills so as to defraud the Exception.

"One Exception must be made; and that is, Either very unequal Matches, as when a Woman of Nineteen Marries an old Man of Seventy; or Women who have infirm Husbands, I mean known and publickly so. To remedy which, Two things are to be done.

"[1.] The Office must have moving Officers without doors, who shall inform themselves of such matters, and if any such Circumstances appear, the Office should have 14 days time to return their Money, and declare their Subscriptions Void.

"2. No Woman whose Husband had any visible Distemper, should claim under a Year after her Subscription.

"One grand Objection against this Proposal, is, How you will oblige People to pay either their Subscription, or their Quarteridge.

"To this I answer, *By no Compulsion* (tho' that might be perform'd too) but altogether voluntary; only with this Argument to move it, that if they do not continue their Payments, they lose the Benefit of their past Contributions.

"I know it lies as a fair Objection against such a Project as this, That the number of Claims are so uncertain, That no Body knows what they engage in, when they Subscribe, for so many may die Annually out of Two Thousand, as may perhaps make my Payment £20 or 25 *per Ann.*, and if a Woman happen to Pay that for Twenty Years, though she receives the £500 at last she is a great Loser; but if she dies before her Husband, she has lessened his Estate considerably, and brought a great Loss upon him.

"*First,* I say to this, That I wou'd have such a Proposal as this be so fair and easy, that if any Person who had Subscrib'd found the Payments too high, and the Claims fall too often, it shou'd be at their Liberty at any Time, upon Notice given, to be released and stand Oblig'd no longer; and if so, *Volenti non fit Injuria;* every one knows best what their own Circumstances will bear.

"In the next Place, because Death is a Contingency, no Man can directly Calculate, and all that Subscribe must take the Hazard; yet that a Prejudice against this Notion may not be built on wrong Grounds, let's examine a little the Probable hazard, and see how many shall die Annually out of 2000 Subscribers, accounting by the common proportion of Burials, to the number of the Living.

"Sir William Petty in his *Political Arithmetick,*[6] by a very Ingenious Calculation, brings the Account of Burials in London, to be 1 in 40 Annually, and proves it by all the proper Rules of proportion'd Computation; and I'le take my Scheme from thence. If then One in Forty of all the People in England should Die, that supposes Fifty to Die every Year out of our Two Thousand Subscribers; and for a Woman to Contribute 5s. to every one, would certainly be to agree to Pay £12 10s. *per Ann.* upon her Husband's Life, to receive £500 when he Di'd, and lose it if she Di'd first; and yet this wou'd not be a hazard beyond reason too great for the Gain.

"But I shall offer some Reasons to prove this to be impossible in our Case; First, Sir William Petty allows the City of London to contain about a Million of People, and our Yearly Bill of Mortality never yet amounted to 25000 in the most Sickly Years we have had, Plague Years excepted, sometimes but to 20000, which is but One in Fifty: Now it is to be consider'd here, that Children and Ancient People make up, one time with another, at

6. William Petty, *Another Essay in Political Arithmetick* (London, 1683), reprinted in Charles H. Hull, ed., *Economic Writings of Sir William Petty* (Cambridge, 1899), II, 451–78. For BF's indebtedness to another work of Petty's, see *A Modest Enquiry into the Nature and Necessity of a Paper Currency,* 1729, below, pp. 140–1.

least one third of our Bills of Mortality; and our *Assurances* lies upon none but the Midling Age of the People, which is the only age wherein Life is any thing steady; and if that be allow'd, there cannot Die by his Computation, above One in Eighty of such People, every Year; but because I would be sure to leave Room for Casualty, I'le allow one in Fifty shall Die out of our Number Subscrib'd.

"Secondly, It must be allow'd, that our Payments falling due only on the Death of Husbands, this One in Fifty must not be reckoned upon the Two thousand; for 'tis to be suppos'd at least as many Women shall die as Men, and then there is nothing to Pay; so that One in Fifty upon One Thousand, is the most that I can suppose shall claim the Contribution in a Year, which is Twenty Claims a Year at 5*s.* each, and is £5 *per Ann.* and if a Woman pays this for Twenty Year, and claims at last, she is Gainer enough, and no extraordinary Loser if she never claims at all: And I verily believe any Office might undertake to demand at all Adventures not above £6 *per Ann.* and secure the Subscriber £500 in case she come to claim as a Widow."

I would leave this to the Consideration of all who are concern'd for their own or their Neighbour's Temporal Happiness; and I am humbly of Opinion, that the Country is ripe for many such *Friendly Societies,* whereby every Man might help another, without any Disservice to himself. We have many charitable Gentlemen who Yearly give liberally to the Poor, and where can they better bestow their Charity than on those who become so by Providence, and for ought they know on themselves. But above all, the Clergy have the most need of coming into some such Project as this. They as well as poor Men (according to the Proverb) generally abound in Children; and how many Clergymen in the Country are forc'd to labour in their Fields, to keep themselves in a Condition above Want? How then shall they be able to leave any thing to their forsaken, dejected, and almost forgotten Wives and Children. For my own Part, I have nothing left to live on, but Contentment and a few Cows; and tho' I cannot expect to be reliev'd by this Project, yet it would be no small Satisfaction to me to see it put in Practice for the Benefit of others. I am, Sir, &c.   SILENCE DOGOOD

Silence Dogood, No. 11

Printed in *The New-England Courant*, August 20, 1722.

Neque licitum interea est meam amicam visere.[7]

To the Author of the *New-England Courant*.

Sir, [No. XI.

From a natural Compassion to my Fellow-Creatures, I have sometimes been betray'd into Tears at the Sight of an Object of Charity, who by a bear [*sic*] Relation of his Circumstances, seem'd to demand the Assistance of those about him. The following Petition represents in so lively a Manner the forlorn State of a Virgin well stricken in Years and Repentance, that I cannot forbear publishing it at this Time, with some Advice to the Petitioner.

To Mrs. Silence Dogood.
The Humble Petition of Margaret Aftercast,
SHEWETH,

"1. That your Petitioner being puff'd up in her younger Years with a numerous Train of Humble Servants, had the Vanity to think, that her extraordinary Wit and Beauty would continually recommend her to the Esteem of the Gallants; and therefore as soon as it came to be publickly known that any Gentleman address'd her, he was immediately discarded.

"2. That several of your Petitioners Humble Servants, who upon their being rejected by her, were, to all Apperance in a dying Condition, have since recover'd their Health, and been several Years married, to the great Surprize and Grief of your Petitioner, who parted with them upon no other Conditions, but that they should die or run distracted for her, as several of them faithfully promis'd to do.

"3. That your Petitioner finding her self disappointed in and neglected by her former Adorers, and no new Offers appearing for some Years past, she has been industriously contracting Acquaintance with several Families in Town and Country, where any young Gentlemen or Widowers have resided, and endeavour'd to appear as conversable as possible before them: She has likewise

7. Source not found.

been a strict Observer of the Fashion, and always appear'd well dress'd. And the better to restore her decay'd Beauty, she has consum'd above Fifty Pound's Worth of the most approved *Cosmeticks*. But all won't do.

"Your Petitioner therefore most humbly prays, That you would be pleased to form a Project for the Relief of all those penitent Mortals of the fair Sex, that are like to be punish'd with their Virginity until old Age, for the Pride and Insolence of their Youth.

"And your Petitioner (as in Duty bound) shall ever pray, &c.

MARGARET AFTERCAST"

Were I endow'd with the Faculty of Match-making, it should be improv'd for the Benefit of Mrs. Margaret, and others in her Condition: But since my extream Modesty and Taciturnity, forbids an Attempt of this Nature, I would advise them to relieve themselves in a Method of *Friendly Society;* and that already publish'd for Widows, I conceive would be a very proper Proposal for them, whereby every single Woman, upon full Proof given of her continuing a Virgin for the Space of Eighteen Years, (dating her Virginity from the Age of Twelve,) should be entituled to £500 in ready Cash.

But then it will be necessary to make the following Exceptions.

1. That no Woman shall be admitted into the Society after she is Twenty Five Years old, who has made a Practice of entertaining and discarding Humble Servants, without sufficient Reason for so doing, until she has manifested her Repentance in Writing under her Hand.

2. No Member of the Society who has declar'd before two credible Witnesses, *That it is well known she has refus'd several good Offers since the Time of her Subscribing,* shall be entituled to the £500 when she comes of Age; that is to say, *Thirty Years.*

3. No Woman, who after claiming and receiving, has had the good Fortune to marry, shall entertain any Company with Encomiums on her Husband, above the Space of one Hour at a Time, upon Pain of returning one half the Money into the Office, for the first Offence; and upon the second Offence to return the Remainder. I am, Sir, Your Humble Servant,

SILENCE DOGOOD

Silence Dogood, No. 12

Printed in *The New-England Courant*, September 10, 1722.

Quod est in cordi sobrii, est in ore ebrii.[8]

To the Author of the *New-England Courant.*

Sir,   [No. XII.

It is no unprofitable tho' unpleasant Pursuit, diligently to in-spect and consider the Manners and Conversation of Men, who, insensible of the greatest Enjoyments of humane Life, abandon themselves to Vice from a false Notion of *Pleasure* and *good Fellow-ship.* A true and natural Representation of any Enormity, is often the best Argument against it and Means of removing it, when the most severe Reprehensions alone, are found ineffectual.

I would in this letter improve the little Observation I have made on the Vice of *Drunkeness,* the better to reclaim the *good Fellows* who usually pay the Devotions of the Evening to Bacchus.

I doubt not but *moderate Drinking* has been improv'd for the Diffusion of Knowledge among the ingenious Part of Mankind, who want the Talent of a ready Utterance, in order to discover the Conceptions of their Minds in an entertaining and intelligible Manner. 'Tis true, drinking does not *improve* our Faculties, but it enables us to *use* them; and therefore I conclude, that much Study and Experience, and a little Liquor, are of absolute Necessity for some Tempers, in order to make them accomplish'd Orators. Dic. Ponder discovers an excellent Judgment when he is inspir'd with a Glass or two of *Claret,* but he passes for a Fool among those of small Observation, who never saw him the better for Drink. And here it will not be improper to observe, That the moderate Use of Liquor, and a well plac'd and well regulated Anger, often pro-duce this same Effect; and some who cannot ordinarily talk but in broken Sentences and false Grammar, do in the Heat of Passion express themselves with as much Eloquence as Warmth. Hence it is that my own Sex are generally the most eloquent, because the most passionate. "It has been said in the Praise of some Men, (says an ingenious Author,) that they could talk whole Hours to-gether upon any thing; but it must be owned to the Honour of the other Sex, that there are many among them who can talk whole

8. Proverbial.

Hours together upon Nothing. I have known a Woman branch out into a long extempore Dissertation on the Edging of a Petticoat, and chide her Servant for breaking a China Cup, in all the Figures of Rhetorick."[9]

But after all it must be consider'd, that no Pleasure can give Satisfaction or prove advantageous to a *reasonable Mind,* which is not attended with the *Restraints of Reason.* Enjoyment is not to be found by Excess in any sensual Gratification; but on the contrary, the immoderate Cravings of the Voluptuary, are always succeeded with Loathing and a palled Appetite. What Pleasure can the Drunkard have in the Reflection, that, while in his Cups, he retain'd only the Shape of a Man, and acted the Part of a Beast; or that from reasonable Discourse a few Minutes before, he descended to Impertinence and Nonsense?

I cannot pretend to account for the different Effects of Liquor on Persons of different Dispositions, who are guilty of Excess in the Use of it. 'Tis strange to see Men of a regular Conversation become rakish and profane when intoxicated with Drink, and yet more surprizing to observe, that some who appear to be the most profligate Wretches when sober, become mighty religious in their Cups, and will then, and at no other Time address their Maker, but when they are destitute of Reason, and actually affronting him. Some shrink in the Wetting, and others swell to such an unusual Bulk in their Imaginations, that they can in an Instant understand all Arts and Sciences, by the liberal Education of a little vivifying *Punch,* or a sufficient Quantity of other exhilerating Liquor.

And as the Effects of Liquor are various, so are the Characters given to its Devourers. It argues some Shame in the Drunkards themselves, in that they have invented numberless Words and Phrases to cover their Folly, whose proper Significations are harmless, or have no Signification at all. They are seldom known to be *drunk,* tho' they are very often *boozey, cogey, tipsey, fox'd, merry, mellow, fuddl'd, groatable, Confoundedly cut, See two Moons,* are *Among the Philistines, In a very good Humour, See the Sun,* or, *The Sun has shone upon them;* they *Clip the King's English,* are *Almost froze, Feavourish, In their Altitudes, Pretty well enter'd,* &c.[1]

9. *The Spectator,* No. 247.
1. With a few exceptions and unimportant variations, these synonyms appear in The Drinker's Dictionary, *Pa. Gaz.,* Jan. 13, 1737.

In short, every Day produces some new Word or Phrase which might be added to the Vocabulary of the *Tiplers:* But I have chose to mention these few, because if at any Time a Man of Sobriety and Temperance happens to *cut himself confoundedly,* or is *almost froze,* or *feavourish,* or accidentally *sees the Sun,* &c. he may escape the Imputation of being *drunk,* when his Misfortune comes to be related. I am Sir, Your Humble Servant,   SILENCE DOGOOD

Silence Dogood, No. 13

Printed in *The New-England Courant,* September 24, 1722.

To the Author of the *New-England Courant.*

Sir,   [No. XIII.

In Persons of a contemplative Disposition, the most indifferent Things provoke the Exercise of the Imagination; and the Satisfactions which often arise to them thereby, are a certain Relief to the Labour of the Mind (when it has been intensely fix'd on more substantial Subjects) as well as to that of the Body.

In one of the late pleasant Moon-light Evenings, I so far indulg'd in my self the Humour of the Town in walking abroad, as to continue from my Lodgings two or three Hours later than usual, and was pleas'd beyond Expectation before my Return. Here I found various Company to observe, and various Discourse to attend to. I met indeed with the common Fate of *Listeners,* (who *hear no good of themselves,*) but from a Consciousness of my Innocence, receiv'd it with a Satisfaction beyond what the Love of Flattery and the Daubings of a Parasite could produce. The Company who rally'd me were about Twenty in Number, of both Sexes; and tho' the *Confusion of Tongues* (like that of Babel) which always happens among so many impetuous Talkers, render'd their Discourse not so intelligible as I could wish, I learnt thus much, That one of the Females pretended to know me, from some Discourse she had heard at a certain House before the Publication of one of my Letters; adding, *That I was a Person of an ill Character, and kept a criminal Correspondence with a Gentleman who assisted me in Writing.* One of the Gallants clear'd me of this random Charge, by saying, *That tho' I wrote in the Character of a Woman, he knew me to be a Man; But,* continu'd he, *he has more need of*

41

endeavouring a Reformation in himself, than spending his Wit in satyrizing others.

I had no sooner left this Set of Ramblers, but I met a Crowd of *Tarpolins* and their Doxies, link'd to each other by the Arms, who ran (by their own Account) after the Rate of *Six Knots an Hour,* and bent their Course towards the Common. Their eager and amorous Emotions of Body, occasion'd by taking their Mistresses *in Tow,* they call'd *wild Steerage:* And as a Pair of them happen'd to trip and come to the Ground, the Company were call'd upon to *bring to,* for that Jack and Betty were *founder'd.* But this Fleet were not less comical or irregular in their Progress than a Company of Females I soon after came up with, who, by throwing their Heads to the Right and Left, at every one who pass'd by them, I concluded came out with no other Design than to revive the Spirit of Love in Disappointed Batchelors, and expose themselves to Sale to the first Bidder.

But it would take up too much Room in your Paper to mention all the Occasions of Diversion I met with in this Night's Ramble. As it grew later, I observed, that many pensive Youths with down Looks and a slow Pace, would be ever now and then crying out on the Cruelty of their Mistresses; others with a more rapid Pace and chearful Air, would be swinging their Canes and clapping their Cheeks, and whispering at certain Intervals, *I'm certain I shall have her! This is more than I expected! How charmingly she talks!* &c.

Upon the whole I conclude, That our *Night-Walkers* are a Set of People, who contribute very much to the Health and Satisfaction of those who have been fatigu'd with Business or Study, and occasionally observe their pretty Gestures and Impertinencies. But among Men of Business, the *Shoemakers,* and other Dealers in Leather, are doubly oblig'd to them, inasmuch as they exceedingly promote the Consumption of their Ware: And I have heard of a *Shoemaker,* who being ask'd by a noted Rambler, *Whether he could tell how long her Shoes would last;* very prettily answer'd, *That he knew how many Days she might wear them, but not how many Nights; because they were then put to a more violent and irregular Service than when she employ'd her self in the common Affairs of the House.* I am, Sir, Your Humble Servant,   SILENCE DOGOOD

Silence Dogood, No. 14

Printed in *The New-England Courant*, October 8, 1722.

Earum causarum quantum quaeque valeat, videamus. Cicero.[2]

To the Author of the *New-England Courant*.

Sir,   [No. XIV.

It often happens, that the most zealous Advocates for any Cause find themselves disappointed in the first Appearance of Success in the Propagation of their Opinion; and the Disappointment appears unavoidable, when their easy Proselytes too suddenly start into Extreams, and are immediately fill'd with Arguments to invalidate their former Practice. This creates a Suspicion in the more considerate Part of Mankind, that those who are thus *given to Change, neither *fear God,* nor *honour the King.* In Matters of Religion, he that alters his Opinion on a *religious Account,* must certainly go thro' much Reading, hear many Arguments on both Sides, and undergo many Struggles in his Conscience, before he can come to a full Resolution: Secular Interest will indeed make quick Work with an immoral Man, especially if, notwithstanding the Alteration of his Opinion, he can with any Appearance of Credit retain his Immorality. But, by this Turn of Thought I would not be suspected of Uncharitableness to those Clergymen at Connecticut, who have lately embrac'd the Establish'd Religion of our Nation, some of whom I hear made their Professions with a Seriousness becoming their Order:[3] However, since they have deny'd the

2. *De Senectute,* 5.
3. The case of the "Connecticut clergymen" caused no little excitement and dismay throughout Puritan New England. All spring rumor had attributed Anglican and Arminian views to Timothy Cutler, rector of Yale College, some of his tutors, and several young clergymen in the vicinity of New Haven. "How is the gold become dim!" lamented one of the orthodox. At the Yale commencement, Sept. 12, Cutler created a sensation by closing his prayer with the Episcopal words, "And let all the people say, Amen." Next day the offending clergymen appeared before the trustees in the college library. Two of them declared they doubted the validity of ordination by ministers, the rest were sure that such ordination was absolutely invalid. On Oct. 17 the trustees relieved Cutler of his duties as rector, and enacted a requirement that henceforth every rector and tutor must declare his assent to the Saybrook confession of faith. Soon afterwards Cutler, Daniel Browne, a tutor, and Samuel Johnson, minister of the Congregational church at West Haven, sailed for England to receive

43

Validity of *Ordination* by the Hands of *Presbyters*, and consequently their Power of Administring the *Sacraments*, &c. we may justly expect a suitable Manifestation of their Repentance for invading the *Priests* Office, and living so long in a Corah-like Rebellion. All I would endeavour to shew is, That an indiscreet Zeal for spreading an Opinion, hurts the Cause of the Zealot. There are too many blind Zealots among every Denomination of Christians; and he that propagates the Gospel among *Rakes* and *Beaus* without reforming them in their Morals, is every whit as ridiculous and impolitick as a Statesman who makes Tools of Ideots and Tale-Bearers.

Much to my present Purpose are the Words of two Ingenious Authors of the Church of England, tho' in all Probability they were tainted with Whiggish Principles; and with these I shall conclude this Letter.

"I would (says one[4]) have every zealous Man examine his Heart thoroughly, and, I believe, he will often find that what he calls a Zeal for his Religion, is either Pride, Interest or Ill-nature. A Man who differs from another in Opinion sets himself above him in his own Judgment, and in several Particulars pretends to be the wiser Person. This is a great Provocation to the Proud Man, and gives a keen Edge to what he calls his Zeal. And that this is the Case very often, we may observe from the Behaviour of some of the most Zealous for Orthodoxy, who have often great Friendships and Intimacies with vicious immoral Men, provided they do but agree with them in the same Scheme of Belief. The Reason is, because the vicious Believer gives the Precedency to the virtuous Man, and allows the good Christian to be the worthier Person, at the same Time that he cannot come up to his Perfections. This we find exemplified in that trite Passage which we see quoted in almost every System of Ethicks, tho' upon another Occasion;

> —— *Video meliore proboque*
> *Deteriora sequor* ——[5]

Anglican ordination. Franklin B. Dexter, *Documentary History of Yale University . . . 1701–1745* (New Haven, 1916), pp. 225-33; Williston Walker, *A History of the Congregational Churches in the United States* (N.Y., 1894), pp. 222–6; Clifford K. Shipton, *Biographical Sketches of those who attended Harvard College*, V (Boston, 1937), 50–2.

4. *The Spectator*, No. 185.   5. Ovid, *Metamorphoses*, VII, 20.

44

On the contrary, it is certain if our Zeal were true and genuine, we should be much more angry with a Sinner than a Heretick, since there are several Cases which may excuse the latter before his great Judge, but none which can excuse the former."

"I have (says another[6]) found by Experience, that it is impossible to talk distinctly without defining the Words of which we make use. There is not a Term in our Language which wants Explanation so much as the Word *Church*. One would think when People utter it, they should have in their Minds Ideas of Virtue and Religion; but that important Monosyllable drags all the other Words in the Language after it, and it is made use of to express both Praise and Blame, according to the Character of him who speaks it. By this means it happens, that no one knows what his Neighbour means when he says such a one is for or against the Church. It has happen'd that he who is seen every Day at Church, has not been counted in the Eye of the World a Churchman; and he who is very zealous to oblige every one to frequent it but himself, has been a very good Son of the Church. This Praepossession is the best Handle imaginable for Politicians to make use of, for managing the Loves and Hatreds of Mankind to the Purposes to which they would lead them. But this is not a Thing for Fools to meddle with, for they only bring Disesteem upon those whom they attempt to serve, when they unskilfully pronounce Terms of Art. I have observed great Evils arise from this Practice, and not only the Cause of Piety, but also the secular Interest of Clergymen, has extreamly suffered by the general unexplained Signification of the Word *Church*." I am, Sir, Your Humble Servant.

SILENCE DOGOOD[7]

6. *The Guardian*, No. 80, June 12, 1713.

7. This was Mrs. Dogood's final appearance in the *New-England Courant*. On Dec. 3, 1722, "Hugo-Grim," writing in care of the printer, appealed to her to break silence. "Is your Common-Place Wit all Exhausted, your stock of matter all spent? We thought you were well stor'd with that. . . ." James Franklin, whether or not he yet knew the identity of the author, was willing to support the entertaining fiction, and appended an advertisement to Hugo's letter: "If any Person or Persons will give a true Account of Mrs. Silence Dogood, whether Dead or alive, Married or unmarried, in Town or Countrey, that so, (if living) she may be spoke with, or Letters convey'd to her, they shall have Thanks for their Pains."

[Elegy on My Sister Franklin]

Copy: University of Pennsylvania Library

The University of Pennsylvania acquired in 1934 an eighty-six line "Elegy on my Sister Franklin," undated but written in an eighteenth-century hand, and signed "B.F."[8] The Elegy opens as follows:

> Warm from my Breast surcharg'd with Grief and Woe
> These melancholly Strains spontaneous flow,
> Flow for a fav'rite Sister's sad Decease,
> Flow for the worthiest of the female Race.

The manuscript is a sheet of four pages and appears to be a copy of an earlier version, for the penman inadvertently skipped lines 35 and 36, but put them in at the bottom of the second page, indicating where they belonged. Although the University librarians admitted that it might prove impossible either to date the verses or to identify the deceased lady, they believed the Elegy "to be the earliest manuscript of Benjamin Franklin, one of his earliest efforts in literary composition."

The difficulties anticipated in 1934 are only too real. The case for Benjamin Franklin's authorship is not conclusive. The manuscript is not in his autograph; apparently it is not even the author's copy. No genealogical data have been found that indicate that the composer's "Sister [-in-law] Franklin" was the wife of any of Benjamin Franklin's brothers. And as for the supposition that the Elegy was composed between 1718 and 1722 because Franklin wrote verses when he was a young man, he wrote them on occasions throughout his life.

More serious objections are raised by a careful study of the Elegy. It is so like the one Franklin satirized in the *New-England Courant*[9] that it has been assumed that if he wrote it, he could have composed it only *before* June 25, 1722, when the Dogood Letter No. 7 appeared: he would not, so runs the argument, have written such a piece after having so heartily ridiculed that type of poetry. Yet it is equally arguable that the composer of the Elegy would not have satirized productions like his own

8. It is described and printed in facsimile in Univ. of Pa. *Lib. Chron.*, 11 (1934), 26–33, and reprinted in part in Van Doren, *Franklin*, pp. 25–6. The MS had once been owned by Luther S. Livingston, who seems not to have discussed it in any of his many writings on BF. It was sold in 1934 in the library of Rev. Dr. Roderick Terry by Amer. Art Assoc.-Anderson Galleries, Inc., Sale No. 4107.

9. Above, p. 23. Compare the Elegy's "We've lost a Mother, Daughter, Sister kind" with the lines to which Mrs. Dogood pointed derisively: "Come let us mourn, for we have lost a Wife, a Daughter, and a Sister."

after having committed his grief to verse, and that therefore Mrs. Dogood's satire and B.F.'s Elegy must be by different hands. Moreover, nothing young Franklin wrote before 1722 has persuaded the editors that he could have written the Elegy, which, though a bad poem, reveals considerable facility with the language. And, they believe, by the time Franklin was sufficiently master of English verse to write such a piece— that is, some time after 1722—he was temperamentally incapable of doing so.

With no evidence that the Elegy was by Benjamin Franklin other than the initials "B.F." at the end in the copyist's hand, and with some reasons that strongly suggest that he did not and could not have written it, the editors have decided not to include it in this edition.

The Printer to the Reader

Printed in *The New-England Courant*, February 11, 1723.

Arrest and imprisonment had not intimidated James Franklin. Probably encouraged by the refusal of the House of Representatives to concur in the Council's proposal to reestablish press censorship, he printed, July 30, Chapter XXIX of Magna Carta, with glosses, on the freeman's right to trial by jury according to the law. On September 17, 1722, appeared a burlesque rhymed account of his case and on January 14, 1723, a long essay on religious hypocrites and some comments on Governor Shute's departure from the colony.[1] As a result James Franklin came under official notice once more. The General Court, censuring the *Courant* for its tendency to mock religion, reflect on the ministers, and affront the magistrates, forbade him "to print or Publish the New England Courant, or any other Pamphlet or Paper of the like Nature, except it be first Supervised by the Secretary of this Province." Franklin ignored the order, printed his next issue without the Secretary's permission, and the week

1. Samuel Shute's governorship, 1716–27, was one of the stormiest in Massachusetts history. The Assembly insulted him when he asked for a fixed salary, as his instructions required; overrode his opposition to issues of paper money; denied his right to adjourn the General Court and designate its place of meeting; refused to provide for defense against Indian attacks; made absurd and unwarranted assertions to control of military operations, even to appointing and dismissing military officers; and claimed the sole right to inquire into the conduct of public officials. Finding compromise with this lawless, opinionated Assembly impossible, Shute sailed to England Jan. 1, 1723, to lay his grievances before the Privy Council; but he never returned to Massachusetts. James T. Adams, *Revolutionary New England, 1691–1776* (Boston, 1923), pp. 102–6, 131; *DAB*.

after that published an ironical letter of advice to himself on how to avoid offending the authorities. Ordered arrested for contempt, he went into hiding, and, as Benjamin remembered it, "there was a Consultation held in our Printing House among his Friends what he should do in this Case. Some Propos'd to evade the Order by changing the Name of the Paper; but my Brother seeing Inconveniencies in that, it was finally concluded on as a better Way to let it be printed for the future under the name of *Benjamin Franklin*." That the paper might not appear as published by the printer's apprentice, it was proposed that Benjamin's indenture be returned to him "with a full Discharge on the Back of it, to be shown on Occasion," and that he sign new indentures for the remainder of his time, "which were to be kept private." This "very flimsy Scheme" was immediately executed; the first issue under the new arrangement appeared on February 11. It opened with an address to the public, only part of which, to judge by its style, was by Benjamin Franklin.[2]

Having thus provided for the continuation of his paper, James Franklin delivered himself up February 12, and gave his bond to keep the peace. One of his sureties was Thomas Fleet, a contributor to the *Courant*. The charges were considered by the Grand Jury in May, but no indictment was returned, and the printer was discharged. The *Courant*, however, continued to appear over Benjamin Franklin's name until it expired in 1726, although the nominal publisher had run away from Boston in September 1723.[3]

The late Publisher of this Paper, finding so many Inconveniencies would arise by his carrying the Manuscripts and publick News to be supervis'd by the Secretary, as to render his carrying it on unprofitable, has intirely dropt the Undertaking. The present Publisher having receiv'd the following Piece, desires the Readers to accept of it as a Preface to what they may hereafter meet with in this Paper.

Non ego mordaci distrinxi Carmine quenquam,
Nulla vonenato Litera onista Joco est.[4]

2. Parton did not "hesitate to attribute the greater part" of this address to BF. *Franklin*, I, 91.

3. Clyde A. Duniway, *The Development of Freedom of the Press in Massachusetts* (Cambridge, Mass., 1906), pp. 100–3, 164–6; Mass. House of Reps., *Journals, 1722–1723*, pp. 208–9.

4. Non ego mordaci destrinxi carmine quemquam
    nec meus ullius crimina versus habet.
Candidus a salibus suffusis felle refugi,
    nulla venenato littera mixta ioco est.   Ovid, *Tristia*, II, 563–6.

Long has the Press groaned in bringing forth an hateful, but numerous Brood of Party Pamphlets, malicious Scribbles, and Billingsgate Ribaldry. The Rancour and bitterness it has unhappily infused into Mens minds, and to what a Degree it has sowred and leaven'd the Tempers of Persons formerly esteemed some of the most sweet and affable, is too well known here, to need any further Proof or Representation of the Matter.

No generous and impartial Person then can blame the present Undertaking, which is designed purely for the Diversion and Merriment of the Reader. Pieces of Pleasancy and Mirth have a secret Charm in them to allay the Heats and Tumors of our Spirits, and to make a Man forget his restless Resentments. They have a strange Power to tune the harsh Disorders of the Soul, and reduce us to a serene and placid State of Mind.

The main Design of this Weekly Paper will be to entertain the Town with the most comical and diverting Incidents of Humane Life, which in so large a Place as Boston, will not fail of a universal Exemplification: Nor shall we be wanting to fill up these Papers with a grateful Interspersion of more serious Morals, which may be drawn from the most ludicrous and odd Parts of Life.

As for the Author, that is the next Question. But tho' we profess our selves ready to oblige the ingenious and courteous Reader with most Sorts of Intelligence, yet here we beg a Reserve. Nor will it be of any Manner of Advantage either to them or to the Writers, that their Names should be published; and therefore in this Matter we desire the Favour of you to suffer us to hold our Tongues: Which tho' at this Time of Day it may sound like a very uncommon Request, yet it proceeds from the very Hearts of your Humble Servants.

By this Time the Reader perceives that more than one are engaged in the present Undertaking. Yet is there one Person, an Inhabitant of this Town of Boston, whom we honour as a Doctor in the Chair, or a perpetual Dictator.

The Society had design'd to present the Publick with his Effigies, but that the Limner, to whom he was presented for a Draught of his Countenance, descryed (and this he is ready to offer upon Oath) Nineteen Features in his Face, more than ever he beheld in any Humane Visage before; which so raised the Price of his Picture, that our Master himself forbid the Extravagance of com-

49

ing up to it. And then besides, the Limner objected a Schism in his Face, which splits it from his Forehead in a strait Line down to his Chin, in such sort, that Mr. Painter protests it is a double Face, and he'll have *Four Pounds* for the Pourtraiture. However, tho' this double Face has spoilt us of a pretty Picture, yet we all rejoiced to see old Janus in our Company.

There is no Man in Boston better qualified than old Janus for a *Couranteer*, or if you please, an *Observator*, being a Man of such remarkable *Opticks*, as to look two ways at once.

As for his Morals, he is a chearly Christian, as the Country Phrase expresses it. A Man of good Temper, courteous Deportment, sound Judgment; a mortal Hater of Nonsense, Foppery, Formality, and endless Ceremony.

As for his Club, they aim at no greater Happiness or Honour, than the Publick be made to know, that it is the utmost of their Ambition to attend upon and do all imaginable good Offices to good Old Janus the Couranteer, who is and always will be the Readers humble Servant.

P.S. Gentle Readers, we design never to let a Paper pass without a Latin Motto if we can possibly pick one up, which carries a Charm in it to the Vulgar, and the learned admire the pleasure of Construing. We should have obliged the World with a Greek scrap or two, but the Printer has no Types, and therefore we intreat the candid Reader not to impute the defect to our Ignorance, for our Doctor can say all the Greek Letters by heart.[5]

5. This issue carried the following announcement: "This Paper having met with so general an Acceptance in Town and Country, as to require a far greater Number of them to be printed, than there is of the other publick Papers; and it being besides more generally read by a vast Number of Borrowers, who do not take it in, the Publisher thinks proper to give this publick Notice for the Incouragement of those who would have *Advertisements* inserted in the publick Prints, which they may have printed in this Paper at a moderate Price."

On Titles of Honor[6]

Printed in *The New-England Courant*, February 18, 1723.

Mero meridie si dixerit illi tenebras esse, credit.[7]

There is nothing in which Mankind reproach themselves more than in their Diversity of Opinions. Every Man sets himself above another in his own Opinion, and there are not two Men in the World whose Sentiments are alike in every thing. Hence it comes to pass, that the same Passages in the Holy Scriptures or the Works of the Learned, are wrested to the meaning of two opposite Parties, of contrary Opinions, as if the Passages they recite were like our Master Janus, looking *two ways at once,* or like Lawyers, who with equal Force of Argument, can plead either for the *Plaintiff* or *Defendant.*

The most absurd and ridiculous Opinions, are sometimes spread by the least colour of Argument: But if they stop at the first Broachers, *they* have still the Pleasure of being wiser (in their own Conceits) than the rest of the World, and can with the greatest Confidence pass a Sentence of Condemnation upon the Reason of all Mankind, who dissent from the peculiar Whims of their troubled Brains.

We were easily led into these Reflections at the last Meeting of our Club, when one of the Company read to us some Passages from a zealous Author against *Hatt-Honour, Titular Respects,* &c. which we will communicate to the Reader for the Diversion of this Week, if he is dispos'd to be merry with the Folly of his Fellow-Creature.[8]

"*Honour,* Friend, *says he,* properly ascends, and not descends; yet the Hat, when the Head is uncover'd, *descends,* and therefore there can be no Honour in it. Besides, Honour was from the *Beginning,* but Hats are an Invention of a *late Time,* and consequently true Honour standeth not therein.

6. Attributed to BF by Parton (*Franklin*, I, 93) and Van Doren (*Franklin*, p. 31) for stylistic reasons. The editors concur.

7. Petronius, *Satyricon*, 37.

8. The quoted material is a parody of William Penn, *No Cross, no Crown: Or several Sober Reasons Against Hat-Honour, Titular-Respects* . . . ([London] 1669), pp. 8, 11–12, as expanded by Penn in subsequent editions of his work. A. Stuart Pitt, "Franklin and William Penn's *No Cross, No Crown*," *Mod. Lang. Notes,* LIV (1939), 466–7.

"In old Time it was no disrespect for Men and Women to be call'd by their own Names: Adam, was never called *Master* Adam; we never read of Noah *Esquire,* Lot *Knight* and *Baronet,* nor the *Right Honourable* Abraham, *Viscount Mesopotamia, Baron of Carran;* no, no, they were plain Men, honest Country Grasiers, that took Care of their Families and their Flocks. Moses was a great Prophet, and Aaron a Priest of the Lord; but we never read of the *Reverend* Moses, nor the *Right Reverend Father in God,* Aaron, by Divine Providence, *Lord Arch-Bishop of Israel:* Thou never sawest *Madam* Rebecca in the Bible, my *Lady* Rachel, nor Mary, tho' a Princess of the Blood after the Death of Joseph, call'd the *Princess Dowager of Nazareth;* no, plain Rebecca, Rachel, Mary, or the *Widow* Mary, or the like: It was no Incivility then to mention their naked Names as they were expressed."

If common civility, and a generous Deportment among Mankind, be not put out of Countenance by the profound Reasoning of this Author, we hope they will continue to treat one another handsomely to the end of the World. We will not pretend an Answer to these Arguments against *modern Decency* and *Titles of Honour;* yet one of our Club will undertake to prove, that tho' Abraham was not styl'd *Right Honourable*, yet he had the Title of *Lord* given him by his Wife Sarah, which he thinks entitles her to the Honour of *My Lady* Sarah; and Rachel being married into the same Family, he concludes she may deserve the Title of *My Lady* Rachel. But this is but the Opinion of one Man; it was never put to Vote in the Society.

P.S. At the last Meeting of our Club, it was unanimously agreed, That all Letters to be inserted in this Paper, should come directed to old Janus; whereof our Correspondents are to take Notice, and conform themselves accordingly.

[Other Courant Essays Possibly by Franklin]

Franklin's contributions to the *New-England Courant* were not limited to the fourteen letters of Mrs. Silence Dogood. After he had revealed himself as their author and "began to be considered a little more by my Brother's Acquaintance," he was doubtless occasionally invited or emboldened to do another piece. When James Franklin was in prison, Franklin "had the Management of the Paper," which meant that he had to see that its columns were filled each week. No doubt the Couranteers helped him. But the young printer composed articles himself. Some of these were well-chosen extracts from English publications calculated to "give our Rulers some Rubs"; in addition young Franklin may have written some news notes and essays in the spirit of Dogood.

The issues of the *Courant* between the last of the Dogood letters and Franklin's departure from Boston in the following fall contain a number of essays the authorship of which cannot now be determined. James Franklin or members of his circle could have written them all; Benjamin Franklin could have written some, and probably did, but the editors have found no evidence to establish an identification. Listed below, by title and date only, are the essays the ascription of which to Benjamin Franklin seems most tempting; other scholars are invited to examine them anew and prove or disprove his authorship.

> High Tide in Boston, March 4, 1723
> Tatlers and Tale Bearers, March 18, 1723
> Timothy Wagstaff, April 15, 1723[9]
> Abigail Twitterfield, July 8, 1723
> On Lecture-Day Visiting, August 19, 1723.

Promissory Note to John Phillips[1]

DS: Historical Society of Pennsylvania

Boston May 5th [?] 1724[2]

I Promise to Pay or Cause to be paid unto John Phillips Bookseller The Just Sum of Three pounds Three Shilling In money by January next as witness my hand BENJAMIN FRANKLIN

9. Believed by Parton (*Franklin*, I, 94) to be "quite in the spirit of Franklin."

1. John Phillips (1701–1763), opened a bookshop on the south side of Boston Town House, 1723. He was subsequently deacon of Brattle Street Church, colonel of the Boston Regiment, captain and treasurer of the Ancient and Honorable Artillery Company, overseer of the poor, moderator of seventeen town meetings between 1749 and 1761, representative to the General Court. George E. Littlefield, *Early Boston Booksellers, 1642–1711* (Boston, 1900), pp. 225–30.

2. BF returned to Boston in late April or early May to lay before his father Governor Keith's proposal that the elder Franklin should set his son up in a printing house and that Keith would use his influence to obtain for the young man the public printing of Pennsylvania and Delaware. Josiah Franklin, puzzled and suspicious that so generous an offer should be made to a lad of eighteen, declined it politely. BF went back to Philadelphia, this time with his parents' knowledge and blessing.

To Sir Hans Sloane[3]

ALS: British Museum

Sir   June 2, 1725

Having lately been in the Nothern Parts of America, I have brought from thence a Purse made of the Stone Asbestus,[4] a Piece of the Stone, and a Piece of Wood, the Pithy Part of which is of the same Nature, and call'd by the Inhabitants, Salamander Cotton. As you are noted to be a Lover of Curiosities, I have inform'd you of these; and if you have any Inclination to purchase them, or see 'em, let me know your Pleasure by a Line directed for me at the Golden Fan in Little Britain, and I will wait upon you with them. I am, Sir Your most humble Servant

                                                        BENJAMIN FRANKLIN

P.S. I expect to be out of Town in 2 or 3 Days, and therefore beg an immediate Answer.[5]

Addressed: For Sir Hans Sloane, in Kingstreet. Bloomsbury

3. Sir Hans Sloane, Bart. (1660–1753), secretary of the Royal Society, 1693–1712, succeeded Newton as its president, 1727; physician to Queen Anne and to George I; president of the Royal College of Physicians, 1719–35; founder of the Chelsea Physic Garden. His books, manuscripts, and natural history specimens, bequeathed to the nation, formed a part of the original collection of the British Museum. G. R. de Beer, *Sir Hans Sloane and the British Museum* (London, 1953).

4. This purse, now in the British Museum (Natural History), was made of roughly plaited tremolite-asbestos, of primitive form, with loops at the top through which an asbestos thread was run. Jessie M. Sweet, "Benjamin Franklin's Purse," *Notes and Records of the Royal Society of London*, IX (1952), 308–9. A picture of it appears in I. Bernard Cohen, *Franklin and Newton* (Phila., 1956), facing p. 248.

5. Nearly fifty years later BF recorded this incident otherwise. Sloane, he wrote in his autobiography, heard of the purse, called on him, took him home to see "all his Curiosities, and persuaded me to let him add that [the purse] to the Number, for which he paid me handsomely."

A

DISSERTATION

ON

Liberty and *Necessity*,

PLEASURE *and* PAIN.

Whatever is, is in its Causes just
Since all Things are by Fate ; but purblind Man
Sees but a part o'th' Chain, the nearest Link,
His Eyes not carrying to the equal Beam
That poises all above.

Dryd.

LONDON:
Printed in the Year MDCCXXV.

A Dissertation on Liberty and Necessity

A Dissertation on Liberty and Necessity, Pleasure and Pain. London: Printed in the Year MDCCXXV. (Yale University Library)

As a journeyman in Samuel Palmer's printing house in Bartholomew's Close Franklin worked on the third edition of William Wollaston's *The Religion of Nature Delineated.*[6] Some of the author's arguments "not appearing ... well-founded," he composed "a little metaphysical Piece" to refute them. This was the *Dissertation on Liberty and Necessity*, which at once increased Palmer's respect for his workman, though he abominated its views. Franklin's essay opened in the same manner as Wollaston's, and its tail-piece was the same vignette Palmer had used on Wollaston's title-page. Only one hundred copies were struck off. Franklin gave a few to friends, but, "conceiving it might have an ill Tendency," destroyed the rest of the edition. The only two copies known to survive are in the Library of Congress and Yale University Library. The pamphlet, apparently pirated, was reprinted at Dublin in 1733, but it is doubtful that it had much influence.[7]

His purpose, Franklin explained in brief summary to Benjamin Vaughan, November 9, 1779, was "to prove the Doctrine of Fate, from the supposed Attributes of God; in some such Manner as this, That in creating and governing the World, as he was infinitely wise, he knew what would be best; infinitely good, he must be dispos'd; and infinitely powerful, he must be able to execute it. Consequently *all is right.*" This doctrine he subsequently refuted in an essay never published and now lost; and he came to regard the writing of the *Dissertation* as one of the "errata" of his life.

6. Not the second, as BF wrote in his autobiography: there had been a private printing in 1722. William Wollaston (1660–1724), schoolmaster and moral philosopher, exercised considerable authority on the moralistic thought of his century. *DNB.*

7. Bernard Faÿ declared that one Lyons replied to BF's pamphlet in the appendix to the fourth edition of his *The Infallibility of Human Judgment ...* (London, 1724). *Franklin, the Apostle of Modern Times* (Boston, 1929), p. 95. Lyons' book, however, was almost certainly published before BF's tract was printed and, though the titles of Lyons' appendix and of BF's essay are alike, Lyons clearly was not answering BF, but replying to the proposition that, "Every effect hath a sufficient Cause, every sufficient Cause must produce its Effect," whence he drew the conclusion "that Man is not a free agent, but all his Actions are Necessary." On the contrary, as BF relates in his autobiography, Lyons was so favorably impressed by the *Dissertation* that he made the author's acquaintance, often talked with him, and introduced him to Dr. Mandeville and to Henry Pemberton, who promised to take him to see Sir Isaac Newton.

In its general syllogistic form the *Dissertation* is indebted to Franklin's study of Ozell's translation of *Logic, or, the Art of Thinking* by the learned doctors of Port Royal, Arnauld and Nicole. (A copy of this book, with Franklin's signature on the title-page, is in the Library Company of Philadelphia.) The content of the essay is a distillation of Franklin's reading of Locke, Shaftesbury, and Anthony Collins.[8]

A DISSERTATION

ON LIBERTY AND NECESSITY, &c.[9]

To Mr. J. R.[1]

Sir,

I have here, according to your Request, given you my *present* Thoughts of the *general State of Things* in the Universe. Such as they are, you have them, and are welcome to 'em; and if they yield you any Pleasure or Satisfaction, I shall think my Trouble sufficiently compensated. I know my Scheme will be liable to many

8. On this see Frank L. Mott and Chester E. Jorgenson, eds., *Benjamin Franklin; Representative Selections* (N.Y., 1936), pp. cxvii–cxxviii; on the pamphlet's position in the whole deistical movement see Alfred Owen Aldridge, "Benjamin Franklin and Philosophical Necessity," *Mod. Lang. Quar.*, XII (1951), 292–309.

9. The verses on the title-page are from John Dryden, *Oedipus*, III, i, 244–8.

1. James Ralph (*c.* 1705–1762), merchant's clerk in Philadelphia, "ingenious, genteel in his Manners, and extreamly eloquent," a member of BF's literary group, 1724, ambitious to become a poet but without enough talent for it. BF blamed himself for unsettling Ralph's religious principles. Abandoning wife and infant, Ralph sailed with BF to London, where he lived on the latter's bounty until he found a place as a schoolmaster in the country. During Ralph's absence from London, BF looked after his mistress but "grew fond of her Company, and, being at this time under no Religious Restraints," he "attempted Familiarities (another Erratum) which she repuls'd with a proper Resentment." Ralph ended the friendship forthwith, not a little to BF's relief.

During the next thirty years Ralph composed some indifferent poems, had a small success as a dramatist, drew Pope's withering scorn, and, becoming "a pretty good Prose Writer," made a career as a political writer in the service of George Bubb Dodington, Frederick, Prince of Wales, and the Duke of Bedford. He assisted Henry Fielding in managing the Little Theater, Haymarket, 1735–37, and collaborated with him in editing *The Champion*, an anti-ministerial weekly. He subsequently edited *The Remembrancer*, described as "a weekly slap in the face for the ministry," and *The Protester*. He was pensioned

Objections from a less discerning Reader than your self; but it is not design'd for those who can't understand it. I need not give you any Caution to distinguish the hypothetical Parts of the Argument from the conclusive: You will easily perceive what I design for Demonstration, and what for Probability only. The whole I leave entirely to you, and shall value my self more or less on this account, in proportion to your Esteem and Approbation.

Sect. i. Of Liberty and Necessity.

i. *There is said to be a* First Mover, *who is called* God, *Maker of the Universe.*

ii. *He is said to be all-wise, all-good, all powerful.*

These two Propositions being allow'd and asserted by People of almost every Sect and Opinion; I have here suppos'd them granted, and laid them down as the Foundation of my Argument; What follows then, being a Chain of Consequences truly drawn from them, will stand or fall as they are true or false.

iii. *If He is all-good, whatsoever He doth must be good.*

iv. *If He is all-wise, whatsoever He doth must be wise.*

The Truth of these Propositions, with relation to the two first, I think may be justly call'd evident; since, either that infinite Goodness will act what is ill, or infinite Wisdom what is not wise, is too glaring a Contradiction not to be perceiv'd by any Man of common Sense, and deny'd as soon as understood.

v. *If He is all-powerful, there can be nothing either existing or acting in the Universe* against *or* without *his Consent; and what He consents to must be good, because He is good; therefore* Evil *doth not exist.*

Unde Malum? has been long a Question, and many of the Learned have perplex'd themselves and Readers to little Purpose in Answer to it. That there are both Things and Actions to which we give

---

in 1753 on condition that he give up political writing. He wrote a good *History of England during the Reigns of King William, Queen Anne, and King George I.*

BF renewed his acquaintance with Ralph when he returned to London, 1757; employed him to assist in preparing for the press *An Historical Review of the Constitution and Government of Pennsylvania,* 1759; and, presumably to help Ralph's daughter, purchased more than fifty titles, for £6 5s., at the sale of Ralph's library, 1762. Robert W. Kenny, "James Ralph: An Eighteenth-Century Philadelphian in Grub Street," *PMHB,* LXIV (1940), 218–42; John B. Shipley, "Franklin Attends a Book Auction," *ibid.,* LXXX (1956), 37–45; *DAB; DNB.*

the Name of *Evil,* is not here deny'd, as *Pain, Sickness, Want, Theft, Murder,* &c. but that these and the like are not in reality *Evils, Ills,* or *Defects* in the Order of the Universe, is demonstrated in the next Section, as well as by this and the following Proposition. Indeed, to suppose any Thing to exist or be done, *contrary* to the Will of the Almighty, is to suppose him not almighty; or that Something (the Cause of *Evil*) is more mighty than the Almighty; an Inconsistence that I think no One will defend: And to deny any Thing or Action, which he consents to the existence of, to be good, is entirely to destroy his two Attributes of *Wisdom* and *Goodness.*

There is nothing done in the Universe, say the Philosophers, *but what God either does, or* permits *to be done.* This, as He is Almighty, is certainly true: But what need of this Distinction between *doing* and *permitting?* Why, first they take it for granted that many Things in the Universe exist in such a Manner as is not for the best, and that many Actions are done which ought not to be done, or would be better undone; these Things or Actions they cannot ascribe to God as His, because they have already attributed to Him infinite Wisdom and Goodness; Here then is the Use of the Word *Permit;* He *permits* them to be done, *say they.* But we will reason thus: If God permits an Action to be done, it is because he wants either *Power* or *Inclination* to hinder it; in saying he wants *Power,* we deny Him to be *almighty;* and if we say He wants *Inclination* or *Will,* it must be, either because He is not Good, or the Action is not *evil,* (for all Evil is contrary to the Essence of *infinite Goodness.*) The former is inconsistent with his before-given Attribute of Goodness, therefore the latter must be true.

It will be said, perhaps, that *God permits evil Actions to be done, for* wise *Ends and Purposes.* But this Objection destroys itself; for whatever an infinitely good God hath wise Ends in suffering to *be,* must be good, is thereby made good, and cannot be otherwise.

VI. *If a Creature is made by God, it must depend upon God, and receive all its Power from Him; with which Power the Creature can do nothing contrary to the Will of God, because God is Almighty; what is not contrary to His Will, must be agreeable to it; what is agreeable to it, must be good, because He is Good; therefore a Creature can do nothing but what is good.*

60

This Proposition is much to the same Purpose with the former, but more particular; and its Conclusion is as just and evident. Tho' a Creature may do many Actions which by his Fellow Creatures will be nam'd *Evil,* and which will naturally and necessarily cause or bring upon the Doer, certain *Pains* (which will likewise be call'd *Punishments;*) yet this Proposition proves, that he cannot act what will be in itself really Ill, or displeasing to God. And that the painful Consequences of his evil Actions *(so call'd)* are not, as indeed they ought not to be, *Punishments* or Unhappinesses, will be shewn hereafter.

Nevertheless, the late learned Author of *The Religion of Nature,* (which I send you herewith) has given us a Rule or Scheme, whereby to discover which of our Actions ought to be esteem'd and denominated *good,* and which *evil:* It is in short this, "Every Action which is done according to *Truth,* is good; and every Action contrary to Truth, is evil: To act according to Truth is to use and esteem every Thing as what it is, &c. Thus if *A* steals a Horse from *B,* and rides away upon him, he uses him not as what he is in Truth, viz. the Property of another, but as his own, which is contrary to Truth, and therefore *evil.*" But, as this Gentleman himself says, (Sect. I. Prop. VI.) "In order to judge rightly what any Thing is, it must be consider'd, not only what it is in one Respect, but also what it may be in any other Respect; and the whole Description of the Thing ought to be taken in:" So in this Case it ought to be consider'd, that *A* is naturally a *covetous* Being, feeling an Uneasiness in the want of *B*'s Horse, which produces an Inclination for stealing him, stronger than his Fear of Punishment for so doing. This is *Truth* likewise, and *A* acts according to it when he steals the Horse. Besides, if it is prov'd to be a *Truth,* that *A* has not Power over his own Actions, it will be indisputable that he acts according to Truth, and impossible he should do otherwise.

I would not be understood by this to encourage or defend Theft; 'tis only for the sake of the Argument, and will certainly have no *ill Effect.* The Order and Course of Things will not be affected by Reasoning of this Kind; and 'tis as just and necessary, and as much according to Truth, for *B* to dislike and punish the Theft of his Horse, as it is for *A* to steal him.

VII. *If the Creature is thus limited in his Actions, being able to do only such Things as God would have him to do, and not being able to*

61

refuse doing what God would have done; then he can have no such Thing as Liberty, Free-will or Power to do or refrain an Action.

By *Liberty* is sometimes understood the Absence of Opposition; and in this Sense, indeed, all our Actions may be said to be the Effects of our Liberty: But it is a Liberty of the same Nature with the Fall of a heavy Body to the Ground; it has Liberty to fall, that is, it meets with nothing to hinder its Fall, but at the same Time it is necessitated to fall, and has no Power or Liberty to remain suspended.

But let us take the Argument in another View, and suppose ourselves to be, in the common sense of the Word, *Free Agents*. As Man is a Part of this great Machine, the Universe, his regular Acting is requisite to the regular moving of the whole. Among the many Things which lie before him to be done, he may, as he is at Liberty and his Choice influenc'd by nothing, (for so it must be, or he is not at Liberty) chuse any one, and refuse the rest. Now there is every Moment something *best* to be done, which is alone then *good*, and with respect to which, every Thing else is at that Time *evil*. In order to know which is best to be done, and which not, it is requisite that we should have at one View all the intricate Consequences of every Action with respect to the general Order and Scheme of the Universe, both present and future; but they are innumerable and incomprehensible by any Thing but Omniscience. As we cannot know these, we have but as one Chance to ten thousand, to hit on the right Action; we should then be perpetually blundering about in the Dark, and putting the Scheme in Disorder; for every wrong Action of a Part, is a Defect or Blemish in the Order of the Whole. Is it not necessary then, that our Actions should be over-rul'd and govern'd by an all-wise Providence? How exact and regular is every Thing in the *natural* World! How wisely in every Part contriv'd! We cannot here find the least Defect! Those who have study'd the mere animal and vegetable Creation, demonstrate that nothing can be more harmonious and beautiful! All the heavenly Bodies, the Stars and Planets, are regulated with the utmost Wisdom! And can we suppose less Care to be taken in the Order of the *moral* than in the *natural* System? It is as if an ingenious Artificer, having fram'd a curious Machine or Clock, and put its many intricate Wheels and Powers in such a Dependance on one another, that the whole might move in the most exact Order and Regularity, had nevertheless plac'd in it several other Wheels endu'd with an independent *Self-Motion,* but ignorant of the general Interest of the Clock; and these would every now and then be moving wrong, disordering the true Movement, and making continual Work for the Mender; which might better be prevented, by depriving them of that Power of Self-Motion, and placing them in a Dependance on the regular Part of the Clock.

VIII. *If there is no such Thing as Free-Will in Creatures, there can be neither Merit nor Demerit in Creatures.*

IX. *And therefore every Creature must be equally esteem'd by the Creator.*

These Propositions appear to be the necessary Consequences of the former. And certainly no Reason can be given, why the Creator should prefer in his Esteem one Part of His Works to another, if with equal Wisdom and Goodness he design'd and created them all, since all Ill or Defect, as contrary to his Nature, is excluded by his Power. We will sum up the Argument thus, When the Creator first design'd the Universe, either it was His Will and Intention that all Things should exist and be in the Manner they are at this Time; or it was his Will they should *be* otherwise i.e. in a different Manner: To say it was His Will Things should be otherwise than they are, is to say Somewhat hath contradicted His Will, and broken His Measures, which is impossible because inconsistent with his Power; therefore we must allow that all Things exist now in a Manner agreeable to His Will, and in consequence of that are all equally Good, and therefore equally esteemed by Him.

I proceed now to shew, that as all the Works of the Creator are equally esteem'd by Him, so they are, as in Justice they ought to be, equally us'd.

SECT. II. Of Pleasure and Pain.

I. *When a Creature is form'd and endu'd with Life, 'tis suppos'd to receive a Capacity of the Sensation of* Uneasiness *or* Pain.

It is this distinguishes Life and Consciousness from unactive unconscious Matter. To know or be sensible of Suffering or being acted upon is *to live;* and whatsoever is not so, among created Things, is properly and truly *dead.*

All *Pain* and *Uneasiness* proceeds at first from and is caus'd by Somewhat without and distinct from the Mind itself. The Soul must first be acted upon before it can re-act. In the Beginning of Infancy it is as if it were not; it is not conscious of its own Existence, till it has receiv'd the first Sensation of *Pain;* then, and not before, it begins to feel itself, is rous'd, and put into Action; then it discovers its Powers and Faculties, and exerts them to expel the Uneasiness. Thus is the Machine set on work; this is Life. We are first mov'd by *Pain,* and the whole succeeding Course of our Lives is but one continu'd Series of Action with a View to be freed from it. As fast as we have excluded one Uneasiness another appears, otherwise the Motion would cease. If a continual Weight is not apply'd, the Clock will stop. And as soon as the Avenues of Uneasiness to the Soul are choak'd up or cut off, we are dead, we think and act no more.

II. *This Uneasiness, whenever felt, produces* Desire *to be freed from it, great in exact proportion to the Uneasiness.*

Thus is *Uneasiness* the first Spring and Cause of all Action; for till we are uneasy in Rest, we can have no Desire to move, and without Desire of moving there can be no voluntary Motion. The Experience of every Man who has observ'd his own Actions will evince the Truth of this; and I think nothing need be said to prove that the *Desire* will be equal to the *Uneasiness,* for the very Thing implies as much: It is not *Uneasiness* unless we desire to be freed from it, nor a great *Uneasiness* unless the consequent Desire is great.

I might here observe, how necessary a Thing in the Order and Design of the Universe this *Pain* or *Uneasiness* is, and how beautiful in its Place! Let us but suppose it just now banish'd the World entirely, and consider the Consequence of it: All the Animal Creation would immediately stand stock still, exactly in the Posture they were in the Moment Uneasiness departed; not a Limb, not a Finger would henceforth move; we should all be reduc'd to the Condition of Statues, dull and unactive: Here I should continue to sit motionless with the Pen in my Hand thus——and neither leave my Seat nor write one Letter more. This may appear odd at first View, but a little Consideration will make it evident; for 'tis impossible to assign any other Cause for the voluntary Motion of an Animal than its *uneasiness* in Rest. What a different Appearance then would the Face of Nature make, without it! How necessary is it! And how unlikely that the Inhabitants of the World ever were, or that the Creator ever design'd they should be, exempt from it!

I would likewise observe here, that the vIIIth Proposition in the preceding Section, viz. *That there is neither Merit nor Demerit,* &c. is here again demonstrated, as infallibly, tho' in another manner: For since *Freedom from Uneasiness* is the End of all our Actions, how is it possible for us to do any Thing disinterested? How can any Action be meritorious of Praise or Dispraise, Reward or Punishment, when the natural Principle of *Self-Love* is the only and the irresistible Motive to it?

III. *This* Desire *is always fulfill'd or satisfy'd.*

In the *Design* or *End* of it, tho' not in the *Manner:* The first is requisite, the latter not. To exemplify this, let us make a Supposition; A Person is confin'd in a House which appears to be in imminent Danger of Falling, this, as soon as perceiv'd, creates a violent *Uneasiness,* and that instantly produces an equal strong *Desire,* the End of which is *freedom from the Uneasiness,* and the *Manner* or Way propos'd to gain this *End,* is *to get out of the House.* Now if he is convinc'd by any Means, that he is mistaken, and the House is not likely to fall, he is immediately freed from his *Uneasiness,* and the *End* of his Desire is attain'd as well as if it had been in the *Manner* desir'd, viz. *leaving the House.*

All our different Desires and Passions proceed from and are reducible to this one Point, *Uneasiness,* tho' the Means we propose to ourselves for expelling of it are infinite. One proposes *Fame,* another *Wealth,* a third *Power,* &c. as the Means to gain this *End;* but tho' these are never attain'd, if the Uneasiness be remov'd by some other Means, the *Desire* is satisfy'd. Now during the Course of Life we are ourselves continually removing successive Uneasinesses as they arise, and the *last* we suffer is remov'd by the *sweet Sleep* of Death.

IV. *The fulfilling or Satisfaction of this* Desire, *produces the Sensation of* Pleasure, *great or small in exact proportion to the* Desire.

Pleasure is that Satisfaction which arises in the Mind upon, and is caus'd by, the accomplishment of our *Desires,* and by no other Means at all; and those Desires being above shewn to be caus'd by our *Pains* or *Uneasinesses,* it follows that *Pleasure* is wholly caus'd by *Pain,* and by no other Thing at all.

65

v. *Therefore the Sensation of* Pleasure *is equal, or in exact proportion to the Sensation of* Pain.

As the *Desire* of being freed from Uneasiness is equal to the *Uneasiness,* and the *Pleasure* of satisfying that Desire equal to the *Desire,* the *Pleasure* thereby produc'd must necessarily be equal to the *Uneasiness* or *Pain* which produces it: Of three Lines, *A, B,* and *C,* if *A* is equal to *B,* and *B* to *C, C* must be equal to *A.* And as our *Uneasinesses* are always remov'd by some Means or other, it follows that *Pleasure* and *Pain* are in their Nature inseparable: So many Degrees as one Scale of the Ballance descends, so many exactly the other ascends; and one cannot rise or fall without the Fall or Rise of the other: 'Tis impossible to taste of *Pleasure,* without feeling its preceding proportionate *Pain;* or to be sensible of *Pain,* without having its necessary Consequent *Pleasure:* The *highest Pleasure* is only Consciousness of Freedom from the *deepest Pain,* and Pain is not Pain to us unless we ourselves are sensible of it. They go Hand in Hand; they cannot be divided.

You have a View of the whole Argument in a few familiar Examples: The *Pain* of Abstinence from Food, as it is greater or less, produces a greater or less *Desire* of Eating, the Accomplishment of this *Desire* produces a greater or less *Pleasure* proportionate to it. The *Pain* of Confinement causes the *Desire* of Liberty, which accomplish'd, yields a *Pleasure* equal to that *Pain* of Confinement. The *Pain* of Labour and Fatigue causes the *Pleasure* of Rest, equal to that *Pain.* The *Pain* of Absence from Friends, produces the *Pleasure* of Meeting in exact proportion. &c.

This is the *fixt Nature* of Pleasure and Pain, and will always be found to be so by those who examine it.

One of the most common Arguments for the future Existence of the Soul, is taken from the generally suppos'd Inequality of Pain and Pleasure in the present; and this, notwithstanding the Difficulty by outward Appearances to make a Judgment of another's Happiness, has been look'd upon as almost unanswerable: but since *Pain* naturally and infallibly produces a *Pleasure* in proportion to it, every individual Creature must, in any State of *Life,* have an equal Quantity of each, so that there is not, on that Account, any Occasion for a future Adjustment.

Thus are all the Works of the Creator *equally* us'd by him; And no Condition of Life or Being is in itself better or preferable to another: The Monarch is not more happy than the Slave, nor the Beggar more miserable than Croesus. Suppose *A, B,* and *C,* three distinct Beings; *A* and *B,* animate, capable of *Pleasure* and *Pain, C* an inanimate Piece of Matter, insensible of either. *A* receives ten Degrees of *Pain,* which are necessarily succeeded by ten Degrees of *Pleasure: B* receives fifteen of *Pain,* and the consequent equal Number of *Pleasure: C* all the while lies unconcern'd, and as he has not suffer'd the former, has no right to the latter. What can be more equal and just than this? When the Accounts come to be adjusted, *A* has no Reason to complain that his Portion of *Pleasure* was five Degrees less than that of *B,* for his Portion of *Pain* was five Degrees less likewise: Nor has *B* any Reason to boast that his *Pleasure* was five Degrees greater than that of *A,* for his *Pain* was proportionate: They are then both on the same Foot with *C,* that is, they are neither Gainers nor Losers.

It will possibly be objected here, that even common Experience shews us, there is not in Fact this Equality: "Some we see hearty, brisk and chearful perpetually, while others are constantly bur- den'd with a heavy Load of Maladies and Misfortunes, remaining for Years perhaps in Poverty, Disgrace, or Pain, and die at last without any Appearance of Recompence." Now tho' 'tis not neces- sary, when a Proposition is demonstrated to be a general Truth, to shew in what manner it agrees with the particular Circumstances of Persons, and indeed ought not to be requir'd; yet, as this is a common Objection, some Notice may be taken of it: And here let it be observ'd, that we cannot be proper Judges of the good or bad Fortune of Others; we are apt to imagine, that what would give us a great Uneasiness or a great Satisfaction, has the same Effect upon others: we think, for Instance, those unhappy, who must depend upon Charity for a mean Subsistence, who go in Rags, fare hardly, and are despis'd and scorn'd by all; not considering that Custom renders all these Things easy, familiar, and even pleasant. When we see Riches, Grandeur and a chearful Countenance, we easily imagine Happiness accompanies them, when oftentimes 'tis quite otherwise: Nor is a constantly sorrowful Look, attended with con- tinual Complaints, an infallible Indication of Unhappiness. In short, we can judge by nothing but Appearances, and they are very apt to deceive us. Some put on a gay chearful Outside, and appear to the World perfectly at Ease, tho' even then, some inward Sting, some secret Pain imbitters all their Joys, and makes the Ballance even: Others appear continually dejected and full of Sorrow; but even Grief itself is sometimes *pleasant,* and Tears are not always without their Sweetness: Besides, Some take a Satisfaction in being thought unhappy, (as others take a Pride in being thought humble,) these will paint their Misfortunes to others in the strongest Colours, and leave no Means unus'd to make you think them thoroughly miserable; so great a *Pleasure* it is to them *to be pitied;* Others retain the Form and outside Shew of Sorrow, long after the Thing itself, with its Cause, is remov'd from the Mind; it is a Habit they have acquir'd and cannot leave. These, with many others that might be given, are Reasons why we cannot make a true Estimate of the *Equality* of the Happiness and Unhappiness of others; and unless we could, Matter of Fact cannot be opposed to this Hypothesis. Indeed, we are sometimes apt to think, that the Uneasinesses we ourselves have had, outweigh our Pleasures; but the Reason is this, the Mind takes no Account of the latter, they slip away unremark'd, when the former leave more lasting Impressions on the Memory. But suppose we pass the greatest part of Life in Pain and Sorrow, suppose we die by Torments and *think no more,* 'tis no Diminution to the Truth of what is here advanc'd; for the *Pain,* tho' exquisite, is not so to the *last* Moments of Life, the Senses are soon benumm'd, and render'd incapable of transmitting it so sharply to the Soul as at first; She perceives it cannot hold long, and 'tis an *exquisite Pleasure* to behold the immediate Approaches of Rest. This makes an Equivalent tho' Annihilation should follow: For the Quantity of *Pleasure* and *Pain* is not to be measur'd by its Duration, any more than the Quantity of Matter by its Extension; and as one cubic Inch may be made to contain, by Condensation, as much Matter as would fill ten thousand cubic Feet, being more expanded, so one single Moment of *Pleasure* may outweigh and compensate an Age of *Pain.*

It was owing to their Ignorance of the Nature of Pleasure and Pain that the Antient Heathens believ'd the idle Fable of their Elizium, that State of uninterrupted Ease and Happiness! The Thing is intirely impossible in Nature! Are not the Pleasures of the

68

Spring made such by the Disagreeableness of the Winter? Is not the Pleasure of fair Weather owing to the Unpleasantness of foul? Certainly. Were it then always Spring, were the Fields always green and flourishing, and the Weather constantly serene and fair, the Pleasure would pall and die upon our Hands; it would cease to be Pleasure to us, when it is not usher'd in by Uneasiness. Could the Philosopher visit, in reality, every Star and Planet with as much Ease and Swiftness as he can now visit their Ideas, and pass from one to another of them in the Imagination; it would be a *Pleasure* I grant; but it would be only in proportion to the *Desire* of accomplishing it, and that would be no greater than the *Uneasiness* suffer'd in the Want of it. The Accomplishment of a long and difficult Journey yields a great *Pleasure;* but if we could take a Trip to the Moon and back again, as frequently and with as much Ease as we can go and come from Market, the Satisfaction would be just the same.

The *Immateriality* of the Soul has been frequently made use of as an Argument for its *Immortality;* but let us consider, that tho' it should be allow'd to be immaterial, and consequently its Parts incapable of Separation or Destruction by any Thing material, yet by Experience we find, that it is not incapable of Cessation of *Thought,* which is its Action. When the Body is but a little indispos'd it has an evident Effect upon the Mind; and a right Disposition of the Organs is requisite to a right Manner of Thinking. In a sound Sleep sometimes, or in a Swoon, we cease to think at all; tho' the Soul is not therefore then annihilated, but *exists* all the while tho' it does not *act;* and may not this probably be the Case after Death? All our Ideas are first admitted by the Senses and imprinted on the Brain, increasing in Number by Observation and Experience; there they become the Subjects of the Soul's Action. The Soul is a mere Power or Faculty of *contemplating* on, and *comparing* those Ideas when it has them; hence springs Reason: But as it can *think* on nothing but Ideas, it must have them before it can *think* at all. Therefore as it may exist before it has receiv'd any Ideas, it may exist before it *thinks.* To remember a Thing, is to have the Idea of it still plainly imprinted on the Brain, which the Soul can turn to and contemplate on Occasion. To forget a Thing, is to have the Idea of it defac'd and destroy'd by some Accident, or the crouding in and imprinting of great variety of other Ideas upon it, so that the Soul cannot find out its Traces and distinguish it. When we have thus lost the Idea of any one Thing, we can *think* no more, or *cease to think*, on that Thing; and as we can lose the Idea of one Thing, so we may of ten, twenty, a hundred, &c. and even of all Things, because they are not in their Nature permanent; and often during Life we see that some Men, (by an Accident or Distemper affecting the Brain,) lose the greatest Part of their Ideas, and remember very little of their past Actions and Circumstances. Now upon *Death*, and the Destruction of the Body, the Ideas contain'd in the Brain, (which are alone the Subjects of the Soul's Action) being then likewise necessarily destroy'd, the Soul, tho' incapable of Destruction itself, must then necessarily *cease to think* or *act*, having nothing left to think or act upon. It is reduc'd to its first inconscious State before it receiv'd any Ideas. And to cease to *think* is but little different from *ceasing to be*.

Nevertheless, 'tis not impossible that this same *Faculty* of contemplating Ideas may be hereafter united to a new Body, and receive a new Set of Ideas; but that will no way concern us who are now living; for the Identity will be lost, it is no longer that same *Self* but a new Being.

I shall here subjoin a short Recapitulation of the Whole, that it may with all its Parts be comprehended at one View.

1. *It is suppos'd that God the Maker and Governour of the Universe, is infinitely wise, good, and powerful.*

2. *In consequence of His infinite Wisdom and Goodness, it is asserted, that whatever He doth must be infinitely wise and good;*

3. *Unless He be interrupted, and His Measures broken by some other Being, which is impossible because He is Almighty.*

4. *In consequence of His infinite Power, it is asserted, that nothing can exist or be done in the Universe which is not agreeable to His Will, and therefore good.*

5. *Evil is hereby excluded, with all Merit and Demerit; and likewise all preference in the Esteem of God, of one Part of the Creation to another.* This is the Summary of the first Part.

Now our common Notions of Justice will tell us, that if all created Things are equally esteem'd by the Creator, they ought to be equally us'd by Him; and that they are therefore equally us'd, we

Little Britain, Aldersgate, London, where Franklin lived in 1725.

might embrace for Truth upon the Credit, and as the true Consequence of the foregoing Argument. Nevertheless we proceed to
confirm it, by shewing *how* they are equally us'd, and that in the
following Manner.

1. *A Creature when endu'd with Life or Consciousness, is made
capable of Uneasiness or Pain.*

2. *This Pain produces Desire to be freed from it, in exact proportion to itself.*

3. *The Accomplishment of this Desire produces an equal Pleasure.*

4. *Pleasure is consequently equal to Pain.*

From these Propositions it is observ'd,

1. *That every Creature hath as much Pleasure as Pain.*

2. *That Life is not preferable to Insensibility; for Pleasure and
Pain destroy one another: That Being which has ten Degrees of Pain
subtracted from ten of Pleasure, has nothing remaining, and is upon an
equality with that Being which is insensible of both.*

3. *As the first Part proves that all Things must be equally us'd by the
Creator because equally esteem'd; so this second Part demonstrates that
they are equally esteem'd because equally us'd.*

4. *Since every Action is the Effect of Self-Uneasiness, the Distinction
of Virtue and Vice is excluded; and* Prop. VIII. *in* Sect. I. *again
demonstrated.*

5. *No State of Life can be happier than the present, because Pleasure
and Pain are inseparable.*

Thus both Parts of this Argument agree with and confirm one
another, and the Demonstration is reciprocal.

I am sensible that the Doctrine here advanc'd, if it were to be
publish'd, would meet with but an indifferent Reception. Mankind
naturally and generally love to be flatter'd: Whatever sooths our
Pride, and tends to exalt our Species above the rest of the Creation,
we are pleas'd with and easily believe, when ungrateful Truths
shall be with the utmost Indignation rejected. "What! bring ourselves down to an Equality with the Beasts of the Field! with the
meanest part of the Creation! 'Tis insufferable!" But, (to use a Piece
of *common* Sense) our *Geese* are but *Geese* tho' we may think 'em
Swans; and Truth will be Truth tho' it sometimes prove mortifying
and distasteful.

Journal of a Voyage, 1726

MS not found; reprinted from WTF, *Memoirs*, 4to edit., I, Appendix, i-xix; also transcript: Library of Congress.

The transcript of this Journal was made from Franklin's manuscript, and from it William Temple Franklin printed the text. Thus the transcript is one step closer to the lost original. The printed text is followed here, however, because of the mutilated state and uncertain punctuation of the longhand transcript. On the other hand, Temple Franklin's version is at variance with both the transcript and Franklin's presumed original in its too-lavish use of hyphens, as in "a-head" and "to-morrow." One difference is that the printed version speaks of "the Snow," which the *Berkshire* met at sea on September 23; this was almost certainly "a snow" (a type of vessel), as it appears in the transcript. In two or three instances Temple Franklin has "improved" on the transcript, which may reproduce his grandfather's language. These differences and changes are noted.

JOURNAL of occurrences in my voyage to Philadelphia on board the Berkshire, Henry Clark Master, from London.

Friday, July 22, 1726

Yesterday in the afternoon we left London, and came to an anchor off Gravesend about eleven at night. I lay ashore all night, and this morning took a walk up to the Windmill Hill, whence I had an agreeable prospect of the country for above twenty miles round, and two or three reaches of the river with ships and boats sailing both up and down, and Tilbury Fort on the other side, which commands the river and passage to London. This Gravesend is a *cursed biting* place; the chief dependence of the people being the advantage they make of imposing upon strangers. If you buy any thing of them, and give half what they ask, you pay twice as much as the thing is worth. Thank God, we shall leave it to-morrow.

Saturday, July 23

This day we weighed anchor and fell down with the tide, there being little or no wind. In the afternoon we had a fresh gale, that brought us down to Margate, where we shall lie at anchor this night. Most of the passengers are very sick. Saw several Porpoises,[2] &c.

2. "Porpusses" in the transcript.

Sunday, July 24

This morning we weighed anchor, and, coming to the Downs, we set our pilot ashore at Deal and passed through. And now whilst I write this, sitting upon the quarter-deck, I have methinks one of the pleasantest scenes in the world before me. 'Tis a fine clear day, and we are going away before the wind with an easy pleasant gale. We have near fifteen sail of ships in sight, and I may say in company. On the left hand appears the coast of France at a distance, and on the right is the town and castle of Dover, with the green hills and chalky cliffs of England, to which we must now bid farewell. Albion, farewell!

Monday, July 25

All the morning calm. Afternoon sprung up a gale at East: blew very hard all night. Saw the Isle of Wight at a distance.

Tuesday, July 26

Contrary winds all day, blowing pretty hard. Saw the Isle of Wight again in the evening.

Wednesday, July 27

This morning the wind blowing very hard at West, we stood in for the land, in order to make some harbour. About noon we took on board a pilot out of a fishing shallop, who brought the ship into Spithead off Portsmouth. The captain, Mr. Denham[3] and myself went on shore, and during the little time we staid I made some observations on the place.

Portsmouth has a fine harbour. The entrance is so narrow that you may throw a stone from fort to fort; yet it is near ten fathom deep and bold close to: but within there is room enough for five hundred, or for aught I know a thousand sail of ships. The town is strongly fortified, being encompassed with a high wall and a deep and broad ditch, and two gates that are entered over drawbridges; besides several forts, batteries of large cannon and other

3. Thomas Denham (d. 1727), Philadelphia merchant, half-owner of the *Berkshire*, sailed on the ship that took BF to England, 1724, and "in this Passage," BF wrote in the autobiography, "Mr. Denham contracted a Friendship for me that continued during his Life." He arranged BF's return to Philadelphia, gave him a job as clerk in his business at £50 current a year, and made him a bequest in his will. His business ledger of 1726–28 is in Hist. Soc. of Pa. *PMHB*, XLIII (1919), 278.

outworks, the names of which I know not, nor had I time to take so strict a view as to be able to describe them. In war time the town has a garrison of 10,000 men; but at present 'tis only manned by about 100 Invalids. Notwithstanding the English have so many fleets of men of war at sea at this time,* I counted in this harbour above thirty sail of 2nd, 3d, and 4th rates that lay by unrigged, but easily fitted out upon occasion, all their masts and rigging, lying marked and numbered in storehouses at hand. The King's yards and docks employ abundance of men, who even in peace time are constantly building and refitting men of war for the King's service. Gosport lies opposite to Portsmouth, and is near as big if not bigger; but except the fort at the mouth of the harbour, and a small outwork before the main street of the town, it is only defended by a mud wall which surrounds it, and a trench or dry ditch of about ten feet depth and breadth. Portsmouth is a place of very little trade in peace time; it depending chiefly on fitting out men of war. Spithead is the place where the fleet commonly anchor, and is a very good riding place. The people of Portsmouth tell strange stories of the severity of one Gibson,[4] who was governor of this place in the Queen's time, to his soldiers, and show you a miserable dungeon by the town gate, which they call *Johnny Gibson's Hole*, where for trifling misdemeanors he used to confine his soldiers till they were almost starved to death. 'Tis a common maxim, that without severe discipline it is impossible to govern the licentious rabble of soldiery. I own indeed that if a commander finds he has not those qualities in him that will make him beloved by his people, he ought by all means to make use of such methods as will make them fear him, since one or the other (or both) is absolutely necessary; but Alexander and Caesar, those renowned generals, received more faithful service, and performed greater actions by means of the love their soldiers bore them, than they could possibly have done, if instead of being beloved and respected they had been hated and feared by those they commanded.

*One gone to the Baltic; one to the Mediterranean; and one to the West Indies.

4. Sir John Gibson (1637–1717), soldier, M.P., lieutenant governor of Portsmouth, 1689–1717. *DNB*.

Thursday, July 28

This morning we came on board, having lain on shore all night. We weighed anchor and with a moderate gale stood in for Cowes in the Isle of Wight, and came to an anchor before the town about eleven o'clock. Six of the passengers went on shore and diverted themselves till about 12 at night; and then got a boat, and came on board again, expecting to sail early in the morning.

Friday, July 29

But the wind continuing adverse still, we went ashore again this morning, and took a walk to Newport, which is about four miles distant from Cowes, and is the metropolis of the island. Thence we walked to Carisbrooke, about a mile farther, out of curiosity to see that castle, which King Charles the First was confined in; and so returned to Cowes in the afternoon, and went on board in expectation of sailing.

Cowes is but a small town, and lies close to the sea-side, pretty near opposite to Southampton on the main shore of England. It is divided into two parts by a small river that runs up within a quarter of a mile of Newport, and is distinguished by East and West Cowes. There is a fort built in an oval form, on which there are eight or ten guns mounted for the defence of the road. They have a post-office, a custom-house, and a chapel of ease; and a good harbour for ships to ride in, in easterly and westerly winds.

All this day I spent agreeably enough at the draft-board. It is a game I much delight in; but it requires a clear head, and undisturbed; and the persons playing, if they would play well, ought not much to regard the *consequence* of the game, for that diverts and withdraws the attention of the mind from the game itself, and makes the player liable to make many false open moves; and I will venture to lay it down for an infallible rule, that if two persons *equal* in judgment play for a considerable sum, he that loves money most shall lose; his anxiety for the success of the game confounds him. Courage is almost as requisite for the good conduct of this game as in a real battle; for if the player imagines himself opposed by one that is much his superior in skill, his mind is so intent on the defensive part that an advantage passes unobserved.

Newport makes a pretty prospect enough from the hills that surround it; (for it lies down in a bottom). The houses are beautifully intermixed with trees, and a tall old-fashioned steeple rises in the midst of the town, which is very ornamental to it. The name of the church I could not learn:[5] but there is a very neat market-house, paved with square stone, and consisting of eleven arches. There are several pretty handsome streets, and many well-built houses and shops well stored with goods. But I think Newport is chiefly remarkable for oysters, which they send to London and other places, where they are very much esteemed, being thought the best in England. The oyster-merchants fetch them, as I am informed, from other places, and lay them upon certain beds in the river, (the water of which is it seems excellently adapted for that purpose) a-fattening, and when they have laid a suitable time they are taken up again, and made fit for sale.

When we came to Carisbrooke, which, as I said before, is a little village about a mile beyond Newport, we took a view of an ancient Church that had formerly been a priory in Romish times, and is the first church, or the mother church of the island. It is an elegant building, after the old Gothic manner, with a very high tower, and looks very venerable in its ruins. There are several ancient monuments about it; but the stone of which they are composed is of such a soft crumbling nature, that the inscriptions are none of them legible. Of the same stone are almost all the tomb-stones, &c. that I observed in the island. From this church, (having crossed over the brook that gives name to the village, and got a little boy for a guide) we went up a very steep hill, through several narrow lanes and avenues, till we came to the castle gate.[6] We entered over the ditch (which is now almost filled up, partly by the ruins of the mouldering walls that have tumbled into it, and partly by the washing down of the earth from the hill by the rains) upon a couple of brick arches, where I suppose formerly there was a drawbridge. An old woman who lives in the castle, seeing us as strangers walk about, sent and offered to show us the rooms if we pleased, which we accepted. This castle, as she informed us, has for many years been the seat of the Governors of the island: and the rooms and hall, which are very large and handsome with high

5. Probably the church of St. Thomas of Canterbury. For a description of Newport, see *Victoria History of Hampshire and the Isle of Wight*, v, 253–65.
6. For a history and description of Carisbrooke Castle, seat of the governors of the Isle of Wight, see *ibid.*, 222–35.

arched roofs, have all along been kept handsomely furnished, every succeeding governor buying the furniture of his predecessor; but Cadogan[7] the last governor, who succeeded General Webb,[8] refusing to purchase it, Webb stripped it clear of all, even the hangings, and left nothing but bare walls. The floors are several of them of plaster of Paris, the art of making which, the woman told us, was now lost. The castle stands upon a very high and steep hill, and there are the remains of a deep ditch round it; the walls are thick, and seemingly well contrived: and certainly it has been a very strong hold in its time, at least before the invention of great guns. There are several breaches in the ruinous walls, which are never repaired, (I suppose they are purposely neglected) and the ruins are almost every where overspread with ivy. It is divided into the lower and the upper castle, the lower enclosing the upper which is of a round form, and stands upon a promontory to which you must ascend by near an hundred stone steps: this upper castle was designed for a retreat in case the lower castle should be won, and is the least ruinous of any part except the stairs before mentioned, which are so broken and decayed that I was almost afraid to come down again when I was up, they being but narrow and no rails to hold by. From the battlements of this upper castle (which they call the coop) you have a fine prospect of the greatest part of the island, of the sea on one side, of Cowes road at a distance, and of Newport as it were just below you. There is a well in the middle of the coop, which they called the bottomless well, because of its great depth; but it is now half filled up with stones and rubbish, and is covered with two or three loose planks; yet a stone, as we tried, is near a quarter of a minute in falling before you hear it strike. But the well that supplies the inhabitants at present with water is in the lower castle, and is thirty fathoms deep. They draw their water with a great wheel, and with a bucket that holds near a barrel. It makes a great sound if you speak in it, and echoed the

7. Lieutenant General William Cadogan (1675–1726), afterwards Baron Cadogan of Reading, soldier, diplomat, M.P., governor of the Isle of Wight, 1715–26. Bishop Atterbury described him as "a big, bad, bold, blustering, bloody, blundering booby." *DNB.*

8. Lieutenant General John Richmond Webb (1667–1724), soldier, M.P., governor of the Isle of Wight, 1710–15. It was he who was "as Paris handsome and as Hector brave." *DNB.*

flute we played over it very sweetly. There are but seven pieces of ordnance mounted upon the walls, and those in no very good order; and the old man who is the gunner and keeper of the castle, and who sells ale in a little house at the gate, has in his possession but six muskets, (which hang up at his wall) and one of them wants a lock. He told us that the castle, which had now been built 1203 years, was first founded by one Whitgert a Saxon who conquered the island, and that it was called Whitgertsburg for many ages.[9] That particular piece of building which King Charles lodged in during his confinement here is suffered to go entirely to ruin, there being nothing standing but the walls. The island is about sixty miles in circumference, and produces plenty of corn and other provisions, and wool as fine as Cotswold; its militia having the credit of equalling the soldiery, and being the best disciplined in England. [Joseph Dudley?][1] was once in King William's time entrusted with the government of this island. At his death it appeared he was a great villain, and a great politician; there was no crime so damnable which he would stick at in the execution of his designs, and yet he had the art of covering all so thick, that with almost all men in general, while he lived, he passed for a saint. What surprised me was, that the silly old fellow, the keeper of the castle, who remembered him governor, should have so true a notion of his character as I perceived he had. In short I believe it is impossible for a man, though he has all the cunning of a devil, to live and die a villain, and yet conceal it so well as to carry the name of an honest fellow to the grave with him, but some one by some accident or other shall discover him. Truth and sincerity have a certain distinguish-

9. Another view is that the word comes from *caer*, the Celtic for stronghold. [Thomas]*Barber's Picturesque Illustrations of the Isle of Wight* [1834], p. 46.

1. The name is omitted from both the printed version and the transcript. The reference may have been to Lieutenant General John Cutts (1661–1707), created Baron Cutts, a brave and reckless soldier whom Swift characterized as "the vainest old fool alive," governor of the Isle of Wight, 1693–1707. *DNB*. More probably, however, it was to Joseph Dudley (1647–1720) of Massachusetts, deputy governor of the Isle of Wight under Cutts, 1693–1701, and actually in charge of the island while his superior was serving with the army. Dudley had been president of the council of the Dominion of New England, 1686–89, and was royal governor of Massachusetts, 1702–15, incurring in these offices the intense dislike of many of his fellow colonists. *DAB;* Everett Kimball, *The Public Life of Joseph Dudley* (N.Y., 1911).

78

ing native lustre about them which cannot be perfectly counter-feited, they are like fire and flame that cannot be painted.

The whole castle was repaired and beautified by Queen Elizabeth and strengthened by a breast-work all round without the walls, as appears by this inscription in one or two places upon it.

1598

E.R.

40

Saturday, July 30

This morning about eight o'clock we weighed anchor, and turned to windward till we came to Yarmouth, another little town upon this island, and there cast anchor again, the wind blowing hard and still westerly. Yarmouth is a smaller town than Cowes; yet the buildings being better, it makes a handsomer prospect at a distance, and the streets are clean and neat. There is one monu-ment in the church which the inhabitants are very proud of, and which we went to see. It was erected to the memory of Sir Robert Holmes, who had formerly been governor of the island.[2] It is his statue in armour, somewhat bigger than the life, standing on his tomb with a truncheon in his hand, between two pillars of porphyry. Indeed all the marble about it is very fine and good; and they say it was designed by the French King for his palace at Versailles, but was cast away upon this island, and by Sir Robert himself in his life-time applied to this use, and that the whole monument was finished long before he died, (though not fixed up in that place); the inscription likewise (which is very much to his honour) being written by himself. One would think either that he had no defect at all, or had a very ill opinion of the world, seeing he was so care-ful to make sure of a monument to record his good actions and transmit them to posterity.

Having taken a view of the church, town, and fort, (on which there is seven large guns mounted) three of us took a walk up further into the island, and having gone about two miles, we headed a creek that runs up one end of the town, and then went to

2. Sir Robert Holmes (1622–1692), governor of the Isle of Wight, 1669–92, is buried in the parish church of St. James, Yarmouth. The monument was described by Thomas Pocock in 1704. John Knox Laughton, *Memoirs Relating to the Lord Torrington*, Camden Society, n.s., XLVI (1889), 180.

Freshwater church, about a mile nearer the town, but on the other side of the creek. Having stayed here some time it grew dark, and my companions were desirous to be gone, lest those whom we had left drinking where we dined in the town, should go on board and leave us. We were told that it was our best way to go straight down to the mouth of the creek, and that there was a ferry boy that would carry us over to the town. But when we came to the house the lazy whelp was in bed, and refused to rise and put us over; upon which we went down to the water-side, with a design to take his boat, and go over by ourselves. We found it very difficult to get the boat, it being fastened to a stake and the tide risen near fifty yards beyond it: I stripped all to my shirt to wade up to it; but missing the cause-way, which was under water, I got up to my middle in mud. At last I came to the stake; but to my great disappointment found she was locked and chained. I endeavoured to draw the staple with one of the thole-pins, but in vain; I tried to pull up the stake, but to no purpose: so that after an hour's fatigue and trouble in the wet and mud, I was forced to return without the boat. We had no money in our pockets, and therefore began to conclude to pass the night in some hay-stack, though the wind blew very cold and very hard. In the midst of these troubles one of us recollected that he had a horse-shoe in his pocket which he found in his walk, and asked me if I could not wrench the staple out with that. I took it, went, tried and succeeded, and brought the boat ashore to them. Now we rejoiced and all got in, and when I had dressed myself we put off. But the worst of all our troubles was to come yet; for, it being high water and the tide over all the banks, though it was moonlight we could not discern the channel of the creek, but rowing heedlessly straight forward, when we were got about half way over, we found ourselves aground on a mud bank, and striving to row her off by putting our oars in the mud, we broke one and there stuck fast, not having four inches water. We were now in the utmost perplexity, not knowing what in the world to do; we could not tell whether the tide was rising or falling; but at length we plainly perceived it was ebb, and we could feel no deeper water within the reach of our oar. It was hard to lie in an open boat all night exposed to the wind and weather; but it was worse to think how foolish we should look in the morning, when the owner of the boat should catch us in that condition, where we must be exposed to the view of all the town.

After we had strove and struggled for half an hour and more, we gave all over, and sat down with our hands before us, despairing to get off; for if the tide had left us we had been never the nearer, we must have sat in the boat, as the mud was too deep for us to walk ashore through it, being up to our necks. At last we bethought ourselves of some means of escaping, and two of us stripped and got out, and thereby lightening the boat, we drew her upon our knees near fifty yards into deeper water, and then with much ado, having but one oar, we got safe ashore under the fort; and having dressed ourselves and tied the man's boat, we went with great joy to the Queen's Head, where we left our companions, whom we found waiting for us, though it was very late. Our boat being gone on board, we were obliged to lie ashore all night; and thus ended our walk.

Sunday, July 31

This morning the wind being moderated, our pilot designed to weigh, and, taking advantage of the tide, get a little further to windward. Upon which the boat came ashore, to hasten us on board. We had no sooner returned and hoisted in our boat but the wind began again to blow very hard at West, insomuch that instead of going any further, we were obliged to weigh and run down again to Cowes for the sake of more secure riding, where we came to an anchor again in a very little time; and the pudding which our mess made and put into the pot at Yarmouth we dined upon at Cowes.

Monday, August 1

This morning all the vessels in the harbour put out their colours in honour of the day, and it made a very pretty appearance.[3] The wind continuing to blow hard westerly, our mess resolved to go on shore, though all our loose corks were gone already. We took with us some goods to dispose of, and walked to Newport to make our market, where we sold for three shillings in the pound less than the prime cost in London; and having dined at Newport, we returned in the evening to Cowes, and concluded to lodge on shore.

Tuesday, August 2

This day we passed on shore, diverting ourselves as well as we could; and the wind continuing still westerly, we stayed on shore this night also.

3. August 1 was the anniversary of the accession of George I.

81

Wednesday, August 3

This morning we were hurried on board, having scarce time to dine, weighed anchor, and stood away for Yarmouth again, though the wind is still westerly; but meeting with a hoy when we were near half way there that had some goods on board for us to take in, we tacked about for Cowes, and came to anchor there a third time, about four in the afternoon.

Thursday, August 4

Stayed on board till about five in the afternoon, and then went on shore and stopped all night.

Friday, August 5

Called up this morning and hurried aboard, the wind being North-West. About noon we weighed and left Cowes a third time, and sailing by Yarmouth we came into the channel through the Needles; which passage is guarded by Hurst Castle, standing on a spit of land which runs out from the main land of England within a mile of the Isle of Wight. Towards night the wind veered to the Westward, which put us under apprehensions of being forced into port again: but presently after it fell a flat calm, and then we had a small breeze that was fair for half an hour, when it was succeeded by a calm again.

Saturday, August 6

This morning we had a fair breeze for some hours, and then a calm that lasted all day. In the afternoon I leaped overboard and swam round the ship to wash myself. Saw several Porpoises this day. About eight o'clock we came to an anchor in forty fathom water against the tide of flood, somewhere below Portland, and weighed again about eleven, having a small breeze.

Sunday, August 7

Gentle breezes all this day. Spoke with a ship, the *Ruby*, bound for London from Nevis, off the Start of Plymouth. This afternoon spoke with Captain Homans in a ship bound for Boston, who came out of the River when we did, and had been beating about in the Channel all the time we lay at Cowes in the Wight.

Monday, August 8

Fine weather, but no wind worth mentioning, all this day; in the afternoon saw the Lizard.

Tuesday, August 9

Took our leave of the land this morning. Calms the fore part of the day. In the afternoon a small gale, fair. Saw a grampus.

Wednesday, August 10

Wind N.W. Course S.W. about four knots. By observation in latitude 48°50'. Nothing remarkable happened.

Thursday, August 11

Nothing remarkable. Fresh gale all day.

Calms and fair breezes alternately.
{ Friday, August 12
{ Saturday, —— 13
{ Sunday, —— 14

No contrary winds, but calms and fair breezes alternately.
{ Monday, —— 15
{ Tuesday, —— 16
{ Wednesday, — 17

Thursday, August 18

Four dolphins followed the ship for some hours: we struck at them with the fizgig,[4] but took none.

Friday, August 19

This day we have had a pleasant breeze at East. In the morning we spied a sail upon our larboard bow, about two leagues distance. About noon she put out English colours, and we answered with our ensign, and in the afternoon we spoke with her. She was a ship of New York, Walter Kippen Master,[5] bound from Rochelle in France to Boston with salt. Our captain and Mr. D. went on board and stayed till evening, it being fine weather. Yesterday complaints being made that a Mr. G——n one of the passengers had with a fraudulent design marked the cards, a Court of Justice was called immediately, and he was brought to his trial in form. A Dutchman who could speak no English deposed by his interpreter, that when our mess was on shore at Cowes, the prisoner at the bar marked all the court cards on the back with a pen.

4. Fizgig was a kind of harpoon.
5. Walter Kipping lost his ship in a hurricane off South Carolina, 1728. Kipping to Cadwallader Colden, Nov. 13, 1729. *Colden Papers*, I (N.-Y. Hist. Soc., *Colls.*, 1917), 301.

I have sometimes observed that we are apt to fancy the person that cannot speak intelligibly to us, proportionably stupid in understanding, and when we speak two or three words of English to a foreigner, it is louder than ordinary, as if we thought him deaf, and that he had lost the use of his ears as well as his tongue. Something like this I imagine might be the case of Mr. G——n; he fancied the Dutchman could not see what he was about because he could not understand English, and therefore boldly did it before his face.

The evidence was plain and positive, the prisoner could not deny the fact, but replied in his defence, that the cards he marked were not those we commonly played with, but an imperfect pack, which he afterwards gave to the cabin-boy. The Attorney-General observed to the court that it was not likely he should take the pains to mark the cards without some ill design, or some further intention than just to give them to the boy when he had done, who understood nothing at all of cards. But another evidence being called, deposed that he saw the prisoner in the main top one day when he thought himself unobserved, marking a pack of cards on the backs, some with the print of a dirty thumb, others with the top of his finger, &c. Now there being but two packs on board, and the prisoner having just confessed the marking of one, the court perceived the case was plain. In fine the jury brought him in guilty, and he was condemned to be carried up to the round top, and made fast there in view of all the ship's company during the space of three hours, that being the place where the act was committed, and to pay a fine of two bottles of brandy. But the prisoner resisting authority, and refusing to submit to punishment, one of the sailors stepped up aloft and let down a rope to us, which we with much struggling made fast about his middle and hoisted him up into the air, sprawling, by main force. We let him hang, cursing and swearing, for near a quarter of an hour; but at length he crying out murder! and looking black in the face, the rope being overtort about his middle, we thought proper to let him down again; and our mess have excommunicated him till he pays his fine, refusing either to play, eat, drink, or converse with him.

Saturday, August 20

We shortened sail all last night and all this day, to keep company with the other ship. About noon Captain Kippen and one of his passengers came on board and dined with us; they stayed till evening. When they were gone we made sail and left them.

Sunday, August 21

This morning we lost sight of the Yorker, having a brisk gale of wind at East. Towards night a poor little bird came on board us, being almost tired to death, and suffered itself to be taken by the hand. We reckon ourselves near two hundred leagues from land, so that no doubt a little rest was very acceptable to the unfortunate wanderer, who 'tis like was blown off the coast in thick weather, and could not find its way back again. We receive it hospitably and tender it victuals and drink; but he refuses both, and I suppose will not live long. There was one came on board some days ago in the same circumstances with this, which I think the cat destroyed.

Monday, August 22

This morning I saw several flying-fish, but they were small. A favourable wind all day.

Fair winds, nothing remarkable.
{ Tuesday, August 23
{ Wednesday, —— 24

Thursday, August 25

Our excommunicated ship-mate thinking proper to comply with the sentence the court passed upon him, and expressing himself willing to pay the fine, we have this morning received him into unity again. Man is a sociable being, and it is for aught I know one of the worst of punishments to be excluded from society. I have read abundance of fine things on the subject of solitude, and I know 'tis a common boast in the mouths of those that affect to be thought wise, *that they are never less alone than when alone.* I acknowledge solitude an agreeable refreshment to a busy mind; but were these thinking people obliged to be always alone, I am apt to think they would quickly find their very being insupportable to them. I have heard of a gentleman who underwent seven years close confinement, in the Bastile at Paris. He was a man of sense, he was a thinking man; but being deprived of all conversation, to what purpose should he think? for he was denied even the instruments of expressing his thoughts in writing. There is no burden so grievous to man as time that he knows not how to dispose of. He was forced at last

85

to have recourse to this invention: he daily scattered pieces of paper about the floor of his little room, and then employed himself in picking them up and sticking them in rows and figures on the arm of his elbow-chair; and he used to tell his friends, after his release, that he verily believed if he had not taken this method he should have lost his senses. One of the philosophers, I think it was Plato, used to say, that he had rather be the veriest stupid block in nature, than the possessor of all knowledge without some intelligent being to communicate it to.

What I have said may in a measure account for some particulars in my present way of living here on board. Our company is in general very unsuitably mixed, to keep up the pleasure and spirit of conversation: and if there are one or two pair of us that can sometimes entertain one another for half an hour agreeably, yet perhaps we are seldom in the humour for it together. I rise in the morning and read for an hour or two perhaps, and then reading grows tiresome. Want of exercise occasions want of appetite, so that eating and drinking affords but little pleasure. I tire myself with playing at draughts, then I go to cards; nay there is no play so trifling or childish, but we fly to it for entertainment. A contrary wind, I know not how, puts us all out of good humour; we grow sullen, silent and reserved, and fret at each other upon every little occasion. 'Tis a common opinion among the ladies, that if a man is ill-natured he infallibly discovers it when he is in liquor. But I, who have known many instances to the contrary, will teach them a more effectual method to discover the natural temper and disposition of their humble servants. Let the ladies make one long sea voyage with them, and if they have the least spark of ill nature in them and conceal it to the end of the voyage, I will forfeit all my pretensions to their favour. The wind continues fair.

Friday, August 26

The wind and weather fair till night came on; and then the wind came about, and we had hard squalls with rain and lightning till morning.

Saturday, August 27

Cleared up this morning, and the wind settled westerly. Two dolphins followed us this afternoon: we hooked one and struck the other with the fizgig; but they both escaped us, and we saw them no more.

Sunday, August 28

The wind still continues westerly, and blows hard. We are under a reefed mainsail and foresail.

Monday, August 29

Wind still hard West. Two dolphins followed us this day; we struck at them, but they both escaped.

Tuesday, August 30

Contrary wind still. This evening the moon being near full, as she rose after eight o'clock, there appeared a rainbow in a western cloud to windward of us. The first time I ever saw a rainbow in the night caused by the moon.

Wednesday, August 31

Wind still West, nothing remarkable.

Thursday, September 1

Bad weather, and contrary winds.

Friday, September 2

This morning the wind changed, a little fair. We caught a couple of dolphins, and fried them for dinner. They tasted tolerably well.[6] These fish make a glorious appearance in the water: their bodies are of a bright green, mixed with a silver colour, and their tails of a shining golden yellow; but all this vanishes presently after they are taken out of their element, and they change all over to a light grey. I observed that cutting off pieces of a just-caught living dolphin for baits, those pieces did not lose their lustre and fine colours when the dolphin died, but retained them perfectly. Every one takes notice of that vulgar error of the painters, who always represent this fish monstrously crooked and deformed, when it is in reality as beautiful and well shaped a fish as any that swims. I cannot think what should be the original of this chimera of theirs, (since there is not a creature in nature that in the least resembles their dolphin) unless it proceeded at first from a false imitation of a fish in the posture of leaping, which they have since improved into a crooked monster with a head and eyes like a bull, a hog's snout, and a tail like a blown tulip. But the sailors give me another reason, though a whimsical one, viz. that as this most beautiful fish is only to be caught at sea, and that very far to the Southward, they say the painters

6. The transcript reads: "They eat indifferent well."

wilfully deform it in their representations, lest pregnant women should long for what it is impossible to procure for them.

Wind still westerly; nothing remarkable.

$\left\{\begin{array}{l}\text{Saturday, September 3}\\ \text{Sunday, ———— 4}\\ \text{Monday, ———— 5}\end{array}\right.$

Tuesday, September 6

This afternoon the wind continuing still in the same quarter, increased till it blew a storm, and raised the sea to a greater height than I had ever seen it before.

Wednesday, September 7

The wind is somewhat abated, but the sea is very high still. A dolphin kept us company all this afternoon: we struck at him several times, but could not take him.

Thursday, September 8

This day nothing remarkable has happened.[7] Contrary wind.

Friday, September 9

This afternoon we took four large dolphins, three with a hook and line, and the fourth we struck with a fizgig. The bait was a candle with two feathers stuck in it, one on each side, in imitation of a flying-fish, which are the common prey of the dolphins. They appeared extremely eager and hungry, and snapped up the hook as soon as ever it touched the water. When we came to open them, we found in the belly of one, a small dolphin half digested. Certainly they were half famished, or are naturally very savage to devour those of their own species.

Saturday, September 10

This day we dined upon the dolphins we caught yesterday, three of them sufficing the whole ship, being twenty-one persons.

Sunday, September 11

We have had a hard gale of wind all this day, accompanied with showers of rain. 'Tis uncomfortable being upon deck; and though we have been all together all day below, yet the long continuance of these contrary winds has made us so dull, that scarce three words have passed between us.

7. The transcript adds: "but I am so indolent that —"

Nothing remarkable; $\left\{\begin{array}{l}\text{Monday, September 12}\\\text{Tuesday, —— 13}\end{array}\right.$
wind contrary.

Wednesday, September 14

This afternoon about two o'clock, it being fair weather and almost calm, as we sat playing Draughts upon deck, we were surprised with a sudden and unusual darkness of the sun, which as we could perceive was only covered with a small thin cloud: when that was passed by, we discovered that that glorious luminary laboured under a very great eclipse. At least ten parts out of twelve of him were hid from our eyes, and we were apprehensive he would have been totally darkened.

Thursday, September 15

For a week past we have fed ourselves with the hopes that the change of the moon (which was yesterday) would bring us a fair wind; but to our great mortification and disappointment, the wind seems now settled in the westward, and shews as little signs of an alteration as it did a fortnight ago.

Friday, September 16

Calm all this day. This morning we saw a *Tropic bird*, which flew round our vessel several times. It is a white fowl with short wings; but one feather appears in his tail, and he does not fly very fast.[8] We reckon ourselves about half our voyage; latitude 38 and odd minutes. These birds are said never to be seen further North than the latitude of 40.

Saturday, September 17

All the forenoon the calm continued, the rest of the day some light breezes easterly; and we are in great hopes the wind will settle in that quarter.

Sunday, September 18

We have had the finest weather imaginable all this day, accompanied with what is still more agreeable, a fair wind. Every one puts on a clean shirt and a cheerful countenance, and we

8. Probably the yellow-billed tropic bird, one of the phaethontidae. Alfred Newton, *A Dictionary of Birds* (London, 1893–96), pp. 990–1; Edward H. Forbush and John B. May, *Natural History of the Birds of Eastern and Central North America* (Boston, 1939), pp. 18–19.

begin to be very good company. Heaven grant that this favourable gale may continue! for we have had so much of turning to
windward, that the word *helm-a-lee* is become almost as disagreeable to our ears as the sentence of a judge to a convicted
malefactor.

Monday, September 19

The weather looks a little uncertain, and we begin to fear the
loss of our fair wind. We see Tropic birds every day, sometimes
five or six together; they are about as big as pigeons.

Tuesday, September 20

The wind is now westerly again, to our great mortification;
and we are come to an allowance of bread, two biscuits and a
half a day.

Wednesday, September 21

This morning our Steward was brought to the geers and
whipped, for making an extravagant use of flour in the puddings,
and for several other misdemeanors. It has been perfectly calm
all this day, and very hot. I was determined to wash myself in the
sea to-day, and should have done so had not the appearance of a
shark, that mortal enemy to swimmers, deterred me: he seemed
to be about five feet long, moves round the ship at some distance
in a slow majestic manner, attended by near a dozen of those
they call pilot-fish, of different sizes; the largest of them is not so
big as a small mackerel, and the smallest not bigger than my little
finger. Two of these diminutive pilots keep just before his nose,
and he seems to govern himself in his motions by their direction;
while the rest surround him on every side indifferently. A shark
is never seen without a retinue of these, who are his purveyors,
discovering and distinguishing his prey for him; while he in
return gratefully protects them from the ravenous hungry dolphin.
They are commonly counted a very greedy fish; yet this refuses
to meddle with the bait we have thrown out for him. 'Tis likely
he has lately made a full meal.

Thursday, September 22

A fresh gale at West all this day. The shark has left us.

Friday, September 23

This morning we spied a sail to windward of us about two

leagues. We shewed our jack upon the ensign-staff, and shortened sail for them till about noon, when she came up with us. She was a snow from Dublin,[9] bound to New York, having upwards of fifty servants on board, of both sexes; they all appeared upon deck, and seemed very much pleased at the sight of us. There is really something strangely cheering to the spirits in the meeting of a ship at sea, containing a society of creatures of the same species and in the same circumstances with ourselves, after we had been long separated and excommunicated as it were from the rest of mankind. My heart fluttered in my breast with joy when I saw so many human countenances, and I could scarce refrain from that kind of laughter which proceeds from some degree of inward pleasure. When we have been for a considerable time tossing on the vast waters, far from the sight of any land or ships, or any mortal creature but ourselves (except a few fish and sea birds) the whole world, for aught we know, may be under a second deluge, and we (like Noah and his company in the Ark) the only surviving remnant of the human race. The two Captains have mutually promised to keep each other company; but this I look upon to be only matter of course, for if ships are unequal in their sailing they seldom stay for one another, especially strangers. This afternoon the wind that has been so long contrary to us, came about to the eastward (and looks as if it would hold), to our no small satisfaction. I find our messmates in a better humour, and more pleased with their present condition than they have been since we came out; which I take to proceed from the contemplation of the miserable circumstances of the passengers on board our neighbour, and making the comparison. We reckon ourselves in a kind of paradise, when we consider how they live, confined and stifled up with such a lousy stinking rabble in this sultry latitude.

Saturday, September 24

Last night we had a very high wind, and very thick weather; in which we lost our consort. This morning early we spied a sail a-head of us, which we took to be her; but presently after we spied another, and then we plainly perceived that neither of them could be the snow, for one of them stemmed with us, and the other bore down directly upon us, having the weather gage of us. As

9. The printed version calls this vessel "the Snow."

the latter drew near we were a little surprised, not knowing what to make of her; for by the course she steered she did not seem designed for any port, but looked as if she intended to clap us aboard immediately. I could perceive concern in every face on board; but she presently eased us of our apprehensions by bearing away a-stern of us. When we hoisted our jack she answered with French colours, and presently took them down again; and we soon lost sight of her. The other ran by us in less than half an hour, and answered our jack with an English ensign; she stood to the eastward, but the wind was too high to speak with either of them. About nine o'clock we spied our consort, who had got a great way a-head of us. She, it seems, had made sail in the night, while we lay-by with our main yard down during the hard gale. She very civilly shortened sail for us, and this afternoon we came up with her; and now we are running along very amicably to-gether side by side, having a most glorious fair wind.

> *On either side the parted billows flow,*
> *While the black ocean foams and roars below.*

Sunday, September 25

Last night we shot a-head of our consort pretty far. About midnight having lost sight of each other, we shortened sail for them: but this morning they were got as far a-head of us as we could see, having run by us in the dark unperceived. We made sail and came up with them about noon; and if we chance to be a-head of them again in the night, we are to show them a light, that we may not lose company by any such accident for the future. The wind still continues fair, and we have made a greater run these last four-and-twenty hours than we have done since we came out. All our discourse now is of Philadelphia, and we begin to fancy ourselves on shore already. Yet a small change of weather, attended by a westerly wind, is sufficient to blast all our blooming hopes, and quite spoil our present good humour.

Monday, September 26

The wind continued fair all night. In the twelve o'clock watch our consort, who was about a league a-head of us, showed us a light, and we answered with another. About six o'clock this morning we had a sudden hurry[1] of wind at all points of the compass, accompanied with the most violent shower of rain I ever saw, insomuch that the sea looked like a *cream dish*. It surprised us with all our sails up, and was so various, uncertain, and contrary, that the mizen topsail was full, while the head sails were all aback; and before the men could run from one end of the ship to the other, 'twas about again. But this did not last long ere the wind settled to the North-East again, to our great satisfaction. Our consort fell astern of us in the storm, but made sail and came up with us again after it was over. We hailed one another on the morrow, congratulating upon the continuance of the fair wind, and both ran on very lovingly together.

Tuesday, September 27

The fair wind continues still. I have laid a bowl of punch that we are in Philadelphia next Saturday sen'night, for we reckon ourselves not above 150 leagues from land. The snow keeps us company still.

Wednesday, September 28

We had very variable winds and weather last night, accompanied with abundance of rain; and now the wind is come about westerly again, but we must bear it with patience. This afternoon we took up several branches of gulf weed (with which the sea is spread all over from the Western Isles to the coast of America); but one of these branches had something peculiar in it. In common with the rest it had a leaf about three quarters of an inch long, indented like a saw, and a small yellow berry filled with nothing but wind; besides which it bore a fruit of the animal kind, very surprising to see. It was a small shell-fish like a heart, the stalk by which it proceeded from the branch being partly of a gristly kind. Upon this one branch of the weed there were near forty of these vegetable animals; the smallest of them near the end contained a substance somewhat like an oyster, but the larger were visibly animated, opening their shells every moment, and thrusting out a set of unformed claws, not unlike those of a crab; but the inner part was still a kind of soft jelly. Observing the weed more narrowly, I spied a very small crab crawling among it, about as big as the head of a ten-penny nail, and of a

1. The transcript describes this as a "burst" of wind.

yellowish colour, like the weed itself. This gave me some reason to think that he was a native of the branch, that he had not long since been in the same condition with the rest of those little embrios that appeared in the shells, this being the method of their generation; and that consequently all the rest of this odd kind of fruit might be crabs in due time. To strengthen my conjecture, I have resolved to keep the weed in salt water, renewing it every day till we come on shore, by this experiment to see whether any more crabs will be produced or not in this manner. I remember that the last calm we had, we took notice of a large crab upon the surface of the sea, swimming from one branch of weed to another, which he seemed to prey upon; and I likewise recollect that at Boston, in New England, I have often seen small crabs with a shell like a snail's upon their backs, crawling about in the salt water; and likewise at Portsmouth in England. It is likely nature has provided this hard shell to secure them till their own proper shell has acquired a sufficient hardness, which once perfected, they quit their old habitation and venture abroad safe in their own strength. The various changes that silk-worms, butterflies, and several other insects go through, make such alterations and metamorphoses not improbable. This day the captain of the snow with one of his passengers came on board us; but the wind beginning to blow, they did not stay dinner, but returned to their own vessel.

Thursday, September 29

Upon shifting the water in which I had put the weed yesterday, I found another crab, much smaller than the former, who seemed to have newly left his habitation. But the weed begins to wither, and the rest of the embrios are dead. This new comer fully convinces me, that at least this sort of crabs are generated in this manner. The snow's Captain dined on board us this day. Little or no wind.

Friday, September 30

I sat up last night to observe an eclipse of the moon, which the calendar calculated for London informed us would happen at five o'clock in the morning, September 30. It began with us about eleven last night, and continued till near two this morning, darkening her body about six digits, or one half; the middle of it being about half an hour after twelve, by which we may discover that we are in a meridian of about four hours and half from London, or 67½ degrees of longitude, and consequently have not much above one hundred leagues to run. This is the second eclipse we have had within these fifteen days. We lost our consort in the night, but saw him again this morning near two leagues to wind-ward. This afternoon we spoke with him again. We have had abundance of dolphins about us these three or four days; but we have not taken any more than one, they being shy of the bait. I took in some more gulf-weed to-day with the boat-hook, with shells upon it like that before mentioned, and three living perfect crabs, each less than the nail of my little finger. One of them had something particularly observable, to wit, a thin piece of the white shell which I before noticed as their covering while they remained in the condition of embrios, sticking close to his natural shell upon his back. This sufficiently confirms me in my opinion of the manner of their generation. I have put this remarkable crab with a piece of the gulf-weed, shells, &c. into a glass phial filled with salt water, (for want of spirits of wine) in hopes to preserve the curiosity till I come on shore. The wind is South-West.

Saturday, October 1

Last night our consort, who goes incomparably better upon a wind than our vessel, got so far to windward and a-head of us, that this morning we could see nothing of him, and 'tis like shall see him no more. These South-Wests are hot damp winds, and bring abundance of rain and dirty weather with them.

Sunday, October 2

Last night we prepared our line with a design to sound this morning at four o'clock; but the wind coming about again to the North West, we let it alone. I cannot help fancying the water is changed a little, as is usual when a ship comes within soundings, but 'tis probable[2] I am mistaken; for there is but one besides myself of my opinion, and we are very apt to believe what we wish to be true.

Monday, October 3

The water is now very visibly changed to the eyes of all except the Captain and Mate, and they will by no means allow it; I

2. The transcript reads: " 'tis like."

JOURNAL OF A VOYAGE, 1726

suppose because they did not see it first. Abundance of dolphins are about us, but they are very shy, and keep at a distance. Wind North West.

Tuesday, October 4

Last night we struck a dolphin, and this morning we found a flying-fish dead under the windlass. He is about the bigness of a small mackarel, a sharp head, a small mouth, and a tail forked somewhat like a dolphin, but the lowest branch much larger and longer than the other, and tinged with yellow. His back and sides of a darkish blue, his belly white, and his skin very thick. His wings are of a finny substance, about a span long, reaching, when close to his body, from an inch below his gills to an inch above his tail. When they fly it is straight forward, for (they cannot readily turn) a yard or two above the water, and perhaps fifty yards is the farthest before they dip into the water again, for they cannot support themselves in the air any longer than while their wings continue wet. These flying-fish are the common prey of the dolphin, who is their mortal enemy. When he pursues them they rise and fly, and he keeps close under them till they drop, and then snaps them up immediately. They generally fly in flocks, four or five, or perhaps a dozen together, and a dolphin is seldom caught without one or more in his belly. We put this flying-fish upon the hook, in hopes of catching one, but in a few minutes they got it off without hooking themselves; and they will not meddle with any other bait.

Tuesday Night

Since eleven o'clock we have struck three fine dolphins, which are a great refreshment to us. This afternoon we have seen abundance of grampuses, which are seldom far from land; but towards evening we had a more evident token, to wit, a little tired bird, something like a lark, came on board us, who certainly is an American, and 'tis likely was ashore this day. It is now calm. We hope for a fair wind next.

Wednesday, October 5

This morning we saw a heron, who had lodged aboard last night. 'Tis a long-legged, long-necked bird, having as they say but one gut. They live upon fish, and will swallow a living eel thrice sometimes before it will remain in their body. The wind is West again. The ship's crew was brought to a short allowance of water.

Thursday, October 6

This morning abundance of grass, rock-weed, &c. passed by us; evident tokens that land is not far off. We hooked a dolphin this morning that made us a good breakfast. A sail passed by us about twelve o'clock, and nobody saw her till she was too far astern to be spoken with. 'Tis very near calm: we saw another sail a-head this afternoon; but night coming on, we could not speak with her, though we very much desired it: she stood to the Northward, and it is possible might have informed us how far we are from land. Our artists on board are much at a loss. We hoisted our jack to her, but she took no notice of it.

Friday, October 7

Last night, about nine o'clock, sprung up a fine gale at North East, which run us in our course at the rate of seven miles an hour all night. We were in hopes of seeing land this morning, but cannot. The water, which we thought was changed, is now as blue as the sky; so that unless at that time we were running over some unknown shoal our eyes strangely deceived us. All the reckonings have been out these several days; though the captain says 'tis his opinion we are yet an hundred leagues from land: for my part I know not what to think of it, we have run all this day at a great rate; and now night is come on we have no soundings. Sure the American continent is not all sunk under water since we left it.

Saturday, October 8

The fair wind continues still; we ran all night in our course, sounding every four hours, but can find no ground yet, nor is the water changed by all this day's run. This afternoon we saw an *Irish Lord*,[3] and a bird which flying looked like a yellow duck. These they say are not seen far from the coast. Other signs of land have we none. Abundance of large porpoises ran by us this afternoon, and we were followed by a shoal of small ones, leaping out of the water, as they approached. Towards evening we spied a sail a-head and spoke with her just before dark. She was bound from New York for Jamaica, and left Sandy Hook yesterday about noon, from which they reckon themselves forty-five leagues distant. By this we compute that we are not above thirty leagues from our capes, and hope to see land to-morrow.

3. Not identified.

Sunday, October 9

We have had the wind fair all the morning: at twelve o'clock we sounded, perceiving the water visibly changed, and struck ground at twenty-five fathoms, to our universal joy. After dinner one of our mess went up aloft to look out, and presently pronounced the long-wished for sound, LAND! LAND! In less than an hour we could descry it from the deck, appearing like tufts of trees. I could not discern it so soon as the rest; my eyes were dimmed with the suffusion of two small drops of joy. By three o'clock we were run in within two leagues of the land, and spied a small sail standing along shore. We would gladly have spoken with her, for our captain was unacquainted with the coast, and knew not what land it was that we saw. We made all the sail we could to speak with her. We made a signal of distress; but all would not do, the ill-natured dog would not come near us. Then we stood off again till morning, not caring to venture too near.

Monday, October 10

This morning we stood in again for land; and we, that had been here before, all agreed that it was Cape Henlopen: about noon we were come very near, and to our great joy saw the pilot-boat come off to us, which was exceeding welcome. He brought on board about a peck of apples with him; they seemed the most delicious I ever tasted in my life: the salt provisions we had been used to, gave them a relish. We had an extraordinary fair wind all the afternoon and ran above an hundred miles up the Delaware before ten at night. The country appears very pleasant to the eye, being covered with woods, except here and there a house and plantation. We cast anchor when the tide turned, about two miles below Newcastle, and there lay till the morning tide.

Tuesday, October 11

This morning we weighed anchor with a gentle breeze, and passed by Newcastle, whence they hailed us and bade us welcome. 'Tis extreme fine weather. The sun enlivens our stiff limbs with his glorious rays of warmth and brightness. The sky looks gay, with here and there a silver cloud. The fresh breezes from the woods refresh us, the immediate prospect of liberty after so long and irksome confinement ravishes us. In short all things conspire to make this the most joyful day I ever knew. As we passed by Chester some of the company went on shore, impatient once more to tread on *terra firma,* and designing for Philadelphia by land. Four of us remained on board, not caring for the fatigue of travel when we knew the voyage had much weakened us. About eight at night, the wind failing us, we cast anchor at Redbank, six miles from Philadelphia, and thought we must be obliged to lie on board that night: but some young Philadelphians happening to be out upon their pleasure in a boat, they came on board, and offered to take us up with them: we accepted of their kind proposal, and about ten o'clock landed at Philadelphia, heartily congratulating each other upon our having happily completed so tedious and dangerous a voyage. Thank God!

Plan of Conduct

MS not found; reprinted from Robert Walsh, "Life of Benjamin Franklin," *Delaplaine's Repository of the Lives and Portraits of Distinguished Americans* (Philadelphia, 1815–17), II, 51–2.

"Perhaps the most important Part" of the foregoing Journal, Franklin wrote in his autobiography, was "the *Plan* to be found in it which I formed at Sea, for regulating my future Conduct in Life." The plan does not appear in the surviving transcript of the Journal, and is probably lost. About 1785, however, Franklin allowed William Rawle, a fellow member of the Society for Political Inquiries, to make a copy of "the preamble and heads of it"; and Rawle, in 1815, gave this material to his friend Robert Walsh of Philadelphia for a sketch of Franklin. Walsh seems to have printed only a part of what Rawle sent him—the part that appears here. Franklin considered his plan "the more remarkable, as being form'd when I was so young, and yet being pretty faithfully adhered to quite thro' to old Age."

[1726]

Those who write of the art of poetry teach us that if we would write what may be worth the reading, we ought always, before we begin, to form a regular plan and design of our piece: otherwise, we shall be in danger of incongruity. I am apt to think it is the same as to life. I have never fixed a regular design in life; by which means it has been a confused variety of different scenes. I am now entering upon a new one: let me, therefore, make some resolutions, and form some scheme of action, that, henceforth, I may live in all respects like a rational creature.

1. It is necessary for me to be extremely frugal for some time, till I have paid what I owe.

2. To endeavour to speak truth in every instance; to give nobody expectations that are not likely to be answered, but aim at sincerity in every word and action—the most amiable excellence in a rational being.

3. To apply myself industriously to whatever business I take in hand, and not divert my mind from my business by any foolish project of growing suddenly rich; for industry and patience are the surest means of plenty.

4. I resolve to speak ill of no man whatever, not even in a matter of truth; but rather by some means excuse the faults I hear charged upon others, and upon proper occasions speak all the good I know of every body.

To Jane Franklin[4]   MS not found; reprinted from Duane, *Works*, VI, 3.

Dear Sister,   Philadelphia, January 6, 1726–7

I am highly pleased with the account captain Freeman[5] gives me of you. I always judged by your behaviour when a child that you would make a good, agreeable woman, and you know you were ever my peculiar favourite. I have been thinking what would be a suitable present for me to make, and for you to receive, as I hear you are grown a celebrated beauty. I had almost determined on a tea table, but when I considered that the character of a good housewife was far preferable to that of being only a pretty gentlewoman, I concluded to send you a *spinning wheel*, which I hope you will accept as a small token of my sincere love and affection.

Sister, farewell, and remember that modesty, as it makes the most homely virgin amiable and charming, so the want of it infallibly renders the most perfect beauty disagreeable and odious.

4. Jane Franklin (1712–1794). BF's youngest and favorite sister married Edward Mecom of Boston, July 27, 1727 (Genealogy, C.17). Van Doren, *Jane Mecom;* Van Doren, *Franklin-Mecom*, which brings together their lifelong correspondence.

5. Isaac Freeman, ship's captain of Boston, friend of the Franklin family.

But when that brightest of female virtues shines among other perfections of body and mind in the same person, it makes the woman more lovely than an angel. Excuse this freedom, and use the same with me. I am, dear Jenny, your loving brother,

B. Franklin

Articles of Belief and Acts of Religion

Autograph MS: Library of Congress; also transcript: Library of Congress

Franklin mentioned this private liturgy in his autobiography. Though he had had a conventional religious upbringing and contributed to the support of the Presbyterian meeting in Philadelphia, he seldom attended public worship, preferring to use Sundays for his own studies. Once, however, persuaded to go to church, he went five successive weeks but, finding no morality in the minister's sermons, "was disgusted, and attended his Preaching no more. I had some Years before compos'd a little Liturgy or Form of Prayer for my own private Use, viz, in 1728. entitled, *Articles of Belief and Acts of Religion*. I return'd to the Use of this, and went no more to the public Assemblies."[6] The manuscript in Franklin's hand survives, except for a few pages, and there is a transcript of the whole by William Temple Franklin.

ARTICLES OF BELIEF

AND

ACTS OF RELIGION

In Two Parts.[7]

Here will I hold—If there is a Pow'r above us
(And that there is, all Nature cries aloud,
Thro' all her Works), He must delight in Virtue
And that which he delights in must be Happy.   Cato.[8]

6. For further discussion see Frank L. Mott and Chester E. Jorgenson, eds., *Benjamin Franklin: Representative Selections* (N.Y., 1936), pp. cxxviii–cxxxv.

7. Part II has not been found.

8. Joseph Addison, *Cato, A Tragedy*, v, i, 15–18. BF used these lines again as one of the mottoes for his "little Book" for daily self-examination in the virtues.

Part I.

Philada.

Nov. 20 1728.

First Principles

I BELIEVE there is one Supreme most perfect Being, Author and Father of the Gods themselves.

For I believe that Man is not the most perfect Being but One, rather that as there are many Degrees of Beings his Inferiors, so there are many Degrees of Beings superior to him.

Also, when I stretch my Imagination thro' and beyond our System of Planets, beyond the visible fix'd Stars themselves, into that Space that is every Way infinite, and conceive it fill'd with Suns like ours, each with a Chorus of Worlds for ever moving round him, then this little Ball on which we move, seems, even in my narrow Imagination, to be almost Nothing, and my self less than nothing, and of no sort of Consequence.

When I think thus, I imagine it great Vanity in me to suppose, that the *Supremely Perfect,* does in the least regard such an inconsiderable Nothing as Man. More especially, since it is impossible for me to have any positive clear Idea of that which is infinite and incomprehensible, I cannot conceive otherwise, than that He, *the Infinite Father,* expects or requires no Worship or Praise from us, but that he is even INFINITELY ABOVE IT.

But since there is in all Men something like a natural Principle which enclines them to DEVOTION or the Worship of some unseen Power;

And since Men are endued with Reason superior to all other Animals that we are in our World acquainted with;

Therefore I think it seems required of me, and my Duty, as a Man, to pay Divine Regards to SOMETHING.

I CONCEIVE then, that the INFINITE has created many Beings or Gods, vastly superior to Man, who can better conceive his Perfections than we, and return him a more rational and glorious Praise. As among Men, the Praise of the Ignorant or of Children, is not regarded by the ingenious Painter or Architect, who is rather honour'd and pleas'd with the Approbation of Wise men and Artists.

It may be that these created Gods, are immortal, or it may be that after many Ages, they are changed, and Others supply their Places.

Howbeit, I conceive that each of these is exceeding wise, and good, and very powerful; and that Each has made for himself, one glorious Sun, attended with a beautiful and admirable System of Planets.

It is that particular wise and good God, who is the Author and Owner of our System, that I propose for the Object of my Praise and Adoration.

For I conceive that he has in himself some of those Passions he has planted in us, and that, since he has given us Reason whereby we are capable of observing his Wisdom in the Creation, he is not above caring for us, being pleas'd with our Praise, and offended when we slight Him, or neglect his Glory.

I conceive for many Reasons that he is a *good Being*, and as I should be happy to have so wise, good and powerful a Being my Friend, let me consider in what Manner I shall make myself most acceptable to him.

Next to the Praise due, to[9] his Wisdom, I believe he is pleased and delights in the Happiness of those he has created; and since without Virtue Man* can have no Happiness in this World, I firmly believe he delights to see me Virtuous, because he is pleas'd when he sees me Happy.

And since he has created many Things which seem purely design'd for the Delight of Man, I believe he is not offended when he sees his Children solace themselves in any manner of pleasant Exercises and innocent Delights, and I think no Pleasure innocent that is to Man hurtful.

I *love* him therefore for his Goodness and I *adore* him for his Wisdom.

Let me then not fail to praise my God continually, for it is his Due, and it is all I can return for his many Favours and great

*See Junto Paper of Good and Evil, &c.[1]

9. On the facing page of the MS "due, to" has been changed to "resulting from."

1. Not found.

Goodness to me; and let me resolve to be virtuous, that I may be happy, that I may please Him, who is delighted to see me happy. Amen.

1. Adoration.   ♓2. Petition.   ♓3. Thanks.

Prel.

> Being mindful that before I address the DEITY, my Soul ought to be calm and Serene, free from Passion and Perturbation, or otherwise elevated with Rational Joy and Pleasure, I ought to use a Countenance that expresses a filial Respect, mixt with a kind of Smiling, that signifies inward Joy, and Satisfaction, and Admiration.

> O wise God,
>   My good Father,
> Thou beholdest the Sincerity of my Heart,
>   And of my Devotion;
> Grant me a Continuance of thy Favour!

Powerful Goodness, &c.[2]   (1)

O Creator, O Father, I believe that thou art Good, and that thou art *pleas'd with the Pleasure*[3] of thy Children.

                    Praised be thy Name for Ever.

(2)

By thy Power hast thou made the glorious Sun, with his attending Worlds; from the Energy of thy mighty Will they first received [their prodigious][4] Motion, and by thy Wisdom hast thou prescribed the wondrous Laws by which they move.

                    Praised be thy Name for ever.

2. The words "Powerful Goodness" are taken from the facing page of the MS. They may represent BF's intention to insert here the words of the "little Prayer, which was prefix'd to my Tables of Examination; for daily Use," and mentioned at the start of his Scheme of Employment in the autobiography, where he planned to begin each day with "Rise, wash, and address *Powerful Goodness.*" The prayer as there given reads: "O Powerful Goodness! bountiful Father! merciful Guide! Increase in me that Wisdom which discovers my truest Interests; Strengthen my Resolutions to perform what that Wisdom dictates. Accept my kind Offices to thy other Children, as the only Return in my Power for thy continual Favours to me."

3. On the facing page appear the words: "i.e., thou delightest in their Happiness."

4. Brackets in the MS.

(3)

By thy Wisdom hast thou formed all Things, Thou hast created Man, bestowing Life and Reason, and plac'd him in Dignity superior to thy other earthly Creatures.

Praised be thy Name for ever.

(4)

Thy Wisdom, thy Power, and thy GOODNESS are every where clearly seen; in the Air and in the Water, in the Heavens and on the Earth; Thou providest for the various winged Fowl, and the innumerable Inhabitants of the Water; Thou givest Cold and Heat, Rain and Sunshine in their Season, and to the Fruits of the Earth Increase.

Praised be thy Name for ever.

(5)

I believe thou hast given Life to thy Creatures that they might Live, and art not delighted with violent Death and bloody Sacrifices.

Praised be thy Name for Ever.[5]

(6)

Thou abhorrest in thy Creatures Treachery and Deceit, Malice, Revenge, [*Intemperance*][6] and every other hurtful Vice; but Thou art a Lover of Justice and Sincerity, of Friendship, Benevolence and every Virtue. Thou art my Friend, my Father, and my Benefactor.

Praised be thy Name, O God, for Ever.

Amen.

After this, it will not be improper to read part of some such Book as Ray's Wisdom of God in the Creation or Blacmore on the Creation, or the Archbishop of Cambray's Demonstration of the Being of a God; &c.[7] or else spend some Minutes in a serious Silence, contemplating on those Subjects.

5. The whole of Art. 5 has been struck out in the MS.
6. Brackets in the MS.
7. The books referred to are John Ray, *The Wisdom of God manifested in the Works of the Creation* (London, 1691, and many subsequent editions); Richard Blackmore, *Creation: A Philosophical Poem* (London, 1712); and Archbishop Fénelon, *A Demonstration of the existence and attributes of God, drawn from the knowledge of nature, from proofs purely intellectual, and from the ideas of the Infinite Himself* (2d edit., London, 1720).

Then Sing
Milton's Hymn to the Creator[8]

These are thy Glorious Works, Parent of Good!
Almighty: Thine this Universal Frame,
Thus wondrous fair! Thy self how wondrous then!
Speak ye who best can tell, Ye Sons of Light,
Angels, for ye behold him, and with Songs,
And Choral Symphonies, Day without Night
Circle his Throne rejoicing. You in Heav'n,
On Earth, join all Ye Creatures to extol
Him first, him last, him midst and without End.
　　Fairest of Stars, last in the Train of Night,
If rather thou belongst not to the Dawn,
Sure Pledge of Day! That crown'st the smiling Morn
With thy bright Circlet; Praise him in thy Sphere
While Day arises, that sweet Hour of Prime.
　　Thou Sun, of this Great World both Eye and Soul
Acknowledge Him thy Greater, Sound his Praise
In thy Eternal Course; both when thou climb'st,
And when high Noon hast gain'd, and when thou fall'st.
Moon! that now meet'st the orient Sun, now fly'st
With the fix'd Stars, fix'd in their Orb that flies,
And ye five other Wandring Fires, that move
In mystic Dance, not without Song, resound
His Praise, that out of Darkness call'd up Light.
Air! and ye Elements! the Eldest Birth
Of Nature's Womb, that in Quaternion run
Perpetual Circle, multiform; and mix
And nourish all Things, let your ceaseless Change
Vary to our great Maker still new Praise.
Ye Mists and Exhalations! that now rise
From Hill or steaming Lake, dusky or grey,
Till the Sun paint your fleecy Skirts with Gold,
In Honour to the World's Great Author rise.
Whether to deck with Clouds th' uncolour'd Sky
Or wet the thirsty Earth with falling Show'rs,

---

8. *Paradise Lost*, v, 153–6, 160–204. A diagram of the solar system on a facing page of the MS appears to be intended to illustrate these lines.

Rising or falling still advance his Praise.
His Praise, ye Winds! that from 4 Quarters blow,
Breathe soft or loud; and wave your Tops ye Pines!
With every Plant, in Sign of Worship wave.
Fountains! and ye that warble as ye flow
Melodious Murmurs, warbling tune his Praise.
Join Voices all ye living Souls, ye Birds!
That singing, up to Heav'n's high Gate ascend,
Bear on your Wings, and in your Notes his Praise.
Ye that in Waters glide! and ye that walk
The Earth! and stately Tread, or lowly Creep;
Witness *if I be silent,* Ev'n or Morn,
To Hill or Valley, Fountain or Fresh Shade,
Made Vocal by my Song, and taught his Praise.

{ Here follows the Reading of some Book or part of a Book
{ Discoursing on and exciting to MORAL VIRTUE

Petition.

Prel.{ In as much as by Reason of our Ignorance We cannot be Certain that many Things Which we often hear mentioned in the Petitions of Men to the Deity, would prove REAL GOODS if they were in our Possession, and as I have Reason to hope and believe that the Goodness of my Heavenly Father will not withold from me a suitable Share of Temporal Blessings, if by a VIRTUOUS and HOLY Life I merit[9] his Favour and Kindness, Therefore I presume not to ask such Things, but rather Humbly, and with a sincere Heart express my earnest Desires that he would graciously assist my Continual Endeavours and Resolutions of eschewing Vice and embracing Virtue; Which kind of Supplications will at least be thus far beneficial, as they[1] remind me in a solemn manner of my Extensive   DUTY.

That I may be preserved from Atheism and Infidelity, Impiety and Profaneness, and in my Addresses to Thee carefully avoid

9. In the margin: "conciliate."
1. "At least . . . they" replaced on the facing page of the MS by "at the same time."

Irreverence and Ostentation, Formality and odious Hypocrisy,
                                    Help me, O Father

That I may be loyal to my Prince, and faithful to my Country, careful for its Good, valiant in its Defence, and obedient to its Laws, abhorring Treason as much as Tyranny,
                                    Help me, O Father

That I may to those above me be dutiful, humble, and submissive, avoiding Pride, Disrespect and Contumacy, Help me, O Father

That I may to those below me, be gracious, Condescending and Forgiving, using Clemency, protecting *Innocent Distress,* avoiding Cruelty, Harshness and Oppression, Insolence and unreasonable Severity,   Help me, O Father

That I may refrain from Calumny and Detraction; that I may avoid and abhor Deceit and Envy, Fraud, Flattery and Hatred, Malice, Lying and Ingratitude,   Help me, O Father

That I may be sincere in Friendship, faithful in Trust, and impartial in Judgment, watchful against Pride, and against Anger (that momentary Madness),   Help me, O Father

That I may be just in all my Dealings and temperate in my Pleasures, full of Candour and Ingenuity, Humanity and Benevolence,
                                    Help me, O Father

That I may be grateful to my Benefactors and generous to my Friends, exerting Charity and Liberality to the Poor, and Pity to the Miserable,   Help me, O Father

That I may avoid Avarice, Ambition, and Intemperance, Luxury and Lasciviousness,   Help me, O Father

That I may possess Integrity and Evenness of Mind, Resolution in Difficulties, and Fortitude under Affliction; that I may be punctual in performing my Promises, peaceable and prudent in my Behaviour,   Help me, O Father

That I may have Tenderness for the Weak, and a reverent Respect for the Ancient; That I may be kind to my Neighbours, good-natured to my Companions, and hospitable to Strangers,
                                    Help me, O Father

That I may be averse to Craft and Overreaching, abhor Extortion, Perjury, and every kind of Wickedness,   Help me, O Father

That I may be honest and Openhearted, gentle, merciful and Good, chearful in Spirit, rejoicing in the Good of Others,

Help me, O Father

That I may have a constant Regard to Honour and Probity; That I may possess a perfect Innocence and a good Conscience, and at length become Truly Virtuous and Magnanimous,

Help me, Good God,
Help me, O Father[2]

And forasmuch as Ingratitude is one of the most odious of Vices, let me not be unmindful gratefully to acknoledge the Favours I receive from Heaven.

Thanks.

For Peace and Liberty, for Food and Raiment, for Corn and Wine, and Milk, and every kind of Healthful Nourishment,

Good God, I Thank thee.

For the Common Benefits of Air and Light, for useful Fire and delicious Water, Good God, I Thank thee.

For Knowledge and Literature and every useful Art; for my Friends and their Prosperity, and for the fewness of my Enemies,

Good God, I Thank thee.

For all thy innumerable Benefits; For Life and Reason, and the Use of Speech, for Health and Joy and every Pleasant Hour,

my Good God, I thank thee.

End of the first Part.

Epitaph

Autograph MS: Yale University Library; another autograph MS: Richard Gimbel, New Haven, Conn. (1959); facsimile printed in Charles John Smith, *Historical and Literary Curiosities* (London, 1840).

Three autograph texts of the Epitaph are known—two in manuscript, one a facsimile of the now lost Upcott holograph. Each differs from

2. The text from this point on is taken from William Temple Franklin's transcript.

the other two, and all vary, significantly or in details, from eighteenth-century transcripts or printed versions. This is not surprising, since Franklin used to make copies of the Epitaph for his friends and, writing from memory, would make changes, either inadvertently or as improvements. His friends in turn gave copies to their friends, and at any point in this process a printer might be allowed to take a copy to brighten his almanac or magazine. No version is known that can be called Franklin's first or corrected draft, and no one can know which of the three holographs listed above Franklin would have chosen as best had he considered them—or whether he might not have preferred yet another version of which no autograph survives. So the three must be regarded as equally authoritative. The text presented here is the one in the Mason Collection at Yale; from its handwriting it seems to be the earliest.

Nor is the date of composition certain. Franklin himself wrote on the Upcott holograph, probably in 1784, that he had composed the piece in 1728. William Temple Franklin accepted this date. And Dr. John Coakley Lettsom, sending a copy to a friend in 1785, declared that it was done "when Dr. Franklin was a printer . . . as each of the club [Junto?] in rotation did the same."[3] On the other hand, Benjamin Vaughan apparently believed that it had been composed earlier than 1728, but his substantiating details are incorrect. When Franklin's friend and admirer Ezra Stiles copied a version in Jane Mecom's possession in 1779, he indicated that it had been "composed 20 years ago" or about 1759. In the absence of stronger evidence to the contrary, Franklin's own statement that he wrote the Epitaph in 1728 seems the most acceptable.

Whether the concept of the Epitaph, comparing a printer's body to an old book, was original with Franklin has also been the subject of discussion and inquiry. He has been charged with plagiarizing a Latin epitaph on Jacob Tonson that was printed in the *Gentleman's Magazine* in 1736. This charge is without foundation, of course, if Franklin composed his Epitaph in 1728. But he could have seen other applications of the simile, not uncommon in his day, such as Benjamin Woodbridge's epitaph on John Cotton, printed in Mather's *Magnalia Christi Americana* (1702).[4]

3. Thomas J. Pettigrew, *Memoirs of the Life and Writings of the Late John Coakley Lettsom* (London, 1817), I, second pagination, 101–2.

4. For an exhaustive discussion of the sources, variations, and sequels of the Epitaph, see L. H. Butterfield, "B. Franklin's Epitaph," *New Colophon*, III (1950), 9–30, where eleven variants are considered.

The Body of
B. Franklin,
Printer;
Like the Cover of an old Book,
Its Contents torn out,
And stript of its Lettering and Gilding,
Lies here, Food for Worms.
But the Work shall not be wholly lost:
For it will, as he believ'd, appear once more,
In a new & more perfect Edition,
Corrected and amended
By the Author.

He was born Jan. 6. 1706.
Died   17

Franklin's Epitaph in his own hand.

The Body of

B. Franklin,

Printer;

Like the Cover of an old Book,

Its Contents torn out,

And stript of its Lettering and Gilding,

Lies here, Food for Worms.

But the Work shall not be wholly lost:[5]

For it will, as he believ'd, appear once more,

In a new & more perfect Edition,[6]

Corrected and amended[7]

By the Author.

He was born Jan. 6. 1706.

Died   17   [8]

Martha Careful and Caelia Shortface

Printed in *The American Weekly Mercury*, January 28, 1728/9.

When Samuel Keimer forestalled Franklin's plan to publish a newspaper by announcing that he would publish one of his own, Franklin expressed his resentment through the satirical essays of The Busy-Body (see below, p. 113). The Busy-Body, however, was not the first to ridicule Keimer. Plodding methodically through the alphabet of Chambers' *Cyclopaedia*, Keimer had unwittingly printed in his fifth issue, January 21, the article on abortion. The following week Bradford's *American Weekly Mercury* carried on its front page letters of protest purportedly

5. "But the Work shall not be lost;" in the Gimbel autograph and Smith facsimile.
6. "new and more elegant" in the Gimbel and Smith versions.
7. "Corrected and improved" in the Gimbel autograph; "Revised and corrected" in the Smith facsimile.
8. These lines, recording the date of birth and providing space for the date of death, are omitted from the Gimbel and Smith versions.

from two outraged females. From the style and circumstance of the letters, however, the editors believe that Martha Careful and Caelia Shortface were probably one, and that Franklin may have been her name. It is probable that, encouraged by the success of the womanly protests, Bradford and Franklin determined that their facetious attacks on Keimer should continue and that Franklin undertook to produce a series in the manner of Mrs. Silence Dogood. It is at least noteworthy that the first Busy-Body letter appeared the next week after Martha and Caelia had voiced their sex's sense of scandal and insult.

Having had several Letters from the Female Sex, Complaining of S.K. I have thought fit to Publish the Two following.

Mr. Andrew Bradford,
   In behalf of my Self and many good modest Women in this City (who are almost out of Countenance) I Beg you will Publish this in your next *Mercury*, as a Warning to Samuel Keimer: That if he proceed farther to Expose the Secrets of our Sex, in That audacious manner, as he hath done in his *Gazette, No. 5.* under the Letters, A.B.O. To be read in all *Taverns* and *Coffee-Houses,* and by the Vulgar: I say if he Publish any more of that kind, which ought only to be in the Repositary of the Learned; my Sister Molly and my Self, with some others, are Resolved to run the Hazard of taking him by the Beard, at the next Place we meet him, and make an Example of him for his Immodesty. I Subscribe on the behalf of the rest of my Agrieved Sex. Yours
24 January, 1728.   MARTHA CAREFUL

Friend Andrew Bradford,
   I desire Thee to insert in thy next *Mercury*, the following Letter to Samuel Keimer, for by doing it, Thou may perhaps save Keimer his Ears, and very much Oblige our Sex in general, but in a more Particular manner. Thy modest Friend,   CÆLIA SHORTFACE

Friend Samuel Keimer,
   I did not Expect when thou puts forth Thy Advertisement concerning Thy *Universal Instructor,* (as Thou art pleas'd to call it,) That, Thou would have Printed such Things in it, as would make all the Modest and Virtuous Women in Pennsilvania ashamed.

I was last Night in Company with several of my Acquaintance, and Thee, and *Thy Indecencies,* was the Subject of our Discourse, but at last we Resolved, That if thou Continue to take such Scraps concerning Us, out of thy great Dictionary, and Publish it, as thou hath done in thy *Gazette,* No. 5, to make Thy Ears suffer for it: And I was desired by the rest, to inform Thee of Our Resolution, which is That if thou proceed any further in that *Scandalous manner,* we intend very soon to have thy right Ear for it; Therefore I advice Thee to take this timely Caution in good part; and if thou canst make no better Use of Thy Dictionary, Sell it at Thy next *Luck in the Bag;* and if Thou hath nothing else to put in Thy *Gazette,* lay it down, I am, Thy Troubled Friend,
27th of the 11th Mo. 1728.   CÆLIA SHORTFACE

The Busy-Body, No. 1

Printed in *The American Weekly Mercury,* February 4, 1728/9.

Franklin and Hugh Meredith[9] decided in 1728 to start a newspaper in opposition to Bradford's *American Weekly Mercury.*[1] Samuel Keimer[2] learned of this plan from George Webb, to whom Franklin incautiously revealed it when the former applied for employment as a journeyman,

9. See below, p. 175 n.

1. Anna Janney DeArmond, *Andrew Bradford, Colonial Printer* (Newark, Del., 1949).

2. Samuel Keimer (1688–1742), printer in London, publisher of the *London Post,* imprisoned several times for debt and seditious publications, migrated to Pennsylvania, 1722, where he set up as a printer, 1723, with BF as journeyman. A man of strange religious enthusiasms, inefficient, suspicious, unattractive, and pitiable, Keimer none the less printed a number of important English works for the American market. BF sketched his character and conduct pretty fully in his autobiography, summing him up as "an odd Fish, ignorant of common Life, fond of rudely opposing receiv'd Opinions, slovenly to extream dirtiness, enthusiastic in some Points of Religion, and a little Knavish withal." Keimer sold his business to David Harry in 1730, and sailed to Barbadoes, where he printed the *Barbadoes Gazette,* 1731–38. Stephen Bloore, "Samuel Keimer: A Footnote to the Life of Franklin," *PMHB,* LIV (1930), 255–87; C. Lennart Carlson, "Samuel Keimer: A Study in the Transit of English Culture to Colonial Pennsylvania," *ibid.,* LXI (1937), 357–86; Chester E. Jorgenson, "A Brand Flung at Colonial Orthodoxy," *Journalism Quar.,* XII (1935), 272–7.

and forestalled the new printing firm by publishing, October 1, proposals for a paper of his own, to be called the *Universal Instructor in all Arts and Sciences: and Pennsylvania Gazette*. Its first issue appeared December 24, 1728. "I resented this," Franklin recalled in his autobiography, "and to counteract them, as I could not yet begin our Paper, I wrote several Pieces of Entertainment for Bradford's Paper, under the Title of the Busy Body which Breintnal[3] continued some Months." These pieces ceased abruptly with Number 32, September 25, 1729, that is, the week Franklin and Meredith bought Keimer's paper.

Manuscript notes in the file of the *Mercury* in the Library Company of Philadelphia indicate the authors of the various essays. Someone, probably Franklin himself, has written in the margin of the issue of February 18, 1729: "The Busy Body was begun by B.F. who wrote the first four Numbers, part of No. 5, part of No. 8. the rest by J. Brintnal"; and other notations in the same hand appear on the fifth and eighth essays. The authority of these notes has been accepted since 1790.[4] Internal evidence offers no compelling reason to assign any of the other Busy-Body letters to Franklin.[5]

Mr. Andrew Bradford,

I design this to acquaint you, that I, who have long been one of your *Courteous Readers,* have lately entertain'd some Thoughts of setting up for an Author my Self; not out of the least Vanity, I

3. Joseph Breintnall (d. 1746), Quaker merchant and copyist for scriveners, one of the first members of the Junto, member of St. John's Masonic Lodge, secretary of the Library Company, 1731–46, sheriff of Philadelphia, 1735–38, described by BF as "good-natur'd, friendly . . . a great Lover of Poetry, reading all he could meet with, and writing some that was tolerable; very ingenious in many little Nicknackeries, and of sensible Conversation." He recommended John Bartram to Peter Collinson as "a very proper person" to furnish seeds and plants, made prints of tree leaves (see below, p. 344 n), and devised an ingenious experiment to test the reflection of the sun's rays by cloths of different colors (see BF to Mary Stevenson, Sept. 20, 1761). His letters to Peter Collinson on the aurora borealis and on his reactions to a rattlesnake bite were printed in the Royal Society's *Philos. Trans.*, XLI (1742), 359; XLIV (1748), 147–50. Stephen Bloore, "Joseph Breintnall, First Secretary of the Library Company," *PMHB*, LIX (1935), 42–56.

4. "History of the Life and Character of Benjamin Franklin," *The Universal Asylum and Columbian Magazine*, V (1790), 5.

5. Elizabeth C. Cook, *Literary Influences in Colonial Newspapers, 1704–1750* (N.Y., 1912), pp. 59–84, is a searching analysis of the Busy-Body, its sources and analogues.

assure you, or Desire of showing my Parts, but purely for the Good of my Country.

I have often observ'd with Concern, that your *Mercury* is not always equally entertaining. The Delay of Ships expected in, and want of fresh Advices from Europe, make it frequently very Dull; and I find the Freezing of our River has the same Effect on News as on Trade. With more Concern have I continually observ'd the growing Vices and Follies of my Country-folk. And tho' Reformation is properly the concern of every Man; that is, *Every one ought to mend One;* yet 'tis too true in this Case, that *what is every Body's Business is no Body's Business,* and the Business is done accordingly. I, therefore, upon mature Deliberation, think fit to take *no Body's Business* wholly into my own Hands; and, out of Zeal for the Publick Good, design to erect my Self into a Kind of *Censor Morum;* proposing with your Allowance, to make Use of the *Weekly Mercury* as a Vehicle in which my Remonstrances shall be convey'd to the World.

I am sensible I have, in this Particular, undertaken a very unthankful Office, and expect little besides my Labour for my Pains. Nay, 'tis probable I may displease a great Number of your Readers, who will not very well like to pay 10s. a Year for being told of their Faults. But as most People delight in Censure when they themselves are not the Objects of it, if any are offended at my publickly exposing their private Vices, I promise they shall have the Satisfaction, in a very little Time, of seeing their good Friends and Neighbours in the same Circumstances.

However, let the Fair Sex be assur'd, that I shall always treat them and their Affairs with the utmost *Decency* and Respect. I intend now and then to dedicate a Chapter wholly to their Service; and if my Lectures any Way contribute to the Embellishment of their Minds, and Brightning of their Understandings, without offending their *Modesty*, I doubt not of having their Favour and Encouragement.

'Tis certain, that no Country in the World produces naturally finer Spirits than ours, Men of Genius for every kind of Science, and capable of acquiring to Perfection every Qualification that is in Esteem among Mankind. But as few here have the Advantage of good Books, for want of which, good Conversation is still more scarce, it would doubtless have been very acceptable to your Readers, if, instead of an old out-of-date Article from Muscovy or Hungary, you had entertained them with some well-chosen Extract from a good Author. This I shall sometimes do, *when I happen to have nothing of my own to say that I think of more Consequence*. Sometimes, I propose to deliver Lectures of Morality or Philosophy, and (because I am naturally enclin'd to be meddling with Things that don't concern me) perhaps I may sometimes talk Politicks. And if I can by any means furnish out a Weekly Entertainment for the Publick, that will give a rational Diversion, and at the same Time be instructive to the Readers, I shall think my Leisure Hours well employ'd: And if you publish this I hereby invite all ingenious Gentlemen and others, (that approve of such an Undertaking) to my Assistance and Correspondence.

'Tis like by this Time you have a Curiosity to be acquainted with my Name and Character. As I do not aim at publick Praise I design to remain concealed; and there are such Numbers of our Family and Relations at this Time in the Country, that tho' I've sign'd my Name at full Length, I am not under the least Apprehension of being distinguish'd and discover'd by it. My Character indeed I would favour you with, but that I am cautious of praising my Self, lest I should be told *my Trumpeter's dead:* And I cannot find in my Heart, at present, to say any Thing to my own Disadvantage.

It is very common with Authors in their first Performances to talk to their Readers thus, *If this meets with a* SUITABLE *Reception;* Or, *If this should meet with* DUE *Encouragement, I shall hereafter publish,* &c. This only manifests the Value they put on their own Writings, since they think to frighten the Publick into their Applause, by threatning, that unless you approve what they have already wrote, they intend never to write again; when perhaps, it mayn't be a Pin Matter whether they ever do or no. As I have not observ'd the Criticks to be more favourable on this Account, I shall always avoid saying any Thing of the Kind; and conclude with telling you, that if you send me a Bottle of Ink and a Quire of Paper by the Bearer, you may depend on hearing further from Sir, Your most humble Servant   THE BUSY BODY

No. 1.

The Busy-Body, No. 2

Printed in *The American Weekly Mercury*, February 11, 1728/9.

THE BUSY-BODY. NO. 2.

All Fools have still an Itching to deride;
And fain would be upon the laughing Side.   Pope.[6]

Monsieur Rochefocaut[7] tells us somewhere in his Memoirs, that the Prince of Conde delighted much in Ridicule; and us'd frequently to shut himself up for Half a Day together in his Chamber with a Gentleman that was his Favourite, purposely to divert himself with examining what was the Foible or ridiculous side of every Noted Person in the Court. That Gentleman said afterwards in some Company, that he thought nothing was more ridiculous in any Body, than this same Humour in the Prince; and I am somewhat inclin'd to be of his Opinion. The General Tendency there is among us to this Embellishment, (which I fear has too often been grossly imposed upon my loving Countrymen instead of Wit) and the Applause it meets with from a rising Generation, fill me with fearful Apprehensions for the future Reputation of my Country: A young Man of Modesty (which is the most certain Indication of large Capacities) is hereby discourag'd from attempting to make any Figure in Life: His Apprehensions of being outlaugh'd, will force him to continue in a restless Obscurity, without having an Opportunity of knowing his own Merit himself, or discovering it to the World, rather than venture to expose himself in a Place where a Pun or a Sneer shall pass for Wit, Noise for Reason, and the Strength of the Argument be judg'd by that of the Lungs. Among these witty Gentlemen let us take a View of Ridentius: What a contemptible Figure does he make with his Train of paultry Admirers? This Wight shall give himself an Hours Diversion with the Cock of a Man's Hat, the Heels of his Shoes, an unguarded Expression in his Discourse, or even some Personal Defect; and the Height of his low Ambition is to put some One of the Company to the Blush, who perhaps must pay an equal Share of the Reckoning with himself. If such a Fellow makes Laughing the sole End and Purpose of his Life, if it is necessary to his Constitution, or if he

6. *Essay on Criticism*, 32–3.
7. Probably François, duc de La Rochefoucauld, prince de Marcillac (1613–1680). The anecdote has not been found.

has a great Desire of growing suddenly fat, let him treat; let him give publick Notice where any dull stupid Rogues may get a Quart of Four-penny for being laugh'd at; but 'tis barbarously unhandsome, when Friends meet for the Benefit of Conversation, and a proper Relaxation from Business, that one should be the *Butt* of the Company, and Four Men made merry at the Cost of the Fifth.

How different from this Character is that of the good-natur'd gay Eugenius? who never spoke yet but with a Design to divert and please; and who was never yet baulk'd in his Intention. Eugenius takes more Delight in applying the Wit of his Friends, than in being admir'd himself: And if any one of the Company is so unfortunate as to be touch'd a little too nearly, he will make Use of some ingenious Artifice to turn the Edge of Ridicule another Way, chusing rather to make even himself a publick Jest, than be at the Pain of seeing his Friend in Confusion.

Among the Tribe of Laughers I reckon the *pretty Gentlemen* that write *Satyrs*, and carry them about in their Pockets, reading them themselves in all Company they happen into; taking an Advantage of the ill Taste of the Town, to make themselves famous for a Pack of paultry low Nonsence, for which they deserve to be kick'd, rather than admir'd, by all who have the least Tincture of Politeness. These I take to be the most incorrigible of all my Readers; nay I expect they will be squibbing at the BUSY-BODY himself: However the only Favour he begs of them is this; that if they cannot controul their over-bearing Itch of *Scribbling*, let him be attack'd in downright BITING LYRICKS; for there is no *Satyr* he Dreads half so much as an Attempt towards a Panegyrick.

The Busy-Body, No. 3

Printed in *The American Weekly Mercury*, February 18, 1728/9.

THE BUSY-BODY. NO. 3.

Non vultus instantis Tyranni
Mente quatit solida—neque Auster
Dux inquieti turbidus Adriae,
Nec fulminantis magna Jovis manus.   Hor.[8]

It is said that the Persians in their ancient Constitution, had publick Schools in which Virtue was taught as a Liberal Art or

8. Horace, *Odes*, III, iii, 3–6.

Science; and it is certainly of more Consequence to a Man that he has learnt to govern his Passions; in spite of Temptation to be just in his Dealings, to be Temperate in his Pleasures, to support himself with Fortitude under his Misfortunes, to behave with Prudence in all Affairs and in every Circumstance of Life; I say, it is of much more real Advantage to him to be thus qualified, than to be a Master of all the Arts and Sciences in the World beside.

Virtue alone is sufficient to make a Man Great, Glorious and Happy. He that is acquainted with Cato, as I am, cannot help thinking as I do now, and will acknowledge he deserves the Name without being honour'd by it. Cato is a Man whom Fortune has plac'd in the most obscure Part of the Country. His Circumstances are such as only put him above Necessity, without affording him many Superfluities; Yet who is greater than Cato? I happened but the other Day to be at a House in Town, where among others were met Men of the most Note in this Place: Cato had Business with some of them, and knock'd at the Door. The most trifling Actions of a Man, in my Opinion, as well as the smallest Features and Lineaments of the Face, give a nice Observer some Notion of his Mind. Methought he rapp'd in such a peculiar Manner, as seem'd of itself to express, there was One who deserv'd as well as desir'd Admission. He appear'd in the plainest Country Garb; his Great Coat was coarse and looked old and thread-bare; his Linnen was homespun; his Beard perhaps of Seven Days Growth, his Shoes thick and heavy, and every Part of his Dress corresponding. Why was this Man receiv'd with such concurring Respect from every Person in the Room, even from those who had never known him or seen him before? It was not an exquisite Form of Person, or Grandeur of Dress that struck us with Admiration. I believe long Habits of Virtue have a sensible Effect on the Countenance: There was something in the Air of his Face that manifested the true Greatness of his Mind; which likewise appear'd in all he said, and in every Part of his Behaviour, obliging us to regard him with a Kind of Veneration. His Aspect is sweetned with Humanity and Benevolence, and at the same Time emboldned with Resolution, equally free from a diffident Bashfulness and an unbecoming Assurance. The Consciousness of his own innate Worth and unshaken Integrity renders him calm and undaunted in the Presence of the most Great and Powerful, and upon the most extraordinary

Occasions. His strict Justice and known Impartiality make him the Arbitrator and Decider of all Differences that arise for many Miles around him, without putting his Neighbours to the Charge, Perplexity and Uncertainty of Law-Suits. He always speaks the Thing he means, which he is never afraid or asham'd to do, because he knows he always means well; and therefore is never oblig'd to blush and feel the Confusion of finding himself detected in the Meanness of a Falshood. He never contrives Ill against his Neighbour, and therefore is never seen with a lowring suspicious Aspect. A mixture of Innocence and Wisdom makes him ever seriously chearful. His generous Hospitality to Strangers according to his Ability, his Goodness, his Charity, his Courage in the Cause of the Oppressed, his Fidelity in Friendship, his Humility, his Honesty and Sincerity, his Moderation and his Loyalty to the Government, his Piety, his Temperance, his Love to Mankind, his Magnanimity, his Publick-spiritedness, and in fine, his *Consummate Virtue,* make him justly deserve to be esteem'd the Glory of his Country.

> ——*The Brave do never shun the Light,*
> *Just are their Thoughts and open are their Tempers;*
> *Freely without Disguise they love and hate;*
> *Still are they found in the fair Face of Day,*
> *And Heaven and Men are Judges of their Actions.* Rowe.[9]

Who would not rather chuse, if it were in his Choice, to merit the above Character, than be the richest, the most learned, or the most powerful Man in the Province without it?

Almost every Man has a strong natural Desire of being valu'd and esteem'd by the rest of his Species; but I am concern'd and griev'd to see how few fall into the Right and only infallible Method of becoming so. That laudable Ambition is too commonly misapply'd and often ill employ'd. Some to make themselves considerable pursue Learning, others grasp at Wealth, some aim at being thought witty, and others are only careful to make the most of an handsome Person; But what is Wit, or Wealth, or Form, or Learning when compar'd with Virtue? 'Tis true, we love the handsome, we applaud the Learned, and we fear the Rich and Powerful; but we even Worship and adore the Virtuous. Nor is it strange; since Men of Virtue, are so rare, so very rare to be

9. Nicholas Rowe, *The Fair Penitent,* II, ii, 34–8.

found. If we were as industrious to become Good, as to make ourselves Great, we should become really Great by being Good, and the Number of valuable Men would be much increased; but it is a Grand Mistake to think of being Great without Goodness; and I pronounce it as certain, *that there was never yet a truly Great Man that was not at the same Time truly Virtuous.*

O Cretico! Thou sowre Philosopher! Thou cunning States-man! Thou art crafty, but far from being Wise. When wilt thou be esteem'd, regarded and belov'd like Cato? When wilt thou, among thy Creatures meet with that unfeign'd Respect and warm Good-will that all Men have for him? Wilt thou never understand that the cringing, mean, submissive Deportment of thy Dependants, is (like the Worship paid by Indians to the Devil) rather thro' Fear of the Harm thou may'st do to them, than out of Gratitude for the Favours they have receiv'd of thee? Thou art not wholly void of Virtue; there are many good Things in thee, and many good Actions reported of thee. Be advised by thy Friend: Neglect those musty Authors; let them be cover'd with Dust, and moulder on their proper Shelves; and do thou apply thy self to a Study much more profitable, The Knowledge of Mankind, and of thy Self.[1]

This is to give Notice that the BUSY-BODY *strictly forbids all Persons, from this Time forward, of what Age, Sex, Rank, Quality, Degree or Denomination soever, on any Pretence to enquire who is the Author of this Paper, on Pain of his Displeasure, (his own near and Dear Relations only excepted).*

'Tis to be observ'd that if any bad Characters happen to be drawn in the Course of these Papers, they mean no particular Person, if they are not particularly apply'd.

Likewise that the Author is no Partyman, but a general Meddler.

N.B. *Cretico lives in a neighbouring Province.*

1. Apparently the Busy-Body's "characters" were recognized: despite BF's disclaimer, the "sowre Philosopher" was probably Keimer; and the latter printed a mild warning that the author should not give way to defamation and scandal. "It requires a great Genius and much good Nature to manage with Decency and Humanity the Way of Writing which the Busy-Body would seem to imitate; feigned and imaginary Characters may excite Vertue and discourage Vice; but to figure out and apply them by gross Descriptions, has the ill Effect which I take this Trouble to persuade the *Busy-Body* to avoid." *Pa. Gaz.*, Feb. 25, 1729.

The Busy-Body, No. 4

Printed in *The American Weekly Mercury*, February 25, 1728/9.

THE BUSY-BODY. NO. 4.

Nequid nimis.

In my first Paper I invited the Learned and the Ingenious to join with me in this Undertaking; and I now repeat that Invitation. I would have such Gentlemen take this Opportunity, (by trying their Talent in Writing) of diverting themselves and their Friends, and improving the Taste of the Town. And because I would encourage all Wit of our own Growth and Produce, I hereby promise, that whoever shall send me a little Essay on some moral or other Subject, that is fit for publick View in this Manner (and not basely borrow'd from any other Author) I shall receive it with Candour, and take Care to place it to the best Advantage. It will be hard if we cannot muster up in the whole Country, a sufficient Stock of Sense to supply the *Busy-Body* at least for a Twelvemonth. For my own Part, I have already profess'd that I have the Good of my Country wholly at Heart in this Design, without the least sinister View; my chief Purpose being to inculcate the noble Principles of Virtue, and depreciate Vice of every kind. But as I know the Mob hate Instruction, and the Generality would never read beyond the first Line of my Lectures, if they were usually fill'd with nothing but wholesome Precepts and Advice; I must therefore sometimes humour them in their own Way. There are a Set of Great Names in the Province, who are the common Objects of Popular Dislike. If I can now and then overcome my Reluctance, and prevail with my self to Satyrize a little, one of these Gentlemen, the Expectation of meeting with such a Gratification, will induce many to read me through, who would otherwise proceed immediately to the Foreign News. As I am very well assured that the greatest Men among us have a sincere Love for their Country, notwithstanding its Ingratitude, and the Insinuations of the Envious and Malicious to the contrary, so I doubt not but they will chearfully tolerate me in the Liberty I design to take for the End above mentioned.

As yet I have but few Correspondents, tho' they begin now to increase. The following Letter, left for me at the Printers, is one of the first I have receiv'd, which I regard the more for that it comes from one of the Fair Sex, and because I have my self oftentimes suffer'd under the Grievance therein complain'd of.

"Sir,   *To the Busy-Body.*

"You having set your self up for a *Censurer Morum* (as I think you call it) which is said to mean a *Reformer of Manners*, I know no Person more proper to be apply'd to for Redress in all the Grievances we suffer from *Want of Manners* in some People. You must know I am a single Woman, and keep a Shop in this Town for a Livelyhood. There is a certain Neighbour of mine, who is really agreeable Company enough, and with whom I have had an Intimacy of some Time standing; But of late she makes her Visits so excessively often, and stays so very long every Visit, that I am tir'd out of all Patience. I have no Manner of Time at all to my self; and you, who seem to be a wise Man, must needs be sensible that every Person has little Secrets and Privacies that are not proper to be expos'd even to the nearest Friend. Now I cannot do the least Thing in the World, but she must know all about it; and it is a Wonder I have found an Opportunity to write you this Letter. My Misfortune is, that I respect her very well, and know not how to disoblige her so much as to tell her I should be glad to have less of her Company; for if I should once hint such a Thing, I am afraid she would resent it so as never to darken my Door again. But, alas, Sir, I have not yet told you half my Afflictions. She has two Children that are just big enough to run about and do pretty Mischief: These are continually along with Mamma, either in my Room or Shop, if I have never so many Customers or People with me about Business. Sometimes they pull the Goods off my low Shelves down to the Ground, and perhaps where one of them has just been making Water; My Friend takes up the Stuff, and cries, *Eh! thou little wicked mischievous Rogue! — But however, it has done no great Damage; 'tis only wet a little;* and so puts it up upon the Shelf again. Sometimes they get to my Cask of Nails behind the Counter, and divert themselves, to my great Vexation, with mixing my Ten-penny and Eight-penny and Four-penny together. I Endeavour to conceal my Uneasiness as much as possible, and with a grave Look go to Sorting them out. She cries, *Don't thee trouble thy self, Neigh-*

123

bour: Let them play a little; I'll put all to rights my self before I go.
But Things are never so put to rights but that I find a great deal
of Work to do after they are gone. Thus, Sir, I have all the Trouble
and Pesterment of Children, without the Pleasure of — calling
them my own; and they are now so us'd to being here that they
will be content no where else. If she would have been so kind as
to have moderated her Visits to ten times a Day, and stay'd but
half an hour at a Time, I should have been contented, and I
believe never have given you this Trouble: But this very Morning
they have so tormented me that I could bear no longer; For
while the Mother was asking me twenty impertinent Questions,
the youngest got to my Nails, and with great Delight rattled them
by handfuls all over the Floor; and the other at the same Time
made such a terrible Din upon my Counter with a Hammer, that
I grew half distracted. I was just then about to make my self a
new Suit of Pinners,[2] but in the Fret and Confusion I cut it quite
out of all Manner of Shape, and utterly spoil'd a Piece of the first
Muslin. Pray, Sir, tell me what I shall do. And talk a little against
such unreasonable Visiting in your next Paper: Tho' I would not
have her affronted with me for a great Deal, for sincerely I love
her and her Children as well I think, as a Neighbour can, and
she buys a great many Things in a Year at my Shop. But I would
beg her to consider that she uses me unmercifully; Tho' I believe
it is only for want of Thought. But I have twenty Things more
to tell you besides all this; There is a handsome Gentleman that
has a Mind (I don't question) to make love to me, but he can't
get the least Opportunity to —: O dear, here she comes again;
I must conclude   Yours, &c.   PATIENCE"

Indeed, 'tis well enough, as it happens, that *she is come,* to
shorten this Complaint which I think is full long enough already,
and probably would otherwise have been as long again. However, I must confess I cannot help pitying my Correspondent's
Case, and in her Behalf exhort the Visitor to remember and consider the Words of the Wise Man, *Withdraw thy Foot from the
House of thy Neighbour least he grow weary of thee, and so hate thee.*[3]
It is, I believe, a nice thing and very difficult, to regulate our

2. Pinners: a form of head-dress; also an apron.
3. Prov. 25:17.

124

Visits in such a Manner, as never to give Offence by coming too seldom, or too often, or departing too abruptly, or staying too long. However, in my Opinion, it is safest for most People, in a general way, who are unwilling to disoblige, to visit seldom, and tarry but a little while in a Place; notwithstanding pressing invitations, which are many times insincere. And tho' more of your Company should be really desir'd; yet in this Case, too much Reservedness is a Fault more easily excus'd than the Contrary.

Men are subjected to various Inconveniences meerly through lack of a small Share of Courage, which is a Quality very necessary in the common Occurences of Life, as well as in a Battle. How many Impertinences do we daily suffer with great Uneasiness, because we have not Courage enough to discover our Dislike? And why may not a Man use the Boldness and Freedom of telling his Friends that their long Visits sometimes incommode him? On this Occasion, it may be entertaining to some of my Readers, if I acquaint them with the Turkish Manner of entertaining Visitors, which I have from an Author of unquestionable Veracity;[4] who assures us, that even the Turks are not so ignorant of Civility, and the Arts of Endearment, but that they can practice them with as much Exactness as any other Nation, whenever they have a Mind to shew themselves obliging.

"When you visit a Person of Quality, (says he) and have talk'd over your Business, or the Complements, or whatever Concern brought you thither, he makes a Sign to have Things serv'd in for the Entertainment, which is generally, a little Sweetmeat, a Dish of Sherbet, and another of Coffee; all which are immediately brought in by the Servants, and tender'd to all the Guests in Order, with the greatest Care and Awfulness imaginable. At last comes the finishing Part of your Entertainment, which is, Perfuming the Beards of the Company; a Ceremony which is perform'd in this Manner. They have for the Purpose a small Silver Chaffing-Dish, cover'd with a Lid full of Holes, and fixed upon a handsome Plate. In this they put some fresh Coals, and upon them a piece of *Lignum Aloes,* and shutting it up, the Smoak immediately ascends with a grateful Odour thro' the Holes of the Cover. This Smoak is held under every one's Chin, and offer'd as it were a Sacrifice to his Beard. The bristly Idol soon receives

4. Not identified.

the Reverence done to it, and so greedily takes in and incorporates the gummy Steam, that it retains the Savour of it, and may serve for a Nosegay a good while after.

"This Ceremony may perhaps seem ridiculous at first hearing; but it passes among the Turks for an high Gratification. And I will say this in its Vindication, that it's Design is very wise and useful. For it is understood to give a civil Dismission to the Visitants; intimating to them, that the Master of the House has Business to do, or some other Avocation, that permits them to go away as soon as they please; and the sooner after this Ceremony the better. By this Means you may, at any Time, without Offence, deliver your self from being detain'd from your Affairs by tedious and unseasonable Visits; and from being constrain'd to use that Piece of Hypocrisy so common in the World, of pressing those to stay longer with you, whom perhaps in your Heart you wish a great Way off for having troubled you so long already."

Thus far my Author. For my own Part, I have taken such a Fancy to this Turkish Custom, that for the future I shall put something like it in Practice. I have provided a Bottle of right French Brandy for the Men, and Citron-Water for the Ladies. After I have treated with a Dram, and presented a Pinch of my best Snuff, I expect all Company will retire, and leave me to pursue my Studies for the Good of the Publick.

Advertisement.

I give Notice that I am now actually compiling, and design to publish in a short Time, the true History of the Rise, Growth and Progress of the renowned Tiff-Club.[5] All Persons who are acquainted with any Facts, Circumstances, Characters, Transactions, &c. which will be requisite to the Perfecting and Embellishment of the said Work, are desired to communicate the same to the Author, and direct their Letters to be left with the Printer hereof.

The Letter sign'd *Would-be-something* is come to hand.

5. To promote his political ambitions after his removal from the governorship of Pennsylvania, 1726, Sir William Keith organized two clubs, one for gentlemen, the other for tradesmen. The latter was known as the Tiff Club. The clubs did their work so well that Sir William was elected to the Assembly. In view of his experience in 1724 BF was not one of Sir William's party. Burton A. Konkle, *The Life of Andrew Hamilton, 1676–1741* (Phila., 1941), p. 41.

The Busy-Body, No. 5

Printed in *The American Weekly Mercury*, March 4, 1728/9.

THE BUSY-BODY. NO. 5.

Vos, O Patricius sanguis, quos vivere fas est
Occipiti caeco, posticae occurrite sannae. Persius.[6]

This Paper being design'd for a Terror to Evil-Doers, as well as a Praise to them that do well, I am lifted up with secret Joy to find that my Undertaking is approved, and encourag'd by the Just and Good, and that few are against me but those who have Reason to fear me.

There are little Follies in the Behaviour of most Men, which their best Friends are too tender to acquaint them with: There are little Vices and small Crimes which the Law has no Regard to, or Remedy for: There are likewise great Pieces of Villany sometimes so craftily accomplish'd, and so circumspectly guarded, that the Law can take no Hold of the Actors. All these Things, and all Things of this Nature, come within my Province as CENSOR, and I am determined not to be negligent of the Trust I have reposed in my self, but resolve to execute my Office diligently and Faithfully.

And that all the World may judge with how much Humanity as well as Justice I shall behave in this Office; and that even my Enemies may be convinc'd I take no Delight to rake into the Dunghill Lives of vicious Men; and to the End that certain Persons may be a little eas'd of their Fears, and reliev'd from the terrible Palpitations they have lately felt and suffer'd, and do still suffer; I hereby graciously pass an Act of general Oblivion, for all Offences, Crimes and Misdemeanors of what Kind soever, committed from the Beginning of Year sixteen hundred and eighty one, until the Day of the Date of my first Paper; and promise only to concern my self with such as have been since and shall hereafter be committed. I shall take no Notice who has, (heretofore) rais'd a Fortune by Fraud and Oppression, nor who by Deceit and Hypocrisy: What Woman has been false to her good Husband's Bed; nor what Man has, by barbarous Usage or Neglect, broke the Heart of a faithful Wife, and wasted his Health

6. Persius, *Satires*, I, 61–2.

127

and Substance in Debauchery: What base Wretch has betray'd his Friend, and sold his Honesty for Gold, nor what yet baser Wretch, first corrupted him and then bought the Bargain: All this, and much more of the same Kind I shall forget and pass over in Silence; — but then it is to be observed that I expect and require a sudden and general Amendment.

These Threatnings of mine I hope will have a good Effect, and, if regarded, may prevent abundance of Folly and Wickedness in others, and at the same Time save me abundance of Trouble. And that People may not flatter themselves with the Hopes of concealing their Misdemeanours from my Knowledge, and in that View persist in Evil-doing, I must acquaint them, that I have lately enter'd into an Intimacy with the extraordinary Person who some Time since wrote me the following Letter; and who, having a Wonderful Faculty that enables him [to] discover the most secret Iniquity, is capable of giving me great Assistance in my designed Work of Reformation.

"Mr. Busy-Body.

"I rejoice Sir, at the Opportunity you have given me to be serviceable to you, and by your Means to this Province. You must know, that such have been the Circumstances of my Life, and such were the marvellous Concurrences of my Birth, that I have not only a Faculty of discovering the Actions of Persons that are absent or asleep; but even of the Devil himself in many of his secret Workings, in the various Shapes, Habits and Names of Men and Women. And having travel'd and conversed much and met but with a very few of the same Perceptions and Qualifications, I can recommend my Self to you as the most useful Man you can correspond with. My Father's Father's Father (for we had no Grandfathers in our Family) was the same John Bunyan that writ that memorable Book *The Pilgrim's Progress,* who had in some Degree a natural Faculty of *Second Sight.*[7] This Faculty (how derived to him, our Family Memoirs are not very clear) was enjoy'd by all his Descendants, but not by equal Talents.

7. Probably a satire on the sensational Duncan Campbell (1680?–1730), "the Dumb Doctor" of London, who claimed the power of second sight and was the subject of a biography by Defoe, 1720. For evidences of Campbell's reputation see *The Censor* (2d edit., London, 1717), I, 81, and titles cited in *DNB.*

'Twas very dim in several of my first Cousins, and probably had been nearly extinct in our particular Branch, had not my Father been a Traveller. He lived in his youthful Days in New England. There he married, and there was born my elder Brother, who had so much of this Faculty, as to discover Witches in some of their occult Performances. My Parents transporting themselves to Great Britain my second Brother's Birth was in that Kingdom. He shared but a small Portion of this Virtue, being only able to discern Transactions about the Time, and for the most Part after their happening. My good Father, who delighted in the *Pilgrim's Progress,* and mountainous Places, took Shipping with his Wife for Scotland, and inhabited in the Highlands, where my Self was born; and whether the Soil, Climate or Astral Influences, of which are preserved divers Prognosticks, restored our Ancestors Natural Faculty of *Second Sight,* in a greater Lustre to me than it had shined in thro' several Generations, I will not here discuss. But so it is, that I am possess'd largely of it, and design if you encourage the Proposal, to take this Opportunity of doing good with it, which I question not will be accepted of in a grateful Way, by many of your honest Readers, Tho' the Discovery of my Extraction bodes me no Deference from your great Scholars and modern Philosophers. This my Father was long ago aware of, and lest the Name alone should hurt the Fortunes of his Children; he in his Shiftings from one Country to another wisely changed it.

"Sir, I have only this further to say, how I may be useful to you and as a Reason for my not making my Self more known in the World: By Virtue of this Great Gift of Nature *Second-Sightedness.* I do continually see Numbers of Men, Women and Children of all Ranks, and what they are doing, while I am sitting in my Closet; which is too great a Burthen for the Mind, and makes me also conceit even against Reason, that all this Host of People can see and observe me, which strongly inclines me to Solitude and an obscure Living; and on the other Hand, it will be an Ease to me to disburthen my Thoughts and Observations in the Way proposed to you by, Sir, your Friend, and humble Servant. ———"

I conceal this Correspondent's Name in my Care for his Life and Safety, and cannot but approve his Prudence in chusing to live obscurely. I remember the Fate of my poor Monkey: He had an ill-natur'd Trick of grinning and chattering at every Thing he saw in Pettycoats. My ignorant Country Neighbours got a Notion that Pugg snarl'd by instinct at every Female who had lost her Virginity. This was no sooner generally believ'd than he was condemn'd to Death; By whom I could never learn, but he was assassinated in the Night, barbarously stabb'd and mangled in a Thousand Places, and left hanging dead on one of my Gate posts, where I found him the next Morning.[8]

The Censor observing that the *Itch of Scribbling* begins to spread exceedingly, and being carefully tender of the Reputation of his Country in Point of *Wit* and *Good Sense,* has determined to take all manner of Writings, in Verse or Prose, that pretend to either, under his immediate Cognizance; and accordingly hereby prohibits the Publishing any such for the future, 'till they have first pass'd his Examination, and receiv'd his *Imprimatur.* For which he demands as a Fee only 6*d.* per Sheet.

N.B. He nevertheless permits to be published all Satyrical Remarks on the Busy-Body, the above Prohibition notwithstanding, and without Examination, or requiring the said Fees: which Indulgence the small Wits in and about this City are advised gratefully to accept and acknowledge.

The Gentleman who calls himself Sirronio, is directed, on the Receipt of this, to burn his great Book of *Crudities.*

P.S. In Compassion to that young Man on Account of the great Pains he has taken; in Consideration of the Character I have just receiv'd of him, that he is really *Good-natured;* and on Condition he shows it to no Foreigner or Stranger of Sense, I have thought fit to reprieve his said *great Book of Crudities* from the Flames, till further Order.

Noli me tangere.[9]

I had resolved when I first commenc'd this Design, on no Account to enter into a publick Dispute with any Man; for I

---

8. Compare *The Spectator,* No. 579.
9. The initials "BF," possibly in Franklin's hand, have been written opposite this section of the essay in the file in Lib. Co. Phila.

judg'd it would be equally unpleasant to me and my Readers, to see this Paper fill'd with contentious Wrangling, Answers, Replies, &c. which is a Way of Writing that is Endless, and at the same time seldom contains any Thing that is either edifying or entertaining. Yet when such a considerable Man as Mr. —— finds himself concern'd so warmly to accuse and condemn me, as he has done in Keimer's last *Instructor,* I cannot forbear endeavouring to say something in my own Defence, from one of the worst of Characters that could be given of me by a Man of Worth. But, as I have many Things of more Consequence to offer the Publick, I declare that I will never, after this Time, take Notice of any Accusations not better supported with Truth and Reason; much less may every little Scribbler, that shall attack me, expect an Answer from the Busy-Body.

The Sum of the *Charge, deliver'd* against me, either directly or indirectly in the said Paper, is this. Not to mention the first weighty Sentence concerning *Vanity and Ill-Nature,* and the shrew'd Intimation *that I am without Charity, and therefore can have no Pretence to Religion,* I am represented as guilty of *Defamation and Scandal, the Odiousness of which is apparent to every good Man, and the Practice of it opposite to Christianity, Morality, and common Justice, and in some Cases so far below all these as to be inhumane.* As a *Blaster of Reputations.* As *attempting by a Pretence to screen my Self from the Imputation of Malice and Prejudice.* As *using a Weapon which the Wiser and better Part of Mankind hold in Abhorrence:* And as *giving Treatment which the wiser and better Part of Mankind dislike on the same Principles, and for the same Reason as they do Assassination.* &c. And all this, is infer'd and concluded from a Character I wrote in my Number 3.

In order to examine the Justice and Truth of this heavy Charge, let us recur to that Character. And here we may be surpriz'd to find what a Trifle has rais'd this mighty Clamour and Complaint, this Grievous Accusation! The worst Thing said of the Person, in what is called my gross Description, (be he who he will to whom my Accuser has apply'd the Character of Cretico) is, that he is a *sower Philosopher, crafty, but not wise:* Few Humane Characters can be drawn that will not fit some body, in so large a Country as this; But one would think, supposing I meant Cretico a real Person, I had sufficiently manifested my impartiality, when

I said in that very Paragraph, *That Cretico is not without Virtue; that there are* MANY *good Things in him, and* MANY *good Actions reported of him;* Which must be allow'd in all Reason, very much to overballance in his Favour those worst Words *sowre Temper'd* and *cunning.* Nay my very Enemy and Accuser must have been sensible of this, when he freely acknowledges, *that he has been seriously considering, and cannot yet determine, which he would chuse to be, the Cato or Cretico of that Paper:* Since my Cato is one of the best of Characters.

Thus much in my own Vindication. As to the *only reasons* there given why I ought not to continue drawing Characters, viz. *Why should any Man's Picture be published which he never sat for; or his good Name taken from him any more than his Money or Possessions at the arbitrary Will of another,* &c? I have but this to answer. The Money or Possessions I presume are nothing to the Purpose, since no Man can claim a Right either to those or a good Name, if he has acted so as to forfeit them. And are not the Publick the only Judges what Share of Reputation they think proper to allow any Man? Supposing I was capable, and had an Inclination to draw all the good and bad Characters in America; Why should a good Man be offended with me for drawing good Characters? And if I draw Ill Ones, can they fit any but those that deserve them? And ought any *but such* to be concern'd that they have their Deserts? I have as great an Aversion and Abhorrence from Defamation and Scandal as any Man, and would with the utmost Care avoid being guilty of such base Things: Besides I am very sensible and certain, that if I should make use of this Paper to defame any Person, my Reputation would be sooner hurt by it than his, and the Busy-Body would quickly become detestable; because in such a Case, as is justly observed, *The Pleasure arising from a Tale of Wit and Novelty soon dies away in generous and Honest Minds, and is followed with a secret Grief to see their Neighbours calumniated.* But if I my self was actually the worst Man in the Province, and any one should draw my true Character, would it not be ridiculous in me to say, *he had defam'd and scandaliz'd me;* unless added, *in a Matter of Truth?* If any Thing is meant by asking, *Why any Man's Picture should be publish'd which he never sate for?* It must be, that we should give no Character without the Owner's Consent. If

I discern the Wolf disguis'd in harmless Wool, and contriving the Destruction of my Neighbour's Sheep, must I have his Permission before I am allow'd to discover and prevent him? If I know a Man to be a designing Knave, must I ask his Consent to bid my Friends beware of him? If so, Then by the same Rule, supposing the Busy-Body had really merited, all his Enemy has charg'd him with, his Consent likewise ought to have been obtain'd before so terrible an Accusation was published against him.

I shall conclude with observing, that in the last Paragraph save one of the Piece now examin'd, much ILL NATURE and some Good Sense are *Co-inhabitants,* (as he expresses it.) The *Ill Nature* appears, in his endeavouring to discover Satyr, where I intended no such Thing, but quite the Reverse: The good Sense is this, *that drawing too good a Character of any one, is a refined Manner of Satyr that may be as injurious to him as the contrary, by bringing on an Examination that undresses the Person, and in the Haste of doing it, he may happen to be stript of what he really owns and deserves.* As I am Censor, I might punish the first, but I forgive it. Yet I will not leave the latter unrewarded; but assure my Adversary, that in Consideration of the Merit of those four Lines, I am resolved to forbear *injuring* him on any Account in that *refined Manner.*

I thank my Neighbour P—w—l for his kind Letter. The Lions complain'd of shall be muzzled.[1]

1. On March 13 Keimer printed three replies to the Busy-Body. One was a spirited answer in verse: * * *

> What a confounded Noise and Racket,
> There is about your Weekly *Pacquet?*
> Some Parts good, and some Parts bad,
> Show it has different Authors had.
> The Author of the Good's unknown,
> But all the *bad ones* are your own;
> And thus your own Stuff does infest,
> And bastardizes all the rest.
>
> * * *
>
> But prithee tell me, art thou mad,
> To mix good Writing with the bad?
> Fie, Sir, let all be of a Piece,
> *Spectators, Swans, or Joseph's Geese:*

The Busy-Body, No. 8[2]

Printed in *The American Weekly Mercury*, March 27, 1729.

THE BUSY-BODY. No. 8.

——*Quid non mortalia Pectora cogis*
Auri sacra Fames! Virgil.[3]

One of the greatest Pleasures an Author can have is certainly the Hearing his Works applauded. The hiding from the World our Names while we publish our Thoughts, is so absolutely necessary to this Self-Gratification, that I hope my Well-wishers will congratulate me on my Escape from the many diligent, but fruitless Enquiries that have of late been made after me. Every Man will own, That an Author, as such, ought to be try'd by the Merit of his Productions only; but Pride, Party, and Prejudice at this Time run so very high, that Experience shews we form our Notions of a Piece by the Character of the Author. Nay there

---

You hinted at me in your Paper,
Which now has made me draw my Rapier.
With scornful Eye, I see your Hate,
And pity your unhappy Fate:
For all those Vices you have shewn,
Are but faint Copies of your own.

* * *

In the second, entitled "Hue and Cry after the *Busy-Body*," the "two separate Heads" of Censor Morum were distinguished. One author was characterized as a "Free-thinker of the Peripatetick Sect," who liked to gaze on the market crowds for an hour or so and then, having purchased some cheap joint of meat, would stroll off "with the Air of a Spanish *Hidalgo* . . . to the venerable Tubb his Mansion." The other, never better than "an Understrapper to a Press" until "that Prodigy of Wit, Mr. B——d," promoted him, seemed to be "not one but every Ape's Epitome." The third thrust was in the form of a fable in which the owls, bats, and other birds of night, discussing their neighbors, turned their criticism on the sun. The sun, overhearing them, retorted that although he could scorch and burn them all in an instant, "the only Answer I shall give you, or the Revenge I shall take of you, is, *to shine on.*"

2. Notes in the margin of the copy in Lib. Co. Phila. indicate that "BF" was the author of the first section, "Breitnal" the author of the letter of Titan Pleiades, and "BF" the author of the remainder of the essay.

3. *Aeneid*, III, 56–7.

are some very humble Politicians in and about this City, who will ask on which Side the Writer is, before they presume to give their Opinion of the Thing wrote. This ungenerous Way of Proceeding I was well aware of before I publish'd my first Speculation; and therefore concealed my Name. And I appeal to the more generous Part of the World, if I have since I appear'd in the Character of the Busy-Body given an Instance of my siding with any Party more than another, in the unhappy Divisions of my Country; and I have above all, this Satisfaction in my Self, That neither Affection, Aversion or Interest, have byass'd me to use any Partiality towards any Man, or Sett of Men; but whatsoever I find nonsensically ridiculous, or immorally dishonest, I have, and shall continue openly to attack with the Freedom of an honest Man, and a Lover of my Country.

I profess I can hardly contain my Self, or preserve the Gravity and Dignity that should attend the *Censorial-Office*, when I hear the odd and unaccountable Expositions that are put upon some of my Works, thro' the malicious Ignorance of some, and the vain Pride of more than ordinary Penetration in others; one Instance of which many of my Readers are acquainted with. A certain Gentleman has taken a great Deal of Pains to write a KEY to the Letter in my *No. 4.* wherein he has ingeniously converted a gentle Satyr upon tedious and impertinent Visitants into a Libel on some in the Government: This I mention only as a Specimen of the Taste of the Gentlemen, I am forsooth, bound to please in my Speculations, not that I suppose my Impartiality will ever be called in Question upon that Account. Injustices of this Nature I could complain of in many Instancies; but I am at present diverted by the Reception of a Letter, which tho' it regards me only in my Private Capacity, as an Adept, yet I venture to publish it for the Entertainment of my Readers.

"To Censor Morum, Esq; Busy-Body General of the Province of Pennsylvania, and the Counties of Newcastle, Kent, and Sussex, upon Delaware.

"Honourable Sir,
    "I judge by your Lucubrations, that you are not only a Lover of Truth and Equity, but a Man of Parts and Learning, and a Master of Science; as such I honour you. Know then, *Most pro-*

found Sir, that I have from my Youth up, been a very indefatigable Student in, and Admirer of that Divine Science, *Astrology*. I have read over Scot, Albertus Magnus, and Cornelius Agrippa above 300 Times; and was in hopes by my Knowledge and Industry, to gain enough to have recompenced me for my Money expended, and Time lost in the Pursuit of this Learning. You cannot be ignorant, Sir, (for your intimate *Second sighted* Correspondent knows all Things) that there are large Sums of Money hidden under Ground in divers Places about this Town, and in many Parts of the Country; But alas, Sir, Notwithstanding I have used all the Means laid down in the *immortal Authors* beforementioned, and when they fail'd, the ingenious Mr. P—d—l with his *Mercurial Wand* and *Magnet*, I have still fail'd in my Purpose. This therefore I send to Propose and desire an Acquaintance with you, and I do not doubt, notwithstanding my repeated Ill-Fortune, but we may be exceedingly serviceable to each other in our Discoveries; and that if we use our united Endeavours, the Time will come when the Busy-Body, his *Second-sighted Correspondent,* and *your very humble Servant,* will be Three of the richest Men in the Province: And then, Sir, what may not we do? *A Word to the Wise is sufficient.* I conclude with all demonstrable Respect, Yours, and Urania's Votary, TITAN PLEIADES."

In the Evening after I had received this Letter, I made a Visit to my *Second-sighted* Friend, and communicated to him the Proposal. When he had read it, he assur'd me, that to his certain Knowledge there is not at this Time so much as one Ounce of Silver or Gold hid under Ground in any Part of this Province, For that the late and present Scarcity of Money had obliged those who were living, and knew where they had formerly hid any, to take it up, and use it in their own necessary Affairs: And as to all the Rest which was buried by Pyrates and others in old Times, who were never like to come for it, he himself had long since dug it all up and applied it to charitable Uses, And this he desired me to publish for general Good. For, as he acquainted me, There are among us great Numbers of honest Artificers and labouring People, who fed with a vain Hope of growing suddenly rich, neglect their Business, almost to the ruining of themselves and Families, and voluntarily endure abundance of Fatigue in a fruitless Search after Imaginary hidden Treasure. They wander thro' the Woods and Bushes by Day, to discover the Marks and Signs; at Midnight they repair to the hopeful Spot with Spades and Pickaxes; full of Expectation they labour violently, trembling at the same Time in every Joint, thro' Fear of certain malicious Demons who are said to haunt and guard such Places. At length a mighty hole is dug, and perhaps several Cartloads of Earth thrown out, but alas, no Cag or Iron Pot is found! no Seaman's Chest cram'd with Spanish Pistoles, or weighty Pieces of Eight! Then they conclude, that thro' some Mistake in the Procedure, some rash Word spoke, or some Rule of Art neglected, the Guardian Spirit had Power to sink it deeper into the Earth and convey it out of their Reach. Yet when a Man is once thus infatuated, he is so far from being discouraged by ill Success, that he is rather animated to double his Industry, and will try again and again in a Hundred Different Places, in Hopes at last of meeting with some lucky Hit, that shall at once Sufficiently reward him for all his Expence of Time and Labour.

This odd Humour of Digging for Money thro' a Belief that much has been hid by Pirates formerly frequenting the River, has for several Years been mighty prevalent among us; insomuch that you can hardly walk half a Mile out of Town on any Side, without observing several Pits dug with that Design, and perhaps some lately opened. Men, otherwise of very good Sense, have been drawn into this Practice thro' an over weening Desire of sudden Wealth, and an easy Credulity of what they so earnestly wish'd might be true. While the rational and almost certain Methods of acquiring Riches by Industry and Frugality are neglected or forgotten. There seems to be some peculiar Charm in the conceit of *finding* Money; and if the Sands of Schuylkil were so much mixed with small Grains of Gold, that a Man might in a Day's Time with Care and Application get together to the Value of half a Crown, I make no Question but we should find several People employ'd there, that can with Ease earn Five Shillings a Day at their proper Trades.

Many are the idle Stories told of the private Success of some People, by which others are encouraged to proceed; and the Astrologers, with whom the Country swarms at this Time, are either in the Belief of these things themselves, or find their Advantage in persuading others to believe them; for they are often consulted about the critical Times for Digging, the Methods of laying the Spirit, and the like Whimseys, which renders them very necessary to and very much caress'd by the poor deluded *Money-hunters*.

There is certainly something very bewitching in the Pursuit after Mines of Gold and Silver, and other valuable Metals; And many have been ruined by it. A Sea Captain of my Acquaintance used to blame the English for envying Spain their Mines of Silver; and too much despising or overlooking the Advantages of their own Industry and Manufactures. For my Part, says he, I esteem the Banks of Newfoundland to be a more valuable Possession than the Mountains of Potosi; and when I have been there on the Fishing Account, have look'd upon every Cod pull'd up into the Vessel as a certain Quantity of Silver Ore, which required only carrying to the next Spanish Port to be coin'd into Pieces of Eight;[4] not to mention the *National Profit* of fitting out and Employing such a Number of Ships and Seamen. Let honest Peter Buckrum, who has long without Success been a Searcher after hidden Money, reflect on this, and be reclaimed from that unaccountable Folly. Let him consider that every Stitch he takes when he is on his Shop-board, is picking up part of a Grain of Gold that will in a few Days Time amount to a Pistole; And let Faber think the same of every Nail he drives, or every Stroke with his Plain. Such Thoughts may make them industrous, and of consequence in Time they may be Wealthy. But how absurd is it to neglect a certain Profit for such a ridiculous Whimsey: To spend whole Days at the George, in company with an idle Pretender to Astrology, contriving Schemes to discover what was never hidden, and forgetful how carelessly Business is managed at Home in their Absence: To leave their Wives and a warm Bed at Midnight (no matter if it rain, hail, snow or blow a Hurricane, provided that be the critical Hour) and fatigue themselves with the Violent Exercise of Digging for what they shall never find, and perhaps getting a Cold that may cost their Lives,

4. In a prospectus for an *Histoire naturelle . . . des poissons* in six volumes (one volume only was published, under a slightly different title, 1815), S.B.J. Noël de la Morinière quoted BF's sentiment: "Tout homme qui pêche un poisson, tire de la mer une pièce monnaie."

or at least disordering themselves so as to be fit for no Business beside for some Days after. Surely this is nothing less than the most egregious Folly and Madness.

I shall conclude with the Words of my discreet Friend Agricola, of Chester-County, when he gave his Son a Good Plantation, *My Son*, says he, *I give thee now a Valuable Parcel of Land; I assure thee I have found a considerable Quantity of Gold by Digging there; Thee mayst do the same. But thee must carefully observe this. Never to dig more than Plow-deep.*[5]

The Nature and Necessity of a Paper-Currency

A Modest Enquiry into the Nature and Necessity of a Paper-Currency. Philadelphia: Printed and Sold at the New Printing-Office, near the Market. 1729.[6] (Historical Society of Pennsylvania)

Pennsylvania's first experience with paper currency came in 1723 with the passage of two acts which provided for issues of bills of credit totaling £45,000. Except for £7,500 allocated to governmental agencies for public expenditure, the new currency was to be loaned to private individuals at 5 per cent interest for specified terms of years on the security of real-estate mortgages. The borrowers were to repay the principal in equal annual installments and the bills of credit received in payment were to be canceled and destroyed. The last of the loans would be repaid and the last bills of credit "sunk" in 1736.[7] But in 1726, when

5. The quarrel with Keimer continued. On March 20 the latter had attacked the Busy-Body, asserting that the only "suitable Reception" of the series was contempt. And in April he printed a broadside or handbill which he tried to make the public believe came from BF and Meredith. The following reply was inserted in Bradford's *American Weekly Mercury*, April 24: "This may inform those that have been induc'd to think otherwise, That the silly Paper, call'd *a Touch of the Times*, &c. was Wrote, Printed and Published by Mr. Keimer; and that his putting the Words NEW PRINTING OFFICE at the Bottom, and instructing the Hawkers to say it was done there is an Abuse."

6. The title page contains a quotation from Persius, *Satires*, III, 69–71:
"—Quid asper
Utile Nummus habet; patriae, carisque; propinquis
Quantum elargiri deceat, —"

7. *Laws of Pa.*, 1742 edit., pp. 230–44, 269–87. For a general account of paper currency in Pennsylvania during this period see William Robert Shepherd, *History of Proprietary Government in Pennsylvania* (N.Y., 1896), chap. IX.

almost £5,000 of the paper money had been retired, complaint about the shrinking currency induced the Assembly to halt the further destruction of the bills and to authorize instead their reissue on new mortgage loans.[8]

During the next few years paper currency became a major issue. Many believed the acts of 1723 and 1726 had greatly promoted the prosperity of Pennsylvania; others, including the more conservative inhabitants, the proprietors in England, and officials of the British government, feared inflation and serious depreciation of the paper money such as had already taken place in New England and South Carolina. The Assembly, acting on several petitions, sent to the governor in February 1729 a bill for a large new emission of bills of credit, with a lower interest rate on the mortgage loans and a longer term for retirement than any earlier Pennsylvania act had provided. Governor Patrick Gordon favored paper currency but objected to the terms of the bill. Prolonged discussions followed between governor and Assembly.[9]

While these negotiations were in progress Franklin joined the debate. He and his friends had discussed the matter in the Junto, he wrote many years later in his autobiography, and he was "on the Side of an Addition." He remembered the stagnant condition of the city when he "first walk'd about the Streets of Philadelphia, eating my Roll," in 1723 just before the first of the currency acts began to take effect, and by contrast the prosperity that had followed. He attributed the great improvement to the more plentiful supply of a circulating medium. "Our Debates possess'd me so fully of the Subject, that I wrote and printed an anonymous Pamphlet on it, entituled, *The Nature and Necessity of a Paper Currency*." This essay was dated April 3, 1729, and was one of the first of the publications issued by the new firm of Franklin and Meredith "at the New Printing-Office near the Market."

The first part of this paper is a discussion of the importance of an adequate supply of money for the successful conduct of a community's business. The treatment is general but has particular application to a colonial area such as Pennsylvania. Some of Franklin's ideas may have been derived from his reading; others doubtless reflected the discussion then going on in the province at large and among his friends in the Junto. The second part of the essay deals with the specific question of how much paper currency might be safe for a community and how it should be secured to avoid the danger of a serious depreciation. Here Franklin relied heavily on his reading, especially on Sir William Petty's

8. *Laws of Pa.*, 1742 edit., pp. 321–33.
9. 8 *Pa. Arch.*, III, *passim*.

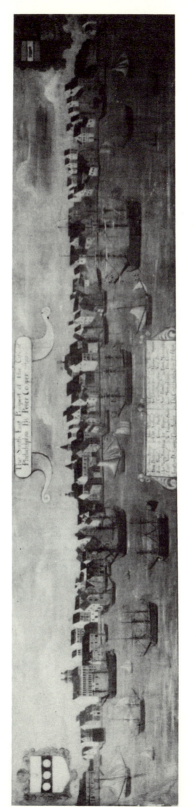

Philadelphia in 1720.

Treatise of Taxes and Contributions, first published in 1662.[1] At one point his presentation of the labor theory of value employs the same argument, the same illustrations, and even some of the same phrases that Petty had used in his pioneer discussion of this matter.[2] And Franklin's statement of the "natural standard" of interest (usury, as he called it) is, with a short interpolation, almost an exact transcription of Petty's words on this subject.[3] Franklin's own contribution here does not derive from its originality but from his ability to apply existing ideas to the immediate problem in language that would be understandable to his Pennsylvania readers.[4]

The pamphlet appeared while the governor and the Assembly were trying to work out a compromise measure. The negotiations were successful and on May 10 Governor Gordon signed a bill providing for the emission of £30,000 in bills of credit on conditions very much like those of the two acts of 1723. Interest was again set at 5 per cent, though the Assembly (and Franklin) had both favored 4 per cent, and the term of the loans was established at sixteen years, though the governor had wanted it to be only ten.[5] Franklin believed that his pamphlet had helped secure this favorable measure. Friends in the Assembly, he wrote later, "who conceiv'd I had been of some Service, thought fit to reward me, by employing me in printing the Money, a very profitable Jobb, and a great Help to me. This was another Advantage gain'd by my being able to write." Here Franklin's memory was somewhat at fault. Actually it was Andrew Bradford who printed the £30,000 voted in 1729,[6] but when the Assembly authorized £40,000 more in 1731 that printing contract did go to Franklin. For this job he received £100.[7]

A MODEST ENQUIRY, &C.

There is no Science, the Study of which is more useful and commendable than the Knowledge of the true Interest of one's Country; and perhaps there is no Kind of Learning more abstruse and intricate, more difficult to acquire in any Degree of Perfection

1. Reprinted in Charles Henry Hull, ed., *The Economic Writings of Sir William Petty* (Cambridge, 1899), I, 1–97.

2. See below, p. 149 and note.

3. See below, p. 153 and note.

4. William A. Wetzel, *Benjamin Franklin as an Economist* (Baltimore, 1895), pp. 18–22, 30–2, discusses this pamphlet and first points out the parallel with Petty's *Treatise*.

5. *Laws of Pa.*, 1742 edit., pp. 364–81; 8 *Pa. Arch.*, III, 1949–64, *passim*.

6. *Ibid.*, pp. 2025, 2043.

7. See below, p. 174.

than This, and therefore none more generally neglected. Hence it is, that we every Day find Men in Conversation contending warmly on some Point in Politicks, which, altho' it may nearly concern them both, neither of them understand any more than they do each other.

Thus much by way of Apology for this present *Enquiry into the Nature and Necessity of a Paper Currency*. And if any Thing I shall say, may be a Means of fixing a Subject that is now the chief Concern of my Countrymen, in a clearer Light, I shall have the Satisfaction of thinking my Time and Pains well employed.

To proceed, then,

There is a certain proportionate Quantity of Money requisite to carry on the Trade of a Country freely and currently; More than which would be of no Advantage in Trade, and Less, if much less, exceedingly detrimental to it.

This leads us to the following general Considerations.

First, *A great Want of Money in any Trading Country, occasions Interest to be at a very high Rate.* And here it may be observed, that it is impossible by any Laws to restrain Men from giving and receiving exorbitant Interest, where Money is suitably scarce: For he that wants Money will find out Ways to give 10 *per Cent.* when he cannot have it for less, altho' the Law forbids to take more than 6 *per Cent.* Now the Interest of Money being high is prejudicial to a Country several Ways: It makes Land bear a low Price, because few Men will lay out their Money in Land, when they can make a much greater Profit by lending it out upon Interest: And much less will Men be inclined to venture their Money at Sea, when they can, without Risque or Hazard, have a great and certain Profit by keeping it at home; thus Trade is discouraged. And if in two Neighbouring Countries the Traders of one, by Reason of a greater Plenty of Money, can borrow it to trade with at a lower Rate than the Traders of the other, they will infallibly have the Advantage, and get the greatest Part of that Trade into their own Hands; For he that trades with Money he hath borrowed at 8 or 10 *per Cent.* cannot hold Market with him that borrows his Money at 6 or 4. — On the contrary, *A plentiful Currency will occasion Interest to be low:* And this will be an Inducement to many to lay out their Money in Lands, rather than put it out to Use, by which means Land will begin to rise in Value and bear a better Price: And at the same Time it will tend to enliven Trade exceedingly, because People will find more Profit in employing their Money that Way than in Usury; and many that understand Business very well, but have not a Stock sufficient of their own, will be encouraged to borrow Money to trade with, when they can have it at moderate Interest.

Secondly, *Want of Money in a Country reduces the Price of that Part of its Produce which is used in Trade:* Because Trade being discouraged by it as above, there is a much less Demand for that Produce. And this is another Reason why Land in such a Case will be low, especially where the Staple Commodity of the Country is the immediate Produce of the Land, because that Produce being low, fewer People find an Advantage in Husbandry, or the Improvement of Land. — On the contrary, *A Plentiful Currency will occasion the Trading Produce to bear a good Price:* Because Trade being encouraged and advanced by it, there will be a much greater Demand for that Produce; which will be a great Encouragement of Husbandry and Tillage, and consequently make Land more valuable, for that many People would apply themselves to Husbandry, who probably might otherwise have sought some more profitable Employment.

As we have already experienced how much the Increase of our Currency by what Paper Money has been made, has encouraged our Trade; particularly to instance only in one Article, *Ship-Building;* it may not be amiss to observe under this Head, what a great Advantage it must be to us as a Trading Country, that has Workmen and all the Materials proper for that Business within itself, to have *Ship-Building* as much as possible advanced: For every Ship that is built here for the English Merchants, gains the Province her clear Value in Gold and Silver, which must otherwise have been sent Home for Returns in her Stead; and likewise, every Ship built in and belonging to the Province, not only saves the Province her first Cost, but all the Freight, Wages and Provisions she ever makes or requires as long as she lasts; provided Care is taken to make This her *Pay Port,* and that she always takes Provisions with her for the whole Voyage, which may easily be done. And how considerable an Article this is yearly in our Favour, every one, the least acquainted with mercantile Affairs, must needs be sensible; for if we could not Build our selves, we must either

143

purchase so many Vessels as we want from other Countries, or else Hire them to carry our Produce to Market, which would be more expensive than Purchasing; and on many other Accounts exceedingly to our Loss. Now as Trade in general will decline where there is not a plentiful Currency, so *Ship-Building* must certainly of Consequence decline where Trade is declining.

Thirdly, *Want of Money in a Country discourages Labouring and Handicrafts Men (which are the chief Strength and Support of a People) from coming to settle in it, and induces many that were settled to leave the Country, and seek Entertainment and Employment in other Places, where they can be better paid.* For what can be more disheartning to an industrious labouring Man, than this, that after he hath earned his Bread with the Sweat of his Brows, he must spend as much Time, and have near as much Fatigue in getting it, as he had to earn it. *And nothing makes more bad Paymasters than a general Scarcity of Money.* And here again is a Third Reason for Land's bearing a low Price in such a Country, because Land always increases in Value in Proportion with the Increase of the People settling on it, there being so many more Buyers; and its Value will infallibly be diminished, if the Number of its Inhabitants diminish. — On the contrary, *A Plentiful Currency will encourage great Numbers of Labouring and Handicrafts Men to come and Settle in the Country,* by the same Reason that a Want of it will discourage and drive them out. Now the more Inhabitants, the greater Demand for Land (as is said above) upon which it must necessarily rise in Value, and bear a better Price. The same may be said of the Value of House-Rent, which will be advanced for the same Reasons; and by the Increase of Trade and Riches People will be enabled to pay greater Rents. Now the Value of House-Rent rising, and Interest becoming low, many that in a Scarcity of Money practised Usury, will probably be more inclined to Building; which will likewise sensibly enliven Business in any Place; it being an Advantage not only to *Brickmakers, Bricklayers, Masons, Carpenters, Joiners, Glaziers,* and several other Trades immediately employ'd by Building, but likewise to *Farmers, Brewers, Bakers, Taylors, Shoemakers, Shop-keepers,* and in short to every one that they lay their Money out with.

Fourthly, *Want of Money in such a Country as ours, occasions a greater Consumption of English and European Goods, in Proportion to the Number of the People, than there would otherwise be.* Because Merchants and Traders, by whom abundance of Artificers and labouring Men are employed, finding their other Affairs require what Money they can get into their hands, oblige those who work for them to take one half, or perhaps two thirds Goods in Pay. By this Means a greater Quantity of Goods are disposed of, and to a greater Value; because Working Men and their Families are thereby induced to be more profuse and extravagant in fine Apparel and the like, than they would be if they were obliged to pay ready Money for such Things after they had earn'd and received it, or if such Goods were not imposed upon them, of which they can make no other Use: For such People cannot send the Goods they are paid with to a Foreign Market, without losing considerably by having them sold for less than they stand 'em in here; neither can they easily dispose of them at Home, because their Neighbours are generally supplied in the same Manner; But how unreasonable would it be, if some of those very Men who *have been a Means* of thus forcing People into unnecessary Expence, should be the first and most earnest in accusing them of *Pride and Prodigality.* Now tho' this extraordinary Consumption of Foreign Commodities may be a Profit to particular Men, yet the Country in general grows poorer by it apace. — On the contrary, As *A plentiful Currency will occasion a less Consumption of European Goods, in Proportion to the Number of the People,* so it will be a means of making the Balance of our Trade more equal than it now is, if it does not give it in our Favour; because our own Produce will be encouraged at the same Time. And it is to be observed, that tho' less Foreign Commodities are consumed in Proportion to the Number of People, yet this will be no Disadvantage to the Merchant, because the Number of People increasing, will occasion an increasing Demand of more Foreign Goods in the Whole.

Thus we have seen some of the many heavy Disadvantages a Country (especially such a Country as ours) must labour under, when it has not a sufficient Stock of running Cash to manage its Trade currently. And we have likewise seen some of the Advantages which accrue from having Money sufficient, or a Plentiful Currency.

The foregoing Paragraphs being well considered, we shall naturally be led to draw the following Conclusions with Regard to what Persons will probably be for or against Emitting a large Additional Sum of Paper Bills in this Province.

1. Since Men will always be powerfully influenced in their Opinions and Actions by what appears to be their particular Interest: Therefore all those, who wanting Courage to venture in Trade, now practise Lending Money on Security for exorbitant Interest, which in a Scarcity of Money will be done notwithstanding the Law, I say all such will probably be against a large Addition to our present Stock of Paper-Money; because a plentiful Currency will lower Interest, and make it common to lend on less Security.

2. All those who are Possessors of large Sums of Money, and are disposed to purchase Land, which is attended with a great and sure Advantage in a growing Country as this is; I say, the Interest of all such Men will encline them to oppose a large Addition to our Money. Because their Wealth is now continually increasing by the large Interest they receive, which will enable them (if they can keep Land from rising) to purchase More some time hence than they can at present; and in the mean time all Trade being discouraged, not only those who borrow of them, but the Common People in general will be impoverished, and consequently obliged to sell More Land for less Money than they will do at present. And yet, after such Men are possessed of as much Land as they can purchase, it will then be their Interest to have Money made Plentiful, because that will immediately make Land rise in Value in *their* Hands. Now it ought not to be wonder'd at, if People from the Knowledge of a Man's Interest do sometimes make a true Guess at his Designs; for, *Interest,* they say, *will not Lie.*

3. Lawyers, and others concerned in Court Business, will probably many of them be against a plentiful Currency; because People in that Case will have less Occasion to run in Debt, and consequently less Occasion to go to Law and Sue one another for their Debts. Tho' I know some even among these Gentlemen, that regard the Publick Good before their own apparent private Interest.

4. All those who are any way Dependants on such Persons as are above mentioned, whether as holding Offices, as Tenants, or as Debtors, must at least *appear* to be against a large Addition; because if they do not, they must sensibly feel their present Interest hurt. And besides these, there are, doubtless, many well-meaning Gentlemen and Others, who, without any immediate private Interest

of their own in View, are against making such an Addition, thro'
an Opinion they may have of the Honesty and sound Judgment of
some of their Friends that oppose it, (perhaps for the Ends aforesaid)
without having given it any thorough Consideration themselves.
And thus it is no Wonder if there is a *powerful* Party on that Side.

On the other Hand, Those who are Lovers of Trade, and delight to see Manufactures encouraged, will be for having a large
Addition to our Currency: For they very well know, that People
will have little Heart to advance Money in Trade, when what they
can get is scarce sufficient to purchase Necessaries, and supply
their Families with Provision. Much less will they lay it out in advancing new Manufactures; nor is it possible new Manufactures
should turn to any Account, where there is not Money to pay the
Workmen, who are discouraged by being paid in Goods, because
it is a great Disadvantage to them.

Again, Those who are truly for the Proprietor's Interest (and
have no separate Views of their own that are predominant) will
be heartily for a large Addition: Because, as I have shewn above,
Plenty of Money will for several Reasons make Land rise in Value
exceedingly: And I appeal to those immediately concerned for the
Proprietor in the Sale of his Lands, whether Land has not risen
very much since the first Emission of what Paper Currency we
now have, and even by its Means. Now we all know the Proprietary has great Quantities to sell.

And since a Plentiful Currency will be so great a Cause of advancing this Province in Trade and Riches, and increasing the
Number of its People; which, tho' it will not sensibly lessen the
Inhabitants of Great Britain, will occasion a much greater Vent
and Demand for their Commodities here; and allowing that the
Crown is the more powerful for its Subjects increasing in Wealth
and Number, I cannot think it the Interest of England to oppose
us in making as great a Sum of Paper Money here, as we, who
are the best Judges of our own Necessities, find convenient. And
if I were not sensible that the Gentlemen of Trade in England, to
whom we have already parted with our Silver and Gold, are mis-
informed of our Circumstances, and therefore endeavour to have
our Currency stinted to what it now is, I should think the Government at Home had some Reasons for discouraging and impov-
erishing this Province, which we are not acquainted with.

It remains now that we enquire, *Whether a large Addition to our Paper Currency will not make it sink in Value very much;* And here it will be requisite that we first form just Notions of the Nature and Value of Money in general.

As Providence has so ordered it, that not only different Countries, but even different Parts of the same Country, have their peculiar most suitable Productions; and likewise that different Men have Genius's adapted to Variety of different Arts and Manufactures, Therefore *Commerce,* or the Exchange of one Commodity or Manufacture for another, is highly convenient and beneficial to Mankind. As for Instance, *A* may be skilful in the Art of making Cloth, and *B* understand the raising of Corn; *A* wants Corn, and *B* Cloth; upon which they make an Exchange with each other for as much as each has Occasion, to the mutual Advantage and Satisfaction of both.

But as it would be very tedious, if there were no other Way of general Dealing, but by an immediate Exchange of Commodities; because a Man that had Corn to dispose of, and wanted Cloth for it, might perhaps in his Search for a Chapman to deal with, meet with twenty People that had Cloth to dispose of, but wanted no Corn; and with twenty others that wanted his Corn, but had no Cloth to suit him with. To remedy such Inconveniences, and facilitate Exchange, Men have invented MONEY, properly called a *Medium of Exchange,* because through or by its Means Labour is exchanged for Labour, or one Commodity for another. And whatever particular Thing Men have agreed to make this Medium of, whether Gold, Silver, Copper, or Tobacco; it is, to those who possess it (if they want any Thing) that very Thing which they want, because it will immediately procure it for them. It is Cloth to him that wants Cloth, and Corn to those that want Corn; and so of all other Necessaries, it *is* whatsoever it will procure. Thus he who had Corn to dispose of, and wanted to purchase Cloth with it, might sell his Corn for its Value in this general Medium, to one who wanted Corn but had no Cloth; and with this Medium he might purchase Cloth of him that wanted no Corn, but perhaps some other Thing, as Iron it may be, which this Medium will immediately procure, and so he may be said to have exchanged his Cloth for Iron; and thus the general Exchange is soon performed, to the Satisfaction of all Parties, with abundance of Facility.

148

For many Ages, those Parts of the World which are engaged in Commerce, have fixed upon Gold and Silver as the chief and most proper Materials for this Medium; they being in themselves valuable Metals for their Fineness, Beauty, and Scarcity. By these, particularly by Silver, it has been usual to value all Things else: But as Silver it self is of no certain permanent Value, being worth more or less according to its Scarcity or Plenty, therefore it seems requisite to fix upon Something else, more proper to be made a *Measure of Values,* and this I take to be *Labour.*

By Labour[8] may the Value of Silver be measured as well as other Things. As, Suppose one Man employed to raise Corn, while another is digging and refining Silver; at the Year's End, or at any other Period of Time, the compleat Produce of Corn, and that of Silver, are the natural Price of each other; and if one be twenty Bushels, and the other twenty Ounces, then an Ounce of that Silver is worth the Labour of raising a Bushel of that Corn. Now if by the Discovery of some nearer, more easy or plentiful Mines, a Man may get Forty Ounces of Silver as easily as formerly he did Twenty, and the same Labour is still required to raise Twenty Bushels of Corn, then Two Ounces of Silver will be worth no more than the same Labour of raising One Bushel of Corn, and that Bushel of Corn will be as cheap at two Ounces, as it was before at one; *cæteris paribus.*

Thus the Riches of a Country are to be valued by the Quantity of Labour its Inhabitants are able to purchase, and not by the Quantity of Silver and Gold they possess; which will purchase more or less Labour, and therefore is more or less valuable, as is said before, according to its Scarcity or Plenty. As those Metals have grown much more plentiful in Europe since the Discovery of America, so they have sunk in Value exceedingly; for, to instance in England, formerly one Penny of Silver was worth a Days Labour, but now it is hardly worth the sixth Part of a Days Labour; because not less than Six-pence will purchase the Labour of a Man for a Day in any Part of that Kingdom; which is wholly to be attributed to the much greater Plenty of Money now in England than formerly. And yet perhaps England is in Effect no richer

8. This paragraph combines in paraphrase two passages in Sir William Petty, *A Treatise of Taxes and Contributions* (1662), chap. IV, secs. 13–14, and chap. V, sec. 10, second paragraph.

now than at that Time; because as much Labour might be purchas'd, or Work got done of almost any kind, for £100 then, as
will now require or is now worth £600.

In the next Place let us consider the Nature of *Banks* emitting
Bills of Credit, as they are at this Time used in Hamburgh, Amsterdam, London and Venice.

Those Places being Seats of vast Trade, and the Payment of
great Sums being for that Reason frequent, *Bills of Credit* are
found very convenient in Business; because a great Sum is more
easily counted in Them, lighter in Carriage, concealed in less
Room, and therefore safer in Travelling or Laying up, and on
many other Accounts they are very much valued. The Banks are
the general Cashiers of all Gentlemen, Merchants and great Traders in and about those Cities; there they deposite their Money,
and may take out Bills to the Value, for which they can be certain to have Money again at the Bank at any Time: This gives the
Bills a Credit; so that in England they are never less valuable than
Money, and in Venice and Amsterdam they are generally worth
more. And the Bankers always reserving Money in hand to answer more than the common Run of Demands (and some People
constantly putting in while others are taking out) are able besides
to lend large Sums, on good Security, to the Government or others, for a reasonable Interest, by which they are paid for their
Care and Trouble; and the Money which otherwise would have
lain dead in their Hands, is made to circulate again thereby among
the People: And thus the Running Cash of the Nation is as it were
doubled; for all great Payments being made in Bills, Money in
lower Trade becomes much more plentiful: And this is an exceeding great Advantage to a Trading Country, that is not over-stock'd
with Gold and Silver.

As those who take Bills out of the Banks in Europe, put in Money for Security; so here, and in some of the neighbouring Provinces, we engage our Land. Which of these Methods will most
effectually secure the Bills from actually sinking in Value, comes
next to be considered.

Trade in general being nothing else but the Exchange of Labour
for Labour, the Value of all Things is, as I have said before, most
justly measured by Labour. Now suppose I put my Money into a
Bank, and take out a Bill for the Value; if this Bill at the Time of

my receiving it, would purchase me the Labour of one hundred Men for twenty Days; but some time after will only purchase the Labour of the same Number of Men for fifteen Days; it is plain the Bill has sunk in Value one fourth Part. Now Silver and Gold being of no permanent Value; and as this Bill is founded on Money, and therefore to be esteemed as such, it may be that the Occasion of this Fall is the increasing Plenty of Gold and Silver, by which Money is one fourth Part less valuable than before, and therefore one fourth more is given of it for the same Quantity of Labour; and if Land is not become more plentiful by some proportionate Decrease of the People, one fourth Part more of Money is given for the same Quantity of Land, whereby it appears that it would have been more profitable to me to have laid that Money out in Land which I put into the Bank, than to place it there and take a Bill for it. And it is certain that the Value of Money has been continually sinking in England for several Ages past, because it has been continually increasing in Quantity. But if Bills could be taken out of a Bank in Europe on a Land Security, it is probable the Value of such Bills would be more certain and steady, because the Number of Inhabitants continue to be near the same in those Countries from Age to Age.

For as Bills issued upon Money Security are Money, so Bills issued upon Land, are in Effect *Coined Land*.

Therefore (to apply the Above to our own Circumstances) If Land in this Province was falling, or any way likely to fall, it would behove the Legislature most carefully to contrive how to prevent the Bills issued upon Land from falling with it. But as our People increase exceedingly, and will be further increased, as I have before shewn, by the Help of a large Addition to our Currency; and as Land in consequence is continually rising, So, in case no Bills are emitted but what are upon Land Security, the Money-Acts in every Part punctually enforced and executed, the Payments of Principal and Interest being duly and strictly required, and the Principal *bona fide* sunk according to Law, it is absolutely impossible such Bills should ever sink below their first Value, or below the Value of the Land on which they are founded. In short, there is so little Danger of their sinking, that they would certainly rise as the Land rises, if they were not emitted in a proper Manner for preventing it; That is, by providing in the Act *That*

Payment may be made, either in those Bills, or in any other Bills made current by any Act of the Legislature of this Province; and that the Interest, as it is received, may be again emitted in Discharge of Publick Debts; whereby circulating it returns again into the Hands of the Borrowers, and becomes Part of their future Payments; and thus as it is likely there will not be any Difficulty for want of Bills to pay the Office, they are hereby kept from rising above their first Value: For else, supposing there should be emitted upon mortgaged Land its full present Value in Bills; as in the Banks in Europe the full Value of the Money deposited is given out in Bills; and supposing the Office would take nothing but the same Sum in those Bills in Discharge of the Land; as in the Banks aforesaid, the same Sum in their Bills must be brought in, in order to receive out the Money: In such Case the Bills would most surely rise in Value as the Land rises; as certainly as the Bank Bills founded on Money would fall if that Money was falling. Thus if I were to mortgage to a Loan-Office, or Bank, a Parcel of Land now valued at £100 in Silver, and receive for it the like Sum in Bills, to be paid in again at the Expiration of a certain Term of Years; before which, my Land rising in Value, becomes worth £150 in Silver: 'Tis plain, that if I have not these Bills in Possession, and the Office will take nothing but these Bills, or else what it is now become worth in Silver, in Discharge of my Land; I say it appears plain, that those Bills will now be worth £150 in Silver to the Possessor; and if I can purchase them for less, in order to redeem my Land, I shall by so much be a Gainer.

I need not say any Thing to convince the Judicious that our Bills have not yet sunk, tho' there is and has been some Difference between them and Silver; because it is evident that that Difference is occasioned by the Scarcity of the latter, which is now become a Merchandize, rising and falling, like other Commodities, as there is a greater or less Demand for it, or as it is more or less Plenty.

Yet farther, in order to make a true Estimate of the Value of Money, we must distinguish between Money as it is Bullion, which is Merchandize, and as by being coin'd it is made a Currency: For its Value as a Merchandize, and its Value as a Currency, are two distinct Things; and each may possibly rise and fall in some Degree independent of the other. Thus if the Quantity of Bullion increases in a Country, it will proportionably decrease in Value; but if at the same Time the Quantity of current Coin should decrease, (supposing Payments may not be made in Bullion) what Coin there is will rise in Value as a Currency, i.e. People will give more Labour in Manufactures for a certain Sum of ready Money.

In the same Manner must we consider a *Paper Currency* founded on Land; as it is Land, and as it is a Currency:

Money as Bullion, or as Land, is valuable by so much Labour as it costs to procure that Bullion or Land.

Money, as a Currency, has an Additional Value by so much Time and Labour as it saves in the Exchange of Commodities.

If, as a Currency, it saves one Fourth Part of the Time and Labour of a Country; it has, on that Account, one Fourth added to its original Value.

When there is no Money in a Country, all Commerce must be by Exchange. Now if it takes one fourth Part of the Time and Labour of a Country, to exchange or get their Commodities exchanged; then, in computing their Value, that Labour of Exchanging must be added to the Labour of manufacturing those Commodities: But if that Time or Labour is saved by introducing Money sufficient, then the additional Value on Account of the Labour of Exchanging may be abated, and Things sold for only the Value of the Labour in making them; because the People may now in the same Time make one Fourth more in Quantity of Manufactures than they could before.

From these Considerations it may be gathered, that in all the Degrees between having no Money in a Country, and Money sufficient for the Trade, it will rise and fall in Value as a Currency, in Proportion to the Decrease or Increase of its Quantity: And if there may be at some Time more than enough, the Overplus will have no Effect towards making the Currency, as a Currency, of less Value than when there was but enough; because such Overplus will not be used in Trade, but be some other way disposed of.

If we enquire, *How much* per Cent. *Interest ought to be required upon the Loan of these Bills;* we must consider[9] what is the Natural

---

9. The passage from "we must consider" through "the Principal it self" follows almost literally the first half of Sir William Petty, *A Treatise of Taxes and Contributions* (1662), chap. v, sec. 3, except that BF has interpolated the words "For it cannot be expected" through "in the world."

Standard of Usury: And this appears to be, where the Security is undoubted, at least the Rent of so much Land as the Money lent will buy: For it cannot be expected that any Man will lend his Money for less than it would fetch him in as Rent if he laid it out in Land, which is the most secure Property in the World. But if the Security is casual, then a kind of Ensurance must be enterwoven with the simple natural Interest, which may advance the Usury very conscionably to any height below the Principal it self. Now among us, if the Value of Land is twenty Years Purchase, Five *per Cent.* is the just Rate of Interest for Money lent on undoubted Security. Yet if Money grows scarce in a Country, it becomes more difficult for People to make punctual Payments of what they borrow, Money being hard to be raised; likewise Trade being discouraged, and Business impeded for want of a Currency, abundance of People must be in declining Circumstances, and by these Means Security is more precarious than where Money is plenty. On such Accounts it is no wonder if People ask a greater Interest for their Money than the natural Interest; and what is above is to be look'd upon as a kind of *Præmium* for the Ensurance of those Uncertainties, as they are greater or less. Thus we always see, that where Money is scarce, Interest is high, and low where it is plenty. Now it is certainly the Advantage of a Country to make Interest as low as possible, as I have already shewn; and this can be done no other way than by making Money plentiful. And since, in Emitting Paper Money among us, the Office has the best of Security, the Titles to the Land being all skilfully and strictly examined and ascertained; and as it is only permitting the People by Law to coin their own Land, which costs the Government nothing, the Interest being more than enough to pay the Charges of Printing, Officers Fees, &c. I cannot see any good Reason why Four *per Cent.* to the Loan-Office should not be thought fully sufficient. As a low Interest may incline more to take Money out, it will become more plentiful in Trade; and this may bring down the common Usury, in which Security is more dubious, to the Pitch it is determined at by Law.

If it should be objected, *That Emitting It at so low an Interest, and on such easy Terms, will occasion more to be taken out than the Trade of the Country really requires:* It may be answered, That, as has already been shewn, there can never be so much of it emitted as to make it fall below the Land it is founded on; because no Man in his Senses will mortgage his Estate for what is of no more Value to him than That he has mortgaged, especially if the Possession of what he receives is more precarious than of what he mortgages, as that of Paper Money is when compared to Land: And if it should ever become so plenty by indiscreet Persons continuing to take out a large Overplus, above what is necessary in Trade, so as to make People imagine it would become by that Means of less Value than their mortgaged Lands, they would immediately of Course begin to pay it in again to the Office to redeem their Land, and continue to do so till there was no more left in Trade than was absolutely necessary. And thus the Proportion would find it self, (tho' there were a Million too much in the Office to be let out) without giving any one the Trouble of Calculation.

It may perhaps be objected to what I have written concerning the Advantages of a large Addition to our Currency, *That if the People of this Province increase, and Husbandry is more followed, we shall overstock the Markets with our Produce of Flower,* &c. To this it may be answered, that we can never have too many People (nor too much Money) For when one Branch of Trade or Business is overstocked with Hands, there are the more to spare to be employed in another. So if raising Wheat proves dull, more may (if there is Money to support and carry on new Manufactures) proceed to the raising and manufacturing of *Hemp, Silk, Iron,* and many other Things the Country is very capable of, for which we only want People to work, and Money to pay them with.

Upon the Whole it may be observed, That it is the highest Interest of a Trading Country in general to make Money plentiful; and that it can be a Disadvantage to none that have honest Designs. It cannot hurt even the Usurers, tho' it should sink what they receive as Interest; because they will be proportionably more secure in what they lend; or they will have an Opportunity of employing their Money to greater Advantage, to themselves as well as to the Country. Neither can it hurt those Merchants who have great Sums out-standing in Debts in the Country, and seem on that Account to have the most plausible Reason to fear it; *to wit,* because a large Addition being made to our Currency, will increase the Demand of our Exporting Produce, and by that

Means raise the Price of it, so that they will not be able to purchase so much Bread or Flower with £100 when they shall receive it after such an Addition, as they now can, and may if there
is no Addition: I say it cannot hurt even such, because they will
get in their Debts just in exact Proportion so much the easier and
sooner as the Money becomes plentier; and therefore, considering
the Interest and Trouble saved, they will not be Losers; because
it only sinks in Value as a Currency, proportionally as it becomes
more plenty. It cannot hurt the Interest of Great Britain, as has
been shewn; and it will greatly advance the Interest of the Proprietor. It will be an Advantage to every industrious Tradesman,
&c. because his Business will be carried on more freely, and Trade
be universally enlivened by it. And as more Business in all Manufactures will be done, by so much as the Labour and Time spent
in Exchange is saved, the Country in general will grow so much
the richer.

It is nothing to the Purpose to object the wretched Fall of the
Bills in New-England and South-Carolina, unless it might be made
evident that their Currency was emitted with the same Prudence,
and on such good Security as ours is; and it certainly was not.

As this Essay is wrote and published in Haste, and the Subject
in it self intricate, I hope I shall be censured with Candour, if, for
want of Time carefully to revise what I have written, in some
Places I should appear to have express'd my self too obscurely,
and in others am liable to Objections I did not foresee. I sincerely
desire to be acquainted with the Truth, and on that Account shall
think my self obliged to any one, who will take the Pains to shew
me, or the Publick, where I am mistaken in my Conclusions, And
as we all know there are among us several Gentlemen of acute
Parts and profound Learning, who are very much against any
Addition to our Money, it were to be wished that they would favour the Country with their Sentiments on this Head in Print;
which, supported with Truth and good Reasoning, may probably
be very convincing. And this is to be desired the rather, because
many People knowing the Abilities of those Gentlemen to manage a good Cause, are apt to construe their Silence in This, as an
Argument of a bad One. Had any Thing of that Kind ever yet appeared, perhaps I should not have given the Publick this Trouble:
But as those ingenious Gentlemen have not yet (and I doubt never

will) think it worth their Concern to enlighten the Minds of their erring Countrymen in this Particular, I think it would be highly commendable in every one of us, more fully to bend our Minds to the Study of *What is the true Interest of* PENNSYLVANIA; whereby we may be enabled, not only to reason pertinently with one another; but, if Occasion requires, to transmit Home such clear Representations, as must inevitably convince our Superiors of the Reasonableness and Integrity of our Designs.

Philadelphia, April 3. 1729.   B. B.

The Printer to the Reader

Printed in *The Pennsylvania Gazette*, October 2, 1729.

The attacks of the Busy-Body, Keimer's business incompetence, the flatness of his paper plodding doggedly through the letter A of Chambers' *Cyclopaedia*,[1] all combined to keep the *Universal Instructor in all Arts and Sciences* from getting either subscribers or advertisers. Keimer's creditors, growing apprehensive, had him seized in June, and the paper missed an issue as a result. Thereafter things worsened rapidly. On September 18 he announced his intention of leaving Pennsylvania, and on September 25—in Number 39, his last—he published his decision to sell the paper. "Yet that his generous Subscribers may not be baulk'd or disappointed, he has agreed with B. Franklin and H. Meredith, at the New Printing-Office, to continue it to the End of the Year, having transfer'd the Property wholly to them, [D. Harry declining it] and probably if farther Encouragement appears, it will continue longer."[2] The first issue under the new management appeared on October 2. Its title was shortened, its layout and typography were improved, it printed more local news, and it began with a statement of editorial policy.

The *Pennsylvania Gazette* being now to be carry'd on by other Hands, the Reader may expect some Account of the Method we design to proceed in.

Upon a View of Chambers's great Dictionaries, from whence were taken the Materials of the *Universal Instructor in all Arts and Sciences*, which usually made the First Part of this Paper, we find

1. See above, p. 111, for the mocking protests of Martha Careful and Caelia Shortface when Keimer printed Chambers' article on Abortion.
2. The brackets are Keimer's.

that besides their containing many Things abstruse or insignificant to us, it will probably be fifty Years before the Whole can be gone thro' in this Manner of Publication. There are likewise in those Books continual References from Things under one Letter of the Alphabet to those under another, which relate to the same Subject, and are necessary to explain and compleat it; these taken in their Turn may perhaps be Ten Years distant; and since it is likely that they who desire to acquaint themselves with any particular Art or Science, would gladly have the whole before them in a much less Time, we believe our Readers will not think such a Method of communicating Knowledge to be a proper One.

However, tho' we do not intend to continue the Publication of those Dictionaries in a regular Alphabetical Method, as has hitherto been done; yet as several Things exhibited from them in the Course of these Papers, have been entertaining to such of the Curious, who never had and cannot have the Advantage of good Libraries; and as there are many Things still behind, which being in this Manner made generally known, may perhaps become of considerable Use, by giving such Hints to the excellent natural Genius's of our Country, as may contribute either to the Improvement of our present Manufactures, or towards the Invention of new Ones; we propose from Time to Time to communicate such particular Parts as appear to be of the most general Consequence.

As to the *Religious Courtship*, Part of which has been retal'd to the Publick in these Papers, the Reader may be inform'd, that the whole Book will probably in a little Time be printed and bound up by it self; and those who approve of it, will doubtless be better pleas'd to have it entire, than in this broken interrupted Manner.

There are many who have long desired to see a good News-Paper in Pennsylvania; and we hope those Gentlemen who are able, will contribute towards the making This such. We ask Assistance, because we are fully sensible, that to publish a good News-Paper is not so easy an Undertaking as many People imagine it to be. The Author of a Gazette (in the Opinion of the Learned) ought to be qualified with an extensive Acquaintance with Languages, a great Easiness and Command of Writing and Relating Things cleanly and intelligibly, and in few Words; he should be able to speak of War both by Land and Sea; be well acquainted with Geography, with the History of the Time, with the several Interests of Princes and States, the Secrets of Courts, and the Manners and Customs of all Nations. Men thus accomplish'd are very rare in this remote Part of the World; and it would be well if the Writer of these Papers could make up among his Friends what is wanting in himself.

Upon the Whole, we may assure the Publick, that as far as the Encouragement we meet with will enable us, no Care and Pains shall be omitted, that may make the *Pennsylvania Gazette* as agreeable and useful an Entertainment as the Nature of the Thing will allow.

Governor Burnet and the Massachusetts Assembly[3]

Printed in *The Pennsylvania Gazette*, October 9, 1729.

His Excellency Governor Burnet died unexpectedly about two Days after the Date of this Reply to his last Message: And it was thought the Dispute would have ended with him, or at least have lain dormant till the Arrival of a new Governor from England, who possibly might, or might not be inclin'd to enter too rigorously into the Measures of his Predecessor. But our last Advices by the Post acquaint us, that his Honour the Lieutenant Governour (on whom the Government immediately devolves upon the Death or Absence of the Commander in Chief) has vigorously renew'd the Struggle on his own Account; of which the Particulars will be seen in our Next.

3. "Our first Papers made a quite different Appearance from any before in the Province," BF recalled in his autobiography; "but some spirited Remarks of my Writing on the Dispute then going on between Governor Burnet and the Massachusetts Assembly, struck the principal People, occasion'd the Paper and the Manager of it to be much talk'd of, and in a few Weeks brought them all to be our Subscribers." This dispute was over the governor's salary. William Burnet (1688–1729), governor of New York and New Jersey, 1720–28, now governor of Massachusetts, had been instructed to obtain from the legislature a "fixed and honorable salary," but was voted only enough "to enable him to manage the public affairs of the government." He rejected the grant; the issue was joined. Both parties advanced constitutional arguments, and the Board of Trade finally recommended that the Assembly's conduct be laid before Parliament. Before a solution was reached Burnet died, Sept. 7, 1729. Leonard W. Labaree, *Royal Government in America* (New Haven, 1930), pp. 360–3; *DAB*.

Perhaps some of our Readers may not fully understand the Original or Ground of this warm Contest between the Governour and Assembly. It seems, that People have for these Hundred Years past, enjoyed the Privilege of Rewarding the Governour for the Time being, according to *their Sense* of his Merit and Services; and few or none of their Governors have hitherto complain'd, or had Reason to complain, of a too scanty Allowance. But the late Gov. Burnet brought with him Instructions to demand a *settled Salary* of £1000 *per Annum*, Sterling, on him and all his Successors, and the Assembly were required to fix it immediately. He insisted on it strenuously to the last, and they as constantly refused it. It appears by their Votes and Proceedings, that they thought it an Imposition, contrary to their own Charter, and to *Magna Charta;* and they judg'd that by the Dictates of Reason there should be a mutual Dependence between the *Governor* and the *Governed,* and that to make any Governour independent on his People, would be dangerous, and destructive of their Liberties, and the ready Way to establish Tyranny: They thought likewise, that the Province was not the less dependent on the Crown of Great-Britain, by the Governour's depending immediately on them and his own good Conduct for an ample Support, because all Acts and Laws which he might be induc'd to pass, must nevertheless be constantly sent Home for Approbation in Order to continue in Force. Many other Reasons were given and Arguments us'd in the Course of the Controversy, needless to particularize here, because all the material Papers relating to it, have been inserted already in our Publick News.

Much deserved Praise has the deceas'd Governour received, for his steady Integrity in adhering to his Instructions, notwithstanding the great Difficulty and Opposition he met with, and the strong Temptations offer'd from time to time to induce him to give up the Point. And yet perhaps something is due to the Assembly (as the Love and Zeal of that Country for the present Establishment is too well known to suffer any Suspicion of Want of Loyalty) who continue thus resolutely to Abide by what *they Think* their Right, and that of the People they represent, maugre all the Arts and Menaces of a Governour fam'd for his Cunning and Politicks, back'd with Instructions from Home, and powerfully aided by the

160

great Advantage such an Officer always has of engaging the principal Men of a Place in his Party, by conferring where he pleases so many Posts of Profit and Honour. Their happy Mother Country will perhaps observe with Pleasure, that tho' her gallant Cocks and matchless Dogs abate their native Fire and Intrepidity when transported to a Foreign Clime (as the common Notion is) yet her Sons in the remotest Part of the Earth, and even to the third and fourth Descent, still retain that ardent Spirit of Liberty, and that undaunted Courage in the Defence of it, which has in every Age so gloriously distinguished Britons and Englishmen from all the Rest of Mankind.

The Printer to the Reader

Printed in *The Pennsylvania Gazette*, October 23, 1729.

The Publishers of this Paper meeting with considerable Encouragement, are determined to continue it; and to that End have taken Measures to settle a general Correspondence, and procure the best and earliest Intelligence from all Parts. We shall from time to time have all the noted Publick Prints from Great Britain, New-England, New-York, Maryland and Jamaica, besides what News may be collected from private Letters and Informations; and we doubt not of continuing to give our Customers all the Satisfaction they expect from a Performance of this Nature.

From this Time forward, instead of publishing a *Whole Sheet* once a Week, as the first Undertaker engag'd to do in his *Proposals,* we shall publish a *Half Sheet* twice a Week, which amounts to the same Thing; only we think it will be more acceptable to our Readers, inasmuch as their Entertainment will by this Means become more frequent. Numb. XLIV. will come out on Monday next.[4]

4. The issue of October 27 repeated the second paragraph of this notice and added the following: "Those Gentlemen that are Subscribers, living in the Country, have their Papers carefully sent them sealed up by the first Opportunity; others that chuse to send for them have them always ready with their Names wrote upon each Paper. And our Country Correspondents are desired to acquaint as soon as possible with every remarkable Accident, Occurence, &c. fit for publick Notice, that may happen within their Knowledge, in Order to make this Paper more universally intelligent."

Affairs of Ireland[5]

Printed in *The Pennsylvania Gazette*, November 20, 1729.

AFFAIRS OF IRELAND

The English Papers have of late been frequent in their Accounts of the unhappy Circumstances of the Common People of Ireland; That Poverty, Wretchedness, Misery and Want are become almost universal among them; That their Lands, being now turn'd to raising of Cattle, the Tilling of which formerly employ'd great Numbers of Poor, there is not Corn enough rais'd for their Subsistence one Year with another; and at the same Time the Trade and Manufactures of the Nation being cramp'd and discourag'd, the labouring People have little to do, and consequently are not able to purchase Bread at its present dear Rate: That the Taxes are nevertheless exceeding heavy, and Money very scarce; and add to all this, That their griping avaricious Landlords exercise over them the most merciless Racking Tyranny and Oppression. Hence it is that such Swarms of them are driven over into America; and notwithstanding the general Disrespect and Aversion to their Nation that they every where meet with among the Inhabitants of the Plantations, and the Hardships they must necessarily undergo before they can be well settled, they are even inexpressibly happy when they can get there: For it is observed, that to compleat their Misfortunes, they have commonly long and miserable Passages, occasioned probably by the Unskilfulness of the Mariners; the People, earnest to be gone, being oblig'd to take up with any Vessel that will go; and 'tis like frequently with such as have before been only Coasters, because they cannot always get those that have been us'd to long Voyages, or to come to these Parts of the World; and being besides but meanly provided, many starve for Want, and many die of Sickness by being crowded in such great Numbers on board one Vessel. The following Particulars are taken entire from several late English Prints.

5. Large-scale immigration of Irish to the colonies was attracting considerable attention in 1729. The *New-England Weekly Journal*, Aug. 25, 1729, for example, carried a report from New-Castle dated Aug. 14, that about 2000 Irish had landed during the past week and more were expected soon. About 6000 had come into the Delaware River since April. Some 200 had died in passage on one ship. Reprinted in 1 *N.J. Arch.*, XII, 185.

From the Casuist: The Case of the Trespassing Horse[6]

Printed in *The Pennsylvania Gazette*, December 16, 1729.

To the Printers of the *Pennsylvania Gazette*.

I send you here an Answer to a *Query* in your last Paper.[7] It is there said *A Man by Night shot a trespassing Horse in his Corn-field, taking the Horse for a Deer.* Then it is *queried Whether he ought to pay for the same, since it was by Mistake, and the Horse a Trespasser.*

I Answer, the Man who kill'd the Horse ought to pay for the same, for two Reasons; First, because the Mistake was not barely accidental, but had more of Rashness in it; And secondly, Because the Law has provided Redress for such as have Damage by trespassing Cattle.

It may be added that the Death of the Horse was a greater Loss to the Owner, than the Damage done in the Corn-field could amount to; and if it were not, the Law (regarding every Man's Property impartially) does not privilege any Man, so injured, to take his own Satisfaction. Besides the ill Practice of Night-watching to shoot Venison is unwarrantable, in as much as a Man by so doing undertakes to perform what he knows he cannot see to do without great Danger of committing worse Mistakes than shooting of Horses, as have heretofore happen'd when Men have been shot for Deer. Yours,   THE CASUIST

6. The *Gazette* of Jan. 18, 1732, printed another query to the Casuist about rights, liabilities, and a horse. It referred to the discussion here reprinted and the Casuist answered it on Jan. 25 (see below, pp. 221–6). Since BF was demonstrably writing as "the Casuist" in 1732 he was probably that character in 1729.

7. The query appeared at the end of a news note from Burlington, N. J., dated Nov. 30, in the *Gazette*, Dec. 9: "On the 15th Instant, at Night, one John Antrum was watching for Venison in his Cornfield, and a Horse happening to come into the Field, he took him for a Deer, and shot him dead; it is said he must pay for the same. *Query*, Whether he ought to pay for the same, since it was by Mistake, and the Horse a Trespasser."

Extracts from the Gazette, 1729

Printed in *The Pennsylvania Gazette*, October 2 to December 30, 1729.

The Pennsylvania Gazette usually printed several columns of intelligence, from out-of-town and foreign newspapers or from private letters; and essays, which might be reprinted from English periodicals, contributed by a member of the Junto or a reader, or written by Franklin himself. But every issue carried local news, reports, advertisements, squibs, and announcements. To illustrate the variety of these materials originating in Philadelphia that Franklin worked with in his paper, short selections will be made for the years 1729–47 and will be grouped together at the end of the calendar year in which they appeared instead of inserted separately in their proper chronological places. They show Franklin, his family and friends, and the people and events which reflected or excited his interests. Pieces perhaps trivial are included in these *Gazette* selections because their style is so like Franklin's that it is probable he wrote them; though to determine now which specific paragraphs are his is impossible. No attempt is made to reproduce the exact typography, especially in the case of advertisements. The imprint of the last issue of the *Gazette* for each year will appear as the final extract for that year.

We hear from Amboy, that all the Persons concern'd with Eanon (the same that dy'd at Sea in his Passage from Dublin to this Place) in counterfeiting the 18*d.* Bills of New Jersey, are apprehended and secur'd in their Prison. It is not found that any other of the New Bills are counterfeited but those of 18*d.* And it is remarkable that all Attempts of this Kind upon the Paper Money of this and the neighbouring Provinces, have been detected and met with ill Success.[8]   [October 2]

[ADVERTISEMENT] Bibles, Testaments, Psalters, Psalm-Books, Accompt-Books, Bills of Lading bound and unbound, Common Blank Bonds for Money, Bonds with Judgment, Counterbonds, Arbitration Bonds, Arbitration Bonds with Umpirage, Bail Bonds, Counterbonds to save Bail harmless, Bills of Sale, Powers of Attorney, Writs, Summons, Apprentices Indentures, Servants

8. On reaching Philadelphia, July 30, 1729, one of the passengers of the *Charming Sally* revealed that counterfeit Jersey bills had been found in the baggage of Thomas Eanon, another passenger, who had died during the voyage. Kenneth Scott, *Counterfeiting in Colonial America* (N.Y., 1957), pp. 76–7.

Indentures, Penal Bills, Promisory Notes, &c. all the Blanks in the most authentick Forms, and correctly printed; may be had at the Publishers of this Paper; who perform all other Sorts of Printing at reasonable Rates. [October 2]

JUST PUBLISHED: TITAN LEEDS's Almanack, for the Year, 1730. in his usual plain Method; being far preferable to any yet published in America. To be sold by David Harry at the late Printing-Office of Samuel Keimer, at Three Shillings and nine-pence per Dozen.

N.B. As this Almanack for its Worth has met with universal Reception, it has rais'd the Price of the Copy to £25 a year, for which Reason the Printer cannot afford them under the abovementioned Price: But gives this Friendly Caution to the Publick, That when they buy Almanacks for 3s. a Dozen, they must not expect Titan Leeds's, or any so valuable.⁹ [October 2]

And sometime last Week, we are informed, that one Piles a Fidler, with his Wife, were overset in a Canoo near Newtown Creek. The good Man, 'tis said, prudently secur'd his Fiddle, and let his Wife go to the Bottom. [October 16]

At present the Foreign News of most Consequence to us seems to be that which relates to the Peace with Spain. The four following Paragraphs concerning it, are taken from four different London Papers, of the latest Date that came in the last Vessel from thence to Philadelphia. The two first are from the *London Journal* and the *British Journal,* both at this time accounted *Government* Papers; the third is from the *Craftsman,* who is suppos'd to be a Whigg Writer, but against the present Administration; the fourth is from *Fog's Journal,* (the same that was formerly called *Mist's Journal*) always reckoned a Tory Paper. When the Reader has allowed for these Distinctions, he will be better able to form his Judgment on the Affair.¹ [October 23]

We are inform'd that the following Accident lately happen'd at Merion, viz. A Man had order'd his Servant to take some Fowls in from Roost every Night for fear of the Fox: But one Evening

9. See note 2 below and p. 280.
1. All the issues were of Aug. 16.

hearing them cry, he look'd out and saw, as he thought, a Fox among them; accordingly he took his Gun, charg'd with Swan Shot, and fir'd at him; when to his Surprize it prov'd to be the Servant's Arm, which taking down the Fowls he had mistaken for a Fox. The Man receiv'd several Shot, some thro' his Arm, but none of them are thought to be dangerous. [November 6]

[ADVERTISEMENT] Whereas William Bradford, of New-York, Printer, has basely and villanously forged an Almanack in my Name, which is not only a considerable Damage to me and my Printer, but also an Imposition upon the Publick: I hereby declare the said Almanack is a base and scandalous Counterfeit, printed without my Consent or Knowledge; and earnestly request all that use to buy Almanacks for the Sake of mine or my Father's Calculations to discourage such a detestable Piece of Villany: And they may be assur'd I will take the most proper Methods to prosecute the said Bradford, in Order to hinder such Male-Practices for the future. *As Witness my Hand,*
Burlington Nov. 3. 1729. TITAN LEEDS[2]

N.B. The *Genuine Leeds*'s *Almanacks* are to be had of David Harry, at the late House of Samuel Keimer, and of William Heurtin, Goldsmith, in New-York. [November 10]

[ADVERTISEMENT] Whereas Titan Leeds has been pleased to send forth a scandalous Advertisement against William Bradford,

2. This is a confusing story, but it is pertinent to BF's publication of *Poor Richard's Almanacks*. William Bradford of New York printed Titan Leeds' *The American Almanack for the Year of Christian Account* of 1715; and his son Andrew of Philadelphia printed it thereafter through 1726. Leeds took his *Almanacks* for 1727 through 1729 to Samuel Keimer of Philadelphia. To offset this loss Andrew Bradford purchased the calculations of Titan's brother Felix, printing them under the same title as Titan's, namely, *The American Almanack for the Year of Christian Account* for 1727 through 1730. Thus for 1729 two Leeds *American Almanacks* appeared in Philadelphia: Titan's printed by Keimer, and Felix's printed by Bradford. To regain customers for the original (Titan) Leeds' *Almanacks* Titan and his printer, now David Harry, Keimer's successor, brought out *The Genuine Leeds' Almanack for the Year of Christian Account, 1730,* while Andrew Bradford continued with Felix Leeds' *American Almanack.* And in New York, as this exchange of letters indicates, William Bradford reprinted, with only unimportant changes, Titan Leeds' *Genuine Almanack* under the title of *The American Almanack.*

saying, *He has forged an Almanack in my* (*Titan Leeds*) *Name, which is a Damage to me, and an Imposition upon the Publick,*

These are therefore to inform all Persons, That the above Assertion of Titan Leeds is a base and notorious Falshood; for altho' his Almanack is Re-printed, upon perusal we find it to be the same with that which is said to be printed at Philadelphia (the Errors in the first Impression excepted) and it is but Justice to the Buyers that the Errors therein should be corrected, the Time of holding Courts in New-York and New-Jersey being all wrong. And whether W. Bradford Re-printed said Almanack or not, he claims a Property in it, because about five Years ago he agreed with Titan for his Copy so long as W.B. liv'd, for a certain Sum of Money, (which Agreement he has under Titan's Hand) and paid him £20 in Part, and the Remainder he sent in 3 Weeks after he wrote for it. But in the interim the famous Sam. Keimer steps in and offers Titan more Money for it, Titan accepts, and sells it a second Time. When William Bradford told Titan he would sue him for the Nonperformance of his Agreement, Titan writes several Letters, *praying W.B. not to sue him, because it would Ruin him, and he would pay back the Money;* and by the Intreaty of some Friends W.B. did forbear to sue him, or reprint the Almanack, altho' (as he told Titan) he claimed a Property in it.

Upon the said Bradford's being thus disappointed, Felix Leeds (Titan's Brother) publishes an Almanack; No sooner came this forth but Titan and Sam. Keimer send out their Advertisements, and tell the World, That *Felix could not write an Almanack, That it was a Counterfeit, a Cheat and Imposition upon the Publick;* and this base and abusive Method they continued Year after Year without any Provocation, and W. and A. Bradford lay under their Scandals without Interruption. This Year his Almanack is Re-printed, and he says W.B. has done it, but perhaps he may find himself mistaken, altho' he claims a Property in it. And perhaps it will be Reprinted until such Time as Titan and Keimer make Satisfaction for the Money, and the gross Lies and Abuses they have cast upon the said Wm. and Andrew Bradford, as well as for Keimer's Reprinting several Books upon them, to their Damage of above £200. And it's but a just Reprizal if they Re-print upon him.

And Friend Titan is hereby advertised, That he may expect to be handled in another Manner than this Advertisement, for his so free Charges of *Villany, Forgery, Counterfeit,* &c.

New-York, Nov. 10. 1729.   WILLIAM BRADFORD

N.B. Felix Leeds's, Titan Leeds's and William Birket's Almanacks, are to be sold by Wholesale and Retail by William Bradford in New-York, and by Andr. Bradford in Philadelphia.
[November 13]

N.B. While the Post to New-York continues his Fortnight Stages, which he has now begun, we shall publish a whole Sheet once a Week as usual, and not a Half Sheet twice a Week, as we have lately done. *The Paper will now come out on Tuesdays.*
[December 9]

We hear from Trenton, that on Friday the 5th Instant, a good new Stable belonging to Mr. John Severn, was burnt down to the Ground, in which was consumed five Load of English Hay, and seven Horses were burnt to Death; occasioned by the Carelessness of a Servant, who let a Candle fall among the Hay.

About the same Time a Barn and Stable was burnt near Allen's-Town: The Owner attempting to save a good Horse he had in the Stable, very narrowly escap'd with his own Life; 'tis observed as something unaccountable in the Nature of Horses, that they are so far from endeavouring to avoid the Danger of Fire, as to stand obstinately and suffer themselves to be burnt; nor will they be led from it unless first made blindfold.   [December 16]

Those Gentlemen and Others who have taken this *Gazette* from the Beginning, and have not yet answered for the same, are desired to take Notice, that the Pay for the first Three Quarters of a Year only is due to Mr. Keimer the former Publisher; and that their Year with us begins on the second of October last, which was the Date of our first Paper, *No. XL.*   [December 23]

PHILADELPHIA: Printed by B. FRANKLIN and H. MEREDITH, at the *New Printing-Office* near the Market, where Advertisements are taken in, and all Persons may be supplied with this Paper, at *Ten Shillings* a Year.

Printer's Errors

Printed in *The Pennsylvania Gazette*, March 13, 1729/30.

To the Publisher of the *Pennsylvania Gazette*.

Sir,   *Printerum est errare.*

As your last Paper was reading in some Company where I was present, these Words were taken Notice of in the Article concerning Governor Belcher, [*After which his Excellency, with the Gentlemen trading to New-England,* died *elegantly at Pontack's*]. The Word *died* should doubtless have been *dined,* Pontack's being a noted Tavern and Eating-house in London for Gentlemen of Condition; but this Omission of the Letter (*n*) in that Word, gave us as much Entertainment as any Part of your Paper. One took the Opportunity of telling us, that in a certain Edition of the Bible, the Printer had, where David says *I am fearfully and wonderfully made,* omitted the Letter (*e*) in the last Word, so that it was, *I am fearfully and wonderfully mad;* which occasion'd an ignorant Preacher, who took that Text, to harangue his Audience for half an hour on the Subject of *Spiritual Madness.* Another related to us, that when the Company of Stationers in England had the Printing of the Bible in their Hands, the Word (*not*) was left out in the Seventh Commandment, and the whole Edition was printed off with *Thou shalt commit Adultery,* instead of *Thou shalt not,* &c.[3] This material *Erratum* induc'd the Crown to take the Patent from them which is now held by the King's Printer. The *Spectator*'s Remark upon this Story is, that he doubts many of our modern Gentlemen have this faulty Edition by 'em, and are not made sensible of the Mistake. A Third Person in the Company acquainted us with an unlucky Fault that went through a whole Impression of Common-Prayer-Books; in the Funeral Service, where these Words are, *We shall all be changed in a moment, in the twinkling of an Eye,* &c. the Printer had omitted the (*c*) in *changed,* and it read thus, *We shall all be hanged,* &c.[4] And lastly, a Mistake of your Brother News-Printer

---

3. This was the so-called "Wicked" Bible of 1631.

4. The anecdote is retold in *Poor Richard's Almanack* for 1750. It was related in *American Museum,* VIII (1790), 24, where it is said that BF deliberately removed the "c" from a line Keimer had set, in order to teach his master the importance of accuracy.

was mentioned, in *The Speech of James Prouse written the Night before he was to have been executed,* instead of *I die a Protestant,* he has put it, *I died a Protestant.* Upon the whole you came off with the more favourable Censure, because your Paper is most commonly very correct, and yet you were never known to triumph upon it, by publickly ridiculing and exposing the continual Blunders of your Contemporary. Which Observation was concluded by a good old Gentleman in Company, with this general just Remark, That whoever accustoms himself to pass over in Silence the Faults of his Neighbours, shall meet with much better Quarter from the World when he happens to fall into a Mistake himself; for the Satyrical and Censorious, whose Hand is against every Man, shall upon such Occasions have every Man's Hand against him. I am, Sir, your Friend, &c.   J.T.

[Two Dialogues between Philocles and Horatio, concerning Virtue and Pleasure]

Printed in *The Pennsylvania Gazette,* June 23 and July 9, 1730.

Duane included these two dialogues and seven other pieces from the *Gazette* in his edition of Franklin's writings (*Works,* IV, 367–405) on the basis of a note, purportedly in Franklin's hand, on the inside cover of a bound volume of the *Gazette* listing the essays and stating that they were "written by B.F." Later editors have followed Duane in printing some or all of them. Franklin specifically mentions in his autobiography having written one of the group, an essay on Self-Denial, and it is included in the present edition in its proper place (Feb. 18, 1735). For the other eight, there is no external evidence of Franklin's authorship; on the contrary, five of them are known to have been published elsewhere before they appeared in the *Gazette.* Neither the style nor the content of the remaining three suggests to the present editors that Franklin wrote them. He took the two dialogues between Philocles and Horatio from the *London Journal,* March 29 and September 20, 1729, as Alfred Owen Aldridge first noted ("Franklin's 'Shaftesburian' Dialogues not Franklin's: A Revision of the Franklin Canon," *American Literature,* XXI [1949], 151–9). The other rejected pieces in this group are listed below according to their dates of appearance in the *Gazette,* but simply by title and with reference back to this note.

To Sarah Davenport[5]   ALS: American Philosophical Society

Dear Sister,   [June? 1730][6]

Your kind and affectionate Letter of May the 15th, was extreamly agreeable to me; and the more so, because I had not for two Years before, receiv'd a Line from any Relation, my Father and Mother only excepted. I am glad to hear your Family are got well thro' the Small Pox, and that you have your Health continu'd to you. I sold your Husbands Watches for about £3 10s. this Money, and I now send him 3 Barrels of Flower (tho' it be long first) which come to about the Money. I reckon my self very much oblig'd to him for not being more urgent with me. The Flower Brother John[7] will deliver to him. Please to give my Respects to him, and excuse my not sending sooner. I am sorry to hear of Sister Macom's Loss, and should be mighty glad of a Line from her; and from Sister Homes,[8] who need be under no Apprehensions of not writing polite enough to such an unpolite Reader as I am; I think if Politeness is necessary to make Letters between Brothers and Sisters agreeable, there must be very little Love among 'em. I am not about to be married as you have heard. At present I am much hurryed in Business but hope to make a short Trip to Boston in the Spring. Please to let me know how Sister Douse[9] is, and remember my kind Love to her, as also to Brother Peter,[1] and Sister Lydia[2] &c. Dear Sister, I love you tenderly, adieu.   B. Franklin

5. Sarah Franklin (C. 12; 1699–1731), married May 3, 1722, James Davenport, baker and keeper of King's Head Tavern, Boston. For further data on all the persons mentioned in this letter, see Genealogy.

6. The date is indicated by "Sister Macom's Loss," which doubtless refers to the death of Jane Franklin Mecom's first child, Josiah, May 18, 1730; and by the reference to BF's unmarried state.

7. John Franklin (C. 8; 1690–1756), a soap-boiler like his father, subsequently postmaster of Boston.

8. Mary Franklin (C. 10; 1694–1731), married Robert Homes, mariner and captain of a ship plying between Boston and Philadelphia.

9. Elizabeth Franklin (C. 1; 1677–1759), BF's half-sister, married as her second husband, 1721, Richard Douse, shipmaster.

1. Peter Franklin (C. 9; 1692–1766), merchant and shipmaster, subsequently postmaster of Philadelphia.

2. Lydia Franklin (C. 16; 1708–1758), married Robert Scott, shipmaster, 1731.

Ledger A & B [Journal and Ledger]

MS Account Book: American Philosophical Society

The earliest of Franklin's surviving business record books is a tall, narrow volume (15 in. by 6 in.) of 380 pages, lettered on the cover "LEIDGERS A & B," and ruled as an account book. It covers in general the years 1730–38, although some entries of both earlier and later dates are included. Only credit transactions are recorded, not "over-the-counter" cash sales and purchases. Except for a few miscellaneous records and memoranda, the entries are of two kinds: "journal" and "ledger."

The flyleaf bears the inscription: "Benja Franklin's Journal, began July 4. 1730." The next 73 pages record a series of transactions, chronologically entered, including such items as goods bought and sold, printing services rendered to customers, payments made or received on account, promissory notes given or received. Nearly all the entries are in Franklin's hand; a very few are by an unknown person, perhaps one of his journeymen, and the rest are by Deborah Franklin. The last regular entry is dated December 7, 1737, and is followed by a memorandum marked only "Feb." The nature of the entries in this Journal can be seen from the following samples selected from the early pages of the record:

1730	July	15	Andrew Hamilton Esq. Dr. To ½ Doz. Powers of Attorney[3]	—	1	3
		25	Morris Trent of Trentown Cr By Cash	2	10	—
	Oct.	9	Dr. John Moore Esq. to printing blank Lists	1	15	—
	Nov.	6	Adjusted Accts with Mr. Whitemarsh to the 26th Day of October past, and I am Dr to Ballance	25	—	—
1731	Jan	1	Province of Pennsylvania Dr To printing Votes of the last Session of the Assembly in Augt 1730. 3 Sheets a 26/	3	18	—
			To printing Laws made that Session relating to Damms and Trustees &c. 2½ Sheets a 25/	3	2	6
			To printing Votes 1½ Sheets of the first Session of this Assembly a 26/ per	1	19	—
	Jan	5	Bought of Wm. Allen 20 Reams of Paper 13 a 12/ & 7 a 15/	13	1	—

The same kinds of entries are also found in a surviving "Shop Book," covering the period November 14, 1735, to August 3, 1739. Most of these are in Deborah Franklin's hand, although her husband's writing

3. That is, blank forms for the execution of powers of attorney.

appears often enough to suggest that during the period when the Journal and the Shop Book overlapped (November 14, 1735, to December 7, 1737) Franklin may have recorded his business transactions in whichever volume happened to be convenient at the moment.

On the 169th page of "Ledger A & B" is a new heading: "Accounts posted or Ledger." Beneath is a memorandum which Franklin wrote shortly before he sailed for England in 1757, that shows his effort to set his records in order: "I have drawn a red Line over all such Accounts in this Book, as are either settled or not like to be recovered. B. FRANKLIN March 5, 1757." Approximately 190 numbered pages of ledger entries follow, recording in debit and credit columns his individual customers' accounts. Some of these were opened in 1728 or 1729, but most start in 1730 or later. Immediately preceding this Ledger is an eight-page alphabetical index of these customers.

By November 1736 he had used up the pages at the back of the book reserved for ledger accounts, so he turned to the blank section between the Journal and the Ledger Index and continued the Ledger, starting at the rear and working toward the front. He numbered these pages from back to front in carefully written, reversed or "mirror" figures, which he also entered opposite the appropriate names in the Index. The last ledger account begins with an entry dated November 18, 1738, and the latest date found for any entry is May 21, 1741.

Many of the individual accounts in both parts of the Ledger are canceled with red lines as indicated in Franklin's note of 1757; others terminate with the words "Carried to Ledger E" (which has not been found), or some similar phrase. A large proportion remain unbalanced as between debit and credit entries, and many show no credit entries at all. Most, but not all, of the separate entries first appear under their respective dates in the Journal or the Shop Book, from which they were posted to the appropriate customer's account in the Ledger. The principal exceptions are charges for *Gazette* advertisements and subscriptions, which are only occasionally entered in either of the daily records. On the other hand, some Journal and Shop Book entries are not found in the Ledger. A few of the final pages of the Ledger contain lists of otherwise unrecorded "Small Debts" and "Advertisements in Gazette not paid for," together with a number of miscellaneous jottings and accounts.

The following examples will illustrate the various kinds of business activities recorded in the Ledger and some of the methods of payment:

1730, I	Feb. 3	Trustees of the Loan Office Dr				Contra	Cr		
		For an Advertisement	–	5	–	For Cash in full	–	5	–
		For Printing & Paper				For Cash at twice[4]	100	–	–
		of 40000£	114	13	5	Abated	14	13	5
			114	18	5		114	18	5

		George Brownell Dr				Contra	Cr		
		For 2 Doz Watts Psalms	3	–	–	For Cash pd Mr.			
1735/6	Feb. 7	For binding a small Book	–	1	6	Heurtin [?]	2	–	6½
		For a Psalmbook	–	1	9	For ½ doz Bibles	1	7	–
	Nov. 27	For a spelling Book	–	1	–	For Cash paid Skelton	–	12	–
1735/6	Jan. 6	For Advt of Schoolkeeping					3	19	6½
		&c	–	5	–				
1737	Sept. 7	For a Sermon	–	1	–				
	20	For 4 quire paper	–	8	–				
		For the Gazette 2 Year & 7				Contra Cr by Cash in			
		months	1	5	10	full	1	4	6½
			5	4	1		5	4	1

		Anthony Nichols	Dr			Contra	Cr		
		For Cash	–	15	–	By Dogs & Pothooks	1	15	6
		For Barclay's Apology	–	8	–				
		For a gilt Bible	–	7	6				
		For Cash	–	5	–				
			1	15	6				
		For a Power Attorney	–	–	4				
1733, 4		For an Account Book	–	8	–				
		For an Almanack 1734	–	–	5				
	No. 443	For Advt in Gazette Owen							
		Evans	–	3	–				
1737	Sept. 6	For a Slate and Pencil	–	2	8				
38	May 11	For a blank Book 6 quire	–	2	–				
		Carried to Ledger E							

This Journal and Ledger and the associated Shop Book provide an extended view of Franklin's business activities during the period they cover. From these pages one can learn a good deal about his commercial printing, the advertising he carried in the *Gazette*, the goods he sold in his shop, and those he bought for business use or sale. But the books do not permit a complete and detailed reconstruction of his financial affairs. There are no records of strictly cash transactions, no inventories of stock and equipment. Wages and most of his other outlays are only hinted at in occasional memoranda or are omitted entirely. Franklin must have kept other books which have not been found. Consequently, neither these volumes nor such other fragmentary records as do survive

4. That is, paid in two installments. On the printing of this paper currency see above, p. 141.

for these years would enable one to prepare even approximately accurate periodic statements of income and expense, of profit and loss, or of assets and liabilities. What information these books do offer on the details of his business is ably illustrated by George Simpson Eddy's study, *Account Books Kept by Benjamin Franklin: Ledger 1728–1729, Journal 1730–1737* (New York, privately printed, Columbia University Press, 1928).

From Hugh Meredith:[5] Dissolution of Partnership

DS: American Philosophical Society

[July 14, 1730]

BE IT REMEMBERED, That Hugh Meredith and Benjamin Franklin have this Day separated as Partners, and will henceforth act each on his own Account. And that the said Hugh Meredith, for a valuable Consideration by him received from the said Benjamin Franklin, hath relinquished, and doth hereby relinquish to the said Franklin, all Claim, Right or Property to or in the Printing Materials and Stock heretofore jointly possessed by them in Partnership; and to all Debts due to them as Partners in the Course of their Business; which are all from henceforth the sole Property of the said Benjamin Franklin. In Witness whereof I have hereunto set my Hand, this fourteenth Day of July, Anno Dom. One Thousand seven Hundred and Thirty.   HUGH MEREDITH

5. Hugh Meredith (*c.*1697–*c.*1749), an apprentice of Samuel Keimer, 1728, and an original member of the Junto, won BF's friendship as an honest, sensible, observant man, a wide reader, though a poor printer and addicted to drink. After BF left Keimer's employ Meredith's father, Simon, grateful for BF's good influence on his son, established the two as partners in a printing business. But Meredith was seldom sober and did his work badly; his father failed to provide all the promised capital; and BF was relieved to have Hugh voluntarily withdraw from the business, though he carried his name on the *Gazette* through May 4, 1732. Douglas C. McMurtrie, *A History of Printing in the United States*, II (N.Y., 1936), 28-9. Meredith moved to North Carolina and wrote a good description of that province, printed in the *Gazette*, May 6 and 15, 1731. As late as 1739 BF was helping him with loans and goods (see Simon Meredith to BF, July 29, 1739); he employed him to collect rags for paper, and noted in Ledger D, Dec. 3, 1749, that since providing Meredith with a stock of books to sell in the country, he had neither seen his former partner nor received any remittance.

[Public Men]

Printed in *The Pennsylvania Gazette*, September 10, 1730.

Although the paragraph in the *Gazette* introducing this essay may be BF's, its entire text is taken, with unimportant excisions, from Edward Bysshe's translation of Xenophon's *The Memorable Things of Socrates* (London, 1712), pp. 107–14. Duane printed it in his edition of BF's writings (*Works*, IV, 401–5), as did Sparks and Bigelow; for its present exclusion see above, p. 170.

On Governor Belcher's Speech[6]

Printed in *The Pennsylvania Gazette*, September 24, 1730.

In our last we gave our Readers the most material Paragraphs of Governor Belcher's Speech to the Assembly of his other Government of New-Hampshire; and in our next shall insert his Speech at large to the Assembly of the Massachusetts, which we have by this Post. It may suffice at present to observe from it, that he has brought with him those very Instructions that occasion'd the Difference between Governor Burnet and that People,[7] which were what he went home commission'd as Agent for the Country, to get withdrawn, as an intolerable Grievance. But by being at Court, it seems, he has had the *advantage* of seeing Things in another Light, and those Instructions do now appear to him highly consistent with the Privileges and Interest of the People, which before, as a *Patriot*, he had very different Notions of.[8]

6. Jonathan Belcher (1682–1757), wealthy merchant, member of the Massachusetts Council, represented the Assembly in England in its salary controversy with Governor Burnet in 1728. While Belcher was still in London Burnet died, and Belcher got the appointment as governor of Massachusetts and New Hampshire, Jan. 8, 1730. His instructions about salary were even more stringent than Burnet's, but he now defended the executive's prerogative. The Assembly remained obdurate and again the issue was joined. Dismissed in 1741, he obtained the governorship of New Jersey, 1746. In 1751 he sought BF's advice about electrical treatment for his palsy. Leonard W. Labaree, *Royal Government in America* (New Haven, 1930), pp. 363–5; *DAB*.

7. See above, p. 159.

8. BF continued his discussion of Belcher's controversy with the Massachusetts Assembly in the *Pa. Gaz.*, July 24, 1732. This account consists of quotations and abstracts from the House's reply of June 30 to the governor's message of June 1. BF's draft of the abstracts is in Hist. Soc. Pa.

On Conversation

Printed in *The Pennsylvania Gazette*, October 15, 1730.

The opinions expressed in this essay are exactly those Franklin is known to have held and which he set down in his autobiography and elsewhere.[9] In addition the style and organization seem very like those of the young Franklin—sometimes colloquial and anecdotal, always clear and competent, though not yet exhibiting that mastery of language and problems of structure which characterized his literary composition a few years later. For these reasons the present editors believe that Franklin probably wrote this piece.

> *Sic vita erat: facile omnes perferre, ac pati,*
> *Cum quibus erat cumque una, iis sese dedere,*
> *Eorum obsequi studiis, adversus nemini,*
> *Numquam præponens se aliis: ita facillime*
> *Sine Invidia invenias laudem, et amicos pares.* Ter.[1]

BF's concern over the controversy is mentioned in a rhymed description of a Junto meeting, composed by Nicholas Scull (1687–1761), a member, probably in the spring of 1731:

> Bargos [Franklin] whos birth is by fair Boston claimd
> And Justly is for a great Genius fam'd
> Proceeded next to sing New Englands fate
> Her case how Des'prate and her foes how great
> How B——r crost the seas to plead her cause
> Secure her freedom and support her laws
> How like a Rock unmovd the Hero stod
> Exposd to danger for his countrys good
> And as the only means for her Reliefe
> Wisely Procurd himself to be her Cheife
> How cloth'd with Power how he Perceives his faults
> Her Power and Granduer gives us strength of thought
> He tells New England now, her cause is wrong
> Thus with her sovreign to contend so long
> Perswades her sons two thousand pound is just
> The King Commands it and obey they must
> Yet they maintain what their forefathers held
> Nor to their monarch will their freedom yeild.

N[icholas] B. W[ainwright], "Nicholas Scull's 'Junto' Verses," *PMHB*, LXXIII (1949), 82–4.

9. See, for examples, the notes in his commonplace book, below, p. 270, and "On Ill Natured Speaking," below, p. 327.

1. Terence, *Andria*, I, i, 35–9.

To *please* in *Conversation* is an Art which all People believe they understand and practise, tho' most are ignorant or deficient in it. The Bounds and Manner of this Paper will not allow a regular and methodical Discourse on the Subject, and therefore I must beg Leave to throw my Thoughts together as they rise.

The two grand Requisites in the Art of Pleasing, are *Complaisance* and *Good Nature*. *Complaisance* is a seeming preference of others to our selves; and *Good Nature* a Readiness to overlook or excuse their Foibles, and do them all the Services we can. These two Principles must gain us their good Opinion, and make them fond of us for their own Sake, and then all we do or say will appear to the best Advantage, and be well accepted. *Learning, Wit,* and *fine Parts,* with *these,* shine in full Lustre, become wonderfully agreeable, and command Affection; but without *them,* only seem an Assuming over others, and occasion Envy and Disgust. The common Mistake is, that People think to please by setting themselves to View, and shewing their own Perfections, whereas the easier and more effectual Way lies quite contrary. Would you win the Hearts of others, you must not seem to vie with, but admire them: Give them every Opportunity of displaying their own Qualifications, and when you have indulg'd their Vanity, they will praise you too in Turn, and prefer you above others, in order to secure to themselves the Pleasure your Commendation gives.

But above all, we should mark out those Things which cause Dislike, and avoid them with great Care. The most common amongst these is, *talking overmuch,* and robbing others of their Share of the Discourse. This is not only Incivility but Injustice, for every one has a natural Right to speak in turn, and to hinder it is an Usurpation of common Liberty, which never fails to excite Resentment. Beside, great Talkers usually leap from one thing to another with so much rapidity, and so ill a Connection, that what they say is a mere Chaos of Noise and Nonsense; tho' did they speak like Angels they still would be disagreeable. It is very pleasant when two of these People meet: the Vexation they both feel is visible in their Looks and Gestures; you shall see them gape and stare, and interrupt one another at every Turn, and watch with the utmost Impatience for a Cough or a Pause, when they may croud a Word in edgeways: neither hears nor cares what the other says; but both talk on at any Rate, and never fail to part highly disgusted with each other. I knew two Ladies, gifted this Way, who by Accident travelled in a Boat twenty Miles together, in which short Journey they were both so extreamly tired of one another, that they could never after mention each others Name with any Temper, or be brought in Company together, but retained a mutual Aversion which could never be worn out.

The contrary Fault to this, and almost as disobliging, is that of seeming wholly unconcerned in Conversation, and bearing no other Part in the Discourse than a *No* or *Yes* sometimes, or an *Hem,* or perhaps a *Nod* only. This Inattention and Indifference appears so like Disrespect, that it affronts the Desire we all possess of being taken Notice of and regarded, and makes the Company of those who practise it tiresome and insipid. Such is the Vanity of Mankind, that minding what others say is a much surer Way of pleasing them than talking well our selves.

Another Error very common and highly disagreeable, is to be ever speaking of our selves and our own Affairs. What is it to the Company we fall into whether we quarrel with our Servants, whether our Children are froward and dirty, or what we intend to have for Dinner to morrow? The Sauciness of a Negro, the Prattle of a Child, the spoiling a Suit of Cloaths, the Expences of House-keeping, or the Preparation for a Journey, may be to ourselves Matters of great Importance, as they occasion us Pain or Pleasure; but wherein are Strangers concerned, or what Amusement can they possibly receive from such Accounts? Opposite to this, but not less troublesome, is the impertinent Inquisitiveness of some People which is ever prying into and asking ten thousand Questions about the Business of others. To search after and endeavour to discover Secrets, is an unpardonable Rudeness; but what makes this Disposition worse, it is usually attended with an ill-natur'd, ungenerous, and mischievous Desire of exposing and aggravating the Mistakes and Infirmities of others. People of this Turn are the Pest of Society, and become both feared and hated. On these two Heads it may be useful always to remember, that we never ought to trouble People with more of our own Affairs than is needful for them to know, nor enquire farther into theirs than themselves think fit to tell us.

Story-telling is another Mistake in Conversation, which should be avoided by all who intend to please. It is impossible to hear a long insipid trifling Tale, void of Wit or Humour, drawn in by Neck and Shoulders, and told meerly for the sake of talking, without being uneasy at it. Besides, People this way given are apt to tell the same String of Stories, with all their rambling Particulars, again and again over; without considering, that whatsoever Pleasure themselves may find in talking, their Hearers wish their Tongues out. Old Folks are most subject to this Error, which is one chief Reason their Company is so often shun'd.

Another very disagreeable Error, is, a Spirit of *Wrangling* and *Disputing*, which some perpetually bring with them into Company: insomuch, that say whate'er you will, they'll be sure to contradict you: and if you go about to give Reasons for your Opinion, however just they be, or however modestly propos'd, you throw them into Rage and Passion. Though, perhaps, they are wholly unacquainted with the Affair, and you have made yourself Master of it, it is no Matter, the more ignorant they are you still find them the more positive, and what they want in Knowledge they endeavour to supply by Obstinacy, Noise and Fury: and when you press hard upon them, instead of Argument they fly to personal Reproaches and Invectives. Thus every Trifle becomes a serious Business, and such People are continually involved in Quarrels.

Raillery is a part of Conversation, which to treat of fully would require a whole Paper; but now, I have only room to observe that it is highly entertaining or exceedingly disobliging, according as it is managed, and therefore we ought to use it with all the Caution possible. Natural Infirmities, unavoidable Misfortunes, Defects, or Deformities of any kind, should never be the Subject of it, for then it is not only impertinent, but affronting and inhuman. It's like Salt, a little of which in some Cases gives a Relish, but if thrown on by Handfuls, or sprinkled on things at random, it spoils all. Raillery supposes Wit; but agreeable as Wit is, when it takes a wrong Turn it becomes dangerous and mischievous. When Wit applies it self to search into, expose, and ridicule the Faults of others, it often inflicts a Wound that rankles in the Heart, and is never to be forgiven. To rally safely, and so as to please, it is requisite that we perfectly know our Company: it's not enough that we intend no Ill, we must be likewise certain what we say shall be taken as we intend it; otherwise, for the sake of a Jest we may lose a Friend, and make an inveterate Enemy. I shall say no more on this Head, but that we ought to use it sparingly; and whatever Opportunities may offer of shewing our Parts this way, so soon as any Body appears uneasy at it, and receives it with a grave Face, both Good Manners and Discretion advise to change the Subject for something else more harmless.

Akin to Raillery, and what oftentimes goes along with it, is *Scandal.* But if People hereby think to gain Esteem, they unhappily are mistaken; for every Body (even those who hear them with a seeming Pleasure) considers them with a kind of Horror. No one's Reputation is safe against such Tongues: all in Turn may expect to suffer by them. Insensible of the Ties of Friendship, or the Sentiments of Humanity, such Creatures are mischievous as Bears or Tygers, and are as much abhorr'd and fear'd.

There are many more Mistakes which render People disagreeable in Conversation, but these are the most obvious; and whosoever avoids them carefully can never much displease. I shall only add, in a few Words, what are the most likely Means to make a Man be well accepted.

Let his Air, his Manner, and Behaviour, be easy, courteous and Affable, void of every Thing haughty or assuming; his Words few, express'd with Modesty, and a Respect for those he talks to. Be he ever ready to hear what others say; let him interrupt no Body, nor intrude with his Advice unask'd. Let him never trouble other People about his own Affairs, nor concern himself with theirs. Let him avoid Disputes; and when he dissents from others propose his Reasons with Calmness and Complaisance. Be his Wit ever guided by Discretion and Good Nature, nor let him sacrifice a Friend to raise a Laugh. Let him not censure others, nor expose their Failings, but kindly excuse or hide them. Let him neither raise nor propagate a Story to the Prejudice of any Body. In short, be his Study to command his own Temper, to learn the Humours of Mankind, and to conform himself accordingly.[2]

2. The author of "An Essay on Conversation" in *American Weekly Mercury,* July 23, 1730, had asserted that the two indispensable things for good conversation were knowledge and good nature.

A Witch Trial at Mount Holly

Printed in *The Pennsylvania Gazette*, October 22, 1730.

This hoax is included here on the authority of John Bach McMaster,[3] though no external evidence that Franklin wrote it has been found; all that can be said is that he could have done so. Smyth printed it without questioning (*Writings*, II, 170–2), as have subsequent editors and biographers. Records of the Court of Quarter Sessions of Burlington County, N.J., for 1730, which might indicate how much fact there was in the *Gazette* account, no longer exist.

BURLINGTON, Oct. 12. Saturday last at Mount-Holly, about 8 Miles from this Place, near 300 People were gathered together to see an Experiment or two tried on some Persons accused of Witchcraft. It seems the Accused had been charged with making their Neighbours Sheep dance in an uncommon Manner, and with causing Hogs to speak, and sing Psalms, &c. to the great Terror and Amazement of the King's good and peaceable Subjects in this Province; and the Accusers being very positive that if the Accused were weighed in Scales against a Bible, the Bible would prove too heavy for them; or that, if they were bound and put into the River, they would swim; the said Accused desirous to make their Innocence appear, voluntarily offered to undergo the said Trials, if 2 of the most violent of their Accusers would be tried with them. Accordingly the Time and Place was agreed on, and advertised about the Country; The Accusers were 1 Man and 1 Woman; and the Accused the same. The Parties being met, and the People got together, a grand Consultation was held, before they proceeded to Trial; in which it was agreed to use the Scales first; and a Committee of Men were appointed to search the Men, and a Committee of Women to search the Women, to see if they had any Thing of Weight about them, particularly Pins. After the Scrutiny was over, a huge great Bible belonging to the Justice of the Place was provided, and a Lane through the Populace was made from the Justices House to the Scales, which were fixed on a Gallows erected for that Purpose opposite to the House, that the Justice's Wife and

---

3. *Benjamin Franklin as a Man of Letters* (Boston, 1887), p. 71. The *Gentleman's Magazine*, I (1731), 29, printed a brief account of the trial, based on the *Gazette* publication, which it accepted as fact.

the rest of the Ladies might see the Trial, without coming amongst the Mob; and after the Manner of Moorfields, a large Ring was also made. Then came out of the House a grave tall Man carrying the Holy Writ before the supposed Wizard, &c. (as solemnly as the Sword-bearer of London before the Lord Mayor) the Wizard was first put in the Scale, and over him was read a Chapter out of the Books of Moses, and then the Bible was put in the other Scale, (which being kept down before) was immediately let go; but to the great Surprize of the Spectators, Flesh and Bones came down plump, and outweighed that great good Book by abundance. After the same Manner, the others were served, and their Lumps of Mortality severally were too heavy for Moses and all the Prophets and Apostles. This being over, the Accusers and the rest of the Mob, not satisfied with this Experiment, would have the Trial by Water; accordingly a most solemn Procession was made to the Mill-pond; where both Accused and Accusers being stripp'd (saving only to the Women their Shifts) were bound Hand and Foot, and severally placed in the Water, lengthways, from the Side of a Barge or Flat, having for Security only a Rope about the Middle of each, which was held by some in the Flat. The Accuser Man being thin and spare, with some Difficulty began to sink at last; but the rest every one of them swam very light upon the Water. A Sailor in the Flat jump'd out upon the Back of the Man accused, thinking to drive him down to the Bottom, but the Person bound, without any Help, came up some time before the other. The Woman Accuser, being told that she did not sink, would be duck'd a second Time; when she swam again as light as before. Upon which she declared, That she believed the Accused had bewitched her to make her so light, and that she would be duck'd again a Hundred Times, but she would duck the Devil out of her. The accused Man, being surpriz'd at his own Swimming, was not so confident of his Innocence as before, but said, *If I am a Witch, it is more than I know.* The more thinking Part of the Spectators were of Opinion, that any Person so bound and plac'd in the Water (unless they were mere Skin and Bones) would swim till their Breath was gone, and their Lungs fill'd with Water. But it being the general Belief of the Populace, that the Womens Shifts, and the Garters with which they were bound help'd to support them; it is said they are to be tried again the next warm Weather, naked.

183

Extracts from the Gazette, 1730

Printed in *The Pennsylvania Gazette*, January 6 to December 29, 1730.

About the End of next Month, a Course of Papers of Speculation and Amusement will begin to be inserted in this *Gazette*, for the Entertainment of our Readers. Those Gentlemen and others, who may be inclined to divert themselves or their Friends by trying their Hands in some little Performance of that Nature, are hereby invited to make use of this Opportunity; and whatever they send, (to be left at the Publishers) that is fit for publick View, will be kindly received, and communicated in the most proper Time and Manner.[4]   [January 6]

This is to inform the Writer of *A certain Letter, giving a certain Account of a late certain Difference between a certain —— and his Wife, with certain Animadversions upon their Conduct*, &c. That, for certain charitable Reasons, the said Letter is at present thought not fit to be published.   [January 27]

The same Day [Saturday last] an unhappy Man one Sturgis, upon some Difference with his Wife, determined to drown himself in the River; and she, (kind Wife) went with him, it seems, to see it faithfully performed, and accordingly stood by silent and unconcerned during the whole Transaction: He jump'd in near Carpenter's Wharff, but was timely taken out again, before what he came about was thoroughly effected, so that they were both obliged to return home as they came, and put up for that Time with the Disappointment.   [February 10]

Last Week some counterfeit Five Shilling Bills of our Currency were passed here; but as they were clumsily done, upon mean Letter and ordinary Paper, and very unlike the Originals, they were soon discovered, and trac'd to One who was lately in Town from New-Castle. Orders are sent down to examine him about them. It is supposed they are come from the *old Quarter;* tho' 'tis surprising that a Course of ill Success is not a sufficient Discouragement to such Practices.[5]   [February 19]

4. There was almost no response to this invitation.
5. The result of the examination is not known. Kenneth Scott, *Counterfeiting in Colonial Pennsylvania* (N.Y., 1955), p. 24.

184

The great Snow we had here, was so much greater in New-England, as to prevent all Travelling on the Roads for a considerable Time; so that the Eastern Post was not come in to York last Thursday; and therefore our Post who waited there for him, is not yet arrived here, tho' he had been expected on Friday Night last. Upon this Account the Publication of our Paper has been so long delayed [two days]. [February 19]

[ADVERTISEMENT] Newydd ei Argraphu ac ar werth yn yr Argraphdy Newydd, gyferbyn a'r Farchnad yn Philadelphia.

Ca'n yn dangos Truenus hanes, Ma'b a Merch, y modd y darfu i'r Ferch Dorri ei Haddewid ag êf, yr hyn a barodd iddo adel ei Dylwyth, a myned ymmaith: a'i dôst Alar o achos ei Rhieni hi.

Fe a wnaeth y Gân ei hûn ac ai gadawodd wrth fyned Ymmaith gyda ei hên Gyfeillion, er Cyngor iddynt hwy ac eraill i beidio a rhoddi eu Bryd ar bethau 'r Byd hwn: Mae yu dangos drwy 'r cyfan ei bûr Gariad at y Ferch; ai sawr Barch a gobaith yn ei Jachawdwr, ai wîr Gariad i'r Grefydd Gristianogol. Prîs 3d.

Yn yr vn Fan y mae ar Werth Cyfraith yr Iâr a'r Mynawyd, rhwng Sion ac Eynion, o Waith Dafydd Manuel. Prîs 4d.

Yn yr vn Lle y gall y nêb a chwennycho, gael Argraphu, yn Gymraeg neu Saefneg yn Dda, ac o weddol Brîs: Ac hefyd Rhwymo hên Lyfrau yn Dda, ac ar Brîs Gweddol.[6] [March 13]

When Mr. Bradford publishes after us, and has Occasion to take an Article or two out of the *Gazette,* which he is always welcome to do, he is desired not to date his Paper a Day before ours, (as last Week in the Case of the Letter containing Kelsey's Speech, &c.) lest distant Readers should imagine we take from him, which we always carefully avoid.[7] [March 19]

6. This announcement informed the *Gazette*'s Welsh readers of the recent printing of two works at the New Printing-Office: a song by a disappointed young man lamenting his broken engagement but affirming his love for the girl and for the Christian religion (price 3d.) and an account of the contract(?) of the hen and the owl between John and Eynion, by David Manuel (price 4d.). Patrons were further advised that they could get good printing done in Welsh or English and have old books well bound, both at reasonable prices.

7. The speech made by one William Kelsey just before his execution March 7 at New Castle, Del., for burglary and setting fire to the county jail, was printed in the *Gazette* March 13. Bradford's printing appeared in

Next Week will be Published, The Votes and Proceedings of the Honourable House of Representatives. Printed and Sold at the New Printing-Office near the Market.

The Laws enacted at the last Session are also in the Press, and will be published with Expedition, and sold at the same Place.

[March 19]

[Advertisement] A Likely Negroe Woman to be Sold. Enquire at the Widow Read's in Market-Street, Philadelphia.[8]

[April 9]

On Friday Night last, about 11 o'Clock, a Fire broke out in a Store near Mr. Fishbourn's Wharff, and before it could be master'd consumed all the Stores, &c. on the Wharff, damaged several Houses on that Side the Street, and crossing the Way, seized the fine House of Mr. J. Dickinson, with two other Houses adjoining towards Walnut-street, which are all ruined. The Loss in the Whole is supposed to be four or five Thousand Pounds. It is thought that if the People had been provided with good Engines and other suitable Instruments, the Fire might easily have been prevented spreading, as there was but little Wind. There is now a Subscription on Foot for supplying the Town with every Thing necessary of that Nature, which meets with great Encouragement. There was much Thieving at the Fire, and several ill Persons are now in Prison on that Account.[9] [April 30]

We hear from New-England, that the Small-Pox spreads in divers parts of the Country. There is an Account published of the Number of Persons inoculated in Boston in the Month of March, amounting to Seventy-two; of which two only died, and the rest have recovered perfect Health. Of those who had it in the common Way, 'tis computed that one in four died. Several Hundreds have been inoculated, and but about four in the Hundred have died un-

---

the issue of the *Mercury* dated March 12 but not actually printed until March 14, as a note apologizing for the delay makes clear: "The Post is not come in Saturday [March 14] 12 a-Clock."

8. Widow Read was BF's mother-in-law.

9. Since 1718 the Common Council had provided fire protection by pumping engines and other equipment. Harrold E. Gillingham, "Philadelphia's First Fire Defences," *PMHB*, LVI (1932), 360–2.

der Inoculation; and even those are supposed to have first taken the Infection in the common Way.[1] [May 14]

[ADVERTISEMENT] JAMES AUSTIN's PERSIAN INK, approved of by the properest Judges in England to be the best of any yet made; Sold only at the New Printing-Office in Philadelphia, at 12*d. per Bottle*. [June 23]

Some of our last Papers were wrought off with the following Transposition. In the 2d Column of the 2d Page, that which is properly the 6th Line is placed as the 9th, so that what is now the 9th Line must be read as the 6th, in order to make Sense of that Part of the Paragraph. The judicious Reader will easily distinguish accidental Errors from the Blunders of Ignorance, and more readily excuse the former which sometimes happen unavoidably.
[July 2]

N.B. Tho' we have the Pleasure to observe that these *Essays* of *Primitive Christianity* are exceedingly acceptable to the generality of our Readers; yet we are concern'd to hear that some worthy and learned Men are dissatisfied with them, as believing them to contain sundry false, heretical and pernicious Positions and Opinions: If such Gentlemen who think these Papers hurtful, are inclined to write any Thing by way of Answer, to manifest the Weakness and Error of the Doctrine contained therein; this may inform them, that any Thing of that Kind will be thankfully received, and faithfully handed to the Publick in *the Gazette*, without putting the Author to one Penny Charge; provided the Answer to each *Essay* be not much longer than the *Essay* it self.[2] [July 30]

From Woodbury Creek on the other Side of the River we hear, that on Sunday Night last a Servant Man belonging to one Tatcham, got out of Bed at Midnight, and telling a Lad who slept with him that he was going a long Journey and should never see him more,

1. The epidemic raged in Boston through the summer, subsiding in August. John Duffy, *Epidemics in Colonial America* (Baton Rouge, La., 1953), pp. 52–4.

2. This note was printed at the end of three essays on the origins of Christianity, reprinted from the *London Journal*. Apparently no one accepted BF's offer.

he went into the Orchard and hanged himself on a Tree: But it seems the Rope broke in the Operation, and towards Morning he found himself alive upon the Ground to his no small Surprize. He then went and hid himself in the Barn among some Straw, for several Hours, while his Master and the rest of the Family were searching and enquiring after him to no Effect. At length having procured a better Rope, he hanged himself again in the Barn, and was there accidentally found by the Maid in the Afternoon: When he was cut down there appeared no sign of Life in him, nor were any Means used to recover him; but by that Time the Coroner and his Inquest were got together and come to View his Body, he was upon his Legs again, and is now living. [August 27]

JUST PUBLISHED: JERMAN'S ALMANACKS for the Year 1731. Containing, beside what is usual, a correct Table of Houses for the Latitude of Forty Degrees, which has been much desired by the Ingenious. Printed and Sold at the New Printing-Office near the Market. [October 15]

JUST PUBLISHED: GODFREY'S ALMANACKS for the Year 1731. Done on a large Sheet of Demi Paper, after the London manner. Containing the Eclipses, Lunations, Judgment of the Weather, the Time of the Sun's Rising and Setting, Moon's Rising and Setting, Seven Stars Rising, Southing and Setting, Time of High-water, Fairs, Courts, and Observable Days. With several other Things useful and curious. Printed and sold at the New-Printing-Office near the Market. [October 29]

***During the three Winter Months, while the Post performs his Stage but once a Fortnight; This Paper will be published on Tuesdays. And as the Winter generally Occasions a Scarcity of News in these Parts; and it being very little Satisfaction to the Reader to have a whole Sheet, when half of it must be fill'd with Trifles, or Things of small Consequence; we shall for the above Time publish it in half Sheets, which we doubt not will be equally entertaining. [December 3]

(*‡*) It is now above 14 Months since we undertook the Publishing this Paper; Those Subscribers who have taken it a Year, are desired to send in their respective Payments. [December 8]

[Advertisement] Ralph Sandiford being bound for England, hath printed a Second Impression of his *Negroe Treatise* to be distributed by him *Gratis,* or by Matthias Aspdin his Attorney; unto whom all Persons indebted to him are desired to pay the same with Speed, to prevent Charge to themselves.

And whereas some Persons would not apply for his Books *Gratis,* the Printer having Leave from the Author, has them ready for Sale at 12*d.* a-piece, at the New Printing-Office near the Market.[3]

[December 22]

Buried in the several Burying-Grounds of this City from December 30, 1729. *to* December 29, 1730.

Church	81	Baptists		18
Quakers	39	Strangers	Whites	41
Presbyterians	18		Blacks	30

In all 227.

[December 29]

Just Published: The Laws made the last Session of the late Assembly, relating to Wears and Damms in Skuylkill, and to the Trustees of the Loan-Office. Printed and sold at the New Printing-Office near the Market. Price *Six-Pence. Where may be had,* Latin Grammars, *and* Dyche's Spelling-Books.   [December 29]

Philadelphia: Printed by B. Franklin and H. Meredith, at the *New Printing-Office* near the Market, where Advertisements are taken in, and all Persons may be supplied with this Paper, at *Ten Shillings* a Year.

3. Ralph Sandiford (1693–1733), Quaker merchant, observed slavery during a visit to the West Indies. Franklin and Meredith printed his *A Brief Examination of the Practice of the Times,* 1729, one of the early anti-slavery tracts, copies of which he distributed in the face of threats of prosecution. A second edition was printed, 1730, as *The Mystery of Iniquity: in a Brief Examination of the Practice of Times* [sic]. Roberts Vaux, *Memoirs of the Lives of Benjamin Lay and Ralph Sandiford* (Phila., 1815), pp. 59–71; BF to John Wright, Nov. 4, 1789; Edward R. Turner, *The Negro in Pennsylvania* (Washington, 1911), p. 71. BF's Ledger A & B (above, p. 172) on Feb. 28, 1733, credits Sandiford with 10*s.* received of Benjamin Lay "for 50 of his Books which he intends to give away."

Advertisement of Godfrey's Almanacs[4]

Printed in *The Pennsylvania Gazette*, January 19, 1730/1.

Godfrey's Almanacks for the Year 1731. Done on a large Sheet of Demi Paper, after the London manner. Containing the Eclipses, Lunations, Judgment of the Weather, the Time of the Sun's Rising and Setting, Moon's Rising and Setting, Seven Stars Rising, Southing and Setting, Time of High-water, Fairs, Courts, and Observable Days. With several other Things useful and curious. Printed and sold at the New-Printing-Office near the Market.

N.B. The 3 Mathematical Questions proposed in *Leeds's Almanack*,[5] were solv'd and answer'd by Godfrey, in less than half an Hour after he saw them, as the Printer hereof can testify; the Solutions and Answers were sent by the Post to the Author of the Questions, together with 3 other Questions for him to Answer; but there being a Pretence that the first Copy of those Questions came not to Hand; and a Second having been sent above 6 Weeks since, concerning which nothing can yet be heard; it is thought proper to publish the said Questions, that there may be no Room for further Excuse. *Note,* A Copy of the aforesaid Solutions is in the Hands of the Printer.

4. Thomas Godfrey (1704–1749), glazier, self-taught mathematician, inventor of the quadrant called Hadley's, an original member of the Junto. BF printed his almanacs for 1730–32, Bradford those for 1733–36. That advertised here was titled *The Pennsylvania Almanack for the Year of Christian Account 1731*. The Godfreys' house and BF's shop were in the same building, and BF boarded with them before his marriage. Of Godfrey BF wrote in his autobiography that "he knew little out of his way, and was not a pleasing Companion, as like most Great Mathematicians I have met with, he expected unusual Precision in every thing said, or was forever denying or distinguishing upon Trifles, to the Disturbance of all Conversation." *DAB.*

5. The questions "proposed to the Sons of Art," to be answered by June 1, 1731, were:

"I. There is a Wall containing 18225 cubical Feet. The Height is five times the Breadth, and the Length eight times the Height. I demand the Breadth of the Wall?

"II. Suppose a Ship sails between the S. and W. till the Sum of the Difference of Latitude and Departure be 7, and her Distance 5. I demand the Difference of Latitude and Departure severally?

"III. Suppose the Area of an equilateral Triangle to be 600. The Sides are required?" *The American Almanack For the Year of Christian Account 1731* (Phila., 1730).

Question I. Suppose 2 Ships being in the same Latitude, distant from each other 100 Leagues, sail directly North 500 Leagues, (20 in a Degree) and then are 70 Leagues a-part: *What are the Latitudes?*

Quest. II. Suppose 2 Roads of = Breadth to cross each other at Right-angles in the Centre of a given circular Piece of Ground, and take up the half or third Part of that circular Piece of Ground: *What is the Proportion of the Breadth of the Roads to the Diameter of the Circle?*

Quest. III. Suppose a Ship in North Latitude, sailing between the North and East,

$$\text{makes her} \left\{ \begin{matrix} 50 \\ 40 \\ 30 \end{matrix} \right\} \text{Minutes more} \left\{ \begin{matrix} \text{Diff. Latitude.} \\ \text{Departure.} \\ \text{Diff. Longitude.} \end{matrix} \right.$$
$$\text{Distance} \qquad\qquad \text{than her}$$

What is the Course, Distance, and both Latitudes?

From James Logan[6]

Letterbook copy: Historical Society of Pennsylvania; also transcript: Harvard College Library (Sparks)

Friend B.F.   1st of May 1731

I did wrong perhaps in bringing out with me the Paper I had from T. G.[7] but on thy Letter I return it. To give my opinion of it is needless, for it Speaks for itself. That method of Locks (as

6. James Logan (1674–1751), a Quaker of Scots ancestry, who came to Philadelphia, 1699, as William Penn's secretary, was for nearly half a century a leading political figure in Pennsylvania, serving variously as provincial secretary; clerk, member, and in time senior member of the Council; mayor of Philadelphia; presiding judge of the Philadelphia County Court of Quarter Sessions; and chief justice of the Supreme Court. The Penn family entrusted him with oversight of their property interests for many years. He was a man of wide intellectual interests, literary, philosophical, and scientific. At Stenton, his country home near Germantown, he assembled a library of 3,000 books, one of the finest in the colonies. After his death his heirs installed the collection, according to his wishes, in a building he had erected for the purpose in Philadelphia, creating thereby the Loganian Library as a public trust. Frederick B. Tolles, *James Logan and the Culture of Provincial America* (Boston, 1957). BF "acknowledged his obligations to him [Logan] in the beginning of his Carreer, and valued himself on his friendship." Deborah Norris Logan to P. S. Du Ponceau, Jan. 17, 1820, APS.

7. "T. G." was Thomas Godfrey (above, p. 190). The paper referred to was probably one by Joseph Morgan, Presbyterian minister of Hopewell, N.J., which BF printed in the *Gazette*, May 18 and 25, 1732.

they are call'd) in Rivers is found of great Use, and comes daily more into practice. There are now vast numbers of them in England: But the authors Proposal of a Side Dam (to me at least) is new, and in some places, I believe, might be advantageously applied, but scarce in [the] Delaware, I doubt; For Such a Wall, as it must be Tight to make it of any Use would be vastly laborious and chargeable. Besides that what we call Falls in our River for the most part are not properly Such, but only ledges of Rocks cross the Stream, which are not near so difficult to remove, as it would be to make such Walls and Gates, that are necessary only where there is a Descent, when with us were the Rocks removed the Stream would be near a Level. His other Proposals, where practicable for the Ground, might doubtless be useful on the great Rivers in Europe, where large Cities and Towns are Seated both below and above, and here perhaps in future Ages may be tried, but scarce under any of our Governments as they are at present established. It would be well I believe to have the Paper made public, for 'tis a pity that such ingenious Thoughts should be lost. But as it is doubtful at least whether any part of it will be putt in practice in these parts during this Age how far an Impression of it might answer the Charge I shall not pretend to judge. I thought to have taken a Copy of it, but for want of a fitt hand here for such purposes have not done it. Thy friend (sign'd only)   J. L.

To B. Franklin

Observations on Reading History[8]

MS Autobiography: Huntington Library

OBSERVATIONS on my Reading History in Library

May 9. 1731.

That the great Affairs of the World, the Wars, Revolutions, &c. are carried on and effected by Parties.

8. These Observations, written on a "little Paper, accidentally preserv'd," and copied by Franklin into his autobiography in August 1788, were the genesis of his *"great and extensive Project"*—never realized—to establish a party of virtue, under the name of The Society of the Free and Easy. Par. Text edit., pp. 236–42.

That the View of these Parties is their present general Interest, or what they take to be such.

That the different Views of these different Parties, occasion all Confusion.

That while a Party is carrying on a general Design, each Man has his particular private Interest in View.

That as soon as a Party has gain'd its general Point, each Member becomes intent upon his particular Interest, which thwarting others, breaks that Party into Divisions, and occasions more Confusion.

That few in Public Affairs act from a meer View of the Good of their Country, whatever they may pretend; and tho' their Actings bring real Good to their Country, yet Men primarily consider'd that their own and their Country's Interest was united, and did not act from a Principle of Benevolence.

That fewer still in public Affairs act with a View to the Good of Mankind.

There seems to me at present to be great Occasion for raising an united Party for Virtue, by forming the Virtuous and good Men of all Nations into a regular Body, to be govern'd by suitable good and wise Rules, which good and wise Men may probably be more unanimous in their Obedience to, than common People are to common Laws.[9]

I at present think, that whoever attempts this aright, and is well qualified, cannot fail of pleasing God, and of meeting with Success.

B. F.

9. An entry in BF's Commonplace Book about 1732 (Hist. Soc. Pa.) shows a development of his ideas for the Society of Virtue:

"R, B T A O Gs Gz

"tht wn I hv 200 clr.

"He may travel, every where endeavouring to promote Knowledge and Virtue; by erecting J[unto]s, promoting private Libr[arie]s, establishing a Society of Virtuous Men in all parts, who shall have an universal Correspondence and unite to support and encourage Virtue and Liberty and Knowledge; by all Methods. make m slf wrth 2 b mpld n s grt nd gd a Dsyn.

"O G M M W."

The shorthand can be expanded to read: "that when I have £200 clear" and "make myself worthy to be employed in so. great and good a Design." The cipher's meaning is not known.

Apology for Printers

Printed in *The Pennsylvania Gazette*, June 10, 1731.

Being frequently censur'd and condemn'd by different Persons for printing Things which they say ought not to be printed, I have sometimes thought it might be necessary to make a standing Apology for my self, and publish it once a Year, to be read upon all Occasions of that Nature. Much Business has hitherto hindered the execution of this Design; but having very lately given extra-ordinary Offence by printing an Advertisement with a certain *N.B.* at the End of it,[1] I find an Apology more particularly requi-site at this Juncture, tho' it happens when I have not yet Leisure to write such a thing in the proper Form, and can only in a loose manner throw those Considerations together which should have been the Substance of it.

I request all who are angry with me on the Account of printing things they don't like, calmly to consider these following Particu-lars

1. That the Opinions of Men are almost as various as their Faces; an Observation general enough to become a common Proverb, *So many Men so many Minds.*

2. That the Business of Printing has chiefly to do with Mens Opinions; most things that are printed tending to promote some, or oppose others.

3. That hence arises the peculiar Unhappiness of that Business, which other Callings are no way liable to; they who follow Print-ing being scarce able to do any thing in their way of getting a Living, which shall not probably give Offence to some, and per-haps to many; whereas the Smith, the Shoemaker, the Carpen-ter, or the Man of any other Trade, may work indifferently for People of all Persuasions, without offending any of them: and the Merchant may buy and sell with Jews, Turks, Hereticks, and Infidels of all sorts, and get Money by every one of them, with-out giving Offence to the most orthodox, of any sort; or suffer-ing the least Censure or Ill-will on the Account from any Man whatever.

---

1. The advertisement has not been found in the *Gazette;* it was probably a handbill.

4. That it is as unreasonable in any one Man or Set of Men to expect to be pleas'd with every thing that is printed, as to think that nobody ought to be pleas'd but themselves.

5. Printers are educated in the Belief, that when Men differ in Opinion, both Sides ought equally to have the Advantage of being heard by the Publick; and that when Truth and Error have fair Play, the former is always an overmatch for the latter: Hence they chearfully serve all contending Writers that pay them well, without regarding on which side they are of the Question in Dispute.

6. Being thus continually employ'd in serving all Parties, Printers naturally acquire a vast Unconcernedness as to the right or wrong Opinions contain'd in what they print; regarding it only as the Matter of their daily labour: They print things full of Spleen and Animosity, with the utmost Calmness and Indifference, and without the least Ill-will to the Persons reflected on; who nevertheless unjustly think the Printer as much their Enemy as the Author, and join both together in their Resentment.

7. That it is unreasonable to imagine Printers approve of every thing they print, and to censure them on any particular thing accordingly; since in the way of their Business they print such great variety of things opposite and contradictory. It is likewise as unreasonable what some assert, *That Printers ought not to print any Thing but what they approve;* since if all of that Business should make such a Resolution, and abide by it, an End would thereby be put to Free Writing, and the World would afterwards have nothing to read but what happen'd to be the Opinions of Printers.

8. That if all Printers were determin'd not to print any thing till they were sure it would offend no body, there would be very little printed.

9. That if they sometimes print vicious or silly things not worth reading, it may not be because they approve such things themselves, but because the People are so viciously and corruptly educated that good things are not encouraged. I have known a very numerous Impression of *Robin Hood's Songs* go off in this Province at 2s. per Book, in less than a Twelvemonth; when a small Quantity of *David's Psalms* (an excellent Version) have lain upon my Hands above twice the Time.

10. That notwithstanding what might be urg'd in behalf of a Man's being allow'd to do in the Way of his Business whatever he is paid for, yet Printers do continually discourage the Printing of great Numbers of bad things, and stifle them in the Birth. I my self have constantly refused to print any thing that might countenance Vice, or promote Immorality; tho' by complying in such Cases with the corrupt Taste of the Majority, I might have got much Money. I have also always refus'd to print such things as might do real Injury to any Person, how much soever I have been solicited, and tempted with Offers of great Pay; and how much soever I have by refusing got the Ill-will of those who would have employ'd me. I have heretofore fallen under the Resentment of large Bodies of Men, for refusing absolutely to print any of their Party or Personal Reflections. In this Manner I have made my self many Enemies, and the constant Fatigue of denying is almost insupportable.[2] But the Publick being unacquainted with all this, whenever the poor Printer happens either through Ignorance or much Persuasion, to do any thing that is generally thought worthy of Blame, he meets with no more Friendship or Favour on the above Account, than if there were no Merit in't at all. Thus, as Waller says,[2a]

> *Poets loose half the Praise they would have got*
> *Were it but known what they discreetly blot;*

Yet are censur'd for every bad Line found in their Works with the utmost Severity.

---

2. BF expressed his policy fully in the autobiography: "In the Conduct of my Newspaper I carefully excluded all Libelling and Personal Abuse .... Whenever I was solicited to insert any thing of that kind, and the Writers pleaded as they generally did, the Liberty of the Press, and that a Newspaper was like a Stage Coach in which any one who would pay had a Right to a Place, my Answer was, that I would print the Piece separately if desired ... but that I would not take upon me to spread his Detraction, and that having contracted with my Subscribers to furnish them with what might be either useful or entertaining, I could not fill their Papers with private Altercation ... without doing them manifest Injustice." Several apocryphal tales appeared soon after BF's death to illustrate his independence as a printer; for two such anecdotes, see New York *Weekly Visitor*, II (Dec. 22, 1810), 109; *PMHB*, XLVIII (1924), 383.

2a. Edmund Waller, *Works* (London, 1729), p. 238.

I come now to the particular Case of the *N.B.* above-mention'd, about which there has been more Clamour against me, than ever before on any other Account. In the Hurry of other Business an Advertisement was brought to me to be printed; it signified that such a Ship lying at such a Wharff, would sail for Barbadoes in such a Time, and that Freighters and Passengers might agree with the Captain at such a Place; so far is what's common: But at the Bottom this odd Thing was added, N.B. *No Sea Hens*[3] *nor Black Gowns will be admitted on any Terms.* I printed it, and receiv'd my Money; and the Advertisement was stuck up round the Town as usual. I had not so much Curiosity at that time as to enquire the Meaning of it, nor did I in the least imagine it would give so much Offence. Several good Men are very angry with me on this Occasion; they are pleas'd to say I have too much Sense to do such things ignorantly; that if they were Printers they would not have done such a thing on any Consideration; that it could proceed from nothing but my abundant Malice against Religion and the Clergy: They therefore declare they will not take any more of my Papers, nor have any farther Dealings with me; but will hinder me of all the Custom they can. All this is very hard!

I believe it had been better if I had refused to print the said Advertisement. However, 'tis done and cannot be revok'd. I have only the following few Particulars to offer, some of them in my Behalf, by way of Mitigation, and some not much to the Purpose; but I desire none of them may be read when the Reader is not in a very good Humour.

1. That I really did it without the least Malice, and imagin'd the *N.B.* was plac'd there only to make the Advertisement star'd at, and more generally read.

3. Sea-hens, or guillemots, a species of auk, make a great uproar in their "loomeries" or nesting grounds; they seem to be pugnaciously and noisily jealous of their respective nesting places. James Fisher and R. M. Lockley, *Sea-Birds: An Introduction to the Natural History of the Sea-Birds of the North Atlantic* (Boston, 1954), p. 269. In Scotland the term sea-hen is sometimes used of the crooner, or lyra, a fish which makes a croaking, plaintive sound when landed. John Jamieson, *An Etymological Dictionary of the Scottish Language* (new edit., Paisley, 1879), I, 536; III, 199. If BF's advertiser had either meaning in mind when he linked "Sea-Hens" with "Black Gowns," the insult to the clergy was the stronger.

2. That I never saw the Word *Sea-Hens* before in my Life; nor have I yet ask'd the meaning of it; and tho' I had certainly known that *Black Gowns* in that Place signified the Clergy of the Church of England, yet I have that confidence in the generous good Temper of such of them as I know, as to be well satisfied such a trifling mention of their Habit gives them no Disturbance.

3. That most of the Clergy in this and the neighbouring Provinces, are my Customers, and some of them my very good Friends; and I must be very malicious indeed, or very stupid, to print this thing for a small Profit, if I had thought it would have given them just Cause of Offence.

4. That if I have much Malice against the Clergy, and withal much Sense; 'tis strange I never write or talk against the Clergy my self. Some have observed that 'tis a fruitful Topic, and the easiest to be witty upon of all others. I can print any thing I write at less Charge than others; yet I appeal to the Publick that I am never guilty this way, and to all my Acquaintance as to my Conversation.

5. That if a Man of Sense had Malice enough to desire to injure the Clergy, this is the foolishest Thing he could possibly contrive for that Purpose.

6. That I got Five Shillings by it.

7. That none who are angry with me would have given me so much to let it alone.

8. That if all the People of different Opinions in this Province would engage to give me as much for not printing things they don't like, as I can get by printing them, I should probably live a very easy Life; and if all Printers were every where so dealt by, there would be very little printed.

9. That I am oblig'd to all who take my Paper, and am willing to think they do it out of meer Friendship. I only desire they would think the same when I deal with them. I thank those who leave off, that they have taken it so long. But I beg they would not endeavour to dissuade others, for that will look like Malice.

10. That 'tis impossible any Man should know what he would do if he was a Printer.

11. That notwithstanding the Rashness and Inexperience of Youth, which is most likely to be prevail'd with to do things that ought not to be done; yet I have avoided printing such Things

as usually give Offence either to Church or State, more than any Printer that has followed the Business in this Province before.

12. And lastly, That I have printed above a Thousand Advertisements which made not the least mention of *Sea-Hens* or *Black Gowns;* and this being the first Offence, I have the more Reason to expect Forgiveness.

I take leave to conclude with an old Fable, which some of my Readers have heard before, and some have not.

"A certain well-meaning Man and his Son, were travelling towards a Market Town, with an Ass which they had to sell. The Road was bad; and the old Man therefore rid, but the Son went a-foot. The first Passenger they met, asked the Father if he was not ashamed to ride by himself, and suffer the poor Lad to wade along thro' the Mire; this induced him to take up his Son behind him: He had not travelled far, when he met others, who said, they were two unmerciful Lubbers to get both on the Back of that poor Ass, in such a deep Road. Upon this the old Man gets off, and let his Son ride alone. The next they met called the Lad a graceless, rascally young Jackanapes, to ride in that Manner thro' the Dirt, while his aged Father trudged along on Foot; and they said the old Man was a Fool, for suffering it. He then bid his Son come down, and walk with him, and they travell'd on leading the Ass by the Halter; 'till they met another Company, who called them a Couple of sensless Blockheads, for going both on Foot in such a dirty Way, when they had an empty Ass with them, which they might ride upon. The old Man could bear no longer; My Son, said he, it grieves me much that we cannot please all these People: Let us throw the Ass over the next Bridge, and be no farther troubled with him."

Had the old Man been seen acting this last Resolution, he would probably have been call'd a Fool for troubling himself about the different Opinions of all that were pleas'd to find Fault with him: Therefore, tho' I have a Temper almost as complying as his, I intend not to imitate him in this last Particular. I consider the Variety of Humours among Men, and despair of pleasing every Body; yet I shall not therefore leave off Printing. I shall continue my Business. I shall not burn my Press and melt my Letters.[4]

4. Thomas Whitmarsh, criticized for something he printed, published a large part of this essay as his defense in the *South-Carolina Gazette*, Oct. 14, 1732.

To Jane Mecom

MS not found; reprinted from Duane, *Works*, VI, 3–5.

Dear Sister,   Philadelphia, June 19, 1731[5]

Yours of May 26, I received with the melancholy news of the death of sister Deavenport, a loss, without doubt, regretted by all that knew her, for she was a good woman.[6] Her friends ought, however, to be comforted that they have enjoyed her so long and that she has passed through the world happily, having never had any extraordinary misfortune or notable affliction, and that she is now secure in rest, in the place provided for the virtuous. I had before heard of the death of your first child, and am pleased that the loss is in some measure made up to you by the birth of a second.[7]

We have had the small pox here lately, which raged violently while it lasted; there have been about fifty persons inoculated, who all recovered, except a child of the doctor's, upon whom the small pox appeared within a day or two after the operation, and who is therefore thought to have been certainly infected before. In one family in my neighbourhood there appeared a great mortality. Mr. George Claypole,[8] (a descendant of Oliver Cromwell) had, by industry, acquired a great estate, and being in excellent business, (a merchant) would probably have doubled it, had he lived according to the common course of years. He died first, suddenly; within a short time died his best negro; then one of his children; then a negro woman; then two children more, buried at the same time; then two more: so that I saw two double buryings come out of the house in one week. None were left in the family, but the mother and one

5. Incorrectly dated 1730 by Duane. For clarity and logic two changes have been made in Duane's rendering of the second paragraph: the comma after "mortality" has been replaced by a period, and the verb "has acquired" is printed here as "had acquired."

6. Sarah Franklin Davenport died May 23, 1731, leaving five children. Her husband remarried November 1731 (Genealogy, C.12).

7. Jane Mecom's first child died May 18, 1730. Her second, Edward, was born March 29, 1731 (Genealogy, C.17.1 and C.17.2).

8. George Claypoole, son of James, whose brother John married Elizabeth, daughter of Oliver Cromwell; merchant, alderman, executor (with Isaac Norris and James Logan) of the estate of the Philadelphia merchant Jonathan Dickinson, 1722; died December 21, 1730, aged 55.

child, and both their lives till lately despaired of; so that all the father's wealth, which every body thought, a little while ago, had heirs enough, and no one would have given six pence for the reversion, was in a few weeks brought to the greatest probability of being divided among strangers: so uncertain are all human affairs: the dissolution of this family is generally ascribed to an imprudent use of quick silver in the cure of the itch; Mr. Claypole applying it as he thought proper, without consulting a physician for fear of charges, and the small pox coming upon them at the same time made their case desperate. But what gives me the greatest concern, is the account you give me of my sister Homes's misfortune: I know a cancer in the breast is often thought incurable: yet we have here in town a kind of shell made of some wood, cut at a proper time, by some man of great skill (as they say,) which has done wonders in that disease among us, being worn for some time on the breast.[9] I am not apt to be superstitiously fond of believing such things, but the instances are so well attested as sufficiently to convince the most incredulous.

This if I have interest enough to procure, as I think I have, I will borrow for a time and send it to you, and hope the doctors you have will at least allow the experiment to be tried, and shall rejoice to hear it has the accustomed effect.

You have mentioned nothing in your letter of our dear parents, but I conclude they are well because you say nothing to the contrary. I want to hear from sister Douse,[1] and to know of her welfare, as also of my sister Lydia, who I hear is lately married.[2] I intended to have visited you this summer, but printing the paper money here has hindered me near two months, and our assembly will sit the 2d of August next, at which time I must not be absent, but I hope to see you this Fall. I am, Your affectionate brother,   B. FRANKLIN

9. Despite this treatment, Mary Franklin Homes died later in 1731 (Genealogy, C.10).

1. Elizabeth Franklin Douse (1678–1759), BF's eldest half-sister (Genealogy, C.1).

2. Lydia Franklin married Robert Scott, 1731 (Genealogy, C.16).

St. John's Lodge, Account[3]

MS Ledger ("Liber B"): Historical Society of Pennsylvania

Benja. Frankline to Stok Dr:

Ao.Dom. 1731		£	s	d
June 24th	To: 5 Lodge days omition at 6d. per diem		2	6
	To: remainder of your £3 Entrance is £2 0 1	2	0	1
July 5	To Stock for this Lodge day			6
August 2	to Stock for this day			6
Septembr. 6th	to your monthly Quota 6d.			6
octobr. 4	to Quota			6
novembr. 5th	for absence 1s. and monthly Quota 6d.		1	6
Decembr. 6th	for Quota			6
		2	6	7
1731/2				
Jany. 3	for Do.			6
febraery 7th	to Do.			6
march 6	for absence 1s. and Quota 6d.		1	6
1732				
april the 3d	to Quota 6d.			6
may the 1	for absence 1s. and Quota 6d.		1	6
June the 5	for Quota 6d.			6
		£2	11	7
July 3	for Quota			6
augst. 7	for Do.			6
Septembr. 4	for Do.			6

Per Contra Cr:

Ao.Dom. 1731		£	s	d
June 24th	To moneys recd. over Pluss of your Expences Entring	£2	2	7
July 5	By moneys to Stock for this Lodge day			6
Augst. 2	By moneys to Stock			6
Septembr. 6th	By moneys you Pd. for monthly Quota			6
octobr. 4	By moneys for Quota			6
decembr. 6th	By moneys Pd.		1	6
		2	6	1
1731/2				
Jany. 3d	By Do.			6
febraery 7th	By Do.			6
1732				
April 3d	By Do. Quota and for Last time absence 2s.		2	0
June 5	By Quota 6d.			6
19	By moneys for absence and Quota			
		£2	9	7
			1	6
		2	11	1
July 3d	By moneys for Quota 6d.			6
aug 7	By Do.			6
Septembr. 4	By Do.			6
			1	6

Dr.

Date	Description	£ s d
novembr. 6	for absence 1s. and Quota 6d.	1 6
decembr. 4	for Ditto	1 6
1732/3		
January 1st	for Quota	6
february 5	for Do.	6
march 5	for Do.	6
		£2 16 7
1733		
april 2d	for absence 1s. and Quota 6d.	1 6
may 7	for Quota	6
June 4	for Do.	6
		£3 10 1
July 2	for Do.	6
augst. 6	for Do.	6
	this day moneys Pd. you for daybook &c.	15 0
Septr. 3	for Quota	6
29	for Quota	6
novembr. 5	for Do.	6
		3 17 7
Xbr.[December]3	for do.	6
[1733/4]		
Janry. 7	for do.	6
feb. 4	for do.	6
March 4	for do.	6
June 3	for do.	1 6
		4 1 1

Cr.

Date	Description	£ s d
1732/3		
march 5	By moneys paid	4 6
	By moneys Lent the Lodge for Wm. Pringle 5s.	5 0
		3 2 1
July 2d	By moneys for Quota	6
Augst. 6th	By Do.	6
novembr. 5th	By Do.	6
	Cr. by Day booke 13s.	3 3 7
Dec. 3	By Do.	13 0
		£3 16 7
[1733/4]		
Jan 7	By Do.	6
Mar 4	By Do.	6
1734	By Cash recd.	£3 18 1
	See new Accot in Folio.[4]	3
		£4 1 1

St. John's Lodge, Account—*Continued*

Date	Debit	£	s	d		Date	Credit	£	s	d
1735 June 2	To One Year's Stock	£		6		1734/5 March 5	By Cash recd. for 3 Qrly. Paymts.	£	4	6
1736 June 7	To Ditto			6		1735 Dec. 1	By Ditto for 2 Ditto			3
		£	12			1736 Apl. 6	By Ditto for 1 Ditto		1	6
1737 June 7	To Ditto	0	6	0		June 24	By Ditto for a payment due the last Year		1	6
Ditto	To the Lodge's gen'rall Accot of Expence		14	7		Do.	By Ditto in full to this Day		1	6
		£1	7					£	12	
1738 June 24	To One Year's Stock	£		6		1737 June 7	By Cash in full	£1		7

3. BF was initiated into St. John's Lodge of Masons in Philadelphia in February 1731. This account book shows that his attendance thereafter was regular: between July 5, 1731 and June 3, 1735, for example, he was present at 28 regular meetings and absent from only six. For each meeting he was charged sixpence as a contribution to the lodge's "stock" or treasury, and for his absences he was fined a shilling in addition. The accounts were kept by at least three different treasurers. They were balanced June 19, 1732, June 1734, and June 7, 1737. For a page in facsimile see Julius F. Sachse, *Benjamin Franklin as a Free Mason* (Phila., 1906), facing p. 34.

4. The accounts are continued on later pages of the volume.

Articles of Agreement with Thomas Whitmarsh[5]

Copy: Land Office, Department of Internal Affairs, Harrisburg, Pa.

[September 13, 1731]

ARTICLES of Agreement made and indented the Thirteenth Day of September Anno Domini one thousand seven hundred and thirty one Between Benjamin Franklin of Philadelphia in the Province of Pennsylvania Printer of the one Part and Thomas Whitemarsh of the same place Printer of the other Part, viz. WHEREAS the said Benjamin Franklin and Thomas Whitemarsh have determined to enter into a Copartnership for the carrying on of the Business of printing in Charlestown in South Carolina, It is hereby covenanted, granted, and agreed by and between the said Parties and each of them the said Benjamin and Thomas for himself, his Heirs, Executors, and Administrators, doth covenant, promise, and grant to and with the other and to and with the Heirs, Executors, and Administrators of the other of them in Manner following, To say, THAT they the said Benjamin Franklin and Thomas Whitemarsh shall be Partners in the said Business of Printing in Carolina for and during the Term of Six Years next ensuing the Day of the Arrival of the said Thomas in the Port of Charlestown aforesaid, if they the said Benjamin and Thomas shall so long live. THAT the said Benjamin Franklin shall be at the sole Charge and Expence of providing a printing Press with all its necessary Appurtenances together with four hundred weight of Letters (if the said Thomas shall think so great a Quantity necessary, and require it) and shall

5. Thomas Whitmarsh (d. 1733), "an excellent Workman," whom BF had known in London, was employed by BF as a journeyman, probably in 1729. He was made a Mason in St. John's Lodge, Philadelphia, July 5, 1731. In response to liberal inducements offered by the Assembly of South Carolina to a printer willing to open a shop in that colony, the two men formed a partnership in 1731. Whitmarsh's purchases of supplies, printed books, and almanacs are recorded in BF's Ledgers A and B (above, p. 172); this information is most readily available in George S. Eddy, *Account Books Kept by Benjamin Franklin* (N.Y., 1928), pp. 14–16. Whitmarsh printed the *South-Carolina Gazette* from Jan. 8, 1732, to Sept. 8, 1733; and died soon afterwards. BF made a similar agreement, Nov. 26, 1733, with another journeyman, Louis Timothée (see below, p. 339). Hennig Cohen, *The South Carolina Gazette, 1732–1775* (Columbia, S.C., 1953), pp. 230–3; Julius F. Sachse, *Old Masonic Lodges of Pennsylvania* (Phila., 1912), I, 44. Punctuation, almost entirely lacking in the manuscript, has been added.

cause the same to be transported at his own Risque to the said Town of Charlestown in South Carolina. THAT the Business of printing and disposing of the Work printed shall be under the Care, Management, and Direction of the said Thomas Whitemarsh and the working Part performed by him or at his Expence. THAT all Charges for Paper, Ink, Balls, Tympans, Wool, Oil, and other Things necessary to printing, together with the Charge of all common and necessary Repairs of the Press and its Appurtenances and also the Charge of Rent for a Shop and for so much Room as is necessary to be used in the Management of the Business aforesaid, shall be divided into three equal Parts of which two Parts shall be disbursed by and paid as due from the said Thomas Whitemarsh and the remaining Third Part shall be allowed to be paid as due from the said Benjamin Franklin and taken out of his Share of the Income next to be mentioned. THAT all Money received or to be received for printing or for any Thing done or to be done relating thereto by the said Thomas Whitemarsh either as Gratuity, Premium, Reward, or Salary from the Government or from others shall be divided into three equal Parts of which the said Thomas for his Care, Management, and Performance shall have two Parts and the said Benjamin Franklin shall have the remaining Third Part. THAT he the said Thomas Whitemarsh for that End and Purpose shall keep fair and exact Book of Accounts of and concerning all Work done and sold by him and all his Receipts and Disbursments relating to the Business of Printing in Copartnership aforesaid with the Day, Month and Year of each Entry and submit the same to the View of the said Benjamin Franklin, his lawful Attorney, Executors, or Administrators as often as there unto required. And the Accounts of the Copartners aforesaid shall be drawn out Fair, communicated to each other and settled once a Year during the Copartnership aforesaid or oftner if either of them require it. And that upon such Settlement the said Thomas Whitemarsh shall remitt the Part by this Agreement belonging to the said Benjamin Franklin in such Wares or Merchandizes or in Bills of Exchange or in Money as the said Benjamin shall direct by Letter or Order under his Hand and on Board such Vessel and to such Port as the said Benjamin shall also require by Letter or Order as aforesaid at the proper Risque of the said Benjamin. THAT the said Thomas Whitemarsh shall not during the Term of the Copartnership aforesaid work with any other printing Materials than those belonging to the said Benjamin Franklin nor follow any other Business but Printing during the said Term, occasional Merchandize excepted. THAT the Loss by bad Debts shall be divided and sustained by both Parties in the same Proportion as the Money ought to have been divided by this Agreement if it had been received. THAT neither of the said Parties shall reap any Benefit or Advantage by his Survivorship if the other of them shall depart this Life before the Expiration of the said Term of six Years as aforesaid, But that if the said Thomas Whitemarsh shall depart this Life before the Expiration of the said Term his Executors or Administrators shall within one Year after such Decease deliver up the Press, Tipes, and all the Materials of printing which have been provided by the said Benjamin Franklin or at his Charge to the said Benjamin, his Heirs, Executors, or lawful Attorney in good Order and good Condition (allowing the usual Ware and Decay of such Things) as also the share of Money, Effects, and Debts belonging to the said Benjamin by this Agreement which shall be in the Hands of the said Thomas Whitemarsh or due at his Decease. AND if the said Benjamin Franklin shall depart this Life before the Expiration of the Term of Copartnership aforesaid the said Thomas Whitemarsh shall continue the Business aforesaid, nevertheless paying and remitting the Part by this Agreement belonging to the said Benjamin Franklin unto the Heirs, Executors, Administrators, or Assigns of the said Benjamin or as they shall [direct?]. PROVIDED the Heirs or Assigns of the said Benjamin perform all Parts of this Agreement to the said Thomas which he the said Benjamin ought to have done had he lived. AND that at the Expiration of the Term of six Years aforesaid the said Thomas shall have the Right of purchasing the abovesaid Printing Press, Materials, and Types if he is so disposed at their first Value in Philadelphia allowing only what shall be judged a reasonable Abatement for the Wear of such Things in the Time they have been used. BUT if the said Thomas shall not be inclined to purchase them at that Price he shall transport or cause to be transported to and delivered at Philadelphia the said printing Press, Materials, and Types at his own proper Risque and Charges to the said Benjamin Franklin, his Heirs, Executors, Administrators, or Assigns. AND if any unusual Damage by bad Usuage, Accident, or Negligence have happened to them he the said

Thomas shall make it good. Provided nevertheless THAT if the first Printing Press, Materials, and Types which shall be sent by the said Benjamin Franklin to Carolina according to this Agreement mis-carry thro' the Dangers of the Sea the Copartnership hereby made shall be disolved and abolished unless the said Benjamin be willing to continue it and provide another Press and Types as aforesaid and send them at his own Risque as before, any Thing herein contained to the Contrary notwithstanding.

Sealed and Delivered   BENJAMIN FRANKLIN [Seal]
  in the Presence of us   THOMAS WHITMARSH [Seal]
  WM. MAUGRIDGE
  NICHOLAS CASSELL

MEMORANDUM the twenty fourth Day of November Ao. Di. One thousand seven hundred and thirty three before me, Edward Roberts Esquire, one of the Justices of the Peace for the City and County of Philadelphia, came William Maugridge and Nicholas Cassell both of the said City, Joiners; And upon their solemn Affirmations according to Law Did declare and say they were present and did see the within named Benjamin Franklin and Thomas Whitmarsh seal and as their respective Act and Deed deliver the within Writing indented, contained in the three preceeding Pages of this Sheet of Paper, And that the Names of them the said William Maugridge and Nicholas Cassell thereunto subscribed as Witnesses are of their these Affirmants own Hands writing respectively. WITNESS my Hand and Seal the Day and Year abovesaid.

EDWARD ROBERTS [L.S.]

RECORDED the 24th Day of November Ao. Di. 1733

Joseph Breintnall to Directors of Library Company

MS Minute Book: Library Company of Philadelphia

The Library Company of Philadelphia was Franklin's "first Project of a public Nature." He drafted its plan, rules, and articles of agreement; the latter were signed July 1, 1731, naming ten directors, a secretary, and a treasurer, and announcing that the Company would be organized when fifty subscriptions were obtained. With the help of the Junto, this took about four months. The secretary then prepared this call to meeting, and Franklin had copies delivered to all concerned.

[November 8, 1731]
The Minutes of me Joseph Breintnall Secretary to the Directors of the Library Company of Philadelphia, with such of the Minutes of the same Directors as they order me to make. Begun the 8th Day of November 1731. By Virtue of the Deed or Instrument of the said Company dated the first Day of July last.

The said Instrument being compleated by fifty Subscriptions I subscribed my Name to the following Summons or Notice, which Benjamin Franklin sent by a Messenger. Vizt.

To

Benjamin Franklin,	Thomas Hopkinson
William Parsons,	Philip Syng Junr.
Thomas Godfrey,	Anthony Nicholas
Thomas Cadwalader,	John Jones Junr.
Robert Grace and	Isaac Penington[6]

"Gentlemen,
"The Subscription to the Library being compleated You the Directors appointed in the Instrument are desired to meet this Eve-

6. William Parsons. See below, p. 359.
Thomas Godfrey. See above, p. 190.
Thomas Cadwalader (c.1707–1779), physician, apprenticed to Dr. Evan Jones, studied medicine in London. Later burgess of Trenton, N.J., physician to the Pennsylvania Hospital, trustee of the Academy, vice-president of the APS, member of the Philadelphia Common Council, member of the Provincial Council, author of *An Essay on the West-India Dry-Gripes*, printed by BF in 1745. *DAB*.

Robert Grace (1709–1766), an original member of the Junto, lent BF money to set up independently as a printer, proprietor of the Warwick Iron Works, where the Pennsylvania fireplaces were cast. Mrs. Thomas Potts James, *Memorial of Thomas Potts, Junior* (Cambridge, Mass., 1874), pp. 375–92.

Thomas Hopkinson (1709–1751), lawyer, member of the Junto, St. John's Lodge, and Union Fire Company. Later clerk of the Orphans Court, Master of the Rolls, Prothonotary of Philadelphia County, Judge of Vice-Admiralty, member of the Philadelphia Common Council, member of the Provincial Council, trustee of the Academy. Thomas H. Montgomery, *A History of the University of Pennsylvania* (Phila., 1900), pp. 100–2.

Philip Syng (1703–1789), silversmith, member of the Junto, St. John's Lodge, Union Fire Company, and the Fishing Company of the Colony in

209

ning at 5 o'Clock, at the House of Nicholas Scull to take Bond of the Treasurer for the faithfull Performance of his Trust, and to consider of, and appoint a proper Time for the Payment of the Money subscribed, and other Matters relating to the said Library.

Philada. 8 Novr. 1731   JOSEPH BREINTNALL, Secy."[7]

Miscellaneous Business Memoranda

MSS: American Philosophical Society

Volume 66 of the Franklin Papers in the American Philosophical Society contains approximately 250 miscellaneous business papers and memoranda. A few are undated; most bear dates between 1729 and 1768, but a few items are of an earlier or later year. They range from torn scraps the size of a playing card or even smaller to single or double sheets of quarto size; and are mounted in the volume on numbered pages in roughly chronological order. The individual papers are not indexed, but a typewritten list set into the volume indicates briefly the nature and date of each. Some of them, especially among those of the earliest years, have no connection with Franklin, but were accidentally mixed with his papers, probably when they were salvaged in 1778 from Joseph Galloway's house Trevose, where they had been stored. The earliest transaction recorded in this volume clearly concerning Franklin is dated 1731.

Over 90 per cent of the papers in Volume 66, however, are directly connected with Franklin's business transactions or those of members of his immediate family. They include statements of his printing and sta-

---

Schuylkill; engraved the seal of the Library Company. Later trustee of the Academy, treasurer of the APS, vestryman of Christ Church, warden and treasurer of Philadelphia. *DAB*.

Anthony Nicholas, or Nichols (d. 1751), blacksmith; built a fire engine and other equipment for Philadelphia, 1735. Harrold E. Gillingham, "Philadelphia's First Fire Defences," *PMHB*, LVI (1932), 362, 365.

John Jones, Jr., cordwainer.

Isaac Penington (1700–1742), a large property-owner in Bucks County. Later justice of Bucks County Court and sheriff of Bucks County. *DAB*, under "Edward Penington."

7. At the meeting the Directors decided to collect twenty-five of the pledges—40s. subscription and 10s. annual payment—at once; this was done by December 14. The remaining twenty-five were solicited after the New Year. With a capital fund of £100 and an annual income of £25, the Library was able to send its first book order to England, March 31, 1732. Austin K. Gray, *Benjamin Franklin's Library* (N.Y., 1937), pp. 8–9. The MS draft of the list of books ordered is in Pierpont Morgan Lib.

tionery accounts; receipts for payments; bills of exchange; promissory notes signed to or by him; stray pages of journal or ledger entries; notes requesting him to deliver books, other articles, or cash to the bearers; merchants' accounts with other men which Franklin settled and in turn credited to himself; and tradesmen's bills for goods and services of all sorts.

This last category is the largest and most representative. The bills show that among the articles supplied to Franklin or his dependents were cloth of various kinds (linen, calico, chintz, cambric, taffeta); mattresses, bolsters, and pillows; tea, both bohea and green; elixirs and bitters; chinaware; hats; paper and parchments; fish and oil; beer; and harness. There are bills to Franklin for such services as the alteration of gowns for Mrs. Franklin and their daughter Sarah; the stabling of his horse; and the repair of his carriage (a "Double chere") on a trip to Boston. Bills from London shopkeepers after 1757 show brass casters for a chair; a shovel, tongs, and coal for Franklin's fire; butter, cream, and spices for his table; steel spindles for his armonica; leather breeches; spectacles; candles; Madeira wine; books; and a variety of articles to send home to his wife and daughter in Philadelphia or to his sister Jane Mecom in Boston.

The papers in Volume 66 do not comprise all the documents of these several varieties that have survived. Others are scattered among the Franklin Papers in the American Philosophical Society, in other collections, and in private possession. A large proportion of the whole are too inconsequential to print in this edition. Those which shed useful light on significant figures or events in Franklin's career will be presented, in full or in abstract, at the appropriate places in the text or footnotes in this and later volumes.

Petition to the Pennsylvania Assembly regarding Fairs[8]

Draft: Historical Society of Pennsylvania

[1731]

To the Honourable House of Representatives of the Province of Pennsylvania

The Petition of divers Inhabitants of the City of Philadelphia Humbly sheweth

That the Fairs which are held in this City twice a Year are of very small Benefit to the Inhabitants the Wares therein sold being

8. Probably suggested by a letter BF printed in *Pa. Gaz.*, Nov. 27, 1731, but it seems not to have been presented to the Assembly.

either such as may be bought at any other Time, or else insignificant Toys and Trifles; and if any Business be then done between People of the Country and of the Town, it is very little, and might as well be done if there were no Fair.

That the said Fairs are the Occasion of much Disturbance in the City; by such a Concourse of rude People many of them intoxicated with strong Liquors, and becoming quarrelsome or mischievous.

That they tend to corrupt the Morals, and destroy the Innocence of our Youth; who are at such Times induc'd to Drinking and Gaming, in mix'd Companies of vicious Servants and Negroes.

That Servants who by Custom think they have a Right to Liberty of going out at those Times, commonly disorder themselves so as to be unfit for Business in some Time after; and what is worse, having perhaps done some Mischief in their Liquor, and afraid of Correction, or getting among ill Companions, they combine to run away more than at any other Time.

That the said Fairs give great Opportunity and Encouragement to Thieving and Pilfering, People not being able effectually to watch their Goods in the Hurry of the Fair; and the Thief by mixing immediately with the Croud, has a greater Advantage of escaping with his Booty.

That the Riot and Confusion of the Rabble after Night gives great Offence to all sober People; and frequently Windows are broke and other Mischief done, no Body knowing by whom; and 'tis apprehended that all these Disorders will increase as the City grows more Populous.

Your Petitioners therefore Pray, that, the said Fairs may either be thoroughly regulated in such Manner as to the Wisdom of this House shall seem meet, or else totally abolished and Your Petitioners shall ever pray &c.

Doctrine to be Preached   Draft: Library of Congress

"From time to time," Franklin wrote in his autobiography, he put down "on Pieces of Paper such Thoughts as occur'd" to him respecting his proposed United Party for Virtue. In 1788 he found one of these slips, containing, he thought, a statement of "the Essentials of every known Religion, and . . . free of every thing that might shock the Professors of any Religion." What follows here may have been another of those "Pieces of Paper," an earlier and fuller draft of the "Essentials" of his creed. At least the substance and penmanship of the notes belong to Franklin's earlier years.

[1731]

Doct. to be prea[che]d

That there is one God Father of the Universe.

That he [is] infinitely good, Powerful and wise.

That he is omnipresent.

That he ought to be worshipped, by Adoration Prayer and Thanksgiving both in publick and private.

That he loves such of his Creatures as love and do good to others: and will reward them either in this World or hereafter.

That Men's Minds do not die with their Bodies, but are made more happy or miserable after this Life according to their Actions.

That Virtuous Men ought to league together to strengthen the Interest of Virtue, in the World: and so strengthen themselves in Virtue.

That Knowledge and Learning is to be cultivated, and Ignnorance dissipated.

That none but the Virtuous are wise.

That Man's Perfection is in Virtue.   [*Remainder lost*]

Extracts from the Gazette, 1731

Printed in *The Pennsylvania Gazette*, January 5 to December 28, 1731.

In our last we gave our Readers an Account of the Number of Burials in this City for a Year past, by comparing which with the Number of Burials of one Year in Boston, Berlin, Colln, Amsterdam and London, (*See our Gazette* No. 64, 77, 78.) a pretty near Judgment may be made of the different Proportions of People in each City. In this Paper we exhibit an Account for one Year, of all the Vessels entered and cleared, from and to what Places, in the Ports of Philadelphia, Amboy, New-York, Rhode-Island, Boston, Salem and New-Hampshire, by which the ingenious Reader may make some Judgment of the different Share each Colony possesses of the several Branches of Trade. At the End we have subjoined an

213

Extract from a new Piece, entituled, *The Trade and Navigation of Great Britain considered,* &c. written by Mr. Joshua Gee,[9] and by him presented within this 12 Month to the King, Queen, Prince, Lords of Trade, and every Member of Parliament; by which the Reader may be informed what Commodities the several Colonies Trade in.

N.B. *Some Vessels enter several Times in a Year.*[1]   [January 5]

Those Subscribers for this Paper, who live on the Post Road to York, and at York, and have taken it a Twelvemonth, are desired to pay in their respective Yearly Payments at those Places where they usually receive their News, that the Money may be transmitted to us by the Post.   [January 12]

The Practice of Inoculation for the Small-Pox, begins to grow among us. J. Growdon, Esq; the first Patient of Note that led the Way, is now upon the Recovery, having had none but the most favourable Symptoms during the whole Course of the Distemper; which is mentioned to show how groundless all those extravagant Reports are, that have been spread through the Province to the contrary. *For an Account of the Method and Usefulness of Inoculation, see our Gazette,* No. 80.[2]   [March 4]

The Country may depend upon it, that there are not more Burials in a Week in this City than we give an Account of.   [March 4]

9. Joshua Gee, English merchant, writer on economics, mortgagee of Pennsylvania, 1708–29, participant in the Principio Iron Works in Maryland, a sort of agent for Pennsylvania in England. The famous treatise from which BF reprinted an extract was first published in 1729. Mabel P. Wolff, *The Colonial Agency of Pennsylvania, 1712–1757* (Phila., 1933), pp. 3–35.

1. A table followed this paragraph. It is condensed herewith:

Port	Dates	Entered In	Cleared Out
Philadelphia	Dec. 4, 1729–Dec. 3, 1730	161	171
Perth Amboy	Dec. 3, 1729–Dec. 2, 1730	39	44
New York	Dec. 1, 1729–Dec. 5, 1730	211	222
Rhode Island	Dec. 1, 1729–Dec. 3, 1730	126	108
Boston	Dec. 1, 1729–Dec. 5, 1730	533	629
New Hampshire	Dec. 1, 1729–Dec. 3, 1730	102	124

2. The *Gazette*, May 28, 1730, printed an account of inoculation from Ephraim Chambers, *Cyclopædia; or, an Universal Dictionary of Arts and Sciences,* II (1728), 390–1.

From Maryland we hear, That Subscriptions have been lately made among the Gentlemen there, for encouraging the Manufacture of Linen: The Mayor and Common Council of Annapolis, have promised to pay as a Reward the Sum of *Five Pounds* to the Person that brings the finest Piece of Linen, of the Growth and Manufacture of Maryland, to next September Fair; for the second Piece in Fineness *Three Pounds,* and for the third, *Forty Shillings;* the Linen to continue the Property of the Maker. Like Rewards are offered in Baltimore County, and 'tis thought the Example will be followed by all the Counties in Maryland. [April 15]

At a Petty Sessions of the Peace, held for the County of Burlington, at Burlington the 16th Day of April, 1731. it was consider'd that FAIRS generally occasion great Concourse of People from the most adjacent Places, and that at present it is not meet for keeping the FAIR at Burlington as usual, by reason of the great Mortality in Philadelphia, and other Parts of Pennsylvania, where the Small-Pox now violently rages: Therefore, to prevent to the utmost Power of the said Justices, the further spreading of so epidemical and dangerous a Distemper, and more especially for that the approaching Heat of Summer may render it more malignant and fatal, It is Order'd, that MAY FAIR next, be, and is hereby prohibited to be kept in the said Town of Burlington; and all Persons are hereby to take Notice accordingly, as they will answer for their Contempt at their Perils. [April 22]

Ferdinando John Paris, Esq; was, at the last Sitting of our Assembly, chosen Agent for this Province at the Court of Great Britain. [April 29]

The new Settlement going forward at Cape Fear, having for these 3 or 4 Years past, been the Subject of much Discourse, especially among Country People; and great Numbers resorting thither continually, from this and the neighbouring Provinces, meerly to view the Place and learn the Nature of the Country, that they may be capable of judging whether it will probably be an advantageous Exchange if they should remove and settle there; and none having at their Return published their Observations for the Information of others; The following *Account of Cape Fear,* (extracted from the private Letters of a judicious and impartial Person, who lately resided there some Time, and who had not the least Interest that might induce him either to commend or discommend the Country beyond strict Truth,) it is thought will not be unacceptable to a great Part of our Readers.[3]   [May 6]

TO-MORROW WILL BE PUBLISH'D, The Votes of the House of Representatives of this Province at their last Session. Containing, the CHARGE brought by the Managers against Mr. Fishbourn late Trustee of the General Loan-Office, with his Answer and Defence at large, and the Proceedings of the House thereupon: The Petition of the Wardens and Vestry of Christ-Church, in which they lay Claim to the Baptist Meeting-house in Philadelphia; with the Remonstrance of the Baptists in Answer thereunto at large: The Proceedings relating to the Brewing-Bill, and several other very curious Things. Sold by B. Franklin, Price 2s. 6d.
[May 27]

All Persons indebted to Benj. Franklin, Printer of this Paper, are desired to send in their respective Payments: (Those Subscribers for the News excepted, from whom a Twelvemonth's Pay is not yet due.)

Gentlemen, It is but a little to each of you, though it will be a considerable Sum to me; and lying in many Hands wide from each other, (according to the Nature of our Business) it is highly inconvenient and scarce practicable for me to call upon every one; I shall therefore think myself particularly obliged, and take it very kind of those, who are mindful to send or bring it in without farther Notice.   [June 10]

From Newcastle we hear, that on Tuesday the 8th Instant, the Lightning fell upon a House within a few Miles of that Place, in which it killed 3 Dogs, struck several Persons deaf, and split a Woman's Nose in a surprizing Manner.   [June 17]

3. The Account of North Carolina thus introduced and concluded in the issue of May 13, was by BF's former partner, Hugh Meredith. Of it BF wrote in his autobiography that it was "the best Account that had been given of that Country . . . and they gave grate [sic] Satisfaction to the Publick."

Friday Night last, a certain St-n-c-tt-r was, it seems, in a fair way of dying the Death of a Nobleman; for being caught Napping with another Man's Wife, the injur'd Husband took the Advantage of his being fast asleep, and with a Knife began very diligently to cut off his Head. But the Instrument not being equal to the intended Operation, much struggling prevented Success; and he was oblig'd to content himself for the present with bestowing on the Aggressor a sound Drubbing. The Gap made in the Side of the St-n-c-tt-r's Neck, tho' deep, is not thought dangerous; but some People admire, that when the Person offended had so fair and suitable an Opportunity, it did not enter into his Head to turn St-n-c-tt-r himself.   [June 17]

Sure some unauspicious cross-grain'd Planet, in Opposition to Venus, presides over the Affairs of Love about this Time. For we hear, that on Tuesday last, a certain C-n-table having made an Agreement with a neighbouring Female, to *Watch* with her that Night; she promised to leave a Window open for him to come in at; but he going his Rounds in the dark, unluckily mistook the Window, and got into a Room where another Woman was in bed, and her Husband it seems lying on a Couch not far distant. The good Woman perceiving presently by the extraordinary Fondness of her Bedfellow that it could not possibly be her Husband, made so much Disturbance as to wake the good Man; who finding somebody had got into his Place without his Leave, began to lay about him unmercifully; and 'twas thought, that had not our poor mistaken Galant, call'd out manfully for Help (as if he were commanding Assistance in the King's Name) and thereby raised the Family, he would have stood no more Chance for his Life between the Wife and Husband, than a captive L---- between two Thumb Nails.   [June 24]

The Small-pox has now quite left this City. The Number of those that died here of that Distemper, is exactly 288, and no more. 64 of the Number were Negroes; If these may be valued one with another at £30 per Head, the Loss to the City in that Article is near £2000.   [July 8]

[ADVERTISEMENT] ALEPPO INK, For the true staining Black, equal to any Sort of Ink whatever; and far exceeding all other

Sorts in the Lastingness of its Colour: So that no Ink is so proper as this for Records, Deeds, and other Writings which ought to endure. Sold at the New Printing-Office, Price 1s. *per* Bottle. Where also you may have good common Ink. [July 8]

[ADVERTISEMENT] Whereas by an Act of Parliament made in the Ninth Year of the Reign of her late Majesty Queen ANNE, entituled *An Act for establishing a General Post-Office for all her Majesty's Dominions,* &c. it is among other Things enacted, That all Masters of Vessels, Sailors and Passengers, shall immediately upon their Arrival in any Port, deliver the Letters and Pacquets on board to the Post-Master, or his Deputy, under the Penalty of *Five Pounds, British Money,* for every several Offence.

And whereas by the same Act it is also Enacted, That if any Master, Sailor or Passenger on board any Boat or Vessel, passing or repassing, on any River or Rivers, in any of her Majesty's Dominions, shall or do collect, carry or deliver any Letters or Pacquets, he or they shall forfeit and pay *Five Pounds,* British Money, for every several Offence, *One Hundred Pounds* of like British Money, for every Week he or they shall continue to carry or deliver any Letters or Pacquets, as aforesaid.

This is therefore to give Notice to all Masters of Vessels, Sailors, Passengers, and others whom it may concern, That they be careful not to offend against the aforesaid Act of Parliament, upon Pain of being prosecuted for the several Penalties therein mentioned, pursuant to the Orders and Instructions of his Majesty's Post-Master General, to the Post-Master of Philadelphia. [July 15]

[ADVERTISEMENT] Good Writing-Parchment. Sold by the Printer hereof, very reasonable. [July 15]

[ADVERTISEMENT] Whereas one John Emmery, by Trade a Cabinet-maker, went from England in the Year 1725 to the West Indies, and from thence to some of the Northern Colonies: This is to inform him, if he be living, that he may apply to the Printer of this Paper, and be informed of something to his Advantage. [July 15]

We are credibly inform'd, that the young Woman who not long since petitioned the Governor, and the Assembly to be divorced from her Husband, and at times industriously solicited most of the Magistrates on that Account, has at last concluded to cohabit with him again. It is said the Report of the Physicians (who in Form examined his *Abilities,* and allowed him to be in every respect *sufficient,*) gave her but small Satisfaction; Whether any Experiments *more satisfactory* have been try'd, we cannot say; but it seems she now declares it as her Opinion, That *George is as good as de best.* [July 29]

[ADVERTISEMENT] The Widow Read, removed from the upper End of Highstreet to the New Printing-Office near the Market, continues to make and sell her well-known Ointment for the ITCH, with which she has cured abundance of People in and about this City for many Years past. It is always effectual for that purpose, and never fails to perform the Cure speedily. It also kills or drives away all Sorts of Lice in once or twice using. It has no offensive Smell, but rather a pleasant one; and may be used without the least Apprehension of Danger, even to a sucking Infant, being perfectly innocent and safe. Price 2s. a Gallypot containing an Ounce; which is sufficient to remove the most inveterate Itch, and render the Skin clear and smooth.

She also continues to make and sell her excellent *Family Salve* or Ointment, for Burns or Scalds, (Price 1s. an Ounce) and several other Sorts of Ointments and Salves as usual.

At the same Place may be had *Lockyer's Pills,* at 3d. a Pill. [August 19]

Thursday last, a certain P——r ['tis not customary to give Names at length on these Occasions] walking carefully in clean Cloaths over some Barrels of Tar on Carpenter's Wharff, the head of one of them unluckily gave way, and let a Leg of him in above his Knee. Whether he was upon the Catch at that time, we cannot say, but 'tis certain he caught a *Tartar.* 'Twas observ'd he sprung out again right briskly, verifying the common Saying, *As nimble as a Bee in a Tarbarrel.* You must know there are several sorts of *Bees:* 'tis true he was no *Honey Bee,* nor yet a *Humble Bee,* but a *Boo bee* he may be allow'd to be, namely *B.F.*

N.B. *We hope the Gentleman will excuse this Freedom.*
[September 23]

We hear from Hopewell in the Jerseys, that on the 4th past, two Bucks were observed fighting near the new Meeting House there; one of them extraordinary large, supposed to be a Roe-Buck; the other small and of the common sort. In company with them was a black Doe, who stood by to see the Engagement. The small Buck proved a full match for the great one, giving him many violent Punches in the Ribs, but in the height of the Battle, they fastned their Horns so strongly together, that they were not able with all their Strength to disengage; and in that condition they were taken. The Doe retreated into the Woods, but being pursued with several Beagle Hounds, she was taken also alive, and they have put her and the large Buck into a boarded Pasture together, in hopes to have a Breed, if the Sizes are not too unsuitable. This is the second Brace of Bucks that have been caught by the Horns this Fall. *Had they not better put 'em up quietly in their Pockets?*   [October 14]

[ADVERTISEMENT] This is to give Notice, that Mr. Louis Timothee, Master of the FRENCH TONGUE, hath settled himself with his Family in this City, in order to keep a publick *French School;* he will also, if required, teach the said Language to any young Gentlemen or Ladies, at their Lodgings. He dwelleth in Front Street, next door to Dr. Kearsley.[4]   [October 14]

***The Second Year is expired since we undertook this Paper: Those Persons who are indebted on that account, are desired to send in their respective Payments.   [October 14]

[ADVERTISEMENT] Lost on Tuesday Night last, on the Road between Marcus Hook and Chester, a Pocket Book with 30*s.* Money, and some Notes. The Finder is desired to leave the Book and Notes with the Printer hereof, and take the Money for his Pains.   [October 21]

[ADVERTISEMENT] A Likely Servant Lad's Time for near Seven Years, to be disposed of; He is fit for Town or Country Business. Enquire of the Printer hereof.   [October 21]

We hear from Cecil County in Maryland, That the Rev. Mr. Ormston, Minister of the Church there, is lately dead. His Man left him in good Health sitting by the Fire, while he went to a Neigh-

4. See below, p. 230.

bour's House; but at his Return, found him lying upon the Hearth, his Pipe by his Side, and his Head burnt off in the Fire. He was formerly Minister of the Church in this City.   [November 18]

JUST PUBLISH'D, The Votes of the Honourable House of Representatives of this Province, in their Three last Sessions. Printed by B. Franklin, and sold either separately or together.

[December 14]

[ADVERTISEMENT] Choice English Quills, just imported, Sold by the Printer hereof. Of whom may be had, Jerman's Almanacks for 1732, and Godfrey's Almanacks, either on large Sheets or in Books, at 3s. 6d. per Dozen.   [December 28]

PHILADELPHIA: Printed by B. FRANKLIN and H. MEREDITH, at the *New Printing-Office* near the Market, where Advertisements are taken in, and all Persons may be supplied with this Paper, at *Ten Shillings* a Year.

Query to the Casuist: The Case of the Missing Horse

Printed in *The Pennsylvania Gazette*, January 18, 1731/2.

To the Printer of the *Gazette*.

In one of your Papers about two Years since, there was an Account of a Horse which by Mistake was shot in a Field in the Night, by a Man who lay watching for Deer. The Account was accompanied with a Query, Whether the Man ought to pay for the Horse, since it was by Misadventure, and the Horse a Trespasser? The Query, I remember, was answered the Week following, very much to my Satisfaction, by one that stil'd himself *The Casuist*.[5] If Mr. Casuist be yet in being, I would by your means communicate to him another *Query* about a Horse; on which I should be glad to have his Opinion. The Case is this: A Man bargained with another, for the Keeping of his Horse six Months, while he made a Voyage to Barbadoes. At his Return, he demands the Horse. The Man who had him to keep, assures the Owner, that his Horse stray'd away, or was stolen, within a few Days after he receiv'd him, and that he has not heard of him since. The Owner then demands the Value of

5. See above, p. 163.

his Horse in Money. *Query,* Whether the Man who took the Horse to keep, may not justly demand a Deduction of so much as the Keeping of the Horse would have amounted to for Six Months, according to the Agreement?   T. P.

From the Casuist: The Case of the Missing Horse

Printed in *The Pennsylvania Gazette,* January 25, 1731/2; also draft: Historical Society of Pennsylvania.[6]

To the Query, propos'd to the Casuist in the last Gazette, I have received two Answers, from different Hands, each of which subscribes himself The Casuist. *As their Opinions are different, 'twill perhaps be more satisfactory to the Querist if I insert them both.*

To the Printer of the *Gazette.*

My Opinion, which is desired by T.P. on his Query in your last Week's Paper, I here send to you.

The Keeper, being accountable for the Value of the Horse, at the end of Six Months, to his Owner, should then ask him if he's willing to sell the Horse, and for what Price. The Owner setting a reasonable Price, may thereout deduct his Charge for Keeping (according to Agreement) and pay the remaining Sum to the Owner in Money.

This I think will be just in so plain a Case. But as the Owner's Consent to the Selling of his Horse, is requisite, and as it may happen he will refuse, and the Case may be attended with other Circumstances; to wit, in the Opinion of the Keeper the Owner sets too great a Price, and will not, when he is told of the Misfortune of the Horse's being stray'd or stolen away, make a moderate Abatement; Or, at first he answers he is not willing to part with his Horse: And, in the Opinion of the Owner, the Keeper has not duly regarded the Performance of his Bargain, has carelessly suffered the Horse to stray or be stolen, or does conceal him in order to purchase him at an under Rate. The Case being thus, I would advise the Parties to refer the Decision of it to two or more honest Men, indifferently chosen between them. Yours,

THE CASUIST

6. The surviving draft, in BF's hand, is of the second letter only. The authorship of the first and third replies is uncertain.

To the Printer of the *Gazette*.

According to the Request of your Correspondent, T.P. I send you my Thoughts on the following Case, by him proposed, viz.

A Man bargained with another, for the Keeping of his Horse six Months, while he made a Voyage to Barbadoes. At his Return, he demands the Horse. The Man who had him to keep, assures the Owner, that his Horse stray'd away, or was stolen, within a few Days after he receiv'd him, and that he has not heard of him since. The Owner then demands the Value of his Horse in Money. Query, *Whether the Man who took the Horse to keep, may not justly demand a Deduction of so much as the Keeping of the Horse would have amounted to for six Months, according to the Agreement?*

It does not appear they had any Dispute about the Value of the Horse, whence we may conclude there was no room for such Dispute, it being well known how much he cost, and that he could not honestly have been sold again for more.

But the Value of the Horse is not express'd in the Case, nor the Sum agreed for keeping him six Months; wherefore in order to our more clear Apprehension of the Thing, let *Ten Pounds* represent the Horse's Value, and *Three Pounds* the Sum agreed for his Keeping.

Now the sole Foundation on which the Keeper can ground his Demand of a Deduction, for Keeping a Horse he did not keep, is this; *Your Horse,* he may say, *which I was to restore to you at the end of 6 Months, was worth* Ten Pounds; *If I now give you* Ten Pounds, *'tis an equivalent for your Horse, and equal to returning the Horse itself: Had I return'd your Horse,* (value £10) *you would have paid me £3 for his Keeping, and therefore would have receiv'd in Fact but £7 clear; you then suffer no Injury if I now pay you £7; and consequently you ought in Reason to allow me the remaining £3 according to our Agreement.*

But the Owner of the Horse may possibly insist upon being paid the whole Sum of Ten Pounds, without allowing any Deduction for his Keeping after he was lost; and that for these Reasons.

1. Unless an express Agreement be made to the contrary, 'tis always suppos'd when Horses are put out to keep, that the Keeper runs the Risque of them, (unavoidable Accidents only excepted, wherein no Care of the Keeper can be supposed sufficient to preserve them, such as their being slain by Lightning, swept away by

sudden Floods, or the like). *This you yourself tacitly allow, when you offer to restore me the Value of my Horse.* Were it otherwise, People, having no Security against a Keeper's Neglect or Mismanagement, would never put Horses out to keep.

2. Keepers, considering the Risque they run, always demand such a Price for keeping Horses, that if they were to follow that Business continually, they may have a living Profit, tho' they now and then pay for a Horse they have lost. And if they were to be at no Risque, they could afford to keep Horses for less than they usually have: So that what a Man pays more for his Horse's Keeping, than the Keeper could afford to take if he ran no Risque, is in the Nature of a Præmium for the Insurance of his Horse. *If I then pay you for the few Days you kept my Horse, you ought to restore me his full Value.*

3. *You acknowledge that my Horse eat of your Hay and Oats but a few Days, 'tis unjust then to charge me for all the Hay and Oats that he* only might have eat if you had kept him, *in the Remainder of the 6 Months, and which you have now good in your Stable.* If, as the Proverb says, 'tis unreasonable to expect a Horse should void Oats, who never eat any; 'tis certainly as unreasonable to expect Payment for those Oats.

4. If Men in such Cases as this, are to be paid for keeping Horses when they were not kept; then they have a great Opportunity of wronging the Owners of Horses: *For, by privately selling my Horse for his Value £10 soon after you had him in Possession, and returning me only £7 at the Expiration of the Time, demanding £3 as a Deduction agreed for his Keeping; you get that £3 clear into your Pocket; beside the Use of my Money 6 Months for nothing.*

5. But, you say, *the Value of my Horse being £10 if you deduct £3 for his Keeping, and return me £7 'tis all I would in fact have receiv'd, had you return'd my Horse; therefore, as I am no Loser, I ought to be satisfied.* This Argument, were there any weight in it, might equally serve to justify a Man in selling, as abovesaid, as many of the Horses he takes to keep, as he conveniently can, putting clear into his own Purse, all that Charge their Owners must have been at for their Keeping, and returning the rest; for this being no Loss to the Owners, he may say, *Where no Man is a Loser, Why may not I be a Gainer?* I need only answer to this, That I allow the Horse cost me but £10 nor could I have sold him for more, had I been dispos'd

to part with him; but this can be no Reason why you should buy him of me at that Price, whether I will sell him or not. 'Tis plain I valued him at £13 otherwise I should not have paid £10 for him, and agreed to give you £3 more for his Keeping till I had Occasion to use him. Thus, tho' you pay me the whole £10 which he cost me (deducting only for his Keeping those few Days) I am still a Loser; I lose the Charge of those Days Keeping, I lose the £3 at which I valued him above what he cost me, and I lose the Advantage I might have made of my Money in 6 Months, either by the Interest, or by joining it to my Stock in Trade in my Voyage to Barbadoes. And all this I lose by your Negligence.

6. And lastly, Whenever a Horse is put to keep, the Agreement naturally runs thus: The Keeper says, *I will feed your Horse 6 Months on good Hay and Oats, if at the End of that Time you will pay me £3.* The Owner says, *If you will feed my Horse 6 Months on good Hay and Oats, I will give you £3 at the End of that Time.* Now we may plainly see, the Keeper's Performance of his Part of the Agreement must be antecedent to that of the Owner; and the Agreement being wholly conditional, the Owner's Part is not in Force till the Keeper has performed his. *You then, not having fed my Horse 6 Months, as you agreed to do, there lies no Obligation on me to pay you for 6 Months Feeding.*

Thus we have heard what can be said on both sides. Upon the whole, I am of Opinion, that no Deduction should be allow'd for the Keeping of the Horse after the Time of his straying. I am Yours, &c.   THE CASUIST

Since the Above, I have also receiv'd the Following.

To the Printer of the Pennsylvania *Gazette.*

Altho' I am not Mr. Casuist, I have presumed to send the following Answer to the Query in your last Week's Paper.

The Loss of the Horse, naturally implies a Neglect of the Keeper; and there is no Reason the Owner should suffer by any Act of the Keeper, either in the Price of the Horse, or Expence of seeking after him. And forasmuch as the Keeper hath fallen short in the Performance of his Contract, he not only doth not deserve any Reward, but hath forfeited the Penalty of the Bargain, if there were any Penalty annexed to it. But it is quite otherwise with the

Owner; for the Performance on his Part, is subsequent to that of the Keeper; nor can he be said to fail till the other hath performed, which he hath put out of his Power ever to do. Therefore he ought to have Satisfaction for no more than the Time he had the Horse in Keeping. Yours, &c.   N.B.

The Palatines' Appeal[7]

Printed in *The Pennsylvania Gazette*, February 15, 1731/2.

Being desired the Week before last, to render into good English an imperfect Translation of the Letter from some Palatines to the Rev. Mr. Weys,[8] I took the Pains to alter the Form of it entirely, and put it in the most advantageous Dress I could, with a View of inserting it afterwards in my *Gazette:* But before the Time of Publishing, the Gentleman from whom I had the Letter, let me know, that there being some Reflections therein upon the Captain, which perhaps were too much aggravated, and he not here to answer any thing in his own vindication, it might be better not to print it till we should be further informed, and allowed me only to make a short Abstract, giving an Account what Distress the poor People had been in, without mentioning the Captain at all. This I did; but was surpriz'd upon sight of Mr. Bradford's next Paper, to find my Version inserted there at length, Word for Word, (excepting a few typographical Errors and his affixing a Date to it whereas there was none in the Original.) It seems some Person, to whom a Copy had been lent, carried it to him. I was displeas'd that I had taken so much pains for my Competitor, and my Subscribers are displeased that I did not in my Paper give as full an Account

7. BF's translation of a letter to the Rev. Mr. George Michael Weiss from some German immigrants who, after an agonizing passage of 24 weeks in *Love and Unity*, Capt. Jacob Lobb, came ashore at Martha's Vineyard.

8. George Michael Weiss (1700–1761), pastor of the German Reformed church in Philadelphia, 1727–32; at Rhinebeck, Dutchess Co., N.Y., 1732–46, and at Goshenhoppen and Great Swamp in Pennsylvania, after 1746. A Presbyterian colleague in the ministry spoke of him as "a bright young man and a fine scholar," who spoke Latin as readily as German. Henry Harbaugh, *The Fathers of The German Reformed Church in Europe and America* (Lancaster, Pa., 1857), I, 265–74; Joseph H. Dubbs, *The Reformed Church in Pennsylvania* (Lancaster, Pa., 1902), pp. 83–90.

as he gave: I have therefore now made a new Version of the Letter, containing some Particulars omitted in the former, and more agreeable to the rude Simplicity of Language and Incoherence of Narrative in the Original. From which the Reader may perhaps be able to make a better Judgment of the Affair than before.[9]

Dear Mr. Weys,

We your poor and abandon'd Sheep, who have no Relief or Assistance to expect of any Body, turn our selves to you as our faithful Pastor, and beseech you to take part of our deplorable Condition, and to represent it to the Spiritual and Temporal Powers in Philadelphia: For this wicked Murderer of Souls, Capt. Labb, has thought to starve us all, (not have taken enough Provision in Rotterdam according to our Agreement) and to make himself Master of all our Goods; for we have seen in the last eight Weeks no Bread at all, and in four of these eight Weeks, a pint of Grouts was the Allowance of Five Persons one Day, and a Quart of Water a Person one Day. Our Time from Rotterdam to the Land here at Homes Hole Marthas Vineyard 16 hours from Rhode-island, has been four and twenty Weeks, and of 150 Persons, more than 100 are died and perished. And the Ship went on only in the Day-time, and Nights commonly the Helm was tied, and twice we awaked them, and asking them why they did not sail, and the Wind was so good; then they loosed the Sails, and went away. And in these last eight Weeks, the Hunger was so great, that we have eat Rats and Mice, so that one Rat cost eight pence, and two Shillings; and a Mouse three pence and four pence, and a Quart of Water four pence, that some of us let others have for their Childrens sake. When it was a little stormy Weather, the whole Voyage from Rotterdam, they did not give us in two and three Days no Victuals, and these last eight Weeks no Water too;

9. This version is longer, more detailed, and more moving than that which Andrew Bradford printed in *American Weekly Mercury*, Feb. 8, 1732, as "Extract and Translation of a Letter from some Palatines . . . dated December 23, 1731." Compare, for example, the passage beginning "so that in one Night seven Persons . . . "with BF's first rendering: "Seven Persons died of Hunger and Thirst in one Night and were thrown naked into the Sea without any thing to sink them, nor durst we ask any thing of the Sailors because upon the least Occasion we were beat and kickt and used like Slaves or Malifactors."

227

so that in one Night seven Persons miserably are starved to Death and thrown into the Sea; one must throw the poor People naked into the Sea, and let them swim, and one could not have a little Sand to sink the Body to the Ground; one dare not ask any thing from the Sailors, for they sent us back with Scolding and Railing, and we were kicked, beat and used as if we were Slaves and maleficent Persons. In this Time, we thought to refresh our selves with our Rhenish Wine, which was about six Awms that we had bought at Worms for our Money got with hard Labour; we would distribute it amongst the People, that they might not all be starved; and we went together to the Captain, and desired that he would give it us out; at last he gave us the Key to the Hold in a great Passion, but sent no body with to show where they had put the Wine: When we had searched a great while, we found some of our Casks, the Bungs drawn out with a Skrew, and the Wine all drunk up. And when we asked the Sailors what they had done with our Wine, we received Scolding and Railing for all Answer. Misery was so great: And we desired the Captain oftentimes to put us on Land, that we might buy us some more Provision; then he has put us off from day to day eight Weeks long. Till at last it pleased Almighty God to send us a Sloop, which brought us to Homes Hole, Marthas Vineyard, where he came to Anchor in the middle of the Sea: He kept us there in the Ship still five or six Days, and we must pay dear for every thing, so that one Loaf of Indian Corn Bread cost 8 Shillings; and he gave out of us, that we were Turks and no Christians: In that time starved yet fifteen Persons more, and if we had been kept there three or four Days longer, we should all have been starved, for not one was able to reach to the other a Drop of Water. And then we were put in a great Hurry in the Sloop, and set on shore, without our Beds, or any thing of our Moveables; so that we did not know what he intended to do with us, nor if we should ever see any thing again of our Moveables; which makes us suffer much, for there are but few Houses, so that we can have no Accommodation, because of the narrowness of the Place. The good People of this Island did whatever they could to refresh us with Bread, Meat and other Victuals. And the Sailors carried away most all our Moveables, and all our Chests broke open and spoliated. They have persuaded us, for dead and living, to pay the whole Freight, as if they had landed us at Philadelphia;

and which we have sign'd to, not understanding what it was; but we are not able to accomplish; for in order to pay for the dead, we should have taken the Goods of the Dead; but in discharging the Vessel we found, that most of their Chests as well as ours were broke open and plundered. The Captain however has obtained that we should pay him in 3 Weeks time, therefore we desire you instantly to have Compassion with us, and to assist us as much as in your Power, and to represent our pitiful State to the Governour; for if no Resistance be made to this wicked Captain, he'll make us all Beggars. What shall be our Duty for your pains, we shall thankfully repay. God Almighty have Mercy upon us, and help us out of this Distress. We would have sent two or three Men with this Letter, but not one is yet able to stir; for we are all very weak and feeble; but assoon as there shall be two or three able to travel, they shall follow: But if the cold Weather should fall in, and hinder them, we desire you to go on in our Name, and recommending you to the Protection of the Almighty we are

JOHANNES GOHR, JACOB DIEFFEBACH, JONAS DANER, JACOB KUNTZ, SAMUEL SCHWACHHAMER[1]

To Library Company Subscribers

MS Minute Book: Library Company of Philadelphia

March 25th 1732.
THE Directors, in Town, met with the Treasurer and Secretary at Nicholas Scull's, as was agreed at last Meeting, B. Franklin having sent a Messenger about with printed Notes in these Words Vizt. "Sir. Next Saturday Evening Attendance will be given at N. Scull's, to receive the Money subscribed to the Library, of

1. The mistreatment of the Palatines aroused widespread sympathy. In Boston a subscription for their relief yielded £200, and the governor of Pennsylvania urged Governor Belcher to prosecute Lobb. *Pa. Gaz.*, Feb. 22, 1732. Captain Lobb was charged with causing the deaths of two young passengers, one an infant, by withholding food; but he was acquitted. *Philadelphische Zeitung*, June 24, 1732. He thereupon brought suit against those who had pressed the murder charge against him. *Pa. Gaz.*, May 18, 1732; Mass. House of Reps., *Journals, 1731-1732*, pp. 340, 341, 344. Meanwhile 34 of the survivors reached Philadelphia, where they took the oath of allegiance May 15. *Pa. Gaz.*, May 18, 1732; 2 *Pa. Arch.*, XVII, 37.

those who have not yet paid; when you are desired to appear without Fail, either to pay or relinquish; that it may then be known who are, and who are not concerned."

Louis Timothée[2] to the German Inhabitants

Printed in *Philadelphische Zeitung*, May 6, 1732.

den 6 Mey 1732[3]

An alle teutsche Einwohner der Provintz Pennsylvanien.

Nachdem ich von verschiedenen teutschen Einwohnern dieses Landes bin ersuchet worden, eine teutsche Zeitung ausgehen zu lassen, und ihnen darinnen das vornehmste und merckwürdigste neues, so hier und in Europa vorfallen möchte, zu communiciren; doch aber hierzu viele mühe, grosse correspondentz und auch Unkosten erfordert werden: Als habe mich entschlossen, denen teutschen zu lieb, gegenwärtiges Specimen davon heraus zu geben, und ihnen dabey die Conditiones welche nothwendig zu der continuation derselben erfordert werden, bekent zu machen.

Erstlich, müsten zum wenigsten, um die unkosten die darauf lauffen, gut zu machen, 300 stücks können gedruckt und debitiret werden, und müste in jeder Township dazu ein mann ausgemachet werden, welcher mir wissen liesse, wie viel Zeitungen jedes mahl an ihn müsten gesandt werden, und der sie dan weiters einen jeglichen zustellen und die bezahlung davor einfordern müste.

Vor jede Zeitung muss jährlich 10 Shillinge erleget, und davon alle quartal 2*sh.* 6*d.* bezahlet werden.

Dagegen verspreche ich auf meiner seite, durch gute Correspondentz die ich in Holland und England habe allezeit das

2. Louis Timothée (later Lewis Timothy), native of Holland, in 1731 migrated with his family to Philadelphia, where he advertised himself as a teacher of French (see above, p. 220); employed by BF as a journeyman and editor, 1732; librarian of the Library Company of Philadelphia, 1732–33; printer of the *South-Carolina Gazette;* died 1738. Hennig Cohen, *The South Carolina Gazette, 1732–1775* (Columbia, S.C., 1953), pp. 233–7; see below, p. 339.

3. This was both a prospectus and the first issue of BF's first German newspaper. It lays down his conditions for continuing publication. The only known copy of this issue is in Yale Univ. Lib.; a facsimile and description are printed in *PMHB*, XXVI (1902), 91. See below, p. 233.

merkwürdigste und neueste so in Europa und auch hier passiret, alle woche einmahl, nemlich Sonnabends in gegenwärtiger form einer Zeitung, nebst denen schiffen so hier abgehen und ankommen, und auch das steigen oder fallen des Preisses der Güter, und was sonst zu wissen dienlich, bekandt zu machen.

Advertissemente oder Bekant machungen, welche man an mich schicken möchte, sollen das erste mahl vor 3 shill. 3 mahl aber vor 5 shil. hinein gesetzet werden.

Und weil ich nützlich erachte die gantze beschreibung der aufrichtung dieser provintz, mit allen derselben privilegien, rechten und gesetzen, bey ermangelung genugsamer Neuigkeiten, darinen bekandt zu machen; solte nicht undienlich seyn, dass ein jeder, zumahl wer kinder hat, diese Zeitungen wohl bewahre, und am ende des jahres an einander heffte; zumahl da solche dann gleichsam als eine Chronica dienen können, die vorigen Geschichte daraus zu ersehen, und die folgende desto besser zu verstehen.

Auch wird anbey zu bedencken gegeben, ob es nicht rahtsam wäre, in jeder grossen Township einen reitenden Boten zu bestellen, welcher alle woche einmahl nach der stadt reiten und was ein jeder da zu bestellen hat, mit nehmen könne.

So bald nun die obgemeldte anzahl der Unterschreiber vorhanden, welche so bald als möglich ersuche in Philadelphia an Caspar Wuster, oder in Germantown an Daniel Mackinet zu übersenden, soll die wöchentliche continuation erfolgen; biss dahin bleibe Euer allerseits Dienstwilliger   L. TIMOTHÉE, Sprachmeister, wohnhafft in Frontstreet, Philad.

Report of a Committee on By-Laws for St. John's Lodge[4]

MS not found; reprinted from Grand Lodge of Pennsylvania, *Abstract of the Proceedings . . . 1885*, pp. 37–9.

Gentlemen of the Lodge   [June 5, 1732]

The Committee you have been pleased to appoint to consider of the present State of the Lodge, and of the properest Methods to improve it, in obedience to your commands have met, and, after

---

4. BF was made a Mason in St. John's Lodge not later than Feb. 1, 1731. Julius F. Sachse, *Old Masonic Lodges of Pennsylvania* (Phila., 1912–13), I, 26–7. Under date of Sept. 9, 1731, he entered a charge of 5s. in his Journal for 100 "Blanks for Masons."

much and mature Deliberation, have come to the following Resolutions:

1. That since the excellent Science of Geometry and Architecture is so much recommended in our ancient Constitutions, Masonry being first instituted with this Design, among others, to distinguish the true and skilful Architect from unskilful Pretenders; total Ignorance of this Art is very unbecoming a Man who bears the worthy Name and Character of MASON; We therefore conclude, that it is the Duty of every Member to make himself, in some Measure, acquainted therewith, as he would honor the Society he belongs to, and conform to the Constitutions.

2. That every Member may have an Opportunity of so doing, the present Cash be laid out in the best Books of Architecture, suitable Mathematical Instruments, &c.

3. That since the present whole Stock is not too large for that purpose, every Member indebted to the Lodge pay what is from him respectively due on Monday night, the nineteenth Instant, that so the whole being ready by the 24th of June, may be sent away by the first Opportunity. And that every one not paying that Night, be suspended till he do pay: For without Care be taken that Rules are punctually observed, no Society can be long upheld in good Order and Regularity.

4. That since Love and Good Will are the best Cement of any Society, we endeavour to encrease it among ourselves by a kind and friendly conversation, so as to make us of ourselves desire to meet, but that all Compulsion, by fining any Person for not Meeting, be utterly taken away and abolished, Except only Persons in Office, and others when a Meeting is call'd upon Extraordinary Occasions.[5]

5. That the use of the Balls be established in its full Force and Vigour; and that no new Member be admitted against the will of any present Member; because certainly more Regard ought to be had in this way to a Brother who is already a Mason, than to any Person who is not one, and we should never in such cases disoblige a Brother, to oblige a Stranger.

6. That any Member of this Lodge having a complaint against any other Member, shall first apply himself to the Wardens, who shall bring the Cause before the Lodge, where it shall be consider'd and made up, if possible, before the Complainant be

5. This paragraph was struck out.

allow'd to make that Complaint publick to the World: the Offender against this Rule to be expell'd.

June 5, 1732

The Members whose Names are underwritten, being a Majority, agree unanimously to the within Proposals of the Committee (except the fourth, which is cross'd out) and accordingly have hereunto set their hands.

WILL. PRINGLE[6]   JOHN EMERSON
THOMAS BOUDE   LAWCE REYNOLDS
B. FRANKLIN   JOHN HOBART
XTOPHER THOMPSON   HENRY PRATT
THOS. HARTT   SAM'L NICHOLAS
DAVID PARRY

[Louis Timothée?] to the Reader

Printed in *Philadelphische Zeitung*, June 24, 1732.[7]

Wiewohl ich geglaubet hätte, dass sich unter denen teutschen Einwohnern dieses Landes mehr Liebhaber solten gefunden haben, die dieses zumahl vor junge Persohnen so nützliche werck, die ausgabe der Zeitungen nehmlich, befördern, und dazu mit anstehen würden; so erstrecket sich doch die anzahl derer die sich dazu unterschrieben haben vor jetzo nicht über 50. Nichts desto weniger

6. William Pringle, believed to have been a Mason in England; Deputy Grand Master of Pennsylvania in 1731 and 1732. Thomas Boude (*c.* 1700–1781), bricklayer; first secretary of St. John's Lodge; Senior Grand Warden, 1732; Deputy Grand Master of Pennsylvania, 1741. Christopher Thompson, an original member of the Lodge. Thomas Hart (d. 1749), bricklayer; warden of St. John's Lodge. David Parry (d. 1748), formerly a teacher in Chester County. John Emerson (d. 1735), lawyer. Lawrence Reynolds, Philadelphia tanner. John Hobart, proprietor of the Sun Tavern, where the Grand Lodge met, 1732. Henry Pratt (d. 1749), Senior Grand Warden, 1737; coroner of the city and county of Philadelphia, 1741–48; proprietor of the Royal Standard Tavern, 1749; director of the Library Company. Samuel Nicholas (d. 1734), bricklayer. Sachse, *Old Masonic Lodges*, I, 29–46.

7. Although BF was disappointed in his aim to obtain 300 subscribers to his German newspaper (see above, p. 230 n), he printed a second issue, apparently confident that subscriptions would come in. They did not, however; and no later issue of this paper has been found. The only known copy of the issue of June 24 is in Hist. Soc. Pa.; it has been described and printed in facsimile in *PMHB*, XXIV (1900), 306–7.

habe auf meiner seiten nicht ermangeln wollen damit einen anfang zu machen, der hoffnung lebende, dass sich noch mehrere einfinden werden selbiges zu befördern, sonsten ich mich genöthiget sehen würde, bald wieder damit auf zu hören.

Ich hatte zwar in meiner ersten Zeitung versprochen dieselbe alle 8 tage zu publiciren, doch die meisten stimmen haben erwählet dieselbe lieber vor 5.schillinge das gantze Jahr alle 14 tage einmahl zu haben; weilen alsdann füglicher zwey und zwey eine zeitung halten, und jede person gemächlt eher die helffte bezahlen könte; Welches ich mir dann auch gefallen lasse, und selbige von nun an alle 14. tage einmal heraus geben will. Die Ansprache des Königes von England, welche ich in meinem vorigen versprochen, weil sie allzulang, und ich einen andern vorrath von Neuigkeiten bekommen, habe lieber wollen auslassen, wie ich auch um der ursachen willen meine erklährungen, die wohl über einige sachen nöthig gewesen wären, lieber auf eine andere gelegenheit verspahre, und nur die brieffe von wort zu wort jetzo mittheile.

Query to the Casuist: A Case of Conscience

Printed in *The Pennsylvania Gazette*, June 26, 1732; also draft: Historical Society of Pennsylvania.

To the Printer of the *Gazette*.

Sir,   New-Castle, June 20
    I am puzzled with a certain Case of Conscience, which I would gladly have well solved; and if the acute Gentleman who has sometimes in your Paper assum'd the Name of *Casuist*, would undertake the Discussion, it will exceedingly oblige, Your Friend and Reader, &c.

The CASE is this;

    Suppose *A* discovers that his Neighbour *B* has corrupted his Wife and injur'd his Bed: Now, if 'tis probable, that by *A*'s acquainting *B*'s Wife with it, and using proper Solicitations, he can prevail with her to consent, that her Husband be used in the same Manner, *is he justifiable in doing it?*

P.S. If you are acquainted with Mr. Casuist, you may give him this privately, and I will cause one to call at your House sometime hence for his Answer: But if you know him not, please to publish it, that he may read it in your Paper.

From the Casuist: A Case of Conscience

Printed in *The Pennsylvania Gazette*, July 3, 1732; also draft: Historical Society of Pennsylvania.

To the Printer of the *Gazette*.

Sir,

The Case of Conscience propos'd to me in you last Gazette, does not require much Consideration to give an Answer.

It should seem that the Proposer of that Case, is either no Christian, or a very ill instructed one; otherwise he might easily have learnt his Duty from these positive Laws of Religion, *Thou shalt not commit Adultery: Return not Evil for Evil, but repay Evil with Good*. But supposing him to be one who would make *Reason* the Rule of his Actions, I am of Opinion he will find himself wholly unjustifiable in such a Proceeding; when he considers That it is a Breach of the Laws of his Country, which every reasonable Man knows he ought to observe: That it is making himself Judge in his own Cause, which all allow to be unreasonable: And, that such Practices can produce no Good to Society, but great Confusion and Disturbance among Mankind.

The Philosopher said, with Regard to an Affront which he was urg'd to revenge, *If an Ass kicks me, should I kick him again?* So may the injured Man of Prudence and Virtue say, "If a Fool has made himself wicked and vicious, and has prevailed with an honest Woman to become as bad as himself; should I also make my self wicked and vicious, and corrupt another honest Woman, that I may be even, or upon a Level, with him?" I am your Friend,

THE CASUIST

Anti-Casuist: A Case of Conscience[8]

Draft: Historical Society of Pennsylvania

[July 3, 1732]

Anti Casuist says: I allow the Heighnousness of the Crime, &c.

Whether I am a Christian or a Man of Reason, I am not unjustifiable in doing it, from these Considerations.

8. This draft of a further argument on the subject by Anti-Casuist appears in BF's Commonplace Book directly after his drafts of the query to the Casuist and of the Casuist's reply. He probably wrote all three about the same time. He revised the first two pieces and printed them in the *Gazette* but never did so with Anti-Casuist's response.

If my Wife commits Adultery with him, she thereby dissolves the Bond of Marriage between her and me, and makes us two separate and single Persons. The Laws of every Country and even of Christianity allow Adultery to be a good Cause of Divorce and tho' the fact be not publickly prov'd it doth nevertheless in its own Nature make this Separation. Also he by committing Adultery dissolves the Bond of Marriage between himself and his Wife, and makes them two separate single Persons; tis plain then, that being all four single; if I afterwards enjoy his Wife, or rather her that was his Wife, I do not commit Adultery for Adultery cannot be committed where both Parties are single and consequently, do not breake that positive Command which he mentions; I am not Lawyer enough to be sure of it, but I question it is a Breach of the Law of the Country either; for I know of no Law that says I shall not use his Wife nor [*illegible*].

But 2ly supposing the Marriages remain undissolved and she is his Wife still; if he has injur'd his Wife and defrauded her of her due Benevolence, bestowing it where it was not due, on my Wife; my Family having receiv'd is properly Debtor, and his Wife is Creditor; if I then bestow on his Wife the Benevolence which was before due to mine; my Wife has no Cause to complain having before receiv'd from him; and with respect to his Wife, tis so far from doing an Injury that 'tis rather righting the injured or paying a just Debt; and then tis also as far from Revenge; for as he took my Wife for his Use, I give myself for his Wife's Use; which is the same thing as if a Man demanded my Bed and I give him the Coverlid also. So that a Man does not thereby as the Casuist asserts, break the Law which forbids Revenge.

Then as to Injury, no Injury can be done where no Body is injur'd; and I believe 'twill puzzle the Casuist, or any Body else to show who is injur'd in this Case, provided the Thing be never made publick.

He says such a Practice would bring nothing but Confusion in the World; and that the Person injuring is a Debtor and tis better &c.[9] If he means that the Practice of B is apt to make Confusion

9. The draft of the Casuist's reply to the original query contains a passage not found in the printed version but referred to here. It reads in part: "That the Person injuring is now as it were his Debtor, and he has a Demand of Justice upon him; and tis better to have an ill Man in our Debt, that [than] either to be equal or in Debt to him."

I agree to it, because some in A's Case would not act so prudently as A is suppos'd to do, but would murder their Wives and perhaps the Agressor also; But the suppos'd Practice of A is apt if things are in Confusion to set all to rights again. B being conscious that he is an Agressor, and has injur'd A; if A does not return him the like; must always be in fear of A's Revenge in a worse Manner; and some instances might be given of Men in B's Case, who have kill'd Persons they have first injur'd meerly to be free from the Fear of their Resentment: But when B knows that A is even with him in the particular abovemention'd he has no further Cause of Suspicion; and they may embrace with open Hearts like Brothers, and be good Friends ever after; For If B might think it an Injury in any other Man to use his Wife; he cannot say tis an Injury in A, because he had first serv'd him so; and If he will say that his Familiarity with A's Wife, was only a Civility; he cannot [*written above:* has no Room to] complain that the Civility was not return'd. I shall conclude by observing that while Mr. Casuist, kept to the Subject of Horses, he seem'd to talk well enough; but now in meddling with Affairs between Man and Wife, it plainly appears that he is but a Horse Casuist. Next Week the Story out of human Prudence. I am Yours.

Anthony Afterwit[1]

Printed in *The Pennsylvania Gazette*, July 10, 1732; also draft: Historical Society of Pennsylvania.

Mr. Gazetteer,

I am an honest Tradesman, who never meant Harm to any Body. My Affairs went on smoothly while a Batchelor; but of late I have met with some Difficulties, of which I take the Freedom to give you an Account.

About the Time I first address'd my present Spouse, her Father gave out in Speeches, that if she married a Man he liked, he

---

1. Study and comparison of drafts of essays like this with their printed versions reveal interesting variations in spelling, capitalization, choice of words, and phrasing. Some of these are important for the light they throw on BF's creative processes and the evolution of his literary style. Only the more significant differences will be noted here.

would give with her £200 on the Day of Marriage. 'Tis true he never said so to me, but he always receiv'd me very kindly at his House, and openly countenanc'd my Courtship. I form'd several fine Schemes, what to do with this same £200 and in some Measure neglected my Business on that Account: But unluckily it came to pass, that when the old Gentleman saw I was pretty well engag'd, and that the Match was too far gone to be easily broke off; he, without any Reason given, grew very angry, forbid me the House, and told his Daughter that if she married me he would not give her a Farthing. However (as he foresaw) we were not to be disappointed in that Manner; but having stole a Wedding, I took her home to my House; where we were not in quite so poor a Condition as the Couple describ'd in the Scotch Song, who had

> *Neither Pot nor Pan,*
> *But four bare Legs together;*

for I had a House tolerably furnished, for an ordinary Man, before. No thanks to Dad, who I understand was very much pleased with his politick Management. And I have since learn'd that there are old Curmudgeons (*so called*) besides him, who have this Trick, to marry their Daughters, and yet keep what they might well spare, till they can keep it no longer: But this by way of Digression; *A Word to the Wise is enough.*

I soon saw that with Care and Industry we might live tolerably easy, and in Credit with our Neighbours: But my Wife had a strong Inclination to be a *Gentlewoman*. In Consequence of this, my old-fashioned Looking-Glass was one Day broke, as she said, *No Mortal could tell which way.* However, since we could not be without a Glass in the Room, *My Dear,* says she, *we may as well buy a large fashionable One that Mr. Such-a-one has to sell; it will cost but little more than a common Glass, and will be much handsomer and more creditable.* Accordingly the Glass was bought, and hung against the Wall: But in a Week's time, I was made sensible by little and little, *that the Table was by no Means suitable to such a Glass.* And a more proper Table being procur'd, my Spouse, who was an excellent Contriver, inform'd me where we might have very handsome Chairs *in the Way;* And thus, by Degrees, I found all my old Furniture stow'd up into the Garret, and every thing below alter'd for the better.

Had we stopp'd here, we might have done well enough; but my Wife being entertain'd with *Tea* by the Good Women she visited, we could do no less than the like when they visited us; and so we got a *Tea-Table* with all its Appurtenances of *China* and *Silver*. Then my Spouse unfortunately overwork'd herself in washing the House, so that we could do no longer without a *Maid*. Besides this, it happened frequently, that when I came home at *One*, the Dinner was but just put in the Pot; for, *My Dear thought really it had been but Eleven:* At other Times when I came at the same Hour, *She wondered I would stay so long, for Dinner was ready and had waited for me these two Hours*. These Irregularities, occasioned by mistaking the Time, convinced me, that it was absolutely necessary *to buy a Clock;* which my Spouse observ'd, *was a great Ornament to the Room!* And lastly, to my Grief, she was frequently troubled with some Ailment or other, and nothing did her so much Good as *Riding;* And *these Hackney Horses were such wretched ugly Creatures, that*—I bought a very fine pacing Mare, which cost £20. And hereabouts Affairs have stood for some Months past.

I could see all along, that this Way of Living was utterly inconsistent with my Circumstances,[2] but had not Resolution enough to help it. Till lately, receiving a very severe Dun, which mention'd the next Court, I began in earnest to project Relief. Last Monday my Dear went over the River, to see a Relation, and stay a Fortnight, because *she could not bear the Heat of the Town*. In the Interim, I have taken my Turn to make Alterations, viz. I have turn'd away the Maid, Bag and Baggage (for what should we do with a Maid, who have (except my Boy) none but our selves). I have sold the fine Pacing Mare, and bought a good Milch Cow, with £3 of the Money. I have dispos'd of the Tea-Table, and put a Spinning Wheel in its Place, which methinks *looks very pretty:* Nine empty Canisters I have stuff'd with Flax; and with some of the Money of the Tea-Furniture, I have bought a Set of Knitting-Needles; for to tell you a Truth, which I would have go no farther, *I begin to want Stockings*. The stately Clock I have transform'd into an Hour-Glass, by which I gain'd a good round Sum; and one of the Pieces of the old Looking-Glass, squar'd and fram'd, supplies the Place of the Great One, which I

2. Draft reads: "this did not at all suit with my Circumstances."

have convey'd into a Closet, where it may possibly remain some Years. In short, the Face of Things is quite changed; and I am mightily pleased when I look at my Hour-Glass, *what an Ornament it is to the Room.*[3] I have paid my Debts, and find Money in my Pocket. I expect my Dame home next Friday, and as your Paper is taken in at the House where she is, I hope the Reading of this will prepare her Mind for the above surprizing Revolutions. If she can conform to this new Scheme of Living, we shall be the happiest Couple perhaps in the Province, and, by the Blessing of God, may soon be in thriving Circumstances. I have reserv'd the great Glass, because I know her Heart is set upon it. I will allow her when she comes in, to be taken suddenly ill with the *Headach,* the *Stomach-ach, Fainting-Fits,* or whatever other Disorders she may think more proper; and she may retire to Bed as soon as she pleases: But if I do not find her in perfect Health both of Body and Mind the next Morning, away goes the aforesaid Great Glass, with several other Trinkets I have no Occasion for, to the Vendue that very Day. Which is the irrevocable Resolution of, Sir, Her loving Husband, and Your very humble Servant,

ANTHONY AFTERWIT[4]

Postscript, You know we can return to our former Way of Living, when we please, if Dad will be at the Expence of it.[5]

Celia Single

Printed in *The Pennsylvania Gazette,* July 24, 1732; also draft: Historical Society of Pennsylvania.

My Correspondent Mrs. Celia, must excuse my omitting those Circumstances of her Letter, which point at People too plainly; *and content herself that I insert the rest as follows.*

3. Draft reads: "and methinks you would smile to see my Hourglass hanging up in the Place of the Clock. What a great Ornament it is to the Room."

4. "Abigail Afterwit" was one of James Franklin's pseudonyms in the *New-England Courant,* Jan. 29, 1722. Anthony Afterwit's essay was reprinted by James Franklin in the *Rhode-Island Gazette,* Jan. 25, 1733, where it elicited a reply on "The Tea Table" from "Patience Teacraft." Miss Teacraft's essay was reprinted in *Pa. Gaz.,* May 31, 1733.

5. The postscript in the draft is a question to the editor and the editor's answer: "I would be glad to know how you approve my Conduct. Answ. I don't love to concern my self in Affairs between Man and Wife."

Mr. Gazetteer,

I must needs tell you, that some of the Things you print do more Harm than Good; particularly I think so of my Neighbour the Tradesman's Letter in one of your late Papers, which has broken the Peace of several Families,[6] by causing Difference between Men and their Wives: I shall give you here one Instance, of which I was an Eye and Ear Witness.

Happening last Wednesday Morning to be in at Mrs. C——ss's, when her Husband return'd from Market, among other Things which he had bought, he show'd her some Balls of Thread. *My Dear*, says he, *I like mightily those Stockings which I yesterday saw Neighbour Afterwit knitting for her Husband, of Thread of her own Spinning: I should be glad to have some such Stockins my self: I understand that your Maid Mary is a very good Knitter, and seeing this Thread in Market, I have bought it, that the Girl may make a Pair or two for me.* Mrs. Careless was just then at the Glass, dressing her Head; and turning about with the Pins in her Mouth, *Lord, Child*, says she, *are you crazy? What Time has Mary to knit? Who must do the Work, I wonder, if you set her to Knitting?* Perhaps, my Dear, *says he,*[7] you have a mind to knit 'em yourself; I remember, when I courted you, I once heard you say you had learn'd to knit of your Mother. *I knit Stockins for you*, says she, *not I truly; There are poor Women enough in Town, that can knit; if you please you may employ them.* Well, but my Dear, *says he,* you know a

6. Draft reads: "which has disoblig'd many of our Sex and broken the Peace of several Families."

7. In this essay BF the author posed a typographical problem for BF the printer. It was his common practice in print to indicate quoted spoken words, whether in direct or indirect discourse, by the use of italics. In printing this essay he followed his practice through the opening speeches of husband and wife, these being conveniently separated by some words of narrative, set in roman. But beginning with the husband's second speech the dialogue follows continuously without interruption, except for such interpolated words as "says he" and "says she." To set all the speeches in italics would be confusing, for there would then have been no breaks to show where the words of one speaker ended and those of the other began. BF solved this problem by setting the wife's speeches as usual in italics, with "says she" and other interpolations in roman, and reversing this procedure for the husband's speeches, thus making it clear to readers where one ended and the other began. Except for the editors' standard practice of normalizing proper names, BF's typographical device is followed in this reprinting.

penny sav'd is a penny got, a pin a day is a groat a year, every little makes a mickle,[8] and there is neither Sin nor Shame in Knitting a pair of Stockins; why should you express such a mighty Aversion to it? As to *poor* Women, you know we are not People of Quality, we have no Income to maintain us, but what arises from my Labour and Industry; methinks you should not be at all displeas'd, if you have an Opportunity to get something as well as myself. *I wonder,* says she, *how you can propose such a thing to me; did not you always tell me you would maintain me like a Gentlewoman? If I had married Capt. ——, he would have scorn'd even to mention Knitting of Stockins.* Prithee, *says he, (a little nettled)* what do you tell me of your Captains? If you could have had him, I suppose you would; or perhaps you did not very well like him: If I did promise to maintain you like a Gentlewoman, I suppose 'tis time enough for that when you know how to behave like one; mean while 'tis your Duty to help make me able. How long d'ye think I can maintain you at your present Rate of Living? *Pray,* says she, (somewhat fiercely, and dashing the Puff into the Powder-Box) *don't use me after this Manner, for I assure you I won't bear it. This is the Fruit of your poison News-papers; there shall come no more here, I promise you.* Bless us, *says he,* what an unaccountable thing is this! Must a Tradesman's Daughter, and the Wife of a Tradesman, necessarily and instantly be a Gentlewoman?[9] You had no Portion; I am forc'd to work for a Living; if you are too great to do the like, there's the Door, go and live upon your Estate, if you can find it,[1] in short, I don't desire to be troubled w'ye.

—— What Answer she made, I cannot tell; for knowing that a Man and his Wife are apt to quarrel more violently when before Strangers, than when by themselves, I got up and went out hastily: But I understood from Mary, who came to me of an Errand in the Evening, that they dined together pretty peaceably, (the Balls of Thread that had caused the Difference, being thrown into the Kitchen Fire) of which I was very glad to hear.

I have several times in your Paper seen severe Reflections upon us Women, for Idleness and Extravagance, but I do not remember to have once seen any such Animadversions upon the Men.

8. Draft omits: "a pin . . . a mickle."
9. Draft reads: "Lady."
1. Draft reads: "and I never had any Thing with ye."

If I were dispos'd to be censorious, I could furnish you with Instances enough: I might mention Mr. Billiard, who spends more than he earns, at the Green Table; and would have been in Jail long since, were it not for his industrious Wife: Mr. Husselcap, who often all day long[2] leaves his Business for the rattling of Half-pence in a certain Alley: Mr. Finikin, who has seven different Suits of fine Cloaths, and wears a Change every Day, while his Wife and Children sit at home half naked: Mr. Crownhim, who is always dreaming over the Chequer-board, and cares not how the World goes,[3] so he gets the Game: Mr. T'otherpot the Tavern-haunter; Mr. Bookish, the everlasting Reader; Mr. Tweedledum, Mr. Toot-a-toot, and several others, who are mighty diligent at any thing beside their Business. I say, if I were dispos'd to be censorious, I might mention all these, and more; but I hate to be thought a Scandalizer of my Neighbours, and therefore forbear. And for your part, I would advise you, for the future, to entertain your Readers with something else besides People's Reflections upon one another; for remember, that there are Holes enough to be pick'd in your Coat as well as others; and those that are affronted by the Satyrs you may publish, will not consider so much who *wrote*, as who *printed:*[4] Take not this Freedom amiss, from Your Friend and Reader, CELIA SINGLE

Alice Addertongue[5]

Printed in *The Pennsylvania Gazette*, September 12, 1732; also draft: Historical Society of Pennsylvania.

Mr. Gazetteer,

I was highly pleased with your last Week's Paper upon SCAN-DAL,[6] as the uncommon Doctrine therein preach'd is agreeable both to my Principles and Practice, and as it was published very sea-

2. Draft reads: "who every Market Day at least, and often all Day long."
3. Draft reads: "how the World goes with his Family."
4. Draft adds: "and treat you accordingly."
5. The draft consists of both BF's first unorganized sentences, paragraphs, and even phrases, and the more coherent version into which he worked them. In the following notes references are made to the latter.
6. An essay on the usefulness of censure, *Pa. Gaz.*, Sept. 7, 1732. In the draft the following syllogism appears:

sonably to reprove the Impertinence of a Writer in the foregoing Thursdays *Mercury*, who at the Conclusion of one of his silly Paragraphs, laments, forsooth, that the *Fair Sex* are so peculiarly guilty of this enormous Crime: Every Blockhead ancient and modern, that could handle a Pen, has I think taken upon him to cant in the same senseless Strain. If to *scandalize* be really a *Crime*, what do these Puppies mean? They describe it, they dress it up in the most odious frightful and detestable Colours, they represent it as the worst of Crimes, and then roundly and charitably charge the whole Race of Womankind with it. Are they not then guilty of what they condemn, at the same time that they condemn it? If they accuse us of any other Crime, they must necessarily *scandalize* while they do it: But to *scandalize* us with being guilty of *Scandal*, is in itself an egregious Absurdity, and can proceed from nothing but the most consummate Impudence in Conjunction with the most profound Stupidity.

This, supposing, as they do, that to scandalize is a Crime; which you have convinc'd all reasonable People, is an Opinion absolutely erroneous. Let us leave then these Ideot Mock-Moralists, while I entertain you with some Account of my Life [and] Manners.

I am a young Girl of about thirty-five, and live at present with my Mother. I have no Care upon my Head of getting a Living, and therefore find it my Duty as well as Inclination, to exercise my Talent at CENSURE, for the Good of my Country folks. There was, I am told, a certain generous Emperor, who if a Day had passed over his Head, in which he had conferred no Benefit on any Man, used to say to his Friends, in Latin, *Diem perdidi*, that is, it seems, *I have lost a Day*. I believe I should make use of the same Expression, if it were possible for a Day to pass in which I had not, or miss'd, an Opportunity to scandalize somebody: But, Thanks be praised, no such Misfortune has befel me these dozen Years.

Yet, whatever Good I may do, I cannot pretend that I first entred into the Practice of this Virtue from a Principle of Publick Spirit; for I remember that when a Child, I had a violent Inclina-

---

He that censures the Crimes of others, is censorious.
If Censoriousness is a Crime,
    Then the Censorious are Criminals;
    Then accusing others of Censoriousness is criminal;
    Then accusing some Vice in others is criminal.

tion to be ever talking in my own Praise, and being continually told that it was ill Manners, and once severely whipt for it, the confin'd Stream form'd itself a new Channel, and I began to speak for the future in the Dispraise of others. This I found more agreable to Company, and almost as much so to my self: For what great Difference can there be, between putting your self up, or putting your Neighbour down? *Scandal*, like other Virtues, is in part its own Reward, as it gives us the Satisfaction of making our selves appear better than others, or others no better than ourselves.

My Mother, good Woman, and I, have heretofore differ'd upon this Account. She argu'd that Scandal spoilt all good Conversation, and I insisted that without it there could be no such Thing. Our Disputes once rose so high, that we parted Tea-Table, and I concluded to entertain my Acquaintance in the Kitchin. The first Day of this Separation we both drank Tea at the same Time, but she with her Visitors in the Parlor. She would not hear of the least Objection to any one's Character, but began a new sort of Discourse in some such queer philosophical Manner as this; *I am mightily pleas'd sometimes,* says she, *when I observe and consider that the World is not so bad as People out of humour imagine it to be. There is something amiable, some good Quality or other in every body. If we were only to speak of People that are least respected, there is* such a one *is very dutiful to her Father, and methinks has a fine Set of Teeth;* such a one *is very respectful to her Husband;* such a one *is very kind to her poor Neighbours, and besides has a very handsome Shape;* such a one *is always ready to serve a Friend, and in my Opinion there is not a Woman in Town that has a more agreeable Air and Gait.* This fine kind of Talk, which lasted near half an Hour, she concluded by saying, *I do not doubt but every one of you have made the like Observations,*[7] *and I should be glad to have the Conversation continu'd upon this Subject.* Just at that Juncture I peep'd in at the Door, and never in my Life before saw such a Set of simple vacant Countenances; they looked somehow neither glad, nor sorry, nor angry, nor pleas'd, nor indifferent, nor attentive; but, (excuse the Simile) like so many blue wooden Images of Rie Doe [rye Dough]. I in the Kitchin had already begun a ridiculous Story of Mr. ——'s Intrigue with his Maid, and his Wife's Behaviour upon the Discovery; at some Passages we laugh'd heartily, and one of the gravest

7. Draft adds: "among your Acquaintance."

of Mama's Company, without making any Answer to her Discourse, got up *to go and see what the Girls were so merry about:* She was follow'd by a Second, and shortly after by a Third, till at last the old Gentlewoman found herself quite alone, and being convinc'd that her Project was impracticable, came her self and finish'd her Tea with us; ever since which *Saul also has been among the Prophets,* and our Disputes lie dormant.

By Industry and Application, I have made my self the Center of all the *Scandal* in the Province, there is little stirring but I hear of it.[8] I began the World with this Maxim, *That no Trade can subsist without Returns;* and accordingly, whenever I receiv'd a good story, I endeavour'd to give two or a better in the Room of it. My Punctuality in this Way of Dealing gave such Encouragement, that it has procur'd me an incredible deal of Business, which without Diligence and good Method it would be impossible for me to go through. For besides the Stock of Defamation thus naturally flowing in upon me, I practice an Art by which I can pump Scandal out of People that are the least enclin'd that way. Shall I discover my Secret? Yes; to let it die with me would be inhuman. If I have never heard Ill of some Person, I always impute it to defective Intelligence; *for there are none without their Faults, no not one.* If she is a Woman, I take the first Opportunity to let all her Acquaintance know I have heard that one of the handsomest or best Men in Town has said something in Praise either of her Beauty, her Wit, her Virtue, or her good Management. If you know any thing of Humane Nature, you perceive that this naturally introduces a Conversation turning upon all her Failings,[9] past, present, and to come. To the same purpose, and with the same Success, I cause every Man of Reputation to be praised before his Competitors in Love, Business, or Esteem on Account of any particular Qualification. Near the Times of *Election,* if I find it necessary, I commend every Candidate before some of the opposite Party, listning attentively to what is said of him in answer: (But Commendations in this latter Case are not always necessary, and should be used judiciously;) of late Years I needed only observe what they said of one another freely; and having for the

8. Draft reads: "Center of all the Intelligence in the Province, and there is no Scandal agoing [?] but I hear of it."
9. Draft reads: "Faults and failings."

Help of Memory taken Account of all Informations and Accusations received, whoever peruses my Writings after my Death, may happen to think, that during a certain Term, the People of Pennsylvania chose into all their Offices of Honour and Trust, the veriest Knaves, Fools and Rascals in the whole Province. The Time of Election used to be a busy Time with me, but this Year, with Concern I speak it, People are grown so good natur'd, so intent upon mutual Feasting and friendly Entertainment, that I see no Prospect of much Employment[1] from that Quarter.

I mention'd above, that without good Method I could not go thro' my Business: In my Father's Life-time I had some Instruction in Accompts, which I now apply with Advantage to my own Affairs. I keep a regular Set of Books, and can tell at an Hour's Warning how it stands between me and the World. In my *Daybook* I enter every Article of Defamation as it is transacted; for Scandals *receiv'd in,* I give Credit; and when I pay them out again, I make the Persons to whom they respectively relate *Debtor.* In my *Journal,* I add to each Story by Way of Improvement, such probable Circumstances as I think it will bear, and in my *Ledger* the whole is regularly posted.[2]

I suppose the Reader already condemns me in his Heart, for this particular of *adding Circumstances;* but I justify that part of my Practice thus. 'Tis a Principle with me, that none ought to have a greater Share of Reputation than they really deserve; if they have, 'tis an Imposition upon the Publick: I know it is every one's Interest, and therefore believe they endeavour, to conceal *all* their Vices and Follies; and I hold, that those People are *ex-*

1. Draft reads: "Hurry" for "Employment." The "Feasting" and "Entertainment" Alice refers to as taking place "this Year" were occasioned by the welcome accorded Thomas Penn on his arrival in the province in August and a conference with the chiefs of the Six Nations in early September.

2. Draft contains a paragraph that was dropped in the printed version: "To this End I have a Book of Lies, the pure Works of Invention, but such as are to all appearance both possible and probable; for they are exactly adapted to the Circumstance Genius or Character of the Persons to whom they relate. In this Affair I have so great Judgement and Address, that none of my Lies miscarry; every one that hears them, believes them. That of the Prophecy of the Burning of Market Street last Winter, was mine, which I father'd, or rather Mother'd upon a very good Woman my Neighbour. I think there has not been one this seven Year relating to People of the least Note which I have not had a Hand in."

247

traordinary foolish or careless who suffer a *Fourth* of their Failings to come to publick Knowledge: Taking then the common Prudence and Imprudence of Mankind in a Lump, I suppose none suffer above *one Fifth* to be discovered: Therefore when I hear of any Person's Misdoing, I think I keep within Bounds if in relating it I only make it *three times* worse than it is; and I reserve to my self the Privilege of charging them with one Fault in four, which, for aught I know, they may be entirely innocent of. You see there are but few so careful of doing Justice as my self; what Reason then have Mankind to complain of *Scandal?* In a general way, the worst that is said of us is only half what *might* be said, if all our Faults were seen.

But alas, two great Evils have lately befaln me at the same time; an extream Cold that I can scarce speak, and a most terrible Toothach that I dare hardly open my Mouth: For some Days past I have receiv'd ten Stories for one I have paid; and I am not able to ballance my Accounts without your Assistance. I have long thought that if you would make your Paper a Vehicle of Scandal, you would double the Number of your Subscribers. I send you herewith Account of *4 Knavish Tricks, 2 crackt M---n--ds, 5 Cu--ld-ms, 3 drub'd Wives,* and *4 Henpeck'd Husbands,* all within this Fortnight; which you may, as Articles of News, deliver to the Publick; and if my Toothach continues, shall send you more; being, in the mean time, Your constant Reader,

ALICE ADDERTONGUE

I thank my Correspondent Mrs. Addertongue for her Good-Will; but desire to be excus'd inserting the Articles of News she has sent me; such Things being in Reality no News at all.

Joseph Breintnall to Peter Collinson[3]

ALS: British Museum; also MS Minute Book: Library Company of Philadelphia

Sir   Philada. 9br. 7th [November 7], 1732

Your Goodness in assisting Mr. Hopkinson in the Choice and Purchase of our Books, and the valuable Present you have so gen-

---

3. According to the minutes BF composed the letter, which Breintnall "copied fair and sent."

erously made us, demand our most grateful Acknowledgements.[4] An Undertaking like ours, was as necessary here, as we hope it will be useful; there being no Manner of Provision made by the Government for publick Education, either in this or the neighbouring Provinces, nor so much as a good Booksellers Shop nearer than Boston.

Every Encouragement to an Infant Design, by Men of Merit and Consideration, gives new Spirit to the Undertakers, strengthens the Hands of all concern'd, and greatly tends to secure and establish their Work; Hence, as well as from the noble Knowledge communicated in the Books you have given us, will arise the lasting Obligation we shall find ourselves under to Mr. Collinson. We wish you every kind of Happiness and Prosperity, and particularly that you may never want Power nor Opportunity of enjoying that greatest of Pleasures to a benevolent Mind, the giving Pleasure to others.

Signed by Order of the Library Company of Philadelphia
JOSEPH BREINTNALL Secry

Endorsed: On sending a present of Books to the Library Company of Pensilvania—Just Establish'd.

Reply to a Complaining Reader

Printed in *The Pennsylvania Gazette*, November 9, 1732.

To the Printer of the *Gazette*.

As you sometimes take upon you to correct the Publick, you ought in your Turn patiently to receive publick Correction. My Quarrel against you is, your Practice of publishing under the Notion of News, old Transactions which I suppose you hope we have forgot. For Instance, in your Numb. 669, you tell us from London of July 20. That the Losses of our Merchants are laid before the Congress of Soissons, by Mr. Stanhope, &c. and that Admiral Hopson died the 8th of May last. Whereas 'tis certain, there has been no Congress at Soissons nor any where else these three Years

4. In a letter to the Library Company, July 22, Collinson announced he was making a gift of Henry Pemberton's *A View of Sir Isaac Newton's Philosophy* (London, 1728), and Philip Miller's *The Gardeners Dictionary* (London, 1731).

at least; nor could Admiral Hopson possibly die in May last, unless he has made a Resurrection since his Death in 1728. And in your Numb. 670. among other Articles of equal Antiquity, you tell us a long Story of a Murder and Robbery perpetrated on the Person of Mr. Nath. Bostock, which I have read Word for Word not less than four Years since in your own Paper.[5] Are these your *freshest Advices foreign and domestick?* I insist that you insert this in your next, and let us see how you justify yourself.   MEMORY

I need not say more in Vindication of my self against this Charge, than that the Letter is evidently wrong directed, and should have been *To the Publisher of the Mercury:* Inasmuch as the Numb. of my Paper is not yet amounted to 669, nor are those old Articles any where to be found in the *Gazette,* but in the *Mercury* of the two last Weeks. I may however say something in his Excuse, viz. That 'tis not to be always expected there should happen just a *full Sheet* of *New* Occurrences for each Week; and that the oftner you are told a good Thing, the more likely you will be to remember it. I confess I once lately offended in this kind my self, but it was *thro' Ignorance;* and that may possibly be the Case with others.

Agreement between Louis Timothée and Directors of Library Company[6]   DS: New York Public Library

[November 14, 1732]

MEMORANDUM of Agreement indented and made the fourteenth Day of November Anno Dom. One thousand seven hundred and thirty two between Louis Timothée of the City of Philadelphia

5. The issues mentioned were the *American Weekly Mercury*, Oct. 26 and Nov. 2, 1732. A European Congress met at Soissons in June 1728; its proceedings were reported in the *Mercury* almost weekly for several months, beginning with the issue of Sept. 19. Vice Admiral Edward Hopsonn, commanding the West India Station, died May 8, 1728. The *Mercury's* report of the murder of Nathaniel Bostock has not been found.

6. See above, p. 230. Timothée left Philadelphia, Nov. 1733, to run a printing-office in Charleston, S.C. (see below, p. 339). BF took his place as librarian until March 14, when the Directors engaged William Parsons (see below, p. 359).

Gentleman Of the one part and Benjamin Franklin Robert Grace Thomas Godfrey William Maugridge John Nicholas John Jones junr Hugh Roberts Anthony Nicholas William Parsons and Henry Pratt a Committee of Directors of the Library Company of Philadelphia for and on Behalf of the said Company Of the other part, Vizt.

THAT the said Louis Timothee shall be the Librarian of the said Company for and during the Space of Three Months from the Date hereof.

THAT he shall give due Attendance in the Library on Wednesdays from two 'till three o'Clock and on Saturdays from the Hours of Ten to four weekly during the said Term and may permit any civil Gentlemen to peruse the Books of the Library in the Library-Room.

THAT he shall lend the said Books to such Subscribers as are Members of the said Company as often as any of them shall orderly require the Loan of any Books then in the Library unlent. But shall not lend to, or suffer to be taken out of the Library by, any Person who is not a subscribing Member any of the said Books, Mr. James Logan only excepted.[7] Taking of every Borrower a promissory Note to pay such a Sum and in such Time as particularly is set down in the Catalogue of the said Books remaining in his Custody in the Library Which Notes are to become void if such Borrowers within the Time limited return undefaced to him the said Louis Timothee the Books so lent, and not otherwise.[8]

THAT as to the Order of lending the said Books He the said Librarian shall not lend at one Time to any one Person more than

7. The Directors excepted Logan in appreciation of his aid in preparing a list of suitable books for the Library to order.

8. On the same day the Directors entered into this agreement with Timothée, they authorized a form of promissory note: "I promise to pay Lewis Timothee or his Order, the Sum of   for Value received. Nevertheless if within   from the Date hereof, I return undefaced to the said Lewis Timothee a Book belonging to the Library Company of Philadelphia entituled   which I have now borrowed of him this Bill is to be void. Witness my Hand the   Day of   ." BF undertook to print these blank forms. Lib. Co. Phila. Minutes, Nov. 14, 1732. With slight modifications this form seems to have served for many years. A printed form in blank, but signed by BF, is in APS.

one Book except such as in the said Catalogue are mentioned to be lent together nor for a longer Time or a less Sum pledg'd by Note as aforesaid than as in the said Catalogue set down.

THAT the said Louis Timothee shall not put any of such promissory Notes as aforesaid (as may become payable) in Suit, nor assign any of the said Notes, without the Order and Direction of a Majority of the said Committee. And that he shall attend the said Committee at any of their Meetings to which he is or shall be warn'd.

AND THAT the said Committee of Directors in Consideration of his the said Louis Timothee's Care and Trouble in the Premises and for the Use of the Room in his House where the said Books are reposited shall pay to the said Louis Timothee at the Expiration of the said Three Months the Sum of Three Pounds lawful Money certain and such a further Allowance as then after such Time of Experience shall by the Parties hereto be thought and concluded on to be a reasonable Reward. IN WITNESS whereof the said Parties to these Presents have interchangeably set their Hands and Seals hereunto. Dated the Day and Year first above written.

Sealed and delivered ⎱
In the Presence of us ⎰
    WM. COLEMAN
    JOSEPH BREINTNALL

B. FRANKLIN [Seal]
ROBT. GRACE [Seal]
THOS GODFREY [Seal]
JNO NICHOLAS [Seal]
JNO. JONES JUNR. [Seal]
HUGH ROBERTS [Seal]
ANTHO NICHOLAS [Seal]

On Colds   Printed in *The Pennsylvania Gazette*, November 30, 1732.

From all Parts of this Province, and even from Maryland, People complain of Colds, which are become more general than can be remember'd in these Parts before. Some ascribe this Distemper to the sudden Change of Weather into hard Frost, which we had about the middle of November; but others believe it contagious, and think 'tis communicated by infected Air, after somewhat the same Manner as the Small-pox or Pestilence. They urge in Support of this Opinion, not only that this Cold was first heard of in the eastermost Parts of New-England, about the End of September and Beginning of October last, from whence it has gradually made its Progress thro' all the English Settlements hitherto, New-Hampshire, Massachusets, Rhode-Island, Connecticut, New-York, New-Jersey, and Pennsylvania; but also the Judgment of Dr. Molineux a noted Physician of Ireland,[9] who gives an Account of an universal Cold very much like this, which happen'd in his Time. This Account, which is to be met with in the *Philosophical Transactions,* seems, however, to favour both Opinions; the following is an Extract of it.

"About the Beginning of November, 1693, after a constant Course of moderately warm Weather for the Season, upon some Snow falling in the Mountains and Country round about the Town, of a sudden it grew extreamly cold, and soon after succeeded some few Days of a very hard Frost; whereupon Rheums of all kinds, such as violent Coughs that chiefly affected in the Night, great Defluction of thin Rheum at the Nose and Eyes, immoderate Discharge of Saliva by Spitting, Hoarseness in the Voice, sore Throats with some Trouble in swallowing, Wheasings, Stuffings, and soreness in the Breast, a dull Heaviness and stoppage in the Head, with such like Disorders, the usual Effects of Cold, seized great Numbers of all sorts of People in Dublin.

"When the Distemper was but moderate, it was usually over in eight or ten Days; but with those in whom it rose to greater Height, it continued a Fortnight or 3 Weeks, and sometimes above a Month; one way or other it universally affected all kinds of Men, those that were in the Country as well as City; those that were much abroad in the Weather and open Air, and those that stayed much within-doors, or even kept close in their Chambers; those that were robust and hardy, as well as those that were weak and tender; Men, Women, Children, of all Ranks and Conditions, the youngest and the oldest.

"It was remarkable for its vast Extent: It seized them at London, Oxford, and all other Places of England, as universally, and

9. Thomas (later Sir Thomas) Molyneux (1661–1733), "Historical Account of the late General Coughs and Colds; with some Observations on other Epidemick Distempers," *Philos. Trans.*, XVIII (1694), 105–11. The quotation is extracted and revised from pp. 105–8.

with the same Symptoms as us at Dublin; but with this observable Difference, that it appeared three or four Weeks sooner at London than at Dublin. It also reached the Continent, and infested the northern Parts of France, as about Paris; also Flanders, Holland, and the rest of the United Provinces, with more Violence than these Countries; so that I believe no other epidemic Distemper was ever observed to extend so far." The Doctor concludes with a Remark, that spreading epidemic Distempers generally take their Progress from East to West.

The curious, perhaps would be glad to know whether this Cold was preceded by a sudden Change of Weather and Frost, throughout its Progress, as well as in Pensilvania.

A Sea Captain's Letter[1]   Draft: Historical Society of Pennsylvania

Franklin drafted private letters, *Gazette* essays, and Junto papers in a commonplace book he kept during 1730–38. Those parts of this manuscript book which can be identified and dated are presented at their proper chronological places in the present work. The remaining materials have been assigned the date 1732, the year in which most of the commonplace book was filled. They include this and the next four items.

[1732?]

We thank the Gentlewoman who favour'd us with the following Copy of Letter, which was written by [a] Sea Captain then at Leghorn to his Wife in Boston. Dated July 17. 1724.

My Dear,

When you sollicited me to give you some Instructions for the Education of our Daughters, I ever thought I said enough, in this single Rule, *Endeavour to make them like your self:* And were I assured that Fate had decreed this present Separation between us to be lasting, which God forbid, I could with Satisfaction leave those dear Pledges of our mutual Love in your Care, whose Prudence could allway advise them to Things that are best, and whose Example would be the most perfect Pattern.

---

1. Presumably an unfinished draft of an unpublished essay on the education of women.

However, when I last had the Pleasure of being with you and them, you obtained from me a Promise, That I would give you my Thoughts on that Subject in Writing. Hurry of Business hinder'd my performing it then, but my Indisposition in this City occasion'd by the unfortunate breaking of my Leg, (of which you have already had an Account) has afforded me Leisure enough to comply with your Request, and my Engagement. [*Unfinished*]

Standing Queries for the Junto[2]

Printed in Benjamin Franklin, *Political, Miscellaneous, and Philosophical Pieces*, ed. Benjamin Vaughan, (London, 1779), pp. 533–6; also draft: Historical Society of Pennsylvania.

In the fall of 1727 Franklin "form'd most of my ingenious Acquaintances into a Club for mutual Improvement, which we called the Junto." An important inspiration for it was the deep influence which Cotton Mather's *Essays to do Good* had had on Franklin.[3] Mather had proposed voluntary associations to promote religion and morality; he outlined their nature and form and even suggested an order of business.[4] Franklin took the suggestion, secularized it, gave it a practical and specific purpose.

"The Rules I drew up," Franklin continued in his autobiography, "requir'd that every Member in his Turn should produce one or more Queries on any Point of Morals, Politics or Natural Philosophy, to be discuss'd by the Company, and once in three Months pronounce and read an Essay of his own Writing on any Subject he pleased." Except as partial drafts, these rules do not survive. There does exist, however,

2. This heading is derived from the MS draft, which is entitled simply "Standing Queries." Vaughan, whose text is reprinted here, called the document "Rules for a Club formerly established in Philadelphia." Duane (*Works*, V, 357) and William Temple Franklin (*Memoirs*, 4to, I, app., xx) followed Vaughan, the latter omitting the adverb. Sparks (*Works*, II, 9), and after him Bigelow (*Works*, I, 331) and Smyth (*Writings*, II, 88), used "Rules for a Club Established for Mutual Improvement." The heading here adopted seems to describe the document more accurately.

3. BF to Samuel Mather, May 12, 1784.

4. [Cotton Mather], *Bonifacius. An Essay Upon the Good, that is to be Devised and Designed, by those Who Desire . . . to Do Good While they Live . . .* (Boston, 1710), pp. 171–3. The running title, *Essays to do Good*, is the one by which the book has been known.

a part of the Junto's ritual—the twenty-four "Standing Queries" which were read and answered at every meeting and the four qualifications which every candidate for admission was required to meet. The idea for these questions probably owes something to Mather's proposed order of business, with its ten "Points of Consideration," which were to be read "from time to time" at the meetings, "with a due Pause upon each of them, for any one to offer what he please upon it."

The Standing Queries were first printed by Vaughan, who probably received them from Franklin. Vaughan described them simply as "an early performance" of their author. Duane and William Temple Franklin reprinted them without assigning a date; but Sparks, apparently without evidence or authority, asserted that they "were drawn up in the year 1728." The year 1732, however, is a more likely date in view of the first draft and its relation to the order of business for the Junto proposed under the hypothetical date June 30, 1732. The regulations of 1732, for example, required all new members to meet the four qualifications, "and all the old ones are to take it [them]"—a requirement that indicates that the Junto had been in existence some time *before* the Standing Queries were drafted.

Franklin's draft was admittedly incomplete and imperfect. In the margin opposite the Standing Queries, for example, he wrote: "Memo these Queries are not plac'd in the order I design 'em."[5] The order and phrasing as printed by Vaughan are both improved. The same is true of the Qualifications, the order in Vaughan ascending logically from love of the Junto to love of truth. Vaughan's version is printed here as being more nearly the final product of the author's thought.

In his edition Duane added to these Queries a list of questions which he said had been discussed at meetings of the Junto. These questions Duane took from the *Eulogium on Benjamin Franklin* by Provost William Smith, who found them in a manuscript book of Junto minutes.[6] The questions are omitted here, however, because Franklin had nothing to do with them: he was in England when they were discussed in the so-called "young Junto" in 1758–59.

Previous question, to be answer'd at every meeting.

Have you read over these queries this morning, in order to con-

---

5. The Queries in Vaughan's edition appeared in the following order in the draft: 1, 12, 3, 4, 5, 9, 10, 2, 13, 11, 6, 23, 14, 15, 16, 17, 18, 19, 20, 21, 7, 8, 22, 24.

6. Smith, *Eulogium* . . . (Phila., 1792), pp. 13–14.

sider what you might have to offer the Junto [touching]⁷ any one of them? viz.

1. Have you met with any thing in the author you last read, remarkable, or suitable to be communicated to the Junto? particularly in history, morality, poetry, physic, travels, mechanic arts, or other parts of knowledge.

2. What new story have you lately heard agreeable for telling in conversation?

3. Hath any citizen in your knowledge failed in his business lately, and what have you heard of the cause?

4. Have you lately heard of any citizen's thriving well, and by what means?

5. Have you lately heard how any present rich man, here or elsewhere,⁸ got his estate?

6. Do you know of any fellow citizen, who has lately done a worthy action, deserving praise and imitation? or who has committed an error proper for us to be warned against and avoid?⁹

7. What unhappy effects of intemperance have you lately observed or heard? of imprudence? of passion? or of any other vice or folly?

8. What happy effects of temperance? of prudence? of moderation? or of any other virtue?

9. Have you or any of your acquaintance been lately sick or wounded? If so, what remedies were used, and what were their effects?

10. Who do you know that are shortly going voyages or journies, if one should have occasion to send by them?

11. Do you think of any thing at present, in which the Junto may be serviceable to *mankind?* to their country, to their friends, or to themselves?¹

12. Hath any deserving stranger arrived in town since last meeting, that you heard of? and what have you heard or observed of his character or merits? and whether think you, it lies

7. So printed by Vaughan.
8. Draft omits: "here or elsewhere."
9. Draft omits: "be warned against and."
1. Draft version is longer: ". . . serviceable to Mankind? to their Country consistent with their Duty to Mankind; to their Friends consistent with their Duty to Mankind and their Country; to themselves consistent with their Duty to Mankind, their Country and their Friends."

in the power of the Junto to oblige him, or encourage him as he deserves?[2]

13. Do you know of any deserving young beginner lately set up, whom it lies in the power of the Junto any way to encourage?

14. Have you lately observed any defect in the laws of your *country*, [of][3] which it would be proper to move the legislature for an amendment? Or do you know of any beneficial law that is wanting?

15. Have you lately observed any encroachment on the just liberties of the people?

16. Hath any body attacked your reputation lately? and what can the Junto do towards securing it?

17. Is there any man whose friendship you want, and which the Junto or any of them, can procure for you?

18. Have you lately heard any member's character attacked, and how have you defended it?

19. Hath any man injured you, from whom it is in the power of the Junto to procure redress?

20. In what manner can the Junto, or any of them, assist you in any of your honourable designs?

21. Have you any weighty affair in hand, in which you think the advice of the Junto may be of service?

22. What benefits have you lately received from any man not present?

23. Is there any difficulty in matters of opinion, of justice, and injustice, which you would gladly have discussed at this time?

24. Do you see any thing amiss in the present customs or proceedings of the Junto, which might be amended?

Any person to be qualified, to stand up, and lay his hand on his breast, and be asked these questions; viz.[4]

1. Have you any particular disrespect to any present members? *Answer*. I have not.

2. Draft reads: "Hath any remarkable Stranger arriv'd in Town since last Meeting that you know of; and what have you heard or observ'd of his Character or Merits? And wherein think you the Junto can oblige him or encourage him as he deserves?"

3. So printed in Vaughan.

4. In the draft the Qualifications are in the form of indirect questions, as: "Whether he loves all Men of What Profession or Religion soever."

2. Do you sincerely declare that you love mankind in general;[5] of what profession or religion soever? *Answ.* I do.

3. Do you think any person ought to be harmed in his body, name or goods, for mere speculative opinions, or his external way of worship? *Ans.* No.

4. Do you love[6] truth for truth's sake, and will you endeavour impartially to find and receive it yourself and communicate it to others? *Answ.* Yes.[7]

Proposals and Queries to be Asked the Junto[8]

Draft: Historical Society of Pennsylvania

Proposals   [1732]

That P S and A N be immediately invited into the Junto.[9]

That all New Members be qualified by the 4 qualifications and all the old ones take it.

That these Queries [be] copied at the beginning of a Book [and] be read distinctly each Meeting [with] a Pause between each while one might fill and drink a Glass of Wine.

That if they cannot all be gone thro' in one Night we begin the next where we left off, only such as particularly regard the Junto to be read every Night.

That it be not hereafter the Duty of any Member to bring Queries but left to his Discretion.

That an old Declamation be without fail read every Night when there is no New One.

That Mr. Brientnals Poem on the Junto be read once a Month, and hum'd in Consort, by as many as can hum it.

5. Draft reads: "all Men."
6. Draft adds: "and seeks."
7. Johann Gottfried Herder (1744–1803) translated these queries into German, adding comments, and presented them to the Friday Club of Weimar, July 5, 1791, to serve as the basis for the club's procedure. J. G. Herder, *Briefe zu Beförderung der Humanität* (Riga, 1793), pp. 10–34; Bernhard Suphan, ed., *Herders Sämmtliche Werke* (Berlin, 1877–1913), XVI, 43n; XVII, 10–16; see also Beatrice Marguerite Victory, *Benjamin Franklin and Germany* (Phila., 1915), p. 119.
8. See above, p. 255.
9. Philip Syng and Anthony Nicholas?

1732

That once a Month in Spring, Summer and Fall the Junto meet of a Sunday in the Afternoon in some proper Place cross the River for Bodily Exercise.

That in the aforesaid Book be kept Minutes thus

Fryday June 30. 1732.

Present ABCDEF &c.

1. HP read this Maxim viz. or this Experiment viz or &c.[1]
5. Lately arriv'd one —— of such a Profession or such a Science &c.
7. XY grew rich by this Means &c.

That these Minutes be read once a Year at the Anniversary.

That all Fines due be immediately paid in, and that penal Laws for Queries and Declamations [be] abolish'd only he who is absent above ten Times in the Year, to pay 10s. towards the Anniversary Entertainment.

That the Secretary for keeping the Minutes be allow'd one Shilling per Night, to be paid out of the Money already in his Hands.

That after the Queries are begun reading, all Discourse foreign to them shall be deem'd impertinent.

When any thing from Reading an Author is mention'd, if it excead   lines and the Junto require it; The Person shall bring the Passage, or an Extract from [*written above:* Abstract of] it, in Writing, the next Night, if he has it not [with] him.

When the Books of the Library come: Every Member shall undertake some Author, that he may not be without Observations to communicate.

Queries to be ask'd the Junto

Whence comes the Dew that stands on the Outside of a Tankard that has cold Water in it in the Summer Time?

Does the Importation of Servants increase or advance the Wealth of our Country?

Would not an Office of Insurance for Servants be of Service, and what Methods are proper for the erecting such an Office?

1. BF's marginal note explains that these numbers refer to the regular Junto Queries (see above, p. 256).

Qu. Whence does it proceed, that the Proselytes to any Sect or Persuasion generally appear more zealous than those who are bred up in it?

Answ. I Suppose that People *bred* in different Persuasions are nearly zealous alike. He that changes his Party is either sincere, or not sincere; that is he either does it for the sake of the Opinions merely, or with a View of Interest. If he is sincere and has no View of Interest; and considers before he declares himself, how much Ill will he shall have from those he leaves, and that those he is about to go among will be apt to suspect his Sincerity: if he is not really zealous he will not declare; and therefore must be zealous if he does declare. If he is not sincere, He is oblig'd at least to put on an Appearance of great Zeal, to convince the better, his New Friends that he is heartily in earnest, for his old ones he knows dislike him. And as few Acts of Zeal will be more taken Notice of than such as are done against the Party he has left, he is inclin'd to injure or malign them, because he knows they contemn and despise him. Hence one Renegade is (as the Proverb says) worse than 10 Turks.

Qu. Can a Man arrive at Perfection in this Life as some Believe; or is it impossible as others believe?

A. Perhaps they differ in the meaning of the Word Perfection.

I suppose the Perfection of any Thing to be only the greatest the Nature of that Thing is capable of;

different Things have different Degrees of Perfection; and the same thing at different Times.

Thus an Horse is more perfect than an Oyster yet the Oyster may be a perfect Oyster as well as the Horse a perfect Horse.

And an Egg is not so perfect as a Chicken, nor a Chicken as a Hen; for the Hen has more Strength than the Chicken, and the C[hicken] more Life than the Egg: Yet it may be a perfect Egg, Chicken and Hen.

If they mean, a Man cannot in this Life be so perfect as an Angel, it is [*written above:* may be] true; for an Angel by being incorporeal is allow'd some Perfections we are at present incapable of, and less liable to some Imperfections that we are liable to.

If they mean a Man is not capable of being so perfect here as he is capable of being in Heaven, that may be true likewise. But that a Man is not capable of being so perfect here, as he is capable of being here; is not Sense; it is as if I should say, a Chicken in the State of a Chicken is not capable of being so perfect as a Chicken is capable of being in that State. In the above Sense if there may be a perfect Oyster, a perfect Horse, a perfect Ship, why not a perfect Man? that is as perfect as his present Nature and Circumstances admit?

Quest. Wherein consists the Happiness of a rational Creature?

Ans. In having a Sound Mind and a healthy Body, a Sufficiency of the Necessaries and Conveniencies of Life, together with the Favour of God, and the Love of Mankind.

Qu. What do you mean by a sound Mind?

A. A Faculty of reasoning justly and truly in searching after [and] discovering such Truths as relate to my Happiness. Which Faculty is the Gift of God, capable of being improv'd by Experience and Instruction, into Wisdom.

Q. What is Wisdom?

A. The Knowledge of what will be best for us on all Occasions and of the best Ways of attaining it.

Q. Is any Man wise at all Times, and in all Things?

A. No; but some are much more frequently wise than others.

Q. What do you mean by the Necessaries of Life?

A. Having wholesome Food and Drink wherewith to satisfie Hunger and Thirst, Cloathing and a Place of Habitation fit to secure against the inclemencies of the Weather.

Q. What do you mean by the Conveniencies of Life?

A. Such a Plenty [*uncompleted*]

And if in the Conduct of your Affairs you have been deceived by others, or have committed any Error your self, it will be a Discretion in you to observe and note the same, and the Defailance, with the Means or Expedient to repair it.

No Man truly wise but who hath been deceived.

Let all your observations be committed to writing every Night before you go to Sleep.[2]

---

2. This section, including an illegible shorthand sentence, struck out in the draft.

Query, Whether it is worth a Rational Man's While to forego the Pleasure arising from the present Luxury of the Age in Eating and Drinking and artful Cookery, studying to gratify the Appetite for the Sake of enjoying healthy Old Age, a Sound Mind and a Sound Body, which are the Advantages reasonably to be expected from a more simple and temperate Diet.[3]

Whether those Meats and Drinks are not the best, that contain nothing in their natural Tastes, nor have any Thing added by Art so pleasing as to induce us to Eat or Drink when we are not athirst or Hungry or after Thirst and Hunger are satisfied; Water for Instance for Drink and Bread or the Like for Meat?

What is the [*written above:* is there any] Difference between Knowledge and Prudence?

If there is any, which of the two is most Eligible?

Is it justifiable to put private Men to Death for the Sake of publick Safety or Tranquility, who have committed no Crime?

As in the Case of the Plague to stop Infection, or as in the Case of the Welshmen he e Executed.

Whether Men ought to be denominated Good or ill Men from their Actions or their Inclinations?[4]

If the Sovereign Power attempts to deprive a Subject of his Right, (or which is the same Thing, of what he thinks his Right) is it justifiable in him to resist if he is able?

What general Conduct of Life is most suitable for Men in such Circumstances as most of the Members of the Junto are; Or, of the many Schemes of Living which are in our Power to pursue, which will be most probably conducive to our Happiness.

Which is best to make a Friend of, a wise and good Man that is poor; or a Rich Man that is neither wise nor good? Which of the two is the greatest Loss to a Country, if they both die?

Which of the two is happiest in Life?

Does it not in a general Way require great Study and intense Application for a Poor Man to become rich and Powerful, if he would do it, without the Forfeiture of his Honesty?

3. This sentence is preceded by an uncompleted query beginning, "Whether Temperance as it preserves."
4. Struck out in the draft.

Does it not require as much Pains, Study and Application to become truly Wise and strictly Good and Virtuous as to become rich?

Can a Man of common Capacity pursue both Views with Success at the same Time?

If not, which of the two is it best for him to make his whole Application to?

On the Providence of God in the Government
of the World   Draft: Historical Society of Pennsylvania

[1732][5]

When I consider my own Weakness, and the discerning Judgment of those who are to be my Audience, I cannot help blaming my self considerably, for this rash Undertaking of mine, it being a Thing I am altogether ill practis'd in and very much unqualified for; I am especially discouraged when I reflect that you are all my intimate Pot Companions who have heard me say a 1000 silly Things in Conversations, and therefore have not that laudable Partiality and Veneration for whatever I shall deliver that Good People commonly have for their Spiritual Guides; that You have no Reverence for my Habit, nor for the Sanctity of my Countenance; that you do not believe me inspir'd or divinely assisted, and therefore will think your Selves at Liberty to assent or dissent agree [*written above:* approve] or disagree [*written above:* disapprove] of any Thing I advance, canvassing and sifting it as the private Opinion of one of your Acquaintance. These are great Disadvantages and Discouragements but I am enter'd and must proceed, humbly requesting your Patience and Attention.

I propose at this Time to discourse on the Subject of our last Conversation: the Providence of God in the Government of the World. I shall not attempt to amuse you with Flourishes of Rhetorick, were I master of that deceitful Science because I know ye are Men of substantial Reason and can easily discern between sound Argument and the false Glosses of Oratory; nor

5. In BF's Commonplace Book the draft of this essay to the Junto follows the draft of rules for the Junto (see above, p. 255), written probably in 1732.

shall I endeavour to impose on your Ears, by a musical Accent in delivery, in the Tone of one violently affected with what he says; for well I know that ye are far from being superstitious [or] fond of unmeaning Noise, and that ye believe a Thing to be no more true for being sung than said. I intend to offer you nothing but plain Reasoning, devoid of Art and Ornament; unsupported by the Authority of any Books or Men how sacred soever; because I know that no Authority is more convincing to Men of Reason than the Authority of Reason itself. It might be judg'd an Affront to your Understandings should I go about to prove this first Principle, the Existence of a Deity and that he is the Creator of the Universe, for that would suppose you ignorant of what all Mankind in all Ages have agreed in. I shall therefore proceed to observe: 1. That he must be a Being of great Wisdom; 2. That he must be a Being of great Goodness and 3. That he must be a Being of great Power. That he must be a Being of infinite Wisdom, appears in his admirable Order and Disposition of Things, whether we consider the heavenly Bodies, the Stars and Planets, and their wonderful regular Motions, or this Earth compounded of such an Excellent mixture of all the Elements; or the admirable Structure of Animal Bodies of such infinite Variety, and yet every one adapted to its Nature, and the Way of Life it is to be placed in, whether on Earth, in the Air or in the Waters, and so exactly that the highest and most exquisite human Reason, cannot find a fault and say this would have been better so or in another Manner, which whoever considers attentively and thoroughly will be astonish'd and swallow'd up in Admiration.

2. That the Deity is a Being of great Goodness, appears in his giving Life to so many Creatures, each of which acknowledge it a Benefit by their unwillingness to leave it; in his providing plentiful Sustenance for them all, and making those Things that are most useful, most common and easy to be had; such as Water necessary for almost every Creature's Drink; Air without which few could subsist, the inexpressible Benefits of Light and Sunshine to almost all Animals in general; and to Men the most useful Vegetables, such as Corn, the most useful of Metals as Iron, and the most useful Animals, as Horses, Oxen and Sheep, he has made easiest to raise, or procure in Quantity or Numbers: each

of which particulars if considered seriously and carefully would fill us with the highest Love and Affection. 3. That he is a Being of infinite Power appears, in his being able to form and compound such Vast Masses of Matter as this Earth and the Sun and innumerable Planets and Stars, and give them such prodigious Motion, and yet so to govern them in their greatest Velocity as that they shall not flie off out of their appointed Bounds nor dash one against another, to their mutual Destruction; but 'tis easy to conceive his Power, when we are convinc'd of his infinite Knowledge and Wisdom; for if weak and foolish Creatures as we are, by knowing the Nature of a few Things can produce such wonderful Effects; such as for instance by knowing the Nature only of Nitre and Sea Salt mix'd we can make a Water which will dissolve the hardest Iron and by adding one Ingredient more, can make another Water which will dissolve Gold and render the most Solid Bodies fluid—and by knowing the Nature of Salt Peter Sulphur and Charcoal those mean Ingredients mix'd we can shake the Air in the most terrible Manner, destroy Ships Houses and Men at a Distance and in an Instant, overthrow Cities, rend Rocks into a Thousand Pieces, and level the highest Mountains. What Power must he possess who not only knows the Nature of every Thing in the Universe, but can make Things of new Natures with the greatest Ease and at his Pleasure!

Agreeing then that the World was at first made by a Being of infinite Wisdom, Goodness and Power, which Being we call God; The State of Things ever since and at this Time must be in one of these four following manners, viz.

1. Either he unchangeably decreed and appointed every Thing that comes to pass; and left nothing to the Course [of] Nature, nor allow'd any Creature free agency. or

2. Without decreeing any thing, he left all to general Nature and the Events of Free Agency in his Creatures, which he never alters or interrupts. or

3. He decreed some Things unchangeably, and left others to general Nature and the Events of Free agency, which also he never alters or interrupts; or

4. He sometimes interferes by his particular Providence and sets aside the Effects which would otherwise have been produced by any of the Above Causes.

266

1732

I shall endeavour to shew the first 3 Suppositions to be inconsistent with the common Light of Reason; and that the 4th is most agreeable to it, and therefore most probably true.

In the 1. place. If you say he has in the Beginning unchangeably decreed all Things and left Nothing to Nature or free Agency. These Strange Conclusions will necessarily follow; 1. That he is now no more a God. 'Tis true indeed, before he had made such unchangeable Decree, he was a Being of Power, Almighty; but now having determin'd every Thing, he has divested himself of all further Power, he has done and has no more to do, he has ty'd up his Hands, and has now no greater Power than an Idol of Wood or Stone; nor can there be any more Reason for praying to him or worshipping of him, than of such an Idol for the Worshippers can be never the better for such Worship. Then 2. he has decreed some things contrary to the very Notion of a wise and good Being; Such as that some of his Creatures or Children shall do all Manner of Injury to others and bring every kind of Evil upon them without Cause; that some of them shall even blaspheme him their Creator in the most horrible manner; and, which is still more highly absurd that he has decreed the greatest Part of Mankind, shall in all Ages, put up their earnest Prayers to him both in private and publickly in great Assemblies, when all the while he had so determin'd their Fate that he could not possibly grant them any Benefits on that Account, nor could such Prayers be any way available. Why then should he ordain them to make such Prayers? It cannot be imagined they are of any Service to him. Surely it is not more difficult to believe the World was made by a God of Wood or Stone, than that the God who made the World should be such a God as this.

In the 2. Place. If you say he has decreed nothing but left all things to general Nature, and the Events of Free Agency, which he never alters or interrupts. Then these Conclusions will follow; He must either utterly hide him self from the Works of his Hands, and take no Notice at all of their Proceedings natural or moral; or he must be as undoubtedly he is, a Spectator of every thing; for there can be no Reason or Ground to suppose the first—I say there can be no Reason to imagine he would make so glorious a Universe meerly to abandon it. In this Case imagine the Deity looking on and beholding the Ways of his Creatures; some Hero's

267

in Virtue he sees are incessantly indeavouring the Good of others, they labour thro vast difficulties, they suffer incredible Hardships and Miseries to accomplish this End, in hopes to please a Good God, and obtain his Favour, which they earnestly Pray for; what Answer can he make them within himself but this; *take the Reward Chance may give you, I do not intermeddle in these Affairs;* he sees others continually doing all manner of Evil, and bringing by their Actions Misery and Destruction among Mankind: What can he say here but this, *if Chance rewards you I shall not punish you, I am not to be concerned.* He sees the just, the innocent and the Beneficent in the Hands of the wicked and violent Oppressor; and when the good are at the Brink of Destruction they pray to him, *thou, O God, art mighty and powerful to save; help us we beseech thee:* He answers, *I cannot help you, 'tis none of my Business nor do I at all regard these things.* How is it possible to believe a wise and an infinitely Good Being can be delighted in this Circumstance; and be utterly unconcern'd what becomes of the Beings and Things he has created; for thus, we must believe him idle and unactive, and that his glorious Attributes of Power, Wisdom and Goodness are no more to be made use of.

In the Third Place. If you say he has decreed some things and left others to the Events of Nature and Free Agency, Which he never alters or interrupts; Still you unGod him, if I may be allow'd the Expression; he has nothing to do; he can cause us neither Good nor Harm; he is no more to be regarded than a lifeless Image, than Dagon, or Baall, or Bell and the Dragon; and as in both the other Suppositions foregoing, that Being which from its Power is most able to Act, from its Wisdom knows best how to act, and from its Goodness would always certainly act best, is in this Opinion supposed to become the most unactive of all Beings and remain everlastingly Idle; an Absurdity, which when considered or but barely seen, cannot be swallowed without doing the greatest Violence to common Reason, and all the Faculties of the Understanding.

We are then necessarily driven into the fourth Supposition, That the Deity sometimes interferes by his particular Providence, and sets aside the Events which would otherwise have been produc'd in the Course of Nature, or by the Free Agency of Men; and this is perfectly agreeable with what we can know of his

Attributes and Perfections: But as some may doubt whether 'tis possible there should be such a Thing as free Agency in Creatures; I shall just offer one Short Argument on that Account and proceed to shew how the Duties of Religion necessary follow the Belief of a Providence. You acknowledge that God is infinitely Powerful, Wise and Good, and also a free Agent; and you will not deny that he has communicated to us part of his Wisdom, Power and Goodness; i.e. he has made us in some Degree Wise, potent and good; and is it then impossible for him to communicate any Part of his Freedom, and make us also in some Degree Free? Is not even his *infinite* Power sufficient for this? I should be glad to hear what Reason any Man can give for thinking in that Manner; 'tis sufficient for me to shew tis not impossible, and no Man I think can shew 'tis improbable, but much more might be offer'd to demonstrate clearly that Men are in some Degree free Agents, and accountable for their Actions; however, this I may possibly reserve for another separate Discourse hereafter if I find Occasion.

Lastly If God does not sometimes interfere by his Providence tis either because he cannot, or because he will not; which of these Positions will you chuse? There is a righteous Nation grievously oppress'd by a cruel Tyrant, they earnestly intreat God to deliver them; If you say he cannot, you deny his infinite Power, which [you] at first acknowledg'd; if you say he will not, you must directly deny his infinite Goodness. You are then of necessity oblig'd to allow, that 'tis highly reasonable to believe a Providence because tis highly absurd to believe otherwise.

Now if tis unreasonable to suppose it out of the Power of the Deity to help and favour us particularly or that we are out of his Hearing or Notice or that Good Actions do not procure more of his Favour than ill Ones. Then I conclude, that believing a Providence we have the Foundation of all true Religion; for we should love and revere that Deity for his Goodness and thank him for his Benefits; we should adore him for his Wisdom, fear him for his Power, and pray to him for his Favour and Protection; and this Religion will be a Powerful Regulater of our Actions, give us Peace and Tranquility within our own Minds, and render us Benevolent, Useful and Beneficial to others.

Miscellaneous Observations[6]

Draft: Historical Society of Pennsylvania

The great Secret of succeeding in Conversation, is, To admire little, to hear much; allways to distrust our own Reason, and sometimes that of our Friends; never to pretend to Wit, but to make that of others appear as much as possibly we can: to hearken to what is said, and to answer to the purpose.[7]

Ut jam nunc dicat jam nunc debentia dici.[8]

In vain are musty Morals taught in Schools
By rigid Teachers, and as rigid Rules,
Where Virtue with a Frowning Aspect Stands,
And frights the pupil with her rough Commands.
But Woman ———
Charming Woman can true Converts make,
We love the Precepts for the Teacher's Sake;
Virtue in them appears so bright and gay
We hear with Transport, and with Pride obey.

You may first write a Letter that may carry good Sense, to your Friend, but let the Lines be wide asunder: Then between these Lines write your Secret Letter with Gall Water only, wherein the Galls have been infused but a little while. Dissolve Copperas in fair Water, dip a pensil in the Water and moisten the Paper in the Interlining.

Pennyworth of Spirit of Vitriol in a Thumb-bottle [and] half as much Spring Water—Write—Fire.

I am about Courting a Girl I have had but little Acquaintance with; how shall I come to a Knowledge of her Fawlts? and whether she has the Virtues I imagine she has?

Answ. Commend her among her Female Acquaintance.

----

6. Grouped here are miscellaneous materials from BF's Commonplace Book, not elsewhere presented. A brief outline of Morals of Chess, which would otherwise be included here, will be treated with the text of that essay, which is usually dated 1779.

7. Compare with BF's essay on conversation (see above, p. 177).

8. Horace, *Ars Poetica*, 43.

If a sound Body and a sound Mind, which is as much as to say Health and Virtue are to be preferred before all other Considerations; Ought not Men in choosing of a Business either for themselves or Children to refuse such as are unwholesome for the Body; and such as make a Man too dependent, too much oblig'd to please others, and too much subjected to their Humours in order to be recommended and get a Livelihood.

Extracts from the Gazette, 1732

Printed in *The Pennsylvania Gazette*, January 4 to December 28, 1732.

*** We have no Entries this Week, the River being full of Ice.
[January 4]

Lost last Saturday Night, in Market Street, about 40 or 50*s*. If the Finder will bring it to the Printer hereof, who will describe the Marks, he shall have 10*s*. Reward. [March 30]

[ADVERTISEMENT] Choice Flour of *Mustard-Seed*, in Bottles, very convenient for such as go to Sea; to a little of which if you put hot Water, and stop it up close, you will have strong Mustard, fit to use, in 15 minutes. Sold at the New Printing-Office near the Market, at 1*s*. per Bot. [April 6]

The Subscribers towards a Library in this City, are hereby advertis'd, That Monday the First of May ensuing, is the Day appointed for the Choice of the proper Officers of the Company, for the following Year; and that the Meeting for that Purpose will be at the House of Nicholas Scull in the Market Street, at Two in the Afternoon. JOSEPH BREINTNALL
Philad. April 20. 1732. [April 20]

I do not love to have the Gazette filled with these *Controversies about Religion*, yet I cannot refuse to insert the following Piece, as it appears to be written in his own Vindication, by a Gentleman who has not been very tenderly used in my Papers.[9] [May 4]

9. The writer of the piece here introduced, who signed himself "Prosit," had formerly presented his thoughts in the *American Weekly Mercury*. "Marcus" customarily replied in the *Gazette*. When "Prosit" sent his defense to BF to publish, "Marcus" found a channel for his rejoinders in Bradford's paper.

Sunday last during Afternoon Service, a Fire broke out in the Brewhouse of Mr. Badcock. All the Congregations broke up in great Surprize; and there was immediately abundance of People present at the Place, yet they could not save the Building. Had it happen'd in the Night time, or had not the Tide been up in the Dock, 'tis thought much more Damage would have been done; for several Houses catch'd at a considerable Distance. The Engines did great Service, and the People were very active: They saved the Dwelling House, but not without damaging the Roof. Some Persons were hurt, tho' none mortally.   [May 4]

[ADVERTISEMENT] A likely young Negro Fellow, about 19 or 20 Years of Age, to be disposed of: He is very fit for Labour, being us'd to Plantation Work, and has had the Small-Pox. Enquire of the Printer hereof.   [May 11]

On Sunday the 28th past, about three Miles from this City, a Clap of Thunder fell upon the House of the Widow Mifflin, struck down part of the Top of the Chimney, and split it down several Feet; tore and shattered the Roof, split a Rafter, and broke it off in two Places: and struck off the Plaistering with part of the Brick Wall in the inside of a lower Room, broke the Window Glass and melted the Lead; another Story lower several Splinters of the Window Frame were broke off, some of the Glass broke, and Lead melted; and a Lad who stood in a Porch near the Window, was struck down, and burnt badly in a Streak about the Breadth of one's Hand, from the Side of his Face down to the Calf of his Leg; but it no way hurt any part of his Clothes: He is also much hurt by a Fall he received down four or five Steps with his Head on a Pavement. There were four or five Children sitting within the House, near the Place where the Lad stood, that were very much surprized and stunn'd with the Thunder, and almost suffocated with the Smoke and sulphurous Smell that fill'd the Room.   [June 1]

[ADVERTISEMENT] There is now in the Press, and for the universal Benefit of Mankind will speedily be published, a most curious Collection of ESSAYS, to wit,

    1. An Essay upon High Nonsense, and Low Nonsense.

272

2. An Essay upon the Nonsense of the Pulpit; under which Title is included, A Dissertation upon mysterious and incomprehensible Nonsense, with some Allusions to the Fathers; the whole supported by the most modern Authorities, taken from the venerable Dean Swift, and other Reverend Divines of the Age.

3. An Essay upon the Nonsense of the BAR; under which Title is included, by way of Digression, a most learned Dissertation upon the following Words in Dyer, fol. 218. *Un de l'Jury a mange un Pere, & boir un haust de Cervois;* proving beyond Contradiction, that whereas it is vulgarly rendered into English, *One of the Jury had eat a Pear, and drunk a Draught of Ale;* it ought to be rendered, *One of the Jury had eat up a Father, and drank a Draught of Hartshorn.* Together with some little Animadversions upon *Matter dehors,* and the inimitable Beauties of an &c. Dedicated to the most incomprehensible Alexander Conundrum, Esq; Barrister at Law.

> *For* THEE *I dim these Eyes, and stuff this Head,*
> *With all such Reading as was never read;*
> *For Thee explain a Thing till all Men doubt it,*
> *And write about it, Goddess, and about it.* Dunciad.

By Timothy Scrubb, Gent. who formerly lived in the Cupola of St. Paul's.[1]   [June 1]

[ADVERTISEMENT] Whereas I am credibly informed, that Alexander Conundrum, Esq; in several Companies both public and private, hath been pleased to give himself strange Airs, in regard to my Character; Now this is to inform the said Alexander, that I intend to be my self personally present in *propria persona* at the next Court of Common Pleas, to be held for the City and County of Philadelphia, where if he happens, as is customary with him, to behave himself any ways impertinently, viz. by standing up and making any of his surprizing Motions, in a Cause wherein he is altogether unconcerned; or if he pop off any of his unaccountable Speeches, such as to the great Astonishment of his

1. Although possibly related to the controversy of Prosit and Marcus, the meaning of this hoax is obscure. No book of this title was printed by BF or any other American printer. Timothy Scrubb was the pseudonym used by an English pamphleteer of the time. The verses are from Pope's *Dunciad* (1728), I, 165–6, 169–70.

Hearers he uttered in Kent County Court; Then, and in such Case, I say, with the same Freedom he hath used me, I shall take the Liberty of making a few Observations on his Conduct.

But if the said Alexander let me alone, and behave himself modestly, I do assure him I shall carry my self towards him with all the Respect due to a Brother of the Quill. TIMOTHY SCRUBB

[June 1]

The *Gazette* will come out again on Monday next, and continue to be published on Mondays.

And on the Saturday following will be published *Philadelphische Zeitung*, or Newspaper in High-Dutch, which will continue to be published on Saturdays once a Fortnight, ready to be delivered at Ten a Clock, to Country Subscribers. Advertisements are taken in by the Printer hereof, or by Mr. Louis Timothee, Language Master, who translates them.[2]

[June 15]

From New-York, we hear, that on Saturday se'nnight, in the Afternoon, they had there most terrible Thunder and Lightning, but no great Damage done. The same Day we had some very hard Claps in these Parts; and 'tis said, that in Bucks County, one Flash came so near a Lad, as, without hurting him, to melt the Pewter Button off the Wasteband of his Breeches. 'Tis well nothing else thereabouts, was made of Pewter.

[June 19][3]

Saturday last, being St. John's Day, a Grand Lodge of the ancient and honourable Society of FREE and ACCEPTED MASONS, was held at the Sun Tavern in Water-street, when, after a hand-

2. See above, p. 230.

3. In this issue of the *Gazette* BF printed a riddle, the author of the best answer to receive a year's subscription. The riddle had appeared in the *South-Carolina Gazette*, Jan. 22, 1732. On June 26 BF printed two answers, and on July 3, after receiving several more replies, he printed the following notice: "Having this Week received several Answers to the *Riddle* proposed in one of these Papers; I must inform the Answerers, that their Performances are not judg'd so well to deserve the Character, *Good Verse*, as those two publish'd in our last; and of those the Publick generally give the Preference to the latter, which was wrote by a *Female Hand*. However, to gratify my Correspondents, I may possibly insert their several Pieces in my next." BF denied his correspondents this gratification, however; nor did the *Gazette* announce the name of the contest winner.

som Entertainment, the worshipful W. ALLEN, Esq; was unanimously chosen *Grand Master* of this Province, for the Year ensuing; who was pleased to appoint Mr. William Pringle Deputy Master. Wardens chosen for the ensuing Year, were Thomas Boude and Benj. Franklin. [June 26]

We hear from Allenstown, that on Tuesday last the House of Mr. James Rogers was struck by Lightning. It split down Part of the Chimney, went through the Room where he was sitting with his Children, but without hurting any of them; and entring into the Cellar, fir'd a full Hogshead of Rum which stood under an Arch, and bursting out the Head, the whole Cellar was instantly fill'd with Flames which pour'd out at the Windows. There was several hundred weight of Butter in Tubs, which melted and took fire also; but by the timely Assistance of abundance of People, and the Help of a large Quantity of Water just gathered from the Rain in a Hollow near by, the House was happily preserved. The Loss however was very considerable; for besides what was consum'd by Fire, all the Goods in his Shop or Store were thrown out in Confusion into the Rain and Dirt. 'Tis said that tho' they fill'd the Cellar with so much Water as to be near a Foot deep, yet, after the Fire was out, it was so hot as not to be tolerable to the Feet and Legs of those who would have gone in. [July 10]

To the Surprize of all the Inhabitants on Delaware, who live above Philadelphia, the Water about a Fortnight since, chang'd to a dark dirty Red, so thick that 'tis said the Fish could scarce see to get out of the Way of Boats, and were frequently struck by the Oars. Those who have lived here above these forty Years, say they never saw or heard of the like before. It was accompanied with a Fresh, 'tis true, but not very considerable when compar'd with such as come down almost every Year without such Change of Colour; and 'tis advis'd from Places 40 Mile above the Falls, that they have had no great Rains there. Those who have caused some of the Water to settle, find a Sort of fine brown Earth at the Bottom; but it must be a prodigious Quantity to colour this vast River in such a Manner. The Conjectures of People are various concerning the Cause of it; some imagine an upper Creek, dam'd by Logs, has chang'd its Course and dug a new Bed; others, (hearing from New York, that about the same Time a Flood came down that River from the Mountains, though they had had no Rain, and overflow'd the low Lands, doing great Damage) conceive, that an Earthquake near the Head of both Rivers, has forced out a Quantity of subterraneous Water into them. These however are only Conjectures, Time may possibly make us wiser. In the Interim, we have the Satisfaction to observe, that the River clears sensibly, and we hope will soon recover its wonted purity.   [July 10]

Thomas Butwell from England, maketh in the newest Fashion, Womens Stays, and Childrens Coats, and maketh crooked Bodies look strait; at the Shop under the New-Printing-Office, where also Men's Work is done reasonably.   [July 17]

[ADVERTISEMENT] Good Live-Geese FEATHERS sold at the Printer's hereof.   [July 31]

We hear that one James Hill, has for some Weeks past travell'd about the Country on foot, pretending to be dumb, and made great Profit of the Charity and Credulity of the People. He has with him a Counterfeit Brief, setting forth, that being taken and kept in Slavery seven Years in Turky, he once attempted to make his Escape, for which they barbarously cut out his Tongue, and burnt him in each Arm; and accordingly he shows two grievous Sores in his Arms, which however are artificial; for at Goshen in Chester County, some People suspecting Fraud, threatned him, &c. so much, that they oblig'd him to speak very well, and confess his Roguery, showing them his Trick of shrinking his Tongue into the back of his Mouth, so as to appear as if it was cut away. They, it seems, were too busy to carry him to a Magistrate, it being Harvest Time, and so they gave him his Liberty; and he continues the same Practice, going from House to House; and having pass'd back of Philadelphia, and through North Wales, 'tis suppos'd he intends to make his Progress in the Jerseys. He came from Annapolis, but avoided Newcastle and Chester as well as this City. 'Tis hop'd this publick Notice may put a Stop to his Proceedings, and prevent good-natur'd People from being further impos'd on by him.   [August 7]

[ADVERTISEMENT] Richard Clements supposed to live in some Part of Maryland, by applying to the Printer hereof may hear of something to his Advantage. [August 28]

Some of the Chiefs of the Five (now Six) Nations, as Ambassadors from their Great Council, having been in Town since a few Days after our Honourable Proprietor's Arrival, a Treaty was entred into with them, in order to renew the ancient Chain of Friendship between them and us; and on Thursday last, at the Great Meeting-House, large Presents were made them on Behalf of our Government, consisting of Blankets, Strouds, Kettles, Guns, Powder, Shot, &c. and in particular, the Proprietor presented six Guns, curiously wrought, and the Stocks japan'd with Gold, the finest that have ever been seen here, to be delivered as a Mark of his Affection, one to the King of each Nation. The oldest Man stood up and made a Speech of Thanks, in behalf of the rest, and they all express'd their Approbation of each Article of the wholesome Advice that was given them, to live in Peace and Unity with their Neighbour Nations, &c. On Saturday they had their last Audience, and took Leave in order to return home. At present they are in Peace with the French, but it seems have sent to forbid their going on with their new Settlement at the Crown Point, and advis'd them to remove thence, least their Proceedings occasion a Rupture.[4] [September 7]

[ADVERTISEMENT] Very good *Sealing-Wax* sold by the Printer hereof, at Wholesale or Retale. [September 12]

On Tuesday the 5th Instant, a small Shock of an Earthquake was felt in this City, about Noon. It was also felt at New-Castle. [September 18]

[ADVERTISEMENT] Whereas some Silver Spoons, about five, much batter'd and bruis'd up together, have been lately offer'd to Sale, and stop'd, as suspected to have been stolen; The Person who has lost them, by applying to the Printer hereof, may hear where they are to be had again. [October 26]

It has been so very cold for this Week past, that our River is

4. For a full account of this conference, see *Pa. Col. Recs.*, III, 435–52.

full of driving Ice, and no Vessels can go up or down, a Thing rarely happening so early in the Year. Many People are ill with violent Colds, and Wood is risen to an excessive Price.

[November 23]

Last Monday Morning a Woman who had been long given to excessive Drinking, was found dead in a Room by her self, upon the Floor. She could not be persuaded to go to Bed the Night before, but would sit up alone, as was her frequent Custom. The Coroners Inquest ascribe her Death to the too great Quantity of Liquor she took at one Time. Her former Husband had many Times put several Sorts of odious Physick into her Drink, in order to give her an Aversion to it, but in vain; for who ever heard of a Sot reclaim'd? If there are any such they are Miracles. People cannot be too cautious of the first Steps that may lead them to be engaged in a Habit the most invincible and the most pernicious of all others.

[December 7]

Last Monday se'nnight in the Evening, three Men went into the Indian Prince Tavern, and having call'd for some Liquor, one of them offer'd a new Twenty Shilling Bill to be chang'd for the Reckoning; Mr. R. Brockden, Master of the House, suspecting it to be a Counterfeit, went with it immediately to A. Hamilton, Esq; (under Pretence of going out to get Change) who caused them presently to be apprehended. Upon Examination, two of them appeared innocent, and were discharged; the third, who offer'd to pass the Bill, being ask'd how he came by it, answer'd that he brought Hogs to Town to sell, and had taken it of a Woman unknown in the Market: Upon searching him, two more of the same sort were found in his Pocket-book, all which he said he had taken for Pork. From the Indian Prince he was carried over to another Tavern, where he had put up his Horse, in order to see if he had any Bags wherein more Bills might be found: While the Examination was continuing there, a Woman Stranger in the outer Room was observed to appear somewhat concern'd; upon which she was call'd in, and ask'd, if she knew that Man? she answer'd Yes, he was her Brother; being ask'd if she had any Money about her, the Man was seen to wink at her, and she answer'd, No; but attempting to slide her Hand into her Pocket, they prevented her, and brought the Woman of the House to search her, who found in her Pocket twenty-three 20s. Bills of the same Sort. The Fellow finding the Story of the Hogs would not answer, nor any other Shuffles avail him any thing, betook himself at last to make an ingenuous Confession. He said that one Grindal who arrived this Summer in Capt. Blair from Ireland, got 600 20s. Bills printed there from a Pattern he carried home last Year; that when he came here, he admitted one Watt into the Secret, and gave him a Number of the Bills to pass and exchange in Pennsylvania, while he went into the Jersies on the same Account, altering his Name to Thomson lest a Wife he had married at New-Garden should hear of him; and that they were to meet next Christmass at Philadelphia, and divide the Profits: That Watt had communicated the Thing to him, and given him Twenty-seven Bills to pass, of which he was to have a Share for himself; telling him, to persuade him to it, that it was no Sin, for it would make Money plentier among poor People. He said he had as yet pass'd but one, of which the Change 19s. was found in his Pocket. He could not tell where Grindal might be at this Time in the Jersies, but he inform'd that Watt was at Eastown in Chester County. Officers were immediately dispatch'd in quest of him, who rid all Night, surpriz'd him in his Bed about Day-break, and guarded him to Town. After Examination he was committed to Prison, to keep company with his Friend the Pork-seller, who it seems has *brought his Hogs to a fine Market.* Tis hoped that by Christmass we shall see Grindal here also, that he may (according to Agreement) *share the Profits with 'em.* The Bills they have attempted to counterfeit are of the last Impression; the Counterfeits might pass with many People who do not take much Notice, but they have imitated the Paper very ill, that of the new Bills being thick and stiff, and the Counterfeits soft and flimsy. What is most surprizing is, that the Counterfeiters, with all their care and exactness, have entirely omitted numbering their Bills; at least none of those are number'd which are seiz'd. Was this Infatuation, or were they afraid they should not number them right?   [December 19]

Tuesday last about Noon, a Fire broke out in Chesnut Street, which had like to have done much Damage; but by a timely and vigorous Assistance was extinguished. The Engines did abundance of Service.   [December 28]

JUST PUBLISHED, FOR 1733: POOR RICHARD: An ALMANACK containing the Lunations, Eclipses, Planets Motions and Aspects, Weather, Sun and Moon's rising and setting, Highwater, &c. besides many pleasant and witty Verses, Jests and Sayings, Author's Motive of Writing, Prediction of the Death of his friend Mr. Titan Leeds, Moon no Cuckold, Batchelor's Folly, Parson's Wine and Baker's Pudding, Short Visits, Kings and Bears, New Fashions, Game for Kisses, Katherine's Love, Different Sentiments, Signs of a Tempest, Death a Fisherman, Conjugal Debate, Men and Melons, H. the Prodigal, Breakfast in Bed, Oyster Lawsuit, &c. by RICHARD SAUNDERS, Philomat. Printed and sold by B. Franklin, Price 3*s.* 6*d.* per Dozen. Of whom also may be had Sheet Almanacks at 2*s.* 6*d.* [December 28]

PHILADELPHIA: Printed by B. FRANKLIN,[5] at the *New Printing-Office* near the Market. *Price* 10*s.* a Year. Where Advertisements are taken in, and BOOK-BINDING is done reasonably, in the best Manner.

Poor Richard, 1733

> *Poor Richard, 1733. An Almanack For the Year of Christ* 1733, ... By Richard Saunders, Philom. Philadelphia: Printed and sold by B. Franklin, at the New Printing-Office near the Market. (Reprinted from the copy of the first impression in the Rosenbach Foundation. A copy of the third impression is in Historical Society of Pennsylvania.)

A successful almanac was a valuable source of income to a provincial printer. Andrew Bradford was printing four and Samuel Keimer one, when Franklin and Meredith opened the New Printing-Office in 1728. Entering this crowded, competitive field, the partners the next year issued Thomas Godfrey's *Pennsylvania Almanack* for 1730; and in the fall of 1730 Franklin added to his line John Jerman's *American Almanack*, formerly printed by Bradford. In 1732, however, both Godfrey and Jerman took their copy to Bradford, who now prepared to issue five almanacs for 1733, leaving Franklin with none. In these circumstances Franklin hastily compiled the first *Poor Richard's Almanack*. It was advertised in the *Gazette* on December 19, 1732, as "just published."[6]

5. Meredith's name was dropped from the imprint beginning with the issue of May 11.

6. Paul L. Ford, ed., "The Sayings of Poor Richard," *The Prefaces, Proverbs, and Poems of Benjamin Franklin* (N.Y., 1890), pp. 1–21.

Eighteenth-century almanacs followed a common pattern, and the new publication displayed originality in no essential feature—not even in its title, which was probably suggested by *Poor Robin's Almanack*, which James Franklin printed at Newport; or in its title-page, which was hardly distinguishable from John Jerman's. The very name of the imaginary compiler of his almanac Franklin borrowed from an actual astrologer and almanac-maker of seventeenth-century England. Richard Saunders was made to address his readers, as all good philomaths did; and sometimes their almanacs, like his, printed epigrammatic verses, proverbs, and aphorisms, occasionally even clever ones. The scope for originality and enterprise was strictly limited by convention and format, but what scope there was Franklin exploited fully.

In advertising his almanacs Franklin offered enticing previews of their contents. He attracted the attention of his competitors and the public with Swiftian hoaxes, predicting to the very hour and minute when his principal rival Titan Leeds would die, and assuring Jerman's readers that the stars themselves foretold that their favorite philomath would rejoin the Church of Rome. He retained the public's interest and won its support by printing a great number of verses, proverbs, and aphorisms, more pointed, humorous, and memorable than those in any other almanac.

Probably none of the verses was original with Franklin; he himself said that most of the proverbs and aphorisms were taken from the wisdom of all ages.[7] But he rarely, if ever, took a line directly from its source, and he never borrowed from his competitors. His relied chiefly on English anthologies, notably James Howell, *Lexicon Tetraglotton* (London, 1660); Thomas Fuller, *Gnomologia* (London, 1732), *Introductio ad Prudentiam* (London, 1726–27), and *Introductio ad Sapientiam* (London, 1731); George Savile, Lord Halifax, *A Character of King Charles the Second: and Political, Moral, and Miscellaneous Thoughts and Reflections* (London, 1750); Samuel Richardson's compilation of "Moral and Instructive Sentiments" as an appendix to *Clarissa*, 1750–

7. Robert Newcomb, The Sources of Benjamin Franklin's Sayings of Poor Richard (unpublished dissertation, Univ. of Maryland, 1957) is the most exhaustive study of its subject and the principal authority for statements in this and the following paragraphs. See also Newcomb's "Poor Richard's Debt to Lord Halifax," *PMLA*, LXX (1955), 535–9, and "Benjamin Franklin and Montaigne," *Mod. Lang. Notes*, LXXII (1957), 489–91; and also Wilfred P. Mustard, "Poor Richard's Poetry," *Nation*, LXXXII (March 22, April 5, 1906), 239, 279; Alan D. McKillop, "Some Newtonian Verses in Poor Richard," *New Eng. Quar.*, XXI (1948), 383–5; Stuart A. Gallacher, "Franklin's *Way to Wealth*: A Florilegium of Proverbs and Wise Sayings," *Jour. of Eng. and Germ. Philol.*, XLVIII (1949), 229–51.

51; and Charles Palmer, *A Collection of Select Aphorisms and Maxims* (London, 1748). Most of the verses at the heads of the months came from similar compilations, especially Sir John Mennes and James Smith, *Wits Recreations* (London, 1640); and the anonymous *Collection of Epigrams* (London, 1735–37). About two-thirds of the sayings and half of the verses have been traced to their sources in one or another of these anthologies. Quite as interesting, for the light it throws on Franklin's methods of work, is his drawing on a particular source for a single year or for consecutive years. Thus Howell was his principal source from 1734 to 1742, and Fuller's *Gnomologia* from 1745 to 1751.

But Richard Saunders was more than a compiler from compilations. He delighted his readers because of the way he carefully selected and skillfully revised the wise sayings and epigrams, eliminating superfluous words, smoothing and balancing awkward phrases, replacing vague and meaningless generalities with his own specific, sharp, and homely terms.[8] In these line-fillers as in formal essays Franklin aimed to be short, clear, and smooth. The following examples illustrate the point:

Halifax: A great Talker may be a man of Sense, but he cannot be one, who will venture to rely on him.

P.R. 1753:   A great Talker may be no Fool, but he is one that relies on him.

Howell: The greatest Talkers are the least doers.

P.R. 1733:   Great Talkers, little Doers.

Halifax: Nothing can be humbler than Ambition, when it is so disposed.

P.R. 1753:   Nothing Humbler than Ambition, when it is about to climb.

Fuller: The Way to be safe, is never to be secure.

P.R. 1748:   He that's secure is not safe.

Though neither the rarest nor typographically the most attractive products of Franklin's press, *Poor Richard's Almanacks* are probably the best known. They sold over 10,000 copies annually for many years, and the name, contents, and format were eagerly and shamelessly imitated and copied until well into the nineteenth century, in England as well as in America. Except the first and third printings of the 1733 almanac, only one copy of each of which is known, and a few other issues of which no more than three copies have been located, each year

8. Charles W. Meister, "Franklin as a Proverb Stylist," *Amer. Lit.*, XXIV (1952–53), 157–66.

of Franklin's authorship is represented by several surviving copies, though many of them are imperfect. Most large collections of Americana have several issues, but none has a complete run.[9] Careful typographical studies of the almanacs will reveal not only the complicated printing history of Franklin's best-seller but actual practices in his shop and, presumably, among American printers generally.[1]

The almanac for 1733 opened with an address to the reader. This was followed by an explanation of astrological signs, a page of calculations of the planets' motions for the year, and an explanation of this particular almanac's format. The months came next, one to a page, each headed by some verse, each with astronomical symbols, weather predictions, and aphorisms intermingled. The almanac ended with a prediction of eclipses for the year, and the dates of courts, Quaker meetings, and fairs in Pennsylvania and neighboring colonies. A list of the kings of England at the front and one of reigning monarchs at the back, a table of distances, and some more verses composed the remainder of the pamphlet. From this and subsequent almanacs the editors will print Franklin's addresses to the reader, the verses and aphorisms of each month, some of the explanations, descriptions, and miscellaneous verses; but not the annual calculations, court lists, and statistical information. A comparison of the illustrations of the complete 1733 almanac (pp. 287–310) with the material which follows in letterpress (pp. 311–8) will indicate clearly what parts of each year's issue will be printed in this edition and how they appear in the original work.

9. Dorothy W. Bridgwater of the Yale University Library is preparing for publication a preliminary checklist of Poor Richard's Almanacs in selected libraries.

1. C. William Miller, "Franklin's Type: Its Study Past and Present," APS *Proc.*, XCIX (1955), 418–32, and "Benjamin Franklin's Philadelphia Type," Bibliographical Soc., Univ. of Va., *Studies in Bibliography*, XI (1958), 179–206.

Poor Richard, 1733

Poor Richard, 1733.

AN

Almanack

For the Year of Christ

1733,

Being the First after LEAP YEAR:

	Years
And makes since the Creation	
By the Account of the Eastern *Greeks*	7241
By the Latin Church, when ☉ ent. ♈	6932
By the Computation of *W.W.*	5742
By the *Roman* Chronology	5682
By the *Jewish* Rabbies	5494

Wherein is contained

The Lunations, Eclipses, Judgment of the Weather, Spring Tides, Planets Motions & mutual Aspects, Sun and Moon's Rising and Setting, Length of Days, Time of High Water, Fairs, Courts, and observable Days.

Fitted to the Latitude of Forty Degrees, and a Meridian of Five Hours West from *London*, but may without sensible Error, serve all the adjacent Places, even from *Newfoundland* to *South-Carolina*.

By *RICHARD SAUNDERS*, Philom.

PHILADELPHIA:

Printed and sold by *B. FRANKLIN*, at the New Printing-Office near the Market.

Courteous Reader,

I Might in this place attempt to gain thy Favour, by declaring that I write Almanacks with no other View than that of the publick Good; but in this I should not be sincere; and Men are now a-days too wise to be deceiv'd by Pretences how specious soever. The plain Truth of the Matter is, I am excessive poor, and my Wife, good Woman, is, I tell her, excessive proud; she cannot bear, she says, to sit spinning in her Shift of Tow, while I do nothing but gaze at the Stars; and has threatned more than once to burn all my Books and Rattling-Traps (as she calls my Instruments) if I do not make some profitable Use of them for the good of my Family. The Printer has offer'd me some considerable share of the Profits, and I have thus begun to comply with my Dame's desire.

Indeed this Motive would have had Force enough to have made me publish an Almanack many Years since, had it not been overpower'd by my Regard for my good Friend and Fellow-Student, Mr. *Titan Leeds*, whose Interest I was extreamly unwilling to hurt: But this Obstacle (I am far from speaking it with Pleasure) is soon to be removed, since inexorable Death, who was never known to respect Merit, has already prepared the mortal Dart, the fatal Sister has already extended her destroying Shears, and that ingenious Man must soon be taken from us. He dies, by my Calculation made at his Request, on *Oct.* 17. 1733. 3 ho. 29 m. *P. M.* at the very instant of the ☌ of ☉ and ☿: By his own Calculation he will survive till the 26th of the same Month. This small difference between us we have disputed whenever we have met these 9 Years past; but at length he is inclinable to agree with my Judgment; Which of us is most exact, a little Time will now determine. As therefore these Provinces may not longer expect to see any of his Performances after this Year, I think my self free to take up the Task, and request a share of the publick Encouragement; which I am the more apt to hope for on this Account

count, that the Buyer of my Almanack may confider himself, not only as purchasing an useful Utenfil, but as performing an Act of Charity, to his poor *Friend and Servant* R. SAUNDERS.

The Anatomy of Man's Body as govern'd by the Twelve Conftellations.

The Head and Face

Neck		Arms
Breaft		Heart
Bowels		Reins
Secrets		Thighs
Knees		Legs

The Feet.

To know where the Sign is,

Firft find the Day of the Month, and againft the Day you have the Sign or Place of the Moon in the 5th Column. Then finding the Sign here, it fhews the part of the Body it governs.

The Names and Characters of the Seven Planets.

♄ Saturn, ♃ Jupiter, ♂ Mars, ☉ Sol, ♀ Venus, ☿ Mercury, ☽ Luna, ☊ Dragons Head and ☋ Tail.

The Five Afpects.

☌ Conjunction, ✶ Sextile, ☍ Oppofition, △ Trine, ☐ Quartile.

Common Notes for the Year 1739.

Golden Number	5	Cycle of the Sun	6
Epaft	25	Dominical Letter	G

Planets Motions for the 1, 8, 15, and 22 days in each Month, 1733.

Mon.	Days	Sun's Place.	♄ ♈	♃ ♍	♂ ♓	♀ ♐	☿ ♑	Mon.	Sun's Place.	♄ ♉	♃ ♏	♂ ♋	♀ ♋	☿ ♋
January	1	22 39	11	7	17	15	27	July	20 ♋ 6	0	0	23	25	25
	8	29 47	12	8	23	23	19		26 36	0	1	26	♌	♌
	15	6 ♒ 55	12	9	28	♑	16		3 ♌ 18	0	1	♌	15	22
	22	14 2	13	9	♈	11	19		10 8	0	2	7	23	♍
February	1	24 9	13	10	11	23	29	August	19 48	1	3	13	♍	16
	8	1 ♓ 13	14	10	16	♒	♒		26 27	1	4	18	14	24
	15	8 15	15	10	21	10	18		3 ♍ 12	0	5	22	23	28
	22	15 16	16	R.	26	19	29		9 58	R	6	27	♎	9
March	1	22 15	17	9	♉	27	♓	September	19 42	0	8	♍	14	23
	8	29 12	18	9	6	♓	24		26 32	♈	9	8	22	16
	15	6 ♈ 8	18	8	11	15	♈		3 ♎ 24	29	10	12	♏	16
	22	13 1	9	8	16	23	22		10 18	28	12	17	9	23
April	1	22 49	21	7	23	♈	♉	October	19 13	28	14	22	25	♎
	8	29 39	21	6	28	14	19		26 12	27	15	27	♐	21
	15	6 ♉ 27	22	5	♊	23	24		3 ♏ 12	26	17	♎	9	♏
	22	13 19	25	4	7	♉	R.		10 12	26	18	5	16	15
May	1	21 54	24	3	13	12	20	Novemb.	20 17	25	20	12	25	28
	8	28 37	25	2	18	21	16		27 21	25	22	16	♑	♐
	15	5 ♊ 20	26	1	23	29	D.		4 ♐ 27	24	23	21	15	20
	22	12 1	27	1	27	♊	19		11 55	24	26	25	23	♑
June	1	21 33	29	0	♋	21	29	December	20 45	24	28	♏	♒	11
	8	28 13	29	0	9	28	♊		27 53	24	28	5	12	13
	15	4 ♋ 59	29	D.	13	♋	21		5 ♑ 12	D.	♐	10	20	12
	22	11 32	29	0	18	16	♋		12 12	24	1	14	28	3

♄ *Saturn* diseas'd with Age, and left for dead;
Chang'd all his Gold to be involv'd in Lead.
♃ *Jove*, Juno leaves, and loves to take his Range;
From whom Man learns to love, and loves to change.
♂ is disarmed, and to ♀ gone,
Where *Vulcan's* Anvil must be struck upon.
That ☽ *Luna's* horn'd, it cannot well be said,
Since I ne'er heard that she was married.

Explanation of this ALMANACK.

THE first Column shews the Days of the Month.
The second shews the Week day, *Sunday* Letter being this Year G.

The third contains the Days observ'd by the Church, the Aspects of the Planets and Judgment of the Weather; the Length, Increase, and Decrease of Days, the rising and setting of the seven Stars, &c.

The fourth is the Time of High Water at *Philadelphia*, (h) signifies *half an hour after*.

The fifth is the Moon's Place.

The sixth is the Sun's rising and setting, thus understood; Against the second Day of *January* you see in the 6th Column these Figures 7 14 5, which show that the Sun rises that Day 14 minutes after 7, and sets 14 minutes before 5. I have chose to put the Sun's rising and setting for every day, rather than the Moon's, because of its constant Use in setting of Clocks and Watches.

In the last Column, with the Changes of the Moon, I have put her rising and setting every five or six Days: If you want to know her rising or setting on a Day or two after That against which I have set it, the common Rule of an hour and half later each day, will be exact enough to direct People in their Travelling, which is the common Use that is made of it.

Profitable Observations and Notes.

ALL Measures of Longitude are deduced from Barley corns: Three Barley-corns make an Inch, 12 Inches a Foot, 3 Feet a Yard, 5 Yards & an half one Pole or Perch, 40 Pearches make a Furlong, 8 Furlongs make a Mile, in a Mile are 320 Perches or Poles, 1066 Paces, 1408 Ells, 1760 Yards, 5280 Feet; 63360 Inches; 190080 Barley corns.

The circumference of the Earth and Sea jointly is 25036 Miles, and the Diameter 7966 Miles, and its Semidiameter 3983 Miles, according to English Mensuration.

A Table of KINGS,

from the Time that *England* was first so called by King *Egbert*.

Kings Names.	Reign began.	Reigned.	Kings Names.	Reign began.	Reigned.
K. Egbert, *Sax.*	818	28	Henry 3.	1216	56
Ethelwolf,	836	21	Edward 1.	274	35
Ethelbald,	857	1	Edward 2.	1307	19
Ethelbert,	858	5	Edward 3.	1326	51
Ethelfred,	863	10	Richard 2.	1377	22
Alfred,	873	27	*Lancaster Line.*		
Edward 1.	900	24	Henry 4.	1399	14
Athelston,	924	16	Henry 5.	1413	9
Edmund 1.	940	6	Henry 6.	1422	38
Eldred,	946	9	*York Line.*		
Edwin,	955	4	Edward 4.	1460	23
Edgar,	959	0	Edward 5.	1483	0
Edward 2.	979	3	Richard 3.	1483	2
Ethelred,	982	34	*Families united.*		
Edmund 2.	1016	1	Henry 7.	1485	24
Danish Line.			Henry 8.	1508	40
Canutus 1.	1017	20	Edward 6.	1547	6
Harold 1.	1037	3	Q. Mary 1.	1553	5
Canutus 2.	1040	2	Q. Elizabeth.	1558	44
Edward *Confessor.*	1042	23	*Kingdoms united.*		
Harold 2.	1065	1	James 1.	1602	22
Norman Line.			Charles 1.	1624	24
W. Conqueror,	1066	21	Charles 2.	1648	36
W. Rufus,	1087	13	James 2.	1684	4
Henry 1.	1100	35	Q. Mary 2.	1688	6
Stephen,	1135	19	William 3.	1688	13
Saxon Line restor'd.			Q. Anne,	1702	12
Henry 2.	1154	35	George 1.	1714	13
Richard 1.	1189	10	GEORGE II.	1727	
John,	1199	17	*Whom God preserve.*		

292

More nice than wise.

Old Batchelor would have a Wife that's wise,
Fair, rich, and young, a Maiden for his Bed;
Not proud, nor churlish, but of faultless size;
A Country Houswife in the City bred.
He's a nice Fool, and long in vain hath staid;
He should bespeak her, there's none ready made.

1	2 Circumcision	12 ♌	R.☉ S. Sun rise 7 15
2	3 7 *sou. 7 51 Ev.	t 24	7 14 5 ☽ rise 4 5 morn
3	4 ☌☉☿ *Windy* &	1h ♍	7 14 5 New ☽ 4 day
4	5 Day 9 h. 34 m.	2h 20	7 13 5 at 8 Aftern.
5	6 *♂☿ *falling wea*	3 ♒	7 12 5 *Never spare the*
6	7 Epiphany □ ♂♃	4 19	7 12 5 *Parson's wine,*
7	G *snow if not too warm*	5 ♓	7 11 5 ☽ sets 8 13 aft.
8	2 *about this time.*	6 17	7 10 5 *nor the Baker's*
9	3 ☉ ent ♒	6h ♈	7 9 5 *pudding.*
10	4 Days incr. 30 m.	7 16	7 8 5 First Quarter.
11	5 *Windy and*	8 ♉	7 8 5 *Visits should be*
12	6 7 *south 7 13	9 14	7 7 5 *short, like a win-*
13	7 *cloudy.*	10 28	7 6 5 *ter's day,* *Lest*
14	G 2 Sund. aft. Ep.	10 ♊	7 5 5 *you're too trouble-*
15	2 7 *so. 6 56	11 25	7 4 5 *som hasten away.*
16	3 *Falling wea. windy*	12 ♋	7 3 5
17	4 □☉♃ *moderate*	1 22	7 2 5 ☽ sets 5 54 mo.
18	5 *snow or rain,*	2 ♌	7 1 5 Full ● 18 day
19	6 Days 10 hours.	2h 19	7 0 5 9 at night.
20	7 *☉♄ *Snow, y Rain*	3 ♍	6 59 6
21	G Septuagesima *fair*	4 13	6 58 6 *A house without*
22	2 7 *south 6 52	5 26	6 57 6 *woman & Fire,*
23	3 *There will be more*	6 ♎	6 56 6 ☽ rises 10 aft.
24	4 □♄♀ *cold rain*	6h 20	6 55 6 *light, is like a*
25	5 Days 10 h. 12 m.	7 ♏	6 54 6 *body without soul*
26	6 *or snow.*	8 14	6 53 6 *or sprite.*
27	7 *Very sharp*	9 26	6 52 6 Last Q. 26 day
28	G Sexages. *Clear but*	10 ♐	6 51 6 ☽ ris. 1 50 mor.
29	2 *sharp and cold,*	10 20	6 50 6 *Kings & Bears*
30	3 K. Cha. I. decol.	11 ♑	6 48 6 *oft worry their*
31	4 *Frosts.*	12 16	6 47 6 *keepers.*

Moderate Weather being soft

hard frost
moderate snow

Very Cold

N. N. of B---s County, pray don't be angry with
poor Richard.

Each Age of Men new Fashions doth invent;
Things which are old, young Men do not esteem:
What pleas'd our Fathers, doth not us content;
What flourish'd then, we out of fashion deem:
And that's the reason, as I understand,
Why Prodigus did sell his Father's Land.

| M. | W. | Remarkable Days, | H. | ☽ | ☉ rises | Lunations, |
D.	D.	Aspects, Weather.	w.	Pl	and sets.	☽ rises & sets.
1	5	Cloudy and some	1	29	6 46 6	☽ rif. 5 2 mor.
2	6	Purification V. M.	2	♒ 6 45 6		
3	7	Spring Tides.	2h	28	6 42 6	New ☽ 9 morn.
4	G	falling weather	3	♓ 6 41 6		Light purse,
5	2	♂ ♄ ☍ this week.	4	27	6 40 6	heavy heart.
6	3	Shrove Tuesday	5	♈ 6 38 6		☽ sets 9 26 aft.
7	4	Ash Wednesday	6	26	6 37 6	He's a Fool that
8	5	☉ enters ♓	6h	♉ 6 36 6		makes his Doctor
9	6	☐ ♃ ☿ Snow or	7	25	6 35 6	his Heir.
10	7	Days incr. 1 36	8	♊ 6 33 6		First Quarter.
11	G	1 Sund. Lent	9	22	6 32 6	☽ sets 1 58 mo.
12	2	Rain.	10	♋ 6 31 6		Ne'er take a wife
13	3	♃ south 5 9	10	19	6 30 6	till thou hast a
14	4	Valentine ✳ ♄ ☿	11	♌ 6 28 6		house (& a fire)
15	5	☐ ♃ ☿ windy &	12	15	6 27 6	to put her in.
16	6	rain perhaps. Rain	1	♍ 6 26 6		☽ sets 5 27 mo.
17	7	△ ☉ ♃ clouds and	1	♍ 6 24 6		♃ set at midn.
18	G	Falling weather,	2h	23	6 23 6	Full ● 17 day,
19	2	✳ ♄ ☿ ✳ ♂ ☿	3	♎ 6 21 6		at 2 Aftern.
20	3	Clear but windy,	4	16	6 20 6	He's gone, and
21	4	in spight of Aspects.	5	28	6 18 6	forgot nothing but
22	5	Days 11 h. 26 m.	6	♏ 6 17 6		to say Farewel—
23	6		6h	22	6 16 6	☽ rif. 11 43 aft.
24	7	St. Matthias	7	♐ 6 15 6		to his creditors.
25	G	3 Sund. in Lent	8	16	6 14 6	Last Quarter.
26	2	♃ set 11 31	9	28	6 13 6	Love well, whip
27	3	rain or snow,	10	♑ 6 12 6		well.
28	4	△ ♃ ☿ and wind.	10	24	6 11 6	☽ rif. 3 morn.

Snow

very cold

old East

Warm

thaw

temperate
but cloudy

cloudy

hard Snow

very bad

a fine day

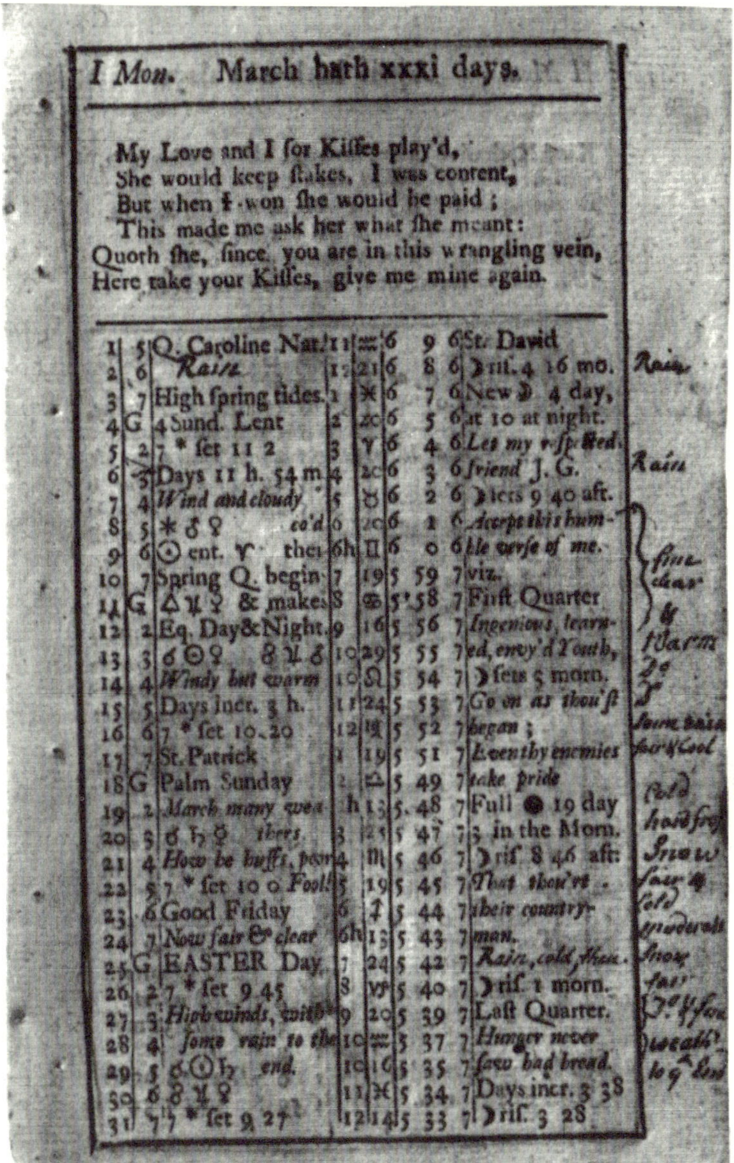

I Mon. March hath xxxi days.

My Love and I for Kiſſes play'd,
She would keep ſtakes, I was content,
But when I won ſhe would be paid;
This made me ask her what ſhe meant:
Quoth ſhe, ſince you are in this wrangling vein,
Here take your Kiſſes, give me mine again.

1	5	Q. Caroline Nat.	11	♒	6	9	6	St. David	
2	6	*Rain*	12	21	6	8	6	☽ ri. 4 16 mo.	*Rain*
3	7	High ſpring tides.	1	♓	6	7	6	New ☽ 4 day,	
4	G	4 Sund. Lent	2	20	6	5	6	at 10 at night.	
5	2	7 * ſet 11 2	3	♈	6	4	6	*Let my reſpected*	
6	3	Days 11 h. 54 m.	4	20	6	3	6	*friend* J. G.	*Rain*
7	4	*Wind and cloudy*	5	♉	6	2	6	☽ ſets 9 40 aft.	
8	5	✱ ♂ ♀ co'd	6	20	6	1	6	*Accept this hum-*	*fine*
9	6	☉ ent. ♈ then	6h	♊	6	0	6	*ble verſe of me.*	*clear*
10	7	Spring Q. begin	7	19	5	59	7	viz.	*&*
11	G	△ ♃ ♀ & makes	8	♋	5	58	7	Firſt Quarter	*Warm*
12	2	Eq. Day & Night.	9	16	5	56	7	*Ingenious, learn-*	
13	3	☌ ☉ ♀ ☍ ♃ ♂	10	29	5	55	7	*ed, envy'd Youth,*	*Do*
14	4	*Windy but warm*	10	♌	5	54	7	☽ ſets 5 morn.	*Do*
15	5	Days incr. 3 h.	11	24	5	53	7	*Go on as thou'ſt*	*d*
16	6	7 * ſet 10 20	12	♍	5	52	7	*began;*	*some rain*
17	7	St. Patrick	1	19	5	51	7	*Even thy enemies*	*fair & cool*
18	G	Palm Sunday	2	♎	5	49	7	*take pride*	*Cold*
19	2	*March many wea-*	h	13	5	48	7	Full ● 19 day	*hard frost*
20	3	☌ ♄ ☿ *thers.*	3	25	5	47	7	3 in the Morn.	
21	4	*How he huffs, poor*	4	♏	5	46	7	☽ riſ. 8 46 aft.	*Snow*
22	5	7 * ſet 10 0 *Fool!*	5	19	5	45	7	*That thou'rt*	*fair &*
23	6	Good Friday	6	♐	5	44	7	*their country-*	*cold*
24	7	*Now fair & clear*	6h	13	5	43	7	*man.*	*moderate*
25	G	EASTER Day	7	24	5	42	7	*Rain, cold, then*	*Snow*
26	2	7 * ſet 9 45	8	♑	5	40	7	☽ riſ. 1 morn.	*fair*
27	3	*High winds, with*	9	20	5	39	7	Laſt Quarter.	*Do & fair*
28	4	*ſome rain to the*	10	♒	5	37	7	*Hunger never*	*weather*
29	5	☌ ☉ ♄ *end.*	10	16	5	35	7	*ſaw bad bread.*	*to g[illegible]*
30	6	☍ ♃ ♀	11	♓	5	34	7	Days incr. 3 38	
31	7	7 * ſet 9 27	12	14	5	33	7	☽ riſ. 3 28	

Kind Katharine to her husband kiſs'd theſe words,
' Mine own ſweet *Will*, how dearly I love thee!
If true (quoth Will) the World no ſuch affords.
And that its true I durſt his warrant be;
For ne'er heard I of Woman good or ill,
  But always loved beſt, her own ſweet Will.

1	G	All Fools.	1	29	5	32	7 Great Talkers,
2	2	*Wet weather, or*	2 ♈	5	31	7 little Doers.
3	3	7 * ſet 9 0	♈h a 9	5	30	7 New ☽ 5 day,
4	4		3 ♉	5	29	7 at 4 morn.
5	5	*Cloudy and likely*	4	29	5	27	7 ☽ ſets 9 29 aſt.
6	6	*for rain.*	5 ♊	5	26	7 *A rich rogue, is*
7	7		6	28	5	24	7 *like a fat hog, who*
8	G	1 Sund. p. Eaſter	6 h ♋	5	25	7 *never does good til*
9	2	☉ enters ♉	7	26	5	22	7 *as dead as a log.*
10	3	7 * ſet 8 50	8 ♌	5	21	7 First Quarter.
11	4	Days 13 h. 20 m	9	22	5	20	7 ☽ ſets 1 46 mo.
12	5	*Wind or Thunder,*	10 ♍	5	19	7 *Relation without*
13	6	8 ☉ ☿	10 16	5	18	7 *friendſhip, friend-*
14	7	8 h ☿	11 28	5	17	7 *ſhip without pow-*
15	G	3 Sund. p. Eaſter	12 ♎	5	16	7 *er, power without*
16	2	7 * ſet 8 21 . *Gous*	1	22	5	15	7 ☽ ſets 4 7 mor.
17	3	*and rain.*	2 ♏	5	14	7 Full ● at 10 at
18	4	*Beware of meat*	2 h 16	5	13	7 night.
19	5	*twice boil'd, & an*	3 28	5	12	7 *will, will while*
20	6	*old foe reconil'd.*	4 ♐	5	11	7 *effect, effect with*
21	7	Days inc. 4 h. 20	5	22	5	10	7 ☽ riſ. 11 aftern.
22	G	4 Sund. p. Eaſter	6 ♑	5	8	7 *out profit, & pro-*
23	2	S George 8 ♃ ♀	6 h	7	7	*fit without ver-*
24	3	Troy burnt	7	6	*tue, are not.*
25	4	St. Mark, Evang.	8	5	Laſt Quarter.
26	5	*Cloudy with high*	9	4	7 *worth a farto.*
27	6	*winds, and perhaps*	10	3	7 ☽ riſ. 1 31 mor.
28	7	7 * ſet 7 47	11	2	7
29	G	Rogation Sunday	12 ♒	0	7 Days 14 hours
05	2	☌ ☉ ♀ *rain.*	12 ♓	4	59	8	7 * ſet 7 54

III Mon. **May hath xxxi days.**

Mirth pleaſeth ſome, to othets 'tis offence,
Some commend plain conceit,ſome profound ſenſe;
Some wiſh a witty Jeſt, ſome diſlike that, (what.
And moſt would have themſelves they know not
Then he that would pleaſe all, and himſelf too,
Takes more in hand than he is like to do.

1	3	Phil. & James.	1	♉	4	58	8	☽ riſ. 3 49 mor.
2	4	*Cloudy and may be*	2	22	4	57	8	New ☽ 2 day,
3	5	Aſcenſion Day,	3	♊	4	56	8	about noon.
4	6	Days 14 h. 10 m.	4	22	4	55	8	*The favour of the*
5	7	*falling weather*	5	♋	4	54	8	*Great is no in-*
6	G	☌ ♀ ☿	6	21	4	53	8	*heritance.*
7	2	*about this time.*	6h	♌	4	52	8	☽ ſets 11 47 aft.
8	3	*Eat to live, and not*	7	18	4	51	8	
9	4	*live to eat.*	8	♍	4	50	8	*Fools make feaſts*
10	5	☉ enters ♊	9	13	4	49	8	Firſt Quarter,
11	6	*But now more clear*	10	25	4	49	8	*and wiſe men eat*
12	7	Days inc. 5 h. 10	11	♎	4	48	8	*em.*
13	G	Whitſunday	12	19	4	47	8	☽ ſets 2 11 mo.
14	2	7 * riſe 3 58 morn	1	♏	4	47	8	*Beware of the*
15	3	*and pleaſant wea-*	2	13	4	46	8	*young Doctor &*
16	4	*ther comes on.*	2h	25	4	46	8	*the old Barber.*
17	5	*March windy, and*	3	♐	4	45	8	Full ● 17 day,
18	6	*April rainy. makes*	4	19	4	44	8	at 2 afternoon.
19	7	May *the pleaſanteſt*	5	♑	4	43	8	☽ riſ. 9 at nigh.
20	G	Trinity Sunday	6	13	4	43	8	*He has chang'd*
21	2	⚹ ♄ ☌	6h	26	4	42	8	*his one ey'd horſe*
22	3	Days 14 h. 58 m.	7	♒	4	41	8	*for a blind one.*
23	4	*month of any.*	8	2	4	41	8	
24	5	7 * riſe 3 14	9	♓	4	40	8	Laſt Quarter.
25	6	*Cloudy wet weather*	10	19	4	40	8	☽ riſ. 12 32 aft.
26	7	△ ♃ ♀	10	♈	4	39	8	*The poor have lit*
27	G	1 Sund. p. Trin.	11	17	4	39	8	*tle, beggars none,*
28	2	*and perhaps Thun-*	12	♉	4	39	8	*the rich too much,*
29	3	K. Cha. II born	1	16	4	39	8	enough *not one.*
30	4	and reſtor'd.	2	♊	4	38	8	Days 14h 46
31	5	*der or high winds.*	2h	17	4	38	8	New ☽ 7 at nig.

Observe the daily circle of the sun,
And the short year of each revolving moon :
By them thou shalt foresee the following day,
Nor shall a starry night thy hopes betray.
When first the moon appears, if then she shrouds
Her silver crescent, tip'd with sable clouds,
Conclude she bodes a tempest on the main,
And brews for fields impetuous floods of rain.

1	6	⚹ rise 2 42	13	♏	4 38	8	After 5 days warm
2	7	More warm though	4	♏	4 38	8	grows sunny, of
3	G	2 Sun. p. Trin.	5	♐	4 38	8	☾ sets 9 38 aft.
4	2	⚹ rise 2 36	6	♐	4 38	8	a womb, a guess,
5	3	it be cloudy.	6h	♑	4 38	8	☌ weather rai-
6	4	☌ ☉ ♀	7	♑	4 38	8	ny.
7	5	⚹ ☉ ♄ △ ♄ ♀	8	♒	4 38	8	
8	6	Pleasant showers	9	♒	4 38	8	First Quarter
9	7	⚹ rise 2 15 △ ♃ ♀	10	♓	4 38	8	☾ set 1 2 57 aft.
10	G	about this time	10	♓	4 38	8	
11	2	St. Barnabas	11	♈	4 38	8	To lengthen thy
12	3	☉ ent. ♋ 10 day	12	♈	4 38	8	Life, lessen thy
13	4	Summer Q. begins	1	♉	4 39	8	Meals.
14	5	☉ makes longest	2	♉	4 39	8	☾ sets 3 morn.
15	6	day 14 h 51 m.	2h	♊	4 39	8	
16	7	K. Geo. II. procla.	3	♊	4 39	8	Full ● 3 morn.
17	G	15 day 1727	4	♊	4 39	8	The proof of gold
18	2	Fair and pleasant	5	♋	4 39	8	is fire, the proof
19	3	⚹ rise 1 44	6	♋	4 39	8	of woman, gold ;
20	4	Edward △ ♃ ♀	6h	♌	4 39	8	☾ rise 10 aftern.
21	5	Showers and likely	7	♌	4 39	8	the proof of man,
22	6	☍ ♄ ♃	8	♍	4 40	8	the woman.
23	7	for more rain,	9	♍	4 40	8	Last Quarter.
24	G	5 Sund. p. Trin.	10	♍	4 40	8	⚹ rise 1 12
25	2	with all a bits	10	♎	4 41	8	☾ rise 1 morn.
26	3	☉ ⚹ ☉ fair	11	♎	4 41	8	After feasts
27	4	Days shorten 5m.	12	♏	4 41	8	wants, the maker
28	5	⚹ rise 12 57	1	♏	4 42	8	scratches his head
29	6	St. Peter & Paul	2	♐	4 42	8	
30	7	New clear again.	3h	♐	4 43	8	New ☾ 3 morn.

V Mon. July hath xxxi days.

‘ Ev'n while the reaper fills his greedy hands,
‘ And binds the golden sheafs in brittle bands:
‘ Oft have I seen a sudden storm arise
‘ From all the warring winds that sweep the skies:
‘ And oft whole sheets descend of slucy rain,
‘ Suck'd by the spungy clouds from off the main;
‘ The lofty skies at once come pouring down,
‘ The promis'd crop and golden labours drown.

1	G	6 Sund. p. Trin.	5	♌	4	43	8	*Many estates are*
2	2	*More windy and*	4	21	4	43	8	☽ sets 8 39 aft.
3	3	□ ♃ ☿ ⚹ ♀ ♄ ☿	5	♍	4	44	8	*spent in the get-*
4	4	☌ ♀ ☿ ☌ ♂ ☿	6	17	4	45	8	*ting, Since wom-*
5	5	*like for rain.*	6h	♎	4	46	8	*en for tea forsook*
6	6	Cornelius	7	12	4	46	8	☽ sets 10 6 aft.
7	7	7 * set 12 21	8	24	4	47	8	First Quarter.
8	G	7 Sund. p. Trin.	9	♏	4	47	8	*spinning & knit-*
9	2	Wind or Thund.	10	17	4	48	8	*ting.*
10	3	□ ♄ ♂	11	29	4	49	8	
11	4	□ ♄ ☉	12	♐	4	50	8	*He that lies down*
12	5	☉ enters ♌	1	13	4	50	8	☽ sets 1 morn
13	6	□ ☉ ♃	2	♑	4	51	8	*with Dogs, shall*
14	7	☌ ☉ ♂ □ ♃ ♂	2h	18	4	52	8	*rise up with fleas*
15	G	8 Sund. p. Trin.	3	♒	4	53	8	Full ● 5 After.
16	2	7 * rise 11 45	4	15	4	54	8	
17	3	*Neither Shame nor*	5	28	4	55	8	☽ rise 8 aftern.
18	4	*Grace yet Bob.*	6	♓	4	56	8	
19	5	Dog Days begin.	6h	16	4	57	8	*A fat kitchin, a*
20	6	△ ♄ ♀	7	♈	4	57	8	*lean Will.*
21	7	⚹ ♃ ☿ Rain	8	24	4	58	8	
22	G	9 Sund. p. Trin.	9	♉	4	58	8	Last Quarter.
23	2	*Thunder with wind*	10	12	4	59	8	☽ ri. 11 38 mo.
24	3	*or falling weather.*	10	♊	5	00	7	*Distrust & cau-*
25	4	St. James	11	20	5	1	7	*tion are the pa-*
26	5		12	♋	5	2	7	*rents of security.*
27	6	△ ♄ ♀ *more rain*	1	18	5	3	7	
28	7	7 * rise 10 54	2	♌	5	4	7	☽ rise 4 morn.
29	G	10 Sund. p. Trin.	2h	17	5	5	7	New ☽ 2 aft.
30	2	*and warm, and*	3	29	5	6	7	*Tongue double,*
31	3	*cloudy.*	4	♍	5	7	7	*brings trouble.*

Rain (beside 17)
fair (beside 19)
Rain (beside 21)

' For us thro' 12 bright figns Apollo guides
' The year, and earth in fev'ral climes divides.
' Five girdles bind the skies, the torrid zone
' Glows with the paffing and repaffing fun.
' Far on the right and left, th' extreams of heav'n,
' To frofts and fnows and bitter blafts are giv'n.
' Betwixt the midft and thefe, God affign'd
' Two habitable feats for humane kind.

1	4 Lammas Day	5	26	5	9	7	☽ fets 8 aftern
2	5 ⁂ ♃ ♀	6	♎	5	10	7	*Take counfel in*
3	6 Day 13 h. 36 m.	6h	20	5	12	7	*wine, but refolve*
4	7 * rife 10 31	7	♏	5	13	7	*afterwards in*
5	G 11 Sund. p. Trin.	8	13	5	14	7	*water.*
6	2 *Sultry hot,*	9	26	5	15	7	First Quarter.
7	3 *perhaps*	10	♐	5	16	7	☽ fet 11 27 aft.
8	4 *Thunder, rain &*	10	19	5	17	7	*He that drinks*
9	5 *wind.*	11	♑	5	18	7	*faft, pays flow,*
10	6 △ ☉ ♄	12	14	5	19	7	*Great famine*
11	7 Days fhort 1h.24	1	16	5	20	7	*when wolves eat*
12	G 12 Sund. p. Trin.	2	♒	5	21	7	☉ enters ♍
13	2	2h	2	5	22	7	☽ fet 4 31 mor.
14	3 Eufebius	3	♓	5	24	7	Full ● 3 morn.
15	4 7 * fouth 5 morn.	4	11	5	26	7	*wolves.*
16	5	5	♈	5	27	7	
17	6 ⁂ ♃ ☉	6	♉	5	28	7	*A good Wife oft*
18	7 *Winds if not wet.*	6h	8	5	29	7	*is God's gift loft.*
19	G 13 Sund. p. Trin.	7	19	5	31	7	☽ rife 9 aftern.
20	2 ♂ ♀ ☿	8	♊	5	32	7	*A taught horfe,*
21	3 Dog-Days end.	9	7	5	33	7	Laft Quarter
22	4 Days 12 h. 52 m.	10	♋	5	34	7	*and a woman to*
23	5 *Pleafant Weather.*	10	14	5	35	7	*teach, and teach-*
24	6 Bartholomew	11	♌	5	36	7	☽ rif. 1 41 mor.
25	7 △ ♄ ♂	12	♌	5	37	7	*ers practifing*
26	G 14 Sund. p. Trin.	1	24	5	38	7	*what they preach*
27	*Thunder & Lights.*	2	♍	5	40	7	*He is ill cloth'd,*
28	*with wind & rain.*	2h	21	5	42	7	New ☽ 3 morn.
29	4 7 * rife 9 ♂	3	♎	5	43	7	*who is bare of*
30	5 Rofa Virg.	4	16	5	45	7	*Virtue.*
31	6 *towards the end.*	5	28	5	46	7	☽ fets 7 46 aft.

Rain ..

Rain

Rain

Death is a Fisherman, the world we see
His Fish-pond is, and we the Fishes be:
His Net some general Sickness; however he
Is not so kind as other Fishers be;
For if they take one of the smaller Fry,
They throw him in again, he shall not die:
But Death is sure to kill all he can get,
And all is Fish with him that comes to Net.

1	7	Giles Abbot	6	10	5	48	7 *Men & Melons*
2	G	☿ ☉ ♀ rain& win	5h	28	5	49	7 London burnt.
3	2	7 * rise 8 46	7	♉	5	50	7 *are hard to know.*
4	3	*The heart of a fool is*	8	14	5	51	7 ☽ set 10 29 aft.
5	4	*in his mouth, but the*	9	27	5	52	7 First Quarter.
6	5	*mouth of a wise man*	10	♊	5	54	7 *He's the best phy-*
7	6	*is in his heart.*	11	22	5	55	7 *sician that knows*
8	7	7 * rise 8 24	12	♋	5	56	7 *the worthlesness*
9	G	16 Sund. p. Trin.	1	18	5	57	7 ☽ sets 2 22 mo
10	2	☉ ent. ♎ 11th day	2	♓	5	58	7 *of the most medi-*
11	3	& makes equ. day	2h	14	5	59	7 *cines.*
12	4	* ♃ ☌ & nigh	3	♈	6	0	6 Full ● 1 aftern.
13	5	8 ☊ ♀ Thunder,	4	14	6	1	6 *Beware of meat*
14	6	*Cloudy with warm*	5	29	6	2	6 *twice boil'd, and*
15	7	7 * rise 8 0 *rains*	6	♉	6	3	6 ☽ rise 8 morn.
16	G	17 Sund. p. Trin.	6h	29	6	4	6 *an old Foe recon-*
17	2	Days short. 2 56	7	♊	6	5	6 *cil'd.*
18	3	*Windy, and like to*	8	28	6	8	6
19	4	*the wet weather.*	9	♋	6	9	6 Last Quarter.
20	5		10	26	6	10	6 ☽ ris. 12 49 nig
21	6	St. Matthew	10	♌	6	11	6 *A fine genius in*
22	7	Maurice B.	11	21	6	13	6 *his own country,*
23	G	18 Sund. p. Trin.	12	♍	6	14	6 *is like gold in*
24	2	7 * rise 7 34	1	17	6	15	6 *the mine.*
25	3	Cleophas 6 ♀ ♀	2	29	6	16	6 ☽ rise 5 morn.
26	4	Days 11 h. 24 m.	2h	6	6	18	6 New ☽ 6 aft.
27	5	*More clear & plea*	3	24	6	19	6 *There is no little*
28	6	7 * south 2 29	4	♏	6	20	6 *enemy.*
29	7	St. Michael *sant.*	5	18	6	21	6 *Flying Clouds.*
30	G	19 Sund. p. Trin.	6	♐	6	22	6 ☽ sets 7 46 aft.

VIII Mon. October hath xxxi days.

Time was my spouse and I could not agree,
Striving about superiority:
The text which saith that man and wife are one,
Was the chief argument we stood upon;
She held, they both one woman should become;
I held they should be man, and both but one.
Thus we contended daily; but the strife
Could not be ended, till both were one Wife.

1	2	Romegius B,	6h	12	6	24	3	The old Man has
2	3	Windy with	7	2	6	26	6	given all to his
3	4	✳ ☌ ♀ Clouds	8	vp	6	27	6	Son; O fool! to
4	5	7 ✳ rise 4 38	9	18	6	28	6	First Quarter.
5	6	Rainy now.	10	♒	6	30	6	☽ sets 12 16
6	7	He has lost his Boots	10	3	6	31	6	undress thy self
7	G	20 Sund. p. Trin.	11	26	6	32	6	before thou art
8	2	but sav'd his spurs,	12	♓	6	33	6	going to bed.
9	3	8 ♄ ☉	1	2	6	35	6	
10	4	7 ✳ sou. 1 48 morn	2	♈	6	36	6	☽ sets 4 42
11	5	K. Geo. II. crown	2h	2	6	37	6	Full ● at 9 Afte
12	6	☉ ent. ♏ ☌ ♄ ☿	3	8	6	38	6	Days 10 h. 44
13	7	d white Frost	4	2	6	39	6	Cheese and salt
14	G	21 Sund. p. Trin	5	Ⅱ	6	40	6	meat, should be
15	2	Edward K. Con.	6	2	6	42	6	sparingly eat.
16	3	Wind, and it's	6h	4	6	43	6	☽ rise 9 42 aft.
17	4	likely for ☌ ☉ ☿	7	2	6	44	6	Doors and walls
18	5	St. Luke Rain	8	♋	6	45	6	have foils paper.
19	6	Days 10 h. 24	9	19	6	46	6	Last Quarter.
20	7	7 ✳ south 1 6	10		6	48	6	
21	G	22 Sund. p. Trin	10	1	6	49	6	☽ rise 1 53 mo.
22	2	Cordula V.	11	2	6	50	6	Anoint & oil him
23	3	Cloudy, with high			6	51	6	head he'll stab you,
24	4	winds	1		6	52	6	stab him & he'l
25	5	Crispin		♍	6	53	6	anoint you.
26	6	Days short. 4h.22	2h	14	6	54	6	New ☽ at noon
27	7	7 ✳ sou. 12 40	3	27	6	55	6	
28	G	23 Sund. p. Trin.	4	♎	6	56	6	☽ sets 6 31 aft.
29	2	cold rain if not snow	5	20	6	57	6	Keep your mouth
30	3	K. Geo. II. Nat.	6	♏	6	58	6	wet, feet dry.
31	4	1684	10h	14	6	59	6	Days 10h. 4m.

IX *Mon.* November hath xxx days.

My neighbour *H---y* by his pleasing tongue,
Hath won a Girl that's rich, wise, fair and young;
The Match (he faith) is half concluded, *he*
Indeed is wondrous willing; but not she.
And reason good, for he has run thro' all
Almost the story of the Prodigal;
Yet swears he never with the hogs did dine;
That's true, for none would trust him with their swine

1	5	All Saints	7	26	7	00	5	☽ sets 10 7 aft.
2	6	All Souls ☌ ☉ ♃	8	♒ 7	1	5	
3	7	Winifred	9	2	7	2	5	First Quarter.
4	G	24 Sund. p. Trin.	10	♓ 7	3	5	*Where bread is*
5	2	PowderPlot 1605	10	18	7	4	5	*wanting, all's to*
6	3	⚹ south 12 0	11	7	5	5	*be sold.*
7	4	⚹ rise achronical.	12	16	7	6	5	☽ sets 3 28 m.
8	5	*Cloudy with Rain,*	1	♉ 7	7	5	*There is neither*
9	6	*or Hail.*	2	16	7	8	5	*honour nor gain,*
10	7	Luther Nat 1483.	2h	♊ 7	9	5	Full ● at 6 mo.
11	G	25 Sund. p. Trin.	3	16	7	10	5	*got in dealing*
12	2	☉ enters ♐	4	♋ 7	10	5	*with a vil-lain.*
13	3	*High winds & cold*	5	16	7	11	5	☽ rise 8 50 aft.
14	4	Machutus B.	6	♌ 7	12	5	*The fool hath*
15	5	⚹ ☌ ☿	6h	♌	7	12	5	*made a vow, I*
16	6	⚹ south 11 11	7	7	13	5	*guess, Never to*
17	7	Hugh Bish.	8	♍ 7	14	5	☽ rise 12 42 m
18	G	26 Sund. p. Trin.	9	7	15	5	Last Quarter.
19	2	☌ ♄ ☽ *windy &*	10	♎ 7	15	5	*let the Fore have*
20	3	Edmund K.	10	7	16	5	*peace.*
21	4	*Falling weather,*	11	♏ 7	16	5	
22	5	⚹ south 10 50	12	12	7	17	5	☽ rise 4 35 mo
23	6	Clement □ ♃ ☽	1	23	7	17	5	*snowy winter, a*
24	7	Day 9h. 24 ⚹ ♃ ☿	2	2	7	18	5	*plentiful harvest.*
25	G	27 Sund. p. Trin.	2h	♐ 7	18	5	New ☽ at 7 mo.
26	2	⚹ south 10 33	3	29	7	19	5	*Nothing more*
27	3	*either rain or snow.*	4	♑ 7	19	5	☽ sets 7 aftern.
28	4	□ ☿ ♀ *pleasant but*	5	12	7	20	5	*like a Fool, than*
29	5	*cloudy at the End.*	6	♒ 7	20	5	*a drunken Man.*
30	6	St. Andrew	6h	18	7	21	5	

She that will eat her breakfast in her bed,
And spend the morn in dressing of her head,
And sit at dinner like a maiden-bride,
And talk of nothing all day but of pride;
God in his mercy may do much to save her,
But what a case is he in that shall have her.

1	3	Unsettled weather	7	♓	7	21	5	☽ sets 11 after.
2	G	Advent Sunday	8	4	7	21	5	First Quarter.
3	2	new,	9	28	7	22	5	God works won-
4	3	△ ☉ ♄ Either rain	10	♈	7	22	5	ders now & then,
5	4	or snow, and then a	10	26	7	22	5	Behold! a Law-
6	5	7 * set 5 10	11	♉	7	23	5	☽ sets 3 15 m.
7	6	frost comes on	11	26	7	23	5	yer, an honest
8	7	snow.	1	♊	7	23	5	Man!
9	G	1 Sund in Adv.	2	26	7	23	5	Full ● 9 at nig.
10	2	☉ enters ♑ then	2h	♋	7	23	5	He that lives
11	3	Wint. Qu. begins	3	14	7	23	5	carnally, won't
12	4	& makes shortest	4	♌	7	23	5	☽ rise 8 8 aft.
13	5	day 9 h. 14 m.	5	23	7	23	5	live eternally.
14	6	Windy and clouds,	6	♍	7	22	5	
15	7	* ♄ ☿	6h	20	7	22	5	Innocence is its
16	G	2 Sund. in Adv.	7	♎	7	22	5	own Defence.
17	2	7 * south 8 58	8	14	7	22	5	Last Quarter.
18	3	like for snow.	9	27	7	22	5	☽ rise 1 15 m.
19	4	* ♄ ♀	10	♏	7	21	5	Time eateth all
20	5	Days incr. 4 mi.	10	20	7	21	5	things, could old
21	6	St Thomas	11	♐	7	21	5	Poets say; The
22	7	High winds and	12	14	7	21	5	Times are
23	G	3 Sund. in Adv.	1	26	7	20	5	☽ rise 5 43 mo.
24	2	* ☿ ♀ □ ♃ ♀	2	♑	7	20	5	chang'd, our
25	3	CHRIST Nativ.	2h 20		7	19	5	New ☽ at 2 mo.
26	4	S. Stephen * ☉ ☍	3	♒	7	19	5	times drink all
27	5	St. John cloudy	4	14	7	18	5	away.
28	6	Innocents weather	5	28	7	18	5	☽ sets 8 29 aft.
29	7	Snow or Rain will	6	♓	7	17	5	Never mind it,
30	G	new appear, and a	6	26	7	17	5	he'll be sober after.
31	2	Frost end the Year.	7	♈	7	16	5	the Holidays.

304

Of the Eclipses, 1733.

THIS Year there will be four Eclipses, two of the Sun and two of the Moon. The first will be an Eclipse of the Sun, *May* 2. visible being about 12 a clock, Digits eclipsed 2 and a half.

The second will be on *May* 17. about two in the Afternoon, wherein the Moon will be eclipsed, not visible here.

The third will be on *Octob.* 26. about 11 in the Morning, a small Eclipse of the Sun, invisible.

The fourth will be on *Novem.* 10. a little after 6 in the Morning it begins, an Eclipse of the Moon, above half of which will be darkned.

Chronology of Things remarkable, 1733.

	Years since,
THE Birth of JESUS CHRIST	1733
Jerusalem taken by the *Romans*	1660
Tower of *London* built	2164
First Mayor of *London*	543
London-Bridge built with Stone	524
The Invention of Guns by a Monk	364
The Art of Printing found out by a Soldier	293
Great Massacre in *France*	161
Spanish Armada burnt	145
K. *James* I. laid the first Stone of *Chelsea Coll.*	124
The Bible new translated	122
Gunpowder Plot	119
The Plague of *London*, whereof died 30900	108
Long Parliament began, *Nov.* 3. 1640.	93
Rebellion in *Ireland*, *Oct.* 23. 1641.	92
King *Charles* I. beheaded	85
Dunkirk delivered to the *English*	75
Oliver Cromwell died, *Sept.* 3. 1658.	75
King *Charles* II. his Return in Peace	73
The great Plague of *London*, whereof died 100000,	67
The great *Seafight* between the *Dutch* & *English*,	68

The Peace between the *English* and *Dutch*   166
Snowed eleven Days together   59
Oates's Plot began, 1678.   55
K. *James* II. declared for Liberty of Conscience   46
The seven Bishops sent to the Tower   45
King *William* III. reduced *Ireland*   43
Gibralter taken, *July* 24.   29
England and *Scotland* united, *May* 1,   26
Three whole Bullocks roasted on the Ice on }
    the *Thames*, Jan. 19. 1716.   } 17
Christopher Columbus found *America*   242
Newfoundland discovered by the *English*   208
The first Use of Coaches in *England*   177
Capt. *Drake's* Voyage round the World   156
Tobacco first taken in *England*   151
Sir *Walter Rawleigh* found and named *Virginia*   147
Virginia first planted by the *English*   127
Newfoundland first planted   124
New York first settled   119
New-England first settled   117
Barbadoes first planted   106
Nevis first planted   105
The building of *Boston*   105
MARYLAND first settled   103
Carolina first planted   85
Jamaica taken from the *Spaniards*   78
New York, *Albany*, and *Newcastle* taken by *Eng.*   71
The Building of *Burlington*   56
Pensylvania first so named   52
Philadelphia first founded   50
The City of *Amboy* laid out   50
The great Flood at *Delaware* Falls   47
The great Earthquake in *Jamaica* 7 *June* 47.   40
The Post-Office erected in *America*   38
The hard Winter which continued till *Mar.* 4.   35
The great Snow about a Yard deep   28
The last wet Harvest, the like not seen here   14
Prince *Frederick Town* laid out   4
King GEORGE II. proclaimed, *June* 15.   6

The

The Benefit of going to LAW.

Dedicated to the Counties of K--t & H-n---rd-n.

TWO Beggars travelling along,
 One blind, the other lame,
Pick'd up an Oyster on the Way
 To which they both laid claim:
The Matter rose so high, that they
 Resolv'd to go to Law,
As often richer Fools have done,
 Who quarrel for a Straw.
A Lawyer took it strait in hand,
 Who knew his Business was,
To mind nor one nor t'other side,
 But make the best o'th' Cause:
As always in the Law's the Case:
 So he his Judgment gave,
And Lawyer-like he thus resolv'd
 What each of them should have:
  Blind Plaintiff, lame Defendant, share
  The Friendly Laws impartial Care,
  A Shell for him, a Shell for thee,
  The Middle is the Lawyer's Fee.

The COURTS.

Supream Courts in Pennsilvania are held

AT Philadelphia, the tenth Day of April, &
 24th Day of September.

 Courts of Quarter Sessions are held

 At Philadelphia, the first Monday in March,
June, September and December.
 At Newtown in Bucks County, on the 11th Day
following (inclusive) in every of Months aforesaid.
 At Chester, the last Tuesday in May, August,
November and February,
 At Lancaster the first Tuesday in each.

 Courts of Common Pleas are held,

 At Philadelphia, the first Wednesday after the
Quarter Sessions, in March, June, September, and
December.
 At Newtown, the 9th Day following (inclusive)
in every of the months aforesaid.

307

At Chester, the last Tuesday in May, August, November, and February.

At Lancaster, the first Tuesday in the Months aforesaid.

At Sussex the first, at Kent the second, and at New-Castle the third Tuesday in the same months.

Mayors Courts in Philadelphia, *are held*

The first Tuesday in January, April, and July, last Tuesday in October.

Supreme Courts in New-Jersey *are held*

AT Burlington, the 1st Tuesday in May, 2d Tuesday in August, 1st Tuesday in Novemb. and 3d in Febr.

At Perth-Amboy, the 2d Tuesday in May, 3d in Aug. the 2d Tuesday in Novemb. and the 4th in February.

In Bergen County, April 3. In Essex, April 10. In Somerset, Octob. 2. In Monmouth, April 24. In Hunterdon, Octob. 23. In Gloucester, June 12. In Salem and Cape-May Counties, June 5. at Salem.

General Sessions and County Courts are held

In Bergen County, Jan. 2. April 3. June 12. Octob. 2.

In Essex, January 9. April 10. June 19. Sept. 25.
In Middlesex, Jan. 16. April 17. July 17. Octob. 9.
In Somerset, Jan. 2. April 3. June 12. Octob. 2.
In Monmouth, Jan. 23. April 24. July 24. Oct. 16.
In Hunterdon, Feb. 6. May 15. Aug. 7. Octob. 23.
In Burlington, Febr. 13. May 6. Aug. 14. Nov. 6.
In Gloucester, March 27. June 12. Sept. 18. Dec. 25.
In Salem, Feb. 20. June 5. Aug. 21. Nov. 27.
In Cape May, Feb. 6. May 12. Aug. 3. Oct. 29.

Supreme Courts in New-York *are held,*

AT the City of New-York, March 13. June 5. October 9. Nov. 27. At Westchester, March 27. At Richmond, April 10. At Orange, April 24. At Suffolk County, July 24. At Albany, August 21. At Ulster, Sept 4. At Dutchess, Sept. 11. At Kings County, Sept. 18. At Queens County, Sept. 25.

Courts of Sessions & Common Pleas are held.
In the City of New-York, May 1. Aug. 1. Nov.
6. Feb. 6. At Albany, June 5. Octob. 2. and Jan.
16. At Westchester, May 27. Octob. 23. In Ul-
ster, May 1. Octob. 2. In Richmond, March 20.
Septemb. 25. In Kings, April 17. Octob. 16. In
Queens, May 15. Sept. 18. In Orange, April 24.
Octob. 30. In Dutches Co. May 15. and Oct. 16.

Provincial Courts in Maryland.

TWO in a Year, held at Annapolis, viz. The
Tuesday of May, & 3d Tuesday of Oct.

County Courts in Maryland.

For Talbot, Baltimore, and St. Mary's Counties on
the 1st Tuesday in March, June, Aug. and Nov. At
Dorchester, Cæcil, Ann Arundel, and Charles Counties, the 2d Tuesday in the same Months. At Kent,
Calvert and Somerset Counties, the third Tuesday
in the same Months. At Queen Ann's and Prince
George's the 4th Tuesdays in the same Months.

QUAKERS General Meetings are kept,

At *Philadelphia*,	March 18.	At *Westbury*,		Aug. 26
At *Salem*,	April 22.	At *Philadelphia*,		Sept. 16
At *Flushing*,	May 27.	At *Jamaica*,		23
At *West River*,	June 5.	At *Cropwell*,	Octob.	7
At *Providence*,	19.	At *Shrewsbury*,		28
At *Newport*,	24.	At *Oyster Bay*,		28
At *Newtown*,	24.	At *Flushing*,	Nov.	25
At *Westchester*,	July 22.	At *Westbury*,	Febr.	25

BAPTISTS General Meetings are kept,

At *Welch-Tract*,	May 13.	At *Piscataway*,	June	3
At *Cohansie*,	20.	At *Philadelphia*,	Sept.	23

FAIRS are kept,

At *Cohansie*,	April 24.	At *Chester*,	Octob.	5
At *N-York* ditto, & Nov. 6.		At *Cohansie*,		16
At *Salem*,	May 1.	At *Salem*,		30
At *New-Castle*,	3.	At *Germantown*,		20
At *Chester*,	5.	At *Bristol*,		29
At *Bristol*,	8.	At *Burlington*,	Nov.	1
At *Burlington*,	10.	At *New-Castle*,		5
At *Philadelphia*,	16.	At *Philadelphia*,		16

A Catalogue of the principal Kings

and Princes in *Europe*, with the Time of their Births and Ages.

	Born	Ag.
George II. K. of *Gr. Brit. &c.*	30 Oct. 1683	50
Wilhelmina-Carolina his Queen	1 Mar. 1682	48
Frederick Prince of *Wales*	19 Jan. 1706	47
Charles 6. Emperor of *Germany*	1 Oct. 1685	48
Louis 15. King of *France*	15 Feb. 1710	23
Mary, Queen of *France*	23 Jun. 1703	30
Leopold 1. Duke of *Lorain*	11 Sep. 1679	54
Philip 5. King of *Spain*	19 Dec. 1683	50
John 5. King of *Portugal*	22 Oct. 1689	44
Fred. W. K. of *Prussia*, El. of *Brand.*	14 Aug. 1688	45
Fred. Augustus K. of *Poland*	12 May 1661	72
Frederick 4. King of *Denmark*	11 Oct. 1671	62
Frederick King of *Sweden*	28 Apr. 1676	57
Charles Frederick, D. of *Holstein*	14 Apr. 1700	33
Prince *Eugene* of *Savoy*	18 Oct. 1663	70
John Gaston, Grand Duke of *Tuscany*	24 May 1671	62

Poor Richard, an American Prince, without Subjects, his Wife being Viceroy over him,	23 Oct. 1684	49

A Description of the Highways & Roads

From *Annapolis* in *Maryland* to *Philadelphia*, 145 Miles, thus accounted;

FROM *Annapolis* M.		To *N-ewcastle*	27
To *Patapsco Ferry*	30	To *Christine Ferry*	5
To *Gunpowder Ferry*	20	To *Brandewyne* Ferry	1
To *Sisquehanah Ferry*	25	To *Naaman's Creek*	9
To *Principio Iron Wor.*	3	To *Chester*	15
To *North-East*	6	To *Derby*	9
To *Elk River*	7	To *Philadelphia*	8

From *Annapolis* to *Williamsburgh*,

FROM *Annapolis* M.		To *Southern's* Ferry	30
To *Lond. T. Ferry*	4	To *Arnold's* Ferry	36
To *Qu. Ann's* Ferry	9	To *Clayborn's* Ferry	22
To *Upper-Marlborough*	9	To *Fernaaux's* Ordina.	12
To *Port Tobacco*	30	To *Williamsburgh*	16
To *Hoo's* Ferry	20	In all	183

185
145 333 *from Phila. to Wmsburg*

310

Courteous Reader,

I might in this place attempt to gain thy Favour, by declaring that I write Almanacks with no other View than that of the publick Good; but in this I should not be sincere; and Men are now a-days too wise to be deceiv'd by Pretences how specious soever. The plain Truth of the Matter is, I am excessive poor, and my Wife, good Woman, is, I tell her, excessive proud; she cannot bear, she says, to sit spinning in her Shift of Tow, while I do nothing but gaze at the Stars; and has threatned more than once to burn all my Books and Rattling-Traps (as she calls my Instruments) if I do not make some profitable Use of them for the good of my Family. The Printer has offer'd me some considerable share of the Profits, and I have thus begun to comply with my Dame's desire.

Indeed this Motive would have had Force enough to have made me publish an Almanack many Years since, had it not been over-power'd by my Regard for my good Friend and Fellow-Student, Mr. Titan Leeds, whose Interest I was extreamly unwilling to hurt: But this Obstacle (I am far from speaking it with Pleasure) is soon to be removed, since inexorable Death, who was never known to respect Merit, has already prepared the mortal Dart, the fatal Sister has already extended her destroying Shears, and that ingenious Man must soon be taken from us. He dies, by my Calculation made at his Request, on Oct. 17. 1733. 3 ho. 29 m. *P.M.* at the very instant of the ♂ of ☉ and ☿ : By his own Calculation he will survive till the 26th of the same Month. This small difference between us we have disputed whenever we have met these 9 Years past; but at length he is inclinable to agree with my Judgment; Which of us is most exact, a little Time will now determine. As therefore these Provinces may not longer expect to see any of his Performances after this Year, I think my self free to take up the Task, and request a share of the publick Encouragement; which I am the more apt to hope for on this Account, that the Buyer of my Almanack may consider himself, not only as purchasing an useful Utensil, but as performing an Act of Charity, to his poor Friend and Servant   R. SAUNDERS

♄ Saturn diseas'd with Age, and left for dead;
Chang'd all his Gold to be involv'd in Lead.
♃ Jove, Juno leaves, and loves to take his Range;

311

From whom Man learns to love, and loves to change.
♂ is disarmed, and to ♀ gone,
Where Vulcan's Anvil must be struck upon.
That ☽ Luna's horn'd, it cannot well be said,
Since I ne'er heard that she was married.

XI Mon. January hath xxxi days.
More nice than wise.
Old Batchelor would have a Wife that's wise,
Fair, rich, and young, a Maiden for his Bed;
Not proud, nor churlish, but of faultless size;
A Country Houswife in the City bred.
He's a nice Fool, and long in vain hath staid;
He should bespeak her, there's none ready made.

Never spare the Parson's wine, nor the Baker's pudding.

Visits should be short, like a winters day,
Lest you're too troublesom hasten away.

A house without woman and Firelight, is like a body without soul
or sprite.

Kings and Bears often worry their keepers.

XII Mon. February hath xxviii days.

N. N. of B---s County, pray don't be angry with poor Richard.

Each Age of Men new Fashions doth invent;
Things which are old, young Men do not esteem:
What pleas'd our Fathers, doth not us content;
What flourish'd then, we out of fashion deem:
And that's the reason, as I understand,
Why Prodigus did sell his Father's Land.

Light purse, heavy heart.

He's a Fool that makes his Doctor his Heir.

Ne'er take a wife till thou hast a house (and a fire) to put her in.

312

He's gone, and forgot nothing but to say *Farewel*—to his creditors.

Love well, whip well.

I Mon. March hath xxxi days.

> My Love and I for Kisses play'd,
> She would keep stakes, I was content,
> But when I won she would be paid;
> This made me ask her what she meant:
> Quoth she, since you are in this wrangling vein,
> Here take your Kisses, give me mine again.

> Let my respected friend J. G.
> Accept this humble verse of me. viz.
> Ingenious, learned, envy'd Youth,
> Go on as thou'st began;
> Even thy enemies take pride
> That thou'rt their countryman.

Hunger never saw bad bread.

II Mon. April hath xxx days.

> Kind Katharine to her husband kiss'd these words,
> "Mine own sweet Will, how dearly I love thee!"
> If true (quoth Will) the World no such affords.
> And that its true I durst his warrant be;
>   For ne'er heard I of Woman good or ill,
>   But always loved best, her own sweet Will.

Beware of meat twice boil'd, and an old foe reconcil'd.

Great Talkers, little Doers.

A rich rogue, is like a fat hog, who never does good til as dead as a log.

Relation without friendship, friendship without power, power without will, will witho[ut] effect, effect without profit, and profit without vertue, are not worth a farto.

313

III Mon. May hath xxxi days.

> Mirth pleaseth some, to others 'tis offence,
> Some commend plain conceit, some profound sense;
> Some wish a witty Jest, some dislike that,
> And most would have themselves they know not what.
>   Then he that would please all, and himself too,
>   Takes more in hand than he is like to do.

Eat to live, and not live to eat.

> March windy, and April rainy,
> Makes May the pleasantest month of any.

The favour of the Great is no inheritance.

Fools make feasts and wise men eat 'em.

Beware of the young Doctor and the old Barber.

He has chang'd his one ey'd horse for a blind one.

The poor have little, beggars none, the rich too much, *enough* not one.

IV Mon. June hath xxx days.

> "Observe the daily circle of the sun,
> And the short year of each revolving moon:
> By them thou shalt forsee the following day,
> Nor shall a starry night thy hopes betray.
> When first the moon appears, if then she shrouds
> Her silver crescent, tip'd with sable clouds,
> Conclude she bodes a tempest on the main,
> And brews for fields impetuous floods of rain."

After 3 days men grow weary, of a wench, a guest, and weather rainy.

To lengthen thy Life, lessen thy Meals.

The proof of gold is fire, the proof of woman, gold; the proof of man, a woman.

After feasts made, the maker scratches his head.

314

V Mon. July hath xxxi days.

> "Ev'n while the reaper fills his greedy hands,
> And binds the golden sheafs in brittle bands:
> Oft have I seen a sudden storm arise
> From all the warring winds that sweep the skies:
> And oft whole sheets descend of slucy rain,
> Suck'd by the spungy clouds from off the main;
> The lofty skies at once come pouring down,
> The promis'd crop and golden labours drown."

Neither Shame nor Grace yet Bob.

> Many estates are spent in the getting,
> Since women for tea forsook spinning and knitting.

He that lies down with Dogs, shall rise up with fleas.

A fat kitchin, a lean Will.

Distrust and caution are the parents of security.

Tongue double, brings trouble.

VI Mon. August hath xxxi days.

> "For us thro' 12 bright signs Apollo guides
> The year, and earth in sev'ral climes divides.
> Five girdles bind the skies, the torrid zone
> Glows with the passing and repassing sun.
> Far on the right and left, th'extreams of heav'n,
> To frosts and snows and bitter blasts are giv'n.
> Betwixt the midst and these, the Gods assign'd
> Two habitable seats for humane kind."

Take counsel in wine, but resolve afterwards in water.

He that drinks fast, pays slow.

Great famine when wolves eat wolves.

A good Wife lost is God's gift lost.

A taught horse, and a woman to teach, and teachers practising
  what they preach.

He is ill cloth'd, who is bare of Virtue.

VII Mon. September hath xxx days.

> Death is a Fisherman, the world we see
> His Fish-pond is, and we the Fishes be:
> His Net some general Sickness; howe'er he
> Is not so kind as other Fishers be;
> For if they take one of the smaller Fry,
> They throw him in again, he shall not die:
> But Death is sure to kill all he can get,
> And all is Fish with him that comes to Net.

The heart of a fool is in his mouth, but the mouth of a wise man is in his heart.

Men and Melons are hard to know.

He's the best physician that knows the worthlessness of the most medicines.

Beware of meat twice boil'd, and an old Foe reconcil'd.

A fine genius in his own country, is like gold in the mine.

There is no little enemy.

VIII Mon. October hath xxxi days.

> Time was my spouse and I could not agree,
> Striving about superiority:
> The text which saith that man and wife are one,
> Was the chief argument we stood upon:
> She held, they both one woman should become;
> I held they should be man, and both but one.
> Thus we contended daily, but the strife
> Could not be ended, till both were one Wife.

He has lost his Boots but sav'd his spurs.

The old Man has given all to his Son: O fool! to undress thy self before thou art going to bed.

Cheese and salt meat, should be sparingly eat.

Doors and walls are fools paper.

Anoint a villain and he'll stab you, stab him and he'l anoint you.

Keep your mouth wet, feet dry.

IX Mon. November hath xxx days.

> My neighbour H---y by his pleasing tongue,
> Hath won a Girl that's rich, wise, fair and young;
> The Match (he saith) is half concluded, he
> Indeed is wondrous willing; but not she.
> And reason good, for he has run thro' all
> Almost the story of the Prodigal;
> Yet swears he never with the hogs did dine;
> That's true, for none would trust him with their swine.

Where bread is wanting, all's to be sold.

There is neither honour nor gain, got in dealing with a vil-lain.

> The fool hath made a vow, I guess,
> Never to let the Fire have peace.

Snowy winter, a plentiful harvest.

Nothing more like a Fool, than a drunken Man.

X Mon. December hath xxxi days.

> She that will eat her breakfast in her bed,
> And spend the morn in dressing of her head,
> And sit at dinner like a maiden bride,
> And talk of nothing all day but of pride;
> God in his mercy may do much to save her,
> But what a case is he in that shall have her.

> God works wonders now and then;
> Behold! a Lawyer, an honest Man!

He that lives carnally, won't live eternally.

Innocence is its own Defence.

> Time *eateth* all things, could old Poets say;
> The Times are chang'd, our times *drink* all away.

Never mind it, she'l be sober after the Holidays.

The Benefit of going to LAW.
Dedicated to the Counties of K--t and H-n---rd-n.

Two Beggars travelling along,
    One blind, the other lame,
Pick'd up an Oyster on the Way
    To which they both laid claim:
The Matter rose so high, that they
    Resolv'd to go to Law,
As often richer Fools have done,
    Who quarrel for a Straw.
A Lawyer took it strait in hand,
    Who knew his Business was,
To mind nor one nor t'other side,
    But make the best o' th' Cause;
As always in the Law's the Case:
    So he his Judgment gave,
And Lawyer-like he thus resolv'd
    What each of them should have:
        Blind Plaintiff, lame Defendant, share
        The Friendly Laws impartial Care,
        A Shell for him, a Shell for thee,
        The Middle is the Lawyer's Fee.

Slippery Sidewalks[2]

Printed in *The Pennsylvania Gazette*, January 11, 1732/3.

Mr. Franklin,

Walking the Street on one of these late slippery Mornings, I caught two terrible Falls, which made me, by way of Precaution for the future, get my Shoes frosted before I went home:[3] for I am a stiff old Fellow, and my Joints none of the most pliant. At the Door before which I fell last, stood a Gentleman-like Looby, with a couple of Damsels, who all made themselves wonderful merry

2. Believed for stylistic reasons to be by BF.
3. To frost a shoe was to attach a pointed piece of iron to the heel, to prevent slipping on ice or frozen ground.

with my Misfortune: And had not a good Woman, whose Door I had just passed, come and helped me up, I might for ought I know, have given them an Hour's Diversion before I found my Legs again. This good Woman, Heaven bless her, had sprinkled Ashes before her Door: I wish her long Life and better Neighbours. I have reason to think the merry People would not have risen so early, and exposed themselves to the Air, that cold Morning, were it not for the sake of enjoying such Entertainments as I afforded them. But they were not alone in the Thing; I saw before I got home, twenty other Gigglers, all employ'd at their Doors in the same Manner. Strange Perverseness of Disposition! to delight in the Mishaps which befal People who have no way disoblig'd us. My Shoes, as I have said, being frosted, I intend the next slippery Time to make a Tour throughout the Town, and take a general List of all the Housekeepers, whom I will divide into three Classes. The humane, kind, compassionate, benevolent Class, I shall easily distinguish by the Ashes at their Doors, as God's People were distinguish'd in Ægypt by the Sprinkling of their Door-posts. The malicious and ill-natured Class I shall know by their Mirth at every Fall or accidental Slip of the Passengers in the Street. The indifferent, thoughtless Class, are the rest. As every Man that walks upon uneven Ice, hazards at each Step his Limbs; methinks some Honours ought to be decreed those of my first Class, proportionate to what the Romans gave him that sav'd the Life of a Fellow-Citizen: They shall, however, be sure of my Respect and Friendship. With regard to those of my two latter Classes, I am resolved, I will not so much as civilly salute one of them, I will not give one of them the Wall, I will not make Room for any of them at a Fire, nor hand them any Thing at a Table, I will not direct a Customer to one of them, if any of my first Class deal in the same Things: In short, I will be as cross-grain'd towards them as 'tis possible for a good-natur'd old Man to be; who is Your Friend and Reader,

N.N.[4]

---

4. In the same issue of the *Gazette* appears an essay on the Family of Boxes, signed by "Chatter-Box" and modeled on Isaac Bickerstaff's piece in the *Tatler*, No. 11, on the Family of Staffs. The editors recognize the possibility that BF was the author, but cannot find sufficient evidence, internal or otherwise, to justify including it here.

Directors of Library Company to Thomas Penn and Reply

ALS: Friends Library, London; also MS Minute Book, Library Company of Philadelphia; printed in *The Pennsylvania Gazette*, May 31, 1733.

Franklin and the Directors of the Library Company had learned that the Proprietor would welcome an address praying his "Countenance and Protection" of their young institution, and on May 14 a committee composed of Franklin, Thomas Hopkinson, William Coleman, and Joseph Breintnall was appointed to draft the address. Next night they presented it, and, although "Some Objections were made to the Style by those who had accustomed themselves to what is called the plain Language," it was approved. Franklin was one of the five Directors who presented the address to Penn on May 24. "The Proprietor received it with great Civility and Kindness, and was pleased to enquire of the Presenters some things concerning the Library and to assure them of his Encouragement."[5]

To the Honourable Thomas Penn Esqr. one of the Proprietors of the Province of Pennsylvania

The Humble Address of the Directors of the Library Company of Philadelphia In Behalf of the Company.

May it please your Honour,   May 16th 1733
All the good People of Pennsylvania rejoice in your happy Arrival and Residence in this your Province, and will continue to rejoice in whatever promotes your Prosperity: Among the Rest, the Subscribers to the Library in Philadelphia beg Leave to assure your Honour, that in the same good Affections they are not behind the warmest of their Countrymen.

Your Province of Pennsylvania, Sir, happy in its Climate and Situation, and in the Constitution of its Government, is thought to be no less happy in the Native Genius of its People; prone as it is to Industry, and capable of every kind of Improvement.

But when Colonies are in their Infancy, the Refinements of Life, it seems, cannot be much attended to. To encourage Agriculture, promote Trade, and establish good Laws must be the principal Care of the first Founders; while other Arts and Sciences, less

5. Lib. Co., Minutes, May 14, 15, 24, 30, 1732.

immediately necessary, how excellent and useful soever, are left to the Care and Cultivation of Posterity. Hence it is that neither in this, nor in the neighbouring Provinces, has there yet been made any Provision for a publick generous Education.

With a View of supplying in some Measure this Deficiency for the present among our Selves we have attempted to erect a COMMON LIBRARY in Philadelphia. And when on this Account we address a Son of the great and good, and ever memorable WILLIAM PENN, we are persuaded than an Endeavour, however small, to propagate Knowledge, and improve the Minds of Men, by rendring useful Science more cheap and easy of Access, will not want his Countenance and Protection.

May your Philadelphia be the future Athens of America: May plenty of her Sons arise, qualified with Learning, Virtue, and Politeness for the most important Offices of Life: And as this must be owing to the Wisdom and Benevolence of your Honourable Family, which gave Being to the Province and its happy Constitution, May every kind of humane Felicity attend the Proprietary House, thro' all Ages, to the latest Posterity.

Signed by Order of the Directors   JOSEPH BREINTNALL Secry.

To which his Honour was pleased to give the following ANSWER.[6]

Gentlemen,

I take this Address very kindly; and assure you, I shall always be ready to promote any Undertaking so useful to the Country, as that of erecting a *common Library* in this City.

Agreement of Directors of Library Company

ADS: Historical Society of Pennsylvania

[May 28, 1733]

We the Subscribers hereto, Directors of the Library Company of Philadelphia, do hereby agree and promise each one of us with

6. Since Penn's reply to the address on May 24 had been oral but the Directors wished to print his response, BF and Hopkinson waited on him, May 31, and received it in writing. The reply is here reprinted from the *Gazette;* it exists also in draft form on the back of the original address and was entered in the minutes of the Library Company.

and to the rest that we will endeavour at all Times hereafter to duly attend at the Monthly Meetings of the said Directors and at such intervening Meetings as shall at such Monthly Meetings be by the Directors present agreed on. And that if it happens We are absent from any of the said Monthly Meetings We will as soon after as we conveniently can repair to the Library in order to know of the Librarian if any intervening Meetings have been agreed on By which we will govern our Selves. And upon every Failure of attending at any of the aforemention'd Meetings We will at our next Appearance in a Meeting of the said Directors either Monthly or by Adjournment forfeit and pay for Each of us One pint of Wine. Witness our Hands hereto the 28th Day of May 1733.

No Reasons shall be pleaded for Absence And the Time of Attendance shall be at or before the Hour of Nine.

B. FRANKLIN[7]	THOS. HOPKINSON
WM. RAWLE	11 June 1733
JNO. JONES JUNR.	WM. PARSONS
HENRY PRATT	THOS. CADWALADER
HUGH ROBERTS	THOS. GODFREY
	ROBT. GRACE

Remarks on a South Carolina Currency Scheme

Printed in *The Pennsylvania Gazette*, May 31, 1733.

As there are frequently Things published in the neighbouring Provinces, which to see would be agreeable to my Readers, but being of too great a Length, I have been obliged either to retail 'em Piecemeal, which disjoints or breaks the Connection of Thoughts, or wholly to omit them; I am therefore lately advised to abstract and give the Substance of them, which I shall do for the future, as often as I imagine it may be any way useful or entertaining.

The *South Carolina Gazette*, of March 24. contains the Beginning of a Discourse upon PAPER CURRENCY, which is continued thro'

7. The text is in BF's hand. Only five Directors were present when this pledge was signed. Hopkinson signed June 11, and the others on that or a later date.

several other Papers.[8] The Author observes, that the principal ObjeΦion against that Currency, is its being so liable to Mutation in its Value: That 'tis now about 30 Years since it first got Footing in the American Plantations; and that altho' it has been design'd only as a present Expedient in Cases of Exigency, yet no Place where it was once establish'd has found itself afterwards in a Condition to do without it. And since (he says) there arises no Benefit to the Publick from cancelling every seven or ten Years Bills issued on Loan or otherwise because the Circumstances of a Country continuing the same, there is still the same Reason for making more, as at first, and much Clamour and some Expence always attends the Periods: He proposes, a *Standing Paper Currency*, to continue till the Country finds the Nature of its Trade will afford Silver and Gold, and *to prevent its sinking in Value*, he would have the Interest be paid in Silver and Gold, and the Bills taken only in Discharge of the Principal.

REMARK upon this SCHEME.

The Subjects of Trade and Money have always occasioned much Speculation, being in themselves, and especially when considered together, extreamly intricate and hard to be understood. And the *Paper Currency* being a Thing of great Importance to these Plantations, whatever is wrote to give us farther Light about it, whatever new Methods are proposed, should be received and examined with Candour.

With regard to this new Scheme, which proposes to fix the Value of the Bills by obliging the Borrowers to pay their Interest in Gold and Silver, the following Difficulties seem to arise, which perhaps if the Author himself were here, he might easily obviate.

1. Interest being now at 10 per Cent. in Carolina, if 50,000 proclamation Money (the Sum he mentions) is issued out upon Loan, £5000 Silver and Gold is yearly necessary to discharge the Interest; and only the Surplus of that Sum can be exported by the Merchant. Now allowing that the yearly Demand of so much Plate in the Country, must prevent its Exportation, Yet must not the Planter outbid the Merchant in order to have it? and if he gives 2 or 4 per Cent. in Paper for it, is not that a Raising their Interest

[8]The discourse was continued in the issues of March 31 and April 7, 1733.

to 12 or 14 per Cent. and does it not lessen the Value of their Bills, compar'd with Silver and Gold?

2. If the Merchant wants Silver and Gold, to make Returns, will he not raise the Price of his Goods till he can afford to purchase it? and the Planter being still oblig'd to have it, will not he be still forced to give more Paper for it?

3. If the Interest be all due at one Time of the Year, will not Silver be at that Time higher and Paper lower than at other Times, and so their Currency continually varying in Value, and very uncertain to Strangers?

These Queries, for ought I know may have little in 'em. If they serve to make a Paper Currency any thing more consider'd, and therefore better understood, it is enough.

Receipted Bill to the Proprietors ADS: Friends Library, London

[June 25, 1733]

The Honourable Proprietor to B. Franklin Dr.[9]

		£		
1. For printing 5 Sheets at 30s. per Sheet		£ 7	10	–
2. For Paper 5 Ream, and 5/6 of a Ream at 20s.		5	16	8
3. For Stitching 500 Books, and pasting the Maps at 6s. per Hund.		1	10	–
4. For cutting the Mapp in Wood		2	–	–
5. For printing and Paper of the Mapps		2	11	8
6. For Printing and Paper of 1000 Coats of Arms at 8s. per Hund.[1]		4	–	–
		£23	8	4

Recd. of James Steel Twenty Pounds in part of this Account. B. FRANKLIN[2]

Endorsed: Receiv'd the Contents of the within Acct. per me June 25. 1733.   B. FRANKLIN

Docketed: Ben Franklin 26th 4 mo. 1733 £23:8:4

9. These charges were probably for printing *Articles of Agreement made and concluded upon between The Right Honourable the Lord Proprietary of Maryland, and The Honourable The Proprietarys of Pensilvania, &c. Touching the Limits and Boundaries of the Two Provinces. With The Commission, Constituting certain Persons to Execute the Same* (Phila., 1733). This was a folio of 19 printed pages. The map, approximately 13 by 15 inches, folded and tipped in, showed the coasts, shores and boundaries of Pennsylvania, Delaware, Maryland, and part of Virginia, roughly from above Philadelphia to Cape Charles.

1. Probably bookplates.

2. BF's name was signed to this receipt by his wife.

A Scolding Wife   Printed in *The Pennsylvania Gazette*, July 5, 1733.

In the copy of this issue of the *Gazette* in the Yale University Library a typographical error in the essay has been corrected in a hand that appears to be Franklin's. The presumed source of this correction and the style of the essay are the reasons why the editors believe it may have been written by Franklin.

To the Printer of the *Gazette*,

Sir,

'Tis an old Saying and a true one, that *there is no Conveniency without an Inconveniency:* For aught I know, there might be a Saying not less true, tho' more new, *That there is no Inconveniency without a Conveniency.*

However, there is the Inconveniency (as 'tis commonly thought) of a Scolding Wife, which has Conveniencies enough in it, to make it (when rightly consider'd) esteem'd a Happiness. For I speak from Experience, (as well as a long Course of Observation) Women of that Character have generally sound and healthy Constitutions, produce a vigorous Offspring, are active in the Business of the Family, special good Housewives, and very Careful of their Husbands Interest. As to the Noise attending all this, 'tis but a Trifle when a Man is us'd to it, and observes that 'tis only a mere Habit, an Exercise, in which all is well meant, and ought to be well taken. For my own Part, I sincerely declare, that the meek whining Complaints of my first Wife, and the silent affected Discontent in the Countenance of my second, gave me (either of them) ten Times the Uneasiness that the Clamour of my present dear Spouse is capable of giving. 'Tis my Opinion, in short, that their Freedom of Speech springs from a Sense they have, that they do their Duty in every Part towards their Husbands, and that no Man can say, *Black is* (the white of) *their Eye.*

There are among my Acquaintance two Maids, that I am confident will make Wives of this Sort: And I wish these Hints may be of any Service towards getting them good Husbands.

A certain French Poet[3] it seems could be so calm in the midst of his Wife's Tempest, as to write the following Lines upon it.

3. Jean Passerat (1534–1602). As printed in his collected works the sonnet is entitled "D'une Hostesse," is addressed to his friend Pierre de Ronsard, and apparently describes a landlady the two poets had known. Prosper

Celui qui n'a pas vû comment la mer Egée,
Heurtant contre sa rive écume en sa fureur:
Comment le Foudre craque, éclatant son horreur,
Sur quelque grosse tour dont la terre est chargée.

Qui n'a pas vû comment la Lionne outragée
D'un rugir gemissant se fend presque le coeur,
Et ce qu'oit le Chasseur à demi mort de peur,
Laissant sur l'autre bord la Tygresse enragée:

Qu'il vienne a mon logis, il entendra souvent
Les meuglemens des boeufs, les orages, le vent,
Les tambours, les canons, la foudre, et la tempete,

Il entendra l'enfer, et ce qu'on peut nommer
D'impetueux au ciel, en la terre, en la mer,
Ma femme, cher ami, seule a tout dans sa tete.

When they were first shown to me, I got a Friend of mine who understands something of the French to translate them; and he gave me the following Version, viz.

He who hath not with Eyes amaz'd beheld
Th' Ægean Sea with foaming Fury swell'd,
Raging against its Banks: Or with [what] Pow'r
The cracking Thunder shivers some huge Tow'r:
Or how the Hunter shudders with his Fears
When the dire roaring Lionness he hears
And the fierce Tygress on the Left appears.
He soon shall hear, if to my House he comes,
The bellowing Bulls, Guns, Hurricanes and Drums,
And piercing Thunder-Crack. He shall hear Hell,
And what impetuous e'er in Heav'n befel,
And what's outragious in the Earth or Seas:
My Wife (dear Friends) hath in her Head all these.

Blanchemain, ed., *Les Poésies de Jean Passerat* (Paris, 1880), I, 172–3. BF almost certainly took the poem from A[bel] Boyer, *The Compleat French-Master, for Ladies and Gentlemen* (10th edit., London, 1729), p. 391. In reprinting it Boyer substituted the title "Sur une Femme Criailleuse" and made several verbal changes, which BF followed, including especially the transformation of the woman described from the two friends' landlady into the speaker's wife.

The Reader perhaps will hardly believe me, if I tell him that this is nothing but *Musick,* and that I think 'tis pity a Man can be allow'd to keep but one Instrument of it in his House at a Time; yet if there were not a Law of this Province prohibiting Poligamy, I should certainly be for marrying the two Girls above-mention'd, in order to compleat my Consort. I am, Sir, Yours, &c.

On Ill-Natured Speaking

Printed in *The Pennsylvania Gazette,* July 12, 1733; also draft: Historical Society of Pennsylvania.

To the Printer of the *Gazette.*

'Tis strange that among Men, who are born for Society and mutual Solace, there should be any who take Pleasure in speaking disagreeable Things to their Acquaintance: But such there are, I assure you, and I should be glad if a little publick Chastisement might be any Means of reforming them. These ill-natur'd People study a Man's Temper, or the Circumstances of his Life, meerly to know what disgusts him, and what he does not love to hear mentioned; and this they take Care to omit no Opportunity of disturbing him with. They communicate their wonderful Discoveries to others, with an ill-natur'd Satisfaction in their Countenances, *Say such a Thing to such a Man, and you cannot mortify him worse.* They delight (to use their own Phrase) in *touching gall'd Horses* that they may see 'em *winch.* Like Flies, a *sore Place* is a Feast to them. Know, ye Wretches, that the meanest Insect, the trifling Musketoe, the filthy Bugg, have, as well as you, the Power of giving Pain to Men; but to be able to give Pleasure to your Fellow Creatures, requires Good-Nature, and a kind and humane Disposition, joined with Talents to which ye seem to have no Pretension.[4]

4. The MS draft of this paragraph begins with the sentence: "There are certain malicious Troublers of good natured Conversation which I should be glad to see publickly corrected." On the page opposite the draft BF has written the following notes, perhaps for a revised and expanded version: "Conversation. the best Method of Instruction. Cicero's Maxim. the Ends of Conv. these all obstructed by Positiveness. the Words certainly, undoubtedly &c. should never be used, but It seems to me, I conceive, I apprehend &c. Reason against being angry for different Opinions." BF expressed some of these sentiments in similar terms in his autobiography, 1784 (Par. Text edit., p. 234).

[A Meditation on a Quart Mugg]

Printed in *The Pennsylvania Gazette*, July 19, 1733.

This essay was first printed by Smyth (*Writings*, II, 198), who considered it a "highly characteristic production." The present editors, however, believe that the essay is not sufficiently characteristic of Franklin's style to be attributed to him. No external evidence of authorship has been found and it is therefore omitted here.

On Literary Style[5]

Printed in *The Pennsylvania Gazette*, August 2, 1733; also draft: Historical Society of Pennsylvania.

To the Printer of the *Gazette*.

There are few Men, of Capacity for making any considerable Figure in Life, who have not frequent Occasion to communicate their Thoughts to others in *Writing;* if not sometimes publickly as Authors, yet continually in the Management of their private Affairs, both of Business and Friendship: and since, when ill-express'd, the most proper Sentiments and justest Reasoning lose much of their native Force and Beauty, it seems to me that there is scarce any Accomplishment more necessary to a Man of Sense, than that of *Writing well* in his Mother Tongue: But as most other polite Acquirements, make a greater Appearance in a Man's Character, this however useful, is generally neglected or forgotten.

I believe there is no better Means of learning to write well, than this of attempting to entertain the Publick now and then in one of your Papers. When the Writer conceals himself, he has the Advantage of hearing the Censure both of Friends and Enemies, express'd with more Impartiality. And since, in some degree, it concerns the Credit of the Province, that such Things as are printed be performed tolerably well, mutual Improvement seems to be the Duty of all Lovers of Writing: I shall therefore frankly communicate the Observations I have made or collected on this Subject, and request those of others in Return.

5. Prepared in response to a query proposed to the Junto. The rough draft notes are printed in Sparks, *Works*, II, 553. On the subject see Chester E. Jorgenson, "Sidelights on Benjamin Franklin's Principles of Rhetoric," *Revue Anglo-Américaine*, XI (1933–34), 208–22.

I have thought in general, that whoever would write so as not to displease good Judges, should have particular Regard to these three Things, viz. That his Performance be *smooth, clear,* and *short:* For the contrary Qualities are apt to offend, either the Ear, the Understanding, or the Patience.

'Tis an Observation of Dr. Swift, that modern Writers injure the Smoothness of our Tongue, by omitting Vowels wherever it is possible, and joining the harshest Consonants together with only an Apostrophe between; thus for *judged,* in it self not the smoothest of Words, they say *judg'd;* for *disturbed, disturb'd,* &c. It may be added to this, says another, that by changing *eth* into *s,* they have shortned one Syllable in a multitude of Words, and have thereby encreased, not only the *Hissing,* too offensive before, but also the great Number of Monosyllables, of which, without great Difficulty, a smooth Sentence cannot be composed. The Smoothness of a Period is also often Hurt by Parentheses, and therefore the best Writers endeavour to avoid them.

To write *clearly,* not only the most expressive, but the plainest Words should be chosen. In this, as well as in every other Particular requisite to Clearness, Dr. Tillotson is an excellent Example. The Fondness of some Writers for such Words as carry with them an Air of Learning, renders them unintelligible to more than half their Countrymen. If a Man would that his Writings have an Effect on the Generality of Readers, he had better imitate that Gentleman, who would use no Word in his Works that was not well understood by his Cook-maid.

A too frequent Use of Phrases ought likewise to be avoided by him that would write clearly. They trouble the Language, not only rendring it extreamly difficult to Foreigners, but make the Meaning obscure to a great number of English Readers. Phrases, like learned Words, are seldom used without Affectation; when, with all true Judges, the simplest Stile is the most beautiful.

But supposing the most proper Words and Expressions chosen, the Performance may yet be weak and obscure, if it has not *Method.* If a Writer would *persuade,* he should proceed gradually from Things already allow'd, to those from which Assent is yet with-held, and make their Connection manifest. If he would *inform,* he must advance regularly from Things known to things unknown, distinctly without Confusion, and the lower he begins the better. It is a common Fault in Writers, to allow their Readers too much Knowledge: They begin with that which should be the Middle, and skipping backwards and forwards, 'tis impossible for any one but he who is perfect in the Subject before, to understand their Work, and such an one has no Occasion to read it. Perhaps a Habit of using good Method, cannot be better acquired, than by learning a little Geometry or Algebra.

Amplification, or the Art of saying Little in Much, should only be allowed to Speakers. If they preach, a Discourse of considerable Length is expected from them, upon every Subject they undertake, and perhaps they are not stock'd with naked Thoughts sufficient to furnish it out. If they plead in the Courts, it is of Use to speak abundance, tho' they reason little; for the Ignorant in a Jury, can scarcely believe it possible that a Man can talk so much and so long without being in the Right. Let them have the Liberty then, of repeating the same Sentences in other Words; let them put an Adjective to every Substantive, and double every Substantive with a Synonima; for this is more agreeable than hauking, spitting, taking Snuff, or any other Means of concealing Hesitation. Let them multiply Definitions, Comparisons, Similitudes and Examples. Permit them to make a Detail of Causes and Effects, enumerate all the Consequences, and express one Half by Metaphor and Circumlocution: Nay, allow the Preacher to to tell us whatever a Thing is negatively, before he begins to tell us what it is affirmatively; and suffer him to divide and subdivide as far as *Two and fiftiethly*. All this is not intolerable while it is not written. But when a Discourse is to be bound down upon Paper, and subjected to the calm leisurely Examination of nice Judgment, every Thing that is needless gives Offence; and therefore all should be retrenched, that does not directly conduce to the End design'd. Had this been always done, many large and tiresome Folio's would have shrunk into Pamphlets, and many a Pamphlet into a single Period. However, tho' a multitude of Words obscure the Sense, and 'tis necessary to abridge a verbose Author in order to understand him; yet a Writer should take especial Care on the other Hand, that his Brevity doth not hurt his Perspicuity.

After all, if the Author does not intend his Piece for general Reading, he must exactly suit his Stile and Manner to the particular Taste of those he proposes for his Readers. Every one observes, the different Ways of Writing and Expression used by the different Sects of Religion; and can readily enough pronounce, that it is improper to use some of these Stiles in common, or to use the common Stile, when we address some of these Sects in particular.

To conclude, I shall venture to lay it down as a Maxim, *That no Piece can properly be called good, and well written, which is void of any Tendency to benefit the Reader, either by improving his Virtue or his Knowledge.* This Principle every Writer would do well to have in View, whenever he undertakes to write. All Performances done for meer Ostentation of Parts, are really contemptible; and withal far more subject to the Severity of Criticism, than those more meanly written, wherein the Author appears to have aimed at the Good of others. For when 'tis visible to every one, that a Man writes to show his Wit only, all his Expressions are sifted, and his Sense examined, in the nicest and most ill-natur'd manner; and every one is glad of an Opportunity to mortify him. But, what a vast Destruction would there be of Books, if they were to be saved or condemned on a Tryal by this Rule!

Besides, Pieces meerly humorous, are of all Sorts the hardest to succeed in. If they are not natural, they are stark naught; and there can be no real Humour in an Affectation of Humour.

Perhaps it may be said, that an ill Man is able to write an ill Thing well; that is, having an ill Design, and considering who are to be his Readers, he may use the properest Stile and Arguments to attain his Point. In this Sense, that is best wrote, which is best adapted to the Purpose of the Writer.

I am apprehensive, dear Readers, lest in this Piece, I should be guilty of every Fault I condemn, and deficient in every Thing I recommend; so much easier it is to offer Rules than to practise them. I am sure, however, of this, that I am Your very sincere Friend and Servant.

Power of Attorney to Deborah Franklin

Printed form with MS insertions in blanks: American Philosophical Society

[August 30, 1733]

KNOW all Men by these Presents, That I *Benjamin Franklin of the City of Philadelphia in Pennsylvania, Printer* have constituted, made and appointed, and by these Presents do constitute, make and appoint my trusty and loving Friend [Friend *struck out*] *Wife Deborah Franklin to be* my true and lawful Attorney, for me and in my Name and Stead, and to my Use, to ask, demand, sue for, levy, recover and receive all such Sum and Sums of Money, Debts, Rents, Goods, Wares, Dues, Accounts, and other Demands whatsoever, which are or shall be due, owing, payable and belonging to me, or detained from me any Manner of Ways or Means whatsoever by *any Persons whatsoever, either in Pennsylvania, Carolina, or any of the Provinces and Governments adjoining to Pennsylvania, or elsewhere* Giving and Granting unto my said Attorney, by these Presents, my full and whole Powers, Strength and Authority, in and about the Premisses, to have, use and take all lawful Ways and Means in my Name, for the Recovery thereof; and upon the Receipt of any such Debts, Dues or Sums of Money aforesaid, Acquittances or other sufficient Discharges, for me and in my Name, to make, seal and deliver; and generally all and every other Act and Acts, Thing and Things, Device or Devices in the Law whatsoever, needful and necessary to be done in and about the Premisses, for me and in my Name to do, execute and perform, as fully, largely and amply, to all Intents and Purposes, as I my self might or could do, if I was personally present, or as if the Matter required more special Authority than is herein given; and Attorneys one or more under *her* for the Purpose aforesaid, to make and constitute, and again at Pleasure to revoke; ratifying, allowing and holding for firm and effectual all and whatsoever my said Attorney shall lawfully do in and about the Premisses, by Virtue hereof. IN WITNESS whereof I have hereunto set my Hand and Seal *this Thirtieth* Day of *August in the Sixth* Year of His Majesty's Reign, *Annoque Domini* One Thousand Seven Hundred and Thirty *three.*

Sealed and Delivered in   B. FRANKLIN
    the Presence of
    EDW. LEWIS
    STEPHEN POTTS

Philadelphia: Printed and Sold at the *New Printing-Office* near the *Market;* where may be had all Sorts of BLANKS.

Half-Hour's Conversation with a Friend

Printed in *The Pennsylvania Gazette*, November 16, 1733.

Andrew Hamilton, speaker of the Assembly, recorder of Philadelphia, and a trustee of the Loan Office, was one of the most powerful public figures in Pennsylvania from 1727 until his death in 1741.[6] Resentful and jealous enemies bitterly attacked him in Bradford's *American Weekly Mercury*, especially during the campaign of 1733.[7] These attacks culminated on October 18 in an anonymous charge that his control of the Assembly, the courts, and the Loan Office was sinister and dictatorial. The *Gazette* printed this defense, which quoted at length Hamilton's own purported comments on the criticism. The style is familiar, and Franklin had long admired and supported Hamilton, who had helped him get the Assembly's printing business and other public work, and the article was probably written at least in part by Franklin.[8]

Mr. Franklin,

As Mr. Bradford was pleased to entertain the Publick with *A true Letter to a Friend in the Country*, as 'tis called, in his Mercury of the 18th of October last, I desire you will give this *Half-hour's Conversation with a Friend* a Place in your Gazette, which may at present serve for an Answer to that Letter. As there is nothing can please every body, so who can tell but this may divert somebody. Sir, Your humble Servant.

To gratify your Curiosity, I shall as far as my Memory will serve me, let you know, as well the Sentiments of the Publick upon the Subject of the Letter published in Mr. Bradford's Mercury of the 18th of October last, as what pass'd between my self and the Person who is supposed to be chiefly pointed out in that Letter.

6. Burton A. Konkle, *The Life of Andrew Hamilton, 1676–1741* (Phila., 1941).

7. Anna Janney DeArmond, *Andrew Bradford, Colonial Journalist* (Newark, Del., 1949), pp. 87–113. Among the Franklin Papers in APS is BF's MS copy of a paper entitled "Advice and Instructions to the Palatines newly arrived in the Province of Pennsylvania. By their Countryman H I Z," which contains a veiled attack on Hamilton's unorthodox religious views. The "Advice" has sometimes been incorrectly attributed to BF. *PMHB*, XVI (1892), 16–17.

8. One response to this article, printed in the *Mercury*, Dec. 14, pointed out that the *Gazette* had unwittingly revealed Hamilton in a not entirely favorable light. Other replies appear in the *Mercury*, Dec. 29, 1733, Jan. 8, Feb. 5, 1734.

I have had the Opportunity of hearing the Sentiments of a great many People concerning that Performance. Some say they are persuaded it was not the Author's Love to his Country induced him to publish those Charges in the Manner he has done, and that it would have been much better to have charged that Man with Particulars, and by Name, and likewise to have subscribed his own, by which the People might at the same Time have known the Criminal and the Accuser; but not having done this, they conclude the whole to be no more than the Effects of some private Resentment. Others, who seem to be very certain against whom all the heavy Charges in that Letter are levelled, and who like the Man no better than the Author does, commend the Letter much, not, they say, that they can agree it is all true, but approve well of that old Saying, *Throw Dirt enough, and some will stick;* and they add, it never having been answered, such who know nothing of the Matter are the more enclin'd to believe it. These Reports made me desirous to see the Person, who is my particular Friend, against whom it seems generally agreed the *true Letter*, as 'tis called, was wrote; And meeting with him last Night, I acquainted him with the various Sentiments of the People upon the Subject: He frankly own'd, that from the particular Description of his Employments, no body could doubt but he was the Man pointed at; but said, seeing it was commonly agreed to be wrote by nobody, he thought no body should regard it. Here I put my Friend in mind, that I had often heard him say very hard Things of an ungrateful Man; and forasmuch as the Letter-writer would have it believed that my Friend was under very great Obligations both to the Proprietor and Governor, and being charged with horrid Ingratitude to both, it might not only draw on him their Resentment, but the Censure of others, who might construe his Silence into a Proof of his Guilt. To which he made me the following Answer, as I can remember, and which I think I am bound in point of Friendship and Justice to his Character, to make as publick as the Letter. "Sir, I am very sensible of the Weight of Power in the Hands of a supreme Magistrate, and how it has been made use of in all Ages, and most Countries of any long standing, to destroy the most innocent Men. I am likewise sensible, that *that* same Power never wants Creatures who are ready to execute Vengeance upon the Heads of those who deserve it

334

least, not always meerly in compliance with the Will of their Superiors, but very frequently because they want his Place or hate his Person. However, I hope no honest Men who understand or have a true Value for that inestimable Blessing of Liberty, which the People here enjoy in a greater Degree than most of their Neighbours, can with just Reason apprehend any Danger from that Quarter of Power. The People of Pennsylvania are too wise to be cheated into an Opinion that a Man is to be destroy'd because his Superiors and a few of their Creatures apprehend that he stands in their Way: No, they know a Man can lose neither Life, Liberty, nor Estate, but by the Judgment of twelve Freemen of Pennsylvania; and being secure of this, and that it is in no Man's Power to prove that he ever deserted the Interest or Cause of his Country, he can laugh at the impotent Efforts of the Great and Powerful." But here I interrupted my Friend and put him in mind, that tho' all he said was most unquestionably true, and that I was pleased to hear him prefer Justice to all Powers and Dependencies whatsoever, yet it did not seem to answer the Charges exhibited against him in the Letter before us: And thereupon he proceeded to the Effect following. "Sir, you know in Law a particular Answer to a general Charge is never required of any Man, and therefore it cannot be expected that I should make a particular Answer to a Number of general Charges, such as, *speaking contemptibly* (I suppose the polite Author means *contemptuously*) *of the Proprietor, abusing and displacing the Governor, endeavouring to put a Stop to the Proceedings of Government and to the Administration of Justice, Partiality in Lending out Money at the Loan-Office, &c.* Now to these I can only make this general Answer, that the Charges are most unjust; and if the worthy Author of that Letter will produce any Person of Credit (but I desire it may be remembred the Author himself is always excepted, for who knows but having once told a Lie he will be so hardy as still to stand to it) that can prove I have wittingly or willingly said or done any Wrong to that honourable Gentleman, or any of his Family, I will in the most publick Manner make such Acknowledgments as all the World shall say are just. Nor have I ever allow'd my self the Freedom with the Propr——r which the Author has seen fit to do, where he (*kind Man*) cautions that Gentleman neither to be wheedled, nor frightned by the Threats of that dangerous Man;

and lest he should faint, for his Encouragement has told him, that all the People will stand by him, and others (no doubt meaning himself) who don't love Trouble, will be roused. Now whether this be decent Treatment of a Gentleman of the Pro——r's Character, in supposing him to want Resolution to resent any Injury done him by any Man, but especially by one out of Favour with his Superiors is most certain, and, as the Author says (and without all doubt wishes it were true) hated by all the People, the Truth of which I leave the World to judge of. As to the displacing the Governor, he said, I don't understand what is meant by that: For, excepting his Majesty, I know none who have a Power to remove him but our Proprietary Family only: and they will bear me Witness, that I never directly nor indirectly made any Application to them for any such Removal; therefore this part of the Charge is utterly false. And as to the Article of Ingratitude, I freely refer the settling the Account of Obligations between the Governor and my self, to his own Honour; and I hope that's fair. As to my putting a stop to the Proceedings of Justice, &c. it is a direct Falshood; neither was I the Person, nor any Acquaintance of the Person's who started those Doubts in the Assembly which gave so great Offence to some folks: yet, whenever the judicious Author shall think fit to enter into that Controversy, I'll venture to say he needs not doubt being favoured with an Answer. As to my ruling all Courts, managing the Assembly at Pleasure, &c. Tho' I have seen the Time within these seven Years, and oftner than once, when my little Interest in those Courts and Councils was esteemed of very great Service to somebody, yet I shall at this time make no other Answer, than to say, these Charges so much concern Men of the best Characters for Integrity and Ability in the Government, that I cannot doubt the Charge will at one time or other meet with a Resentment adequate to the Injury done the Persons concern'd. But as to my great Pride and other personal Vices, I shall only say, *Lord I have sinned, have Mercy upon me a miserable Sinner!*" And then taking up the Letter in his Hand, he merrily said, "Was this fine Letter but stript of all the affected simplicities and disguises the Author has been at the pains to dress it up in (for he used to write in the same stile against Sir William) and put into plain English, methinks it would read pretty much to the following purpose; '*Loving, Loving, Loving*

336

Friends, hear and believe, and then you will see, there is risen up amongst us a dangerous, proud, wicked, witty Fellow, whose Life is inconsistent with your Lives and Liberties, as by the following Instances will to you my dearest Countrymen be most manifest. He speaks contemptibly of the Pr——r, for I my self have heard him swear terribly, that Gentleman was not tall enough to touch the Moon, nor strong enough to remove a Mountain: He abuses the Go——r, and has endeavoured to displace him, for it is commonly reported, that he should say in a certain Place, that his Honour don't see now so well as when he was but one and twenty; and I my self with these very Eyes of mine, saw him once offer the arm'd Chair to the Pro——r when the Gov——r was present; Now if this was not a plain Attempt to displace his Honour, judge ye. He's proud and revengeful to the last Degree, for he will not be thankful to his Betters for abusing him; and upon a certain Time publickly exposed me for insinuating he had taken greater Fees in his Office than by Law he was entitled to. He is a great Lawyer, and will not be fool'd out of a good Cause; he is so cunning too, that he will rarely be concerned in a Case but what he believes to be just, he speaks to it with great Zeal, the Court is oblig'd to do right, and often give Judgment for his Client, and thus it is he rules them as he pleases. He has so much Wit as to propose nothing in Assembly but what he thinks reasonable, and so crafty he will always agree with them in what is just, and by these Methods it is that he manages the Whole at Pleasure. Some of us of late never ask his Advice but when We can't well do without it, which the cunning Rogue knows very well, and for that Reason he is so wayward, that before We can have his Opinion, We are oblig'd to truckle and pretend a mighty regard for his Judgment. When Matters of Government are done without his Advice, he has such a malicious Way of faulting and abusing us who are concerned, that when we blunder, he like the unlucky Boy, upon seeing a Ploughman mount the managed Horse which soon laid the Rider on his Back, laugh'd aloud and cried out, *Well fare you, Countryman, you sit well, e faith!* This terrible Man has had much Power for these last seven Years, and you shall hear the Use he has made on't. I'll assure you what I tell you is true, tho' no body alive knows it. About six Years ago he eat up your Privileges at a Breakfast;

it is but three Years since he made a Dinner of your Liberties; and if you suffer him to live one Year longer, he'll swallow all your Estates for his Supper. In short, he's a Witch; for with his Breath he blows Men blind, and with his Wit and Raillery he strikes them dumb: Is this Man fit to live? I pray you good People do, as a Reward for these my Labours, and that this dangerous Man may be pull'd down, for the love of God, do, chuse me to represent you but one Year, and you shall see —o [no?]—Paper-Money, but Russet Shoes enough,[9] And in the mean Time, let me have the Pleasure to hear you confess what a seasonable Discovery I have made of the Danger your Liberties, Privileges and Properties are in. I hope my Word is sufficient Proof for all these Things; and if you presume to doubt the Truth of what I have said, you are no better than the Courts and Assemblies I have been speaking of, that is, a parcel of Idiots, Fools and Miscreants; and what is still worse, I'll take my Oath on't, you are sworn Enemies to the Prop——r and G——r.' " And here my Friend said he was weary of talking, and would conclude by begging Pardon for putting a few *paw* Words in the Mouth of the worthy Author; but at the same time excused himself by saying, That as the Author had taken the Liberty to lie a great deal, he hoped to be forgiven for making him swear a little; which last Sin, he said, in respect to the Peace of a Neighbourhood, was in his Opinion by far the least of the two. And so he ended. And so I conclude with my own best Advice to our Friend the Author of the *true Letter*. Go on, most excellent Author and Patriot; and having got the Government on your side, spare no Man, who after having been most injuriously treated by you, shall dare to resent, nay, or to deny the Charge, tho' never so unjust. Tell the People again and again, that nothing but that Humanity and Generosity which is so natural to you, and the *tender* Regard you have for their Liberties and Privileges, but above all the Love you have for their Properties, could have rous'd you from your beloved Retirement. And for Proof of all this, appeal to the *Bricklayer*, the *Carpenter*, the *Shipwright*, *Tanner* and *Tax-gatherer*, who will every one of them be Witnesses of the Truth of what I mean. Sir, your humble Servant.

9. Russet shoes, made of unblackened leather, were a mark of countrymen and the lower classes.

Articles of Agreement with Louis Timothée[1]

Draft: Historical Society of Pennsylvania

[November 26, 1733]

ARTICLES of Agreement indented [and] made the 26th Day of November Ao. Di. 1733 Between Benjamin Franklin of the City of Philadelphia in the Province of Pensilvania Printer of the one Part and Lewis Timothée of the said City Printer (now bound on a Voyage to Charlestown in South Carolina) Of the other Part: WHEREAS the said BF and LT have determined to enter into a Copartnership for the Carrying on the Business of Printing in Charles Town aforesaid, It is therefore covenanted, granted and agreed by and between the said Parties to these Presents and the said BF and LT do mutually covenant and agree each with the other of these each to each with the Heirs Executors and Administrators of the other of them in Manner following, That is to say, THAT they the said Benjamin Franklin and LT shall be Partners in carrying on the Trade and Business of Printing in Charlestown aforesaid for and during the Term of 6 Years from the Day on which the said L shall be put in Possession of a Printing Press, Types and Materials in the Town of Charlestown in S. Carol. provided by BF if they the said B and L shall so long live. THAT the said BF shall be at the sole Charge and Expence of providing a Printing Press with all its necessary Appurtenances together with 400 Weight of Letters (if the said L shall require so great a Quantity) and shall cause the same to be delivered into the possession of the said LT in Charlestown aforesaid. THAT the Business and working part of Printing and of Disposing of the Work printed shall be under the Care, Management and Direction of and performed by the said LT or at his Expence. THAT all Charges for Paper, Ink, Balls, Tympans, Wool, Oil and other Things necessary to printing, Together with the Charge of all common and necessary Repairs of the Press and its Appurtenances and also the Charge of Rent for a Shop and for so much Room as is necessary to be used in the man-

---

1. See above, p. 230. Timothée succeeded Thomas Whitmarsh as BF's South Carolina partner (see above, p. 205), resumed publication of the *Gazette*, Feb. 2, 1734, became official printer, and was prominent in local affairs until his death, 1738. Punctuation, largely lacking in the MS, has been added for the sake of clarity.

agement of the Business of Printing aforesaid shall be divided into 3 equal Parts, 2 of which said Parts shall be disbursed [defrayed *written above*] by and paid as due from the said LT; And the remaining 3rd Part shall be defrayed and allowed to be paid as due from the said BF and deducted out of the Income next herein after mentioned. THAT all Money received or to be received for printing or for any Thing done or to be done relating to the Business of printing aforesaid by the said LT, either as Gratuity, Premium, Reward or Salary from the Government or from Others shall be divided into 3 equal Parts, 2 of which said Parts the said LT shall have for his Care, Management and Performance aforesaid, and the said BF shall have the remaining 3rd Part thereof. THAT for the regular transacting the Affairs in Copartnership aforesaid the said LT shall keep fair and exact Books of Accounts of and concerning all Work done and sold by him and of all his Receipts and Disbursments relating to the Business of Printing in Copartnership aforesaid, with the Day, Month and Year of each Entry and submit the same to the View of the said BF, his lawful Attorney, Executors or Administrators as often as thereunto required And that all the Accounts of the Copartners in Copartnership aforesaid shall be drawn out Fair comunicated to each other and settled once a Year during the Copartnership aforesaid or oftner if either of them the said Copartners shall require it. And that upon such Settlement the said LT shall remit the Part by this Agreement belonging to the said BF in such Wares or Merchandizes or in Bills of Exchange or in Money as the said B shall direct by Letter or Order under his Hand on board such Vessell and to such Port as the [said] B shall also require by Letter or Order as aforesaid at the proper Risque of the said B. THAT the said LT shall not work with any other printing Materials than those belonging to the said BF nor follow any other Business but Printing during the Continuance of the Copartnership aforesaid, occasional Merchandize excepted. THAT the Loss by bad Debts shall be divided and sustained by both Parties in the same Proportion as the Money ought to have been divided by this Agreement if it had been received. THAT neither of the said Parties shall reap any Benefit or Advantage by Survivorship if the other of them shall depart this Life before the Expiration of the said Term of 6 Years as aforesaid. But that if the said LT shall depart this Life before the Expiration of the said Term his

Executors or Administrators shall deliver up the Press, Types and all other Materials of printing which have been provided by the said BF or at his Charge to the said B, his certain Attorney, Executors or Administrators upon Demand in good Order and Condition (allowing for the usual Wear and Decay of such things) as also the Share of Money, Effects and Debts belonging to the said B by this Agreement. PROVIDED nevertheless That if PT, Son of the said LT, shall be capable of carrying on and will carry on the Business of Printing aforesaid as it ought to be carried on and shall also give sufficient Security for his complying with and performing all Things relating thereto which by this Agreement the said LT ought to have done had he lived, It shall be in the Power of the said PT to keep and improve the Materials of Printing so provided by the said BF as aforesaid until the Term of Copartnership aforesaid is expired, Any thing herein before contained to the Contrary notwithstanding. But if the said P shall relinquish this Agreement and shall be unwilling to continue the Copartnership hereby made, Then he shall not work at the Business of printing at all in the province of Carolina aforesaid until the Term of Copartnership aforesaid be compleatly expired. AND if the said BF shall depart this Life before the Expiration of the Term of Copartnership aforesaid the said LT shall continue the Business nevertheless, paying and remitting the Part by this Agreement belonging to the said BF unto the Executors, Administrators or Assigns of the said B or as they shall direct, they performing all parts of this Agreement to the said L which he the said B ought to have done if he had lived. And that at the Expiration of the Term of 6 Years aforesaid the said L or his Son P shall have the preference of purchasing the said printing Press, Materials and Types, if they shall be so disposed, at their present Value,[2] allowing only what shall be adjudged a reasonable Abatement for the Wear of such Things in the Time they have been used.[3] But if the said L nor P shall not be enclined to purchase them

2. Originally: "at their first Value in Philadelphia."

3. Mrs. Elizabeth Timothy (as the family later spelled the name) fulfilled the terms of the agreement by continuing the printing business, including publication of the *Gazette*, in her son Peter's name. Unlike her husband, who, though educated and honest, had no taste for business, Mrs. Timothy sent BF exact quarterly accountings, managed the business so well that she supported six children, and at the expiration of the six years' term bought out BF's interest and gave the business to her son. Peter Timothy con-

at that Price they shall transport or cause to be transported to and delivered at Philadelphia the said printing Press, Materials and Types at their own proper Risque and Charges, to the said BF, his Executors, Administrators or Assigns, and if any unusual Damage by bad usuage or Negligence shall have happened to them they the said L or P shall make it good but if any Damage shall happen to the said Printing Press, Types, and Materials by some unavoidable Accident, the Loss shall be divided and sustained by both Parties in the same Manner as the Loss by bad Debts is by this Agreement to be divided and sustained. PROVIDED NEVERTHELESS that if the printing Press, Materials and Types which the said B provides shall be consumed and destroyed by Fire or otherwise rendred unfit for Use before the said LT shall have them in possession, then the Loss thereby shall be wholly sustain'd by the said BF, and the Co-partnership hereby made shall be disolved and abolished, Unless the said B be willing to continue it, and provide another Press and Types as aforesaid and send them at his own Risque to Charlestown aforesaid to be there delivered to the said LT, any thing herein before contained to the Contrary in any wise Notwithstanding. IN WITNESS &c.

Endorsed: Articles of Agreemt. between Printers abt. carrying their Trade viz int. B. Franklin and L. Timothee.

Extracts from the Gazette, 1733

Printed in *The Pennsylvania Gazette*, January 4 to December 31, 1733

Yesterday, being Market Day, Watt who was concern'd in the Counterfeit Money, as mentioned in one of our late Papers, receiv'd part of his Punishment, being whipt, pilloried and cropt. He behaved so as to touch the Compassion of the Mob, and they did not fling at him (as was expected) neither Snow-balls nor any Thing else. We hear that Grindal, the Importer of the Bills, and chief

---

tinued it until his death, 1781, when it was continued by his widow and son Benjamin Franklin Timothy. Hennig Cohen, *The South-Carolina Gazette* (Columbia, S.C., 1953), pp. 230–3, 238–41; Par. Text edit., pp. 246, 248. Ledgers A and B contain some of BF's accounts with Lewis Timothy, his widow, and their son (see above, p. 172).

Person concern'd, was taken in the Jersies, but afterwards made his Escape. In his Pocket-Book was found the Account of Charge, so much to the Printer, so much for engraving the Plates, so much for Paper, &c.[4]   [January 11]

[ADVERTISEMENT] Saturday next will be Published, for 1733: *The Second Edition of* POOR RICHARD: An ALMANACK[5] containing the Lunations, Eclipses, Planets Motions and Aspects, Weather, Sun and Moon's rising and setting, Highwater, &c. besides many pleasant and witty Verses, Jests and Sayings, Author's Motive of Writing, Prediction of the Death of his Friend Mr. Titan Leeds, Moon no Cuckold, Batchelor's Folly, Parson's Wine and Baker's Pudding, Short Visits, Kings and Bears, New Fashions, Game for Kisses, Katherine's Love, Different Sentiments, Signs of a Tempest, Death a Fisherman, Conjugal Debate, Men and Melons, H. the Prodigal, Breatfast in Bed, Oyster Lawsuit, &c. By RICHARD SAUNDERS, Philomat. Printed and sold by B. Franklin, Price 3s. 6d. per Dozen. Of whom also may be had Sheet Almanacks at 2s. 6d.
    A few of the first that were printed had the Months of September and October transpos'd; but that Fault is now rectified. [January 11]

On the 20th past, at a special Court of Common-Pleas held here, came on a Tryal between A. Hamilton, Esq; Plaintiff, and Robert Gregory with Mary his Wife, Defendants; when the Plaintiff recovered £500 Damage against the Defendants, for conspiring to charge him with the unnatural Abuse of the Body of the said Mary Gregory. It appear'd upon the Tryal, from a great Number of Witnesses, that the whole was a villanous Forgery, contriv'd against the said A. Hamilton to extort Money from him: that the said Mary is a Person of a most abandoned and infamous Character, and that she had made the like Attempts against sundry other Persons of unblemished Reputation in this City.   [February 8]

The Ice grows very rotten in the River, and 'tis hop'd will drive in a few Days.   [February 15]

4. See above, p. 278.
5. No copy of this edition is known to have survived.

Sunday Morning last, the Ice in Skuylkyl, tho' prodigious thick and strong, broke up with a Fresh, and came down in Heaps, vast Cakes rouling over and over, in a terrible Manner, breaking great Trees where the Flood came over the low Land. Such a great Quantity of Ice being apt to damn [sic] the River in some Places, it rais'd the Water exceedingly, and drove with greater Violence when those Dams were broken. It carried away the Flats of two Ferries, and did other considerable Damage. The Water was near two Foot and a half high on the Ground Floor of Joseph Grey's House at the middle Ferry; which is much higher than any Fresh is known to have been before in that River: But the House was not *four foot under Water,* as another Account says, meaning, 'tis like, that *four foot of the House was under Water.* [February 22]

[ADVERTISEMENT] Good Rhode-Island CHEESE, and Cod-Fish, sold by the Printer hereof. [March 15]

[ADVERTISEMENT] Lost about four Weeks since, suppos'd in or near the Market-House, a Sheet and half of Prints of Leaves, being Part of a compleat Set. Whoever brings them to the Printer hereof, shall be well rewarded.[6] [April 26]

[ADVERTISEMENT] The Subscribers of the Library Company of Philadelphia, are hereby advertised, that Monday the Seventh of May ensuing, is the Day appointed for the Choice of Directors and Treasurer for the succeeding Year; And for the Subscribers to bring in their first annual Payment of Ten Shillings a piece,

6. BF, Joseph Breintnall, John Bartram, and their friends at this time experimented with making impressions of leaves of trees, shrubs, ferns, and grasses. When the leaves were fresh and skillfully inked and pressed, exceedingly accurate and decorative prints were produced. European botanists asked for examples. Breintnall made impressions for the French traveler M. Aubrey de la Mottraye, whom Dr. Samuel Chew brought to call in June 1733; and in October supplied Peter Collinson with some 130 prints. Leaves were also printed on New Jersey paper currency to make counterfeiting more difficult. *Poor Richard's Almanack* for 1737 carried the leaf of the rattlesnake herb, with Breintnall's description of it. The Library Company of Philadelphia contains two volumes of Breintnall's prints and, in its Du Simitière Papers, several lists of leaf prints, and a poem on a species of wild raspberry which Nicholas Scull discovered near Reading, Pa., 1740, with a print of the leaf.

Advance-Money. And that the Place and Time for this Meeting on the said 7th of May, will be at the House of Mr. Louis Timothee, where the Library is kept, in the Ally next the Boar's-Head Tavern, at Two in the Afternoon.   JOSEPH BREINTNAL, Secr.

N.B. The Subscribers are desired to remember the Penalty upon Non-payment of the Ten-Shillings upon the Day appointed.

[April 26]

[ADVERTISEMENT] There is to be sold a very likely Negro Woman aged about Thirty Years who has lived in this City, from her Childhood, and can wash and iron very well, cook Victuals, sew, spin on the Linen Wheel, milk Cows, and do all Sorts of House-work very well. She has a Boy of about Two Years old, which is to go with her. The Price as reasonable as you can agree.

And also another very likely Boy aged about Six Years, who is Son of the abovesaid Woman. He will be sold with his Mother, or by himself, as the Buyer pleases. Enquire of the Printer. [May 3]

Stolen out of a Shop in Market-Street, a Child's Silver Whistle and Bells, without the Coral. Whoever brings it to the Printer hereof, shall have Five Shillings Reward, and no Questions ask'd.

[May 10]

Monday last a Grand Lodge of the Ancient and Honourable Society of Free and accepted Masons in this Province, was held at the Tun Tavern in Water-Street, when Humphry Murray, Esq, was elected Grand Master for the Year ensuing, who appointed Mr. Thomas Hart his Deputy, and Mr. Peter Cuff and Mr. James Bingham were chosen Wardens. A very Elegant Entertainment was provided upon the Occasion, at which the Proprietor, the Governor, the Mayor of this City, and several other Persons of Distinction honour'd the Society with their Presence. [June 28]

We hear from Richland in Bucks County, that on the 15th Instant, Elizabeth the Wife of Marmaduke Jackson was found Dead in their own Field. The Circumstances relating to her Death are told as follows; None liv'd in the House with the old Couple, except a Child about 3 Years old which they had taken to bring up: The Man used to go out to work in the Country, and leave Home for some Days; accordingly he took leave of his Wife the 14th in the Morning about 8 o'Clock, and left her in good Health. The next Morning about the same Hour a neighbouring Woman going by, call'd in to see how they did, and found only the Child, who told her that Granny (as it used to call her) was asleep in the Field, and it could not wake her: And so it went and shewed the Place where the Woman lay dead. The Coroner's Inquest being call'd, examin'd the Child how its Granny came to lie there, and it said, she was going to cut some Bushes to cover the Tobacco Plants; and then shewed by Motions how she staggered before she fell down; it appeared by the Grass that she had scrambled along some small Distance, and a few Strawberry's were found lying by her, which it was suppos'd she was picking for the Child. They ask'd the Child, where it slept the last Night; and it answer'd, *that it stay'd by Granny all day, but could not wake her; and when 'twas dark, it went home to bed, and came again in the Morning and try'd to wake her, but could not:* Accordingly the Print of the Child alone was found in the Bed.   [June 28]

Yesterday a Marriage was consummated between Charles Read, Esq; one of the Trustees of the Loan-Office of this Province, and the Relict of Mr. Joseph Harwood, Gent. A Lady of considerable Fortune.   [October 18]

The Week before last died here, after a short Illness, Mr. Joseph Norris, eldest Son of Isaac Norris, Esq; He was a young Gentleman of considerable Learning, yet a most facetious and agreeable Companion; and notwithstanding a polite Education, was a sincere Friend. His uncommon Good-Nature alone were sufficient to make his Death regretted by all that had the Pleasure of his Acquaintance.
                                                   [October 18]

¶The Printer of this Paper returned but on Saturday last, from a Journey on which he was absent near seven Weeks: If in that Time any Passages have appeared in the Gazette, that may be construed into Personal Reflection, it was without his Knowledge or Approbation, and must be ascribed to the Inadvertence of those who carried on his Business.[7]   [October 18]

7. In the autobiography there is a short account of BF's visit this fall to his family in Boston and his brother James in Newport.

We hear from Bristol, that on Monday Morning last, two young Men were out a Hunting in the Woods near that Place, one of them being a little before the other, saw something thro' the Bushes on the other Side of the Creek; upon which he stepped back to his Companion, and said, *Lend me that Gun, for I see a fine Deer;* accordingly he took Aim, and gave Fire; but when he came to the Place, he found a Boy about nine Years of Age, (who had just been sent out by his Mother for a Can of Water) strugling for Life: the Child never spoke another Word, being shot in the Breast; and dyed immediately. Scarce a Year passes without one or more of these unhappy Accidents, which ought to make People more careful in their Hunting than they commonly are.

[October 25]

JUST PUBLISH'D FOR 1734. POOR RICHARD: An ALMANACK containing the Lunations, Eclipses, Planets Motions and Aspects, Weather, Sun and Moon's Rising and Setting, High-water, &c. Besides many Pleasant and Witty Verses, Jests and notable Sayings. Thanks to the Publick for his last Years Encouragement. Of His Wife's good Humour. Of his Prediction concerning the Day, Hour, and Minute of Titan Leeds's Death. Mr. Leeds's Character. Remarks upon the Almanack published for 1734 in Leeds's Name. Gelding Time. Good Women, Stars and Angels. Poor Dick's *Litany.* What Death is. What spoils the Teeth. The Travellers Improvement. Blind Fortune. Wedlock. Lawyers, Preachers and Tomtit's Eggs. Robin bit. How to perswade. Lawyer's Will, Bucephalus and his Master. Crowing Hen. S---l the Smith, and J---h the Tapster. The Teacher. Heirs and Widows. John's Wit. The Dutch Maxim. Verses by Mrs. Bridget Saunders, in Answer to the December Verses of last Year. Short Dialogue between a Lawyer and his Client, &c. By Richard Saunders Philom. Philadelphia, Printed and sold by B. Franklin, Price 3s. 6d. per Doz.[8]

[November 16]

8. Following this advertisement BF printed some verses which begin, "I'm not High-Church, nor Low-Church, nor Tory, nor Whig," and are signed Richard Saunders. They have sometimes been ascribed to BF, but were in fact first printed by Thomas Whitmarsh in the *South-Carolina Gazette,* Jan. 8, 1732.

Taken not long since out of a House in Town an oldfashion'd Silver Spoon with a flat flower'd Handle mark'd I.C. the Bottom of the Bowl also flower'd. Taken also a Silver Snuff-Box mark'd M. W. the Lid shuts on without a Hinge. Also some time before, a Child's Silver Whistle and Bells, (the Coral lost.) Whoever will leave either of these Things with the Printer hereof shall have *Five Shillings* Reward for each of them and no Questions ask'd. Or whoever can inform where they are so that they may be had again, shall have the same Reward. [November 22]

LATELY IMPORTED. A Parcel of superfine CROWN SOAP. It cleanses fine Linens, Muslins, Laces, Chinces, Cambricks, &c. with Ease and Expedition, which often suffer more from the long and hard Rubbing of the Washer, through the ill Qualities of the *Soap* they use, than the Wearing. It is excellent for the Washing of Scarlets, or any other bright and curious Colours, that are apt to change by the Use of common *Soap*. The Sweetness of the Flavor and the fine Lather it immediately produces, renders it pleasant for the Use of Barbers. It is cut in exact and equal Cakes, neatly put up, and sold at the New Printing-Office, at 1s. per Cake.[9] [November 22]

Jerman's ALMANACKS are in the Press, and will speedily be published. [November 22]

On Monday Evening last, Mr. Thomas Meakins fell off a Wharff into the Delaware, and before he could be taken out again, was drowned. He was an ancient Man, and formerly liv'd very well in this City, teaching a considerable School; but of late Years was reduc'd to extream Poverty. The following Lines were made by himself some time since.

Some purchase Land, some stately Buildings raise,
To memorize their Names to future Days;

9. From Josiah Franklin at the beginning of the century to Jane Mecom and Peter Collas at its end, members of the family manufactured soap, stamping the green cakes with a crown as a sign of quality. Apparently BF gave the recipe to his mother-in-law. He sent directions for making this soap to his sister, 1771; they are printed in Van Doren, *Franklin-Mecom*, pp. 129–32. Crown soap was much approved and often imitated. For its importance to the family see the Franklin-Mecom correspondence.

But I've a lasting Monument will stand,
When Building's fall, and Sales are made of Land:
A certain Rock on Skuylkill's eastern Side,
Which bears my Name, for Ages will abide;
This Rock, well-known, which Angler's do frequent,
When I am gone, will be my Monument.[1]

[November 29]

NEXT WEEK WILL BE PUBLISHED, The Laws of the Province of New-Jersey, which were enacted the last Sessions of Assembly. Printed and sold by B. Franklin.   [November 29]

PHILADELPHIA: Printed by B. FRANKLIN, at the *New Printing-Office* near the Market. *Price* 10s. a Year. Where Advertisements are taken in, and BOOK-BINDING is done reasonably, in the best Manner.

Poor Richard, 1734

Poor Richard, 1734. An Almanack For the Year of Christ 1734 . . . By Richard Saunders, Philom. Philadelphia: Printed and sold by B. Franklin, at the New Printing-Office near the Market (Yale University Library).

Courteous Readers,   Octob. 30. 1733

Your kind and charitable Assistance last Year, in purchasing so large an Impression of my Almanacks, has made my Circumstances much more easy in the World, and requires my grateful Acknowledgment. My Wife has been enabled to get a Pot of her own, and is no longer oblig'd to borrow one from a Neighbour; nor have we ever since been without something of our own to put in it. She has also got a pair of Shoes, two new Shifts, and a new warm Petticoat; and for my part, I have bought a second-hand Coat, so good, that I am now not asham'd to go to Town or be seen there. These Things have render'd her Temper so much more pacifick than it us'd to be, that I may say, I have slept more, and more quietly

1. Thomas Meakins (or Makin), clerk of the Assembly, teacher in the Friends' Academy, author of a poetical description of Pennsylvania and other verses. *PMHB*, XXXVII (1913), 369–74.

349

within this last Year, than in the three foregoing Years put together. Accept my hearty Thanks therefor, and my sincere Wishes for your Health and Prosperity.

In the Preface to my last Almanack, I foretold the Death of my dear old Friend and Fellow-Student, the learned and ingenious Mr. Titan Leeds, which was to be on the 17th of October, 1733, 3 h. 29 m. P.M. at the very Instant of the ♂ of ☉ and ☿. By his own Calculation he was to survive till the 26th of the same Month, and expire in the Time of the Eclipse, near 11 a clock, A.M. At which of these Times he died, or whether he be really yet dead, I cannot at this present Writing positively assure my Readers; forasmuch as a Disorder in my own Family demanded my Presence, and would not permit me as I had intended, to be with him in his last Moments, to receive his last Embrace, to close his Eyes, and do the Duty of a Friend in performing the last Offices to the Departed. Therefore it is that I cannot positively affirm whether he be dead or not; for the Stars only show to the Skilful, what will happen in the natural and universal Chain of Causes and Effects; but 'tis well known, that the Events which would otherwise certainly happen at certain Times in the Course of Nature, are sometimes set aside or postpon'd for wise and good Reasons, by the immediate particular Dispositions of Providence; which particular Dispositions the Stars can by no Means discover or foreshow. There is however, (and I cannot speak it without Sorrow) there is the strongest Probability that my dear Friend is *no more;* for there appears in his Name, as I am assured, an Almanack for the Year 1734, in which I am treated in a very gross and unhandsome Manner; in which I am called *a false Predicter, an Ignorant, a conceited Scribler, a Fool, and a Lyar.* Mr. Leeds was too well bred to use any Man so indecently and so scurrilously, and moreover his Esteem and Affection for me was extraordinary: So that it is to be feared that Pamphlet may be only a Contrivance of somebody or other, who hopes perhaps to sell two or three Year's Almanacks still, by the sole Force and Virtue of Mr. Leeds's Name; but certainly, to put Words into the Mouth of a Gentleman and a Man of Letters, against his Friend, which the meanest and most scandalous of the People might be asham'd to utter even in a drunken Quarrel, is an unpardonable Injury to his Memory, and an Imposition upon the Publick.

350

Mr. Leeds was not only profoundly skilful in the useful Science he profess'd, but he was a Man of *exemplary Sobriety,* a most *sincere Friend,* and an *exact Performer of his Word.* These valuable Qualifications, with many others so much endear'd him to me, that although it should be so, that, contrary to all Probability, contrary to my Prediction and his own, he might possibly be yet alive, yet my Loss of Honour as a Prognosticator, cannot afford me so much Mortification, as his Life, Health and Safety would give me Joy and Satisfaction. I am, Courteous and kind Reader, Your poor Friend and Servant,   R. SAUNDERS

> Here I sit naked, like some Fairy Elf,
> My Seat a Pumpkin; I grudge no Man's Pelf;
> Though I've no Bread, nor Cheese upon my Shelf;
>   I'll tell thee *gratis,* when it safe is,
> To purge, to bleed, or *cut,* thy Cattle, or—*thy self.*[2]

> Good Women are like STARS in darkest Night,
> Their Virtuous Actions shining as a Light
> To guide their ignorant Sex, which oft times fall,
> And falling oft, turns diabolical.
> Good Women sure are Angels on the Earth,
> Of those good Angels we have had a Dearth;
> And therefore all you Men that have good Wives,
> Respect their Virtues equal with your Lives.

XI Mon. January hath xxxi days.

> From a cross Neighbour, and a sullen Wife,
> A pointless Needle, and a broken Knife;
> From Suretyship, and from an empty Purse,
> A Smoaky Chimney and a jolting Horse;
> From a dull Razor, and an aking Head,
> From a bad Conscience and a buggy Bed;
> A Blow upon the Elbow and the Knee,
> From each of these, *Good L--d deliver me.*

2. These lines were printed directly above the figure representing the zodiac, to which they refer. The same figure appeared in the 1733 Almanac, without the verses. The verses were repeated in some later years.

Would you live with ease,
Do what you ought, and not what you please.

Better slip with foot than tongue.

You cannot pluck roses without fear of thorns,
Nor enjoy a fair wife without danger of horns.

Without justice, courage is weak.

Many dishes many diseases,
Many medicines few cures.

Where carcasses are, eagles will gather,
And where good laws are, much people flock thither.

XII Mon. February hath xxviii days.

What Death is, dost thou ask of me;
    Till dead I do not know;
Come to me when thou hear'st I'm dead;
    Then what 'tis I shall show.
To die's to cease to be, it seems,
    So Learned Seneca did think;
But we've Philosophers of modern Date,
    Who say 'tis Death to cease to Drink.
[*In inner margin, vertically*:] Excuse me ⊙

Hot things, sharp things, sweet things, cold things
All rot the teeth, and make them look like old things.

Blame-all and *Praise-all* are two blockheads.

Be temperate in wine, in eating, girls, and sloth;
Or the Gout will seize you and plague you both.

I Mon. March hath xxxi days.

Some of our Sparks to London town do go
Fashions to see, and learn the World to know;
Who at Return have nought but these to show,
New Wig above, and new Disease below.

Thus the Jack Ass a Traveller once would be,
And roam'd abroad new Fashions for to see;
But home returned, Fashions he had none,
Only his Main and Tail were larger grown.

No man e'er was glorious, who was not laborious.

What pains our Justice takes his faults to hide,
With half that pains sure he might cure 'em quite.

In success be moderate.

Take this remark from Richard poor and lame,
Whate'er's begun in anger ends in shame.

What one relishes, nourishes.

II Mon. April hath xxx days.

When Fortune fell asleep, and Hate did blind her,
Art, Fortune lost; and Ignorance did find her.
Since when, dull Ignorance with Fortune's Store
Hath been inrich'd, and Art hath still been poor.
Poets say Fortune's blind, and cannot see,
But certainly they must deceived be;
Else could it not most commonly fall out
That Fools should have and wise Men go without.

Fools multiply folly.

Beauty and folly are old companions.

Hope of gain
Lessens pain.

All things are easy to Industry,
All things difficult to *Sloth*.

If you ride a Horse, sit close and tight,
If you ride a Man, sit easy and light.

A new truth is a truth, an old error is an error,
Tho' Clodpate wont allow either.

Don't think to hunt two hares with one dog.

353

III Mon. May hath xxxi days.

> Wedlock, as old Men note, hath likened been,
> Unto a publick Crowd or common Rout;
> Where those that are without would fain get in,
> And those that are within would fain get out.
> Grief often treads upon the Heels of Pleasure,
> Marry'd in Haste, we oft repent at Leisure;
> Some by Experience find these Words misplac'd,
> Marry'd at Leisure, they repent in Haste.

> Astrologers say,
> This is a good Day,
> To make Love in May.

> Who pleasure gives,
> Shall joy receive.

Be not sick too late nor well too soon.

Where there's Marriage without Love, there will be Love without Marriage.

Lawyers, Preachers, and Tomtits Eggs, there are more of them hatch'd than come to perfection.

Be neither silly, nor cunning, but wise.

Neither a Fortress nor a Maidenhead will hold out long after they begin to parly.

IV Mon. June hath xxx days.

> When Robin now three Days had married been,
>   And all his Friends and Neighbours gave him Joy;
> This Question of his Wife he asked then,
>   Why till her Marriage Day she prov'd so coy?
> Indeed (said he) 'twas well thou didst not yield,
>   For doubtless then my Purpose was to leave thee:
> *O Sir, I once before was so beguil'd,*
> *And was resolv'd the next should not deceive me.*

Jack Little sow'd little, and little he'll reap.

All things are cheap to the saving, dear to the wasteful.

Would you persuade, speak of Interest, not of Reason.

> Some men grow mad by studying much to know,
> But who grows mad by studying good to grow.

Happy's the Wooing, that's not long a doing.

V Mon. July hath xxxi days.

> A Lawyer being sick and extream ill
> Was moved by his Friends to make his Will,
> Which soon he did, gave all the Wealth he had
> To frantic Persons, lunatick and mad;
> And to his Friends this Reason did reveal
> (That they might see with Equity he'd deal).
> From Madmen's Hands I did my Wealth receive,
> Therefore that Wealth to Madmen's Hands I'll leave.

Don't value a man for the Quality he is of, but for the Qualities he possesses.

Bucephalus the Horse of Alexander hath as lasting fame as his Master.

> Rain or Snow,
> To Chili go,
> You'll find it so,
> For ought we know.
> Time will show.

There have been as great Souls unknown to fame as any of the most famous.

Do good to thy Friend to keep him, to thy enemy to gain him.

A good Man is seldom uneasy, an ill one never easie.

Teach your child to hold his tongue, he'l learn fast enough to speak.

VI Mon. August hath xxxi days.

> Some envious (speaking in their own Renown)
> Say that my Book was not exactly done:

> They wrong me; Yet like Feasts I'd have my Books
> Rather be pleasing to the Guests than Cooks.
>   Ill thrives that hapless Family that shows
> A Cock that's silent, and a Hen that crows:
> I know not which lives more unnatural Lives,
> Obeying Husbands, or commanding Wives.

He that cannot obey, cannot command.

An innocent *Plowman* is more worthy than a vicious *Prince*.

Sam's *Religion* is like a *Chedder Cheese*, 'tis made of the *milk* of one and twenty Parishes.

> Grief for a dead Wife, and a troublesome Guest,
> Continues to the *threshold*, and there is at rest;
> But I mean such wives as are none of the best.

As Charms are nonsense, Nonsence is a Charm.

VII Mon. September hath xxx days.

> S----l the Smith hath lately sworn and said,
> That no Disease shall make him keep his Bed;
> His reason is, I now begin to smell it,
> He wants more Rum, and must be forc'd to sell it.
> Nor less meant J----h when that Vow he made,
> Than to give o'er his cousening Tapster's Trade,
> Who, check'd for short and frothy Measure, swore
> He never would from thenceforth fill Pot more.

An Egg today is better than a Hen to-morrow.

Drink Water, Put the Money in your Pocket, and leave the *Dry-bellyach* in the *Punchbowl*.

He that is rich need not live sparingly, and he that can live sparingly need not be rich.

If you wou'd be reveng'd of your enemy, govern your self.

A wicked Hero will turn his back to an innocent coward.

> *Laws* like to *Cobwebs* catch small Flies,
> Great ones break thro' before your eyes.

356

VIII Mon. October hath xxxi days.

> Altho' thy Teacher act not as he preaches,
> Yet ne'ertheless, if good, do what he teaches;
> Good Counsel, failing Men may give; for why,
> He that's aground knows where the Shoal doth lie.
> My old Friend Berryman, oft, when alive,
> Taught others Thrift; himself could never thrive:
> Thus like the Whetstone, many Men are wont
> To sharpen others while themselves are blunt.

Strange, that he who lives by Shifts, can seldom shift himself.

As sore places meet most rubs, proud folks meet most affronts.

The magistrate should obey the Laws, the People should obey the magistrate.

When 'tis fair be sure take your Great coat with you.

He does not possess Wealth, it possesses him.

Necessity has no Law; I know some Attorneys of the name.

Onions can make ev'n Heirs and Widows weep.

IX Mon. November hath xxx days.

> Dorothy would with John be married;
> > Dorothy's wise, I trow:
> But John by no means Dorothy will wed;
> > John's the wiser of the two.
>
> Those are my Verses which Tom reads;
> > That is very well known:
> But if in reading he makes 'em Nonsense,
> > Then they are his own.

Avarice and Happiness never saw each other, how then shou'd they become acquainted.

> The thrifty maxim of the wary Dutch,
> Is to save all the Money they can touch.

He that waits upon Fortune, is never sure of a Dinner.

A learned blockhead is a greater blockhead than an ignorant one.

Marry your Son when you will, but your Daughter when you can.

357

X Mon. December hath xxxi days.

By Mrs. Bridget Saunders, my Dutchess, in Answer to the December Verses of last Year.

> He that for sake of Drink neglects his Trade,
> And spends each Night in Taverns till 'tis late,
> And rises when the Sun is four hours high,
> And ne'er regards his starving Family;
> God in his Mercy may do much to save him,
> But, woe to the poor Wife, whose Lot it is to have him.

He that knows nothing of it, may by chance be a Prophet; while the wisest that is may happen to miss.

> If you wou'd have Guests merry with your cheer,
> Be so your self, or so at least appear.

> Famine, Plague, War, and an unnumber'd throng
> Of Guilt-avenging Ills, to Man belong;
> Is't not enough Plagues, Wars, and Famines rise
> To lash our crimes, but must our Wives be wise?

> Reader, farewel, all Happiness attend thee:
> May each *New-Year* better and richer find thee.

Of the ECLIPSES, 1734.

There will be but two: The first April 22, 18 min. after 5 in the morning; the second Octob. 15, 36 min. past 1 in the afternoon. Both of the SUN; and both, like Mrs. ---s's Modesty, and old Neighbour Scrape-all's Money, *Invisible.* Or, like a certain Storekeeper late of ---- County, *Not to be seen in these Parts.*

Since the Eclipses take up so little space, I have room to comply with the new Fashion, and propose a *Mathematical Question* to the *Sons of Art;* which perhaps is not more difficult to solve, nor of less Use when solved, than some of those that have been proposed by the ingenious Mr. G----y. It is this,

A certain rich Man had 100 Orchards, in each Orchard was 100 Appletrees, under each Appletree was 100 Hogsties, in each Hogstie was 100 Sows, and each Sow had 100 Pigs. Question, How many Sow-Pigs were there among them?

Note, *The Answer to this Question won't be accepted without the Solution.*

Felix quem faciunt aliena pericula cautum.[3]
To such a height th'Expence of COURTS is gone,
That poor Men are redress'd—*till they're undone.*

William, your Cause is good, give me my Fee, and I'll defend it. But
alas! William is cast, the Verdict goes against him. *Give me another
Fee, and I'll move the Court in Arrest of Judgment.* Then Sentence is
confirmed. *T'other Fee, and I'll bring a Writ of Error.* But Judgment
is again confirm'd, and Will condemn'd to pay Costs. What shall
we do now, Master, says William. *Why since it can't be helpt, there's
no more to be said; pay the Knave his Money, and I'm satisfied.*

Of Disposition they're most sweet,
Their Clients always kindly greet;
And tho' at Bar they rip old Sores,
And brawl and scold like drunken Wh---s,
Their Angers in a moment pass
Away at Night over a Glass;
Nay often laugh at the Occasion
Of their premeditated Passion.
*O may you prosper as you treat us,
Until the D---l sign your* Quietus.

Agreement between Directors of Library Company and William Parsons[4]   DS: Historical Society of Pennsylvania

[March 14, 1734]
MEMORANDUM of Agreement indented [and] made the Fourteenth
Day of March Ao.Di. 1733/4   BETWEEN Benjamin Franklin

3. Proverbial. Many years later BF's friend Jan Ingenhousz, writing from
Vienna, reminded him of this "old proverb"; Feb. 26, 1783. The line and the
remaining material here reprinted precede immediately the almanac's Court
Calendar.
4. William Parsons (1701–1757), served as librarian until 1746. A shoemaker by trade, he was an original member of the Junto, studied mathe-
matics, and was surveyor-general of the province, 1741–48. He moved to
Lancaster, 1748, and to Northampton County, 1752, and held various local
offices in both counties; laid out the town of Easton, 1750; member of the
Assembly, 1753; major in the provincial service, 1755. John W. Jordan,
"William Parsons," *PMHB*, XXXIII (1909), 340–6.

Wm. Rawle   Thos. Godfrey   Hugh Roberts   Anthony Nicholas
Thos. Cadwallader   John Jones   Henry Pratt and Thos. Hopkin-
son a Committee of Directors of the Library Company of Phila-
delphia for and on Behalf of the said Company Of the one Part
and Wm. Parsons of the City of Philadelphia Scrivener Of the other
Part Viz. THAT the said Wm. Parsons shall be the Librarian of the
said Company for and during such Time and for such Salary or
Reward as shall from Time to Time be agreed on between the
Directors of the said Company, for the Time being, and the said
Librarian, The Salary at present agreed on being at the Rate of
Six Pounds per Annum.

THAT on the last Day of every Week he shall attend at the
Library from 4 o'Clock in the Afternoon till 8, to lend out and receive in Books of the said Company.

THAT of every Borrower of Books who is of the Company he
shall at every Time of Borrowing take a Note of Hand of such Form
and for such Sum and Time as customary.

THAT for the Books he shall lend to Persons who are not of the
Company he shall take a Pledge in Money equal to the Sum mentioned in the Notes of Hand of Subscribers in Partnership And
shall also take Notes of Hand of such Persons expressing the Time
of the Loan and Forfeiture of the Money upon their Default And
that they shall pay 8*d*. per Week for all Folios, 6*d*. per Week for all
Quartos and 4*d*. per Week for others and make good all Damages
And that such Books only as are of the first Parcel and have been
given to the Company shall be lent to such Persons, until further
Order.

THAT the said Librarian shall not put any of the Notes in Suit
nor assign any of them without Order of a Committee of Directors.

THAT he shall not lend any Books or Book to any Person who
has made Default and has not made Satisfaction.

THAT he shall attend the Directors at any of their Meetings to
which they shall warn him.

THAT he shall yield up and deliver to the said Directors, for the
Time being, or their Order all the said Books, or Notes of Hand
for such as are lent out, and all Cash, Papers and Effects whatsoever
which shall be in his Custody belonging to the said Company within the Space of one Month after the same shall be demanded of him

by the Directors for the Time being, Damage by Fire and other unavoidable Accidents excepted.[5]

AND the said Directors do hereby agree for themselves and their Successors That they will be at the Charge of Printing the Notes to be given by all Borrowers of Books out of the said Library as aforesaid. And that they will receive of the said Librarian, at any Time within the Space of one Month after requested, all such Books Notes of Hand Cash Papers and Effects whatsoever which shall be in his Custody belonging to the said Company and shall give him proper Discharges for the same. IN WITNESS whereof the said Parties to these Presents have interchangeably set their Hands and Seals hereunto.

Dated the Day and Year first within written.

Sealed and Delivered	B. FRANKLIN	[Seal]
In the presence of us	WM. RAWLE	[Seal]
JOHN ROBERTS	THOS. CADWALADER	[Seal]
JOSEPH BREINTNALL	THOS. GODFREY	[Seal]
	JOHN JONES JUNR	[Seal]
	HENRY PRATT	[Seal]
	THOS. HOPKINSON 1733	[Seal]

MEMO. the 14th March 1733/4 That the Books delivered to the within mentioned Librarian are 29 Folios 20 Quartos 107 Octavos and 88 Duodecimos amounting in the Whole to 239 Volumes Besides Notes of Hand for 3 Folios 1 Quarto 7 Octavos and 5 Duodecimos Together with 19 Historia Litterarias[6] 6 Magazines and a few other Pamphlets and papers.

Witnesses at Signing	THOS. HOPKINSON 1733
JOHN ROBERTS	HENRY PRATT
JOSEPH BREINTNALL	B. FRANKLIN
	JNO. JONES JUNR
	THOS. GODFREY
	WM. RAWLE
	THOS. CADWALADER

5. Compare Louis Timothée's duties only eighteen months before; see above, p. 250.

6. *Historia Litteraria* was a London periodical review of publications. Books are identified as folios, quartos, and the like because they were customarily classified and filed by size.

Sarah Read to Benjamin and Deborah Franklin: Bargain and Sale

DS: American Philosophical Society

This document and the two which immediately follow record the first transactions in the drawn-out process by which Franklin put together the various parcels of land on the south side of Market Street (also called High Street) between Third and Fourth Streets which became the site of his home.[7] The plot involved here, corresponding to the later No. 318 Market Street, was granted by William Penn to Henry Hayes, April 7, 1707.[8] It was 33 ft. broad and 306 deep and lay between a lot on the west which Penn had granted to Samuel Carpenter and others in 1705 and one on the east he had granted to William Boulding in 1706,[9] parts of both of which Franklin later acquired. Hayes sold the eastern half of his lot (16½ ft.) to William Davis, April 12, 1711, and on May 24 of the same year Davis transferred it to John Read, carpenter, father of Franklin's future wife, Deborah.[1] By two documents dated December 10 and 11, 1716, Hayes sold the western half (16½ ft.) to John Read,[2] and, because Davis' transfer of the eastern half to Read had been insufficient in legal form, Hayes confirmed Read's possession by an instrument dated December 12, 1716.[3]

On February 18, 1723/4, John Read mortgaged the entire property to the Trustees of the General Loan Office for £56 5s. in bills of credit of the first Pennsylvania issue (see above, p. 139) with surety in double the amount of the loan. He died September 2 of the same year without having paid the loan; in time the Trustees brought an action in the Court of Common Pleas for the default against his administratrix and widow, Sarah Read, and secured execution on the property for £115 1s. 1d., representing principal, interest, and damages. At the sheriff's auction sale which followed, Sarah Read bought the property in for £354 and received a sheriff's deed dated September 3, 1729. She now

7. The "Chain of Title" is summarized, with the omission of a few minor links, but with the inclusion of useful maps, by Edward M. Riley in a (typescript) Preliminary Historical Report, Franklin Court, Philadelphia, Pennsylvania, pp. 2–8, on file in the headquarters of Independence National Historical Park Project. See also deed, Jan. 14, 1812, among Sarah Bache's heirs, Philadelphia, Recorder of Deeds, Book I. C. no. 19, pp. 1–22.

8. Recorder of Deeds, Patent Book, A, vol. 4, p. 10; original in APS.

9. Patent Book A, vol. 4, pp. 4–14, 123.

1. Neither instrument was recorded in Philadelphia. The deed from Davis to Read is written on the back of the deed from Hayes to Davis. The parchment original is in APS.

2. The original parchment indentures of lease and release are in APS.

3. The parchment original is in APS.

had clear title to what had been her husband's land, on each half of which there apparently stood at the time a small house near the street.[4]

On April 9–11, 1734, Mrs. Read entered into a series of transactions with her son John and her two sons-in-law and daughters, Benjamin and Deborah Franklin and John and Frances Croker, by which she transferred title to the western half-lot and its dwelling house to John Read, Junior,[5] and title to the eastern half-lot and its dwelling house in equal undivided half-interest to the Franklins and Crokers, but received back from the latter couples a lease for 99 years or life at the nominal annual rental of "one Pepper corn only if demanded." The first two documents here printed record the transfer of one half-interest to the Franklins; similar documents, not here printed, conveyed the other half-interest to the Crokers.[6] These indentures follow the cumbersome form of conveyancing commonly used in England in the seventeenth and eighteenth centuries. An indenture of "bargain and sale," leasing the property for a specific term, often one year, placed the lessee in actual possession, as permitted by the Statute of Uses of 1535. The lessor, who now had only a reversionary interest, could sign, ostensibly on the next day, an indenture of "release," which operated at common law to convey that interest, and with it the freehold, to the lessee. This procedure of "lease and release," awkward as it seems today, became popular because it avoided the costly medieval requirement of livery of seisin.[7]

The third document here printed, dated April 11, 1734, is a lease from the Franklins and Crokers to Mrs. Read restoring to her the life use of their half-lot and dwelling house.

[April 9, 1734]

THIS INDENTURE made the Ninth day of April in the Seventh Year of the Reign of our Sovereign Lord George the Second by the

4. The mortgage, foreclosure, and sheriff's sale are recited in the deed from Charles Read, high sheriff of the city and county of Philadelphia, to Sarah Read. Office of the Recorder of Deeds, Philadelphia Deeds, H7, pp. 431–3. Parchment original in APS.

5. Philadelphia Deeds, H7, pp. 439–40. John Read sold this half-lot to his brother-in-law BF for £300, Nov. 15, 1751. Philadelphia Deeds, H7, pp. 440–3.

6. The indenture or bargain and sale to the Crokers, April 9, has not been located; the indenture of release, April 10, 1734, is recorded in Philadelphia Deeds, H7, pp. 435–6; parchment original in APS. On Oct. 12, 1745, John Croker sold his undivided half-interest to BF for £80. Philadelphia Deeds, H7, pp. 437–9.

7. William S. Holdsworth, *An Historical Introduction to the Land Law* (Oxford, 1927), pp. 288–95.

Grace of God of Great Britain France and Ireland King Defender
of the Faith &c Annoque Domini One thousand Seven hundred and
Thirty Four BETWEEN Sarah Read of the City of Philadelphia
Widow of the one part and Benjamin Franklyn of the same Place
Printer and Deborah his Wife of the other part WITNESSETH That
the said Sarah Read in Consideration of Five Shillings to her paid
by the said Benjamin Franklyn and Deborah his Wife HATH Bargained and Sold and by these Presents DOTH Bargain and Sell unto
the said Benjamin Franklyn and Deborah his Wife One full Equal
and undivided half part the whole into two Equal parts to be divided of ALL THAT Messuage or Tenement and Lott of Land thereto
belonging Scituate on the South side of High Street in the City of
Philadelphia aforesaid Containing in Breadth Sixteen Foot and a
half and in Length Three hundred and Six foot bounded Northward with the said High Street Eastward with a Lott late of
William Boulding deceased Southward with the Ends of Chesnutt
Street Lotts and Westward with a Messuage and Lott now or late
of the said Sarah Read Together with all and Singular the Buildings
Improvements Rights Members Hereditaments and Appurtenances whatsoever thereunto belonging and the Revertion and
Revertions Remainder and Remainders Rents Issues and Profits
thereof TO HAVE AND TO HOLD the said One full Equal and undivided half part the whole in two Equal parts to be divided of the
said Messuage or Tenement Lott of Land and Premisses hereby
Bargained and Sold with their and every of their Appurtenances
unto the said Benjamin Franklyn and Deborah his Wife their Executors Administrators and Assigns from the day next before the
day of the date hereof for and during and unto the full End and
Term of one whole Year from thence next Ensuing and fully to
be compleat and Ended YEILDING AND PAYING therefore the
Rent of a Pepper corn only if demanded at the End of the said
Term To the Intent that by virtue of these Presents and of the Statute made for transferring Uses into Possession the said Benjamin
Franklyn and Deborah his Wife may be in the Actual Possession
of all and Singular the Premisses with the Appurtenances and
thereby be Enabled to Accept a Grant and Release thereof and
of the Revertion and Inheritance thereof to them and their Heirs
to the only proper Use and Behoof of them their Heirs and Assigns for Ever. IN WITNESS whereof the Parties to these Presents

have hereunto Sett their Hands and Seals the day and Year First
above written.   SARAH READ [Seal]

Sealed and Delivered in the Presence of Us

JOHN JONES JUNR
THOS. HOPKINSON 1734

Endorsed: Lease for a Year Read to Franklyn et ux
Datd April 9th 1734.

Sarah Read to Benjamin and Deborah Franklin: Release

DS: American Philosophical Society; also copy: Office of Recorder
of Deeds, Philadelphia

[April 10, 1734]
THIS INDENTURE made the Tenth day of April in the Seventh Year
of the Reign of our Sovereign Lord George the Second by the
Grace of God of Great Britain France and Ireland King Defender
of the Faith &c Annoque Domini One thousand Seven hundred
and Thirty Four BETWEEN Sarah Read of the City of Philadelphia
Widow of the one part and Benjamin Franklyn of the same Place
Printer and Deborah his Wife which said Deborah is one of the
Daughters of the said Sarah Read of the other part WITNESSETH
That the said Sarah Read for and in Consideration of the Natural
Love and Affection which she hath and beareth unto the said
Deborah Franklyn and for her better Preferment and Advance-
ment in the World and also in Consideration of Five Shillings to
her the said Sarah Read in hand Paid by the said Benjamin Franklyn
at or before the Sealing or delivery of these Presents the Receipt
whereof She doth hereby Acknowledge HATH Given Granted
Aliened Enfeoffed and Confirmed and by these Presents DOTH Give
Grant Alien Enfeoff and Confirm unto the said Benjamin Franklyn
and Deborah his Wife in their Actual Possession now being by Vir-
ture of a Bargain and Sale to them thereof made for one whole
Year by Indenture bearing date the day next before the day of the
date of these Presents and by Force of the Statute made for transferring Uses into Possession and to their Heirs and Assigns One
full Equal and undivided half part the whole in two equal parts to

be divided of ALL THAT Messuage or Tenement and Lott of Land thereto belonging Scituate on the South side of High Street in the City of Philadelphia aforesaid Containing in breadth Sixteen Foot and a half and in Length Three hundred and Six Feet bounded Northward with the said High Street Eastward with a Lott late of William Boulding deceased Southward with the Ends of Chesnutt Street Lotts and Westward with a Messuage and Lott now or late of the said Sarah Read Together with all and Singular the Buildings Improvements Rights Members Hereditaments and Appurtenances whatsoever thereunto belonging and the Revertion and Revertions Remainder and Remainders Rents Issues and Profits thereof and all the Estate Right Title Interest Property Claim and demand whatsoever of her the said Sarah Read of in and to the same TO HAVE AND TO HOLD the said One full Equal and undivided half part the whole in two Equal parts to be divided of the said Messuage or Tenement Lott of Land and Premises hereby granted or mentioned to be granted with their and every of their Appurtenances unto the said Benjamin Franklyn and Deborah his Wife their Heirs and Assigns for Ever To the only proper Use and Behoof of the said Benjamin Franklyn and Deborah his Wife their Heirs and Assigns for Ever AND THE SAID Sarah Read doth for herself her Heirs Executors and Administrators Covenant Promise and Grant to and with the said Benjamin Franklyn and Deborah his Wife their Heirs and Assigns That the said Benjamin Franklyn and Deborah his Wife their Heirs and Assigns shall and lawfully may from time to time and at all times hereafter Peaceably and Quietly have hold Use Occupy Possess and Enjoy the said Moiety or half part of the said Messuage or Tenement Lott and Premises with the Appurtenances hereby granted without any Lett Suit Trouble Hindrance or Interruption whatsoever of her the said Sarah Read her Heirs Executors or Administrators or any Person or Persons claiming or to claim by from or under her AND THAT She the said Sarah Read her Heirs Executors or Administrators Shall and will at any time or times hereafter upon the Request and at the Costs and Charges in the Law of the said Benjamin Franklyn and Deborah his Wife their Heirs or Assigns make do and Execute or cause to be made done and Executed all and every such further or other lawful Act or Acts Deed or Deeds Conveyances and Assurances in the Law for the further better more Perfect and absolute Granting

Releasing and confirming the said Moiety or half part of the said Messuage or Tenement and Lott of Land and Premisses herein granted with the Appurtenances unto the said Benjamin Franklyn and Deborah his Wife their Heirs and Assigns for Ever as by the said Benjamin Franklyn and Deborah his Wife their Heirs or Assigns or his or their Counsil learned in the Law shall be devised or advised and required IN WITNESS whereof the parties to these Presents have hereunto sett their Hands and Seals the day and Year first above written.   SARAH READ [Seal]

Sealed and Delivered in the Presence of Us

JOHN JONES JUNR
THOS. HOPKINSON 1734

Endorsed: Deed of Gift from Sarah Read to Benjamin Franklyn and his Wife of ½ a Messuage &c. in High Street   Dat 10 Apl 1734

Also Endorsed: Memorandum the 14th Day of February Ao. Di. 1757 Before me Charles Brockden One of the Justices of the Peace &c. personally appeared Sarah Read within named [and did Acknowledge] the within written Indenture to be her Deed and desired that the Same may be Recorded as her Act In Witness whereof I have hereunto Set my Hand and Seal the Day and Year aforesaid.   C. BROCKDEN [Seal]

RECORDED in the Office for Recording of Deeds for the City and County of Philadelphia in Book H vol. 7. p. 433 &c. the 21st of February Ao. Di. 1757, As Witnesseth my Hand and Seal of my Office.   C. BROCKDEN RECR.

Acd. 14 Feb. 57 C B

Benjamin and Deborah Franklin and John and Frances Croker to Sarah Read: Lease

DS: Morris Duane, Philadelphia, on deposit in Historical Society of Pennsylvania (1957)

[April 11, 1734]

THIS INDENTURE made the Eleventh day of April in the Seventh Year of the Reign of our Sovereign Lord George the Second by

the Grace of God of Great Britain France and Ireland King Defender of the Faith &c Annoque Domini One thousand Seven
hundred and Thirty Four BETWEEN Benjamin Franklyn of the City
of Philadelphia Printer and Deborah his Wife and John Croker of
the said City Taylor and Frances his Wife of the one part and
Sarah Read of the said City of Philadelphia Widow of the other
part WITNESSETH That the said Benjamin Franklyn and Deborah
his Wife John Croker and Frances his Wife for and in Consideration of Five Shillings apeice to them paid by the said Sarah Read
at or before the Sealing or delivery of these Presents and for diverse
other good Causes and Considerations them hereunto moving HAVE
demised Granted and to Farm letten and by these Presents DO
Demise Grant and to Farm lett unto the said Sarah Read ALL THAT
Messuage or Tenement and Lott of Land thereto belonging Scituate on the South side of High Street in the City of Philadelphia
aforesaid containing in breadth Sixteen foot and a half and in length
Three hundred and Six foot bounded Northward with the said
High Street Eastward with a Lott late of William Boulding de-
ceased Southward with the Ends of Chesnutt Street Lotts and
Westward with a Lott now or late of the said Sarah Read Together
with all and Singular the Rights Members and Appurtenances whatsoever thereunto belonging or in any wise Appertaining TO HAVE
AND TO HOLD the said Messuage or Tenement Lott of Land and
Premises hereby demised with the Appurtenances unto the said
Sarah Read and her Assigns from henceforth for and during and
unto the full End and Term of Ninety Nine Years if She the said
Sarah Read shall so long Live YEILDING AND PAYING therefore
Yearly and every Year during the Continuance of the Term hereby
granted unto the said Benjamin Franklyn and Deborah his Wife
and John Croker and Frances his Wife their Heirs Executors Administrators and Assigns the Rent of one Pepper corn only if demanded AND THE SAID Benjamin Franklyn for himself and for the
said Deborah his Wife their Heirs Executors Administrators and
Assigns and the said John Croker for himself and for the said
Frances his Wife their Heirs Executors Administrators and Assigns
do covenant Promise and Grant to and with the said Sarah Read
[and?] her Assigns That She the said Sarah Read and her Assigns
shall and lawfully may from time to time and at all times during
the Continuance of the Term hereby granted Peaceably and qui-

etly have hold Use Occupy Possess and Enjoy the said Messuage or Tenement Lott of Land and Premises hereby demised with the Appurtenances without any Lett Suit hindrance or denial whatsoever of or by the said Benjamin Franklyn and Deborah his Wife their Heirs Executors Administrators or Assigns or of or by the said John Croker and Frances his Wife their Heirs Executors Administrators or Assigns any or either of them or any other Person or Persons claiming or to claim by from or under them any or either of them AND THE SAID Sarah Read doth for herself and her Assigns Covenant Promise and Grant to and with the said Benjamin Franklyn and Deborah his Wife their Heirs Executors Administrators and Assigns and to and with the said John Croker and Frances his Wife their Heirs Executors Administrators and Assigns respectively in manner following that is to say that She the said Sarah Read and her Assigns shall and will from time to time and at all times during the continuance of the Term hereby granted at her and their own proper Costs and Charges well and Sufficiently Repair Uphold Support Maintain amend pave glaze fence and keep the said Messuage or Tenement Lott of Land and Premises hereby demised with their Appurtenances Accidents by Fire Excepted AND THAT it shall and may be lawful to and for the said Benjamin Franklyn and Deborah his Wife their Heirs Executors Administrators and Assigns John Croker and Frances his Wife their Heirs Executors Administrators and Assigns any or either of them at any time or times during the said Term hereby granted to Build or make Improvements on any part of the Lott of Land hereby demised and to have Receive Possess and Enjoy such Buildings and Improvements so by them any or either of them to be made or Built and the Rents Issues and Profits thereof to their own proper Use and Behoof without any Lett hindrance or Interruption of her the said Sarah Read or her Assigns This Indenture or any thing herein contained to the contrary thereof in any wise Notwithstanding IN WITNESS whereof the Parties to these Presents have hereunto interchangeably Sett their Hands and Seals the day and Year First above written.

Sealed and Delivered in the Presence of Us	B. FRANKLIN [Seal]
	DEBORAH FRANKLIN [Seal]
JOHN JONES JUNR	JOHN CROKER [Seal]
THOS. HOPKINSON 1734	FRANCES CROKER [Seal]

Endorsed: Franklyn et ux & Croker et ux to Sarah Read Lease of a Messuage &c. in High Street for 99 Yrs. if Lessee so long Live

Dat 11 April 1734

[*In another hand*] Expired

From a Reader to the Printer

Printed in *The Pennsylvania Gazette*, April 11, 1734.

The following I have just now received exactly as I here give it.

Mr. Franklin,

Tho' your News-paper is sometimes as empty as those of others, yet I think you have for the most part (tho' you were once in one particular a sad Offender) had the Modesty to keep it pretty clear of SCANDAL, a Subject that others delight to wallow in. These People, probably from some Corruption in themselves, and possibly from their own Stench, seem to think every thing around them tainted: But that they may see their own Picture, and learn to know what they are doing weekly, pray let your Paper hold the following Glass to them, and as they like the Figure they may proceed for the future; others, however, will find by it what Judgment to make of them. It is a Performance of the immortal Mr. Addison, who to his own and the lasting Honour of the English Nation, labour'd hard, and sometimes with Success, to reform the Follies and Vices of his Country.[8] You may leave out that part of the third Paragraph from the third Line to the End, as foreign to the Subject. Yours, &c.

8. The enclosure was *The Spectator*, No. 451, on defamation in newspapers and pamphlets.

370

Davis Pinx. 1751.   Martin. Sc.

Thomas Penn Esqr.

one of the Proprietors of Pensilvania. 1751.

Bill to Thomas Penn

AD: American Philosophical Society

Honorable Thos. Penn Esq. Dr.[9]

1734				
May 18.	For printing and Paper of 200 Cases at 2*d*. per.	£ 1	13	4
	For a Supplement to the same		5	
	For 300 Warrants a 1*d*. per.	1	5	
Mr. Steel[1]	6 quire Paper a 1*s*. 3*d*.		7	6
	For binding a Book		10	
	For 2 Sermons		3	
Augt.	For printing 200 Bonds at 1*d*.		16	8
	Paper 4 quire a 12*d*.		4	
	For printing 1000 Bonds and Warrants at 1*d*. each	4	3	4
	Paper 20 quire at 1*s*. a quire	1		
	For Large Advertisements		10	
	Ditto in Gazette[2]		5	
Oct. 20	For a Sheet Pasteboard			9
	For Dutch Advts		5	
		11	8	7
	For the Gazette 2 Years	1		
	For binding Catesby's Birds[3] and gilding	1	10	
	D[itt]o A. Arscot[4]		2	6
	For a Book of Constitutions[5]		6	
		[£14	7*s*.	1*d*.]

Thomas Godfrey to the Printer of the Gazette

Printed in *The Pennsylvania Gazette*, August 15, 1734.

Mr. Franklin,

The Germans, an industrious and indefatigable People, have been always famous for their Penetration into the more dark and

9. This is only BF's memorandum of Penn's account, not the bill sent to the proprietor. Two similar memoranda, containing most of the same items and a few additional ones, are also in APS.

1. James Steel, receiver-general of Pennsylvania and the proprietors' agent.

2. Probably the advertisement, signed by Steel and dated Sept. 5, summoning all persons to make payment for lands surveyed to them; it was printed in the *Gazette* Sept. 12.

3. Mark Catesby's *Natural History of Carolina*, of which the first part appeared in London, 1731.

4. Alexander Arscot, *Some Considerations relating to the Present State of the Christian Religion*, first printed by BF, 1731, reprinted, 1732.

5. James Anderson, *The Constitutions of the Free-Masons*, first printed at London, 1723, printed by BF "for the Use of the Brethren in North America," 1734.

abstruse Parts of Learning, such as border upon Magic not excepted. Of this Nation was the renowned Agrippa, Dr. Faustus, and several others that might be named. Their Skill in the most subtle and mischievous Arts, not being at all doubted of by their Enemies, who by frequent Experience have been made too sensible of it, I admire that any Prince in Europe has the Courage to engage in War with them. I have been formerly told of a certain Virtuoso of that Country, then living, who made himself a Gun (under a particular Configuration of the Heavenly Bodies) which had this wonderful Property, That if walking in the Woods at any Time without it, he happened to see a Deer, or any other Creature that fled from him, he could go home and fire his Piece up the Chimney, when the Shot, by an inevitable Necessity, would proceed directly to the Game, at whatever Distance, and kill it dead. Such a Philosopher as this (I thought) could never fail of Encouragement and Promotion; but it seems throughout the late long Peace he has been neglected. I, who am in my Heart on the Side of the Emperor, was afraid lest so useful a Marksman might be dead: But, to my great Satisfaction, I perceive by an Article of News in Mr. Bradford's Paper of the first Instant, that he is still living, and prefer'd to the Post of Gunner of the important Fortress of Philipsburgh; For no one but he could have kill'd the Duke of Berwick, upon the Rhine, and the Duke of Savoy in Italy, Countries so vastly distant, both with the same Shot.[6] I am Yours, &c.   T.G.

P.S. It were to be wish'd the Public had been informed how long the King of Sardinia surviv'd the Duke of Savoy: For he it seems is also kill'd with a Cannon Shot, doubtless by the same Gunner.

6. The *American Weekly Mercury*, under a New York dateline of July 29, reported, "That the Dukes of Berwick and Savoy were both shot by a random shot from the Town of Philipsburg . . . That the King of Sardinia was kill'd by a Cannon shot in Italy." Godfrey's thrust at Bradford is based on the report's carelessness in identifying these persons. Probably the report meant to say "the Duke of Berwick and the Prince of Savoy"; although even in these terms the report was partly false. The Duke of Berwick was indeed killed by a cannon-shot at Philipsburg on the Rhine, June 12, 1734; Prince (not Duke) Eugene of Savoy was "strongly intrenched on the Rhine" nearby at this time, but was not killed; while the Dukes (not Princes) of Savoy had been Kings of Sardinia since 1718, and Charles Emmanuel III, King of Sardinia and Duke of Savoy, was waging war in northern Italy in June 1734.

Admission of John Mifflin to Library Company[7]

ADS: Historical Society of Pennsylvania

27th of Augst. 1734

Such of the Directors of the Library Company as approve of John Mifflin's being admitted a Member are desired to shew their Consent by subscribing their Names hereto

B. FRANKLIN	HUGH ROBERTS
JOHN JONES JUNR	THOS. HOPKINSON 1734
FRAS. RICHARDSON	THOS. CADWALADER
WM RAWLE	PHILIP SYNG JUNR
THOS GODFREY	WM. COLEMAN

To the Grand Lodge of Massachusetts[8]

MS not found; reprinted from Grand Lodge of Massachusetts, *Abstract of the Proceedings . . . 1871*, pp. 356–7.

Philadelphia, Nov. 28, 1734[9]

Right Worshipful Grand Master and Most Worthy and Dear Brethren,

We acknowledge your favor of the 23d of October past, and rejoice that the Grand Master (whom God bless) hath so happily recovered from his late indisposition: and we now, glass in hand, drink to the establishment of his health, and the prosperity of your whole Lodge.

7. John Mifflin (1715–1759), Quaker merchant; later a member of the Philadelphia Common Council, 1747; alderman, 1751; and member of the Provincial Council, 1755; father of Thomas Mifflin, president of the Continental Congress in 1783. Charles P. Keith, *Provincial Councillors of Pennsylvania, 1733–1776* (Phila., 1883), p. 362. This note, in BF's hand, is printed as an example of the procedure followed in admitting members to the Library Company.

8. This and the following letter were apparently written on "one sheet of common letter paper . . . folded as a letter," the first on page one, the second on page three, and the address on page four. Grand Lodge of Massachusetts, *Proc.*, *1871* (Boston, 1872), pp. 358–9.

9. BF was elected Junior Grand Warden of the Pennsylvania Grand Lodge, June 24, 1732; Grand Master, June 24, 1734.

We have seen in the Boston prints an article of news from London,[1] importing that at a Grand Lodge held there in August last, Mr. Price's[2] deputation and power was extended over all America, which advice we hope is true, and we heartily congratulate him thereupon, and though this has not been as yet regularly signified to us by you, yet, giving credit thereto, we think it our duty to lay before your Lodge what we apprehend needful to be done for us, in order to promote and strengthen the interest of Masonry in this Province (which seems to want the sanction of some authority derived from home, to give the proceedings and determinations of our Lodge their due weight) to wit, a Deputation or Charter granted by the Right Worshipful Mr. Price, by virtue of his commission from Britain, confirming the Brethren of Pennsylvania in the privileges they at present enjoy of holding annually their Grand Lodge, choosing their Grand Master, Wardens and other officers, who may manage all affairs relating to the Brethren here with full power and authority, according to the customs and usages of Masons, the said Grand Master of Pennsylvania only yielding his chair, when the Grand Master of all America shall be in place. This, if it seem good and reasonable to you to grant, will not only be extremely agreeable to us, but will also, we are confident, conduce much to the welfare, establishment, and reputation of Masonry in these parts. We therefore submit it for your consideration, and, as we hope our request will be complied with, we desire that it may be done as soon as possible, and also accompanied with a copy of the R. W. Grand Master's first Deputation, and of the instrument by which it appears to be enlarged as above-mentioned, witnessed

1. Not found.

2. Henry Price (1697–1780), tailor, storekeeper, man of business, came from England to Boston, 1723; about 1730 he returned to England where, April 13, 1733, he was deputed "Provincial Grand Master of New England and Dominions and Territories thereunto belonging"; organized Grand Lodge of Massachusetts, July 30, 1733. His authority was extended, 1734, to cover all British North America. Melvin M. Johnson, *The Beginnings of Freemasonry in America* (N.Y., 1924), pp. 28–31, 74–103; J. Hugo Tatsch, *Freemasonry in the Thirteen Colonies* (N.Y., 1929), pp. 20, 22. See David McGregor, "Franklin's Masonic Letters to Price," *The Master Mason*, N.J. edit., II (1926), 955–62, for the Pennsylvania interpretation of Price's appointment.

by your Wardens, and signed by the Secretary; for which favors this Lodge doubt not of being able to behave as not to be thought ungrateful.[3]

We are, Right Worshipful Grand Master and Most Worthy Brethren, Your Affectionate Brethren and obliged humble Servants,

Signed at the request of the Lodge,   B. FRANKLIN, G.M.

Addressed: To Mr. Henry Price At the Brazen Head Boston, N.E.

To Henry Price

MS not found; reprinted from Grand Lodge of Massachusetts, *Abstract of the Proceedings . . . 1871,* p. 357.

Dear Brother Price,   Philadelphia, Nov. 28, 1734

I am glad to hear of your recovery. I hoped to have seen you here this Fall, agreeable to the expectation you were so good as to give me; but since sickness has prevented your coming while the weather was moderate, I have no room to flatter myself with a visit from you before the Spring, when a deputation of the Brethren here will have an opportunity of showing how much they esteem you. I beg leave to recommend their request to you, and to inform you, that some false and rebel Brethren, who are foreigners, being about to set up a distinct Lodge in opposition to the old and true Brethren here, pretending to make Masons for a bowl of punch, and the Craft is like to come into disesteem among us unless the true Brethren are countenanced and distinguished by some such special authority as herein desired. I entreat, therefore, that whatever you shall think proper to do therein may be sent by the next post, if possible, or the

3. The result of this appeal seems to have been that Price appointed BF Provincial Grand Master for Pennsylvania, Feb. 21, 1735. *American Weekly Mercury,* March 27, 1735, printed in facsimile in Johnson, *The Beginnings of Freemasonry in America,* p. 130.

In 1742 one Mr. * * * printed, ostensibly at The Hague, *Apologie Pour l'Ordre des Francs-Maçons. Avec deux Chansons composées par Le Frère Américain.* Anderson Galleries *Catalogue* 1633 (Feb. 28—March 1, 1922), item 265, asserted that "the American brother" was BF, but no evidence supporting this attribution has been found.

next following. I am, Your affectionate Brother and humble Servant   B. FRANKLIN, G.M. Pennsylvania

P.S. If more of the Constitutions are wanted among you, please hint it to me.[4]

Addressed: To Mr. Henry Price At the Brazen Head Boston, N. E.

Extracts from the Gazette, 1734

Printed in *The Pennsylvania Gazette*, January 8 to December 26, 1734.

[ADVERTISEMENT] A Servant Lad's Time for near Five years to be disposed of, on Reasonable Terms. He is by Trade a Taylor, and can work very well. Enquire of the Printer hereof.
[January 30]

Saturday last a Marriage was consummated between Wm. Allen, Esq; one of the Principal Merchants of this City; and Mrs. Margaret Hamilton, only daughter of Andrew Hamilton, Esq; a young Lady of great Merit.   [February 20]

On Tuesday last a Widow of this Town was married in her Shift, without any other Apparel; upon a Supposition that such a Procedure would secure her Husband in the Law from being sued for any Debts of his Predecessor.[5]   [February 27]

JUST PUBLISHED; The Laws of this Province which were passed in the last Sitting of Assembly; viz. The Excise Act, the Flour Act, and two others. Sold by the Printer hereof; Price 1s. 6d.
[March 21]

4. James Anderson, *The Constitutions of the Free-Masons* ... "Re-printed [by BF] in Philadelphia by special Order, for the Use of the Brethren in North-America"; *Pa. Gaz.*, May 16, 1734, advertised it as "just published." In August BF sent 70 copies to Boston.
5. The reference is to the custom which made the second husband responsible for the debts of the first, unless the bride were married in her chemise in the King's highway. Peter Kalm described it fully in 1748 (*Peter Kalm's Travels in North America*, ed. A. B. Benson, N.Y., 1937, I, 225), and several cases are mentioned in Alice Morse Earle, *Customs and Fashions in Old New England* (London, 1893), pp. 77–9.

To be Sold by the Printer hereof, the following Books. Westindia Coasting Pilot. Newhouse's Navigation. Pattoun's Navigation. Key of Commerce. Lex Mercatoria. Euclid's Elements by William Whiston. Burnet's Theory of the Earth, 2 Vols. Lock on Human Understanding, 2 Vols. Blackmore's Prince Arthur. London Dispensatory. Blancard's Physical Dictionary. Geo. Fox's Journal. Basnages History of the Jews. Van Helmont's Works. Cowley's Works. Cambden's Britannia. Raleigh's History of the World. Builders Vademecum. Trader's Vademecum. Barclay's Apology. Willard on the Catechism. Ditton on the Resurrection. English Liberties. Accidences, Nomenclator's, Cato's, and other School Books of various Sorts. Account Books of large Demi Paper and small Paper. Beavan's Primitive Christianity. Honour of the Gout. Greek Lexicon. Latin Dictionary. Bibles of several Sorts, and several Sorts of Histories.

Where may be also had, Quadrants, Forestaffs, Nocturnals, Mariner's Compasses. [March 21]

[ADVERTISEMENT] Ready Money for old RAGS, may be had of the Printer hereof. [April 11]

On Monday last in the Forenoon a Fire broke out in a Pot-house near Walnut-Street; and the Weather having been extream dry a great while together, it burnt very furiously, and by the Flakes of burning Shingles that were carried thro' the Air, several of the neighbouring Houses, and some at a considerable Distance were set on fire also. The Pot-House and a Carpenter's Shop adjoining were both consumed; but by the Diligence and Activity of the People, and especially by the Assistance of the Engines, it was prevented from spreading further. It is thought by some that the Engines sav'd the Town several Thousand Pounds that Day. [April 18]

[ADVERTISEMENT] Very good Live Geese Feathers to be sold at the Printers hereof. [April 25]

[ADVERTISEMENT] The Subscribers to the Library in Philadelphia are hereby advertised, that Monday the 6th of May ensuing, at Two in the Afternoon, is the Time appointed for the

377

Choice of Directors and a Treasurer for the succeeding Year, and for making the second annual Payment, at the House of John Roberts in High-street near the Market.   J. BREINTNAL, Secr.
[April 25]

[ADVERTISEMENT] To be Sold, Nine Thousand Foot of seasoned Merchantable *Boards*, at a Reasonable Price. Inquire of the Printer.   [May 2]

[ADVERTISEMENT] Very good single Refin'd Loaf Sugar sold reasonable by the great or small Quantity, at the Printer's hereof. Also Coffee, and Cases of Bottles.   [May 9]

Last Night a Fire broke out in a back Building behind Dr. Jones's in Market-Street but was soon extinguish'd. It being difficult at first to get Water for the Engines, 'tis thought the Fire would have risen to a great Head there abouts, if so much Rain had not fallen Yesterday as made every Thing very wet. Where there is not Pumps in Yards, it is to be wish'd that People would keep Hogsheads of Water always ready for such Occasions, as they are obliged by Law to do in some Cities.   [May 23]

[ADVERTISEMENT] Two likely young Negroes, one a Lad about 19: The other a Girl of 15, to be sold. Inquire of the Printer.
[May 23]

Monday last a Young Child fell into a Tub of Water in Chesnut-Street, and was unhappily drowned before any body perceiv'd it.

The same Day Ralph Hoy of New-Castle, fell out of a Boat coming up from thence hither, within Sight of this Town, and was drowned.

And the same Day, a Woman offering to pawn the Case of a Watch, it was carried to a Silversmith's in order to be valued, and there discover'd to belong to the Watch late-advertised in this Paper as stolen out of the House of Richard Smith during the Hurry of the late Fire; upon which the Woman was taken up, confess'd the Fact, restor'd the rest of the Watch, and was committed to Prison.   [June 6]

Monday last, a Grand Lodge of the Ancient and Honourable Society of Free and Accepted Masons in this Province, was held at the Tun Tavern in Water-Street, when Benjamin Franklin being elected Grand-Master for the Year ensuing, appointed Mr. John Crap, to be his Deputy; and James Hamilton, Esq; and Thomas Hopkinson, Gent. were chosen Wardens. After which, a very elegant Entertainment was provided, and the Proprietor, the Governor, and several other Persons of Distinction honour'd the Society with their Presence. [June 27]

[ADVERTISEMENT] Lately imported and to be sold by the Printer hereof, large Bibles with the Common Prayer, Apocrypha, and Concordance; small gilt Bibles with the Common Prayer and new Version of Psalms; Common Bibles; Testaments of a large print; Psalters; Account Books of all Sizes; Demi Royal, large Post, and Common Paper; Sealing-wax superfine and common; Ink powder the best; with several other Sorts of Stationary Ware.

Where may be had all sorts of Blanks in the most authentick Forms, and correctly printed. [July 4]

The Weather has been so excessive hot here for a Week past, that a great Number of People have fainted and fallen into Convulsions, and several have died in a few Hours after they were taken. From the Country round about we hear that a great many of the Harvest People faint in the Fields, and 'tis said that in some Places a multitude of Birds are found dead. Excepting the Hot Summer about 7 Years since, such Weather has not been known in this Country in the memory of Man. [July 11]

[ADVERTISEMENT] Very good LAMPBLACK made and sold by the Printer hereof. [July 11]

[ADVERTISEMENT] In Second Street over against the Sign of the Bible, is taught the Arts Mathematical, viz. *Arithmetic* in all its Parts, *Geometry, Mensuration, Surveying, Gauging, Trigonometry, Navigation, Dialling* and *Astronomy*, the use of the *Globes* and other *Mathematical Instruments*, according to the most approv'd Methods, by Theophilus Grew. He also teaches *Algebra* or the *Analytical Art*, with the *Laws* and *Properties* of *Motion*, a thing

379

absolutely necessary to a right understanding of the *Modern Philosophy*. He designs, if he finds Encouragement, to make it his whole business, in order to instruct the young Gentlemen and Youth of the Town, and will give Attendance in his Room up one pair of Stairs from nine to twelve in the Morning, from two to five in the Afternoon, and from Six to Nine in the Evening, as it shall suit each ones conveniency.[6]   [July 25]

By being too nice in the Choice of the little Pieces sent me by my Correspondents to be printed, I had almost discouraged them from writing to me any more. For the Time to come, and that my Paper may become still more generally agreeable, I have resolved not to regard my own Humour so much in what I print; and thereupon I give my Readers the two following Letters.   [August 8]

Last Saturday Morning died here, the Lady of our worthy Governor,[7] at his Country-House near this City, after an Illness which for some Months past had seized her, tho' she was confined to her Bed four days only before her Death: Her Corpse being brought to Town early on Sunday Morning was decently and honourably interred in our Church about Eight in the Evening. She was descended of an honourable Family in the Southern part of Scotland, which suffered much thro' their too great Attachment to that unhappy Prince King James the Second: Her two Brothers bred up by their Father in the Protestant Religion, being afterwards seduced from it, the Eldest, dead some years since, held an high Office in the Court of the late Duke of Tuscany, and the other is now Confessor to His most Catholick Majesty. This Lady was much esteemed by all that knew her, for her solid good Sense, exemplary Piety and extensive Charity, in which last few were more private, or according to their Circumstances more bountiful to the unfortunate. She died a true Protestant of the Communion

6. In his *Gazette* advertisement, Oct. 10, Grew omitted reference to instruction in "Modern Philosophy," but promised "to furnish any One with sufficient Knowledge in any of the foregoing Branches, in Three Months Time, provided the Person have a tolerable Genius, and observe a constant Application."

7. Isabella Clarke Gordon, wife of Patrick Gordon, lieutenant-governor since 1726. Charles P. Keith, *Chronicles of Pennsylvania* (Phila., 1917), II, 686–7.

of the Church of England, for which she had so great an Esteem and Veneration, that very advantageous Offers made to her by her Brothers could not draw her aside from a strict Adherence to the Principles of that excellent Church. Her Death is universally lamented here, and she has left behind her a numerous Family to deplore their irreparable Loss. [September 19]

An Express from New-Castle having late last Thursday Night brought the agreeable News, that the Honourable John Penn, Esq; the eldest of our Proprietors, with his Brother-in-Law Mr. Freame, his Lady and Family were on board a Ship from London, then off New-Castle, and standing up this River; The Honourable Thomas Penn, Esq, with several Gentlemen of this City, hasted early next Morning to Chester (the late afflicting Loss in our Governor's Family, preventing him from making one of the Number). Mr. Penn, Mr. Freame and his Lady came on Shore at that Place about Four in the Afternoon, and after passing that Night there, set out for this City about Nine in the Morning. They were met at Skuylkil River by several Ladies, who came to pay their Compliments to Mrs. Freame on her Arrival, and passing that Ferry, were received by the Mayor, Recorder, and Commonalty of the City, in whose Name the Recorder made the following Speech: [*Text is not reproduced here*]. Then proceeding forward with a Train of several Coaches, Chaises, and a very numerous Company on Horseback, they were saluted at their Entrance into the City, with a Discharge of the Guns on Society-Hill, and afterwards by most of the Ships in our River; about Three in the Afternoon, they alighted at their Brother's House, where an elegant Entertainment was provided for the Ladies, and also for the Gentlemen of the Council of this Province. [September 25]

Yesterday Morning Michael Welfare, one of the *Christian Philosophers* of Conestogoe, appeared in full Market in the Habit of a Pilgrim, his Hat of Linnen, his Beard at full Length, and a long Staff in his Hand. He declared himself sent by Almighty God, to denounce Vengeance against the Iniquity and Wickedness of the Inhabitants of this City and Province, without speedy Repentance. The Earnestness of his Discourse, which continu'd near a quarter of an Hour; the Vehemence of his Action, and the Importance of what he delivered, commanded the Attention of a Multitude of People. And when he had finished he went away unmolested.[8] [September 25]

‡‡‡This present Paper, No. 303, finishes the Fifth Year, since the Printer hereof undertook the *Gazette;* no more need be said to my generous Subscribers, to re-mind them, that every one of those who are above a Twelvemonth in Arrear, has it in his Power to contribute considerably towards the Happiness of his most obliged humble Servant, B. FRANKLIN
[September 25]

JUST PUBLISH'D, POOR RICHARD: An ALMANACK for the Year 1735; containing the Lunations, Eclipses, Planets Motions and Aspects, Weather, Sun and Moon's Rising and Setting, Highwater, &c. Besides many pleasant and witty Verses, Jests and notable Sayings, as usual. Proofs of Titan's Death, predicted in 1733. Titan's Ghost. Saturn, Mars, and Penn's People. Receipt how to make Cuckolds. Bad Commentators. Impudent Hibham. Ignorant Politicians. Eyes and Priests. William's Wife. Well-bred Sally. Cunning and Wisdom. The Miser. Lewis the Great prov'd to be little. Unlearned wise Men. Sam's Wife's Curse. Great Wits jump. Hal's Management. Abstinent Tim. Halfwitted Railers at all Women. The Orator. Habit of Lying. Sally's Teeth. The generous Sun. What makes Folks amiable. The Lawyer's Saint, &c. By RICHARD SAUNDERS, *Philomat.* Printed and Sold by B. Franklin. Price 3*s.* 6*d.* per Dozen.

Note, Jerman's Almanacks are in the Press, and will speedily be published. [November 7]

[ADVERTISEMENT] Any Gentleman that has any Occasion for a Book-Keeper, may be informed of one by the Printer hereof.
[December 12]

8. Michael Wohlfahrt (1687–1741), known as Brother Agonius in the Seventh Day Baptist community at Ephrata, frequently visited Philadelphia to exhort the Quaker Yearly Meeting to his views of truth. Denied admission to the Meeting in 1734, he spoke from the courthouse. BF printed the sermon, 1737. Julius F. Sachse, *The German Sectarians of Pennsylvania* (Phila., 1899), I, 216, 391–4; *Pa. Gaz.,* Jan. 6, 1737.

*₊*Lent at different Times (and forgot to whom) the following Books, viz. Whiston's Astronomical Principles of Religion; Croxall's Esop; Watts's Lyric Poems sacred to Piety, Virtue and Friendship; Steel's Dramatick Works; Discourse of Free-Thinking: The Persons that borrow'd them are desired to return them to the Printer of this Paper.

He has in his Hands the 2d Vol. of Cowley's Works in Octavo, of which he does not know the Owner. [December 12]

Any Person who has a Servant to dispose of that is a Scholar, and can teach Children Reading, Writing and Arithmetick, may hear of a Purchaser by enquiring of the Printer hereof.

[December 26]

PHILADELPHIA: Printed by B. FRANKLIN, at the *New Printing-Office* near the Market. *Price* 10s. a Year. Where Advertisements are taken in, and BOOK-BINDING is done reasonably, in the best Manner.

Index

Compiled by David Horne

Abert, Henrietta Constantia Bache (1822–87), genealogy, lxv

Account books of BF, Ledger A and B, description, and extracts from, 172–5

Adams, Matthew, and *New-England Courant*, 8

Addertongue, Alice. *See* Alice Addertongue

"Affairs of Ireland," article in the *Pa. Gaz.*, 162

Afterwit, Anthony. *See* Anthony Afterwit

Aldridge, Alfred Owen, identifies purported BF essay, 170

Alexander, Marianne (1764–1845). *See* Williams, Marianne Alexander

Alice Addertongue (pen-name of BF), letter by, 243–8

All, Elizabeth Franklin (m. 1761; niece of BF), genealogy, lx

All, Isaac (m. 1761), genealogy, lx

Allen, Isaac, genealogy, lx

Allen, Mary Franklin (m. 1752; niece of BF), genealogy, lx

Allen, William (m. 1752), genealogy, lx

Allen, William (1704–80): entry for, in BF account book, 172; elected Masonic Grand Master, 275; marriage, 376

Almanacs: complications in publishing of, 166 n.; number and form, 280–1

American Almanacks, comp. Jerman, 188, 280, 281, 348, 382

American Philosophical Society, BF papers in, xxii, xxvii

American Weekly Mercury: rivalry with Keimer, 111–13; stale news in, 250 and n.; Hamilton attacked in, 333; erroneous reporting of, 372 n.

Anderson, Allen G., on BF ballad, 6 n.

Annis, Ann (m. 1751). *See* Davenport, Ann Annis

Anthony Afterwit (pen-name of BF), letter by, 237–40

"Apology for Printers," 194–9

Arnauld, Antoine, and Pierre Nicole, BF indebted to work of, 58

Arscot, Alexander, *Some Considerations relating to the Present State of the Christian Religion*, BF charge for work on, 371 and n.

Articles of agreement with Thomas Whitmarsh, 205–8

"Articles of Belief and Acts of Religion," 101–9

Atterbury, Bishop, quoted, 77 n.

Aurora (Philadelphia), B. F. Bache publisher of, lxiii

Autobiography: on Dogood papers, 8; on Sir Hans Sloane, 54 n.; on *Liberty and Necessity*, 57 n.; on Plan of Conduct, 99; on BF's private liturgy mentioned in, 101; on Samuel Keimer, 113 n., 114; on paper currency, 140; on Mass. gubernatorial salary dispute, 159 n.; mentions BF authorship of essay on self-denial, 170; on conversation, 177; on reading history, 192–3; on libel, 196 n.; quoted, 212, 216 n.

Bache, Alexander Dallas (1806–67), genealogy, lxv

Bache, Benjamin (1796–1853), genealogy, lxiii

Bache, Benjamin Franklin (1769–98; grandson of BF), genealogy, lxiii

Bache, Benjamin Franklin (1801–81), genealogy, lxiv

Bache, Catharine Wistar (1770–1820), genealogy, lxiv

Bache, Catharine Wistar (1805–86), genealogy, lxiii

Bache, Deborah (1781–1863). *See* Duane, Deborah Bache

Bache, Elizabeth (1807–37). *See* Burnett, Elizabeth Bache

Bache, Elizabeth Franklin (1777–1820). *See* Harwood, Elizabeth Franklin Bache

Bache, Emma Mary (1803–13), genealogy, lxiv

Bache, Esther Egee (b. 1801), genealogy, lxiv

Bache, Franklin (1792–1864): and BF papers, xxii; genealogy, lxiii

Bache, George Mifflin (1811–46), genealogy, lxv

Bache, Hartman (1798–1872), genealogy, lxiii

Bache, Henrietta Constantia (1822–87). *See* Abert, Henrietta Constantia Bache
Bache, Louis (1779–1819; grandson of BF), genealogy, lxiv
Bache, Margaret Hartman Markoe (1770–1836), genealogy, lxiii
Bache, Marie. *See* McLane, Marie Bache
Bache, Mary, genealogy, lxiii
Bache, Mary Ann Swift (d. *c.* 1812), genealogy, lxiv
Bache, Mary Blechynden (1808–73). *See* Walker, Mary Blechynden Bache
Bache, Matilda Wilkins (b. 1819). *See* Emory, Matilda Wilkins Bache
Bache, Richard (1737–1811; son-in-law of BF), genealogy, lxiii
Bache, Richard, Jr. (1784–1848; grandson of BF), genealogy, lxv
Bache, Richard (1794–1836), genealogy, lxiii
Bache, Richard, 4th, genealogy, lxv
Bache, Sarah (1775–76; granddaughter of BF), genealogy, lxiv
Bache, Sarah (1788–1863). *See* Sergeant, Sarah Bache
Bache, Sarah (1798–1849). *See* Hodge, Sarah Bache
Bache, Sarah Franklin (1743–1808; daughter of BF): genealogy, lxii, lxiii; mentioned, 211
Bache, Sarah Franklin (b. 1824). *See* Wainwright, Sarah Franklin Bache
Bache, Sophia Arabella (1816–1904). *See* Irwin, Sophia Arabella Bache
Bache, Theophylact, I (1809–16), genealogy, lxiv
Bache, Theophylact, II (1817–75), genealogy, lxiv
Bache, William (father of Richard), genealogy, lxiii
Bache, William (1773–*c.* 1820; grandson of BF), genealogy, lxiii
Bache, William (1811–97), genealogy, lxiv
Baker, Rebecca (d. 1746). *See* Folger, Rebecca Baker
Baptism record of BF, 3
Barbadoes Gazette, started by Keimer, 113 n.
Barnard, Bethia Folger (d. 1669; aunt of BF), genealogy, liii, lix
Barnard, John (d. 1669), genealogy, liv
Barnard, Mary (*c.* 1667–1737). *See* Folger, Mary Barnard
Bartram, John: recommended by Breintnall to Collinson, 114 n.; makes prints of leaves, etc., 344 n.
Beaudri, Sarah (m. 1748). *See* Franklin, Sarah Beaudri

Bedford, Duke of, James Ralph in service of, 58 n.
Belcher, Jonathan: biographical note, 176 n.; misprint in news story on, 169; salary controversy with Mass. Assembly, 176, 177 n.; urged to prosecute Capt. Lobb, 229 n.
Berkshire (ship), BF journeys from London to Philadelphia on, 72–99
Berry, Elizabeth Franklin (1678–1759). *See* Douse, Elizabeth Franklin Berry
Berry, Joseph (m. 1707), genealogy, lvii
Biddle, Christine Williams, genealogy, lviii
Bigelow, John: edits BF papers, xxvi; on Dogood papers, 8; editing of Junto queries, 259
Billings, Sarah (d. 1751). *See* Davenport, Sarah Billings
Bingham, James, appointed Masonic officer, 345
Birket, William, almanac of, 168
Birth record of BF, 3
Blackbeard, Defoe on, 7 n. *See also* "Taking of Teach the Pirate"
Blackmore, Richard, book of, mentioned, 105 and n.
Boston: BF's departure from, 53; BF visits (1724), 53 n.; (1733), 346 n.
Boston Post, on BF ballad, 6
Boude, Thomas: signs Masonic by-laws, 233 and n.; appointed Masonic officer, 275
Boulding, William, granted land, 362
Bradford, Andrew: publishes *American Weekly Mercury,* 111, 112, 113; prints paper money, 141; prints Leeds' almanac, 166 n., 167, 168; prints Godfrey's almanac, 190 n.; prints account of Palatines, 226, 227 n.; as printer of almanacs, 280
Bradford, William, prints Leeds' almanac, 166 and n., 167, 168
Breintnall, Joseph: biographical note, 114 n.; writes Busy-Body papers, 114, 134 n.; calls meeting of the Lib. Co., 208–10, 271, 378; sends Collinson letter composed by BF, 248–9; witness to Lib. Co. agreement, 252, 361; poem of, to be read at Junto, 259; helps draft address to Thomas Penn, 320; signs Penn address as Lib. Co. secretary, 321; makes prints of leaves, etc., 344 n.
Browne, Daniel, ordination, 43 n.
Browne, Mehitabel. *See* Kittle, Mehitabel Browne
Brownell, George, entry for, in BF account book, 174

Buckingham, Joseph T., on Dogood papers, 8
Buckmaster, Abiah Franklin (c. 1726–54; niece of BF), genealogy, lix
Buckmaster, George (m. 1743), genealogy, lix
Bunker, Deborah Paddock (d. 1750). See Folger, Deborah Paddock Bunker
Buried treasure, search for, in Pa., 135–9
Burnet, William: biographical note, 159 n.; dispute between Assembly and, 159–61, 176 and n.
Burnett, Elizabeth Bache (1807–37), genealogy, lxiv
Business memoranda of BF, 210–11
Busy-Body papers, 113–39
Butwell, Thomas, staymaker, 276
Bysshe, Edward, trans. of Xenophon, The Memorable Things of Socrates, BF's use of, 176

Cadogan, William (Baron Cadogan of Reading): biographical note, 77 n.; mentioned, 77
Cadwalader, Thomas: biographical note, 209 n.; director of Lib. Co., 209; signs Lib. Co. agreement, 322, 360, 361; approves new member for Lib. Co., 373
Caelia Shortface. See Martha Careful
Caillot, "Blanchette," genealogy, lxiii
Campbell, Duncan, biographical note, 128 n.
Cape Fear, account of, 216
Card-cheat, punished by shipmates, 83–4
Careful, Martha. See Martha Careful
Carisbrooke, Isle of Wight, BF visits, 75, 76–9
Carpenter, Samuel, granted land, 362
Cassell, Nicholas, witness of BF agreement with Whitmarsh, 208
Casuist (BF pen-name): questions put to, 163, 221–2, 234; answers from, 163, 222–5, 235; another answer, 225–6; from "Anti-Casuist," 235–7
Catesby, Mark, Natural History of Carolina, BF binding charge for, 371 and n.
Celia Single (pen-name of BF), letter by, 240–3
Chambers' Cyclopaedia, Keimer's use of, 111, 157 and n.
Champion, edited by Ralph and Fielding, 58 n.
Champlost, Pa. (home of George Fox), BF papers at, xxi–xxii
Chandler, Hannah (m. 1778). See Williams, Hannah Chandler

Charming Sally (ship), counterfeit bills found on passenger of, 164 n.
Chase, Priscilla (d. 1753). See Folger, Priscilla Chase
Checkley, John, and New-England Courant, 8
Chew, Samuel, brings Mottraye to call, 344 n.
Child, Ann (d. 1689). See Franklin, Ann(e) Child
Child, Robert (of Ecton), genealogy, lvi
Chronology of BF's life through 1734, lxxxvii–lxxxviii
Church, Sarah (d. 1745). See Folger, Sarah Church
Clark, Henry, master of Berkshire, 72
Clark, Jerusha (d. 1778). See Folger, Jerusha Clark
Clarke, Anne (Nancy) Johnson (d. 1805), genealogy, lviii
Clarke, Peter (d. c. 1777), genealogy, lviii
Claypoole, Elizabeth Cromwell, married John Claypoole, 200 n.
Claypoole, George: biographical note, 200 n.; dies of smallpox, 200–1
Claypoole, James, father of George, 200 n.
Claypoole, John, married dau. of Cromwell, 200 n.
Cocker, Edward: biographical note, 5 n.; arithmetician, 5
Coffin, Abigail (d. 1770). See Folger Abigail Coffin
Coffin, Dinah (d. 1793). See Folger, Dinah Coffin Starbuck
Coffin, John (d. 1788), genealogy, liv
Coffin, Judith. See Folger, Judith Coffin
Coffin, Keziah Folger (1723–98), genealogy, liv, lxii
Coffin, Ruth Brown (m. 1770). See Stickney, Ruth Brown Coffin
Colds, BF essay on, 252–4
Cole, Hannah Franklin Eddy (1683–1723; half-sister of BF), genealogy, lvi
Cole, Thomas (m. 1710), genealogy, lvii
Coleman, Abiah (m. 1753). See Folger, Abiah Coleman
Coleman, Joanna Folger, (c. 1643–1719), genealogy, liii
Coleman, John (d. 1715), genealogy, liii
Coleman, William: witness to Lib. Co. agreement, 252; helps draft address to Thomas Penn, 320; approves new member for Lib. Co., 373
Collas, Jane Mecom (1745–1802; niece of BF), genealogy, lxii
Collas, Peter (m. 1773): genealogy, lxii; makes soap, 348 n.

Collection of Epigrams (anon.), BF's use of, 282

Collins, Anthony, works studied by BF, 58

Collinson, Peter: and BF's experiments, xxv; Breintnall's letters to, 114 n.; letter to, 248–9; assists Lib. Co., 248–9; receives leaf prints, 344 n.

Collyer, Hannah (d. 1846). *See* Franklin, Hannah Collyer

Commonplace book of BF, extracts from (1732), 270–1

Compton, Elizabeth Franklin (d. 1773; niece of BF), genealogy, lvii

Compton, William (d. 1786), genealogy, lvii

Conversation, BF essay on, 177–81

Cotton, John, epitaph of, 110

Counterfeiting, in Pa., 184, 278–9, 342–3

Courant. See *New-England Courant*

Cowes, Isle of Wight, BF visits, 75, 81, 82

Crane, Verner W., edits BF writings, xxiv, xxvii

Crap, John, appointed Masonic officer, 379

Croker, Frances, real estate transactions of, 363–70

Croker, John, real estate transactions of, 363–70

Cromwell, Oliver, dau. of, married John Claypoole, 200 and n.

Cuff, Peter, appointed Masonic officer, 345

Currency question. *See* Paper currency

Cutler, Timothy, ordination, 43 n.

Cutts, John (Baron Cutts), biographical note, 78 n.

Dallas, Sophia Burrell (1785–1860). *See* Duane, Sophia Burrell Dallas

Daner, Jonas, signs Palatine appeal, 229

Davenport, Abiah (b. 1729). *See* Griffith, Abiah Davenport

Davenport, Ann Annis (m. 1751), genealogy, lx

Davenport, Dorcas (1724–74). *See* Stickney, Dorcas Davenport

Davenport, Elizabeth (b. 1723). *See* Ingersoll, Elizabeth Davenport

Davenport, Franklin (1755–1832), genealogy, lxi

Davenport, James (m. 1722): biographical note, 171 n.; genealogy, lx

Davenport, Josiah [Franklin] (b. 1727; nephew of BF), genealogy, lx

Davenport, Mary (b. 1725/6). *See* Rogers, Mary Davenport

Davenport, Sarah Barton Zantzinger (m. 1804), genealogy, lxi

Davenport, Sarah Billings (d. 1751), genealogy, lx

Davenport, Sarah Franklin (1699–1731; sister of BF): genealogy, lvi, lx; letter to, 171; death of, 200 n.

Davis, William, buys land, 362

Dawes, Rebecca (m. 1740). *See* Homes, Rebecca Dawes

Debts, second husband responsible for wife's, 376 and n.

Defoe, Daniel: quoted, 20, 32–6; writes biography of Duncan Campbell, 128 n.

Denham, Thomas: biographical note, 73 n.; BF's traveling companion, 73

D'Evelin, Ellen Johnson, genealogy, lxiii

D'Evelin, Mary (d. 1811). *See* Franklin, Mary D'Evelin

Dickinson, John, house of, burned, 186

Dieffebach, Jacob, signs Palatine appeal, 229

Dilly, Charles, publishes BF's writings, xxv

Dissertation on Liberty and Necessity, 57–71

"Doctrine to be Preached," 212–13

Dodington, George Bubb, James Ralph in service of, 58 n.

Dogood, Silence. *See* Silence Dogood papers

Dolphins, observed by BF, 87, 88, 96

Douglass, William, and *New-England Courant,* 8

Douse, Elizabeth Franklin Berry (1678–1759; half-sister of BF): genealogy, lvi, lvii; mentioned, 171; marriage, 171 n.; BF inquires for, 201 and n.

Douse, Richard (m. 1721): genealogy, lvii; marriage, 171 n.

Downes, Elizabeth (d. 1777). *See* Franklin, Elizabeth Downes

Drunkenness, synonyms for, 40–1

Dryden, John, quoted, 58

Duane, Benjamin Franklin (1827–93), genealogy, lxv

Duane, Catherine (1814–36), genealogy, lxiv

Duane, Deborah Bache (1781–1863; granddaughter of BF), genealogy, lxiv

Duane, Elizabeth (1821–1901). *See* Gillespie, Elizabeth Duane

Duane, Ellen (1816–46). *See* Satterthwaite, Ellen Duane

Duane, Franklin Bache (1819–20), genealogy, lxv

Duane, Mary (1812–45). *See* Williams, Mary Duane

Duane, Richard Bache (1823–75), genealogy, lxv

Duane, Sarah Franklin (1810–50), genealogy, lxiv
Duane, Sophia Burrell Dallas (1785–1860), genealogy, lxv
Duane, William (1760–1835): genealogy, lxiii, lxiv; edits BF papers, xxv, xxvi; incorrectly attributes essays to BF, 170; mistakenly dates letter, 200 n.; editing of Junto queries, 255 n., 256
Duane, William (1808–82), genealogy, lxiv
Duane, William John (1780–1865), genealogy, lxiv
Dubourg, Barbeu, edits BF's writings, xxv
Dudley, Joseph: biographical note, 78 n.; attack on, 31 n.

Eclipse, lunar, observed by BF, 94–5
Eddy, Hannah Franklin (1683–1723). See Cole, Hannah Franklin Eddy
Eddy, Joseph, genealogy, lvii
Education of women, BF on, 254–5
Egee, Esther (b. 1801). See Bache, Esther Egee
Elegies, satirized, 23–6
"Elegy on My Sister Franklin," authorship of, 46–7
Elegy upon the much Lamented Death of Mrs. Mehitebell Kitel..., quoted, 24, 25
Emerson, John, signs Masonic by-laws, 233 and n.
Emmery, John, Pa. Gaz. advertises for whereabouts, 218
Emory, Matilda Wilkins Bache (b. 1819), genealogy, lxv
Epitaph of BF, composed by himself, 109–11
Extravagance, essays on, 237–40, 240–3
Eyre, John, and New-England Courant, 8

Fabian, Lewis, genealogy, lx
Fabian, Sarah Ingersoll, genealogy, lx
Fairs: petition regarding, 211–12; prohibited during epidemic, 215
Farrow, Ann Franklin (c. 1686–1771), genealogy, lii
Farrow, Hannah (b. 1724). See Walker, Hannah Farrow
Farrow, Henry (d. before 1759), genealogy, lii
Faÿ, Bernard, on Liberty and Necessity, 57 n.
Fénelon, Archbishop, book of, mentioned, 105 and n.
Fielding, Henry, James Ralph collaborates with, 58 n.

Fires, news reports of, 168, 186, 272, 377, 378
Fishbourn, William, trustee of Loan Office, 216
Fisher, Eleanor (d. c. 1728), genealogy, li
Fisher, J. Francis, quoted, xxix
Fisher, Mary Franklin (1673–1758; first cousin of BF), genealogy, li
Fisher, Richard (d. 1758), genealogy, li
Five Nations. See Iroquois
Flagg, Dolly Thurston (m. 1789), genealogy, lxii
Flagg, Jane (c. 1757–82). See Greene, Jane Flagg
Flagg, Josiah (1760–1840), genealogy, lxi
Flagg, Sarah Mecom (1737–64; niece of BF), genealogy, lxi
Flagg, William (d. 1775), married, lxi
Fleet, Thomas, surety for James Franklin, 48
Folger, Abiah (1667–1752). See Franklin, Abiah Folger
Folger, Abiah Coleman (m. 1753), genealogy, liv
Folger, Abigail (m. 1721). See Pinkham, Abigail Folger
Folger, Abigail (1703–87). See Pinkham, Abigail Folger Folger
Folger, Abigail Coffin (d. 1770), genealogy, lvi
Folger, Abisha (1700–88), genealogy, liv
Folger, Bathsheba (m. c. 1676). See Pope, Bathsheba Folger
Folger, Bethia (d. 1669). See Barnard, Bethia Folger
Folger, Bethia Gardner (1676–1716), genealogy, liv
Folger, Daniel (1701/2–44), genealogy, liv, lvi
Folger, Deborah Paddock Bunker (d. 1750), genealogy, lv
Folger, Dinah Coffin Starbuck (d. 1793), genealogy, liv
Folger, Dorcas (m. 1674/5). See Pratt, Dorcas Folger
Folger, Eleazer (1648–1716; uncle of BF), genealogy, liii, liv
Folger, Eleazer, Jr. (1672–1753), genealogy, liv
Folger, Experience (c. 1661–1739). See Swain, Experience Folger
Folger, Jerusha Clark (d. 1778), genealogy, lv
Folger, Jethro (1689–1772), genealogy, lv
Folger, Joanna (c. 1643–1719). See Coleman, Joanna Folger
Folger, Jonathan (1696–1777), genealogy, lv

Folger, John (1659–1732; uncle of BF), genealogy, liii, liv, lv
Folger, John (b. *c.* 1714), genealogy, lv
Folger, John (*c.* 1745–1780), genealogy, lv
Folger, Judith Coffin (m. Peter Folger, first cousin of BF), genealogy, liv
Folger, Keziah (1723–98). *See* Coffin, Keziah Folger
Folger, Margaret Gardner (d. 1727), genealogy, lv
Folger, Mary Barnard (*c.* 1667–1737), genealogy, lv
Folger, Mary Marshall (d. 1765), genealogy, liv
Folger, Mary Morrils (Morrill) (d. 1704), genealogy, liii
Folger, Mary Starbuck (d. 1763), genealogy, lv
Folger, Nathan (1678–1747), genealogy, liv
Folger, Nathaniel (1694/5–1774), genealogy, lv
Folger, Patience (d. 1717). *See* Harker, Patience Folger
Folger (Foulger), Peter (1617–90; grandfather of BF), genealogy, liii, lvi
Folger, Peter (1674–1707), genealogy, liv
Folger, Priscilla Chase (d. 1753), genealogy, lv
Folger, Rebecca Baker (d. 1746), genealogy, lv
Folger, Richard (1698–1782), genealogy, lv
Folger, Sarah Church (d. 1745), genealogy, liv
Folger, Sarah Gardner (m. 1671), genealogy, liv
Folger, Sarah Mahew (d. 1734), genealogy, liv
Folger, Sarah Pease (d. 1783), genealogy, lv
Folger, Shubael (1700–76), genealogy, lv
Folger, Susan Goreham Paddock (d. 1777), genealogy, lv
Folger, Timothy (1732–1814), genealogy, liv
Folger, Zaccheus (1706–79), genealogy, lvi
Ford, Paul Leicester, BF bibliographer, xxvii
Ford, Worthington C.: compiler of list of BF papers, xxvii; on identification of ballad, 6 and n.
Fothergill, John, and BF's experiments, xxv
Foulger, Peter. *See* Folger, Peter
Foulgier, John (*c.* 1593–1660), genealogy, liii
Foulgier, Meribah (Merible) Gibbs (d. *c.* 1664), genealogy, liii
Fox, Charles Pemberton, and BF papers, xxii

Fox, George, and BF papers, xxi
Fraeme, Thomas, and wife, land at Chester, 381
Francklyne, Thomas (fl. 1563–73), genealogy, l
Franklin, Abiah (*c.* 1726–54). *See* Buckmaster, Abiah Franklin
Franklin, Abiah Folger (1667–1752; mother of BF): genealogy, liii, lvi; BF's birth and baptism, 3
Franklin, Ann (*c.* 1686–1771). *See* Farrow, Ann Franklin
Franklin, Ann (*c.* 1728–30; niece of BF), genealogy, lix
Franklin, Ann(e) (1687–1729). *See* Harris, Ann(e) Franklin
Franklin, Ann(e) Child (d. 1689), genealogy, lvi
Franklin, Ann Jeffs (married John Franklin, BF's uncle), genealogy, li
Franklin, Ann Smith (d. 1763), genealogy, lix
Franklin, Benjamin, the Elder (1650–1727; uncle of BF): genealogy, li, lii; verses of, 3–6
Franklin, Benjamin: chronology of life through 1734, lxxxvii–lxxxviii; birth, 3; baptism, 3; contributions to the *New-England Courant*, 8–53; publishes *Courant*, 27, 48; *Courant* essays possibly by, 53; leaves Boston for Philadelphia (1723), 48, 53 and n.; visits Boston (1724), 53 n., (1733), 346 n.; asbestos purse to Sloane, 54 and n.; goes to London (1724), 58 n., (1757), 59 n.; friendship with James Ralph, 58–9 n.; shipboard journal, London to Philadelphia, 72–99; experiments with seaweed and shellfish, 93–4; religious beliefs and ritual of worship, 101–9; quarrels with Keimer, 111–39; decides to start newspaper, 113–14; with Meredith, buys the *Pa. Gaz.*, 114, 157; forms printing firm with Meredith, 140; and Keimer, printer's errors, 169 n.; enters into partnership with Timothée, 205 n., 230 n., 339; becomes partner of Whitmarsh, 205–8; plans and establishes the Lib. Co., 208–10; religious doctrine, 213; falls into tar barrel, 219; issues German newspaper, 230–1, 233–4; composes letter to Collinson, sent by Breintnall, 248–9; replies to a complaining reader of the *Pa. Gaz.*, 249–50; signs Lib. Co. agreement, 252, 322, 359, 361; on education of women, 254–5; compiles first *Poor Richard*, 280–1; helps draft address to Thomas Penn, 320; waits on Penn, 321 n.; makes prints of leaves, etc.,

344 n.; real estate documents, 362–70; active in Masonry, 373 n.; writes note of admission for J. Mifflin to the Lib. Co., 373; elected Masonic Grand Master, 379

Franklin, Deborah Read Rogers (1708–74; wife of BF): genealogy, lxii; entries of, in BF's ledgers, 172; mentioned, 211; power of attorney to, 331–2; real estate documents, 362–70

Franklin, Ebenezer (1701–03; brother of BF), genealogy, lvi

Franklin, Eleanor or Helen (d. 1711), genealogy, li

Franklin, Elizabeth (second wife of BF's grandfather), genealogy, l

Franklin, Elizabeth (1678–1759). See Douse, Elizabeth Franklin Berry

Franklin, Elizabeth (b. 1694), genealogy, liii

Franklin, Elizabeth (d. 1773). See Compton, Elizabeth Franklin

Franklin, Elizabeth (m. 1761). See All, Elizabeth Franklin

Franklin, Elizabeth Downes (d. 1777), genealogy, lxii

Franklin, Elizabeth Gooch Hubbart (Hubbard), genealogy, lviii

Franklin, Elizabeth Tyng (m. 1705), genealogy, lvii

Franklin, Ellen (b. 1798). See Hanbury, Ellen Franklin

Franklin, Eunice Greenleaf (m. 1756), genealogy, lii

Franklin, Francis Folger (1732–36; son of BF), genealogy, lxii, lxiii

Franklin, Hannah (1654–1712). See Morris, Hannah Franklin

Franklin, Hannah (1683–1723). See Cole, Hannah Franklin Eddy

Franklin, Hannah (Anna) Collyer (d. 1846), genealogy, lxii

Franklin, Hannah Kellineck (m. 1719), genealogy, lii

Franklin, Hannah Welles (d. 1705), genealogy, lii

Franklin, Helen (d. 1711). See Franklin, Eleanor

Franklin, James (1696/7–1735; brother of BF): genealogy, lvi, lix; and New-England Courant, 8, 11 n., 48; and Dogood papers, 9; imprisoned, 27, 47, 52; pseudonym of, 240 n.; printer of Poor Robin's Almanack, 281; BF visits, 346 n.

Franklin, James, Jr. (c. 1730–1732; nephew of BF), genealogy, lix

Franklin, Jane (d. c. 1757; cousin of BF). See Page, Jane Franklin

Franklin, Jane (1712–94; sister of BF). See Mecom, Jane Franklin

Franklin, Jane White (1617–62), genealogy, l

Franklin, John (1643–91; uncle of BF), genealogy, li, lvi

Franklin, John (1690–1756; brother of BF): biographical note, 171 n.; genealogy, lvi, lviii, lxii; mentioned, 170

Franklin, John (b. 1716; nephew of BF), genealogy, lviii

Franklin, Joseph (1646–83; uncle of BF), genealogy, li, lii

Franklin, Joseph, I (b. 1688, d. 1688; half-brother of BF), genealogy, lvi

Franklin, Joseph, II (b. 1689, d. 1689; half-brother of BF), genealogy, lvi

Franklin, Josiah (1657–1745; father of BF): genealogy, li, liii, lvi; BF's birth and baptism, 3; house of, 11 n.; rejects Keith's offer to help BF, 53 n.; makes soap, 348 n.

Franklin, Josiah (1685–c. 1715; half-brother of BF), genealogy, lvi, lvii

Franklin, Lydia (1708–58). See Scott, Lydia Franklin

Franklin, Mary (1673–1758; cousin of BF). See Fisher, Mary Franklin

Franklin, Mary (1694–1731; sister of BF). See Homes, Mary Franklin

Franklin, Mary (m. 1752; niece of BF). See Allen, Mary Franklin

Franklin, Mary D'Evelin (d. 1811), genealogy, lxii

Franklin, Mary Gooch, genealogy, lviii

Franklin, Mary Harman (m. 1714), genealogy, lix

Franklin, Peter (1692–1766; brother of BF): biographical note, 171 n.; genealogy, lvi, lix; mentioned, 171

Franklin, Samuel (1641–64; uncle of BF), genealogy, li

Franklin, Samuel (1681–1720; half-brother of BF), genealogy, lvi, lvii

Franklin, Samuel (b. 1684; cousin of BF; genealogy, lii; father lives with, 3–4

Franklin, Samuel, Jr. (1721–75), genealogy, lii

Franklin, Sarah (daughter of Peter and Mary), genealogy, lix

Franklin, Sarah (1699–1731; sister of BF). See Davenport, Sarah Franklin

Franklin, Sarah(?) (m. 1740; niece of BF). See Hall, Sarah(?) Franklin

Franklin, Sarah (1743–1808; daughter of BF). See Bache, Sarah Franklin

Franklin, Sarah (c. 1753–1781). See Pearce, Sarah Franklin

Franklin, Sarah Beaudri (m. 1748), genealogy, lii
Franklin, Sarah Sawyer, genealogy, lii
Franklin, Thomas (1598–1682; grandfather of BF), genealogy, l
Franklin, Thomas (1637–1702; uncle of BF), genealogy, li
Franklin, Thomas (1683–c. 1752; cousin of BF), genealogy, li
Franklin, Thomas (1703–06; brother of BF), genealogy, lvi
Franklin, Thomas (living in 1791), genealogy, li
Franklin, William (c. 1731–1813; son of BF), genealogy, lxii
Franklin, William Temple (1762–1823; grandson of BF): genealogy, lxii; and BF papers, xxi, xxii, xxv, 72; and date of BF's epitaph, 110; editing of Junto queries, 255 n., 256
Franklyn, Agnes Joanes (or James) (d. 1646), genealogy, l
Franklyn, Henry (1573–1631), genealogy, l
Frederick, Prince of Wales, James Ralph in service of, 58 n.
Freedom of speech, defended, 27–30
Freeman, Isaac, friend of Franklin family, 100 n.
Fuller, Anne Harris (b. 1714; niece of BF), genealogy, lvii
Fuller, Anne Walker (m. 1817), genealogy, lvii
Fuller, Jacob (m. 1734), genealogy, lvii
Fuller, Joseph (1746–1822), genealogy, lvii
Fuller, Thomas, *Gnomologia, Introductio ad Prudentiam*, and *Introductio ad Sapientiam*, BF's use of, 281, 282

Galloway, Joseph, BF papers at house of, xxi, 210
Gardner, Mr., and *New-England Courant*, 8
Gardner, Bethia (1676–1716). See Folger, Bethia Gardner
Gardner, Margaret (d. 1727). See Folger, Margaret Gardner
Gardner, Sarah (m. 1671). See Folger, Sarah Gardner
Gee, Joshua: biographical note, 214 n.; cited, 214
General Advertiser (Philadelphia), Benjamin Franklin Bache, publisher of, lxiii
Gibbs, Meribah (Merible) (d. c. 1664). See Foulgier, Meribah Gibbs
Gibson, Sir John: biographical note, 74 n.; severity of, as commander, 74
Gillespie, Elizabeth Duane (1821–1901), genealogy, lxv

God, BF writes on providence of, 264–9
Godfrey, Thomas: biographical note, 190 n.; mentioned, 191 and n.; director of Lib. Co., 209; signs Lib. Co. agreement, 252, 322, 360, 361; compiler of almanacs, 280, *see also Pennsylvania Almanacks;* communication to the *Pa. Gaz.*, 371–2; approves new member for Lib. Co., 373
Gohr, Johannes, signs Palatine appeal, 229
Gooch, Elizabeth. See Franklin, Elizabeth Gooch Hubbart
Gooch, Mary. See Franklin, Mary Gooch
Gordon, Isabella Clarke, death, 380 and n.
Gordon, Patrick: favors paper currency, 140; death of wife, 380 n.
Gordon, Thomas, quoted, 31–2
Goreham, Susan (d. 1777). See Folger, Susan Goreham Paddock
Grace, Robert: biographical note, 209 n.; director of Lib. Co., 209; signs Lib. Co. agreement, 252, 322
Grand Lodge of Mass., BF writes to, 373–5
Gravesend, BF visits, 72
Greene, Catharine Ray, genealogy, lix
Greene, Elihu (m. 1775), genealogy, lxi
Greene, Jane Flagg (c. 1757–1782), genealogy, lxi
Greene, Nathaniel, genealogy, lxi
Greene, William, genealogy, lxi
Greenleaf, Eunice (m. 1756). See Franklin, Eunice Greenleaf
Grew, Theophilus, offers instruction in many fields, 379–80
Griffith, Abiah Davenport (b. 1729; niece of BF), genealogy, lxi
Griffith, John (m. 1751), genealogy, lxi
Growdon, J., smallpox patient, 214
Guardian, quoted, 45

Hale, Edward Everett, on BF ballad, 7
"Half-hour's Conversation with a Friend," 333–8
Hall, Samuel (1740–1807), genealogy, lix
Hall, Sarah(?) Franklin (m. 1740; niece of BF), genealogy, lix
Hamilton, Andrew: entry for, in BF account book, 172; acts as magistrate, 278; defense of, by BF, 333–8; accusation against, 343; marriage of dau., 376
Hamilton, James, appointed Masonic officer, 379
Hamilton, Margaret, marriage, 376
Hanbury, Capel (m. 1818), genealogy, lxiii
Hanbury, Ellen Franklin (b. 1798), genealogy, lxiii
Harker, Ebenezer, genealogy, lv
Harker, Patience Folger (d. 1717; aunt of BF), genealogy, liii, lv

Harman, Mary (m. 1714). *See* Franklin, Mary Harman

Harris, Anne (b. 1714). *See* Fuller, Anne Harris

Harris, Ann(e) Franklin (1687–1729; half-sister of BF), genealogy, lvi, lvii

Harris, Grace (1718–90). *See* Williams, Grace Harris

Harris, Martha (b. 1729). *See* Johnson, Martha Harris

Harris, William (m. 1712), genealogy, lvii

Harry, David: buys Keimer's printing-office, 113 n.; declines to buy Keimer's paper, 157; offers Leeds' almanac for sale, 165, 166 n.

Hart, Thomas: signs Masonic by-laws, 233 and n.; appointed Masonic officer, 345

Harvard College, satirized, 14–18

Harwood, Andrew Allen (1802–84), genealogy, lxiv

Harwood, Benjamin Franklin (1801–02), genealogy, lxiv

Harwood, Elizabeth (great-granddaughter of BF), genealogy, lxiv

Harwood, Elizabeth Franklin Bache (1777–1820; granddaughter of BF), genealogy, lxiv

Harwood, John Edmund (1770–1809), genealogy, lxiv

Harwood, Joseph, widow of, 346

Harwood, Mary (1806–15), genealogy, lxiv

Hayes, Henry, granted land, 362

Hays, I. Minis, comp. calendar of BF papers, xxvii

Hayward, George, on BF ballad, 7

Herder, Johann Gottfried, translates Junto queries, 259 n.

Heurtin(?), Mr., entry for, in BF account book, 174

Hill, James, imposter, 276

Historical Society of Pennsylvania, BF papers in, xxii

Hobart, John, signs Masonic by-laws, 233 and n.

Hodge, Sarah Bache (1798–1849), genealogy, lxiv

Holmes, Sir Robert: biographical note, 79 n.; mentioned, 79

Holyoke, Edward, elegy by, 26 n.

Homans, Capt., mentioned, 82

Homes, Abiah (1718–29; niece of BF), genealogy, lix

Homes, Elizabeth Whitwell (m. 1764), genealogy, lix

Homes (Holmes), Mary Franklin (1694–1731; sister of BF): genealogy, lvi, lix; mentioned, 171; marriage, 171 n.; death of, 201 n.

Homes, Rebecca Dawes (m. 1740), genealogy, lix

Homes (Holmes), Robert (m. 1716): biographical note, 171 n.; genealogy, lix

Homes, Robert (b. 1720; nephew of BF), genealogy, lix

Homes, William (1716/17–1785; nephew of BF), genealogy, lix

Homes, William, Jr. (b. 1742), genealogy, lix

Honor, titles of. *See* "Titles of Honor"

Hopkinson, Thomas: biographical note, 209 n.; director of Lib. Co., 209; helps draft address to Thomas Penn, 320; waits on Penn, 321 n.; signs Lib. Co. agreement, 322, 360, 361; witnesses real estate documents, 365, 367, 370; approves new member for Lib. Co., 373; appointed Masonic officer, 379

Howell, James, *Lexicon Tetraglotton*, BF's use of, 281, 282

Hubbart, Elizabeth (1728–1814). *See* Partridge, Elizabeth Hubbart

Hubbart, Elizabeth Gooch. *See* Franklin, Elizabeth Gooch Hubbart

Hubbart (Hubbard), John, genealogy, lviii

Hubbart, Judith Ray (m. 1747), genealogy, lix

Hubbart, Thomas (1717–96), genealogy, lix

Hubbart, Tuthill (1720–c. 1808), genealogy, lix

Hypocrisy, satirized, 30–2

Ill-natured speaking, paper on, 327

Indians. *See* Iroquois

Ingenhousz, Jan, quotes "old proverb," 359 n.

Ingersoll, Elizabeth. *See* Jarvis, Elizabeth Ingersoll

Ingersoll, Elizabeth Davenport (b. 1723; niece of BF), genealogy, lx

Ingersoll, Joseph (d. c. 1789), genealogy, lx

Ingersoll, Sarah. *See* Fabian, Sarah Ingersoll

Inoculation controversy in Boston, Mathers vs. *Courant* on, 8

Ireland, BF reports on condition of, 162

Irish, immigration to the colonies, 162 n.

Iroquois, treaty with, 277

Irwin, Sophia Arabella Bache (1816–1904), genealogy, lxv

Isle of Wight, BF visits, 75–81

Jarvis, Elizabeth Ingersoll, genealogy, lx

Jeffs, Ann. *See* Franklin, Ann Jeffs

Jerman, John, comp. *American Almanacks*, 280, 281
Joanes (or James), Agnes (d. 1646). *See* Franklyn, Agnes Joanes
Johnson, Anne (d. 1805). *See* Clarke, Anne Johnson
Johnson, Martha Harris (b. 1729; niece of BF), genealogy, lviii
Johnson, Samuel (1696–1772; Conn. clergyman), ordination, 43 n.
Johnson, Samuel (d. *c.* 1783; grand-nephew of BF), genealogy, lviii
Jones, Evan, Thomas Cadwalader apprenticed to, 209 n.
Jones, John, Jr.: director of Lib. Co., 209, 210 n.; signs Lib. Co. agreement, 252, 322, 360, 361; witnesses real estate documents, 365, 367, 370; approves new member for Lib. Co., 373
"Journal of occurrences in my voyage to Philadelphia," 72–99
Junto: BF essay ("Good and Evil") for, 103 n.; discusses currency question, 140; essays in *Pa. Gaz.* by members of, 164; Meredith an original member, 175 n.; Scull's rhymed description of meeting, 177 n.; Godfrey an original member, 190 n.; assists in formation of the Lib. Co., 208; formation of, 255; standing queries for, 255–9; proposals and queries to be asked, 259–64; BF essay, "Providence of God," written for, 264–9; paper in response to query put to, 328 n.; Parsons original member, 359 n.

Kearsley, Dr., mentioned in *Pa. Gaz.*, 220
Keimer, Samuel: biographical note, 113 n.; BF quarrels with, 111–39; use of Chambers' *Cyclopaedia*, 111, 157 and n.; satirized by BF, 121 n.; replies to Busy-Body, 133–4 n.; sells his newspaper to BF and Meredith, 157; mentioned, 165; prints Leeds' almanac, 166 n., 167; mentioned, 169 n.; Meredith apprentice of, 175 n.; printer of almanacs, 280
Keith, Sir William: offers to obtain public printing for BF, 53 n.; organizes political clubs, 126 n.
Kellineck, Hannah (m. 1719). *See* Franklin, Hannah Kellineck
Kelsey, William, speech by, before execution, 185 and n.
Kinsman, Jane Mecom (b. *c.* 1765), genealogy, lxi
Kinsman, Simeon (m. 1800), genealogy, lxi
Kipping, Walter: master of the *Yorker*, 83, 84; loses ship, 83 n.

Kittle, John, wife of, subject of elegy, 24 n.
Kittle, Mehitabel Browne, subject of elegy, 24 n.
Kuntz, Jacob, signs Palatine appeal, 229

La Rochefoucauld, François, duc de, cited, 117 and n.
Lay, Benjamin, entry for, in BF account book, 189 n.
Ledgers of BF. *See* Account books
Leeds, Felix, almanac of, 166 n., 167, 168
Leeds, Titan: almanac of, 165, 166 and n., 167–8, 190 and n.; death of, predicted, 280, 281, 343, 347, 350–1; death of, "proven," 382
Leeds' Almanacks, mathematical questions in, 190 and n.
Lettsom, John Coakley, dates BF's epitaph, 110
Lewis, Edward, witnesses document, 332
Liberty and Necessity. See Dissertation on Liberty and Necessity
Library Company of Philadelphia: formed and called to meeting, 208–10; notice of meeting, 229–30, 271, 344 and n., 377–8; agreement between Timothée and, 250–2; address to Thomas Penn, with reply, 320–1; agreement of directors, 321–2; agreement between Parsons and, 359–61
Library of Congress, BF papers in, xxiii
"Lighthouse Tragedy," lost ballad, 6
Lightning, news reports of houses struck by, 216, 272, 275
Linen, manufacture encouraged, 215
Liquor, abuse of, 39–41
Literary style, essay on, 328–31
Livingston, Luther S., BF MS owned by, 46 n.
Lobb, Jacob, Capt., charged with abusing Palatines, 226 n., 229 n.
Locke, John, works studied by BF, 58
Logan, James: biographical note, 191 n.; letter from, 191–2; mentioned, 200 n.; given Lib. Co. privileges, 251 and n.
London Journal: reprint from, 27–30; on hypocrisy, 31 and n.
London Post, Keimer publisher of, 113 n.
Love and Unity (ship), Palatines passengers on, 226 n.
Lyons, author of *The Infallibility of Human Judgment*, not an answer to BF's *Liberty and Necessity*, 57 n.

Mahew, Sarah (d. 1734). *See* Folger, Sarah Mahew
Mandeville, Bernard, BF introduced to, 57 n.

Manuel, David, essay by, 185 n.

Markoe, Margaret Hartman (1770–1836). *See* Bache, Margaret Hartman Markoe

Marshall, Mary (d. 1765). *See* Folger, Mary Marshall

Martha Careful and Caelia Shortface, papers, 111–13

Masons: BF initiated, lxxxviii, 204 n.; BF's lodge accounts, 202–4; by-laws for lodge, 231; elections in lodge, 274–5, 345; BF writes Grand Lodge of Mass., 373–5; BF elected Grand Master, 379

Massachusetts, dispute between governors and Assembly, 159–61, 176–7

Mather, Cotton, *Essays to Do Good*, influence on BF, 255

Mather, Samuel, replies to Dogood satire of Harvard, 18 n.

Mather family, controversy with, 8

Maugridge, William: witness of BF agreement with Whitmarsh, 208; party to Lib. Co. agreement, 251

McLane, Marie Bache, genealogy, lxv

McMaster, John Bach, attributes piece on witch trial to BF, 182

Meakins (Makin), Thomas, drowned, 348–9

Mecom, Abiah (1751–52; niece of BF), genealogy, lxii

Mecom, Benjamin (1732–c. 1776; nephew of BF), genealogy, lxi

Mecom, Catherine Ouke (Oakey) (m. 1765), genealogy, lxii

Mecom, Ebenezer (1735–62; nephew of BF), genealogy, lxi

Mecom, Edward (1704–65), genealogy, lxi

Mecom, Edward (1731–58; nephew of BF): genealogy, lxi; birth of, 200 n.

Mecom, Elizabeth Ross (m. c. 1757), genealogy, lxi

Mecom, James (b. 1746, d. 1746; nephew of BF), genealogy, lxii

Mecom, Jane (1745–1802). *See* Collas, Jane Mecom

Mecom, Jane (b. c. 1765). *See* Kinsman, Jane Mecom

Mecom, Jane Franklin (1712–94; sister of BF): genealogy, lvii, lix, lx, lxi; tells of prediction, 6 n.; letters to, 100–1, 200–1; BF's favorite sister, 100 n.; and BF epitaph, 110; death of first child, 171 and n.; makes soap, 348 n.

Mecom, John (1741–70; nephew of BF), genealogy, lxii

Mecom, Josiah, I (1729–30; nephew of BF): genealogy, lxi; death of, 171 n.

Mecom, Josiah, II (1743–74; nephew of BF), genealogy, lxii

Mecom, Mary (Polly) (1748–67; niece of BF), genealogy, lxii

Mecom, Peter Franklin (b. 1739; nephew of BF), genealogy, lxii

Mecom, Ruth Whittemore (m. 1755), genealogy, lxi

Mecom, Sarah (1737–64). *See* Flagg, Sarah Mecom

"Meditation on a Quart Mugg" attributed to BF, 328

Memoirs. *See* Autobiography

Mennes, Sir John, and James Smith, *Wits Recreations*, BF's use of, 282

Meredith, Hugh: biographical note, 175 n.; decides to start newspaper with BF, 113; with BF, buys Keimer's newspaper, 114, 157; quarrel with Keimer, 139 n.; and Franklin, printing firm, 140, 280; dissolution of partnership with BF, 175; writes account of North Carolina, 216 n.

Meredith, Simon (father of Hugh), sets son up in business with BF, 175 n.

Mifflin, John: biographical note, 373 n.; admitted to Lib. Co., 373 and n.

Mifflin, Thomas, mentioned, 373 n.

Milton, *Paradise Lost*, quoted, 106–7

Misprints. *See* Printer's errors

Modest Enquiry into the Nature and Necessity of a Paper-Currency, 139–57

Molyneux, Thomas, quoted, 253 and n.

Moore, John, entry for, in BF account book, 172

Morgan, Joseph, paper by, 191 n.

Morrils (Morrill), Mary (d. 1704). *See* Folger, Mary Morrils

Morris, Eleanor (first cousin of BF), genealogy, liii

Morris, Hannah (first cousin of BF), genealogy, liii

Morris, Hannah Franklin (1654–1712; aunt of BF), genealogy, li, liii

Morris, Jane (first cousin of BF), genealogy, liii

Morris, John (d. 1695), genealogy, liii

Mottraye, Aubrey de la, calls on Breintnall, 344 n.

Mount Holly, witch trial. *See* Witch trial at Mount Holly

Mugridge, Donald H., on BF ballad, 6 n.

Murray, Humphrey, elected Masonic Grand Master, 345

National Archives, BF papers in, xxiii

Nature and Necessity of a Paper-Currency. *See* *Modest Enquiry into the Nature and Necessity of a Paper-Currency*

New-England Courant: account of, 8, 9; publication ordered suspended, 47; published by BF, 48
Newport, Isle of Wight, BF visits, 75–6, 81
Newport, Rhode Island, BF visits brother in, 346 n.
News-Letter (Boston), on Capt. Teach, 7
Newton, Sir Isaac, mentioned, 54 n., 57 n.
Nicholas (Nichols), Anthony: biographical note, 210 n.; entry for, in BF account book, 174; director of Lib. Co., 209; signs Lib. Co. agreement, 252; party to Lib. Co. agreement, 360
Nicholas, John, signs Lib. Co. agreement, 252
Nicholas, Samuel, signs Masonic by-laws, 233 and n.
Nichols, Anthony. *See* Nicholas, Anthony
Nicole, Pierre. *See* Arnauld, Antoine
Night-walkers, essay on, 41–2
Noël de la Morinière, S. B. J., quotes BF on value of fish, 138 n.
Norris, Isaac: mentioned, 200 n.; death of son, 346
Norris, Joseph, death, 346

Oakey (Ouke), Catherine (m. 1765). *See* Mecom, Catherine Ouke
"Observations on my Reading History in Library," 192–3
Ormston, Rev., dies, 220–1
Ouke (Oakey), Catherine (m. 1765). *See* Mecom, Catherine Ouke
Ovid, quoted, 48
Ozell, John, trans. *Logic, or, the Art of Thinking,* studied by BF, 58

Paddock, Deborah (d. 1750). *See* Folger, Deborah Paddock Bunker
Paddock, Susan Goreham (d. 1777). *See* Folger, Susan Goreham Paddock
Page, Jane Franklin (d. c. 1757), genealogy, lii
Page, Robert, genealogy, lii
Palatine immigrants, mistreatment of, 226–9
Palmer, Charles, *A Collection of Select Aphorisms and Maxims,* BF's use of, 282
Palmer, Samuel, BF in printing house of, 57
Paper currency, issue of, 140–1, 322–4. See also *Modest Enquiry into the Nature and Necessity of a Paper-Currency*
Parry, David, signs Masonic by-laws, 233 and n.

Parsons, William: biographical note, 359 n.; director of Lib. Co., 209; engaged as librarian, 250 n.; party to Lib. Co. agreement, 251; signs Lib. Co. agreement, 322; agreement between Lib. Co. and, 359–61
Parton, James, on Dogood papers, 8
Partridge, Elizabeth Hubbart (1728–1814), genealogy, lix
Partridge, Samuel (m. 1768), genealogy, lix
Passerat, Jean, quoted, 325–6
Pearce, James (m. 1773), genealogy, lii
Pearce, Sarah Franklin (c. 1753–81), genealogy, lii
Pease, Sarah (d. 1783). *See* Folger, Sarah Pease
Pemberton, Henry, BF introduced to, 57 n.
Penington, Isaac: biographical note, 210 n.; director of Lib. Co., 209
Penn, John, lands at Chester, 381
Penn, Thomas: address of Lib. Co. to, 320–1; BF account with, 371; greets John, arriving at Chester, 381
Penn, William: *No Cross, no Crown,* BF parodies, 51–2; James Logan secretary of, 191 n.; grant of land from, 362
Pennsylvania Almanacks: advertised, 188, 190–1; issued by BF, 280
Pennsylvania Gazette: BF and Meredith buy, 157; statement of editorial policy, 157–9, 161; extracts from (1729), 164–8, (1730), 184–9, (1731), 213–21, (1732), 271–80, (1733), 342–9, (1734), 376–83
Perry, Frances Sergeant (1817–1903), genealogy, lxv
Peter, Hugh, Mary Morrils bond servant of, liii
Petition to the Pennsylvania Assembly regarding fairs, 211–12
Petticoats, satirized, 22–3
Petty, Sir William, cited, 35; *Treatise of Taxes and Contributions,* BF's use of, 140–1, 149 n., 153 n.
Philadelphische Zeitung, 230–1, 233–4, 274
Phillips, John, BF's promissory note to, 53 and n.
Philocles and Horatio, dialogue between, erroneously attributed to BF, 170
Pinkham, Abigail Folger (m. 1721), genealogy, liv
Pinkham, Abigail Folger Folger (1703–87), genealogy, lv
Pinkham, Daniel (m. 1748), genealogy, lvi
"Plan of Conduct," 99–100
Plum cake, at Harvard commencements, 16 n.
Pocock, Thomas, mentioned, 79 n.

Poor Richard's Almanacks: in relation to other almanacs, 166 n.; anecdote of misprint told in, 169 n.; advertised, 280, 343, 347, 382; circumstances attending first issue, 280–1; contents, 281; sales devices, 281; sources for material, 281–2; extant copies, 283; summary of contents of first issue, 283; facsimile pages, 287–310; extracts (1733), 311–18, (1734), 349–59

Poor Robin's Almanacks, issued by James Franklin, 281

Pope, Bathsheba (dau. of Bathsheba Folger Pope), lv

Pope, Bathsheba (Bethshua) Folger (m. *c.* 1676; aunt of BF), genealogy, liii, lv

Pope, Joseph (d. 1712), genealogy, lv

Portsmouth, England, BF visits, 73–4

Potts, Stephen, witnesses document, 332

Pratt, Dorcas Folger (m. 1674/5; aunt of BF), genealogy, liii, liv

Pratt, Henry: signs Masonic by-laws, 233 and n.; party to Lib. Co. agreement, 251; signs Lib. Co. agreement, 322, 360, 361

Pratt, Joseph (d. 1712), genealogy, liv

Prayer, of BF, 104

Price, Henry: biographical note, 374 n.; prominent Mason, 374; BF writes, 375–6

Pride, satirized, 20–2

Pringle, William: signs Masonic by-laws, 233 and n.; appointed Masonic officer, 275

"Printer to the Reader" (1723), 47–50; (Oct. 2, 1729), 157–9; (Oct. 23, 1729), 161

Printer's errors, BF on, 169–70

Printers, BF's apology for, 194–9

Printing account with Thomas Penn, 371

Proprietors of Pa., bill to, 324. *See also* Penn, John; Penn, Thomas

Prosit and Marcus, hoax of, 271 n., 273 n.

Protester, edited by James Ralph, 58 n.

"Providence of God in the Government of the World," 264–9

Queries for Junto. *See* Junto

Ralph, James: biographical note, 58–9 n.; addressed, 58–9

Rawle, William (d. 1741): signs Lib. Co. agreement, 322, 360, 361; approves new member for Lib. Co., 373

Rawle, William (1759-1836), copies part of BF Plan of Conduct, 99

Ray, Catharine. *See* Greene, Catharine Ray

Ray, John, book of, mentioned, 105 and n.

Ray, Judith (m. 1747). *See* Hubbart, Judith Ray

Read, Charles: marriage, 346; sheriff of Philadelphia, 363 n.

Read, Deborah (1708–74). *See* Franklin, Deborah Read Rogers

Read, John (1677–1724; father of Deborah Franklin): genealogy, lxii; buys land, 362

Read, John, Jr. (brother of Deborah Franklin), receives title to land, 363

Read, Sarah (d. 1761; mother of Deborah Franklin): genealogy, lxii; sells slave, 186 and n.; advertises ointment, 219; real estate documents of, 362–70

Reader, communication of, to the printer of the *Pa. Gaz.* (1734), 370

Receipted printing bill, 324

Remembrancer, edited by James Ralph, 58 n.

Reply of BF to a complaining reader, 249–50

Reynolds, Lawrence, signs Masonic by-laws, 233 and n.

Richardson, Francis, approves new member for Lib. Co., 373

Richardson, Samuel, *appendix to Clarissa,* BF's use of, 282

Ridicule, criticism of, 117–18

Roberts, Edward, drafts and witnesses BF agreement with Whitmarsh, 208

Roberts, Hugh: signs Lib. Co. agreement, 252, 322, 361; approves new member for Lib. Co., 373

Rogers, Deborah Read (1708–74). *See* Franklin, Deborah Read Rogers

Rogers, John (m. 1745/6), genealogy, lx

Rogers, John, Jr. (b. 1748), genealogy, lx

Rogers, Mary Davenport (b. 1725/6; niece of BF), genealogy, lx

Ronsard, Pierre de, mentioned, 325 n.

Ross, Elizabeth (m. *c.* 1757). *See* Mecom, Elizabeth Ross

St. John's Lodge: BF's account with, 202–4; by-laws, 231–3; elections, 274–5, 345

Salary of Mass. governor, BF paper on, 159–61

Sandiford, Ralph: biographical note, 189 n.; prints *Negroe Treatise,* 189

Satterthwaite, Ellen Duane (1816–46), genealogy, lxv

Saunders, Richard (pen-name of BF), compiler of *Poor Richard's Almanacks,* 280

Savile, George, Lord Halifax, *A Character of King Charles the Second,* BF's use of, 282

Sawyer, Sarah. *See* Franklin, Sarah Sawyer

Scandal, essay on, 243–9
Schwachhamer, Samuel, signs Palatine appeal, 229
Scolding wife, essay on, 325–7
Scott, Lydia Franklin (1708–58; sister of BF): biographical note, 171 n.; genealogy, lvii, lxi; marriage, 171, 201 and n.
Scott, Robert (m. 1731): genealogy, lxi; marriage, 171 n., 201 n.
Scrubb, Timothy, signs "advertisements" in Pa. Gaz., 273 and n., 274
Scull, Nicholas: composes rhymed description of Junto meeting, 177 n.; Lib. Co. meets at house of, 229, 271
Sea captain's letter, written by BF, 254–5
Second sight, letter on, 128–9
Self-denial, BF essay on, 170
Sergeant, Frances (1817–1903). See Perry, Frances Sergeant
Sergeant, Henry Jonathan (1815–58), lxv
Sergeant, Sarah Bache (1788–1863; granddaughter of BF), genealogy, lxv
Sergeant, Thomas (1782–1860), genealogy, lxv
Sergeant, Thomas, Jr. (1819–78), genealogy, lxv
Sergeant, William (1821–23), genealogy, lxv
Shaftesbury, 3d Earl of, works studied by BF, 58
Shark, observed by BF, 90
Shortface, Caelia. See Martha Careful
Shute, Samuel: James Franklin publishes comments on, 47; quarrel with Mass. Assembly, 47 n.
Silence Dogood papers, 8–45
Single, Celia. See Celia Single
Skelton, Mr., entry for, in BF account book, 174
Slippery sidewalks, BF essay on, 318–19
Sloane, Sir Hans: biographical note, 54 n.; letter to, 54; buys asbestos purse, 54 n.
Smallpox: epidemics of, 186–7, 200, 215, 217, 252; inoculation against, 8, 186–7, 214 and n.
Smith, Ann (d. 1763). See Franklin, Ann Smith
Smith, William, Provost, 256
Smyth, Albert Henry: edits BF papers, xxvi–xxvii; editing of Junto queries, 255 n.; attributes essay to BF, 328
Soapmaking activities of Franklin family, 348 n.
Society for Political Inquiries, BF a member, 99
Society of the Free and Easy, project of BF's, 192–3
Solitude, BF's observations on, 85–6

South Carolina, currency question in, 322–4
South-Carolina Gazette: printed by Whitmarsh, 205 n.; paper-currency article quoted, 322
Spain, peace with, reported by Pa. Gaz., 165
Sparks, Jared: visits Champlost, xxii; edits BF papers, xxvi; editing of Junto queries, 255 n., 256
Spectator: BF's indebtedness to, 9; quoted, 44–5
Spinsters, relief of, 37–8
Starbuck, Dinah Coffin (d. 1793). See Folger, Dinah Coffin Starbuck
Starbuck, Mary (d. 1763). See Folger, Mary Starbuck
Stark, Mary (d. 1828). See Stickney, Mary Stark
Steel, James, printing charges of, 371 and n.
Stevens, Henry, acquires BF papers, xxiii
Stickney, Anthony (1727–74), genealogy, lx
Stickney, Anthony Somersby (1747–1819), genealogy, lx
Stickney, Benjamin Franklin (1775–1852), genealogy, lx
Stickney, Dorcas Davenport (1724–74; niece of BF), genealogy, lx
Stickney, Mary Matilda Way (m. 1835), genealogy, lx
Stickney, Mary Stark (d. 1828), genealogy, lx
Stickney, Ruth Brown Coffin (m. 1770), genealogy, lx
Stiles, Ezra: prediction told to, 6 n.; dates BF's epitaph, 110
Style. See Literary style
Swain, Experience Folger (c. 1661–1739; aunt of BF), genealogy, liii, lvi
Swain, John (c. 1664–1738/9), genealogy, lvi
Swift, Jonathan: quoted, 78 n.; cited, 329
Swift, Mary Ann (d. c. 1812). See Bache, Mary Ann Swift
Syng, Philip, Jr.: biographical note, 209–10 n.; director of Lib. Co., 209; approves new member for Lib. Co., 373

"Taking of Teach the Pirate," lost ballad, 7
Taylor, Capt., and New-England Courant, 8
Terry, Roderick, BF MS owned by, 46 n.
Thompson, Christopher, signs Masonic by-laws, 233 and n.
Thurston, Dolly (m. 1789). See Flagg, Dolly Thurston
Tiff Club, mentioned, 126 and n.

Tillotson, Archbishop John, cited, 329
Timothée, Louis (Lewis Timothy): biographical note, 230 n.; BF becomes partner of, 205 n., 339–42; teaches French, 220; writes prospectus for the *Philadelphische Zeitung*, 230–1; writes explanation to the readers of the *Zeitung*, 233–4; agreement between Lib. Co. and, 250–2; translator for the *Philadelphische Zeitung*, 274; entered in BF account book, 342 n.; Lib. Co. meets at house of, 345
Timothy, Benjamin Franklin, son of Peter, 342 n.
Timothy, Elizabeth (wife of Louis Timothée), continues husband's business, 341 n.
Timothy, Lewis. *See* Timothée, Louis
Timothy, Peter (son of Louis Timothée), continues father's newspaper, 341–2 n.
"Titles of Honor," BF essay, 51–2
Tonson, Jacob, epitaph by, 110
Treasure. *See* Buried treasure
Trent, Morris, entry for, in BF account book, 172
Trevose (Bucks County, Pa., home of Joseph Galloway), BF papers at, xxi, 210
Turner, Thomas, genealogy, lxii
Tyng, Elizabeth (m. 1705). *See* Franklin, Elizabeth Tyng

Universal Instructor in all Arts and Sciences: and Pennsylvania Gazette, Keimer's newspaper, 113–14
University of Pennsylvania, BF papers in, xxii

Vaughan, Benjamin: edits BF's writings, xxv; letter to, quoted, 57; dates BF's epitaph, 110; editing of Junto queries, 255 n., 256
Virtue, essay in praise of, 118–21
Visiting, etiquette of, 122–6
Voyage from London to Philadelphia. *See* "Journal of . . . occurrences"

Wainwright, Sarah Franklin Bache (b. 1824), genealogy, lxv
Walker, Anne (m. 1817). *See* Fuller, Anne Walker
Walker, Hannah Farrow (b. 1724), genealogy, lii
Walker, Henry (b. 1756), genealogy, lii

Walker, John (b. 1755), genealogy, lii
Walker, Mary Blechynden Bache (1808–73), genealogy, lxv
Walker, Thomas, genealogy, lii
Waller, Edmund, quoted, 196
Walsh, Robert, BF's Plan of Conduct used by, 99
Watts, Isaac, quoted, 24
Way, Mary Matilda (m. 1835). *See* Stickney, Mary Matilda Way
Webb, George, reveals BF newspaper plans to Keimer, 113
Webb, John Richmond: biographical note, 77 n.; mentioned, 77
Weiss, George Michael: biographical note, 226 n.; appeal to, 227–9
Welles, Hannah (d. 1705). *See* Franklin, Hannah Welles
White, Jane (1617–62). *See* Franklin, Jane White
Whitmarsh, Thomas: biographical note, 205 n.; entry for, in BF account book, 172; reprints BF paper on printers, 199 n.; BF becomes partner of, 205–8; verses of, 347 n.
Whittemore, Ruth (m. 1755). *See* Mecom, Ruth Whittemore
Whitwell, Elizabeth (m. 1764). *See* Homes, Elizabeth Whitwell
Widows, relief of, 31–6
Williams, Alexander John (d. 1814), genealogy, lviii
Williams, Christine. *See* Biddle, Christine Williams
Williams, Grace Harris (1718–90; niece of BF), genealogy, lvii
Williams, Hannah Chandler (m. 1778), genealogy, lviii
Williams, Henry Jonathan, genealogy, lviii
Williams, John ("the inspector"; brother of Jonathan Williams, Sr.), genealogy, lvii n., lviii
Williams, John (b. 1756; son of Jonathan Williams, Sr.), genealogy, lvii n., lviii
Williams, Jonathan, Sr. (1719–96), genealogy, lvii and n.
Williams, Jonathan, Jr. (1750–1815), genealogy, lvii n., lviii and n.
Williams, Jonathan (d. 1780; nephew of Jonathan Williams, Sr.), genealogy, lvii n.
Williams, Josiah (1747–72), genealogy, lviii
Williams, Josiah (b. c. 1776), genealogy, lviii
Williams, Marianne Alexander (1764–1845), genealogy, lviii
Williams, Mary Duane (1812–45), genealogy, lxiv

Witch trial at Mount Holly, piece on, attributed to BF, 182–3
Wohlfahrt, Michael (Brother Agonius): biographical note, 382 n.; preaches in Philadelphia, 381
Wollaston, William: biographical note, 57 n.; *Religion of Nature Delineated*, BF refutes, 57
Women: foibles, 18–21; apparel, 21–3; education, 254–5
Woodbridge, Benjamin, epitaph by, 110

Writing. *See* Literary style

Yale College, religious crisis in, 43 n.
Yarmouth, Isle of Wight, BF visits, 79–81
Yorker (ship), BF's ship meets, 83, 84, 85

Zantzinger, Sarah Barton (m. 1804). *See* Davenport, Sarah Barton Zantzinger
Zeal, religious, criticized, 43–5